CRACKING LATIN AMERICA

A COUNTRY-BY-COUNTRY GUIDE TO DOING BUSINESS IN THE WORLD'S NEWEST EMERGING MARKETS

ALLYN ENDERLYN
OLIVER C. DZIGGEL

PROBUS PUBLISHING COMPANY
Chicago, Illinois
Cambridge, England

ISBN 1-55738-432-0

Printed in the United States of America

BB

1 2 3 4 5 6 7 8 9 0

CB/BJS

Dedication

This book is dedicated to those corporations with vision who are accepting their role as leaders, and as powerful resources of human energy and money, to effect social change and raise the quality of lives in countries around the world. Their decisions, based on an awareness of global ethical responsibility, can positively affect our basic problems of hunger and poverty, the environment, and the lives of children.

This book is dedicated above all to our children, Oliver and Alexandra.

Table of Contents

Preface

This book has been prepared as a "travel companion" for business people contemplating or pursuing opportunities in Latin America. Virtually every major economy is covered—from the largest and most accessible, Mexico, to the least accessible, Guyana.

For the most part, the source material which comprises the book is derived from official government sources, including American embassy reports and "cables" from each post, U.S. Department of Commerce trade and investment profiles, U.S. Department of State diplomatic advisories and directories, Central Intelligence Agency statistics, and political analyses. In addition, current economic information was often provided by the host government or its central bank.

The Introduction provides a regional overview. It compares and contrasts the individual country situations and highlights a few of the common themes to be encountered.

In the chapters that follow, each country is profiled separately. The same basic topical outline is covered for each country: historic and geographic contexts; socioeconomic and market demographics; and important business contacts and statistics.

The appendices cover additional regional business contacts and resources, as well as comparative statistics.

ACKNOWLEDGMENTS

The authors wish to thank our colleagues, friends, family, and the people at Probus Publishing Company who have been so supportive during the creation of this book. We are especially grateful for the assistance of the many people of the Latin American countries whom we have met and worked with throughout our travels. We appreciate the help given to us by Robert Taft, regional director for all the Foreign Commercial Service posts throughout Latin America, and by his assistant, Brien Smith. We are also grateful to Ysabella Lopez-Bowen, whose work and dedication were invaluable.

Introduction

FORTRESSES AND REGIONAL ECONOMIC INTEGRATION

In the United States, the North American Free Trade Agreement (NAFTA) has been a source of controversy and media attention, particularly in the context of the 1992 presidential campaign and the "first 100 days" of the Clinton administration. In reality, NAFTA merely codifies existing and emerging trade relations between the United States and the economies of Canada and Mexico. Precious little new ground is covered, except in the political realm; when NAFTA is enacted in some form in the fall of 1993, U.S. trade representatives will have a new tool in their arsenal in negotiations with representatives from the European Community (EC). Fortress North America?

But the process of regional economic integration in Latin America has already advanced much further than Mexico and NAFTA. Besides its free trade agreement with the United States, Mexico also has concluded agreements with all of the countries of South America (ALADI), as well as separate bilateral and multilateral agreements with Colombia, Chile, and Venezuela. Other regional pacts already in place are the Central American Common Market (Costa Rica, El Salvador, Guatemala, Honduras, and Nicaragua), the Andean Free Trade Zone (Venezuela, Colombia, Bolivia, Peru, and Ecuador), Mercosur (Argentina, Brazil, Paraguay, Uruguay, with Chile under negotiations), and Caricom (including most of the Caribbean countries). Each of these arrangements is discussed in greater detail in Appendix 1.

The significance of these market clusters is that by the end of the decade, a unified market encompassing all of North, South and Central America, and the Caribbean is quite conceivable—even if nothing more initially than a loose confederation of regional pacts. A political forum for such a process already exists and has been in operation since 1948—the Organization of American States (OAS), which is headquartered in Washington, D.C.

For certain industrial categories—notably communications equipment and services—the OAS has already established standing committees to promote regional trade and market harmonization.

In addition, a specialized multilateral financial institution, the Inter-American Development Bank (also headquartered in Washington, D.C.), has been operating since 1959 to provide funding for key large-scale infrastructure projects such as ports, roads, communications, and energy grids. The IDB also provides financing for capital investments at the enterprise level.

NARCO-TERRORISM, WHITE-GLOVE MILITARISM, AND RUN-AWAY INFLATION

At the regional level, Latin America only recently has been able to break with the images of the recent past—which was, admittedly, a period of rather rough sledding.

The best thing to be said about this "lost decade," as it is called in many of the Latin American countries, is that it is now solidly behind us. Taking great care to not trivialize the personal hardship which accompanied the "devolution" experiment in terms of outrageous inflation rates, economic stagnation, loss of world competitiveness, and deferral of capital investment, the end result is that today a substantial business opportunity exists in the "catch-up" which is being implemented.

For example, the widespread nationalization of productive enterprises which was so fashionable in the early 1970s has now been replaced by wave after wave of privatizations. In some countries, such as Paraguay, virtually all economic activity was in the form of government-owned and operated monopolies, and often even the import/export channels were monopolized under government trading companies. Normal market functions of supply and demand all but disappeared.

The privatizations have been wildly successful—adding much-needed foreign exchange to the national treasuries as well as opening the markets to global suppliers who had previously been excluded. What is most notable about the privatizations is their global governance. Since most of the actions were supported, at least in part, by the World Bank (headquartered in Washington, D.C.), which sets strict rules of conduct, virtually every phase of the privatization process has been competitive and supported with advisors from around the globe (typically with vast experience in past privatizations). Consequently, massive opportunities exist in supplying a wide range of goods and services to these enterprises, now "under new ownership," with billions of dollars to spend.

The nationalized industries were a huge drain on the national budget, which in turn fueled spiraling, high inflation rates as governments simply resorted to printing money to pay the bills. The privatizations, together with other austerity measures imposed by the World Bank and the International Monetary Fund (headquartered in Washington, D.C.), have now brought inflation under control throughout most of the region.

Another casualty of the "lost decade" is the "white glove military" institution. Once a highly prestigious vestige of the break from the colonial past, as well as to some degree a public employment (and administration) mechanism, the military persona is being replaced by the "yuppie" mentality.

A lingering problem is the economic role of trade in drugs which are illegal in the United States, principally cocaine and marijuana. If the staggering multi-billion dollar demand for these drugs were to be eliminated in the United States, several Latin American economies would teeter and collapse. Just as the economic "multiplier effect" is observed in other agrobusiness and service sectors, the drug trade is today thoroughly interwoven with the national and international economic processes. Since it is highly unlikely that the United States will liberalize or legalize the drug trade in the foreseeable future—imagine the balance of payments nightmare if the "invisible" trade suddenly became quantifiable—a country's stability will depend on the fine line between the "political correctness" of combating the smugglers (resulting in continued narco-terrorism) and condoning a proven "cash crop" with worldwide demand.

EMERGING MARKETS

The collapse of the former Soviet Union has had fiscal as well as ideological impacts throughout Latin America. During the past two decades, several countries looked toward the Soviet Union as an alternative to the pervasive influence of the United States Overtly, this included expanded trade relations; covertly, this included "whip-sawing" between the two Cold War adversaries in order to obtain increased foreign and economic aid. Since 1989, however, the Newly Independent States (NIS) are no longer centrally controlled from Moscow, nor are they favorably disposed to subsidizing foreign economies when there is much greater need at home. Further, neither the rubles nor the military equipment face much of an import demand in Latin America.

Based on observations around the world, the predictable result will be that political terrorist activities will gradually diminish as these foreign funds evaporate.

Chapter 1

ARGENTINA

	Total	Urban	
Population (1993)	33,023,000	86.0%	

Main Urban Areas	Population	Percentage of Total	International Calling Code
BUENOS AIRES	2,923,000	8.9	54-1
Cordoba	984,000	3.0	54-51
Rosario	957,000	3.0	54-41
Mendoza	606,000	1.8	54-61
La Plata	565,000	1.7	54-21
San Miguel de Tucuman	499,000	1.5	54-81
Mar del Plata	415,000	1.3	54-23
Santa Fe	292,000	0.9	54-42
San Juan	292,000	0.9	54-64
Salta	261,000	0.8	54-87
Bahia Blanca	224,000	0.7	54-91

Land Area   2,736,690 square kilometers
   Comparable U.S. State   Size of the United States east of the Mississippi River or four times the size of Texas

Language
Spanish	96%
Italian	2%
Amerindian	1%
Other	1%

   Common Business Language   Spanish, English

Currency   1 peso = 100 centavos
   Exchange Rate (May 1993)   U.S. $1.00 = 0.99 peso

Best Nonstop Air Connection via U.S.
Miami to Buenos Aires: 8.5 hours
New York to Buenos Aires: 10.5 hours
Los Angeles to Buenos Aires: 16 hours
Aerolines Argentinas (800) 333-0276
American Airlines (800) 433-7300
Two nonstops daily via Miami.

Best Hotel
Plaza Hotel (U.S. $200)
Florida 1005, 1005 Buenos Aires
Tel   (541) 311-5011 or 312-6001
Fax   (541) 313-2912

INTRODUCTION AND REGIONAL ORIENTATION

The Argentine nation has been built by the fusion of diverse national and ethnic groups. Waves of European immigrants arrived in the late 19th and early 20th centuries. Today, descendants of Italian and Spanish immigrants predominate, but many trace their origins to British and European ancestors. Middle Eastern immigrants number about 500,000 and are concentrated in urban areas. In recent years, there has been a substantial influx of immigrants from neighboring Latin American countries. The native Indian population, estimated at 50,000, is concentrated in the peripheral provinces of the north, northwest, and south.

The Argentine population has one of the lowest growth rates in Latin America (1.5 percent). Eighty percent of the population reside in urban areas of over 2,000, with more than one-third of the population living in the metropolitan Buenos Aires area. The sprawling capital, with more than 10 million inhabitants, serves as the focus for national life.

Argentines have enjoyed comparatively high standards of living; half the population considers itself middle class.

More than 90 percent of Argentines are Roman Catholic. Religious freedom is allowed, although all non-Catholic denominations are required to register with the government. The Protestant community is small but active. Argentina's Jewish community of 350,000 (estimate) is concentrated in Buenos Aires.

The Argentine educational system is compulsory for grades one to seven. The adult literacy rate is 92 percent—one of the highest in Latin America. Literary and artistic tastes have been influenced mainly by Western Europe and, more recently, by the United States.

A large number of Spanish daily newspapers are published in the greater Buenos Aires area; a dozen community newspapers are published in English, French, German, Greek, Hungarian, Italian, Japanese, Polish, Ukrainian, and Yiddish. All the community newspapers are periodicals except the daily English-language Buenos Aires Herald.

Geographical Background

Argentina shares land borders with Bolivia, Brazil, Chile, Paraguay, and Uruguay. It is bounded to the east by the Atlantic Ocean and to the south by the Antarctic Ocean. Extending 3,705 kilometers (2,302 miles) from north to south and with an Atlantic coastline 2,850 kilometers (1,600 miles) long, Argentina is the second largest country in South America, after Brazil, and the eighth largest in the world. Its topography, as varied as that of the United States, ranges from subtropical lowlands in the north to the towering Andean Mountains in the west and the bleak, windswept Patagonian steppe and Tierra del Fuego in the south.

History and Political Conditions

What is now Argentina was discovered in 1516 by the Spanish navigator Juan de Solis. The formal declaration of independence from Spain was made on July 9, 1816.

In 1943, a military coup—led by Colonel Juan Domingo Peron (1895–1974)—ousted the constitutional government. In 1946, Peron was elected president. He pursued a dynamic policy aimed at giving an economic and political voice to the working class. The number of unionized workers increased significantly, which helped consolidate the powerful General Confederation of Labor (CGT). In 1947, Peron announced the first five-year plan based on nationalization and industrialization. He was aided by his energetic wife, Eva Duarte Peron (1919–52). She enhanced his appeal to labor and women's groups and helped women obtain the right to vote in 1947.

Peron, re-elected in 1952, was ousted by the military in 1955, and went into exile. In the 1950s and 1960s, the government passed between military and civilian administrations, as each sought to deal with diminished economic growth and continued social and labor demands. When the military government of Juan Carlos Ongania (et al., 1966–73) brought economic failure and escalating terrorism, Peronism returned to popularity.

On March 11, 1973, general elections were held for the first time in 10 years. Peron was prevented from running, and his stand-in, Dr. Hector J. Campora, was elected. The Peronists also commanded a strong majority in both houses of the National Congress, which assumed office on May 25, 1973. Campora resigned in July 1973, and Raul Lastiri, a Peronist Party loyalist, assumed the presidency and called for new elections. Peron won a decisive victory and returned as president in October 1973 with his third wife, Maria Estela (Isabel) Martinez de Peron, as vice-president.

Even after Peron's dramatic return, extremists on the left and right continued to threaten public order. The government resorted to a number of emergency decrees, including the implementation of special executive authority to deal with violence. This allowed the government to imprison persons indefinitely without charge.

On July 1, 1974, Peron died and was succeeded by his wife, the first woman president in the Western Hemisphere. Mrs. Peron's administration was undermined by economic problems, Peronist intraparty struggles, and persistent terrorism from both the left and the right. As a result, Mrs. Peron was removed from office by a military coup on March 24, 1976. Until December 10,

1983, power was formally executed by the armed forces through a military president and a three-man junta composed of the three service commanders.

The military quashed terrorists and their sympathizers, silenced armed opposition, and restored basic order. The costs were high in terms of lives lost and basic human rights violated. These events were termed the "dirty war," and remain controversial and divisive in Argentine politics, having fueled military discontent that produced three aborted military uprisings against President Raul Alfonsin (1983–89).

Serious economic problems, defeat by the British in June 1982 after an attempt to take control over the Falkland/Malvinas Islands, human rights abuses, and charges of growing corruption combined to discredit the military regime, which moved to a period of gradual transition leading the country toward democratic rule. Bans on political parties were lifted and other basic political liberties restored. The military implemented a successful and generally peaceful process for the return of elected government.

In 1983, Argentines voted for a president, vice president, and 14,000 other national, provincial, and local officials in fair, open, and honest elections. Raul Alfonsin, candidate of the Radical Civic Union (UCR), was elected, winning 52 percent of the popular vote. He began a six-year term of office on December 10, 1983. In 1985 and 1987, large turn-outs for mid-term elections demonstrated continued public support for a strong and vigorous democratic system. The Radical Civic Union-led government took steps to resolve some of the nation's most pressing problems, including accounting for the "disappeared," establishing civilian control of the armed forces, and consolidating democratic institutions. Its effectiveness was hindered by constant friction with the military and chronic economic problems.

In May 1989, Carlos Saul Menem, the Peronist candidate, was elected president with 47 percent of the popular vote and a clear majority in the nation's electoral college. The Peronists and their allies also won control of both houses of the new Congress, which took office in December 1989. President Menem was to have succeeded Alfonsin in December 1989, but a rapidly deteriorating economy and resulting loss of confidence in the national government led Alfonsin to resign, and Menem to succeed him in July. Although the transition came five months earlier than planned, the transfer of power was the first between democratically elected presidents in over 60 years.

Menem surprised most observers, including members of his own party, by adopting economic policies antithetical to Peronism's traditional statist approach. He initiated economic emergency and state reform legislation to cut government spending, increase revenues, and reduce state involvement in the economy. Menem has chosen to battle inflation through conservative fiscal and monetary policies, and he has moved quickly to privatize government-owned industries such as Aerolineas Argentinas and the telephone company. These policies have generated resistance among sectors historically allied to Peronism as well as the Radical Party. However, the opposition remains fragmented, and the President's personal popularity remains relatively high.

CRACKING THE MARKET

Demographics

Ethnic groups: European 97%, mostly Spanish and Italian.

Religions: Roman Catholic 92%, Protestant 2%, Jewish 2%, other 4%.

Languages: Spanish (official), English, Italian, German, French.

Work force: agriculture 19%; industry and commerce 36%; services 20%; Transport and communications 6%; other, 19%.

Economy

Argentina has impressive human and natural resources, but political conflict and uneven economic performance since World War II have impeded full realization of its potential. Nonetheless, it remains one of the richest countries in Latin America.

Among the reasons for the military coup of March 1976 was the deteriorating economy, caused by declining production and rampant inflation. Under the leadership of Minister of the Economy Martinez de Hoz, the military government, in 1978, embarked on a new developmental strategy to move away from the closed-economy model and establish a free-market economy. The strategy also featured the removal or reduction of restrictions in the manufacturing sector and financial markets as well as the search for foreign and domestic investment. Despite those efforts, by late 1980, Argentina entered a period of recession, with declines in production and real wages. After a notable economic recovery in 1986, economic growth again has slowed. Argentina has recorded successive declines in economic activity in 1988 and 1989.

Faced with healing a scarred society, the Alfonsin administration was slow to tackle the root causes of the economic problems. In an attempt to control inflation and set the country on a prudent fiscal course, in June 1985, the government introduced a "shock" plan (the Austral Plan), which succeeded temporarily. Inflation in 1986 slowed to double digits (86 percent) for only the second time since 1972. But in 1987, with a significant increase in the public sector deficit accompanied by very large price and wage increases, inflation climbed 175 percent and reached 386 percent in 1988.

Another economic plan, the Spring Plan, was announced in 1988; its collapse in February 1989 marked the start of a rapid deterioration of the economy which was worsened by political and economic uncertainties surrounding the May 1989 elections.

President Menem, who took office in July 1989, moved quickly to change expectations and to combat rapidly escalating prices. Inflation reached 198 percent in July, a Western Hemisphere one-month record. In contrast with earlier reform efforts, Menem's economic program includes a serious effort to reduce the government's role in the economy. Menem's economic team has reduced import barriers, slashed subsidies and transfers, and privatized public sector firms (e.g., the telephone company and the national airline).

On October 31, 1991, Menem signed a "Deregulation Decree" that gave new impetus to his administration's efforts to remove the manifold governmental devices—regulations, nontariff barriers and the like—that have long protected the interests of privileged minorities at the expense of the majority. Menem speaks often of the need for greater "transparency," wherein governmental decisions are taken subject to public review, thereby reducing the opportunity for corruption.

Behind the welcome economic stability that Argentina now enjoys is the public confidence engendered by the Convertibility Law, which took effect April 1, 1991. The law in essence fixed the local currency (then the austral; as of January 1, 1992, the peso) to the U.S. dollar.

An equally important and closely interrelated factor in the present stability has been the government's success in bringing balance to the fiscal accounts. The privatization of virtually all productive assets in government hands is proceeding well; and the proceeds of the sales (along with the accumulation of arrears to the commercial banks) were once very important in financing the fiscal deficit. Continued improvements in tax collections and the creation of new, more progressive taxes have eased the burden on companies while helping to bring the budget to a sustainable balance by 1993.

The heartland of Argentina is the rich temperate plains known as the pampas, which fan out for almost 800 kilometers (500 miles) from Buenos Aires. Argentina's richest natural resource is this farmland, producing large quantities of wheat, corn, sorghum, soybeans, and sunflower seeds and providing year-round pasturage for Argentina's cattle industry. The country is one of the world's largest exporters of foodstuffs. The crops and livestock of the fertile pampas have long provided it with abundant food for domestic consumption in addition to unusually plentiful exports.

Agricultural products constitute the major source of foreign exchange earnings. In a good year, grains and oilseed harvests can total some 40 million metric tons. The cattle industry, with an estimated 50 million animals, provides for domestic consumption and export markets.

Argentina exports to a variety of buyers. In the early 1980s, the Soviet Union became the major purchaser of grains, while, more recently, Iran, Brazil, and China have served as major markets. Argentina also exports agricultural goods to the United States, primarily canned, precooked, and frozen beef; sugar; and fruits and fruit products.

Argentina obtains about 21 percent of its imports from the United States. Total imports in 1989 were $4.2 billion, of which $9 million was from the United States. Capital equipment, computers and peripherals, telecommunications, chemicals, and electronic components were the principal items sold to Argentina. In 1980, Argentina exported $9.5 billion worth of goods and services; $8 million (12 percent) went to the United States.

Argentina was a net energy importer in

ARGENTINA
Key Economic Indicators

	1989	1990	1991[1]
Income, Production, Employment			
GDP (1991 U.S. $ billions)	134	133	140
Real GDP growth rate (%)	−4.6	−0.7	5.0
GDP growth by sector			
Agriculture[2]	−2.9	9.8	7.0
Industry[2]	−7.1	−4.6	10.0
Minerals[2]	3.2	−1.5	3.0
Services[2]	−2.6	0.9	2.0
Real per capita GDP (1991 U.S. $)	4,133	4,048	4,203
Size of labor force (millions)	12.1	12.3	12.5
Unemployment rate (%)	7.6	8.8	6.4
Money and Prices			
Money supply (M1)[3]	4,960	886	115
Commercial interest rates[4]	40.0	6.7	1.2
Savings rate[2]	7.6	10.2	11.0
Investment rate[2]	9.4	8.6	13.8
Consumer price index[3]	4,923	1,344	75
Wholesale price index[3]	5,386	798	63
Exchange rate (australes per U.S. $)	1,314	5,122	9,950
Balance of Payments and Trade (U.S. $ billion)			
Exports FOB	9,573	12,339	10,500
Imports CIF	−4,149	−4,078	−6,500
U.S. Exports (FAS)[5]	1,037	1,179	785
U.S. Imports (Customs value)[5]	1,398	1,509	684
Aid from other countries	N/A	N/A	N/A
External public debt[5]	58.4	56.2	57.5
Debt service payments paid[6]	650	1,511	1,582
Foreign exchange reserves[7]	3,419	5,874	6,243
Balance of payments	−6,258	679	−719

1. Estimated
2. As percent of GDP
3. Percent—measured year end to year end
4. Nominal monthly rate in percent at year end
5. U.S. $ billions; including interest arrears
6. Includes net service paid by public sector to international financial institutions and on BONEX
7. Estimated—includes gold, SDRs, foreign exchange and outstanding ALADI balances

Source: U.S. Department of Commerce (December 1992).

ARGENTINA
Key Economic Indicators

	1990	1991	1992
Income, Production, Employment			
(U.S. $ millions, unless noted)			
GDP (1992)	104,100	134,700	153,000
Real GDP (% chg)	0.4	6.4	6.5
GDP (projected average growth rate thru 1994, %)	0.1	3.1	4.0
Inflation (%/year)	798	57	6
Unemployment rate (Oct.)	6.0	5.3	5
Foreign exchange reserves	6,170	10,137	11,000
Average exchange rate for U.S. $1	0.4888	0.9552	1
Foreign debt (U.S. $ millions)	60,973	65,097	55,000
U.S. economic assistance	0.16	1.1	1.3
U.S. military assistance	—	—	—
Trade (U.S. $ millions)			
Exports FOB	12,354	12,000	12,900
Imports CIF	4,079	8,100	11,800
Exports to the U.S.	1,626	1,368	1,300
Imports from the U.S.	1,123	1,897	2,800
U.S. share of Argentine import market	25	29	24
Imports of manufactured goods (from all countries)	4,199	4,060	5,000
Projected average growth rate thru 1994 (%)	−34	20	30
From the U.S.	1,500	1,950	2,150
Projected average growth rate thru 1994 (%)	15	73.4	45
U.S. share of manufactured imports (%)	50	43	55
Trade balances with leading partners (1990)			
United States	−361	−330	−300
Brazil	403	689	200
Germany	20	170	80

Source: U.S. Department of Commerce (March 1993).

ARGENTINA
Key Economic Indicators

	1990	1991	1992
Investment			
Total foreign direct investment (U.S. $ millions)	7,200	8,200	N/A
U.S. direct investment (U.S. $ millions)	3,100	3,600	N/A
U.S. share of total foreign investment	43	44	—

Principal foreign investors:
  United States
  Brazil
  Italy
  Germany
  Spain
  France

Source: American Embassy Buenos Aires, Economics Section, and U.S. Department of Commerce (November 1992).

Balance of Payments
(in $ millions)

	1989	1990	1991	1992
Current account	1,305	1,789	−2,818	−4,200
Trade balance	5,374	8,275	3,900	1,900
Exports FOB	9,573	12,354	12,000	12,900
of which, agricultural	5,901	7,311	7,500	7,600
Imports CIF	−4,199	−4,079	−8,100	−11,000
of which, consumption goods	−210	−314	−990	N/A
capital goods	−717	−618	−1,540	N/A
fuels	−359	−319	−400	N/A
other	−2,914	−2,828	−5,170	N/A
Net services	−4,069	−6,486	−6,718	−6,100
Capital account	−5,484	−1,110	3,538	5,093
Overall balance	−6,789	679	720	881

Source: International Monetary Fund, American Embassy Buenos Aires estimates (March 1993).

1987. However, it has reserves of petroleum and natural gas and was self-sufficient in crude oil in 1989. An effort begun under the Alfonsin administration to open the petroleum sector to private investment and increase petroleum production has expanded since July 1989. In addition, significant deregulation of the petroleum sector, including an end to price controls, took effect January 1, 1991. Argentina also has large electrical production capacity, mostly from hydroelectric sources. It has indicated it wants to reduce the size and cost of the massive Yacyreta hydroelectric project (2,400 megawatts) being jointly constructed with Paraguay and scheduled for completion in the mid-1990s.

Natural resources: Fertile plains (pampas). Minerals—lead, zinc, tin, copper, iron, manganese, oil, uranium.

Agriculture (15% of GNP, about 70% of exports by value):
Products—grains, oilseeds and byproducts, livestock products.

Industry (23% of GNP): Types—food processing, motor vehicles, consumer durables, textiles, metallurgy, chemicals.

Political/Institutional Infrastructure

The Republic of Argentina gained its independence from Spain on July 9, 1816.

The 1853 Argentine constitution, similar to that of the United States, mandates a separation of powers into executive, legislative, and judicial branches at the national and provincial level. Each of its 22 provinces, capital district (Buenos Aires) and territory (Tierra del Fuego) also has its own constitution.

The federal legislature is a bicameral Congress (46-member Senate, 254-member Chamber of Deputies). The federal Supreme Court is the final legal arbiter.

The president and vice-president are elected to a six-year single term and cannot immediately run for reelection. Senators are elected by provincial legislatures (with the exception of the two senators representing Buenos Aires, who are elected by an electoral college) for nine-year terms, with one-third standing for reelection every three years. Deputies are elected for four years in alternate terms, with half up for reelection every two years. Cabinet ministers are appointed by the president. Considerable power, including a line item veto power, is granted to the president by the constitution.

The Argentine judiciary functions as a separate and independent entity of the government. The apex of the court system is the Supreme Court, whose nine judges are appointed by the president with the consent of the Senate. The Supreme Court has the power, first asserted in 1854, to declare legislative acts unconstitutional.

Principal Government Officials

President
Carlos Saul Menem

Vice-President
Eduardo Duhalde

President Pro Tempore of the Senate
Eduardo Menem

Speaker of the Lower House (Chamber of Deputies)
Alberto Pierri

Chief Justice of the Supreme Court
Ricardo Levene

Ministers

Interior
Julio Mera Figueroa

Foreign Relations and Worship
Domingo Cavallo

National Defense
Humberto Romero

Economy
Antonio Erman Gonzalez

Education and Justice
Antonio Francisco Salonia

Labor and Social Security
Jorge Alberto Triaca

Health and Social Action
Eduardo Bauza

Public Works and Services
Jose Roberto Dromi

Ambassador to the U.S.
Guido Jose Maria di Tella

Ambassador to the OAS
Juan Pablo Lohle

Ambassador to the UN
Jorge Vasca

Political parties: Justicialista (Peronist), Radical Civic Union, numerous smaller national and provincial parties.

Suffrage: Universal.

Flag: Horizontal blue and white bands emblazoned with "Sun of May."

Defense

The armed forces of Argentina (army, navy, air force) are organized under the control of the president, who is commander-in-chief of the armed forces, and the Ministry of Defense, which is headed by a civilian; three undersecretaries are also civilians. The joint staff, established in 1984, is directly under the Ministry of Defense and is staffed by officers of all services. The joint staff is an advisory and planning body with no operational or command responsibilities. The senior military officer of each of the armed services is the chief-of-staff. The paramilitary forces under the control of the Ministry of Defense are the Gendarmeria and the Naval Prefectura (Coast Guard).

Since the return of democratic government, the U.S. and Argentine armed forces have developed a growing, mutually beneficial defense relationship through an exten-sive range of contacts, including professional exchanges, visits, training, and joint exercises. There are modest international military education, training, and foreign military sales programs. Argentina has offered its Pampa trainer aircraft as a candidate for U.S. Air Force adoption. The Argentine armed forces also maintain defense cooperation and military supply relationships with a number of other countries, principally Israel, Germany, France, Spain, and Italy. The lack of budgetary resources is the most serious problem facing the Argentine armed forces.

Current economic conditions and the government's commitment to reduce public sector spending have slowed modernization and restructuring efforts.

Current Political Conditions

Argentina is going through a period of profound and rapid change, both politically and economically. On the political front, President Menem has worked hard to reassert Argentina as a respected member of the international community. The country has pursued improved political relations with its former adversaries, Chile, Brazil, and the United Kingdom. It also contributes troops to United Nations peace-keeping forces.

The Argentine public has enjoyed new levels of political participation, with five rounds of national balloting being held since the reestablishment of democratic government in 1983. The most recent of these occurred at the provincial and municipal levels in late 1991. Progressive candidates, supportive of the reform program spearheaded by President Menem, won in over 80 percent of the races. This indicates a fundamental realignment of political forces in the country.

The alternative to reform has become unpalatable to the average Argentine. Resistance could come from those who are losing lucrative privileges or from many who will have to find new jobs, as grossly overmanned enterprises and bureaucracies make painful but necessary reductions. On the whole, there is broad support for reform.

Foreign Relations

Argentina pursues a pragmatic foreign policy and maintains relations with almost all countries. Maintaining political sovereignty and encouraging trade and foreign investment in Argentina are major priorities. Relations traditionally have been closest with Western Europe and Latin American neighbors. President Menem is publicly committed to improving relations with the United States and Europe, while encouraging Latin American regional integration.

Having settled its Beagle Channel dispute with Chile in 1984–85, Argentina currently has only one active territorial dispute; this is with the United Kingdom over a group of islands some 480 miles northeast of Cape Horn. The Argentines refer to the islands as the "Malvinas Islands"; the British call them the "Falkland Islands."

Historically, European powers, notably Britain and Spain, made competing claims to sovereignty over the islands. In the early 1800s, Spanish and then Argentine authorities administered the islands. However, in January 1833, Britain reasserted sovereignty, and the islands first became a crown colony and later a self-governing dependency.

In an effort to establish its sovereignty claim, Argentine military forces occupied the islands on April 2, 1982. After a brief, costly war, the Argentine forces were defeated. Direct talks between Argentina and the UK began in September 1989 in an attempt to reestablish normal relations, which were severed following the Falklands/Malvinas conflict. The talks took place under a formula that separated the sovereignty question from discussions on bilateral relations. The two countries reestablished formal rela-

tions in February 1990. Argentina continues to press its sovereignty claim in a variety of forms. The United States has taken no position on the merits of the two countries' sovereignty claims.

U.S.-Argentine Relations

The United States and Argentina have maintained diplomatic relations since 1823. Both countries have sought a constructive relationship based on reciprocal respect and understanding, but bilateral relations often have been turbulent.

In the 1970s, U.S.-Argentine relations entered a particularly difficult period. Concerned about serious human rights violations by the Argentine military government in the campaign against terrorism, the United States restricted both military assistance and the sales of military and other controlled-export items to Argentina. Congress prohibited both military sales and assistance. Argentina consistently maintained that these actions were attempts to influence domestic politics. In the early 1980s, better relations seemed possible as Argentina demonstrated some improvements in human rights. The Falklands/Malvinas war, however, placed additional strains on bilateral relations. The U.S. position on the nonuse of force for the resolution of disputes led the United States to impose new sanctions on Argentina and to provide limited assistance to the United Kingdom in its campaign to regain the islands.

U.S.-Argentine relations improved after the Falklands/Malvinas war. Sanctions imposed during the fighting were lifted, and the United States supported Argentine-sponsored UN resolutions on the Falklands/Malvinas calling for renewed negotiations.

The Argentine human rights situation and political climate improved dramatically following the military's mid-1982 decision to return the country to democracy. During 1983, all remaining political prisoners being held without trial under state-of-siege powers were released.

Also in 1983, the nine-year-old state of siege was lifted, and restrictions on trade union activities and press censorship virtually ceased. Legal prohibitions on military sales were removed upon the inauguration of the democratically elected government of President Alfonsin in December 1983.

Argentina maintains its independent stance in world affairs but cooperates with the United States in resolving bilateral differences.

The countries consult regularly on hemispheric issues. Argentina's relatively advanced economy prompted the United States to phase out its bilateral economic assistance program in 1971, although some training assistance continues. While the program existed, the Agency for International Development (AID) and its predecessor agencies authorized development loans and grants to finance such projects as road building, housing, feasibility studies, and agriculture.

There are no Peace Corps volunteers in Argentina.

Many U.S. industrial firms and banks maintain subsidiaries in Argentina. Licensing agreements with local companies are common. U.S. private investment totals more than $2.6 billion (1991), primarily in manufacturing, chemicals, agricultural manufacturing, transportation equipment, and banking. Several thousand U.S. citizens reside in Argentina.

Trade

Major trading partners are the European Community (EC), the former Soviet Union (predominantly Russia), the U.S., and Brazil.

Principal U.S. Exports (1991):

1. Aircraft/associated equipment ($83 million)
2. Automatic data processing machines and units ($75M)
3. Parts for office and ADP machines ($65M)
4. Nitrogen function compounds ($42M)
5. Estimated low value shipments ($40M)

Principal U.S. Imports (1991):

1. Oil from petrol and bitum minerals ($246M)
2. Bovine or equine leather ($166M)
3. Prepared or preserved meat ($154M)
4. Fruit and vegetable juices ($83M)
5. Crude oil ($75M)

Trade and Investment Policies

Overall, the government has taken significant steps to open the economy to imports during the latter part of 1992.

Import licensing requirements have been removed. Most goods entering Argentina are taxed at one of three rates. A tariff of 22 percent is applied to most finished products, intermediate products are taxed at 13 percent, and raw materials enter at the rate of 5 percent. The average tariff has fallen from 22 percent early in 1991 to the current level of 11 percent.

The government is moving toward the removal of quantitative limits on imports. Imports of electronics goods face a price reference system, which is run by Argentine customs. While the system was designed to counter the practice of underinvoicing, it can also be used to value goods at an artificially high level. There is also a discriminatory tariff on the import of Spanish language books printed in non-Spanish speaking countries, although legislation has been introduced to remedy this situation.

Barriers to U.S. services: While there are plans to open the insurance sector, currently 60 percent of reinsurance must still be placed with the national reinsurance company. The insurance registry for new firms is closed, because the government determined the market was "saturated." Marine insurance for exports and imports is reserved for Argentine companies. U.S. airlines must pay high fees for poor ground handling services provided by a government-designated monopoly at Argentine airports. All public works projects must be insured by the government-owned insurance company. While U.S. banks are well represented in the local market and operate on the basis of national treatment, the establishment of a new bank is not a transparent process, leaving open the possibility of discrimination. Goods imported by the government or receiving special tariff exemptions had to be shipped on Argentine-flagged ships (or U.S. flag ships in our bilateral trade) until President Menem's omnibus deregulation decree of November 1, 1991. This decree and subsequent measures appear to have eliminated these cargo reserve requirements and are opening trucking and port services to private, competitive providers. Argentina's postal service (ENCOTEL) requires applicants for a domestic courier service license to make substantial investments. In addition ENCOTEL charges a high fee on outbound international courier shipments, although it did eliminate the fee on inbound shipments.

Investment barriers: The Argentine government has few restrictions on foreign investors, since the restrictions were reduced in 1989. Foreign investors enjoy national treatment in all sectors except air transportation, shipbuilding, nuclear energy, fishing,

and establishment in border areas. Even these sectors are not immune to policy reform and privatization; e.g., the government of Argentina in November 1991 sold the Tandanor shipyards to a Dutch-French consortium. The U.S. and Argentina signed a bilateral investment treaty on November 14, 1991. The treaty awaits ratification by both congresses.

Government procurement practices: The "Buy Argentine" restrictions have been modified. A preference for Argentine suppliers will be shown only when all other factors (price, quality, etc.) are equal.

Current Customs Regime

The administrative procedures for customs are extensive and time consuming, raising costs for importers.

Argentina has virtually removed all trade barriers and reduced the average tariff. Customs duties have now been set at five different levels, depending on the goods being imported; in general, these are 35 percent ad valorem for electronic equipment, 22 percent ad valorem in the case of consumer goods, 13 percent in the case of semiprocessed products and raw materials for industry. It is 5 percent for certain capital goods and some raw materials, and 0 percent mainly for capital goods for production purposes.

In general, products originating in LAFTA countries are entitled to preferential duty. The customs duty rates may be modified by the Ministry of Economy, which raises or lowers them in a general manner based on economic conditions and, particularly in the case of certain goods, taking into consideration international market prices and local needs. These changes have occurred frequently in the past.

In addition to customs duties, imports are also subject to the taxes totaling approximately 19 percent plus excise taxes for certain goods. The automotive industry is one of very few sectors still protected by import quotas and higher duties.

International Air Courier Tariff Rates

Argentina imposes a high and discriminatory tax on U.S. air couriers providing service to Argentina. The government of Argentina is committed to reducing the tax, but has yet to do so. The government promised to resolve this issue in May 1989. The Section 301 case originally filed in 1984 remains suspended, awaiting the implementation of the government's decision to rescind the discriminatory treatment.

Impact of "Mercosur" on U.S. Exports

Argentina is in the process of forming a common market—Mercosur—with Brazil, Paraguay, and Uruguay by 1995. Bi-annual automatic tariff reductions continue on schedule. Some sectors have moved ahead and are approaching zero. This has already hurt some U.S. exporters who cannot compete with shipping costs plus 11–22 percent duties. The effects of the movement towards a common market in the Southern Cone are already evident, with Brazil now Argentina's largest export market and exports to Paraguay and Uruguay also on the increase. The Mercosur may work to the advantage of U.S. companies which invest in production or license their products, due to the much larger market becoming available. Exporters may also be able to benefit by having one warehouse or stocking distributor instead of four. Eventually, the Mercosur countries are expected to negotiate a Free Trade Agreement with the United States. The most difficult hurdle for consolidating the Mercosur remains macroeconomic policy coordination. Brazilian inflation remains well above that of Argentina.

Policies to Attract New Business

On September 20, 1991, the United States and Argentina signed an agreement committing the Argentine government to the elimination of its few remaining subsidies for industrial exports.

Trade Financing Environment and Options

Basics of the import payment process: There are no government restrictions on payments for imports. Buyer and seller are free to decide terms.

Foreign exchange: The peso is freely convertible, and there are no limitations on foreign exchange. The government must back every peso with hard currency reserves, and the rate is fixed by law at one-to-one.

Payment schedules and deferred payment practices: None required by law.

Most new importers operate via letter of credit due to lack of financing and credit history. The cost of letters of credit is between 2 and 3 percent for first-class firms with a long established relationship with the bank. For other firms, generally smaller and new to the trade, the cost ranges from 4½ to 5 percent. Validity of the letter of credit is generally up to one year.

For the rest, buyers and sellers are limited only by their creativity.

Countertrade requirements: There are no statutory requirements.

Banking system correspondent relationships with U.S. banks: There are a number of major U.S. banks with subsidiaries, branches, or representatives in Argentina. Major Argentine banks also have representatives or correspondents in the U.S.

Local financing possibilities were still limited as of January 1993, but prospects were improving steadily. Credit has grown by over 50 percent since the enactment of the Convertibility Law, from $15.6 billion ($7.4 billion-equivalent in australes and $8.1 billion in dollars) in March 1991 to $23.6 billion ($11.5 billion in pesos and $12.1 billion in dollars) in March 1992. This growth of credit has brought the cost of financing down, and much has been channeled to the relatively new market of consumer credit, boosting demand for final goods still further. Banks are once again making limited consumer loans, but credit for long-term investment remains expensive and difficult to obtain for all but the blue-chip companies.

Sources of financing: Entry into the Brady Plan should make more commercial credits available. The U.S. Export-Import Bank is on cover for medium-term (5–7 years), private sector lending and short-term public lending. OPIC looks favorably on Argentina as a credit risk and has extensive insurance cover here, but has only limited funds available for loans. The World Bank and the Inter-American Development Bank are very active in Argentina.

APPROACHING THE MARKET

Commercial Environment

Argentina has become a model for Latin American economic reform. During the latter half of 1992, the initial successes of the April 1991 Convertibility Law have been consolidated, and other important advances in deregulation, opening the economy, and regularizing Argentina's financial situation have occurred.

President Carlos Menem and Economy Minister Domingo Cavallo continue their policies of extensive public sector reform, rapid privatization of state enterprises, and reliance on market forces.

Economic stability followed from the government's balancing its budget and maintaining confidence in the domestic currency (as of January 1, 1992, the peso). With its "Deregulation Decree" (enacted on October 31, 1991), the government has started unraveling the myriad regulations that favored select interests, distorted relative prices, and permitted corruption.

The benefits of the government's recent successes are readily apparent. Inflation in both retail and wholesale prices is down to levels not seen in Argentina for decades. Production and demand for labor are both growing. Argentines seem uniformly optimistic regarding the trends, and surveys show that political support for both Menem and Cavallo are high.

Higher domestic demand and lower tariffs have resulted in higher imports. A lower volume of agricultural exports at a higher average value will bring export revenues in 1992 close to those of 1991. In the capital account, income from new privatizations and other inflows of private capital will result in a continued growth in reserves. The recently announced Brady Plan agreement with the commercial banks was to be in effect by the end of 1992, "regularizing" Argentina's debt service payments and facilitating greater access to international capital markets.

A significant threat to sustained domestic demand is the persistent retail price inflation of 1–2 percent per month in the first quarter of 1992. This might be coming down, however; inflation in May 1992 fell below 1 percent. If price increases return to the 1–2 percent per month range, the government will be hard pressed to contain wage pressures and to eliminate structural inefficiencies fast enough to guarantee the continued competitiveness of Argentine tradeable goods.

The scope of the reform task facing Argentina should not be underestimated. Many impediments to sustainable growth still need to be overcome. The long list of "Argentine costs," those unique costs that make Argentine goods so uncompetitive internationally, need to be addressed. Although on the road to sustainable economic prosperity, Argentina's journey is by no means over.

Demand for Goods and Services

A burst of domestic demand has left local producers and importers scrambling to meet it. Industrial output is up around 30 percent over 1991's levels. Sales of cement—a good proxy for investment in plant and housing—are up 26 percent over the period February 1991/February 1992. Demand for labor in March 1992 is nearly three times that of March 1991. After declining in 1988–89 and holding near flat in 1990, GDP is growing in 1991–92 at a rate of over six percent. Pent-up demand for consumer goods has led to a surge of buying of both imports and domestically produced goods.

The strength of consumer demand is clearly evident in Table 1-1.

These higher figures of consumption do not infer a universally higher level of output, however. Many sectors that were once protected through import substitution schemes are simply not competitive in international terms.

Argentina's ports today are jammed with goods flowing in from low-cost producers abroad. For some—particularly for the metallurgic and petrochemical industries—survival is at stake.

The higher demand at home and the virtually across-the-board lowering of tariffs boosted imports in 1991 to double their 1990 level; in 1992, they may increase another 50 percent. On one hand, the "boom" in imports shows signs of reaching a plateau as salaries remain stable and modest available credits are used up. On the other hand, the government announced in late June further liberalization of two "sacred cows": automobiles and domestic electronics. Prices of electronics are expected to fall by 20 percent over the next three months, leading to a renewed surge of demand in this sector.

Implications for U.S. Exporters

The short- and medium-term opportunities for exporters are manifold for those willing to do the research and the market development. U.S. goods enjoy a high reputation here. Nearly 300,000 Argentines visited the United States during 1992 and came back loaded with purchases. The current value of the dollar vis-a-vis other major currencies makes our prices attractive.

Imports of capital goods have increased, but at a somewhat slower rate than other

Table 1-1
Sales of Consumer Goods
(thousands of units sold annually)

	1988	1989	1990	1991	1992
Washing machines	90	90	100	140	220
Video cassette recorders	215	154	140	320	420
Color televisions	481	320	330	550	900
Refrigerators	380	360	300	410	530
Automobiles	142	112	90	145	250

Source: Argentine Ministry of Economy (March 1993).

sectors. Despite the expectation for continued stability, most businessmen feel it is too early to invest in new productive capacity; many are only now reaching the limits of their installed capacity. The continuation of stability and the rise in demand will soon force domestic companies to invest in expansion and modernization or lose markets to imports. U.S. capital goods companies should use the interim to position themselves for sales. The Embassy also encourages U.S. services companies to explore opportunities in Argentina immediately.

Given the enormous changes occurring, there is uncertainty over just what the Argentine economy will look like in five years. Nevertheless, there is strong indication that the remarkable transformation of this economy is not a "flash in the pan." For example, this reform has lasted longer (2–3 years), has cut deeper (privatization of state enterprises), and enjoys broader public support (reformist candidates of all parties triumphed in the 1991 mid-term election) than previous reform plans. Furthermore, Argentina's reforms are consistent with a worldwide trend towards open markets and free enterprise, though few countries can boast of having moved so far so fast.

U.S. companies interested in exporting should take a good look at Argentina at once. This is the moment for many companies to get in on the ground floor of an economy with very impressive growth prospects over the next few years. The overall trends have not been so positive in the last 40 years. Waiting to see what will happen risks letting your competitors establish strong positions in a booming market before you enter.

INVESTMENT CLIMATE

Price Stability Results in Economic Growth

Monthly inflation has dropped dramatically,

Evolution of Installed Industrial Capacity
(in percentages)

	1991					
	Jan	Feb	Mar	Apr	May	June
Non-durable consumer products	52.8	50.7	55.6	61.1	59.9	50.6
Durable consumer products	30.5	14.5	31.8	50.3	56.2	49.6
Intermediate goods	67.7	60.0	69.2	67.7	70.4	72.9
Capital goods	36.0	3.7	26.4	36.9	45.1	43.8

Source: Instituto de Investigaciones Economicas (UADE).

	1992					
	Jan	Feb	Mar	Apr	May	June
Non-durable consumer products	81.8	62.7	65.1	64.2	64.5	66.4
Durable consumer products	82.6	29.3	86.8	96.9	94.1	102.5
Intermediate goods	61.8	62.7	68.2	71.1	68.4	71.9
Capital goods	51.9	33.5	76.0	70.3	74.3	72.4

Source: Instituto de Investigaciones Economicas (UADE).

Extent of U.S. Investment in Goods-Producing Sectors
U.S. Direct Investment Position Abroad on a Historical-Cost Basis—1990
(millions of U.S. dollars)

Category		Amount
Petroleum		437
Total manufacturing		1,566
Food and kindred products	345	
Chemicals and allied products	450	
Metals, primary and fabricated	110	
Machinery, except electrical	325	
Electric and electronic equipment	52	
Transportation equipment	−64	
Other manufacturing	348	
Wholesale trade		121
TOTAL PETROLEUM/MANUFACTURING/WHOLESALE TRADE		2,124

Source: U.S. Department of Commerce, Survey of Current Business, August 1991, vol. 71, no. 8, table 11.3.

to an increase in the Consumer Price Index (CPI) of only 10 percent over the six months ending May 31, 1992. The CPI increased by only 22 percent over the 12 months ending March 31, its lowest level of accumulated increase in almost 20 years. A virtually fixed exchange rate and the doubling of imports over the last year have helped limit the increase in wholesale prices to only three percent over the year ending May 1992.

The difference in the increase of prices at the retail and wholesale levels is partly due to the inclusion of services in the former and not in the latter. Services and other nontradeables have not been subject to increasing international competition. Their continued increase might be due to a residual inflationary mentality or even to a natural adjustment of their relative prices, which became distorted during hyperinflation. The presently high level of consumer demand also contributes to the continuing inflation.

Privatization Activities

The privatization process has already resulted in the sale of the national airlines, the telephone company, and a number of oil leases. Other utilities, more leases, and the state petroleum company itself will be sold in the near future. The substantial proceeds from the privatizations and the accumulation of arrears to the commercial banks equal to $8 billion are significant sources of financing for the public sector.

FINANCING AND CAPITAL MARKETS

General Policy Framework

Shortly after Menem took office in July 1989, during an acute economic crisis, the Congress passed two laws that cut the government's fiscal deficit and began the process of deregulation and privatization. In April 1991, the Congress passed the Convertibility Law, which introduced an exchange rate tightly linked to the U.S. dollar, and placed even greater emphasis on fiscal discipline. In October 1991, Menem signed a decree to remove the vestiges of the statist controls that have inhibited the Argentine economy, although implementation of this decree will take time. These four laws, and many other less dramatic actions, have succeeded in bringing inflation down to below 2 percent per month.

A deficit in the fiscal current account is due to continued deficits run by state enterprises (which are to be privatized) and to ongoing deficits in the social security system. These deficits are financed through a combination of the sale of state assets through privatization, borrowings from international financial institutions, and limited sales of sovereign bonds on the Eurobond market. The central government itself is running a slight surplus in its cash flow, due to the fact that it is not fully servicing its external debt to commercial banks.

Under the Convertibility Law, the government can only issue local currency that is fully backed by international reserves. Thus, the central bank controls the money supply by either buying or selling dollars.

Debt Management Policies

During the 1980s the federal government assumed the medium- and long-term external debt obligations of the private sector. Presently, 92 percent of the total debt is the responsibility of the public sector. The government has serviced its debt with the international financial institutions and has managed its obligations to official creditors through partial payments and four Paris Club reschedulings. It has, however, not fully serviced its commercial bank debt which has consequently generated some $7–8 billion in arrears. A Brady Plan-type restructuring of this commercial bank debt, involving both the arrears and some $25 billion in principal outstanding at end-1991, could occur in the future.

The International Monetary Fund (IMF) approved a stand-by agreement for Argentina in November 1989; however, a second bout of hyperinflation caused Argentina to fall short of negotiated targets, and the program was revised in May 1990. An IMF stand-by arrangement was again concluded in July 1991. Argentina is a major debtor country; foreign debt stands at about $60 billion. In June 1990, for the first time since April 1988, the government made an interest payment on its foreign commercial debt. Interest arrears on the debt are currently over $6 billion.

Argentina in July 1992 began negotiations for a three-year Extended Funding Facility. The World Bank has several policy-based loan programs approved and is disbursing against them.

Foreign debt servicing ability: The government has restructured its obligations under the Brady Plan rather like a balloon mortgage; i.e., with a single amortization payment in year 30. For the short and medium term, the government and other Argentine debtors should be able to meet their commitments.

External financing: IBRD and IDA— $887 million in FY 1989 (July 1, 1988–June 30, 1989); IDB—$12 million in CY 1989.

The Currency and Exchange Rate Mechanisms

Under the Convertibility Law, the central bank is required to sell dollars on demand at the exchange rate of 10,000 australes per one U.S. dollar. It has also chosen to buy dollars at the bottom of a 1 percent intervention range, thereby ensuring that the exchange rate never drops below 9,900 australes per one U.S. dollar. With the large inflow of foreign exchange from abroad attracted by the high return on financial instruments denominated in australes and the normal remonetization of the domestic economy following hyperinflationary periods, the market lately has tended to trade at the bottom of this range.

The fixed exchange rate and the differential in rates of inflation between Argentina and its trading partners, including the United States, has tended to make imports increasingly competitive in the domestic market.

Exchange rate developments: Over the long term, price increases of 1 or 2 percent a month are inconsistent with what is essentially a fixed exchange rate. Recent inflation has shown signs of falling below 1 percent, but efforts to cut the "Argentine costs" (that group of inefficiencies and laws that make production in Argentina so costly) have had only limited success.

The dollar has remained weak locally (due to the enormous inflows of capital from abroad) since April 1991, with only repeated Central Bank purchases keeping it within 1 percent of the fixed 1:1 parity. Right now, the market is betting on the government holding the rate at parity; but the market is watching everything closely, prepared to hedge its bets if the reform program shows signs of coming undone.

Foreign exchange reserves are very strong by historical standards and still growing, due principally to the inflow of dollars to purchase state-owned assets and Argentine equities and bonds.

Tapping International Aid Institutions

Both the International Bank for Reconstruction and Development—IBRD (World Bank) and the Inter-American Development Bank (IDB) have active programs in Argentina totaling over $3 billion. These cover a wide range of government projects in areas like public enterprise reform; tax modernization; social security reform; health development; and specific projects such as electric power generation, hydrocarbon engineering, and others.

Contact points in the U.S. Department of Commerce for both banks are:

- World Bank: Janice Mazur, Trade Development Office
  Tel: (202) 482-1246
- IDB: Michelle Miller, Trade Development Office
  Tel: (202) 482-1246

Financial Market Operations and Structural Policies

Argentina is still in the early phase of what will likely be a long and difficult process of structural reform. The problem of "Argentine costs," those unique costs that have made Argentine goods uncompetitive in the face of international competition, is being addressed but has not been eliminated. This process of reform will likely encourage imports from the United States and elsewhere, as companies invest in capital goods to remain competitive and consume larger amounts of inputs to meet rising demand both at home and abroad. Companies should also import more finished goods to satisfy rising effective demand at home.

Few prices remain in Argentina that are not set by market forces. Present trends, if continued, will be for the government to provide fewer subsidies and to lift controls, leaving increasingly fewer regulated prices; controls will likely remain, however, on prices where market imperfections exist (such as natural monopolies).

The government is forced by prevalent evasion and inefficient tax administration to focus principally on taxes that are easily collected.

Thus, it has come increasingly to rely on the value-added tax and other taxes on consumption, as well as import tariffs for revenue. It recently eliminated the last export tax, in part to make up for the appreciation pressures resulting from the inflation differentials.

VISITING AND LOCATING

General Travel Checklist

Visas: Visas are not required of U.S. citizens entering Argentina for tourism for periods up to 90 days. Visas are required for visits to Argentina for all other purposes.

Currency: On January 1, 1992, the austral was replaced by the peso at a conversion rate of 10,000 australes to one peso.

Climate and clothing: Climate ranges from the hot, subtropical lowlands of the north to cold and rainy Tierra del Fuego in the south.

The seasons are reversed: The weather in January in Buenos Aires is like July in Washington, D.C.; weather in July is similar to that of San Francisco in January.

Health: Competent doctors, dentists, and specialists are available in Buenos Aires. No particular health risks exist, and no special precautions are required. Tap water is safe.

Transportation: Buenos Aires' Ezeiza Airport is serviced by many international carriers, with flights originating in the U.S., Europe, and Latin American cities. Buenos Aires has an extensive subway and bus system. Taxis are plentiful. Outside Buenos Aires, travel by train, air, bus, or auto.

Time zones: Argentina is one hour later than U.S. Eastern Standard Time (EST). Daylight savings time is observed from October to April, during which time clocks are set one hour ahead.

Telecommunications: International services are adequate; however, long delays in placing international calls may occur due to the overburdened system. Most provincial cities and Uruguay also can be dialed directly from home and business phones.

Chapter 2
THE BAHAMAS

	Total	Urban	
Population (1993)	259,000	75.0%	

Main Urban Areas	Population	Percentage of Total	International Calling Code
NASSAU	135,000	52.1	809
Freeport	24,000	9.2	809

Land Area	10,070 square kilometers
Comparable U.S. State	Slightly larger than Connecticut
Language	Creole English 85% Creole French 15%
Common Business Language	English
Currency	1 dollar (B$) = 100 cents
Exchange Rate (May 1993)	US$ 1.00 = 0.97 dollar
Best Nonstop Air Connection via U.S.	Miami to Nassau: 1 hour American Airlines: (800) 433-7300 Nonstop every hour on the hour
Best Hotel	Sheraton Grand (US$150) P.O. Box SS 6307 Casino Drive Paradise Island Tel (809) 326-2011 (305) 444-3636 (800) 334-8484

INTRODUCTION AND REGIONAL ORIENTATION

The Bahamas islands are the second most popular foreign destination for American tourists, owing to their Caribbean tropical allure, proximity to the U.S. (one hour flight from Miami), and value.

The Bahamas has much to offer the potential investor: a stable democratic environment, relief from personal and corporate income taxes, timely repatriation of profits, proximity to the United States, extensive air links, good communications networks, designation under the Caribbean Basin Initiative (CBI), and a ready pool of skilled professionals. However, excessive government red tape continues to deter some investors.

More than 75 percent of the population of the Bahamas lives on either New Providence or Grand Bahama. Eighty-five percent of Bahamians are of African descent. Many of their ancestors arrived in the Bahamas when it was a staging area for the slave trade or were brought there by the thousands of British loyalists who fled the American colonies during the Revolutionary War.

Education is compulsory between ages 5 and 14. Of the 225 schools, 187 (83 percent) are fully maintained by the government; the rest are private. In 1985, enrollment for state and private primary, grammar, and secondary schools was 60,744.

The College of the Bahamas, established in Nassau in 1974, provides two or three-year programs leading to an associate of arts degree in seven academic divisions. Several college programs are offered in cooperation with the Universities of Miami and of the West Indies.

Geographical Background

Located immediately off the eastern coast of Miami, the islands' combined land mass is slightly larger than New Jersey and Connecticut combined. The Bahamas is also a popular destination for cruise ships departing from New York and Miami, as well as a popular site for off-shore conferences and conventions.

History and Political Conditions

Christopher Columbus discovered the Bahamas in 1492, when he first landed in the Western Hemisphere. The islands became a British crown colony in 1717. The first royal governor was Captain Woodes Rogers, an ex-pirate who brought law and order to the Bahamas in 1718 by expelling the buccaneers who had used the islands as hideouts. During the American Civil War, the Bahamas prospered as a center of Confederate blockade-running. The islands served as a base for American prohibition rumrunners after World War I. World War II Allied flight training and antisubmarine operations in the Caribbean were centered in the Bahamas. Since the war, the Bahamas has become a major tourist and banking center.

Bahamians achieved self-government through a series of constitutional and political steps, culminating in independence on July 10, 1973.

CRACKING THE MARKET

Demographics

Ethnic groups: Black African 85%; European 15%.

Religions: Baptist, Anglican, Roman Catholic, Methodist.

Literacy rate: 93%.

Work force—124,320 (1988): Majority employed in government, hotel and restaurant, and financial sectors.

Economy

The Bahamas is a politically stable, middle-income developing country. The economy is based on tourism and financial services, which account for approximately 60 percent and 10 percent of Gross Domestic Product (GDP) respectively. The Bahamas was a vacation destination for over 3.6 million tourists in 1991, 83 percent from the United States. Nearly 400 banks and trusts were licensed and over 10,000 offshore companies registered in the Bahamas as of mid-

1992. The agricultural and industrial sectors, while small, have recently been the focus of government efforts to produce economic growth and diversification in the economy.

The Bahamian economy grew at an average rate of 3 percent annually during the 1980s, due largely to continued development in the tourism industry. Per capita income, estimated at U.S. $10,000 in 1991, was among the highest in the Caribbean region. The U.S. recession of 1990–91 and the drop of tourism resulting from the Persian Gulf conflict in 1991 slowed the Bahamian economy. The unofficial inflation rate exceeded 9 percent in 1991, due largely to increased import duties.

The United States remains the Bahamas' major trading partner. U.S. firms exported over U.S. $750 million worth of goods and services to the Bahamas in 1991.

U.S. goods are preferred because of quality, savings in transportation costs, and suitability for the tourist market. The 254,685 Bahamians (1990 figures) living on the 29 inhabited islands of the Bahamian Archipelago import nearly all foodstuffs and manufactured goods.

The Bahamian government actively encourages foreign investment, with free trade zones in Grand Bahama and New Providence. Capital and profits are freely repatriated, and investors are free from personal and corporate income taxes. The government of the Bahamas is committed to maintaining parity between the Bahamian and U.S. dollars. Designation under the Caribbean Basin Initiative (CBI) trade program allows qualified Bahamian goods to enter the United States duty-free.

The Bahamas 1992 recurrent budget totaled U.S. $627.5 million, an increase of U.S. $27.5 million (4.5 percent) over 1991. The budget reflected continuing government priorities on education, health, police, and tourism. The Bahamas continues to run a fiscal deficit due to investment in capital projects by the government and public corporations. Deficits are financed through bond issues, treasury bills, short-term advances from the banking system, and Central Bank financing. The government was forced to implement emergency tax and borrowing measures in November 1991 needed to cover a U.S. $96 million revenue shortfall, however. Austerity measures remain in force, including limiting capital expenditures to projects approved directly by the Ministry of Finance. Total 1991 national debt was in excess of U.S. $1 billion.

Tourism

Tourism provides an estimated 60 percent of GDP and employs 127,000. In 1991 a total of 3.6 million tourists (83 percent from the United States) visited the Bahamas. Total tourist expenditures were an estimated 1.08 billion during 1991. The main tourism centers are New Providence, including the capital of Nassau and Paradise Island, and Grand Bahama, whose main city is Freeport. The number of hotel rooms in the Bahamas increased to 13,165 in 1991, and the average length of stay of stopovers reached 6.2 nights.

Cruise ship traffic to the Bahamas has increased considerably in recent years. Cruise ship calls increased by 1.4 percent in 1991 to 2,372, and nearly half were to Nassau. In 1990, the government began extensive harbor improvement projects for the Family Islands and Nassau Harbor; the harbor can now accommodate up to 13 cruise ships.

However, tourism revenue dropped by an estimated 15 percent in 1991, in large part due to the U.S. recession and the Persian Gulf War; total visitor nights fell by 3.5 percent. Most of the luxury hotels in New Providence experienced financial difficulties. Over 3,000 hotel employees lost their jobs in 1991 as hotels sought to cut operating expenses. Hotel occupancy rates averaged approximately 50 percent for the year (a 65 percent rate is needed by most hotels to break even). At least four of the Bahamas' major hotels—Carnival's Crystal Palace, Resorts International, the Lucaya Beach, and Princess Resort and Casino—are currently up for sale.

Delta Airlines, American Eagle, and US Air are among the U.S. airlines offering scheduled service to the Bahamas. BahamasAir, the national flag carrier, flies to the United States and among the Bahamian Islands. The government is completing a $58 million refurbishing and expansion project at Nassau International Airport. Five airlines suspended service to the Bahamas in 1991: British Airways, Eastern, Midway, US Air Express, and Pan Am Express. TWA Express ceased operation in 1992.

In an effort to increase tourist arrivals, the government has concluded a series of "package" agreements to bring in visitors from Canada and Europe, which together account for 13 percent of tourist traffic to the Bahamas.

Financial Services

The Bahamas' status as a tax haven and its bank secrecy laws make financial services the second leading economic sector. There are 399 banks and trust companies licensed in the Bahamas in 1992, in addition to six major retail banks and several mortgage institutions. Nassau is also home to several investment companies and mutual funds. The financial sector accounted for nearly 10 percent GDP in 1991 and employs 3,300 people, 95 percent of whom are Bahamian.

The Bahamas promulgated the International Business Companies (IBC) Act in January 1990 to simplify and reduce the cost of incorporating offshore companies in the Bahamas. The act was one of several measures to make the Bahamas more competitive in offshore finance. As of mid-1992, over 10,000 IBC-type companies have been established. In February 1991, the House of Assembly passed a measure to allow the establishment of asset protection trusts.

Legislation to refine insurance regulation and enhance local capital markets is also being drafted.

Manufacturing/Industrial

This sector accounted for 3 percent of GDP in 1991, and merchandise exports totaled an estimated U.S. $306.1 million. Under the Caribbean Basin Initiative (CBI), approved products manufactured in the Bahamas qualify for duty-free entry into the United States. Two large chemical companies in Freeport and several citrus growers on Abaco are among the businesses currently exporting under CBI. With no Tax Information Exchange Agreement (TIEA) in place, however, the Bahamas doesn't qualify for 936 (QPSII) funds under CBI. The Canadian government offers similar trade incentives under the CARIBCAN office. Under the Lome IV Convention, a wide range of goods manufactured in the Bahamas may be imported in the European Community duty-free.

Agriculture/Fisheries

These sectors account for 5 percent of GDP and employ 5 percent of the labor force in 1991. Agricultural output totalled $18.5 million in 1991, with an additional $51 million in fisheries exports. The fact that the Bahamas imports over $250 million in foodstuffs each year (80 percent of its food consumption) has led the government to look to these sectors to reduce imports and generate foreign exchange.

There are approximately 240,000 acres of prime agricultural land which remain uncultivated. The primary agricultural islands are Abaco, Andros, Eleuthera, and Grand Bahama. The Bahamian Department of Agriculture has identified areas as potentially the most profitable for investors: beef cattle and pork production and processing, tree food crops, dairy production and processing, winter vegetables, aquaculture, and mariculture. Recognizing the potential of fisheries, the government has plans to develop aquaculture/mariculture into a U.S. $150 million annual business employing 15,000 people over the next decade. Training programs on the fisheries industry are being conducted for Bahamian fishermen and the Ministry of Education will soon introduce "Fisheries" as a topic in the school syllabus. Fish and shrimp farms currently in operation are located in Long Island, Grand Bahama, and in Nassau.

Current country figures for meat production are not available. Meat production in New Providence (Nassau) totaled over 207,000 pounds in 1991. Production of broiler chickens reached 10.7 million pounds in 1991. The Bahamian government moved to protect local poultry producers by imposing a ban on foreign chicken December 4, 1991. This restriction potentially shuts down an annual U.S. $3.5 million market for U.S. poultry producers. Local egg production totalled 4.2 million dozen in 1991, an increase of 3.1 percent over 1990.

Construction

Activity in this sector, which recently accounted for approximately ten percent of GDP, declined in 1991. The value of construction projects undertaken in Nassau fell from U.S. $399.3 million in 1990 to U.S. $251.6 million in 1991. Value of actual construction starts fell from U.S. $335 million in 1990 to U.S. $130.6 million in 1991. The U.S. $58 million expansion of terminal and ancillary facilities at Nassau International Airport is expected to be completed in late 1992. Work was to begin in the fall of 1992 on a new airport on the island of San Salvador. While work continues on Family Islands' electrification and road projects, government funds are tight and only U.S. $100 million was allocated in the 1992 budget for capital development.

Current Economic Situation

Despite optimism that 1992 would be a banner year because of celebrations related to the Quincentennial anniversary of Columbus's encounter with the New World, the government and private sector tourism interests have failed to tap the potential market through a comprehensive advertising campaign. Instead, the focus has been on promoting the Bahamas as a duty-free shopping destination. The 1992 budget abolished customs duties on luxury items normally purchased by tourists.

The government has been attempting to diversify the economy and attract new industries but with little success. The Industries Encouragement Act offers manufacturers relief from import duties and taxes. Tourism, however, remains the major industry, and the Bahamas is affected by the cyclical influences of the U.S. economy.

The United States, from which most food and manufactured goods are imported, is the Bahamas' most important trading partner. Principal Bahamian exports to the United States are pharmaceuticals (hormones), petroleum products, rum, crawfish, and salt. Developing industries include fish farming, citrus growing, and tropical fruits. The Bahamas benefits from being below the frost belt and having no agricultural pests not already present in Florida, permitting certification of fruit exports to the U.S. market.

Political/Institutional Infrastructure

The Commonwealth of the Bahamas is an independent commonwealth, with executive authority vested in the British monarch. Independence from the United Kingdom was achieved on July 10, 1973. The current constitution was adopted on that same date.

THE BAHAMAS
Key Economic Indicators

	1989	1990	1991
Income, Production and Employment (Millions of U.S. Dollars)			
Real GDP	2,497	2,522	N/A
GDP growth rate	2.0	1.0	N/A
GDP by sector (% of total):			
Tourism	50.0	60.0	N/A
Finance	8.0	10.0	N/A
Manufacturing	1.4	3.0	N/A
Agriculture	4.0	5.0	N/A
GDP per capita (U.S. dollars)	9,987	9,902	N/A
Labor force	127,400	N/A	N/A
Unemployment rate (%)	12.4	14.0	16.0
Money and Prices			
Money supply (M1)	300.7	328.4	324.6
Commercial interest rate (%)	9.0	9.0	9.0
Savings rate	N/A	N/A	N/A
Investment rate	N/A	N/A	N/A
Consumer price index	112.6	120.4	129.0
Consumer price index (% change)	4.4	6.9	7.3
Wholesale price index	N/A	N/A	N/A
Exchange rate (U.S. $:B$)	1:1	1:1	1:1
Balance of Payments and Trade			
Total exports FOB	2,567.4	2,813.5	N/A
Nonoil (est)	250.1	287.8	N/A
Exports to U.S.	462.2	506.1	550.3
Total imports CIF	3,005.2	3,022.5	N/A
Nonoil (est)	1,109.3	1,036.2	N/A
Imports from U.S.	773.3	800.7	750.0
Aid from U.S.	0	0	0
Aid from other countries	0	0	0
External public debt	151.5	188.2	201.5
Debt repayment	55.4	51.0	60.3
Gold reserves	N/A	N/A	N/A
Foreign exchange reserves	146.9	159.5	170.1
Balance of payments			
Current account	−170.6	−180.1	−183.0
Merchandise exports FOB	259.6	281.3	306.1
Merchandise imports CIF	1,151.9	1,131.5	1,142.2
Services (net)	650.8	701.6	727.4

Source: American Embassy Nassau.

The Bahamas is a multiparty parliamentary democracy with regular elections. As a Commonwealth country, its political and legal traditions are similar to those of the United Kingdom. The British monarch is still recognized as the head of state, and an appointed governor general is the Queen's representative in the Bahamas. Laws under the 1973 Bahamian constitution are enacted by a bicameral parliament.

The House of Assembly consists of 49 members elected from each constituency for five-year terms. As under the British system, elections may be called at any time. The House performs all major legislative functions.

The leader of the majority party serves as prime minister and head of government. The Cabinet, composed of the prime minister and at least nine other ministers of executive departments, is answerable to the House.

The Senate is an appointive body with limited functions. It comprises 16 members appointed by the governor general, 9 on the advice of the prime minister, 4 at the recommendation of the leader of the opposition in the House, and 3 with the advice of the prime minister after consultations with the opposition leader.

The Progressive Liberal Party (PLP), headed by Prime Minister Sir Lynden O. Pindling, controls the Bahamas' politically stable government. The PLP won 31 of the 49 parliamentary seats in the June 1987 general election.

The PLP was formed in 1953 by blacks discontented with the policies of a group of white businessmen, the "Bay Street Boys," who had controlled the political and economic life of the Bahamas for decades. The PLP first came to power in 1967. The "Bay Street Boys" have been replaced by the "Sunshine Group," although the latter are not as prominent in the political arena.

The Free National Movement (FNM) was created in 1971 by a coalition of the former members of the defunct, white-dominated United Bahamian Party and PLP dissidents. The FNM has 16 seats in the House of Assembly and is recognized officially as the opposition party.

The only other party in the Bahamas is the left-of-center Vanguard Party, which carries no weight in Bahamian politics and has no representatives in parliament.

The chief justice of the Supreme Court is appointed by the governor general on the advice of the prime minister and the leader of the opposition. Other justices are appointed by the governor general with the advice of a judicial commission.

The Family Islands (all those other than New Providence) are administered internally by local commissioners appointed by the government and supervised from Nassau.

Suffrage: Universal over 18; 84,235 registered voters in 1982; about 100,000 in 1987.

Central government revenue (1990 estimate): $581,500,000.

Flag: Black equilateral triangle on stripes of aquamarine and gold, representing land, sea, and sun.

Fiscal year: Calendar year.

Principal Government Officials

Acting Governor General
Sir Henry M. Taylor

Prime Minister and Minister of Finance
Sir Lynden O. Pindling

*Deputy Prime Minister
and Minister of Tourism*
Clement T. Maynard

Minister of Foreign Affairs
E. Charles Carter

Minister of Employment and Immigration
Alfred T. Maycock

*Minister of National Security
and Minister of Education*
Paul L. Adderley

Attorney General
Sean G. A. McWeeney

Minister of Works and Utilities
Darrell E. Rolle

Minister of Health
Norman R. Gay

Minister of Transport,
Minister of Civil Aviation,
and Minister of Local Government
Philip M. Bethel

Minister of Consumer Affairs
Bernard Nottage

Minister of Agriculture, Trade, and Industry
Perry Christie

Minister of Youth, Sports, and Community
Affairs
Peter J. Bethel

Minister of Housing and National Insurance
George W. Mackey

Ambassador to the United States
and Organization of American States
Margaret McDonald

Ambassador to the United Nations
James Multrie

Consul General, Miami
Winston Munnings

Defense

National defense, which includes mostly civilian police forces, accounts for about 11 percent of the government budget (1990 estimate).

Foreign Relations

Foreign affairs are handled by the Ministry of Foreign Affairs. The Commonwealth of the Bahamas became a member of the United Nations in 1973 and the Organization of American States in 1982. The Bahamas has a high commissioner in London and an ambassador in Ottawa.

U.S.-Bahamian Relations

The United States historically has had close economic and trade relations with the Bahamas. The two countries cooperate on meteorology, civil aviation, maritime safety, law enforcement, and agricultural matters. Ethnic and cultural ties, especially in education and sports, are especially strong.

The U.S. Navy and Air Force operate facilities for underwater research, missile tracking, and aids to navigation on Andros and Grand Bahama.

The U.S. preclearance facilities (U.S. Customs, Immigration, and Agriculture) for travelers to the United States operate at the international airports in Nassau and Freeport.

Trade

U.S.-Bahamian trade: The United States is the Bahamas' major trading partner, with U.S. firms exporting $750 million in goods and services to the Bahamas in 1991. American goods are preferred due to quality, savings in transportation costs, and suitability for the tourist market. The Bahamian dollar is traded on par with the U.S. dollar.

Import/export opportunities: The best prospects for U.S. exports to the Bahamas continue to be in foodstuffs, manufactured goods, vehicles and automobile parts, hotel, restaurant, and medical supplies, computers and consumer electronics, petroleum products, and chemicals. In 1991, Bahamian exports to the United States totaled 465.3 million. Bahamian exports to the United States included pharmaceuticals, rum, crawfish, salt, and petroleum products.

Balance of payments and trade: The Bahamas is an import economy and relies on tourism for foreign exchange. The balance of payments fell by $53 million in 1991 and increased the deficit to $238 million. Merchandise exports, however, increased to an estimated $306 million for 1991. Foreign reserves at year end were estimated at $170 million, as banks imported funds to boost reserves.

Trade (1988)

Nonoil exports—$1 billion: salt, aragonite, timber, beverages, chemicals. Oil exports— $2.3 billion.

Major markets: U.S., UK, other EC countries, Canada.

Imports—$1.6 billion: manufactured goods, oil, chemicals, machinery and transport equipment, food, live animals, beverages, tobacco. Major suppliers—U.S., UK, other EC countries, Canada.

Official exchange rate: 1 Bahamian dollar = U.S. $1.

Trade and Investment Policies

Caribbean Basin Initiative: The Bahamas was designated a beneficiary of the Caribbean Basin Initiative (CBI) in 1985. Products manufactured in the Bahamas qualify for duty-free entry into the United States. However, the Bahamas' high wage rates, coupled with small agricultural and manufacturing sectors, have made it difficult to exploit these benefits under CBI.

The government's principal source of revenue is customs duties, which range from 1 to 200 percent. The Tariff Act provides sliding scales of duties which favor development of the tourism industry and Bahamian-financed investment projects. The CY 1992 budget extended protection to local industries by increasing duties 15–60 percent on imported items such as paint, bottled water, bleach, and juices. The 1991 budget also increased tariffs up to 40 percent on many of these same items. In addition, the Bahamian government banned the importation of foreign chicken effective December 4, 1991. The budget also implemented a provision to repeal Section 7 of the Tariff Act, which

allows producers in Freeport, Grand Bahama to export duty-free to the rest of the Bahamas.

Import Situation

The United States is the Bahamas' major trading partner, with U.S. firms exporting over U.S. $773 million worth of goods and services to the Bahamas in 1989. U.S. exports reached U.S. $800 million in 1990, but slipped to U.S. $750 million in 1991, reflecting the economic slump and Bahamian government policies aimed at import substitution and restricting credit. With the exception of the recent ban on foreign-produced chicken, there are no barriers to U.S. imports. A substantial duty is levied on most imported products, however. Customs duties generate nearly 70 percent of government income. Since the previous two budgets included tariff increases aimed at protecting local industries, diversification into the agricultural and manufacturing sectors may signify a smaller market share for U.S. producers. Bahamian regional trade remains small, with CARICOM exports to the Bahamas totaling only $3.7 million in 1990. Total Bahamas-CARICOM trade in 1990 amounted to U.S. $16.3 million (no new figures are available).

Policies to Attract New Businesses

In October 1991, the government implemented legislation to attract and promote investment. The Investment Incentives Act (IIA) divides the Bahamas into four economic zones for the purposes of development. The act simplifies the foreign investment approval process and provides that approved developers are eligible for duty exemptions on supplies for manufacturing and administrative purposes. It also grants exemption from real property tax and license fees over a scheduled period.

Other trade and investment incentives

include the International Business Companies Act, the Industries Encouragement Act, the Hotels Encouragement Act, the Agricultural Manufactories Act, the Spirit and Beer Manufacture Act, and the Tariff Act. The International Business Companies Act simplifies procedures and reduces costs for incorporating companies.

The Industries Encouragement Act provides duty exemption on machinery, equipment, and raw materials used for manufacturing purposes. The Hotels Encouragement Act grants refunds of duty on materials, equipment, and furniture required in construction or furnishing of hotels.

The Agricultural Manufactories Act provides exemption for farmers from duties on agricultural imports and machinery necessary for food production. The Spirit and Beer Manufacture Act grants duty exemptions for producers of beer or distilled spirits on imported raw materials, machinery, tools, equipment, and supplies used in production. The Tariff Act grants one-time relief from duties on imports of selected products deemed to be of national interest. The newly implemented investment promotion program for the twenty-first century is designed to attract individuals and groups of persons with special skills who will establish enterprises offering employment and joint venture business opportunities for Bahamians. It provides permanent residence status to investors who meet its terms.

Under the Hawksbill Creek Agreement, most of the area within Freeport on Grand Bahama island has been designated a free trade zone. Investors are guaranteed exemption from any income, capital gains, real estate, property, emergency, and stamp taxes, and customs duties on imports to be used in their businesses. In the Freeport free zone, tax and duty-free storage of goods is granted, as well as transshipment, manufacturing, processing, and warehousing activities. This agreement was to expire in 1992.

Although the Bahamas encourages foreign investment, specific businesses are reserved exclusively for Bahamians and others for joint ventures which include Bahamian owners.

APPROACHING THE MARKET

Commercial Environment

The Bahamas continues to be a lucrative market for U.S. producers, since U.S. goods are preferred because of quality, savings in transportation costs, and suitability for the tourist market (85 percent of which is comprised of tourists from the United States). The 255,000 Bahamians living on the 29 inhabited islands of the Bahamian archipelago import nearly all foodstuffs and manufactured goods. Geographical proximity to the United States and a Bahamian dollar traded on par with the U.S. dollar helped to make the Bahamas a vacation destination for some 3 million U.S. tourists in 1990.

Despite optimism that 1992 would be a banner tourist year because of the Quincentennial anniversary of Columbus's encounter with the new world, the only new hotel projects are a Club Med Resort on San Salvador Island and the 150-room Comfort Suites on Paradise Island. To attract more visitors and boost the image of the Bahamas as a duty-free shopping destination, the 1992 budget abolished customs duties on luxury items usually purchased by tourists. A U.S. $58 million upgrading and expansion project of Nassau International Airport was expected to be completed in 1992.

The Bahamian government has also focused attention on expanding the cruise ship industry, with harbor expansion projects underway on several Family Islands. Cruise ship calls to Bahamian ports increased by 1.4 percent in 1991 to a total of 2,372. Nearly half of these calls (1,059) were to Nassau. Freeport, with 975 visits, was the next destination of choice. In order to increase government revenues from this traffic, the 1992 budget raised the departure tax for the estimated 2.1 million cruise ship visitors from U.S. $13 to U.S. $20 per person.

The unofficial inflation rate exceeded 9 percent in 1991, compared to 7.2 percent in 1990. The increase was due largely to increased duties on foodstuffs and a host of other items. Emergency tax and borrowing measures were instituted in November 1991 to cover a U.S. $96 million government revenue shortfall. The Bahamas' primary monetary consideration continues to be foreign exchange reserves, needed to purchase essential imports and finance the repatriation of corporate profits. Profits and investment capital may be freely repatriated once the foreign investor or nonresident receives approval from the Central Bank. Liquidity constraints dating from 1987 are still in force in order to maintain a desired level of foreign reserves. Bank lending came to a virtual halt in 1991 and the government advised Bahamians to institute savings programs.

Demand for Goods and Services

Exporters should realize that a country population of approximately 1/4 million people does not represent a substantial export market. While the Bahamian government encourages new industries such as agriculture/fisheries and manufactures, tourism will remain the dominant sector for years to come.

Implications for U.S. Exporters

Exporters to the Bahamas should be aware of the unusual business climate of the country. The majority of exports to the region will not be marketed toward the Bahamians, but the tourists vacationing there. Therefore, any market strategy should include servicing these tourists. Products demanded to facili-

tate their short stay abroad are the primary marketable good. These products may range from hotel restaurant equipment to sunglasses. Exports in goods and services for U.S. citizens, who comprise the majority of the tourists, will be highly receptive in the Bahamian market.

Export Subsidies Policies

The Bahamian government does not provide direct subsidies to industry. The export manufacturing Industries Encouragement Act provides exemptions to approved export manufacturers from duty for raw materials, machinery, and equipment, and the approved product is not subject to any export tax.

Leading Trade Opportunities

Because of its proximity to the Bahamas, the United States is the principal source for imports to the country which include such items as foodstuffs, clothing, dry goods, motor vehicles, building supplies, hardware, and general merchandise of every description, both for local consumption and in support of the tourist, commercial, and industrial sectors. The best prospects for U.S. exports remain food, manufactured goods, machinery, petroleum products, and chemicals. The United States likewise consumes over half of Bahamian exports. The Bahamas exports to the United States include spiny lobster, pharmaceutical products, rum, salt, and aragonite.

Although there are customs duties on virtually all imported products, competition for U.S. exporters is low.

The following sectors are ranked according to market strength:

(1) Foodstuffs and Manufactured Goods

The Bahamas will continue to represent an excellent opportunity for U.S. food exporters. According to current estimates, the Bahamas' annual food consumption is $250 million, 80 percent of which is imported. U.S. foods exports account for about $170 million of this total.

Most promising subsectors: Meats, fruits, and vegetables, food preparations, juices, rice, and breads.

(2) Automobiles and Parts

High customs duty (45–60) is the only trade barrier to the importation of automobiles. There are approximately 39 auto repair shops and dealers on New Providence alone. U.S. car parts are easier to obtain than non-U.S.-made cars and parts.

Most promising subsectors: Tires, paints and air brushing equipment, body repair materials, prefab auto shop, rust proofing equipment, and Japanese car parts.

(3) Hotel and Restaurant Equipment

The dominant tourist sector furnishes a steady demand for these manufactures. There are over 13,000 hotel rooms in the Bahamas.

Most promising subsectors: Kitchen appliances, linen, bulk wholesale food items.

(4) Computers and Electronics

The government's emphasis on expanding the manufacturing sector includes the need for new technology from developed countries. The nearly 400 banks and trust companies in the Bahamas are continually upgrading equipment, as are the public corporations. Many Bahamian technicians and managers are trained in the United States and are familiar with U.S. products and standards.

Possible privatization of national air carrier, BahamasAir, Bahamas Electric Corporation, and Bahamas Telecommunication Corporation may signal increased opportunities for U.S. exporters.

Most promising subsectors: Data processing equipment, automatic teller machines, computerized cash registers.

(5) Discount Items

Discount items may be the market of the future in the Bahamas. Because of high import duties, many Bahamians shop in southern Florida for common items.

Bahamians spend an estimated U.S. $60 million in southern Florida each year. Locally available discount items may attract those who are unable to travel to the United States to shop.

Most promising subsectors: Baby products, including diapers, generic toiletries, and cleaning products.

INVESTMENT CLIMATE

Price Stability

The rate of inflation was estimated at 9 percent in 1991, up from 7.2 percent in 1990. While current unemployment figures are not available, it is estimated that unemployment runs between 20 and 25 percent. It is slightly higher in Nassau and among youth. There are an estimated 127,500 workers in the Bahamas.

Extent of U.S. Investment in Goods-Producing Sectors

Investment: The Bahamian government actively encourages foreign investment, particularly in tourism and banking, but more recently the focus has been on the agricultural and manufacturing sectors. Certain businesses are reserved exclusively for Bahamians, however. Restaurants, construction, and small hotels are all reserved businesses. Other categories of businesses are designated for possible joint ventures between Bahamians and foreigners.

Investment benefits include political stability, proximity to the United States with air links to the United States and Canada, absence of personal or corporate income taxes, designation for duty-free entry of goods under CBI, sophisticated financial services and good communications networks, and easy repatriation of profits. However, some foreign investors have seen their proposals become wrapped up in red tape.

Investment promotion: In October 1991, the government implemented the Investment Incentives Act, which simplifies the foreign investment approval process and provides that approved developers are eligible for duty exemptions on manufacturing and administrative supplies. The Industries Encouragement Act provides duty exemptions on machinery, equipment, and raw materials used for manufacturing. The Agricultural Manufactories Act provides exemptions from import duties on agricultural imports and machinery used for food production. The Hotels Encouragement Act grants refunds of import duties on hotel construction materials and furnishings. In addition, the Investment Promotion Program for the Twenty-First Century (IPP) grants permanent residence status to investors who establish enterprises offering employment and joint venture opportunities to Bahamians. The Bahamas Agricultural and Industrial Corporation (BAIC) is the central agency for all potential private investors seeking advice, information, or assistance on investment opportunities in the Bahamas. The Financial Services Secretariat (FSS) was established in 1990 to promote and assist investors to enter the financial services sector.

Government approval must be obtained for foreign investors to own and operate a business in the Bahamas. Under the Immovable Property Act, foreigners must obtain approval from the Foreign Investment Board before purchasing real property in the Bahamas. The Immigration Act requires foreign personnel to obtain work permits before they can be employed in the Bahamas. In theory, the government will permit foreign employees to work in a technical, supervisory, or managerial capacity to initiate and operate industries, provided no similarly qualified Bahamians are available for the job. In practice, however, foreign investors are often confronted with lengthy and unexplained delays in obtaining work permits.

United States government assistance: The Bahamas has signed an OPIC (Overseas Private Investment Corporation) agreement. OPIC offers political risk insurance as well as direct financing and loan guarantee programs. OPIC also maintains a computerized investment opportunity bank which matches potential foreign investment projects with U.S. investors seeking opportunities overseas. Two OPIC-financed projects in the Bahamas totaling $12.4 million were approved in 1991.

The U.S. Export-Import Bank (EX-IM) offers export financing and guarantees for U.S. exports to the Bahamas. The U.S. Trade and Development Agency (TDA) conducts feasibility study financing for projects with large U.S. export components.

Privatization Activities

The utility companies in the Bahamas are government-owned, as is the national carrier—BahamasAir. The government is considering privatizing some public corporations and BahamasAir to raise capital.

The Bahamian government has never expropriated a business and has stated that "nationalization will not be an instrument of government policy." Profits and investment capital may be freely repatriated.

FINANCING AND CAPITAL MARKETS

General Policy Framework

The Bahamas government continues to run

a fiscal deficit due to investment in capital projects by the government and public corporations. (The recurrent deficit for 1990 was U.S. $59.7 million, while the overall budget deficit in 1990 was U.S. $101.5 million.)

Deficits are financed through bond issues, treasury bills, short-term advances from the banking system, and Central Bank financing. On November 6, 1991, the government enacted legislation to increase revenue by further increasing some import duties, the gasoline tax, taxes on remittances of foreign currency, and the departure tax on cruise ship visitors.

Debt Management Policies

The Bahamas' national debt reached U.S. $912.8 million in 1990, with debt service of $51 million accounting for 10.5 percent of total government revenues. The Bahamas maintains a good international credit rating.

The Currency and Exchange Rate Mechanisms

The Bahamian dollar is pegged to the U.S. dollar at an exchange rate of 1:1, and the Bahamian government is committed to maintaining parity. The Central Bank monitors, but does not impede, the flow of foreign exchange into and out of the Bahamas. Foreign exchange reserves rose to U.S. $159 million in 1990, due partly to tighter liquidity.

Banking and Other Financial Institutions

Domestic financing through commercial bank loans and the issuance of government securities continued to increase in 1991. The National Insurance Board, a Bahamian pension fund, purchased $317.5 million in treasury bills and government-registered stock through August 1991.

The Bahamas' primary monetary consideration is foreign exchange reserves, needed to purchase essential imports and finance the repatriation of corporate profits. The Central Bank has asked banks to limit credit expansion in order to preserve foreign exchange reserves, and liquidity remained tight in 1991. Bank lending came to a virtual halt between January and September 1991.

Financial Market Operations and Structural Policies

Price controls exist on 13 breadbasket items, gasoline, utility rates, public transportation, automobiles, and auto parts. Inflation accelerated from 3.8 percent in June 1990 to 7.6 percent in June 1991.

Recognized internationally as a tax haven, the Bahamas does not impose income, inheritance, or sales taxes. Customs duties range from 1 to 200 percent and are a principal source of government revenue, as they are applied to nearly all imported goods. Other revenue sources include fees on business licenses and work permits, property taxes, and airport and harbor departure taxes. A gambling tax is also levied. To increase revenues, the airport departure tax was raised from U.S. $7 to U.S. $13 per person in 1991, and the government raised the harbor departure tax from U.S. $7 to U.S. $20 per person in 1992.

Chapter 3
BOLIVIA

	Total	Urban
Population (1993)	7,505,000	50.0%

Main Urban Areas	Population	Percentage of Total	International Calling Code
LA PAZ	1,057,000	14.1	591-2
Santa Cruz	628,000	8.4	591-33
Cochabamba	81,000	5.1	591-42
Oruro	96,000	.6	591-52
Potosi	114,000	1.5	591-62
Sucre	96,000	1.3	591-64
Tarija	66,000	0.9	591-66

Land Area   1,098,580 square kilometers
     Comparable U.S. State   Texas and California together

Language
* Quechua   37%
* Spanish   35%
* Aymara   24%
Other   4%
(*) Official languages

     Common Business Language   Spanish, English

Currency   1 Boliviano ($B) = 100 centavos
     Exchange Rate (May 1993)   U.S. $1.00 = 3.37 Bolivianos

Best Nonstop Air Connection via U.S.   Miami to La Paz: 6.5 hours
American Airlines (800) 433-7300
Lloyd Aereo Bolivano (800) 327-3098

Best Hotel   Hotel Plaza Paseo El Prado (U.S. $100)
PO Box 8733
La Paz
Tel: (591-2) 378-311 or 378-317
Fax: (591-2) 343-391

INTRODUCTION AND REGIONAL ORIENTATION

Bolivia is the least developed country in South America. About two-thirds of its people, many of whom are subsistence farmers, live in poverty. Population density ranges from less than one person per square kilometer in the southeastern plains to about 10 per square kilometer (25 per square mile) in the central highlands. Bolivia's high mortality rate prevents the annual population growth rate from exceeding 2.8 percent.

La Paz is the highest capital city in the world—3,600 meters (11,800 feet) above sea level. The fastest growing major city is Santa Cruz, the commercial and industrial hub of the eastern lowlands.

Bolivia's ethnic distribution is estimated to be 60 percent indigenous Aymara and Quechua peoples, 25–30 percent mixed Indian and Spanish (mestizo), and 5–15 percent European (primarily Spanish). Among the limited number of foreign residents are about 700 Japanese and Okinawan families, who emigrated to Bolivia after World War II and settled in the Santa Cruz area. A small Mennonite community resides in the same region.

Almost 95 percent of Bolivians are Roman Catholic, although a number of Protestant denominations are also well represented. Many Indian communities interweave pre-Columbian and Christian symbols in their religious practices. Approximately half of the people speak Spanish as their first language. About 90 percent of the children attend primary school but often for one year or less. The literacy rate is low in many rural areas.

Geographical and Historical Background

Land boundaries: 6,743 kilometers total; Argentina 832 kilometers, Brazil 3,400 kilometers, Chile 861 kilometerss, Paraguay 750 kilometers, Peru 900 kilometers. Bolivia is landlocked, but shares control of Lago Titicaca, world's highest navigable lake, with Peru. Bolivia has wanted a sovereign corridor to the South Pacific Ocean since the Atacama area was lost to Chile in 1884; a dispute with Chile over Rio Lauca water rights remains unresolved.

History and Political Conditions

During most of the Spanish colonial period, modern day Bolivia was called "Upper Peru" or "Charcas" and was governed from Lima. Bolivian silver mines produced much of the Spanish empire's wealth, and Potosi, site of the famed "cerro rico" (rich mountain), was for many years the largest city in the Western Hemisphere. Independence from Spain was proclaimed in 1809, but 16 years of struggle followed before the establishment of the republic, named for Simon Bolivar, on August 6, 1825.

Independence did not bring stability. For nearly 60 years, coups and short-lived constitutions dominated Bolivian politics. Bolivia's weakness was demonstrated during the War of the Pacific (1879–84) when it lost its seacoast and the adjoining rich nitrate fields to Chile.

An increase in the world price of silver brought Bolivia a measure of relative prosperity and political stability in the late 1800s. During the early part of the twentieth century, tin replaced silver as the country's most important source of wealth. Political parties that reflected the interests of the mine owners ruled until the 1930s.

The lot of the Indians, who constituted most of the population, remained deplorable. Forced to work under primitive conditions in the mines and in nearly feudal status on large estates, they were denied access to education, economic opportunity, or political participation.

Bolivia's defeat by Paraguay in the

Chaco War (1932–35) marked a turning point. Great loss of life and territory discredited the traditional ruling classes, while service in the army produced stirrings of political awareness among the Indians. From the end of the Chaco War until the 1952 revolution, the emergence of contending ideologies and the demands of new groups convulsed Bolivian politics.

The Nationalist Revolutionary Movement (MNR) emerged from the ferment as a broadly based party. Denied its victory in the 1951 presidential elections, the MNR led the successful 1952 revolution. Under President Victor Paz Estenssoro, the MNR introduced universal adult suffrage, carried out a sweeping land reform, promoted rural education, and nationalized the country's largest tin mines.

Twelve years of tumultuous rule left the MNR divided, and in 1964, a military junta overthrew President Paz at the outset of his third term. In 1969, the death of President Rene Barrientos, a former member of the junta elected president in 1966, led to a succession of weak governments. Alarmed by public disorder, the military, the MNR, and others installed Colonel (later General) Hugo Banzer Suarez as president in 1971. Banzer ruled with MNR support from 1971 to 1974. Then, impatient with schisms in the coalition, he replaced civilians with members of the armed forces and suspended political activities. The economy grew impressively during Banzer's presidency, but demands for greater political freedom undercut his support. His call for elections in 1978 plunged Bolivia into turmoil once again.

Elections in 1978, 1979, and 1980 were inconclusive and marked by fraud. There were coups, countercoups, and caretaker governments. In 1980, General Luis Garcia Meza carried out a ruthless and violent coup. His government was notorious for human rights abuses, narcotics trafficking, and economic mismanagement.

After a military rebellion forced out Garcia Meza in 1981, three other military governments in 14 months struggled with Bolivia's growing problems. Unrest forced the military to convoke the Congress elected in 1980 and allow it to choose a new chief executive. In October 1982—22 years after the end of his first term of office (1956–60)—Hernan Siles Zuazo again became president. Severe social tension, exacerbated by economic mismanagement and weak leadership, forced him to call early elections and relinquish power a year before the end of his constitutional term.

In the 1985 elections, the Nationalist Democratic Action Party (ADN) of General Banzer won a plurality of the popular vote, followed by Victor Paz Estenssoro's MNR and former Vice-President Jaime Paz Zamora's Movement of the Revolutionary Left (MIR). However, in the congressional run-off, the MIR sided with MNR, and Paz Estenssoro was chosen for a fourth term as president.

When Paz Estenssoro took office in 1985, he faced a staggering economic crisis. Economic output and exports had been declining for several years. Hyperinflation had reached an annual rate of 24,000 percent. There was widespread social unrest, chronic strikes, and unfettered operation by drug dealers.

In four years, his administration achieved an economic and social stability that remains the envy of Bolivia's neighbors. The military stayed out of politics, and all major political parties publicly and institutionally committed themselves to democracy. Human rights violations, which badly tainted some governments earlier in the decade, were not a problem.

However, Paz Estenssoro's remarkable

accomplishments were not won without sacrifice. The collapse of tin prices in October 1985, coming just as the government was moving to nationalize its mismanaged mining company, forced the government to lay off over 20,000 miners. The highly successful shock treatment that restored Bolivia's financial system also led to unrest and temporary social dislocation in some cases. His government's achievements remain fragile in the face of Bolivia's poverty and the country's history of political instability, but they are no less remarkable for that.

President Jaime Paz Zamora took office August 6, 1989, following an electoral contest whose results were only determined early in the morning of the previous day. Election results were: MNR 23.1 percent; ADN 22.7 percent; MIR 19.6 percent. (Paz finished third in the May 7, 1989, elections.) Bolivia's constitution, however, mandates congressional determination of the victor in presidential races where no candidate obtains a majority vote.

In negotiations preceding congressional voting, Paz hammered out a deal with the second place finisher, General Hugo Banzer, to share the leadership. Paz's center-left MIR assumed the presidency and half the ministries. Banzer's center-right ADN gained control of the National Political Council (CONAP), in addition to its ministries.

The 1989 elections were the cleanest in recent Bolivian history. Nonetheless, the MNR asserted that electoral court invalidation of key voting tables gave the ADN/MIR three of its congressional seats.

Paz Zamora has been a moderate president who, despite his Marxist origins and his self-proclaimed "leftist nationalism," has learned from experience that pragmatic approaches to problems are those most likely to bring solutions. Having seen Bolivia experience the hyperinflation (24,000 percent) of the Siles Zuazo administration as vice president, he now supports orthodox economics.

CRACKING THE MARKET

Demographics

Distribution: Roughly 50 percent of the population live in urban areas.

Language: Spanish and Quechua. Aymara is also used in northern parts of the altiplano.

Labor: Total employment is estimated at 1.66 million, of which 47 percent is in agriculture (1989). The estimated urban unemployment rate is 8 percent (1991), although the underemployment rate is considerably higher.

Education: The literacy rate is estimated to be 63 percent (1990).

Ethnic Groups: Indian 48%; Mestizo 39%; Caucasian 12%; other 1%.

There are small Japanese and South Korean communities. Also important economically are the relatively smaller Jewish and Arab (mainly Lebanese) communities.

Economy

Real economic growth resumed in 1987 after five years of decline. While the annual output of goods and services has grown in real terms between 2–3 percent starting in 1987, it has not yet regained the level achieved in 1981. GDP is estimated to have grown another 2.6 percent in 1990, with inflation increasing to around 18 percent for the year. Economic growth has been mainly from new investment by the private sector, which has benefited by the elimination of price controls, import permits, and currency controls. The Bolivian government successfully com-

BOLIVIA
Key Economic Indicators

	1989	1990	1991[p]	Percent Change
(Millions of dollars except where indicated)				
Population (thousands)[1]	6,547	6,693	6,300	2.2
Exchange rate (Bs/$)				
year-end	2.98	3.40	3.75	10.3
average	2.69	3.17	3.58	12.3
National Accounts—GDP				
GDP Growth % (constant Bs.)	2.83	2.62	4.10	
Nominal GDP (millions of $)	5,497.0	5,547.0	6,067.0	
Nominal per capita income $	839.6	828.8	886.7	
Real per capita income % change	0.6	0.4	1.9	
Unemployment rate %[2]	8.7	9.0	7.0	
Finance, Money, and Prices (Millions of Bolivianos)				
Money supply (M1)	706.0	988.0	1,313.5	32.9
Money supply (M2)	2,244.6	3,338.5	5,193.8	35.6
Net domestic credit	4,226.4	5,419.7	6,645.3	22.6
Dollar deposits (millions U.S. $)	453.7	638.3	967.4	51.6
Fiscal deficit (% of GDP)	5.1	3.3	3.6	
Inflation (year-end)	16.5	18.0	14.5	
Trade and Balance of Payments				
Total exports	821.8	926.5	848.6	−8.4
Exports—minerals	403.4	407.1	356.1	−12.5
Exports—hydrocarbons	214.0	226.9	241.2	6.3
Exports—others[3]	204.3	292.5	251.3	−14.1
Total imports	619.9	702.7	941.7	34.0
Trade balance	201.9	223.8	−93.1	
Imports from the U.S.[4]	144.3	138.6	189.7	36.9
Exports to the U.S.[5]	120.0	203.3	208.7	2.7
Current account balance	−13.6	39.2	−262.8	
Capital account balance	147.3	114.0	121.6	
Central Bank gross reserves (year-end)	373.3	375.7	393.0	4.6
Central Bank net international reserves (year-end)	18.6	132.3	200.3	51.4

Sources: Central Bank of Bolivia/National Institute of Statistics (INE)/Economic Policies Analysis Unit (UDAPE).
p. Preliminary figures released by the Central Bank
1. 1992 population number reflects adjusted 1992 census figure. The population growth rate is now assumed to be 2 percent per year.
2. Based on urban areas, with no adjustment for underemployment
3. Data for 1990 and 1991 include re-exports from Bolivia
4. U.S. Department of Commerce, U.S. exports to Bolivia
5. U.S. Department of Commerce, U.S. imports from Bolivia

pleted in 1990 the second year of a three-year International Monetary Fund (IMF) "Economic Structural Adjustment Facility Program" and managed to keep the budget deficit to less than 3.5 percent of GDP.

Agriculture still accounts for about 21 percent of GDP and employs almost half the 1.7 million people in the labor force. Total agricultural production declined slightly in 1989 and 1990 due to drought, but cultivation of wheat, barley, cotton, sunflower, and other nontraditional crops all expanded in the Santa Cruz area. The extraction of minerals and hydrocarbons accounts for more than 15 percent of GDP, followed by manufacturing and commerce, each with 13 percent.

New contracts for oil exploration by several foreign firms should spur the economy, especially if one of them discovers oil (as opposed to gas) so that oil exports can be renewed. Exploitation of Bolivia's large salt flats of the altiplano should also increase export earnings.

Political/Institutional Infrastructure

The constitution promulgated in February 1967 provides for traditional executive, legislative, and judicial powers. The traditionally strong executive, however, tends to overshadow the Congress, whose role is generally limited to debating and approving legislation initiated by the executive. The judiciary consists of the Supreme Court and departmental and lower courts. Bolivia's nine departments have limited autonomy, although departmental officials have been appointed by the central government for many years.

As a result of the July 14, 1985, elections, Bolivian cities and towns are now governed by elected majors and councils for the first time since 1951.

Executive branch: president, vice-president, cabinet

Legislative branch: bicameral National Congress (Congreso Nacional) consists of an upper chamber or Chamber of Senators (Camara de Senadores) and a lower chamber or Chamber of Deputies (Camara de Diputados)

Judicial branch: Supreme Court (Corte Suprema)

Principal Government Officials (July 1992)

President
Jaime PAZ Zamora

Vice-President
Luis OSSIO Sanjines

Minister of Foreign Affairs
Carlos ITURRALDE

Ambassador to the U.S.
Jorge CRESPO Velasco

Ambassador to the UN
Hugo NAVAJAS Mogro

Ambassador to the OAS
Mario ROLON Anaya

Political Parties and Leaders:

Movement of the Revolutionary Left (MIR), Jaime PAZ Zamora; Nationalist Democratic Action (ADN), Hugo BANZER Suarez; Nationalist Revolutionary Movement (MNR), Gonzalo SANCHEZ de Lozada; Christian Democratic Party (PDC), Jorge AGREDO; Free Bolivia Movement (MBL), led by Antonio ARANIBAR; United Left (IU), a coalition of leftist parties which includes Patriotic National Convergency Axis (EJE-P) led by Walter DELGADILLO, and Bolivian Communist Party (PCB) led by Humberto RAMIREZ; Conscience of the Fatherland (CONDEPA), Carlos PALENQUE Aviles; Revolutionary Vanguard-9th of April (VR-9), Carlos SERRATE Reich; Civic Union Solidarity (UCS), Max FERNANDEZ.

Suffrage: Universal and compulsory at age 18 (married) or 21 (single).

Defense

Bolivia's armed forces have played a major and often controversial role in the country's history. Defeated in the 1952 revolution, the army was at first drastically reduced in size and influence. Later, however, the MNR rebuilt the armed forces to counter the power of unruly military leaders. The corrupt, albeit short-lived, tenure of Gen. Luis Garcia Meza from 1980 to 1981 did much to discredit military rule. The armed forces adhered strictly to their constitutional role during the term of elected President Hernan Siles Zuazo (1982–85) and supported fully the constitutional transition to elected presidents, Dr. Paz Estenssoro (1985) and Jaime Paz Zamora (1989). Despite the country's occasionally uncertain political climate, Bolivia's military in recent years has contributed responsibly to strengthening the country's still fragile democracy.

Estimates of Bolivian armed forces troop strength are 22,000 army, 4,000 air force, and 4,000 navy, which patrols Lake Titicaca (the world's highest navigable lake) and various rivers. In addition to its mission of external defense and internal security, the military participates in civic action programs and provides transportation services. Bolivia is a signatory of the Inter-American Treaty of Reciprocal Assistance (Rio Treaty), an agreement among the American states for mutual support against aggression.

Foreign Relations

Bolivia traditionally has maintained normal diplomatic relations with all hemispheric states except Chile. Relations with Chile, strained since Bolivia's defeat in the War of the Pacific (1879–83) and its loss of the coastal province of Atacama, were severed from 1962 to 1975 in a dispute over the use of the waters of the Lauca River. Relations were resumed in 1975 but broken again in 1978 over the inability of the two countries to reach an agreement that might have granted Bolivia a sovereign access to the sea. In the 1960s, relations with Cuba were broken following Castro's rise to power but resumed under the Paz Estenssoro administration in 1985.

During the Garcia Meza regime, Bolivia's relations with many countries, including the United States, were strained. Principal concerns focused on the narcotics problem, human rights abuses, and interruption of the democratic process. The restoration of constitutional democracy in 1982 alleviated some of these concerns and greatly improved Bolivia's diplomatic standing.

From 1970 until 1991, Bolivia notably expanded its links with the former Soviet Union, various East European nations, and the People's Republic of China. (Note: Taiwan maintains a trade/commercial office in La Paz.) These include diplomatic relations, trade, cultural exchanges, and limited economic assistance.

President Paz is an active participant in the formulation and execution of Bolivia's foreign policy. He has shown interest in improving Bolivia's historically poor relationship with Chile.

U.S.-Bolivian Relations

The normally friendly relations between the United States and Bolivia were interrupted during the Garcia Meza regime. Following the unusually violent and repressive coup of July 17, 1980, the United States withdrew its ambassador, cut off security assistance and arms sales, and suspended a substantial portion of economic assistance.

In November 1981, after Garcia Meza's replacement by a more moderate military leader, the U.S. ambassador returned to La Paz. U.S. economic and security assistance programs resumed after Bolivia's return to constitutional democracy. The United States has a longstanding aid relationship with Bolivia. Between 1945 and 1990, economic assistance totaled more than U.S. $1.5 billion; grants made up almost half this sum.

The current major issue in bilateral relations is that Bolivia produces 30–40 percent of the world's coca and is second only to Colombia in production of cocaine. For generations, the traditional practice of chewing coca leaves served to alleviate the rigors of life on the altiplano, but during the past decades, an increasing percentage of coca cultivation has been diverted to the illegal market for the production of cocaine. The corruption and disregard for law that accompanied the growth of the illegal trade have made narcotics trafficking not only a major domestic but an international problem for Bolivia. President Bush's Andean strategy, announced in February 1990, has started cooperative programs in Bolivia and with neighbors Peru and Colombia to help combat the menace of narcotics production and trafficking.

Trade

Imports (CIF, U.S.

$ millions)	1989	619.9
	1990	702.7
	1991	941.7

Import market shares

(percent, 1991)	U.S.	18
	Brazil	14
	Chile	10
	Argentina	9
	Japan	9

Main imports—capital goods, 43 percent; raw materials and intermediary products, 38 percent; and consumer goods, 18 percent.

Exports (CIF, U.S.

$ millions)	1989	821.7
	1990	917.9
	1991	840.3

Major exports: Natural gas, minerals, sugar, soya, and coffee.

Trade and Investment Policies

Bolivia was the first Latin American country, with the exception of Mexico, to sign a bilateral framework agreement establishing the U.S.-Bolivian Trade and Investment Council (TIC). This agreement, signed in May 1990, established, a high-level commission of U.S. and Bolivian government officials who meet yearly to attempt to resolve outstanding trade and investment concerns. As a companion to the TIC's efforts, the U.S. and Bolivian governments are negotiating a Bilateral Investment Treaty (BIT) to establish clear ground rules for foreign investors. Bolivia acceded to the General Agreement on Tariffs and Trade (GATT) in August 1990.

Bolivia is also a member of several regional trade and economic associations, the most prominent being the Andean Pact (Pacto Andino). Bolivia has agreed to participate (under certain conditions) in the pact's free trade area and common external tariff. In addition, Bolivia participates in ALADI (Latin American Integration Association), the Rio Piata Agreement (Cuenca del Plata), URPABOL (a regional trade association between Uruguay, Paraguay, and Bolivia), and has observer status in the Mercosur (Southern Common Market, consisting of Brazil, Argentina, Paraguay, and Uruguay). Bolivia initiated free trade discussions with Mexico in August 1992.

Registered exports exceeded U.S. $1 billion in 1980 and then declined for seven years in a row reflecting the collapse of the economy and falling mineral prices. From a low of U.S. $570 million in 1987, exports have grown steadily and exceeded U.S. $900 million in 1990. Registered imports fell from over U.S. $900 million in 1981 to $490 million in 1984. Imports have grown slowly

(U.S. $716 million in 1990), leaving Bolivia with a positive trade balance in 1989 and 1990.

The IMF estimated that an additional U.S. $250 million of goods were smuggled into Bolivia in 1989. This was probably offset by smuggled exports of coca paste, cocaine, and gold.

Up until the early 1970s, most of Bolivia's trade was with the United States. As Bolivia's economy has diversified and opened during the past two decades, trade with other countries has grown sharply.

The United States remained Bolivia's major supplier in 1990, providing U.S. $139 million, or 19 percent, of Bolivia's imports. The United States was the second largest market for Bolivia, buying U.S. $203 million, or 22 percent, of Bolivia's exports.

Bolivia's major exports to the United States are tin, gold jewelry, and wood products. Its major imports from the United States are wheat, flour, motor vehicles, and all sorts of machinery.

Import Tariffs

In 1990 Bolivia instituted a two-tier tariff system: 5 percent for a defined list of capital goods (largely falling in the Harmonized System—HS—categories of 84 to 87), and 10 percent for all imports (including most agricultural items). These rates are among the lowest in Latin America.

The tariff is calculated on the CIF (cost-insurance-freight) value of the import.

Import taxes are applied, with an additional import tax (a consumption tax) assessed as follows:

- 2 percent ad valorem for books, brochures, and other printed materials
- 10 percent on electrical apparatus, pottery, chinaware, automotive vehicles, and jewelry
- 20 percent on soft drinks and electricity

consumption by commercial and domestic users of excess of 120 kwh

- 30 percent on perfumes, cosmetics, and locally produced and imported alcoholic beverages (excluding beer)
- 50 percent on all tobacco products
- 60 percent on locally produced and imported beer.

The valued-added tax (V.A.T., or I.V.A. in Spanish) is 13 percent.

Duty Exemptions and Reductions

Exemptions/reductions are permitted for:

- imports made under current international agreements and government contracts
- imports under intraregional agreements that specifically provide for duty exemptions
- imports made by diplomatic and consular corps
- travelers' personal effects not exceeding U.S. $300
- imports of gold, except jewelry.

Andean Pact Tariffs

One of the principal objectives of the Cartagena Agreement, which established the Andean Pact, is the formation of a customs union. A common external tariff (CET) has been proposed and accepted by four of the five pact members. (Peru has suspended its pact commitments until the end of 1993.) The CET, which is to be applied to all imports not originating in the Andean Pact (including those from the United States), is 5 to 20 percent, with capital goods and inputs receiving the 5, 10, and 15 percent rates, and consumer goods charged the 20 percent rate. As Bolivia maintains lower rates of 5 and 10 percent, the country has been granted an exception allowing it to maintain those rates.

Price Controls

The government sets the prices for only two commodities, petroleum and the most commonly sold bread rolls.

APPROACHING THE MARKET

Commercial Environment

The United States remains Bolivia's major trading partner, consistently accounting for over one-fifth of its imports and exports. U.S. exports to Bolivia rose by 37 percent during 1991 to a total of U.S. $190 million, according to official U.S. Department of Commerce statistics. U.S. imports from Bolivia also increased slightly to U.S. $209 million, with tin, gold, and wood products representing the largest proportion of imports. In contrast, a wide array of products, from heavy industrial machinery to processed foods, make up the bulk of U.S. sales to Bolivia.

U.S. exports to Bolivia were expected to show strong growth in 1992, particularly in the mining and petroleum sectors, resulting from a major swing in investment in these areas. This accelerated rate of investment should guarantee solid growth for several years. Moreover, most Bolivians turn to the U.S. for the disproportionate share of Bolivia's imports, based on quality, and in some cases, price considerations. U.S. products are now price competitive with Japanese and European products, but some items can still be purchased more cheaply from Brazil and Argentina. However, the increasing number of U.S. investors in Bolivia will likely generate more opportunities for U.S. exporters; exporters can enhance their sales chances through competitive and creative financing.

With regard to product promotion and distribution, Bolivia's small market requires that most agents represent more than one line of merchandise. The amount of effort given to promoting a particular product line is determined in part by the interest and support expressed by the supplier, as well as by the agent's ability and interest. Given the key role played by local representatives, the importance of occasional personal visits from company representatives, as well as prompt, responsive handling of communications, cannot be overstated. After a firm business relationship has been established, local distributors and agents generally expect to be extended an offer to visit the foreign company's plant facilities and head offices in order to become more familiar with the company's personnel and operating techniques.

Although privatizing, Bolivia's economy remains heavily public-sector oriented, and many of the most promising sales and investment opportunities are to be found in the large state-owned corporations. Therefore, business persons should be prepared to deal with government officials and with usual governmental procedures. U.S. exporters or shippers should adhere to the instructions of the Bolivian importer, as well as to the instructions outlined in the Trade Regulations section of this report regarding shipment of goods, so as to avoid difficulties and customs fines.

Mining

Mining equipment sales to Bolivia totaled approximately $100 million in 1991. Estimated sales in 1992, 1993, and 1994 are expected to more than double the 1991 figure to reach a projected U.S. $250 million, U.S. $270 million, and U.S. $290 million, respectively. Historically, about 50 percent of all mining equipment sold in Bolivia was purchased by the state-owned mining company, COMIBOL. Since 1990, private sector sales comprise about 90 percent of total sales.

Best sales prospects for mining equipment in Bolivia include equipment for medium-sized open pit mines and heap leaching operations and for small and medium-sized alluvial gold mining cooperatives. For medium-sized open pit operations, best prospects are drills (open pit production drills), crushers and pulverizers, conveyors, compressors, front loaders, bulldozers, 15 to 30 ton heavy-duty trucks, gravimetric or flotation concentrators, and pumps.

For small mines, best prospects include small drills, front loaders, crushers, concentration tables, flotation concentrators, hand tools, and explosives.

Agricultural Machinery

Bolivia's agricultural sector, including livestock and lumber production, accounted for 21 percent of its GDP in 1991 and employed approximately half the work force. In the Santa Cruz region alone, 20,000 to 40,000 new hectares come into production each year. Nevertheless, over 80 percent of the agricultural land under cultivation is farmed without modern machinery and equipment.

Bolivia's agricultural potential is vast, as less than four percent of the country's usable land is under cultivation. The agricultural sector expanded by 7.2 percent in 1991. Wheat production increased by 90 percent, soybeans by 65 percent, and cotton by 295 percent.

As hectares under cultivation increase, so does the demand for modern agricultural imports such as farm machinery and equipment, cultivators, silos, harvesting machines, spraying machines, irrigation equipment, and tractors.

Hydrocarbons

The oil and gas industry accounted for 6 percent of Bolivia's GDP and 27 percent of exports in 1991. Natural gas sold to Argentina represented over 96 percent of the U.S. $241 million of hydrocarbon exports.

The enactment of the new Hydrocarbons Law in November 1990 has attracted a number of foreign investors, including U.S. producers Chevron, Mobil, Santa Fe, Texaco, Exxon, and Maxus. These companies have recently signed exploration/exploitation contracts, and others are in the negotiating stage. Most of the foreign oil companies currently only need exploration equipment and drilling equipment, but demand for additional equipment and services will expand quickly if large oil fields are discovered.

The chief potential trade opportunity in the hydrocarbons sector is the planned U.S. $400 million gas pipeline to Brazil. The 28-inch, 584-kilometer long pipeline will extend from Santa Cruz, Bolivia, to Sao Paulo, Brazil. A portion of the project will be financed by the Japanese Export-Import Bank and will require the use of Japanese equipment and services; however, the share of the project financed by multilateral development banks (e.g., Inter-American Development Bank (IDB), World Bank) will be tendered via international public bid. Additional major pipeline projects also are being considered to Chile, Paraguay, and Peru.

Road/Railroad Construction

Bolivia's Ministry of Transportation and Communications has an ambitious 10-year road construction plan, which includes the construction of 8,000 kilometers of new roads, 50 percent of which will be paved roads, with a total estimated investment of U.S. $2.6 billion. Many of the projects already have been promised funding by the Spanish, German, and Japanese governments, as well as by donor countries and the IDB. The IDB has pledged to asphalt three major roads in Bolivia, at a cost of just over U.S. $300 million.

In addition, the World Bank has authorized a U.S. $60 million project to be carried out between 1992–96 to rehabilitate railroad tracks, facilitate better transport for exports, and acquire new rolling stock.

Electrical Energy Generation Equipment

The average annual growth rate for electricity consumption is about 7 percent. Estimated annual investment by the Bolivian government for power generation during the next three years will be about U.S. $90 million. A U.S. $20 million World Bank loan will enable the state electricity company, ENDE, to connect the existing eastern and western grid systems. In addition, COBEE, the U.S.-owned private firm that generates and distributes electricity to La Paz and Oruro, is planning a U.S. $120 million investment to substantially increase its hydro-generating capacity. This last project alone will entail equipment purchases totaling approximately U.S. $60 million. In general, excellent opportunities exist for suppliers of power generation equipment and electrical cabling.

Telecommunications Equipment

Steady investment in the Bolivian telecommunications network has resulted in strong growth in the country's telecommunications market. The market was estimated at almost U.S. $26 million in 1990. With virtually no domestic production, Bolivia relies heavily on imports to supply its telecommunications needs. In 1991, U.S. companies exported just over U.S. $5 million to Bolivia for a 22 import market share. Continued growth is expected following the state-owned telecommunications company (ENTEL)'s announcement of plans to construct digital microwave links with Paraguay, Chile, and Argentina.

Best sales prospects continue to be in digital network equipment and satellite earth station equipment, as well as cellular infrastructure equipment and telephones.

Medical Equipment

Ambitious plans for large investments in the health sector are underway in both the public and private health sectors. Most of these projects are being financed by foreign donors, bilateral agreements, and grants supplied by international health organizations. Estimated annual investment over a five-year period (1991–96) will be about U.S. $30 million per year for new hospital construction, equipment, and services.

Best sales prospects include general surgical instruments and supplies, X-ray equipment, electro-medical equipment, and surgical beds.

Other Top Prospects

Other up-and-coming prospects include computers and peripherals, food processing and packaging equipment, cars and automotive parts, and consumer goods and electronics.

Implications for U.S. Exporters

Government activities traditionally represent approximately 70 percent of Bolivia's GNP. The government and its publicly owned corporations and agencies are the main buyers of machinery, equipment, materials, and other products. They are legally required to call for bids when proposed purchases are above 100,000 Bolivianos (notated as "Bs.," and equivalent to approximately U.S. $24,570 at early December 1992's 4.07 Bs./U.S. $ exchange rate). Only those firms legally established under Bolivian laws may bid for government purchases. Thus, it is essential that U.S firms be formally represented in Bolivia through import houses, commission or independent sales agents, or local subsidiaries.

It is important not only to select the type of distribution system most suitable for the exporting firm and its product, but also to appoint an experienced, aggressive, financially solvent representative. Capital goods exporters should ensure that potential representatives have access to key decision-makers among the buyers. Periodic visits by representatives of U.S. suppliers are essential in order to provide assistance to the distributor or agent and to establish personal contact with customers.

Most heavy equipment, machinery, and general merchandise must be delivered through seaports in Peru, Chile, Brazil, and Argentina. Occasionally, bad weather, landslides, port congestion, or other factors may block all import channels. It is important to cooperate closely with Bolivian importers in arranging transportation and preparing and submitting shipping documents. Air cargo transportation may at times be desirable even for heavy items.

There are four principal types of commercial import channels: commission or independent sales agents or representatives, import houses, subsidiaries of foreign firms, and direct importation by government agencies.

Manufacturers may distribute products through international trade fairs. When this channel is used, capital goods destined for the production sector enter under temporary import permission for an exhibition period of 90 days, with a bank guarantee note of 1 percent over the CIF value. Within this period the goods may be nationalized or reexported. If nationalized, duties for certain capital goods may be discounted by 50 percent under the preferential customs policy granted to international trade fairs.

Foreign Trade and Investment Decision-Making Infrastructure

Thus far, Bolivia has established six free trade zones, three of which are now in operation in El Alto, Puerto Aguirre, and Oruro. Bolivian free trade zones are regulated by the National Council of Free Trade Zones (CONZOF), created by Article 20 of the 1990 Investment Law and FTZ Regulations promulgated under Supreme Decree 22526. These FTZs are operated by private companies which are selected by the Government of Bolivia through public bids. There are special procedures which must be followed to obtain approval to operate within these zones. As of December 1992, the zones of Santa Cruz, Cochabamba, and Tarija had yet to open.

Setting Up Business Operations

Agents, Distributors, and Representatives

The majority of the numerous agents, distributors, and representatives in Bolivia are very effective in dealing with government agencies, as well as with private industry. Commission agents take orders on a direct shipment basis. Some specialize in certain products or in supplying customers engaged in specific activities. These agents and representatives do not stock products. Agents are required to have a minimum paid-in capital of U.S. $2,000 to initiate a business activity in Bolivia. They must also meet certain other requirements and register with the Bolivian Chamber of Commerce, the Internal Revenue Service, the Ministry of Industry and Commerce, the National Directory of Commerce, and the local municipality.

Import Houses

Import houses in Bolivia are normally large, although there are some small well-established importers. These firms import for their own use and also represent foreign firms on a commission basis. Many operate general merchandise outlets. Larger importers have subsidiaries and branches throughout the country, as well as subdistributors, and a sales force to canvass retailers, wholesalers, and consumers. This method offers the U.S. exporter a degree of financial security, as the importer assumes the risk of importing general merchandise. More importantly, they are authorized to sell to government agencies in response to tenders.

Wholesale and Retail Merchandising

Thousands of Bolivians are engaged in merchandising, usually in small facilities or as street vendors. Although many goods are available through wholesalers, a significant percentage enter the country as contraband, thus avoiding the usual tax and tariff regulations. In addition, many wholesalers import directly and then distribute goods through their own retail outlets. Many import houses maintain such outlets in Bolivia's major cities, in addition to distributing to other firms.

Government Procurement

All government purchases are regulated by Supreme Decree 21060 and Annex III of Supreme Decree 21660, which establish the requirements for the procurement of goods and services for public sector entities, companies, and institutions. The Bolivian government signed a contract with the Office for Project Services (OPS) of the United Nations Development Program (UNDP) on January 29, 1988; on March 31, 1988, with a British government corporation, Crown Agents; and on February 1, 1990, with the French government corporation C3D. All three contracting offices currently are arranging purchases for government entities.

When a project is financed by an international institution (for example, the World Bank or Inter-American Development Bank), the bids will follow that institution's own rules. Otherwise, the qualifying agency will call for an international public tender when the amount is over U.S. $200,000. The agency may direct invitations to suppliers when the amount is less. OPS publishes all international tenders through the United Nations' publication, *Development Business*.

Bolivian law specifies that American or other foreign firms interested in providing goods and services to the Bolivian government must have a local address in Bolivia and a legal representative or a local agent in order to bid. Foreign bidders may register their firm by sending its name, address, and a list of its products to the qualifying agency's computerized list of suppliers. Interested firms must send an introductory letter with a complete package of catalogs to one of the addresses in the box on the next page.

Advertising

The Bolivian advertising industry has grown and is now more professional and competitive. The tremendous increase in private television channels now in operation prompted the industry to devote special attention to television commercial spots. La Paz remains the principal advertising center.

Nineteen advertising agencies operate in Bolivia. All companies are members of the Association of Advertising Agencies. The association's address is:

Asociacion Boliviana de Agencias de Publicidad
Av. 6 de Agosto, Pasaje Caracas 5
La Paz, Bolivia
  Tel: (591-2) 35-1154
  Cable: ABAP, La Paz
Contact: Eduardo Siles, Vice-President

Television is the principal forum for advertising, followed by the press and radio. According to the latest statistics supplied by the Association of Advertising Agencies, television accounts for 80 percent of advertising expenditures. Eight percent of expenditures are for newspapers and magazine advertisements and 7 percent for radio spots. Other media such as movie theaters, neon signs, billboards, and direct mailing account for the remaining 5 percent.

Head Offices

Offices in Bolivia

CROWN AGENTS
Saint Nicholas House
Saint Nicholas Road
Sutton Surrey SM1 1EL
United Kingdom
Tel: (44-81) 643-3311

CROWN AGENTS
Av. 20 de Octubre 2475
P.O. Box 11393
La Paz, Bolivia
Contact: John Bell
Tel: (591-2) 39-0696

CROWN AGENTS SERVICES LTD.
910 Ponce de Leon Blvd.
Suite 601
Coral Gables, FL 33134
Tel: (305) 448-9866

OFFICE OF PROJECT SERVICES
304 East 45 St., Room 952
New York, NY 10017
Contact: Jorge Claro
International Coordinator

OFICINA DE SERVICIOS PARA
PROYECTOS (OSP)
Edf. Santa Isabel, bloque C
2do. Mezanine
La Paz, Bolivia
Contact: Carlos Fernandez
Tel: (591-2) 32-9156

C3D International
27 Rue Louis Vicat
75738 Paris Cedex 15
Tel: (33-1) 4638-3475/76
Tlx: 250620
Fax: (33-1) 4638-3482

C3D
Calle Hnos. Manchego 2571
Tel: 591-2/379-428
Tlx: 3347 Bv
Fax: (591-2) 391-614
Contact: Ma. Eugenia Ayala

Television: There are 38 television stations in Bolivia, two of which operate from 7 a.m. to midnight. There are five private TV channels in La Paz. One also reaches to Oruro, Cochabamba, Santa Cruz, Potosi, Sucre, and other smaller cities.

All TV stations have color transmission using the U.S. system (NTSC) with 525 lines and 50 cycles. There are approximately 250,000 black and white TV sets and 400,000 color TV sets in use throughout the country.

Radio: There are 125 radio stations ranging in size from 25KW (Radio Illimani) to 1/2 KW in rural areas. La Paz has 40 stations (28 AM, 10 FM, 2 Stereo). The approximately 3.5 million radios in Bolivia reach an audience of some 4.5 million people. Radio stations are very effective in reaching rural populations, particularly given the proliferation of programs in the two native languages, Aymara and Quechua.

Newspapers: Newspapers are the second most important advertising media. The six newspapers in La Paz have a daily circulation of between 30,000 and 80,000.

Theaters: There are about 25 motion picture theaters in La Paz, with an estimated total seating capacity of 20,000.

Market Research and Trade Organizations

Only one U.S. "brand-name" firm, Coopers & Lybrand, currently operates in Bolivia and offers market research services. However, 10 Bolivian market research firms represent foreign consulting companies. Most of these firms also provide engineering and industry feasibility studies. An updated list of consulting firms and their services is available in the Economic/Commercial Section of the American Embassy in La Paz.

All market research and consulting companies are required to register with the National Association of Consulting Companies. All correspondence to the association may be addressed as follows:

Asociacion Nacional de Empresas
    Consultoras (ANEC)
Casilla 8560
Edif. Batallon Colorados Piso 4
La Paz, Bolivia
    Tel: (591-2) 32-4532
Contact: Hernan Zeballos H., President

The engineering consultants association, the Society of Consulting Engineers, may be contacted at the following address:
Sociedad de Ingenieros Consultores
Casilla 6113
La Paz, Bolivia

INVESTMENT CLIMATE

Economic Factors: Reform, Stability, and Growth

The Paz Zamora administration is commit-
ted to attracting foreign investment as the quickest way to spur economic growth. This is particularly true in the administration's final year in office. A higher level of investment, both public and private, contributed to strong economic growth in 1991. The government estimates that private investment grew by 52 percent that year, 50 percent of which was foreign investment. Half the private investment went into the mining and hydrocarbons industries. Public investment, including that of the government-owned corporations, increased by 19 percent.

Bolivia provides excellent investment opportunities for U.S. companies. Liberal trade and investment practices are in force which allow free flow of currencies; no restrictions are placed on remittances or ownership; and price controls or subsidies to local production are limited. Three recently passed investment laws solidify Bolivia's commitment to an open market.

Investment guarantee law: Bolivia enacted a liberal investment law on September 26, 1990. The investment law permits 100 percent foreign ownership and imposes no screening procedures nor requires any registration. Guarantees that investors can own property, remit dividends, interest, and royalties, import and export freely, contract insurance, and make payments or contracts in any currency are also basic tenets of the law. Joint ventures and free zones are granted legal recognition. Only the mining and hydrocarbons sectors have restrictions on foreign investment.

Hydrocarbons law: The Bolivian government enacted a new hydrocarbons law on November 1, 1990. According to this law, YPFB is assigned the responsibility for exploration and exploitation of hydrocarbons in the country. YPFB performs the role of an integrated oil company, performing operations ranging from exploration to development/production of oil and gas fields. YPFB has been given the authority to enter into operational contracts, petroleum services contracts, and joint venture operations with foreign and domestic private firms.

Mining Law: Bolivia enacted a mining law on April 4, 1991, which contains two major changes that concern foreign investment in the mining sector: foreign firms can now operate within the 50-kilometer border belt in joint venture or service contracts with Bolivian miners (with the exception of firms from the country adjacent to the concession; and all new investments in the mining sector will have to comply with a new taxation system replacing a royalties tax with a tax on profits. The change should permit most foreign firms paying taxes in Bolivia to obtain tax credits in their home countries, thus eliminating the danger of double taxation.

Special note for investors: Andean Trade Preference Act (ATPA). This U.S. program, a ten-year, unilateral trade benefits scheme, provides duty-free access to a wide range of products imported into the U.S. from the Andean region. The program, similar to the trade component of the Caribbean Basin Initiative (CBI), is designed to promote economic development through private sector initiative in Bolivia, Colombia, Peru, and Ecuador. The ATPA is referred to as the trade pillar of President Bush's "war on drugs." One of the goals of the ATPA is to encourage alternatives to coca cultivation and production by offering broader access to the U.S. market.

Bolivia and Colombia were officially designated as ATPA beneficiaries in July 1992, with benefits granted immediately thereafter. Leading ATPA-eligible Bolivian exports include fresh cut roses, leather wallets/attache cases/handbags/apparel (receive duty reduction only, not duty elimination), wild rice, and silk products. For complete background information on the ATPA, including a complete list of products ineligible for benefits, consult the Guidebook to the Andean Trade Preference Act, published by the U.S. Department of Commerce's Latin America/Caribbean Business Development Center.

Price Stability

The consumer price index rose only 14.5 percent during 1991, the lowest rate in South America. This was 3.5 points lower than in 1990 but still above the 12 percent target set with the IMF. The government has been in one program or another with the IMF since mid-1985 when, faced with hyperinflation, the newly inaugurated government of Paz Estenssoro signed an IMF standby agreement and allowed the currency to float while eliminating the budget deficit. During 1985, the consumer price index rose by 8,170 percent. In 1987, the CPI rose only 10.7 percent. During the past five years, inflation has averaged 16.3 percent.

The consumer price index rose 5 percent during the first quarter of 1992 mostly as a result of a 13 percent fuel price increase in January. Fuel prices are the only ones still controlled by the central government. The municipal governments try to control prices of bus fares and bread with mixed success.

Privatization

The Bolivian government has developed an aggressive privatization program, with plans to sell 66 companies presently owed by the Regional Development Corporations, as well as the national airline, Lloyd Aereo Boliviano. Due to the fact that these companies have received little investment capital over the last several years, prospects for selling machinery and supplies to these companies will be strong. U.S. accounting and auditing companies are presently employed assisting the Bolivian government in determining the companies' financial worth and in locating prospective purchasers.

FINANCING AND CAPITAL MARKETS

General Policy Framework

Credit is extremely difficult to obtain at the present time, and is generally extended only on a short-term basis. Interest rates range from 16 to 20 percent for loans in U.S. dollars and 32 to 36 percent for Boliviano loans without maintenance of value provisions. (Note: These rates were as of March 1992.) Collateral requirements for all but the most valued clients are very high. Interest rates are influenced by Central Bank of Bolivia certificate of deposit rates, as well as high administrative costs resulting from bank operational inefficiency. Foreign companies are eligible to borrow from the local financial system.

International and bilateral organizations provide some credit lines at lower interest rates. These lines include lines from the Inter-American Development Bank, the World Bank, the Andean Development Corporation, and the U.S. Agency for International Development (USAID). They are channeled through the Central Bank for lending to private Bolivian banks that make loans for productive purposes to the private sector.

Overseas Private Investment Corporation (OPIC) financing is available for U.S. firms wishing to invest in Bolivia.

Debt Management Policies

The government of Bolivia remains heavily dependent on foreign assistance to finance development projects. As of September 1990, the government owed over U.S. $3.6 billion to its foreign creditors. However, most of those loans have very low interest rates with long repayment schedules. The government owed more than U.S. $1.6 billion to the multilateral development banks and was servicing those debts on schedule. It owed almost U.S. $2 billion to other gov-

ernments, but those governments agreed, at the March 1990 Paris Club meeting, to reschedule all of the bilateral debt payments falling due in 1990 and 1991 under the concessional "Toronto terms." Most of the payments that should have been made in 1990 and 1991 instead will be paid in installments between the years 2005–15. The U.S. government reduced 80 percent of Bolivia's bilateral debt on food assistance loans and all the debt (U.S. $341 million) owed to USAID. France and the Netherlands also have canceled one-third of the debt owed by Bolivia.

The government stopped making payments on its debts to foreign banks in the early 1980s. In 1987, those banks agreed to allow the government to buy back its commercial debt claims at 11 cents on the dollar. Through this procedure and the exchange of investment bonds for debt claims, the Bolivian government was able to reduce its commercial debt from U.S. $678 million at the end of 1987 to U.S. $209 million by September 1990.

The government reduced its debt further through a debt swap with Argentina and by renegotiating its debt with Brazil. Debt payments are a burden, but every year since 1985, disbursements of new loans have exceeded repayments. In 1989, the government paid U.S. $221 million on its external debts, almost 28 percent of registered export earnings, but received U.S. $327 million of new loans plus a significant amount of grant assistance.

The Currency and Exchange Rate Mechanism

The national currency is the Boliviano (Bs). The Boliviano is freely convertible for all transactions.

The official exchange rate is set daily by the government's exchange house, the Bolsin, which is under the supervision of the

Central Bank. The Bolsin holds daily auctions of dollars. The directors of the Bolsin meet every day to decide the minimum rate and the number of dollars to offer for sale, with five million the average offered in the course of a day. Sealed bids are then collected and opened with dollars going to those bidding at or above the minimum rate. With this mechanism the Central Bank has slowly devalued the Boliviano in line with domestic inflation and inflation in Bolivia's major trading partners. The rates set by the Bolsin cannot ignore market forces because currency exchanges in banks, hotels, exchange houses, and on the street corners are legal and active. The parallel market exchange rates are seldom more than 1 percent different from the official rates.

Banking and Other Financial Institutions

Bolivia's banking system includes the Central Bank (Banco Central) and three state owned banks for agriculture, housing, and mining. The government also has a large interest in the State Bank (Banco del Estado) and a part interest in the Industrial Bank (Banco Industrial). In addition, there are 19 privately owned commercial banks, including 15 locally owned and 4 foreign banks. The First National City Bank of New York (Citibank) is the only U.S. bank with a branch office in Bolivia. Commercial banks account for over 90 percent of the deposits and loan portfolio of the formal Bolivian financial system. The remaining 10 percent is concentrated in savings and loans, credit unions, and other financial institutions.

All commercial banks provide regular banking services, accepting deposits for both checking and savings accounts and offering loans at short and medium term. Foreign banks generally do not accept foreign currency time and demand deposits, nor do they issue small personal loans at more than short term (one year). The government has

authorized local banks to hold dollar-denominated time deposits. The Central Bank performs the function of the U.S. Federal Reserve Bank. It also provides government guarantees on loans to official agencies.

Several money exchange houses legally operating in Bolivia offer prompt conversion of several currencies at legal rates, in addition to transfers. Travelers checks, dollars, and other currencies can be readily exchanged in exchange houses, banks, and major hotels. It is difficult to cash personal checks in Bolivia as a nonresident.

For more detailed information on Bolivia's financial system, including information on securities exchanges, debt-equity investment bonds, export financing lines for Bolivian exporters, project facilities, and financing for private enterprise development, consult the Financing Guide published by the U.S. Department of Commerce's Latin America/Caribbean Business Development Center.

Tapping International Aid Institutions

Foreign aid: The U.S. government alone planned to provide over U.S. $200 million in 1992 in economic, Peace Corps, and military and drug-related bilateral assistance. The Inter-American Development Bank (IDB) projected U.S. $340 million in soft loans for 1992 and 1993, primarily for infrastructure development.

The International Monetary Fund (IMF) currently provides about U.S. $60 million annually in balance of payments (BOP) support.

VISITING AND LOCATING

General Travel Checklist

A business traveler or tourist needs a valid passport to enter Bolivia. U.S. citizens traveling on nonofficial passports do not require visas for stays up to 30 days. Travelers wishing to extend their stay must pay 70 Bolivianos (notated as Bs., and equivalent to U.S. $17.20 at the early December 1992 exchange rate of 4.07 Bs./U.S. $) for the first 30-day renewal, Bs. 100 (U.S. $24.57) for the second 30-day renewal, and Bs. 150 (U.S. $36.86) for each 30-day extension thereafter.

Travelers intending to conduct business in Bolivia which might require juridical sanction, such as the signing of contracts or the payment or collection of fees, must obtain a Special Purpose Visa (Visa de Objeto Determinado) from the Under Secretary of Immigration following arrival in the country. The applicant must present a document prepared and legalized by a Bolivian attorney stating the exact purpose of the visit. The Special Purpose Visa is valid for 90 days upon the payment of U.S. $50. It can be extended for an additional 90 days upon the payment of Bs. 150 (U.S. $36.86).

Travelers may obtain the Special Purpose Visa before traveling to Bolivia at a Bolivian Consulate in the United States for U.S. $25.

Certain foreign companies doing business in Bolivia have special agreements with the Bolivian government that permit their workers and supervisory personnel to reside in Bolivia for up to one or two years without obtaining permanent residence. In these cases the fees vary with the agreement made with the Bolivian government.

Inquiries concerning entry into Bolivia should be directed to one of the Bolivian consular offices located in the United States.

Transportation is hindered by lack of a developed infrastructure. Bolivia has roughly 41,000 kilometers of roads, but only the roads between Oruro, La Paz, and Lake Titicaca; the road to Cochabamba; and the new road under construction between Cochabamba and Santa Cruz are paved. Road links to other countries, except for Peru, are either nonexistent or virtually impassable during wet weather. Rail links exist to Chile, Brazil, and Argentina, and are to be extended to Peru.

The railroads are generally in bad condition; however, a World Bank financed project is designed to improve them. Bolivia uses the ports of Arica, Antofagasta, and Iquique in Chile.

Grain export facilities on the Paraguay River near Brazil are being improved.

Airline connections to other Latin American capitals and to Miami are reasonable. High air transport costs are an important factor in expensive Bolivian production and export costs.

Utilities are adequate to good. Electric power is reliable in the major cities. Residential current in La Paz is 120 and 220 volts, 50 cycles. Cochabamba, Santa Cruz, and most other cities operate on 220 volts, 50 cycles. Water shortages occur during the dry season in La Paz.

Water may not be considered potable by American standards in any Bolivian city, although the major cities have improved their water supply systems in recent years.

Health: La Paz's altitude of 12,500 feet may cause headaches or more serious problems for persons with heart or lung ailments. Persons with health problems may wish to consult a doctor before coming to La Paz. Recent arrivals are advised to limit their activities. Community sanitary conditions are such that it is advisable to boil water at least 20 minutes or to consume bottled water. There are, however, many good and safe restaurants in the major cities. Hepatitis and rabies are endemic diseases in Bolivia, although with proper caution both can easily be avoided.

Telecommunications: National and international telephone and cable services are available in La Paz and in other major cities. Direct telephone dialing is available between the cities of La Paz, Santa Cruz, Cochabamba, Oruro, Tarija, Potosi, and Sucre. Many business establishments operate telex machines. Direct dialing is available between the United States and Bolivia.

Transportation: Taxi fares from the El Alto airport to La Paz vary according to the number of passengers, but generally the charge is Bs. 5 per person (U.S. $1.23) for a collective taxi. Fares for individual taxis average Bs. 20–25 (U.S. $4.91–U.S. $6.14). Within the city, fares average about Bs. 1.50 (U.S. $0.37) during the day and at night Bs. 2 (U.S. $0.49). Rental cars are available, but this service is very expensive and frequently includes a driver who also must be paid. U.S. drivers licenses are valid in Bolivia for 90 days after arrival.

The major cities of Bolivia offer a radio-taxi service with special fares.

Climate: All of Bolivia experiences a rainy season during the summer months (December-March) and a dry season during the winter-spring (March-November). The average daytime temperature is 60 degrees Fahrenheit for most of the year, but evenings are always much cooler. Cochabamba, at a lower altitude, has a milder climate than La Paz. Santa Cruz is a tropical city, generally hot and humid; occasional winds from the southeast can be very cold, however.

Chapter 4
BRAZIL

	Total	Urban
Population (1993)	160,999,000	75.0%

Main Urban Areas	Population	Percentageof Total	International Calling Code
Sao Paulo	10,063,000	6.3	55-11
Rio de Janeiro	5,603,000	3.5	55-21
Belo Horizonte	2,114,000	1.3	55-31
Salvador	1,804,000	1.1	55-71
Fortaleza	1,584,000	1.0	55-85
BRASILIA	1,568,000	1.0	55-61
Nova Iguacu	1,319.000	0.8	55-21
Recife	1,288,000	0.8	55-81
Curitiba	1,279,000	0.8	55-41
Porto Algere	1,272,000	0.8	55-512
Belem	1,117,000	0.7	55-91
Goiania	923,000	0.6	55-62
Campinas	841,000	0.5	55-192
Manaus	810,000	0.5	55-02
Sao Goncalo	728,000	0.5	55-21

Land Area	8,456,510 square kilometers
Comparable U.S. State	Slightly smaller than total USA

Language	Portuguese	97%
	Amerindian	1%
	Other	2%
Common Business Language	Portuguese, English	

Currency	1 cruzeiro (Cr$) = 100 centavos
Exchange Rate (May 1993)	US$ 1.00 = 3810 cruzeiros

Best Nonstop Air Connection via U.S.

Miami to Rio: 8.25 hours
New York to Rio: 9.5 hours
Los Angeles to Rio: 12 hours
Varig (800) 468-2744
One daily nonstop via Miami.
Miami to Sao Paulo: 8.5 hours
Brasilia to Washington, D.C.: 8.5 hours
TransBrazil Airlines (800) 872-3153

Best Hotel

Sheraton Hotel & Towers (U.S. $165)
Av. Niemeyer 121
Rio de Janeiro 22070
Tel: (55-21) 274-1122

INTRODUCTION AND REGIONAL ORIENTATION

With an estimated population of 150 million, Brazil is the most populous country in Latin America and ranks sixth in the world. Most of the people live in the south-central area, which includes the industrial cities of Sao Paulo, Rio de Janeiro, and Belo Horizonte.

Urban growth has been rapid; by 1984 the urban sector included more than two-thirds of the total population. Increased urbanization has aided economic development but, at the same time, has created serious social and political problems in the major cities.

Four major groups make up the Brazilian population: indigenous Indians of Tupi and Guarani language stock; the Portuguese, who began colonizing in the sixteenth century; Africans brought to Brazil as slaves; and various European and Asian immigrant groups that have settled in Brazil since the mid-nineteenth century. The Portuguese often intermarried with the Indians; marriage with slaves was common. Although the basic ethnic stock of Brazil was once Portuguese, subsequent waves of immigration have contributed to a rich ethnic and cultural heritage.

From 1875 until 1960, about five million Europeans emigrated to Brazil, settling mainly in the four southern states of Sao Paulo, Parana, Santa Catarina, and Rio Grande do Sul. The largest Japanese community outside Japan is in Sao Paulo. Despite class distinctions, national identity is strong, and racial friction is a relatively new phenomenon.

Indigenous full-blooded Indians, located mainly in the northern and western border regions and in the upper Amazon Basin, constitute less than 1 percent of the population. Their numbers are rapidly declining as contact with the outside world and commercial expansion into the interior increase. Brazilian government programs to establish reservations and to provide other forms of assistance have been in effect for years but are increasingly controversial.

Brazil is the only Portuguese-speaking nation in the Americas. About 90 percent of the population belongs to the Roman Catholic Church, although many Brazilians adhere to Protestantism and spiritualism.

As its geography, population size, and ethnic diversity would imply, Brazil's cultural profile and achievements are extensive, vibrant, and constantly changing. Popular culture predominates, with a thriving popular music industry, relatively active cinema, and a highly developed television empire, producing an enormous number of soap operas (telenovelas) that have found a world market. The visual arts, especially painting, are lively, while literature and the theater, although important, play a less prominent role in this fast-moving, media-oriented society.

Traditionally, Brazilian culture has developed around regional subjects, with the country's northeast normally identified with national themes, both nativist and Afro-Brazilian, while the urban centers of Sao Paulo and Rio de Janeiro have demonstrated a tendency toward a more international, and European-oriented expression. With the post-1964 push to a more integrated national culture, these tendencies have diminished somewhat but remain central to understanding the uniqueness of this vast nation.

History and Political Conditions

From 1889 to 1930, the government was a constitutional democracy with a limited franchise. The presidency alternated between the dominant states of Sao Paulo and Minas Gerais. This period ended with a military coup by Getulio Vargas, who remained as dictator until 1945. From 1945 to 1961, Eurico Dutra, Vargas, Juscelino Kubitschek, and Janio Quadros were the elected presidents. When Quadros resigned in 1961, he was succeeded by Vice-President Joao Goulart.

Goulart's years in office were marked by high inflation, economic stagnation, and the increasing influence of radical political philosophies. The armed forces, alarmed by these developments, staged a coup on March 31, 1964. The coup leaders chose as president Army Marshal Humberto Castello Branco, who was elected by the National Congress on April 11, 1964. Castello Branco was followed by retired Army Marshal Arthur da Costa e Silva (1967–69), General Emilio Garrastazu Medici (1969–74), and retired General Ernesto Geisel (1974–79). Geisel began the political liberalization process, known as abertura or "opening," which was carried further by his successor, General Joao Baptista de Oliveira Figueiredo (1979–85).

Figueiredo not only permitted the return of politicians exiled or banned during the 1960s and early 1970s but also allowed them to run for state and federal offices in 1982, including the first direct elections for governor since 1966.

However, the electoral college, consisting of all members of Congress and six delegates chosen from each state, continued to choose the president. In January 1985, the electoral college picked Tancredo Neves from the opposition Brazilian Democratic Movement Party (PMDB). However, Tancredo Neves became ill in March and died a month later. His vice-president, the former Senator Jose Sarney, who had been acting president since inauguration day, became president upon Neves's death.

Brazil completed its transition to a popularly elected government in 1989, when Fernando Collor de Mello won 53 percent of the vote in the first direct presidential elections in 29 years.

CRACKING THE MARKET

Demographics

Brazil has a population of 155 million on a landmass which constitutes 48 percent of South America.

Ethnic groups: Portuguese, Italian, German, Japanese, African, Indians, principally Tupi and Guarani linguistic stock.

Religion: Roman Catholic (89%).

Literacy rate: 78% of adult population.

Work force: 62.5 million (1989): agriculture 35%; industry 25%; services 40%.

Trade union membership: about 6 million.

Economy

Brazil is a country rich in resources and natural advantages. To date, however, its economic performance has lagged behind its potential. Economically, it is a country of contrasts ranging from sophisticated economic centers around Sao Paulo to relatively undeveloped trading outposts on the Amazon. Industrial development has been concentrated in the southeastern states of Rio de Janeiro, Sao Paulo, Parana, and Rio Grande do Sul but is now expanding to include the northeast and center west.

In 1988, Brazil's gross domestic product (GDP) totaled U.S. $352 billion, with an estimated per capita GDP of U.S. $2,434. During the 1950s, GDP rose at an annual rate of more than 6 percent, but averaged above 11 percent annually during the 1968-73 "economic miracle." Growth slowed between 1974–80, and from 1981 to 1983 was either negative or nominal. In 1984, the economy began to improve again, and during 1985–86, GDP grew more than 8 percent per year. After slowing in 1987, growth dropped in 1988 to a negative –0.3 percent but climbed again in 1989 to 3–4 percent.

Agriculture, Industry, and Natural Resources

About one-half of Brazil is covered by forests. The largest rain forest in the world is located in the Amazon Basin and is so impressive in character and extent that the entire Amazon region is identified with it. Recent migrations into the Amazon region and controversial large-scale burning of forest areas placed the international spotlight on Brazil. The government has since reduced incentives for such activity and has begun to implement an ambitious environmental plan.

Eastern Brazil has tropical and semideciduous forests and soil of limited agricultural value; the nutrients in the small amount of humus usually are exhausted after only a few years of farming. The softwood forests of the southern highlands still provide a substantial portion of the construction timber used in Brazil. However, fears that these forests are being cut down so fast that they are in danger of extinction within the next few decades have led the industry to move north. Major timber supplies for domestic and export markets now come from the tropical hardwoods of the Amazon. The thorn forests of the northeastern interior contain dry, cactus-infested, drought-resistant vegetation, its sparseness due as much to overgrazing and overcultivation as to the unreliability of rainfall.

In central Brazil, the states of Mato Grosso, Mato Grosso do Sul, Goias, and parts of Minas Gerais and Sao Paulo contain substantial areas of grassland, with only scattered trees. Unlike the plains of North America, the Brazilian grasslands are less fertile, and large areas of these grasslands are best suited to pastures.

The agricultural sector employs 35 percent of Brazil's population and accounts for about 12 percent of its GDP and almost 40 percent of the country's exports. Except for wheat, Brazil is largely self-sufficient in food. It is the world's leading exporter of coffee and orange juice concentrate; the second largest exporter of cocoa and soybeans; and a major exporter of sugar, meat, and cotton. During the past decade, in an effort to expand its agricultural exports, Brazil began opening new regions to cultivation. The most important of these are devoted to soybean production in Mato Grosso do Sul, Rio Grande do Sul, Sao Paulo, Parana and, more recently, Minas Gerais and Goias. Brazil also has expanded cultivation of sugarcane, the raw material used to produce the ethyl alcohol fuel that powers more than half the nation's cars.

Brazil's power, transportation, and communications systems generally have kept pace with development, but, in recent years, facilities in some areas have not met demand due to lack of investment and maintenance funds. The country has a large and increasingly sophisticated industrial base, producing basic industrial products such as steel, chemicals and petrochemicals, and finished consumer goods and aircraft. A computer industry is also emerging.

Within the past decade, industry has been the greatest contributor to economic growth. Today, it accounts for nearly 35 percent of GDP and 60 percent of exports.

Brazil is one of the world's leading producers of hydroelectric power, with a potential of 106,500 megawatts. Existing hydroelectric plants provide 90 percent of the nation's electricity. Two large hydroelectric projects, the 12,600-megawatt Itaipu Dam on the Parana River—the world's largest dam—and the Tucurui Dam in Para in northeast Brazil are in operation.

Proven mineral resources are extensive, and additional exploration is expanding the resource base. Large iron and manganese reserves provide important sources of indus-

BRAZIL
Key Economic Indicators

	1989	1990	1991
Income, Production, Employment			
GDP (U.S. $ billion)	370.0	355.0	358.0[13]
Real GDP growth (%)	3.6	−4.0	0.8 [1]
Real GDP sectoral growth (%)			
Agriculture	2.2	1.0	3.0 [1]
Industry	3.9	−8.0	−0.8 [1]
Service	3.7	1.5	1.6 [1]
GDP per capita (U.S. $)	2,593.0	2,489.0	N/A
Unemployment rate (year-end %)	2.4	4.8	4.04 [2]
Money and Prices			
M-1 (Bil.cruz. year-end)	103.1	1,651.0	6,139 [3]
Commercial interest rate (average monthly rate)	62.2	28.5	24.0 [4]
Gross savings rate (% of GDP)	22.5	21.0	N/A
Gross domestic investment (% of GDP)	22.4	20.5	N/A
Consumer price increase (CPI) (%)	1,764.9	1,650	382 [5]
Wholesale price increase (%)	1,748.8	1,509	359 [6]
Official exchange rate (Cruzeiro/U.S. $)	1,401.3	1,091	505 [7]
(annual % increase)			
Parallel exchange rate (annual% increase)	2,039.9	470	617 [8]
Balance of Payments and Trade			
Total exports (U.S. $ billion)	34.4	31.3	21.9 [9]
Total imports (U.S. $ billion)	18.3	20.1	13.4 [9]
Total exports to U.S. (U.S. $ billion)	8.0	7.2	N/A
Total imports from U.S. (U.S. $ billion)	4.8	5.1	N/A
U.S. aid (U.S. $ million)	8.9	9.4	N/A
Total U.S. investment (U.S. $ billion)	11.4	11.6	N/A
Total foreign debt (year-end U.S. $ billion)	115.1	124.0	118.4[10]
Annual debt service (U.S. $ billion)	15.5	9.2	N/A
Foreign exchange, less gold (U.S. $ billion)	7.3	8.7	8.1[11]
Current account (U.S. $ billion)	1.6	2.2	1.8[12]

1. Forecast by the IPEA/Ministry of Economy.
2. As of September 1991.
3. As of September 1991.
4. Cost of money for working capital for 30 days average for October 1991.
5. National consumer price index (INPC-FIBGE) last 12 months ending in September 1991.
6. Wholesale price index (IPA-FGV) last 12 months ending in September 1991.
7. Commercial dollar rate, last 12 months ending in October 1991.
8. Parallel dollar (Sao Paulo market), last 12 months ending in October 1991.
9. January-August 1991.
10. As of March 1991.
11. As of August 1991.
12. January-June 1991.
13. Estimate.

trial raw materials and export earnings. Deposits of nickel, tin, chromite, bauxite, beryllium, copper, lead, tungsten, zinc, and gold, as well as lesser known minerals, are exploited. Oil exploration is less urgent now, because of Brazil's reduced dependence on oil and lower world prices.

High-quality coal, especially of the coking grade required in the steel industry, is in short supply. The government is beginning to implement coal extraction and gasification projects to tap Brazil's ample deposits of low-grade coal in the south.

Brazil's first commercial nuclear reactor, Angra I, located near Rio de Janeiro, began operating in early 1982. Site preparations began the same year for Angra II and III. With a combined capacity of 1,245 megawatts, these are the first of eight nuclear plants envisioned under the 1975 nuclear accord between the Federal Republic of Germany and Brazil. However, continued troubles with Angra I and scarce funds have slowed construction of nuclear plants, limiting expansion for the foreseeable future to the two reactors already under construction. Brazil also is engaged in research to master the nuclear fuel cycle.

The Brazilian government has undertaken an ambitious program to reduce dependence on imported oil. Imports previously accounted for more than 70 percent of the country's oil needs but now account for only 50 percent. In addition to developing hydroelectric, nuclear, and coal resources, Brazil has become a world leader in the development of alcohol fuel derived from sugarcane. Brazilian automotive gasoline is a mixture containing up to 22 percent ethyl alcohol. Its auto manufacturers began large-scale production of 100 percent alcohol-powered cars in 1979, and today more than 1.5 million are on the road. Alcohol production has not kept pace, however, leading to alcohol shortages in 1989–90. The Collor government cut alcohol subsidies, and car makers have responded by increasing production of gasoline-powered automobiles.

Political/Institutional Infrastructure

The Federative Republic of Brazil gained its independence from Portugal on September 7, 1822.

A Constituent Assembly drafted a new constitution in late 1988 with broad powers granted to the federal level. At the national level, the constitution establishes a presidential system with three "independent and harmonious powers"—executive, legislative, and judicial. It forbids delegation of powers and provides for a series of checks and balances.

The president is assisted by a vice-president (elected with the president), a presidentially appointed cabinet, and specialized administrative and advisory bodies.

The bicameral National Congress consists of 81 senators (three for each state and the federal district) elected to eight-year terms, and 495 deputies elected at large in each state to four-year terms. The elections are based on proportional representation weighted in favor of less populous states. The last congressional elections were held in October 1990.

The apex of the judicial system is the Supreme Federal Tribunal. Its 11 justices, including the chief justice, are appointed by the president to serve until age 70.

Brazil is divided administratively into 26 states and a federal district, Brasilia. The framework of state and local governments closely parallels that of the federal government. Governors, elected for four-year terms, have more limited powers than do their counterparts in the United States. This is due to the highly centralized nature of the Brazilian system. The limited taxing authority granted to states and municipalities— the only territorial subdivisions of the states— further weakens their power.

The federal district, which moved from Rio de Janeiro to Brasilia in April 1960, is governed by a governor and vice-governor, both of whom were chosen in direct elections in 1990.

Principal Government Officials

President
Fernando COLLOR de Mello

Vice-President
Itamar FRANCO

Foreign Affairs
Jose Francisco REZEK

Ambassador to the U.S.
Marcilio M. MOREIRA

Ambassador to the UN
Paulo NOGUEIRA

Current Political Conditions

Following the 1964 military coup, the 13 existing political parties were abolished, and two political organizations, the pro-government National Renewal Alliance (ARENA) and the opposition Brazilian Democratic Movement (MDB), were formed. In 1979, under a government-sponsored bill approved by the congress, this two-party system was abolished, and a multiparty system was allowed to reemerge. In 1989, more than 20 political parties participated in the campaign. The major parties are:

PMDB—Brazilian Democratic Movement Party (Partido do Movimento Democratico Brasileiro). The country's largest party suffered defections in the 1989 campaign. Known as the MDB from 1966 to 1979, under military-dominated governments, the PMDB includes politicians ranging from conservative to left of center. Most state governors and almost all PMDB cabinet members belong to the conservative wing of the party. PMDB popular support is strongest in urban areas.

PFL—Liberal Front Party (Partido da Frente Liberal). The country's second largest party; defeated in the 1989 presidential campaign, it is now aligned with President Fernando Collor de Mello. The PFL espouses views similar to those of the PDS, but looks to different political leaders and maintains fewer ties to the military establishment.

The PFL is strongest in medium-sized towns and the more conservative cities, especially in the northeast. It was founded in 1985 by Democratic Social Party (PDS) dissidents.

PSDB—Brazilian Social Democracy Party (Partido da Social Democracia Brasileira). Led by Senator Mario Covas, the PSDB was founded in 1988 and includes prominent politicians who quit the PMDB, PFL, and PDT over political differences with national or state leaders of those parties. The PSDB advocates adoption of a parliamentary system of government in Brazil.

PDS—Democratic Social Party (Partido Democratico Social). Founded in 1982, the PDS is the modern version of the ARENA party, which represented the government of Brazil's interests during 21 years of military-dominated governments (1964–85). It advocates using foreign capital for economic development. Its popular support is greatest in certain rural strongholds and among upper/middle class in urban areas.

PDT—Democratic Workers Party (Partido Democratico Trabalhista). The PDT is a populist party led by Leonel Brizola. It is strongest in Rio de Janeiro and Rio Grande do Sul, where Brizola was governor. Much of its support comes from slum dwellers and the rural poor. Founded in 1980 by former members of the Brazilian Labor Party (PTB).

PTB—Brazilian Labor Party (Partido Trabalhista Brasileiro). The PTB, founded in 1945, is a populist party without a major national leader. It strongly supports organized labor but advocates center-right positions on many economic issues. PTB was the party of Getulio Vargas, one of Brazil's most popular presidents. For several decades, beginning in 1945, the PTB exercised political control over Brazil's labor sector. PTB support currently is strongest among urban working class, professionals, and small shopkeepers, particularly in Sao Paulo and Parana states.

PT—Workers' Party (Partido dos Trabalhadores). Formed in 1978, the PT is Brazil's "European-style" leftist party, with a clearly defined ideology and program and strict party discipline.

PL—Liberal Party (Partido Liberal). The PL is a center-right party that is popular among small businessmen and has growing strength in Sao Paulo and Rio de Janeiro.

PRN—National Reconstruction Party (Partido da Reconstrucao Nacional). The PRN was created by Collor in 1989 and served as the vehicle for his 1989 presidential campaign. Collor and his advisers generally advocate free-market solutions to Brazil's economic problems.

Brazil also boasts several dozen small parties, some of which (e.g., National Mobilization Party—PMN, Christian Democratic Party—PDC) are significant in specific regions or states.

Flag: A yellow diamond on a green field; a blue globe with 23 white stars and a band with "Ordem e Progresso" centered on the diamond. The globe represents the sky and the vastness of the states and capital, and green and yellow signify forest and mineral wealth.

Foreign Relations

Traditionally, Brazil has been a leader in the inter-American community and has played an important role in collective security efforts as well as in economic cooperation in the Western Hemisphere. Brazil aligned with the allies in both world wars and, during World War II, its expeditionary force in Italy played a key role in the allied victory at Monte Castello. It is a party to the Inter-American Treaty of Reciprocal Assistance (Rio treaty) and the Organization of American States (OAS). In recent years, Brazil has given high priority to expanding relations with its South American neighbors and is a founding member of the Amazon Pact and the Latin American Integration Association (ALADI), the successor to the Latin American Free Trade Association (LAFTA).

Brazil is a charter member of the United Nations and participates in many of its specialized agencies. It has contributed troops to UN peacekeeping efforts in the Middle East, the former Belgian Congo, and Cyprus.

As Brazil's domestic economy has grown and diversified, the country has become increasingly involved in international politics and economics. The United States, Western Europe, and Japan are primary markets for Brazilian exports and sources of foreign lending and investment. Brazil's dependence on imported petroleum has resulted in more intensive political and economic ties with Middle Eastern countries. In the 1970s, Brazil expanded its relations with black African countries. In 1986, it introduced a proposal at the UN General Assembly to establish a Zone of Peace and Cooperation in the South Atlantic. As an indication of Brazil's broader international role, trade with other developing countries increased from 9 percent of the total in the 1970s to nearly 30 percent in 1983.

The Brazilian government has diplomatic relations with the former U.S.S.R., China, all of the Eastern European countries, and Cuba but not with Vietnam, Cambodia, or North Korea.

U.S.-Brazilian Relations

In the 1950s and 1960s, Brazil received about U.S. $2.4 billion in U.S. economic assistance—U.S. $1.4 billion under the auspices of the U.S. Agency for International Development (AID) and the remainder under PL 480 (Food for Peace) and Peace Corps programs. After 1972, U.S. programs stressed training Brazilians in technology and physical and social sciences (in the United States), especially at the graduate level. Some 14,000 persons were trained by AID during this period, 22,000 from all U.S. government sources. In view of Brazil's impressive economic development and its increased ability to obtain loans and technical assistance from private and multilateral sources, U.S. assistance programs were phased out in the 1970s, major AID activities in Brazil ended in 1979, and the Peace Corps program was ended in 1980. Currently, AID maintains a small advanced developing country program that emphasizes cooperation in science and technology and family planning and responds to endemic disease, emergencies, and natural disasters.

The United States is Brazil's most important commercial partner and largest investor. The U.S. share of Brazilian trade averages 22 percent, and two-way trade amounted to U.S. $14.3 billion in 1988. The growing diversification of U.S.-Brazil trade has led to trade disputes. Brazilian trade practices, including prohibition of some imports and difficult import licensing procedures, market reserve requirements on computer products, and the lack of intellectual property protection (especially patents in certain areas)— led to frictions with the United States and other major trading partners. These culminated in 1988 and 1989, when the United States named Brazil in a number of formal trade action, and took retaliatory steps against some Brazilian imports under U.S. trade law. The U.S. objective was to stimulate negotiations as well as action by the government of Brazil to reduce the trade barriers in question. For its part, Brazil was critical of the United States for singling it out and of high U.S. tariffs on products of inter-

est to Brazil such as steel and orange juice. Efforts by both sides during the middle and latter part of 1989 began to reduce the tensions arising from these issues.

The agreements between Brazil and the United States include a treaty of peace and friendship; an extradition treaty; a joint participation agreement on communication satellites; and scientific cooperation, civil aviation, and maritime agreements. Brazil and the United States exchange professors under Fulbright and other academic programs and carry out university cooperation projects.

Trade (1988)

Exports: $33.8 billion.
   Major markets: U.S. 26%; Japan 7%; Netherlands 8%; Germany 4%; Italy 4%; Argentina 3%.
   Imports: $14.7 billion.
   Major suppliers: U.S. 21%; Germany 10%; Japan 7%; Argentina 5%; France 4%.

Trade and Investment Policies

Import licenses: Although Brazil requires licenses for virtually all imports, the Collor administration has generally abandoned the country's long-standing practice of using them as a nontariff barrier to protect domestic industry except in the case of computer and digital electronics equipment which were subject to restrictive licensing until October 29, 1992. After that time, licensing was expected to become automatic. Licenses are now used for statistical and exchange-control purposes and are issued automatically within five days by the Banco do Brasil. All private banks were to be authorized to issue import licenses by March 1992; a pilot program already allowed five private bank branches to do so.

Services barriers: Restrictive investment laws, lack of administrative transparency, legal and administrative restrictions on remittances, and the occasionally arbitrary application of regulations and laws limit U.S. service exports to Brazil. Service trade possibilities are also affected by limitations on foreign capital participation in many service sectors. Foreign companies are prevented from providing technical services unless Brazilian firms are unable to perform them. Brazilian cargo reserve laws restrict maritime competition.

Financial services, in particular, are severely restricted under the 1988 constitution. As of November 1991, no new foreign banking investments were allowed, and existing foreign banks were prevented from doing business with para-statal companies or from acting as depositories for federal tax receipts.

Foreign participation in the insurance industry is impeded by limitations on foreign investment, market reserves for Brazilian firms in areas such as import insurance, and the requirement that para-statals purchase insurance only from Brazilian-owned firms. Further, the lucrative reinsurance market is reserved for the state monopoly, the Reinsurance Institute of Brazil (IRB).

Investment barriers: In addition to the restrictions on insurance and financial services investments mentioned above, foreign investment is prohibited in other sectors, including petroleum production and refining, public utilities, media, real estate, shipping, and various "strategic industries." In still other sectors, Brazil limits foreign equity participation (such as in computer and digital electronics equipment), imposes local content requirements and links incentives to export performance.

In September 1991, the Collor administration proposed several amendments to the national constitution, two of which, if passed by Congress, would rescind state monopolies in the petroleum sector and remove the limit on foreign equity participation in mining. It is presently still uncertain whether the amendments will have a significant impact on U.S. interest.

Brazil restricts dividend and profit remittances in an effort to spur domestic reinvestment. Annual remittances by foreign firms exceeding 12 percent of registered capital are taxed at steeply graduated rates to a maximum of 60 percent. As of November 1991, the Brazilian Congress was considering a major revision of the law governing foreign remittances which would considerably reduce the overall tax rate. As with the proposed amendments on state monopolies, the situation was inconclusive, but with indications that the revision would eventually be approved.

As part of the Collor I economic stabilization plan, almost all Brazilian financial accounts were frozen in March 1990. The government also blocked an estimated U.S. $1.5 billion in deposits awaiting foreign remittance for a period of six weeks, then allowed their release over the following six months. The government has stated its intention not to impose another remittance block despite increasing inflationary pressures.

Brazilian governments in the past have not hesitated to apply price controls on a wide range of industrial products in attempts to fight inflation. Established foreign investors in Brazil, notably in the auto and pharmaceutical industries, have complained that formerly inflexible price controls forced them into unprofitable production and resulted in lower investment levels. Although the Collor administration has abolished controls on most items, it has threatened to impose selective price controls on those products having increases out of proportion to production costs.

Informatics: In 1984 Brazil approved a law codifying and extending policies followed since the 1970s to promote a national computer industry.

The informatics sector is broadly defined to include not only computers and parts, but all other devices incorporating digital technology. The law granted Brazil's executive branch the authority to restrict imports and foreign investment in this sector through October 1992. U.S. export and investment losses resulting from Brazil's restrictive informatics policies have been substantial, although no reliable quantitative estimates are available.

The restrictive Brazilian informatics law was the subject of a U.S.-initiated Section 301 investigation between 1985 and 1989. Upon assuming office, the Collor administration undertook to revise the informatics policy with the aim of lowering domestic acquisition costs and improving user access to imported or locally manufactured foreign technology. The administration proposed a new law which was passed by Congress in September 1991 and signed by President Collor in October. The law upholds the October 1992 date for ending the restriction on imported informatics products and allows foreign firms to enter the market (although full foreign ownership is still limited by the new law) without being compelled to set up Brazilian majority-owned joint ventures, as required under the previous informatics law.

Data processing and telecommunications: In July 1991, Brazil partially opened up the market for telecommunications, allowing private sector use of public telephone lines for domestic and international data communications, and the installation of private satellite receivers. Other changes during 1991 include the expiration of the market reserve for telephone switching equipment, and the new informatics law, which will make it easier to import telecom-related computing equipment both immediately and after 1992.

Common Market of the South (Mercosul): In August 1990, Brazil, Argentina, Paraguay, and Uruguay jointly signed a treaty establishing a timetable for creation of the Mercosul common market. The target date for complete economic integration is 1995, by which time the four countries aim to harmonize tariffs, industrial and transportation standards, intellectual property, and consumer protection codes, and institute similar tax regimes. The Brazilian Congress ratified the treaty in October 1991.

The United States has encouraged the creation of Mercosul and, in June 1991, embraced it as part of the Enterprise of the Americas Initiative under the "Four plus One" agreement, whereby the U.S. and the four countries in Mercosul will consult closely on trade and investment relations. However, the effects that Mercosul might have on U.S. exporters and investors are still unclear. Manufacturers with local operations may find advantages in rationalizing production facilities among the four countries and welcome harmonization of tariffs, consumer codes, and other laws to the extent that it simplifies access to the larger market. Others, particularly exporters to the Mercosul countries, fear that possible "upward" harmonization of nontariff barriers could restrict their access to existing markets.

Government procurement: Federal, state and municipal governments in Brazil, as well as related agencies and companies, follow a "buy national" policy. Brazil rescinded a law prohibiting foreign-owned firms from bidding on public sector contracts financed by international financial institutions. However, some state-controlled firms still specify contracts as open only to "national" firms.

Although Brazil now applies "buy national" policies informally, the Brazilian constitution mandates government discrimination in favor of "Brazilian companies with national capital." However, these constitutional provisions have not been implemented. The Collor administration has proposed a constitutional amendment which would substantially alter the definition of "national capital," which might reduce or eliminate the threat of discrimination against subsidiaries of foreign companies in government procurement contracts.

While federal agencies and para-statals have been given additional leeway under the Collor administration to import foreign manufactured goods, there is still evidence of the tendency to exclude non-Brazilian suppliers whenever possible. One example is the new informatics law, which calls for government procurement from non-Brazilian companies only if nationally made equipment/services are not competitive.

Brazil is not a signatory to the GATT Code on Government Procurement.

Policies to Attract New Business

Collor has put into place the administrative machinery to implement an ambitious privatization program and has opened Brazil's markets to foreign goods.

Foreign direct investment represents a relatively small but important part of Brazil's capital base. The share of foreign direct investment and reinvestment registered with the central investments totaled U.S. $8.7 billion, largely in manufacturing and finance. The constitution restricts the entry of new foreign investors in the financial services area, although the U.S. and other foreign institutions established before the prohibition continue to have a prominent role. The constitution also contains provisions that restrict investment in petroleum and minerals exploration, health care, chemicals, biotechnology, and new materials. The Congress has not yet completed legislation on foreign investment.

Trade Financing Environment and Options

While Brazil had a broad range of export subsidy programs for manufactured goods and processed agricultural products, all were abolished in mid-1990 with the advent of the Collor administration.

In 1991 the government established PROEX, an export-import financing fund. In October 1991, interest rates for export credits were 8.0 and 8.5 percent for, respectively, developing and developed countries. These rates, and other rules affecting export incentives, are considered to broadly conform to the Organization for Economic Cooperation and Development (OECD) guidelines.

FINANCING AND CAPITAL MARKETS

General Policy Framework

Upon assuming office in March 1990, President Collor immediately announced his intention to implement sweeping economic reforms designed to stop inflation and integrate Brazil into the developed world economy.

Although Collor's first two economic programs have significantly reduced trade barriers, the failure to reduce substantially Brazil's large fiscal deficit has resulted in the continual resurgence of inflation and a lack of confidence in the government's economic policy.

Inflation ran at a monthly rate near 25 percent in October 1991. The government hoped to implement a tax reform program prior to the end of 1991 which would substantially reduce the fiscal deficit, enable Brazil to obtain an IMF program, reschedule its external debts owed to commercial banks and Paris Club creditors, and regain private-sector confidence in the ability of the government to maintain a stable economic environment.

Given Brazil's history and the current lack of support for President Collor in the Congress, the domestic and external financial markets are highly skeptical that the government will be able to achieve all of these objectives and that structural inflation

INVESTMENT CLIMATE
Extent of U.S. Investment in Goods-Producing Sectors
U.S. Direct Investment Position Abroad
on a Historical-Cost Basis—1990
(U.S. $ million)

Category		Amount
Petroleum		650
Total manufacturing		11,286
Food and kindred products	870	
Chemicals and allied products	2,172	
Metals, primary and fabricated	1,232	
Machinery, except electrical	2,169	
Electric and electronic equipment	742	
Transportation equipment	1,520	
Other manufacturing	2,581	
Wholesale trade		302
TOTAL PETROLEUM/MANUFACTURING/WHOLESALE TRADE		12,238

Source: U.S. Department of Commerce, *Survey of Current Business* (August 1991, vol. 71, no. 8, table 11.3).

Foreign direct investment and reinvestment in Brazil (registered with Central Bank as of June 1988): U.S. $30.7 billion. Sources—U.S., U.S. $8.7 billion (28%); Germany, U.S. $4.8 billion (16%); Japan, U.S. $2.9 billion (10%); Switzerland, U.S. $2.9 billion (9%); UK U.S. $1.9 billion (6%); and Canada, $1.4 billion (5%).

can be reduced from the monthly double-digit range.

Monetary policy: Brazil has made many attempts during the 1980s to tighten monetary policy in an effort to reduce inflation. However, these attempts were compromised by the failure of the government to correct a large fiscal deficit, forcing the Central Bank to soften its policies. In March 1990, the Collor government introduced a stabilization program (Collor I) which included price controls and the blocking of about two-thirds of the financial assets in the economy for a period of 18 months.

These measures initially stopped inflation (then approximately 90 percent per month) and substantially slowed economic activity. Concerns about negative growth led

the government to prematurely release a large portion of the blocked assets.

By mid-1990 the monthly inflation rate was around ten percent and by the end of the year it was in the 20 percent range.

On January 31, 1991, the Collor government introduced another package of measures designed to reduce inflation (Collor II). The package included wage and price controls. It also eliminated the generalized "overnight" market, which was complicating monetary policy, through the imposition of a graduated tax on early withdrawals. The program initially brought monthly inflation below 10 percent. However, the failure to reduce the structural fiscal deficit, intermittent tightening and loosening of monetary policy, the unfreezing of prices and wages by the third quarter, and the unfreezing of remaining blocked accounts resulted in monthly inflation rising above 20 percent by the fourth quarter.

Large fiscal deficits and uneven monetary policy are the underlying factors causing inflation in Brazil. During the first Collor plan, the government managed to reduce the operational fiscal deficit from nearly 7 percent of GDP in 1989 to a surplus of 1.3 percent of GDP. However, the bulk of the improvement was made through a series of one-time measures that did not address the structural deficit. Among such measures were the payment of negative real interest rates on the blocked financial assets and government securities, the payment of low real wages to public-sector employees, and a one-time financial assets tax. The operational deficit in 1991 was expected to be on the order of 3 percent of GDP and was on a rising trend. The government has presented a series of tax reform proposals designed to simplify and increase revenues in an effort to improve its fiscal position. This program passed the Congress at the end of 1991.

Debt Management Policies

Brazil's external debt totaled about U.S. $120 billion at the end of 1990. About half this amount represents commercial bank medium- and long-term loans. In July 1989, Brazil stopped servicing payments on medium- and long-term debts owed to commercial banks. By the end of 1990, interest arrears owed to banks totaled nearly U.S. $9 billion. In January 1991, Brazil resumed paying 30 percent of interest payments falling due to banks.

In April 1991, Brazil and its commercial bank creditors agreed on a program that involved payment in cash of 25 percent of the arrears outstanding as of December 1990 and the issuance of 10-year bonds for the remainder.

Brazil is currently negotiating with its creditor banks on a Brady Plan package that would reschedule medium- and long-term debts and eliminate remaining arrears. Brazil also wants to renegotiate its bilateral official debt under a Paris Club accord. Both, however, are contingent on an agreement with the IMF on a stabilization program which was approved in January 1992. A major condition for IMF approval was the passage by the Brazilian Congress of a tax package to help close the fiscal deficit.

As of November 1991, Brazil's debt service ratio (total external debt service payments to exports) was approximately 45 percent, while the ratio of interest payments to exports of goods and services was about 24 percent; Brazil's debt ratio (total external debt to GNP) was about 30 percent.

The Currency and Exchange Rate Mechanisms

Brazil has three exchange rates: a commercial rate, the tourist rate, and the underground, but officially tolerated, parallel rate. Import-export transactions utilize the commercial rate, while the tourist and parallel rates are generally for individual transactions. During 1991, the Central Bank intervened in the commercial market on a daily basis to allow the cruzeiro to depreciate against the dollar in small, uneven increments. The Central Bank also strived to maintain the spread between the parallel and commercial rates at about 12 percent. Private arbitrage generally keeps the tourist rate slightly below the parallel rate.

Increases in the spread between the parallel and commercial rates had generally been seen as an indicator of future expectations of inflation and depreciation of the commercial rate, but the parallel rate is heavily influenced by short-term speculative movements.

During most of 1991, depreciation of the

various rates was not enough to offset increasing inflation; throughout most of the year the Brazilian currency was viewed by many economists to be at least 20 percent overvalued in relation to the U.S. dollar. However, in the last quarter of 1991, the commercial rate was devalued by 15 percent in real terms, so that, as of November, the exchange rate became more closely aligned with international purchasing power parities. However, the spread between the parallel and commercial rates has widened, reaching a peak of 42 percent in late October, indicating future volatility in the exchange markets.

Financial Market Operations and Structural Policies

In August 1991, the government began to return the remaining blocked financial assets, and, in the third quarter, reduced price controls decreed under the two Collor plans. Although the government has spoken of the possibility of selectively reimposing some price controls, prices are now largely determined by market demand.

Tax policies were undergoing a major review at the end of 1992. The Collor administration has proposed a four-tier personal income tax that would raise the marginal rate to 35 percent and eliminate many exemptions.

At the same time, other bills in Congress could establish a unitary personal income tax and a comprehensive value-added tax.

While Brazilian tariffs remain relatively high, rates were substantially reduced in March 1991, especially for machinery and raw materials. The current trade-weighted average tariff rate is approximately 32 percent, with a maximum rate of 85 percent, down from 105 percent in 1990. At present, only 600 items of traded goods enjoy bound Most Favored Nation (MFN) status in Brazil, about 5 percent of the total, compared to

an average of 90 percent among GATT members.

VISITING AND LOCATING

General Travel Checklist

Entry requirements: Visas are required of U.S. citizens. No inoculations are required for entry. Within Brazil, travelers may be required to present a yellow fever certificate when transiting between certain cities.

Climate and clothing: In most parts of the country, days range from warm to hot, except during the rainy period from November through February. The extreme south of Brazil does get cold during the winter (June-August). Wear spring or summer clothes.

Health: Sanitation facilities in many places are being expanded. Carefully prepared and thoroughly cooked foods are safe for consumption. Tap water is not recommended. Yellow fever, rabies, gamma globulin, typhoid, and polio immunizations are recommended.

Telecommunications: Telegraph and long distance telephone services are good. Brasilia is two time zones ahead of eastern standard time; however, time differences vary, due to daylight savings time, in both Brazil and the United States.

Transportation: Direct air service is available. Rio is the normal point of entry, but Sao Paulo, Manaus, Recife, and Belem also have international flights. Domestic flights are expensive. Trains are limited. Inter-city buses run frequently and are inexpensive but often crowded. Metered taxis with red license plates have relatively low rates after 11 p.m. and on weekends. Tipping is the same as in the U.S. The highway system in southeastern Brazil and as far north as Salvador is adequate, but road maintenance is sometimes incomplete.

Security: Street crime is common in Brazil's larger cities and tourists should take precautions such as not wearing jewelry, flashing money, or otherwise calling attention to expensive personal belongings. For more information, check the Department of State's Tips for Travelers.

Chapter 5
CHILE

	Total	Urban	
Population (1993)	13,689,000	84.0%	

Main Urban Areas	Population	Percentage of Total	International Calling Code
SANTIAGO	4,858,000	35.5	56-2
Vina Del Mar	297,000	2.2	56-32
Concepcion	294,000	2.1	56-41
Valparaiso	279,000	2.0	56-32
Talcahuano	231,000	1.7	56-41
Temuco	218,000	1.6	56-45
Antofagasta	205,000	1.5	56-83
Rancagua	172,000	1.3	56-72
Arica	170,000	1.2	56-80
Talca	164,000	1.2	56-71
Puerto Montt	113,000	0.8	56-65
Punta Arenas	112,000	0.8	56-61

Land Area	748,800 square kilometers
Comparable U.S. State	Slightly smaller than twice the size of Montana
Language	Spanish 92%
	Mapudungun 4%
	Other 4%
Common Business Language	Spanish, English
Currency	1 Chilean peso (Ch$) = 100 centavos
Exchange Rate (May 1993)	U.S. $1.00 = 393.20 pesos
Best Nonstop Air Connection via U.S.	Miami to Santiago: 8.5 hours
	New York to Santiago: 12 hours
	Los Angeles to Santiago: 12 hours
	American Airlines (800) 433-7300
	LAN Chile Airlines (800) 735-5526
	Both offer one nonstop daily via Miami
Best Hotel	Hyatt Regency Santiago (U.S. $200)
	Av. Kennedy 4601
	Santiago
	Tel: (56-2) 218-1234
	(800) 33-1234
	Fax: (56-2) 218-3155

INTRODUCTION AND REGIONAL ORIENTATION

About 82 percent of Chile's population live in urban centers, including the 39 percent of the total population who live in the Santiago metropolitan area. The largest population group is of Spanish ancestry, but a small, yet influential, number of Irish and English immigrants came to Chile during the colonial era. German immigration began in 1848 and lasted for 90 years; the southern provinces of Valdivia, Llanquihue, and Osorno have a strong German imprint. Other significant immigrant groups are Italian, Yugoslav, French, and Arab.

About 400,000 persons of predominantly Indian descent, mostly of the Mapuche tribe, reside in the south-central area around Temuco.

Geographical Background

Northern Chile is desert and contains great mineral wealth, primarily copper and nitrates. The relatively small central area dominates the country in terms of population and agricultural resources. This is also the historical center from which Chile expanded until the late nineteenth century, when it incorporated its northern and southern extremes. Southern Chile is rich in forests and grazing lands and has a string of volcanoes and lakes. The southern extreme of this region is a labyrinth of fjords, inlets, canals, twisting peninsulas, and islands. It also has modest but rapidly declining petroleum resources, supplying only about one-fifth of Chile's domestic crude petroleum requirements during the first half of 1989.

History and Political Conditions

Although Chile established a representative democracy in the early twentiethth century, it soon became unstable and degenerated into a system protecting the interests of the ruling oligarchy. By the 1920s, the newly emergent middle- and working-classes were powerful enough to elect a reformist president, but his program was frustrated by a conservative Congress. Continuing political and economic instability resulted in the quasi-dictatorial rule of Gen. Carlos Ibanez (1924–32).

When constitutional procedures were restored in 1932, a strong middle-class party, the Radicals, formed. The Radical Party became the key force in coalition governments for the next 20 years. The 1920s saw the emergence of Marxist groups with strong popular roots. During the period of radical dominance (1932–52), the state increased its role in the economy. However, presidents generally were more conservative than the parties supporting them, and conservative political elements continued to exert considerable power through their influence over the economy and control of rural voters.

The 1964 presidential election of Christian Democrat Eduardo Frei by an absolute majority initiated a period of major reform. Under the slogan "Revolution in Liberty," the Frei administration—the first Christian Democratic government in Latin America—embarked on far-reaching social and economic programs, particularly in education, housing, and agrarian reform (including rural unionization of agricultural workers). By 1967, however, Frei was encountering increasing opposition from leftists who alleged his reforms were inadequate and from conservatives who found them excessive. At its term's end, the Frei administration had made noteworthy accomplishments but had not achieved the party's ambitious goals.

The 1970 presidential election was won narrowly by Dr. Salvador Allende, a Marxist and member of Chile's Socialist Party, who headed the "Popular Unity" (UP) coalition of socialists, communists, radicals, and dissident Christian Democrats. His program included the takeover of many of Chile's private industries and banks, massive land expropriation and collectivization, and the nationalization of American interests in Chile's major copper mines.

Elected with only 36 percent of the vote and by a plurality of 36,000 votes, Allende never enjoyed majority support in the Chilean Congress or broad-based support for his policies. By 1973, most domestic production had declined, and severe shortages of consumer goods, food, and manufactured products were widespread. There were mass demonstrations against the government, recurring strikes, violence by both government supporters and opponents, and widespread rural unrest. Chilean society became polarized into two hostile camps.

These factors, plus public censure of the Allende government by the Chilean Congress, judiciary, and comptroller general for many abuses—including violations of the constitution—brought about a military coup on September 11, 1973. The new military regime, led by General Augusto Pinochet, severely repressed perceived opponents, especially those it believed to be Marxist. The Congress was abolished, and all political parties were banned. Thousands of Chileans were imprisoned and later released or expelled from the country. About 700 others disappeared after arrest by the security forces and are presumed dead.

During its 16 years in power, the military moved Chile away from economic statism toward a largely free market economy, fostering an increase in domestic and foreign private investment. The government slowly reinstitutionalized political life after years of repression and permitted broad freedom of assembly, speech, and association, including trade union activity.

General Pinochet was denied another eight-year term as president in a national plebiscite on October 5, 1988. On December 14, 1989, Christian Democrat Patricio Aylwin, running as the candidate of a 17-party coalition, was elected president. In addition, 38 senators and 120 deputies were elected, and nine appointed senators were named in December. The new government and Congress took office in March 1990. General Pinochet remained commander-in-chief of the army, as permitted in the 1980 constitution. The commander-in-chief of the air force and the director general of carabineros (police) were asked by President Aylwin to remain in their posts. Cabinet ministers are appointed by the president, and regional administrators of the larger cities (intendants), provincial governors, mayors, and rectors of the state universities are also appointed by the central government.

CRACKING THE MARKET

Demographics

Ethnic groups: Spanish-Indian (mestizo), European, Indian.

Religions: Roman Catholic, 89%; Protestant 11%, small Jewish population.

Language: Spanish.

Work force: 4,674,600 (December 1989): agriculture, forestry and fishing 19.3%; industry and commerce 34.1%; services (including government) 30.3%; construction 6.7%; mining 2.3%.

Central government budget (1989): $6.5 billion.

Economy

Chile is rich in natural and human resources. Over much of Chile's history, this resource base had provided a life of relative luxury for the nation's elites but little for the rest of the population. During the last several decades, a politically active middle class has emerged.

This new class demanded a reexamination of how the nation's wealth is managed and shared. From 1925 to 1973, Chile experimented with various economic philosophies, but the general trend was toward increasing state intervention in the economy and protecting or isolating the Chilean economy from outside competition.

In 1970–73, the Allende regime experimented with consumption-oriented state socialism. This produced enormous fiscal deficits fed in part by large consumer subsidies and financed by explosive money growth. By 1973, real per capita gross domestic product (GDP) and real wages had fallen well below the levels of 1970; agricultural production had dropped to the level of the early 1960s; monthly inflation had reached an annual rate above 1,000 percent; the central government deficit expanded to 20 percent of GDP; the black market exchange rate rose to more than 10 times the official rate; and net international reserves were negative.

In mid-1975, in the face of a severe international recession, sharply lower copper prices, quadrupling of oil prices, and lingering damage from Allende's policies, Chile turned to a set of monetarist policies. The key objectives were to eliminate inflation and to allow market forces greater sway. Tariffs were reduced, foreign investment was welcomed, and capital controls were liberalized. Hundreds of nationalized companies were sold to the private sector, although the government retained control of certain companies, notably the large copper mining and refining enterprise CODELCO. Most markets were freed from government controls, and prices were allowed to seek their own levels.

Under these policies, from 1976–81, GDP increased in real terms by an annual average of over 7 percent, inflation declined dramatically, and significant improvements were registered in the general health and welfare of the people. By mid-1981, however, Chile began to suffer the effects of the economic slowdown of its major trading partners. Prices for Chile's exports, such as copper, forest products, and fishmeal, declined sharply. In addition, a fixed peso/dollar exchange rate seriously eroded the competitiveness of Chilean products. To compensate for a lack of competitiveness, Chile borrowed heavily from foreign banks and multilateral financial institutions. In 1982, in part because of events elsewhere, foreign banks stopped lending, creating a serious liquidity shortage. Domestic interest rates rose quickly.

By mid-1982, in the face of a serious decline in domestic production, a sharp rise in unemployment, increasing bankruptcies, and financial deterioration, the Chilean government devalued the peso. In the ensuing recession, GDP fell by 14.1 percent in 1982. The government temporarily took over several large banks with serious economic difficulties, renegotiated the large foreign debt coming due in 1983–84, and supported the renegotiation of domestic bank loans.

In early 1983, Chile agreed to a two-year International Monetary Fund (IMF) macroeconomic austerity program to begin in early 1983. As a result of the IMF measures, the economy declined by 0.7 percent in 1983. In 1984, however, the economy grew 6.3 percent. Continuing foreign exchange shortages limited growth to 2.4 percent in 1985, but in 1986, 1987, and 1988 it recovered to 5.7 percent, 5.4 percent, and 7.4 percent respectively.

In 1988 and 1989, the Pinochet government broke with its austerity program and pursued a set of policies designed to boost economic activity before the 1988 plebiscite and subsequent election in 1989.

Growth soared in 1989 to 10 percent. Inflation nearly doubled to 21.4 percent, and imports jumped 30 percent. Although these expansive policies complicated subsequent adjustment efforts, Chile's economy remains fundamentally sound.

Under the IMF macroeconomic program for 1985–88, Chile continued to achieve strong economic growth while skillfully managing its large external debt-servicing burden. Good performance under the IMF program has assured private commercial lenders that Chile will continue to follow rational economic policies. Long-term prospects for the Chilean economy are heavily influenced by Chile's large external debt ($18 billion as of June 1989) and the low but increasing level of domestic savings and investment. The innovative use of debt for equity swaps has reduced the public sector's medium- to long-term debt with private international banks from $14 billion in 1985 to about $5 billion in June 1990. At the very end of the Pinochet government, Chile took a major step towards establishing a modern banking system. In a unique agreement between the military junta and the political opposition, the central bank became an autonomous institution. The Pinochet government and the political opposition each named two of the five members of the board of governors. The president of the central bank was chosen as a mutually agreed-upon neutral. The central bank is now independent of the rest of government, but its leadership has worked closely with the government of Chile to coordinate policies.

Agriculture

Since the 1982 devaluation, the Chilean agricultural sector experienced a major expansion. Fruit production, in particular, grew 68 percent over the last 6 years and became a principal foreign exchange earner—$0.8 billion in 1989, 166 percent more than in 1983.

The United States is Chile's main agricultural trading partner. In 1989, the United States bought 47 percent of Chile's agricultural exports, mostly fruit, while providing 34 percent of the country's imports. Wheat was Chile's principal agricultural import from the United States, although sales have declined substantially due to Chile's growing self-sufficiency in domestic production.

Most farming occurs in the 1,127 kilometer (700 mi.) stretch of central Chile extending from just north of Santiago to Puerto Montt in the south. Chile's agricultural land is only 30 percent of its territory as compared to the United States, where 76 percent of the land is fit for agricultural uses. Wheat, corn, grapes (wine and table varieties), beans, sugar beets, and fruits are the major crops. Crop yields tend to be higher than in most Latin American countries. Livestock production consists primarily of beef and poultry; beef is pasture fed, and poultry production is much the same as in the United States.

Chile is now a net agricultural exporter but will continue to import tropical products. Chilean agricultural exports consist principally of fresh and processed fruits, pulses, vegetables, wine, and wool.

Exports of these products are growing and will help promote an agricultural trade balance.

Minerals and Mining

Although mining accounts for only 7.6 percent of GDP, mineral products accounted for 55.4 percent of the country's merchandise exports in 1989. Despite the growth of non-copper exports, copper as a percentage of total export earnings has remained roughly the same because of growing production and higher prices. In 1989, copper exports reached a record $4 billion, accounting for almost 50 percent of total exports. Chile is the world's largest producer and exporter of copper, with reserves estimated at about 20 percent of the world total. Most of the ore is processed into refined or blister copper before export, with the remainder being exported in the form of copper concentrate. The country's largest copper producer is the state-owned CODELCO, which produces about 1.2 million metric tons of copper annually.

Chile also exports important quantities of gold, silver, iron ore, molybdenum, natural nitrate, and iodine, and is a growing producer of strategic materials such as rhenium, lithium, selenium, tellurium, and vanadium.

Chile mines bituminous coal in the Gulf of Arauco region, south of Concepcion, in the area around Valdivia, and in the area north of the Strait of Magellan, where modern, low-cost, open-pit mining techniques are applicable. Because of declining petroleum production and an increasing dependence on imported petroleum, coal is expected to play a greater role in meeting Chile's energy needs in future years.

All of Chile's domestic petroleum production comes from the Strait of Magellan and the island of Tierra del Fuego at the southern tip of the country. The state-owned petroleum company, ENAP, is the country's only producer of crude petroleum and natural gas. Because of resource depletion and growing domestic consumption, petroleum production fell to about one-fifth of domestic crude petroleum consumption during 1989, down two-fifths from 1982. Barring unexpected discoveries, Chile's crude petroleum imports, currently running at $600 million per year, will increase.

Industry

Most of Chile's industrial infrastructure was built during the 1930s and 1940s in an effort to replace imported consumer goods, which were in short supply. Manufacturing grew under the protection of high tariffs, and no effort was made to enter into international competition for markets. As a result, much of Chilean industry was inefficient. After 1973, when tariff reductions exposed the Chilean economy to foreign competition, the manufacturing sector was one of the most seriously affected. Fixing the peso to the dollar from 1979 to 1982 hurt manufacturing even more. During the 1982–83 recession,

capacity utilization fell dramatically, and many industries collapsed.

With the adoption of a more realistic exchange rate in 1984–85, the manufacturing sector has been one of the engines leading Chile's export growth. At the same time, efficient domestic industries have replaced imports, boosting employment in the manufacturing sector.

Manufacturing output as a share of GDP has started to increase again from a low of 19 percent in 1982 to over 21 percent in 1989.

Natural resources: Copper, timber, fish, iron ore, nitrates, precious metals, and molybdenum.

Agriculture and fisheries (10% of GDP): Products—wheat, potatoes, corn, sugar beets, onions, beans, fruits, livestock. Arable land—6.6%. Cultivated land—2.5%.

Industry (21% of GDP): Types—textiles, metal manufacturing, food processing, fish processing, pulp, paper, and wood products.

Political/Institutional Infrastructure

The Republic of Chile gained independence on September 18, 1810.

The constitution was approved in a 1980 national plebiscite by a two-thirds majority. Following discussions between the minister of interior, the leader of the coalition of parties opposing Pinochet, and the president of the center-right National Renewal Party, a list of amendments to the constitution was submitted to a plebiscite, and endorsed by over 85 percent of the electorate. Although critics of the 1980 constitution contended the reforms were not sufficiently far-reaching, they eased provisions for amending the constitution; increased the number of elected senators; diminished the role of the national security council and equalized the number of civilian and military members;

CHILE
Key Economic Indicators
(Billions of 1977 Chilean Pesos, Unless Otherwise Noted[1])

	1989	1990	1991
Income, Production, and Employment			
Real GDP	470	480	504[9]
GDP (billions of dollars)	25.5	26.0	27.3[9]
Real GDP growth rate	10	2.1	5[9]
Agriculture, livestock, and forestry	38	40	N/A
Fishing	5	4	N/A
Mining	36	35	N/A
Manufacturing	99	99	N/A
Electricity, gas, and water	12	12	N/A
Construction	27	28	N/A
Trade	85	86	N/A
Transportation/communication	30	33	N/A
Services	139	141	N/A
Real per capita income (thousands of Chilean pesos)	36	36	38[9]
Real per capita income (thousands of dollars)	1.9	1.9	2.0[9]
Labor force (millions)[3]	4.7	4.7	4.7[2]
Unemployment rate[3]	6.3	5.7	7.0[4]
Money and Prices			
Money supply (M1) (billion Chilean pesos)	412	484	688[9]
Commercial interest rates			
Deposits (nominal monthly rate)	2.05	2.83	1.46[5]
Loans and discounts (nominal monthly rate)	2.58	3.34	1.87[5]
Gross domestic saving	16.20	17.20	17.50
Investment rate (% of GDP)	17.2	17.5	16.2[9]
Consumer price index	21.4	27.30	20.0[9]
Wholesale price index	22.8	25.7	18.0[9]
Exchange rate (official)	267	313	360[9]
Exchange rate (parallel)	261	305	350[9]
Balance of Payments and Trade			
(billions current U.S. $ unless noted)			
Total exports FOB	8.1	8.3	8.7[9]
Total exports to U.S.	1.5	1.5	N/A
Total imports CIF	6.5	7.0	7.2[9]
Total imports from U.S.	1.5	1.4	N/A
Aid from U.S.[6]	0.1	0.9	N/A
Aid from other countries	N/A	N/A	N/A
External public debt	16.3	17.5	17.4[7]
Annual debt service payments (paid)	1.6	1.5	N/A
Gold and foreign exchange reserves	2.9	5.3	5.7[8]
Balance of payments	0.4	2.4	0.4[8]

1. National accounts available only in 1977 Chilean pesos. Translation of these figures into 1977 dollars distorts the structure of GDP. (Exchange rate: U.S. $1 = Ch pesos 26.54)
2. As of July 1991
3. Year-end values
4. June-August 1991
5. January-June 1991
6. May 1991
7. As of July 1991
8. As of August 1991
9. Projection

and shortened the presidential period beginning March 1990 to four years, although subsequent presidential terms will be eight years.

The bicameral national Congress is composed of 47 senators (38 elected members and nine designated ones) and 120 deputies. Senators serve for eight years, with staggered terms. Deputies are elected for four years. The new Congress took office on March 11, 1990. Current law provides for the location of the new Congress in the port city of Valparaiso, about 140 kilometers (84 mi.) west of the capital, Santiago.

Chile's congressional elections are governed by a unique binominal majority system in which political parties or groupings form pacts and permit slates (two candidates per slate), from which two senators and two deputies are elected from each district. To determine the winner under this system, a total vote count is made for each individual candidate as well as for each party list. If a leading pact or list receives more than double the vote of the second place list, it wins both seats in that particular district. If the top list's vote is equal to or less than double that of the runner-up list, then the leading candidate from each party in the top two lists is elected.

The political parties with the largest representation in the Chilean Congress are the center-left Christian Democrat Party followed by the center-right National Renewal Party. No communists were elected in either chamber. The center-left coalition supporting President Aylwin captured about 60 percent of the elected seats in both the Senate and the Chamber of Deputies. However, with nine designated senators, the center-right has a 25–22 advantage in the Senate.

Administrative subdivisions: 12 numbered regions, plus Santiago metropolitan region, administered by intendants; regions are divided into provinces, administered by governors; and provinces into municipalities, administered by mayors.

Principal Government Officials (July 1992)

President
Patricio Aylwin

Foreign Affairs
Enrique Silva Cimma

Ambassador to the U.S.
Patricio Silva Echenique

Ambassador to the OAS
Heraldo Munoz Valenzuela

Ambassador to the UN
Juan Somavia Altamirano

Chile maintains an embassy in the United States at:
1732 Massachusetts Avenue, NW
Washington, DC 20036
Tel: (202) 785-1746

Political parties: Major parties include the Christian Democratic Party; the National Renewal Party; the Socialist Party; Party for Democracy; Radical Party; Independent Democratic Union. The Communist Party was proscribed by law under the previous military regime, but initiated proceedings to register as a legal party after the new government assumed power in March 1990.

Suffrage: Everyone 18 and over, including foreigners who have been legally residing for more than five years.

Flag: Divided in half horizontally—the upper left third blue with a white star; upper right two-thirds white; lower half red.

Defense

Defense expenditures (1989): $800 million or 3.2 percent of GDP.

The armed forces are subject to civilian control, exercised by the president through his minister of defense. However, each service is headed by a commander-in-chief.

Army: 55,000 troops under Gen.

Augusto Pinochet. The army is organized into six divisions and one separate brigade. There is an air wing.

Navy: Adm. Jorge Martinez Busch directs the 29,000-person navy. The Chilean marine corps, with a strength of 5,200, is an arm of the navy. The Chilean fleet of 11 surface combatants and four submarines is based in Valparaiso. The navy operates its own aircraft.

Air Force: Air General Fernando Matthei Aubel heads the air force of 12,000. Air assets are distributed among four air brigades headquartered in Iquique, Santiago, Puerto Montt, and Punta Arenas. The Air Force also operates an air base on King George Island, Antarctica.

After the military coup in September 1973, the Chilean national police, or carabineros, were incorporated into the ministry of defense. The carabineros are led by General Stange, who directs a paramilitary force of 27,000 engaged in law enforcement, traffic management, narcotics suppression, border control, and counterterrorist activities. The carabineros maintain operational units in over 1,000 locations throughout Chile.

Foreign Relations

The Chilean government maintains diplomatic relations with more than 70 countries. When the military regime came to power in 1973, the communist countries, except for China and Romania, broke diplomatic relations. Mexico and Italy also severed relations with Chile. In the final months of the military regime, Italy reestablished relations; following the inauguration of the Aylwin government, the Soviet Union, several Eastern and Central European countries, and Mexico reestablished relations.

Relations with Argentina were strained by a boundary dispute at the southern tip of the continent until 1985 when a peaceful settlement was reached with Papal mediation. The loss of territory by Peru and Bolivia to Chile during the War of the Pacific (1879–83) continues to influence national attitudes and policies. Bolivia continues to seek an outlet to the sea and broke relations with Chile in 1978, following a breakdown of negotiations. By treaty, any Bolivian-Chilean agreement involving former Peruvian territory also would require Peru's agreement.

U.S.-Chilean Relations

Despite some improvement in the later years of the Pinochet regime, the full normalization of U.S.-Chilean relations had been affected by continuing human rights problems, including the right of citizens to change their government. The 1976 car-bomb assassination in Washington, DC, of Orlando Letelier, a former Chilean ambassador to the United States and a member of President Allende's cabinet, and Ronni Moffitt, a U.S. citizen, caused a sharp deterioration in relations and led the U.S. Congress to ban security assistance and arms sales to Chile.

In 1979, the Chilean supreme court denied extradition for three Chilean ex-intelligence officials under U.S. indictment in the Letelier/Moffitt case. The United States continues to press for justice, and prospects for resolution of the case are promising under the democratically elected government inaugurated in March 1990, which seeks to transfer prosecution of the case in Chile from the military to the civilian court system.

Meanwhile, the two governments signed a compensation agreement in June 1990 for the Letelier and Moffitt families. The agreement, which must be approved by the Chilean Congress, establishes an international commission to determine the size of the ex gratia payment.

In 1987, Chile was excluded from the Generalized System of Preferences (GSP) and suspended from the Overseas Private Investment Corporation (OPIC) program for its failure to observe international standards of workers' rights. With the restoration of democracy, the government of Chile petitioned to restore those policies. OPIC benefits were restored in October 1990.

The U.S. government supported and welcomed the return of democracy to Chile and has been actively working with the new government to remove remaining legal impediments to a full bilateral relationship. The U.S. Agency for International Development (AID) mission in Chile was formally closed in May 1981. However, in August 1988, a small AID office was reestablished in Chile as part of AID's new advanced developing country program. The United States maintains a bilateral food assistance program which provides dietary supplements to the children of low-income families. This program operates through both official and private voluntary agencies. The U.S. Export-Import Bank helps finance U.S. exports to Chile.

Trade

Exports (1989, FOB) $8.1 billion: copper, molybdenum, iron ore, fishmeal, fruits, forestry products.

Major markets: U.S. 17.8%; Japan 13.7%; Germany 11.2%; Brazil 6.4%.

Imports (1989, CIF.) $7.1 billion: petroleum, machinery, vehicles, electronic equipment, consumer durables.

Major suppliers: U.S. 20.0%; Japan 10.9%; Brazil 10.4%; Argentina 5.0%; Germany 7.2%.

Trade and Investment Policies

Chile generally has few barriers to U.S. exports. Additionally, foreign firms operating in Chile enjoy the same protection and operate under the same conditions as local firms. Nevertheless, treatment in some areas, especially agricultural commodities, diverges from this norm.

To limit under- and overinvoicing of exports and imports, the Central Bank keeps reference prices on a large number of items. It thus can detect gross underinvoicing (in the case of large scale exports) or gross overinvoicing (in the case of large-scale imports).

Import licenses: According to the new legislation governing the Central Bank, there are no legal restrictions on licensing. Import licenses are granted as a routine procedure.

Investment barriers: Trade-related investment measures are applied only to the automobile industry. Manufacturers from the United States (GM) and France (Renault) are assisted by a differential tax provided in exchange for agreeing to meet export targets to stay in business in Chile.

Automobiles and trucks are charged a tax that varies with the vehicle's value and number of cylinders.

Principal nontariff barriers: Chile generally has few barriers to imports. All tariff levels are GATT-bound at 35 percent, and the Chilean rate is currently 11 percent. Chile moved to a unified tariff system in 1975. The original ad valorem rate of 35 percent was gradually reduced to 10 percent after 1979. During the recession of 1982–83, the government hiked tariffs back to 30 percent. With the recovery, rates were again reduced. The Aylwin government has continued to reduce tariffs. It has cut these rates from 15 to 11 percent. Tariffs are lower than 11 percent for certain products from member states of the Latin American Integration Association (ALADI), most products from Mexico (which has a free trade agreement with Chile), products imported by diplomats and the Chilean military, a few products subject to GATT bindings of zero, and 10 products of developing countries under the global system of trade preferences (GSTP) among developing countries.

One of Chile's most egregious nontariff barriers is the import price band system for certain agricultural commodities. Wheat, vegetable oils, and sugar imports are levied with specific duties (on top of the across-the-board 11 percent duty) in the form of an "import price band system." An additional surtax is also applied in some cases. The combined effect of the specific duty and the 11 percent general duty varies according to international price levels. Currently, the wheat ad valorem tariff derived from the price band exceeds the GATT-bound tariff rate of 35 percent. These duties have discouraged Chilean importers from purchasing higher priced, higher quality U.S. wheat.

For sugar, when international prices fall below the import price floor, the price band calculations (specific duty) plus the 11 percent tariff and 18 percent Value Added Tax (VAT) are applied to imports. When international prices are within the price band, the 11 percent tariff and the 18 percent VAT are applied. When international prices exceed the price ceiling, only the VAT is charged for sugar imports.

For vegetable oil, a complex specific duty system is derived from the price band. The government of Chile assesses the specific duty to imported oil according to the current lowest international FOB price. In addition, the 11 percent tariff is applied.

Chilean wheat producers and some milling groups are actively lobbying for the establishment of a wheat flour price band (wheat flour imports are already subject to a 10 percent surtax). The agricultural sector claims that, in the absence of a price band system, wheat flour imports from Argentina will overwhelm the local industry.

Chilean rice producers also continue to lobby for a price band. A price band would discriminate in favor of inefficient small-grain rice producers at the expense of long-grain rice imports that consumers prefer.

Duty surcharges determined by the Comision de Distorsion de Precios (Price Distortion Commission) apply on products that receive a subsidy from the exporting country. Once determined, the surcharge normally applies to all countries, not only to offenders. Dried milk powder imports are an exception to this rule. During 1990, only imports from Poland were required to pay a surtax of $240 per ton. In 1991, all imports from Eastern Europe paid a surtax of $160 per ton. Imports from other countries are not required to pay this surtax because their FOB export prices conform more closely with international market prices.

Potential surcharges range from 5 to 20 percent, well under the bound tariff ceiling established by the GATT. In practice, raw cotton must pay an 8 percent surcharge, and the following products have surcharges of 5 percent: corduroy cloth, tires and inner tubes, floor coverings, and sacking cloth.

Animal health and phytosanitary requirements: Chile occasionally uses animal health and phytosanitary requirements in a nontransparent manner that has the effect of impeding imports. The Chilean government is slow to respond to requests for phytosanitary and animal health requirements for products or commodities new to Chile. No public comment process or announcement of proposed rule changes precedes the promulgation of these requirements.

Government procurement practices: The government has a "Buy Chile" policy only when conditions of sale of locally produced goods (price, delivery times, etc.) are equal to or better than those of equivalent imports. In practice, given that a large number of product categories are not manufactured in Chile, purchasing decisions by state-owned companies are made among competing imports. Requests for public and private bids are published in the local newspapers.

Trade Financing Environment and Options

The Chilean government generally does not provide exporters with direct or indirect support such as preferential financing or export promotion funds. The Chilean government does, however, offer some nonmarket incentives to export. For example, paperwork requirements are simplified for nontraditional exporters. Small nontraditional exporters also qualify for the government's simplified duty drawback system. Through this mechanism, the government returns to producers an amount equivalent to 3 to 10 percent of the value of their exports. This figure represents an estimate of the duties actually paid for imported components in the exported merchandise. Alternatively, qualifying exporters can apply for the return of all paid duties. The government also provides exporters with quicker tax returns on the VAT than other producers receive. The U.S. government has found Chile's subsidies for nontraditional exports countervailable under U.S. countervailing duty law.

All Chilean exporters may also defer tariff payments on capital imports for a period of seven years. If the capital goods are used to produce exported products, deferred du-

---

INVESTMENT CLIMATE
Extent of U.S. Investment in Goods-Producing Sectors
U.S. Direct Investment Position Abroad on a Historical-Cost Basis—1990
(Millions of U.S. dollars)

Category	Amount	
Petroleum		(D)
Total manufacturing		275
Food and kindred products	42	
Chemicals and allied products	144	
Metals, primary and fabricated	−143	
Machinery, except electrical	0	
Electric and electronic equipment	(D)	
Transportation equipment	(D)	
Other manufacturing	180	
Wholesale trade		54
TOTAL PETROLEUM/MANUFACTURING/WHOLESALE TRADE		(D)

(D) Suppressed to avoid disclosing data of individual companies

Source: U.S. Department of Commerce, *Survey of Current Business* (August 1991, vol. 71, no. 8, table 11.3).

ties can be reduced by the ratio of export sales to total sales. If all production is exported, the exporter pays no tariff on capital imports.

FINANCING AND CAPITAL MARKETS

General Policy Framework

Chile has been successful in recent years in maintaining the confidence of the international financial community.

Significantly, these gains were achieved during a period of major political transition. In its first year in power, Chile's new government worked successfully on several fronts to advance its integration in the world economy. Chile restructured its 1991–94 debt maturities on commercial terms and obtained a $200 million Eurobond issue that was subscribed by 20 of the world's most prominent banks. The economy attracted $1.1 billion in direct foreign investment in 1990, and posted a trade surplus of $1.3 billion with the dynamic economies of East Asia. The internationalization of the economy has not been painless. The foreign investment boom and the country's generally liberal foreign exchange regulations unleashed a dollar inflow that has complicated monetary and exchange rate policy.

High copper prices and a tax increase in 1990 enabled the Aylwin government to cover its expenses during 1990 and 1991. The first two budgets prepared by the Aylwin government (for 1991 and 1992) reflect the continuation of generally sound fiscal policies. President Aylwin's economic team has taken pains to ensure that its budget projections are based on conservative economic estimates, and that new expenditures are financed with new sources of revenue. The absolute size of the government relative to the total economy continues to shrink; in the 1992 budget proposal, both revenues and

expenditures were slated to increase more slowly than the expected rate of economic growth. At the same time, however, the government has attempted to fulfill its campaign pledges to increase social spending. The 1991 budget increased real spending on social programs by 15 percent, and the 1992 budget proposal envisions another real increase of 9 percent. Although most estimates of the 1991 central government budget deficit did not exceed 1 percent of GDP, the government will be hard pressed to contain the deficit unless the state copper company (CODELCO) continues to make substantial contributions to the revenue base.

If transfers to the state's Copper Stabilization Fund are included, CODELCO's contribution to government revenues equaled 6 percent of GDP in 1990, the equivalent of 23 percent of government spending.

Debt Management Policies

Chile's debt management remains effective. The government negotiated a favorable rescheduling with its creditor banks of its 1991–94 debt maturities.

As of July 1991, Chile's external debt stock stood at $17.4 billion (this figure includes $1 billion of Central Bank debt to the International Monetary Fund). The value of this debt on the secondary market has climbed over the last few years, and surged again after the conclusion of the rescheduling. It now sells for 90 cents on the dollar (at the beginning of the debt swap program in 1985, Chilean debt sold for only 30 cents on the dollar).

The appreciation of Chilean debt's value signals an end to the country's pioneering Chapter XIX "debt swap" program. Operations authorized by Chapter XIX of the Central Bank's Foreign Exchange Regulations totaled $15.8 million in the first semester of 1991, compared to a first semester 1989 figure of $723.1 million. The decreasing stock of swappable debt partly explains this decline. The rising value of Chilean debt is even more important. Because they reduce the profit realized in a swap operation, rising debt values attenuate foreign investors' motivation to conduct a Chapter XIX operation. In June 1991, Chile became the first country in the region to qualify for and receive a reduction of its PL-480 debt owed to the U.S. government under the Enterprise for the Americas Initiative, which offers reduction of bilateral debt in exchange for economic reform by debtor countries. The total stock of Chile's PL-480 debt was reduced by 40 percent, eliminating approximately $16 million in obligations owed to the United States. Currently under negotiation is the Environment Framework Agreement, which will allow interest payments on the new EAI obligation to be paid in local currency to fund environmental and conservation projects in Chile.

The Currency and Exchange Rate Mechanisms

To maintain the competitiveness of its export-driven economy, Chile uses a crawling peg to determine the official foreign exchange rate. Each month's peg is based on a formula that measures inflation differentials between Chile and its major trading partners in the preceding month.

Inflation trends in the United States are particularly important. This is true not only because the United States is Chile's largest trading partner, but also because Chile conducts virtually all of its international trade in dollars.

Parallel market and interbank rates are allowed to float freely within a band of 5 percent above and below a midpoint. This midpoint, called the "acuerdo" rate, is the Central Bank's reference point, and is adjusted daily to reflect the inflation differentials noted above. When the parallel and interbank rates fall below the band's lower limit (implying an appreciating peso), the Central Bank is obliged to buy the market's excess dollars. When they exceed the band's upper limit, the Bank must sell dollars to maintain its rate. With few interruptions since October 1990, the peso has been at the limits of the band, forcing the Central Bank to buy dollars.

Tapping International Aid Institutions

Economic aid received from the U.S. (grants and loans, 1949–87): Total—$3.5 billion, of which only a small amount was for disaster relief and surplus food in recent years.

Financial Market Operations and Structural Policies

Pricing policies: In general, the government of Chile does not interfere in Chile's markets and does not have specific pricing policies.

State enterprises purchase at the lowest possible price, regardless of the source of the material. U.S. exports enter Chile and compete freely with other imports and Chilean products. Import decisions are generally related to price competitiveness and product availability.

Chile has used loans from the World Bank and Inter-American Development Bank to improve its economic infrastructure (roads, electric generation, etc.) which offer direct support to exporters by lowering in-country transportation costs and by providing reliable low-cost energy supplies.

Tax policies: The most significant tax is the 18 percent value added tax, which affects all sales transactions carried out within Chilean borders and accounts for 10.5 percent of total government revenue. There is an 11 percent ad valorem duty on all imports. In general, personal taxes are relatively low. Business taxes are similar to those levied in the United States.

Regulatory policies: Government regulation of the Chilean economy is limited. The most heavily regulated areas of the economy are the banking sector, utilities, the securities market, and pension funds. There are no government regulations per se that affect the market for U.S. exports to Chile (although other government programs, like the price band system for some agricultural commodities described below, do indeed displace U.S. exports). The sector most directly affected by Chilean government programs is construction. Large infrastructure projects and government-financed housing programs affect the direction and scope of investment in this sector. Government efforts in this regard are likely to intensify because President Aylwin recently announced that the government of Chile will spend the equivalent of $2.3 billion on infrastructure improvements over the 1991–94 period.

Monetary policy: Inflation increased to 27 percent in the Aylwin government's first year, but the economic team reduced the rate to about 20 percent in 1991. Control over the money supply is complicated by the existence of large "quasi-fiscal" deficits associated with the Central Bank's bailout of the Central Government and private banks in 1982–83.

These underperforming assets are valued at more than $11 billion, about 43 percent of the Central Bank's asset base.

VISITING AND LOCATING

General Travel Checklist

Customs: A valid passport and a tourist card (issued by the carrier) are required for entry. Requirements for entry and exit by car are numerous, and obtaining necessary documents can be time-consuming.

Climate and clothing: Seasons are the reverse of those in the U.S. It seldom rains in summer (Dec.-Mar.), and humidity is low. Middays reach 32 C (90 F); nights are cool. Winter (June-Sept.) is cold and rainy, with snow in the surrounding mountains. Sweaters and woolens are recommended April-Nov. A topcoat or lined raincoat is useful in winter.

Health: Conditions are good in Santiago, except for prevalent smog. Allergic conditions, especially those respiratory related, will worsen in the city, particularly during the winter season. Tap water is generally potable except after occasional winter floods. It has a high mineral content which affects some, so it is recommended to accustom the body to the tap water by drinking the easily accessible bottled water initially, and slowly increase the intake of tap water over a 2-week period. Do not eat unwashed fruits and vegetables.

Although no immunizations are required for travel to Chile, typhoid, gamma globulin, and current tetanus-diphtheria toxoid vaccines are recommended.

Telecommunications: The telephone system in Santiago and elsewhere is excellent. International telephone and wire services are good.

Transportation: Flights from the U.S. take 8–10 hours. Overland travel by car or bus from neighboring countries is possible, although winter snows may close the main mountain pass from Argentina for weeks.

The only regular U.S. passenger shipping line is Lykes Line, with embarkation from the ports of Houston and New Orleans. Taxi and bus service in Santiago is good, and fares are reasonable.

Tourist attractions: Beautiful beaches are located within a 2–4 hour drive from Santiago. Some, however, are dangerous because of strong undertows and lack of lifeguards. Because of the cold water, sunbathing is more popular than swimming at most beaches. Other popular summer resorts are found in the lake region, about 500 miles south of Santiago. Known as the "Switzerland of South America," this area offers excellent trout fishing and some of the most magnificent scenery on the continent. Other summer activities include boat trips through the channels and fjords of the south, from Puerto Montt to Punta Arenas on the Strait of Magellan at the tip of the continent, and an excursion to the Juan Fernandez Islands, 400 miles off the coast at Valparaiso.

The northern desert offers isolated beaches, access to the Andean highland Indian culture, and numerous but hard to reach archaeological sites. The museum at San Pedro de Atacama is famous for its pre-Columbian mummies and artifacts. In the Central Region, Chile's world famous mountain resorts offer first-class skiing during the Northern Hemisphere summer.

Chapter 6

COLOMBIA

	Total	Urban	
Population (1993)	35,212,000	68.0%	

Main Urban Areas	Population	Percentage of Total	International Calling Code
BOGOTA	3,975,000	11.3	57-1
Medellin	1,419,000	4.0	57-4
Cali	1,400,000	4.0	57-23
Barranquilla	897,000	2.5	57-5
Cartagena	491,000	1.4	57-59
Pereira	390,000	1.1	57-61
Cucuta	357,000	1.0	57-70
Bucaramanga	342,000	1.0	57-73
Manizales	330,000	0.9	57-69
Ibague	269,000	0.8	57-82

Land Area	1,038,700 square kilometers
Comparable U.S. State	Slightly less than three times the size of Montana
Language	Spanish 99%
	Amerindian —
	Other 1%
Common Business Language	Spanish
Currency	1 Colombia peso (Col$) = 100 centavos
Exchange Rate (May 1993)	U.S. $1.00 = 663 pesos
Best Nonstop Air Connection via U.S.	Miami to Bogota: 3.5 hours
	American Airlines (800) 433-7300
	Two nonstops daily
Best Hotel	Hotel Bogota Royal (U.S. $200)
	At the World Trade Center
	P.O. Box 094077
	Avda. 100 No. 8A-01
	Tel: (57-1) 218-9911 or 218-3261
	Fax: (57-1) 218-3362

INTRODUCTION AND REGIONAL ORIENTATION

Colombia is the fourth most populous country in Latin America. Movement from rural to urban areas has been heavy. The urban population increased from 57 percent of the total population in 1951 to about 70 percent by 1987. The nine eastern departments and territories, constituting about 54 percent of Colombia's area, have less than 3 percent of the population and a density of fewer than 1 person per square kilometer (two persons per square mile). The country has 30 cities with 100,000 or more inhabitants.

The diversity of ethnic origins results from the intermixture of indigenous Indians, Spanish colonists, and African slaves. Today, only about 1 percent of the people can be identified as fully Indian on the basis of language and customs. Few foreigners have immigrated to Colombia. In 1988, an estimated 18,000 U.S. citizens were living there.

Geographical Background

Located in the northwest corner of South America, Colombia is bordered by Venezuela, Brazil, Peru, Ecuador, and Panama. It is the continent's fourth largest country and has a coastline of more than 1,448 kilometers (900 miles) on the Pacific Ocean and 1,760 kilometers (1,100 miles) on the Caribbean Sea.

The Andes Mountains enter Colombia in the southwest and fan out into three distinct ranges running through the country from southwest to north and northeast. Sprinkled throughout the ranges are some 30 volcanoes. In November 1985, Volcano Nevado del Ruiz, near the town of Manizales and about 50 miles west of Bogota, erupted and caused severe mud slides as the glacier atop the volcano melted. The town of Armero was completely inundated, and more than 20,000 persons were killed.

Colombia has three main topographical regions:

- flat coastal areas broken by the high Sierra Nevada de Santa Marta mountain range;
- central highlands; and
- sparsely settled eastern plains (llanos) drained by tributaries of the Orinoco and Amazon Rivers.

The climate varies from tropical heat on the coast and the eastern plains to cool, springlike weather with frequent light rains in the highlands, which experience two dry seasons, from December to February and from June to August. Bogota is 2,630 meters (8,630 ft.) above sea level. The average daily high temperature is between 18 C and 20 C (64 F–67 F); lows range from 9 C to 11 C (48 F–51 F).

History and Political Conditions

After the defeat of the Spanish Army in 1819, the republic included all the territory of the former viceroyalty. Simon Bolivar was elected first president and Francisco de Paula Santander vice-president. In 1822, the United States became one of the first countries to recognize the new republic and to establish a resident diplomatic mission. Ecuador and Venezuela withdrew from the republic in 1830 and became independent states. Panama remained part of Colombia until 1903.

Since then, two political parties that grew out of conflicts between the followers of Bolivar and Santander—the Conservatives and the Liberals—have dominated Colombian politics. Bolivar's supporters, who later formed the nucleus of the Conservative Party, advocated a strong centralized government, a close alliance between the government and the Roman Catholic Church, and a limited franchise.

Santander's followers, forerunners of the

Liberals, wanted a decentralized government, state rather than church control over education and other civil matters, and a broadened suffrage. Those were the principal topics of political debate throughout the nineteenth and early twentieth centuries. The Conservatives established a highly centralized government. The Liberals eventually won universal adult suffrage and a large measure of separation of church and state, although the Catholic Church still retains some important powers, such as the right to give religious instruction in all public schools.

Competitively elected Liberal administrations were in power from 1860 to 1884, from 1930 to 1946, from 1974 to 1982, and from 1986 to the present. The Conservative Party held office from 1884 to 1930, from 1946 to 1953, and from 1982 to 1986.

Colombia, unlike many Latin American countries, established early a solid tradition of civilian government and regular free elections. The military has seized power only three times in Colombian history—in 1830, 1854, and 1953. On the first two occasions, the military dictator was overthrown and civilian rule restored in less than a year.

Colombia has had only one full-fledged civilian dictatorship (1884–94).

Notwithstanding the country's commitment to democratic institutions, Colombia's history has been characterized by periods of widespread violent conflict. Two particularly tragic civil wars (1899–1902 and in the 1940s and 1950s) resulted from bitter rivalry between the Conservative and Liberal Parties.

In 1957 Colombian voters approved the "Declaration of Sitges" which formed a "National Front," under which the Liberal and Conservative Parties would jointly govern. Through regular elections, the presidency would alternate between the parties every four years; the parties also would have parity in all other elective and appointive offices.

The first three National Front presidents brought an end to La Violencia and the blind partisanship that had afflicted both parties. They committed Colombia to the far-reaching social and economic reforms proposed in the charter of the Alliance for Progress and, with assistance from the United States and the international lending agencies, achieved major economic development.

In December 1968, after two years of effort, President Lleras Restrepo won congressional ratification of important constitutional reforms, which abolished a requirement of a two-thirds majority of Congress for passage of major legislation, increased the powers of the executive branch in economic and development matters, and provided for a carefully measured transition from the National Front to traditional two-party competition.

The parity arrangement for other offices has since been phased out. In departmental (state) legislatures and city councils, it ended in 1970, and in the Congress, in 1974. Parity in the appointment of the cabinet, governors, and mayors continued until 1978. Although the parity system established by the Sitges agreement is no longer in effect, the Colombian Constitution requires that the losing major political party be given adequate and equitable participation in the government.

Leftist parties, including the Communist Party of Colombia, rarely have obtained more than a few percentage points of total votes cast.

In mid-1985, the Pro-Soviet Revolutionary Armed Forces of Colombia (FARC) established a political party, the Patriotic Union (UP). In the 1986 congressional elections, the UP won six seats in the Senate and nine in the House; it received 4.3 percent of the votes in the presidential elections. The UP, which has tried to distance itself from direct identification with the FARC, won 16 of the 1,009 mayoral positions contested in Colombia's first popular election of mayors on March 13, 1988, according to Colombian government statistics.

CRACKING THE MARKET

Demographics

Ethnic groups: Mestizo 58%, white 20%, Mulatto 14%, black 4%, mixed black-Indian 3%, Indian 1%.

Religion: Roman Catholic 95%.

Language: Spanish.

Education: Five years compulsory (primary school). Attendance—77% of children enter, but only one-half of the schools offer the full five-year cycle. Only 28% finish primary school. Literacy—80%.

Central government budget: $4.5 billion.

Work force (14 million): agriculture 26%; industry 21%; services 58%.

Economy

During the 1970s, Colombia's industrial development policy shifted from an emphasis on import substitution toward export expansion and diversification. The export share of nontraditional goods such as clothing, yarns, cut flowers, cardboard, cement, emeralds, sugar, rice, and cotton has continued to grow.

The economy experienced a real gross domestic product (GDP) growth rate of 6.1 percent between 1970 and 1978. After 1979, GDP growth declined due to a combination of external and internal factors that included world economic recession, low prices for many export goods, depressed domestic demand, increasingly uncompetitive domestic industry, and high domestic interest rates. Real GDP growth bottomed out in 1982 at 1 percent. In 1984–85, the government initiated a wide ranging structural adjustment program, including trade liberalization, a sharp currency devaluation, and budget and fiscal reforms. The economy responded vig-

orously, with GDP growth jumping from 2.4 percent in 1985 to 5.1 percent in 1986 and 5.4 percent in 1987. The decrease of the GDP growth rate for 1988 to 3.7 percent reflects a reduced coffee harvest, guerrilla disruption of petroleum production, and the government's tight money policy to control inflation. The government is projecting a return to 5 percent growth for 1989. Inflation continues to be one of the chief economic problems with annual rates in the 25 percent to 30 percent range.

Although Colombia's net international reserves grew to $5.6 billion in 1981, a sharp decline in coffee earnings and a continued rise in energy import costs caused reserves to drop to roughly $1.8 billion by the end of 1984. A sharp improvement in the trade balance—aided by improved coffee prices and commencement of oil exports—helped bring the reserve level back up to $3.8 billion by the end of 1988. The total foreign debt of $16 billion ($13 billion public) is low by regional standards. The debt service ratio is estimated at 42 percent of exports. In 1985, the government sought new external financing of $4.1 billion from multilateral institutions and commercial banks for 1985–86. In December 1985, Colombia signed a $1 billion syndicated loan with foreign commercial banks, followed by a similar loan in 1987, and a final syndication of $1.7 billion to round out requirements for 1989–90. The purpose of these loans was to refinance a bulge in principal repayments occurring during 1987–90.

Long-range prospects for settlement of the country's current external financing problems appear good, given the promise of major earnings from energy exports, rapid growth in other exports, and the country's reputation for conservative financial management.

Mining and Energy

Colombia has substantial mineral and energy resources, including petroleum, coal, nickel, gold, emeralds, natural gas, and hydroelectric power. Colombia became a petroleum exporter in mid-1986. Total production has since grown rapidly to more than 430,000 barrels per day (b/d) in early 1989 (when not disrupted by guerrilla attacks), leaving about 200,000 b/d for export after domestic consumption.

Coal also is becoming an important energy source and export commodity. Excellent thermic quality, low sulphur and ash content, and geographic location make Colombian coal an attractive energy source for world consumers. From 1 million tons in 1984, exports have increased to 11 million in 1988. Exports were expected to continue rising to 20 million tons a year by 1993. At the same time, coal was expected to play an increasingly important role in meeting domestic energy needs. Colombia has an estimated 4 percent of world nickel production and 15 percent of world ferronickel production. Earnings from exports of ferronickel totaled $180 million in 1988, due to a sharp price increase but may drop again as prices decline.

Colombia produces 90 percent of the world's supply of emeralds and is an important producer of gold and platinum. Other mineral resources include iron ore, phosphate rock, limestone, gypsum, and salt.

Agriculture, Natural Resources, and Industry

Agriculture employs 26 percent of Colombia's labor force while contributing 22 percent of total GDP. Because of Colombia's diverse climate and topography, various crops can be grown. Cacao, sugarcane, coconuts, bananas, plantains, rice, cotton, tobacco, cassava, and most of the nation's cattle are produced in the hot regions—from sea level to 1,000 meters (3,300 feet). The temperate regions—1,000–2,000 meters (3,300–6,600 feet)—are better suited for coffee, flowers, corn, and other vegetables,

and fruits such as citrus, pears, pineapples, and tomatoes. The cold regions—2,000–3,000 meters (6,600–9,900 feet)—produce wheat, barley, potatoes, cold-climate vegetables, dairy cattle, and poultry. All of these regions yield various forest products, ranging from tropical hardwoods in the hot country to pine and eucalyptus in the colder areas.

The most industrialized member of the five-nation Andean Pact, Colombia has four major industrial centers—Barranquilla, Cali, Medellin, and Bogota—located in distinct geographical regions. The most important manufacturing industries are textiles and clothing, food processing (including beverages), paper and paper products, chemicals and petrochemicals, cement and construction, iron and steel products, and metalworking.

Natural resources: Coal, petroleum, natural gas, iron ore, nickel, gold, copper, emeralds.

Agriculture (21 percent of GDP): Products—coffee, bananas, cut flowers, cotton, sugarcane, livestock, rice, corn, tobacco, potatoes, soybeans, sorghum. Cultivated land—5 percent of total land area.

Industry (21 percent of GDP): Types—textiles and garments, chemicals, metal products, cement, cardboard containers, plastic resins and manufactures, beverages, tourism.

Political/Institutional Infrastructure

The Republic of Colombia gained its independence on July 20, 1810.

The 1886 constitution has been amended frequently and substantially. Major revisions were approved in December 1979, and a revision enacted in January 1986 provided for the direct election of mayors. The Barco administration has presented further major constitutional amendments to the 1988 session of Congress. Freedom of religion, speech, and assembly, along with other basic

COLOMBIA
Key Economic Indicators

	1989	1990	1991
		(projected in 1990)	
Income, Production, Employment			
(Billions of 1975 pesos; 1975 peso rate: 32.96 = U.S. $1)			
Real GDP	703.8	733.4	744.4
Real GDP growth rate	3.2	4.2	1.5
GDP by sector:			
Agriculture	152.0	162.2	167.0
Mining	31.4	33.9	34.2
Manufacturing	146.6	156.3	157.8
Construction	26.6	24.8	25.1
Commerce	65.2	66.9	67.3
Transportation	49.6	50.8	51.8
Government services	62.9	65.3	66.9
Other sectors	162.2	167.1	170.3
Real per capita GDP (pesos)	21,718	21,894	22,152
Labor force (millions)	11.9	12.0	12.1
Unemployment rate (%)	8.9	10.0	10.5
Money and Prices (Percentages)			
Money supply growth (M1)	29.1	25.8	30.0
Commercial interest rates	36–42	34–38	35–39
Savings rate	33.9	36.7	37.8
Investment rate	19.6	19.0	N/A
CPI increase	26.1	32.4	27.0
WPI increase	25.6	25.0	24.0
Exchange rate (peso/U.S. $)[1]			
Official	430.0	564.0	700.0
Parallel	435.0	550.0	625.0
Balance of Payments and Trade (millions U.S. $)			
Total exports (FOB)	6,028	6,675	7,476
to U.S.	2,477	2,793	2,990
Total imports (CIF)	4,548	5,149	6,100
from U.S.	1,719	1,861	2,196
Aid from U.S	4	15	50
Aid from others	N/A	N/A	N/A
Total U.S. investment	2,340	2,360	2,473
External public debt	13,296	13,680	13,700
Debt service payments	2,906	3,150	3,330
International reserves (net)	3,867	4,501	7,100
Balance of payments			
Current account	(192)	530	1,500
Trade balance	1,480	1,526	1,376
Net services and trns	(1,481)	(1,450)	(650)
Capital account	480	(180)	430

1. Year end.
Source: Central Bank, National Planning Department, National Department of Statistics.

rights, is guaranteed by the constitution. The national government has separate executive, legislative, and judicial branches. Elected for a four-year term, the president may not serve consecutive terms. The president's extensive powers include appointing cabinet ministers and departmental and territorial governors without congressional confirmation.

No vice-president as such exists. Every two years, congress elects a "designate" from the president's party to become acting president in the event of the president's resignation, illness, or death. If the president is unable to serve, the acting president must call new elections within three months.

Colombia's bicameral Congress consists of a 114-member Senate and a 199-member Chamber of Representatives, all elected on the basis of proportional representation. Members and alternates are elected within a few months of or at the same time as the president but may be reelected indefinitely. If a member of Congress is absent temporarily or permanently, the seat is taken by the alternate.

Congress meets annually from July 20 to December 16, and the president may call it into special session at other times.

Judicial power is exercised by the 24-member Supreme Court of Justice, subordinate courts, and the Council of State. New Supreme Court justices are selected by justices already in office. Appointments are lifetime until mandatory retirement at age 65.

The country is divided into 23 departments, the Federal District of Bogota, four intendencias, and five comisarias (territories of lesser rank not having local legislatures). Presidentially appointed governors are considered agents of the national government, although their powers are somewhat limited by elected departmental legislatures, which are elected to two-year terms.

Flag: Top half yellow, bottom half blue and red stripes of equal width.

Principal Government Officials

President
Gaviria

Ministers

Agriculture
Gabriel Rosas Vega

Communications
Enrique Danies

Economic Development
Maria Mercedes Cuellar de Martinez

Finance and Public Credit
Luis Fernando Alarcon Mantilla

Foreign Relations
Julio Londono Paredes

Government
Carlos Lemos Simmonds

Justice
Roberto Salazar

Labor and Social Security
Maria Teresa Forero De Saade

Mines and Energy
Margarita Mena de Quevedo

National Defense
Gen. Oscar Botero Restrepo

Education
Manuel Francisco Becerra

Health
Eduardo Diaz Uribe

Public Works and Transport
Priscila Ceballos Ordonez

Ambassador to the U.S.
Victor Mosquera Chaux

Ambassador to the OAS
Leopoldo Villar Borda

Ambassador to the UN
Enrique Penaloza Camargo

Colombia maintains an embassy in the United States at:
2118 Leroy Place, NW
Washington, D.C. 20008
Tel: (202) 387-8338

Colombian Consulates are located in Atlanta, Boston, Chicago, Detroit, Ft. Lauderdale, Houston, Los Angeles, Miami, Minneapolis, New Orleans, New York, Philadelphia, San Diego, San Juan, St. Louis, Tampa, Washington, and Wheeling.

Defense

National defense constitutes 14 percent of the government budget and 1.9 percent of GDP.

Colombia's Ministry of Defense is charged with the country's internal and external defense and security. The army, navy, air force, and national police are under the leadership of the Minister of National Defense (normally an army general). A small marine corps is part of the navy. Jointly they serve as the country's armed forces and number about 220,000 uniformed personnel—135,000 military; 85,000 police.

Many Colombian military personnel have received training in the United States or in U.S. military schools in the former Panama Canal Zone. Over the years, the United States has provided equipment to the Colombian military through the military assistance program or through foreign military sales.

Current Political Conditions

The Liberals failed in their attempt to win three consecutive presidencies when they lost the 1982 election behind Alfonso Lopez Michelsen. Conservative candidate Belisario Betancur won 47 percent of the popular vote to Lopez's 41 percent. Luis Carlos Galan, who had split from the Liberal Party and formed his own New Liberal Party, took 10 percent of the vote. The Liberals won a majority of House and Senate seats from the Conservatives, with leftist front and independent candidates winning only two seats in each chamber. In 1988, the New Liberals were reincorporated into the Liberal Party.

President Betancur raised Colombia's international profile with his often outspoken opinions on events in Central America through his position as a member of the Contadora group. He also stressed combating Colombia's insurgency through a cease-fire arrangement that included the release of many guerrillas imprisoned during the Turbay years. The cease-fire was signed in 1984 but began to unravel when the M-19 guerrillas resumed fighting in 1985, by which time violence had reached levels prior to the cease-fire. Meanwhile, the growing wealth of Colombian narcotics chiefs in the early 1980s, from the sale of cocaine to the United States and other industrialized countries, was accompanied by a marked increase in the wealth of guerrilla groups, especially the FARC, through their participation in the illicit cocaine industry. This wealth has led to a marked growth in the power of these two illegal entities to operate with impunity in Colombia.

A vicious attack on the Supreme Court by the M-19 in 1985 shocked Colombia. Of the 115 people killed, 11 were Supreme Court justices. Although the government and the FARC, the largest guerrilla group, renewed their truce indefinitely in March 1986, peace with the M-19, the EPL, and dissident factions of other guerrilla groups seemed remote as Betancur left office. In September 1988, President Barco unveiled a new peace plan requiring insurgents to cease antigovernment violence as a condition to negotiations. As of June 1989, the only group to accept this requirement was the M-19, which currently is negotiating with the government.

Voters elected Liberal Virgilio Barco to the presidency in 1986 by the largest margin of victory ever. The Barco administration has found that its greatest challenge is from narcotics producers/ processors and guerrillas. Violence emanating from both groups has increased sharply. Like the Betancur administration from 1984 to 1986, the Barco government places a high priority on combating the production and trafficking of illegal narcotics.

Statistics for drug and chemical seizures and cocaine labs destroyed have steadily risen over time. In 1986, 4.3 metric tons of cocaine were seized; in 1988, that figure had reached 15.5 metric tons; as of April 1989, 23 metric tons had been seized. Between 1981 and September 1988, 60 metric tons of cocaine, 17,760 metric tons of marijuana, and more than 4,000 cocaine labs were destroyed. Lab seizures on the Magdalena River in April and May 1988 and January and February 1989 rivaled the Tranquilandia raids of 1984. Police and military units have destroyed numerous other significant labs.

Their antinarcotics activity has grown in scope and effectiveness over time, spearheaded by a special National Police Anti-Narcotics Unit. Narcotics activity is responsible for most of the violence in Colombia.

Narco-traffickers are at war with the police and the military, with guerrilla groups (some of which also are involved in narcotics), and with other drug lords. Narcotics-related violence includes the murders of Attorney General Carlos Mauro Hoyos-Jimenez and UP President Jaime Pardo Leal. Narco-traffickers also have subverted and intimidated the Colombian judicial system, and they remain a pervasive influence in much of Colombian society.

To address the problems of guerrilla violence and political and economic underdevelopment, the Barco administration has pursued long-range policies designed to deliver resources to the poorest areas of the country while bringing them into the political mainstream of the nation. The first popular election of mayors in Colombia's more than 1,000 municipalities took place on March 13, 1988. This political reform is expected to extend real power and decision making to the local level in order to spread the country's democratic institutions to all areas of the country. By the early 1980s, it had become obvious to Colombia's political elite that many democratic institutions were atrophying; that for democracy to work it had to be infused with new life through real political competition at the local level in order to make national level parties more responsive. The mayoral elections were carried out peacefully with the Liberals winning 445 mayoralties, the Conservatives 413, the UP 16, and other candidates 135.

Major political parties: Liberal Party, Social Conservative Party, and Patriotic Union Party (UP)—a political movement formed by the Revolutionary Armed Forces of Colombia (FARC) and the Communist Party (PCC). Suffrage: Universal age 18 and over.

Foreign Relations

Colombia traditionally has sought friendly diplomatic and commercial relations with all countries, regardless of their ideologies or political or economic systems. In 1983, Colombia joined Venezuela, Mexico, and Panama in the Contadora group, which has attempted to find a comprehensive peace settlement in Central America, and assumed a role as mediator between creditor countries and Latin American debtor nations. In 1982, Colombia joined the Nonaligned Movement.

President Barco has pursued a less dramatic role in foreign affairs than his predecessor. He has stressed the continued pursuit of peaceful relations with all countries, increased cooperation and consultation with other Latin American countries, especially regarding increased international cooperation in the fight against illicit narcotics trafficking through membership in the Group of Eight. Colombia was elected by consensus of the Latin American group to a two-year term on the UN Security Council. Through Foreign Minister Julio Londono, President

Barco also is pursuing reforms in the structure of the Foreign Ministry designed to improve the implementation of foreign policy.

Colombia has played an active role in the United Nations and the Organization of American States (OAS) and their subsidiary agencies.

It was the only Latin American country to contribute troops to the UN force in the Korean War. Former President Alberto Lleras Camargo was the first Secretary General of the OAS (1948–54). President Betancur also played a role in improving international trade conditions for developing countries through the International Coffee Organization (which he helped found), the Latin American Integration Association (ALADI), the Inter-American Economic and Social Council, and other international economic forums.

Colombia led negotiations that resulted in the signing at Bogota, on May 26, 1969, of an agreement for the gradual development of the Andean Common Market, a subregional grouping within ALADI, whose goal is to reduce trade barriers among the Andean countries and coordinate economic policies. Other members are Ecuador, Peru, Bolivia, and Venezuela.

U.S.-Colombian Relations

Under President Barco, Colombia and the United States have maintained good relations in general and have increased bilateral cooperation in the area of illicit narcotics.

Generally, the record of U.S.-Colombian relations has been one of constructive cooperation. Between 1961 and 1974, the United States provided Colombia $1.4 billion in development assistance—much of it through the Alliance for Progress—for land reform, education, health, housing, transportation, and electrification. More recently, the two governments have closely cooperated in narcotics control efforts. A long-standing problem between the United States and Colombia was the status of three small, uninhabited islands in the Caribbean. It was finally resolved in 1981 with the ratification of the Quita Sueno treaty, in which the United States renounced all claims to the islands without prejudicing the claims of third parties.

Trade

Trade (1988):

Exports—$5.3 billion: coffee, petroleum, gold, bananas, flowers, chemicals and pharmaceuticals, ferronickel, textiles and garments, coal and coke, sugar, cardboard containers, printed matter, cement, plastic resins and manufactures, emeralds.

Major markets—U.S., Germany, Netherlands, Japan.

Imports—$4.5 billion: machinery/equipment, grains, chemicals, transportation equipment, mineral products, consumer products, metals/metal products, plastic/rubber, paper products.

Major suppliers—U.S., Venezuela, Japan, Germany, France.

Coffee remains the single most important item in Colombia's export sector, although its share in total export earnings has dropped sharply in recent years, from more than half to 30 percent in 1988. The world's second largest coffee producer, Colombia produces 11–13 million bags (60 kilograms each) a year, or 12–15 percent of the world's coffee. Coffee normally earns Colombia about $1.5 billion a year; due to drought in Brazil, such earnings in 1986 exceeded $2.7 billion.

Colombian exports (FOB) in 1988 were $5.3 billion, only slightly higher than $5.25 billion in 1984, due to lower oil export volume and prices. The United States receives the largest share of Colombia's exports, followed by Germany, Venezuela, Netherlands, Japan, and Sweden.

Colombian imports (FOB), consisting primarily of wheat, aircraft, transportation equipment, electric generators, iron, steel, and aluminum, were $4.5 billion in 1988, up from $3.8 billion in 1987.

More than one-third of Colombian imports come from the United States. Other major suppliers (none with more than 10 percent share) are Japan, Germany, Venezuela, Brazil, and France.

Trade and Investment Policies

Import licensing: Colombia's prior import licensing requirement was previously the country's most significant import restriction. In 1991, the government of Colombia eliminated most prior import licensing requirements.

Some 98 percent of tariff lines are now under the free import regime, same-day automatic registration. The remaining 2 percent product categories subject to prior import licensing include certain chemicals which could be used to produce cocaine, munitions, some agricultural commodities, and medicines which require Ministry of Health certification. Government imports, donations, and nonrefundable imports also require prior permit approval.

Import duties: Colombia substantially reduced import duties in 1990 and 1991. There are presently four duty levels (with limited exceptions): 0, 5, 10, and 15 percent. The zero duty level (which now comprises 40 percent of total tariff items) includes raw materials, intermediate and capital goods not produced in Colombia, and certain consumer goods. The 5 and 10 percent levels include raw materials, plus intermediate and capital goods with registered production in the country. The 15 percent level is composed essentially of finished consumer goods. Exceptions to these tariff levels include automobiles (75 percent, to be progressively reduced to 50), pick-up trucks and

jeeps (50 percent), and agricultural products subject to the "price-band" system. In addition, Colombia provides preferential tariff rates for wines from countries belonging to the Latin American Integration Association (ALADI). By the end of January 1992, Colombia revamped its tariff structure to correspond with the just-established Andean Pact common external tariff range.

Import surcharges: The import surcharge was cut in half during 1991, from 16 percent to 8 percent on the CIF value of the import. A value added tax of 12 percent is also assessed against most imports. Higher VAT rates (usually 20 or 35 percent) are applied to a few items, such as automotive vehicles and pleasure boats.

The average total duty (tariff plus import surcharge) is now 14 percent (down from the previous 25 percent); 21 percent for consumer goods, 12 percent for raw materials and intermediate goods, and 12 percent for capital goods. By sectors, average effective protection to local industry as a result of the above measures is 45 percent for consumer goods, 21 percent for raw materials and intermediate goods, and 18 percent for capital goods.

Services barriers:

a. Motion pictures: In June 1989, the Colombian government adopted a resolution enforcing and implementing an agreement with the United States on film, video, and television imports and royalty remittances. The agreement reformed the film royalty remittance system, setting an annual budget for film remittances and providing for automatic approval of film remittances up to $40,000, videos up to $5,000, and television programs up to $4,000 per 60 minutes of transmission. As a practical matter, however, requests to exceed the remittance levels are regularly approved.

b. Banking: Law 9 and Conpes Resolution

49 (January 1991) opened up Colombia's financial sector to foreign investment. The new laws permit foreign investors to own up to 100 percent of financial institutions.

c. Franchising: Colombian laws impede franchising by requiring disclosure of trade secrets and other confidential information and requiring that the franchising agreement be approved by the exchange authority in order to secure remittances. Levels of royalty remittances depend on the level of know-how transferred to the franchisee in the contract.

d. Maritime transportation: As a result of the apertura program, cargo reserve requirements have been reduced and the government will likely implement further reforms in early 1992. At present there are no cargo reserve requirements for exports, with the exception of green coffee. (A minimum of 50 percent of green coffee must be transported on Colombian flag ships.) Ten percent of bulk imports and 50 percent of general cargo imports are subject to the same requirement, with the exception of items required for national defense, those under the Plan Vallejo drawback system, and for free industrial zones, newsprint, and minor imports.

Previous measures designed to restrict the availability of permits to offer shipping services to few companies have been lifted, and permits are now given to small shippers with minimum requirements.

e. Insurance: Insurance for all Colombian imports must be placed in the Colombian market; this restricts market access to foreign insurers and reinsurers for this class of business.

Investment barriers: Colombia, a leader within the Andean Pact to liberalize foreign investment rules, has implemented liberalized foreign investment regulations. Conpes Resolutions 49 and 51 provide for national treatment of foreign investment. The measure also increases the level of allowable annual remittances, which had been limited to 25 percent of the previous year's registered capital but which now may equal all net profits.

Postremittance review by the Superintendent of Foreign Exchange automatically takes place when remittances exceed 25 percent of the previous year's registered capital to ensure that the remittances were indeed net profits. Additionally, the Colombian government may also place restrictions on remittances if the level of international reserves falls below the equivalent of three months' imports. Remittance taxes will be reduced over the next four years from 20 to 12 percent.

The Colombian government has approved regulations for the operation of country investment funds, allowing foreign capital to invest directly in the Colombian stock market.

Some barriers to foreign investment remain. Foreign direct investments in certain fields (mining and petroleum exploration and extraction, public services) require prior authorization from the National Planning Department and/or the Ministry of Mines and Energy. The Colombian government maintains trade related investment measures (TRIMs) only in the automobile assembly sector, but these were liberalized in 1991 to permit assemblers to choose an optimal mix of export and local content requirements for "trade balancing" purposes.

At present, Colombia does not have bilateral investment treaties with other countries, but these are under consideration. The Colombian government has signed investment insurance agreements such as that with the U.S. Overseas Private Investment Corporation (OPIC). OPIC provides political risk and currency convertibility coverage to U.S. firms investing in Colombia. The Colombian government signed on to the World Bank's Multilateral Investment Guarantee Agency (MIGA), but the Colombian Congress has not yet ratified the agreement.

The new Colombian constitution permits expropriation by administrative means in specific cases where the Congress has determined the public good will be served. The articles were included to avoid problems with eminent domain which have hampered large public works projects in the past. However, not until implementing legislation is passed by the new Congress will the parameters of this type of expropriation be clearly defined.

Price controls: The government of Colombia maintains price ceilings for selected consumer and essential goods such as cooking oil, coffee, and pharmaceuticals, based on studies of production costs. The government has also established a "price-band" system, which sets floor and ceiling prices for wheat, barley, corn, milled rice, sorghum, soybeans, sugar, and dry milk. Reference prices, which fall between floor and ceiling prices, are determined each week by the Ministry of Agriculture. If imported agricultural products are priced below reference levels, Colombia uses variable levies to offset the difference, thus protecting local producers.

Government procurement practices: In 1987, Colombia enacted law 222, requiring government-to-government contracting for some major public works projects. Because the U.S. government cannot participate in commercial contracts with foreign countries, U.S. businesses have been prevented from participating as primary contractors. Other barriers imposed by law 222 include: requiring that a foreign contractor associate or subcontract with a Colombian firm for at least 40 percent of the value of the contract; increasing the value of the foreign proposal by 20 percent when evaluating it and comparing it with other proposals; and requiring foreign bidders to list all costs and expenses while local bidders are exempt from this requirement.

U.S. bidders on certain infrastructure projects and equipment sales have been unable to compete with other foreign bidders due to maximum financing rates set below U.S. Ex-Im Bank rates by the Ministry of Finance.

In recent cases where U.S. firms have presented a package of mixed credits (Ex-Im Bank/suppliers) with overall rates that meet government requirements, the packages were still deemed unacceptable by governmental entities.

The elimination or modification of Decree 222 continues to be a high priority. Although pressure from the Colombian contractors' association has made modification of Decree 222 difficult, the Colombian government is nonetheless preparing draft legislation to revise the restrictive rules of the law.

Trade Financing Environment and Options

The Colombian government assists exporters of manufactured and processed agricultural products via tax rebates (CERT), duty exemptions on import of capital goods, and raw materials used for export production (Plan Vallejo).

These measures have been rendered less important in light of the significant import duty reductions during 1991. Preferential rates for export financing are being phased out, and Proexpo, the export financing fund, was converted into an import-export bank offering market rates. The Colombian government, as part of its commitment to gain

U.S. support for accession to the GATT Subsidies Code in 1990, has pledged to phase out these subsidies over a five-year period.

INVESTMENT CLIMATE

The government actively promotes foreign investment. As of December 1988, total registered direct foreign investment was $3 billion, excluding petroleum activities, of which the U.S. share was $2.5 billion.

FINANCING AND CAPITAL MARKETS

General Policy Framework

Colombian economic policy is traditionally conservative, generally based on free-market principles. During 1991, the Colombian government accelerated the economic liberalization plan ("apertura") which had been initiated in February 1990 under former President Barco. The chief achievements of the program include substantial tariff reductions, the virtual elimination of prior import license requirements, liberalized foreign investment regulations, reform of the labor code and decentralization of the financial sector. A new Ministry of Foreign Trade was created to coordinate foreign trade policy and began operation in January 1992. Further significant components of apertura are beginning to be implemented, including privatization of ports and railroads, and de-monopolization of the telecommunication sector. Under the administration of President Gaviria, the pace of apertura has accelerated substantially.

Extent of U.S. Investment in Goods-Producing Sectors
U.S. Direct Investment Position Abroad
on a Historical-Cost Basis—1990
(Millions of U.S. dollars)

Category	Amount	
Petroleum		(D)
Total manufacturing		799
Food and kindred products	201	
Chemicals and allied products	198	
Metals, primary and fabricated	(D)	
Machinery, except electrical	(D)	
Electric and electronic equipment	(D)	
Transportation equipment	(D)	
Other manufacturing	306	
Wholesale trade		18
TOTAL PETROLEUM/MANUFACTURING/WHOLESALE TRADE		(D)

(D) = -Suppressed to avoid disclosing data of individual companies

Source: U.S. Department of Commerce, *Survey of Current Business* (August 1991, vol. 71, no. 8, table 11.3).

Two state-owned companies dominate the petroleum and coal industries (ECOPETROL and CARBOCOL), but operate in partnership with domestic and foreign private companies rather than as monopolies. The Gaviria administration plans to reduce its fiscal deficit and create greater economic efficiency through a vigorous privatization program. Among the projects already well advanced are: abolition of the monopoly of the state telecommunication company (Telecom) concerning domestic telephone and value-added services; reprivatization of five state banks (three have been sold in the period July-October 1991) in which the government intervened during the 1982–83 financial sector crisis; elimination of monopolistic management of the nation's ports (Law 1 of 1991) by the Colombian port company (Colpuertos), and drafting of a privatization plan which targeted December 1992 for the sale of the ports it now manages; separation of maintenance and operation from administration functions of the country's rail system, and opening the former to private or mixed company management in conjunction with the Colombian railroad company, Ferrovias; concentrated efforts to sell the state's equity in 27 companies over the next four years, under the direction of the Industrial Development Institute (IFI) (six have already been sold, another 10 are in negotiation); and the scheduled sale of over 20 hotels owned by the Colombian government.

Additionally, the new foreign investment regulations (Law 9 of 1991 and CONPES Resolution 51) permit foreign investment in public utilities with the prior approval of the National Planning Department.

The Colombian government's fiscal, monetary, and debt management policies have remained conservative. Colombia has not restructured its commercial bank debt; instead, the country has successfully refinanced maturing principal payments. In April 1991, the Colombian government signed a four-year, U.S. $1.775 billion "Hercules" refinancing package with its commercial creditors.

The Colombian government initiated a program to reduce the consolidated public sector fiscal deficit to 0.5 percent of GDP in 1991 through a combination of revenue increases and limiting expenditures. (The fiscal deficit in 1990 was 2.0 percent of GDP, down sharply from 7.0 percent reached in 1986.) Tax revenues have increased 61 percent over 1990 levels, primarily by means of improved collection, an increase in the value-added tax from 10 to 12 percent, expanding the range of transactions subject to the VAT, and by imposing a 3 percent tax on some foreign exchange transactions. These new fiscal revenues offset the reduction in import duty and surcharge revenues resulting from the Colombian government's economic liberalization program. The government avoids money creation to finance the deficit, using instead a flexible combination of domestic and external borrowing.

Following the collapse of the International Coffee Agreement in 1989, Colombian coffee export volume grew by 26 percent in the 1989–90 crop year.

However, 1990–91 exports have leveled off. The continued relatively low price of coffee has caused a severe fiscal drain on the national coffee fund, from which producers are paid the difference between the internal support price and the world export price. The fund could have been depleted within one year if coffee prices did not rise to the $1.00/lb. level. The increase in oil prices due to the Gulf Crisis caused the value of oil exports to surpass those of coffee in 1990 for the first time. Coal exports also increased, as did those of nontraditional products such as bananas, flowers, and leather goods.

Financial sector reforms enacted in 1991 resulted in a complete liberalization of Colombia's foreign exchange regime. On June

21, the Central Bank closed its foreign exchange window and turned over all transactions with the public to the commercial financial system. To slow down the monetization of foreign exchange inflows, the Central Bank began emitting 90-day exchange certificates by which it purchased the excess of foreign exchange balances from the commercial banks. The maturity on these certificates was later extended to 365 days.

Inflation remains a persistent problem in Colombia, reaching 32.4 percent in 1990. Despite maintaining a highly restrictive monetary policy, the government has had difficulty reducing inflation primarily due to the massive inflows of capital attracted by high real interest rates, a limited tax amnesty, and tight internal credit policies. At the end of the third quarter of 1991, reserves reached $7.1 billion, an increase of $2.4 billion from December 1990. Monetary authorities have experimented with various restrictive monetary policies, including a 100 percent marginal reserve requirement (imposed for nine months), an increase in average reserve requirements, large open market operations, and real appreciation of the peso.

Debt Management Policies

Colombia has not had to reschedule its official external debt. Total external debt fell slightly by mid-year 1991 to $16.3 billion; public debt accounted for $13.7 billion of the total. Most of the public debt is to the World Bank and Inter-American Development Bank ($5.7 billion) or to other governments ($2.5 billion). Debt service on public external debt was $3.1 billion in 1990, equivalent to about 46 percent of export earnings.

Colombia has consistently paid interest and principal on its official debt.

However, certain sectors, primarily the public electrical utilities and the state coal company, Carbocol, are experiencing problems in servicing debts.

In April 1991, the Colombian government signed a four-year, $1.757 billion refinancing package with its commercial bank creditors. The "Hercules" syndicated loan/bearer bond issue represented a major success of the Gaviria administration in refinancing 90 percent of commercial bank debt maturing in 1991–94 at favorable terms.

The Currency and Exchange Rate Mechanisms

Decree Law 9, approved in January 1991, completely revised Colombia's foreign exchange regime. Colombia now has essentially a free-market exchange system. Although the Central Bank establishes an official exchange rate, based on a crawling-peg daily devaluation of the peso, it is basically only a reference rate. This crawling-peg devaluation of the official exchange rate is intended to adjust for the relative inflation rates between Colombia and its major trading partners in order to maintain the real exchange rate. However, all commercial transactions are now conducted at free exchange rates determined by the financial markets. The discount on the foreign exchange certificates issued by the Central Bank is the best indicator of the free market exchange rate. The Colombian government may intervene in the financial markets to keep the peso within a 10 percent band of the official rate by buying and selling exchange certificates.

Financial Market Operations and Structural Policies

Taxation: Colombia enacted a comprehensive tax reform in December 1990, which lowered corporate and remittance taxes, increased the value added tax, and tightened up tax collection procedures. These reforms have substantially increased tax revenues.

Major sources of government revenue consist of personal and corporate income taxes, a value added tax, and taxes on international trade. Taxes on income account for one-quarter of total revenues, those on goods and services for about 45 percent, and those on foreign trade for about 28 percent. Draft tax reforms to be introduced to the new Congress in December 1991 will likely increase the VAT again another two or three percentage points.

Colombia maintains certain tax incentives in order to promote investment and nontraditional exports. These include an exemption of duties on free trade zone imports and imports for use in export industries (the Vallejo Plan for capital goods), and a tax rebate for exporters of certain products in the form of a certificate representing a percentage of the value of an export sale which can be used to pay indirect taxes (CERT).

However, the tax incentive for capital goods imports under the Vallejo Plan mechanism has lost importance in light of the recent dramatic duty reductions on capital goods. The number of export products to which these rebates apply, and the applicable rates have been sharply reduced during 1991. The Colombian government committed to phasing out both the Vallejo Plan and the CERT program in its subsidy commitment with the United States.

Colombia acceded to the GATT Subsidies Code in July 1990.

Regulatory policies: The import licensing regime, which previously constituted the greatest impediment to increased imports from the United States, has been virtually eliminated as a result of the apertura program.

Of the 6,828 tariff lines in the Colombian harmonized schedule, only 2 percent now require a prior import license. The government has made an effort to legalize a massive black market in smuggled consumer goods by offering a duty amnesty on existing contraband inventories in addition to beginning a program designed to collect value added taxes on the informal sector of the economy. The contraband market is estimated to be in the range of one billion dollars annually, a very high proportion of which consists of consumer products from the United States and Asia.

VISITING AND LOCATING

General Travel Checklist

Travel advisory: Because of sporadic guerrilla activity, travel in certain areas may be hazardous. Before traveling to Colombia, it is recommended that persons check with the nearest U.S. Consulate or with the U.S. Department of State, Bureau of Consular Affairs, in Washington, DC, for the latest information.

Climate and clothing: Climatic variations depend on altitude. Knits and lightweight woolens are suitable in Bogota.

Customs: A passport is required for travel to Colombia. Tourists may enter and stay in Colombia for 30 days on a tourist card provided by the airlines serving Colombia, providing the tourist has a booked round trip passage. For a stay beyond 30 days, tourists must obtain a visa from the nearest Colombian Embassy or Consulate.

Health: Medical facilities are satisfactory; many doctors have been trained in the United States and speak English. Common medicines are available. Tap water is not always safe in large cities; food should be prepared carefully.

Telecommunications: Long-distance telephone and telegraph service is available. Colombia is in the eastern standard time zone but does not use daylight saving time during the summer.

Transportation: Flights to Bogota, Barranquilla, Cali, Medellin, and Cartagena are easy to arrange from the United States,

Europe, and Latin America. Local air service is also available. Buses provide service throughout the country. Taxis provide the most reliable public transportation in cities.

Tourist attractions: The Bogota Gold Museum and the Caribbean resort of Cartagena, with its seventeenth century fortifications.

Chapter 7
COSTA RICA

	Total	Urban	
Population (1993)	3,268,000	45.0%	

Main Urban Areas	Population	Percentage of Total	International Calling Code
SAN JOSE (Metro)	1,200,000	36.7	506
SAN JOSE	279,000	8.5	506
Alajuela	147,000	4.5	506
Cartago	101,000	3.1	506
Puntarenas	86,000	2.6	506
Limon	63,000	1.9	506
Heredia	63,000	1.9	506
Liberia	33,000	1.0	506

Land Area   50,660 square kilometers
    Comparable U.S. State   Slightly smaller than West Virginia

Language   Spanish   97%
    Creole English   2%
    Caribbean lang.   1%
    Common Business Language   Spanish

Currency   1 colon (C) = 100 centimos
    Exchange Rate (May 1993)   U.S. $1.00 = 122 colons

Best Nonstop Air Connection via U.S.   Miami to San Jose: 2.75 hours
    American Airlines (800) 433-7300
    Lacsa Airlines (800) 225-2272
    Both offer four nonstops daily

Best Hotel   Cariari Golf Country Club & Casino
    P.O. Box 737-1007 (U.S. $95)
    Centro Colon, San Jose
    Tel: (506) 390-222
    Fax: (506) 392-803

INTRODUCTION AND REGIONAL ORIENTATION

Unlike most of their Central American neighbors, Costa Ricans are largely of European rather than mestizo descent, and Spain is the primary country of origin. The indigenous population today numbers no more than 25,000. Blacks, descendants of nineteenth-century Jamaican immigrant workers, constitute a significant English-speaking minority of about 30,000, concentrated around the Caribbean port city of Limon.

Geographical Background

Costa Rica is a rugged, tropical country known as "the Switzerland of Latin America" for its solid tradition of economic, political and cultural stability since the 1930s. It is located in the middle of Central America, sharing a 309-kilometer border with Nicaragua to the north and a 330-kilometer border with Panama to the south. It features beautiful and unspoiled shorelines—the Pacific Ocean to the west and the Caribbean to the east.

In has long been a retreat for avid sports fishermen and naturalists, and much of its territory is protected or national park land. It has active volcanoes, tropical rain forests, and attractive scenery. Its Isla del Coco has been popularized by the recent Hollywood film based on the Michael Crichton book, *Jurassic Park.*

History and Political Conditions

In 1502, on his fourth and last voyage to the New World, Christopher Columbus made the first European landfall in the area. Settlement of Costa Rica began in 1522, and for nearly three centuries the region was administered as part of the Captaincy General of Guatemala, under a military governor.

In 1821, Costa Rica joined other Central American provinces in a joint declaration of independence from Spain. Although the newly independent provinces formed a federation, border disputes broke out among them. Costa Rica's northern Guanacaste Province was annexed from Nicaragua in one such regional dispute. In 1838, long after the Central American federation ceased to function in practice, Costa Rica formally withdrew and proclaimed itself sovereign.

The modern era of peaceful democracy in Costa Rica began in 1889, in a remarkable change of political power, considering the region's turbulent history and conditions. The elections of 1889, considered the first truly free and honest ones in the country's history, began a trend maintained with only two lapses: in 1917–18, Federico Tinoco ruled as a dictator, and in 1948, Jose Figueres led a popular revolution in the wake of a disputed presidential election. With more than 2,000 dead, the revolution was the bloodiest event in Costa Rican history, but the victorious junta drafted a constitution guaranteeing free elections with universal suffrage and the abolition of the army. Figueres became a national hero, winning the first election under the new constitution.

Since that time, Costa Rica has held 11 presidential elections. Only twice, in 1974 and in 1986, was the candidate of the party in power elected. The next elections are scheduled for February 1994.

CRACKING THE MARKET

Demographics
Ethnic composition: White (including mestizo) 96%; Black 2%; Indian 1%; Chinese 1%.

Religion: Roman Catholic 95%.

Language: Spanish (official), English spoken around Puerto Limon.

Literacy: 93% (male 93%, female 93%) age 15 and over can read and write (1990 estimate).

Labor force: 868,300 (1985 estimate): industry and commerce 35.1%; government and services 33%; agriculture 27%; other 4.9%.

Organized labor: 15.1% of labor force.

Economy

The economy will probably not begin to show improvement in GDP growth and inflation containment before the middle of 1993, reacting slowly to a lowering of interest rates that started in late 1991 and to a reduction in government and Central Bank bond sales. Continuing tariff reductions plus the need to restock will maintain a balance of trade deficit, hopefully made smaller by a rise in world coffee and banana prices as well as a general improvement in the terms of foreign trade. Finally, a much improved foreign currency cash flow situation as a result of bilateral and multilateral debt rescheduling agreements will permit Costa Rica to resume modest investments in public health infrastructure, road repair, and public education. With resumed investment in the private sector as well, resulting from the reduced presence of the government and Central Bank in the bonds market and lower interest rates, it is expected that GDP growth will reach 2.5 percent by the end of 1993.

Since its economic crisis of the early 1980s, Costa Rica's economic orientation has supported structural adjustment, focusing on internal stability and growth through increasingly diversified exports. The gross domestic product (GDP) grew an average 5 percent since 1986, nontraditional exports increased 20 to 30 percent annually, official unemployment fell below 6 percent, and inflation is relatively low. These trends slowed in 1990: growth diminished to 36 percent, inflation to over 25 percent, and government deficits increased. A debt buy-back program under the U.S. "Brady Plan" was completed in May 1990, enabling Costa Rica to repurchase 60 percent of its commercial bank debt, cover interest for bonds issued in exchange for part of debt, and cover payments on debt not repurchased. Costa Rica also became the hundredth member of the General Agreement on Tariffs and Trade (GATT) in 1990.

The successful macroeconomic performance of the late 1980s masked serious fiscal imbalances, including a large public-sector deficit and declining international reserves. Immediately after taking office, the Calderon administration began implementing a fiscal austerity program, including revenue increases and expenditure reductions. The programs of the International Monetary Fund, World Bank, the Inter-American Development Bank, and the U.S. Agency for International Development in Costa Rica are aimed at maintaining stability and promoting trade and investment liberalization.

The Costa Rican government actively supports the Enterprise for the Americas Initiative (EAI) announced by President Bush in June 1990. The United States and Costa Rica signed a bilateral trade and investment framework agreement in November 1990 under the EAI as a mechanism to discuss trade and investment issues. In January 1991, the Costa Ricans joined the other Central American countries in committing to discuss the creation of a free trade zone with Mexico by 1996. Later in 1991, Costa Rica and Venezuela began discussions for a free trade arrangement. Further liberalization of Costa Rica's trade and investment regimes and greater access to foreign markets by the country's exporters would provide promising opportunities for foreign and local investors and increased prosperity for Costa Rica.

The two bright spots in the 1991 economy were a reduction in the fiscal budget deficit and, for the first time in several years, a substantial increase in the level of foreign reserves. The latter resulted from a reduction in the foreign trade deficit and increases in the capital account resulting from increased tourism, foreign investment, and repatriation of Costa Rican controlled funds from offshore.

Prospects for the near future look good, despite continuing pressure from international institutions and creditor countries to meet foreign debt payments and to maintain tight monetary and fiscal policies. Prices (CPI) are expected to rise 20 percent, while unemployment stays at the same level as 1991 (5.6 percent). The Central Bank announced a relative freeing of foreign currency restrictions starting March 1, 1992, and followed this with a freeing of the capital account on May 1. These changes are expected to ease import restrictions, improve the investment climate, and set a more realistic exchange rate. The government of Costa Rica continues to lower tariff rates, planning for most tariffs to be in the range of 5–20 percent by mid-1993.

Political/Institutional Infrastructure

Costa Rica is a democratic republic with a strong system of checks and balances. Executive responsibilities are vested in a president who, though somewhat more constrained than most Latin American heads of state, is without question the center of power. The president and 57 Legislative Assembly deputies are elected for four-year terms. A constitutional amendment approved in 1969 limits both the president and the deputies to one term, although a deputy may be returned to the assembly after sitting out a term.

The electoral process is supervised by an independent Supreme Electoral Tribunal, a commission of three principal magistrates, and six alternates selected by the Supreme Court of Justice. Judicial power is exercised by the Supreme Court of Justice, composed of 22 magistrates selected for eight-year terms by the Legislative Assembly, and sub-

COSTA RICA
Key Economic Indicators

	1990	1991	1992
GDP (current dollars—millions)	5,552	5,604	5,706
GDP projected average through 1992 Real annual growth rate	3.7	1.0	2.3
GDP per capita (U.S. $)	1,883	1,810	1,867
Government spending as % of GNP	19.8	18.9	N/A
Inflation (%) (CPI growth—Dec–Dec)	27.3	25.3	20.0
Unemployment (%)	4.6	5.6	5.6
Foreign-exchange reserves (U.S.$—millions)	463.2	648.0	588.0
Average exchange rate (colones per U.S. $1)	104.6	136.8	140.0
Foreign debt (U.S. $—millions)	2,982	3,157	3,365
U.S. economic assistance (U.S. $—millions)	74.2	51.6	22.0
U.S. military assistance* (U.S. $) —Training only	225,000	330,000	240,000

Source: USAID/Office of Economic Analysis.

*   Office of the Defense Representative, U.S. Embassy

COSTA RICA
Key Economic Indicators

	1989	1990	1991[1]
Income, Production, Employment (millions U.S. dollars)			
Real GDP	11,827.3	12,228.8	12,408.6
Real GDP growth (%)	5.7	3.4	1.5
Agriculture	2,265.9	2,362.6	2,421.7
Industry	2,609.8	2,647.2	2,692.2
Electricity/water	356.8	378.9	391.0
Construction	489.7	487.1	433.5
Commerce	2,004.5	2,047.9	2,072.5
Transportation/communication	989.5	1,056.8	1,082.2
Financial	773.2	858.7	879.3
General government	1,048.7	1,059.3	1,075.7
Others	1,289.2	1,330.3	1,360.5
Real GDP per capita (1966 colones)	4,142.0	4,183.0	4,136.0
Real GDP per capita (U.S. $/1990 rate)	1825	1892	N/A
Labor force (thousands)	987.0	1,017.0	1,090.0
Unemployment (%)	3.8	4.6	5.0
Money and Prices			
Money supply (M1) (millions of colones)	63,057.0	67,804.0	77,787.0
Lending rate (%)[2]	33.1	41.6	40.1
Deposit rate (%)[3]	25.0	34.6	30.0
Gross domestic investment (% of GDP)	23.1	22.1	20.8
Consumer price index (% change Dec–Dec)	10.0	27.3	25.0
Wholesale price index (% change Dec–Dec)	10.7	25.9	23.0
Colon to U.S. $ exch rate (Yearly average official)	82.1	92.3	120.0
Colon to U.S. dollar exchange rate (yearly average parallel market)	84.2	98.2	125.0
Balance of Payments and Trade (millions U.S. dollars)			
Exports to U.S.	578.5	586.1	N/A
Imports CIF	1,746.6	2,037.0	1,871.0
Assistance from U.S.	114.8	74.2	51.6
Assistance from other countries	25.2	25.5	117.1
Foreign investment	88.9	135.0	N/A
U.S. investment	66.7	101.2	N/A
Foreign public debt	3,800.9	3,269.2	N/A
Annual debt service paid	282.0	225.0	285.0
Gold reserves	3.1	4.2	N/A
Net international reserves	756.9	470.8	730.4[4]
Current account balance	−439.0	−583.8	−276.4

1. Estimate based on October 1991 data.
2. Average of private and state-owned banks.
3. Average of six month deposit rates of private and state-owned banks and government bonds.
4. As of July 15, 1991.

sidiary courts. A constitutional chamber of the Supreme Court, established in 1989, reviews the constitutionality of legislation and executive decrees and all habeas corpus warrants.

The country's seven provinces are headed by governors appointed by the president, but they exercise little power. There are no provincial legislatures. Autonomous state agencies enjoy considerable operational independence; they include the nationalized commercial banks, the state insurance monopoly, and the Social Security Agency.

Principal Government Officials

(September 1992)

President
Rafael Angel Calderon Fournier

Foreign Minister
Bernd Niehaus Quesada

Ambassador to the U.S.
Gonzalo J. Facio Segrada

Ambassador to the OAS
Carlos Pereira Garro

Ambassador to the UN
Cristian Tattenbach Yglesias

Political Parties and Leaders

National Liberation Party (PLN), Rolando ARAYA Monge; Social Christian Unity Party (PUSC), Rafael Angel CALDERON Fournier; Marxist Popular Vanguard Party (PVP), Humberto VARGAS Carbonell; New Republic Movement (MNR), Sergio Erick ARDON Ramirez; Progressive Party (PP), Isaac Felipe AZOFEIFA Bolanos; People's Party of Costa Rica (PPC), Lenin CHACON Vargas; Radical Democratic Party (PRD), Juan Jose ECHEVERRIA Brealey.

Suffrage is universal and compulsory at age 18.

Defense

The 1949 constitution prohibited the establishment of a standing army in Costa Rica. The country relies on small Civil and Rural Guard forces which patrol the borders and perform internal police functions. Costa Rica faces no serious external or internal threats and looks to the collective security provisions of the 1947 Rio Treaty for defense against external aggression.

The president is the commander-in-chief of the public security forces. The primary organization is the Civil Guard. It is essentially a constabulary force responsible for law and order in urban areas and for land, air, and maritime border surveillance. The secondary organization, the Rural Guard, is responsible for rural police functions throughout Costa Rica's seven provinces. Both organizations fall under the Ministry of Government and Public Security.

Current Political Conditions

Throughout its history, Costa Rica's political system has contrasted sharply with those of its neighbors. The nation has steadily developed and maintained democratic institutions and an orderly, constitutional scheme for government succession. Several elements have contributed to this situation, including educational opportunities, enlightened government leaders, comparative prosperity, flexible class lines, and the absence of a politically intrusive military.

In the elections of 1990, Rafael Angel Calderon Fournier, of the Social Christian Unity Party (PUSC), was elected to succeed Oscar Arias Sanchez of the National Liberation Party (PLN) as Costa Rica's president.

The private-sector oriented and populist PUSC also won a slim majority in the Legislative Assembly—29 of 57 seats. The PUSC is aligned to Christian Democratic and conservative parties in the Western Hemisphere and Europe. The PLN has been the dominant party in Costa Rica since 1948. It is a social democratic party affiliated with the Socialist International. The 1990 elections marked the first time in over 30 years that the PLN lost control of the Legislative Assembly. Overall, Costa Rican governments have swung from moderately conservative to moderately progressive as the PLN and various anti-PLN coalitions have tended to alternate control of the presidency. This pattern was broken in 1974 and 1986, when a PLN candidate succeeded a PLN incumbent. Three minor parties are represented in the 1990–94 Legislative Assembly.

Costa Rica has not been insulated from regional conflicts. Instability in neighboring Nicaragua and Panama in the 1980s discouraged new investment and tourism in Costa Rica. In addition, many Nicaraguans and Salvadorans sought refuge in Costa Rica, further burdening the country's educational and health facilities.

In 1987, President Oscar Arias authored a regional peace plan that became the basis for the peace agreement signed by the presidents of the other Central American countries (excluding Belize and Panama). Arias's efforts earned him the 1987 Nobel Peace Prize. The Esquipulas Process, as the peace plan became known, contributed to bringing about free and open elections in Nicaragua and the subsequent end of the civil war in that country.

Under President Calderon, Costa Rica continues to play a prominent role in the Esquipulas Process. The Costa Ricans have hosted negotiations between the Salvadoran government and the Farabundo Marti guerrilla faction and are key participants in efforts toward regional cooperation on political and economic development and demilitarization.

Foreign Relations

Costa Rica is an active member of the international community. Its record in such areas as human rights and advocacy of peaceful settlement of dispute gives it a weight in world affairs far beyond its size. The country lobbied strenuously for the establishment of the UN High Commissioner for Human Rights and was the first nation to recognize the jurisdiction of the Inter-American Human Rights Court, which is based in San Jose.

Costa Rica expressed a firm commitment to the letter and spirit of the Rio Treaty.

With the establishment of democratically elected governments in all Central American nations in 1990, Costa Rica was able to turn its focus from regional conflicts to the pursuit of democratic and economic development on the isthmus. Costa Rica was instrumental in drawing Panama into the Central American development process and key to the establishment of the multinational Partnership for Democracy and Development in Central America, a partnership of the Central American nations, industrialized democracies, Colombia, Mexico, and Venezuela, and international organizations.

Costa Rica broke relations with Cuba in 1961 to protest Cuban support of leftist subversion in Central America.

U.S.-Costa Rican Relations

The United States and Costa Rica have enjoyed close and friendly relations based on mutual respect for democratic government, human freedoms, social and economic rights, and other shared values. U.S. and Costa Rican views on foreign policy have not always coincided: Costa Rica aligned itself with other Latin American countries against the U.S. position during the 1982 Malvinas-Falkland War and against U.S. military operations in Grenada in 1983. Former President Arias was critical of U.S. policy in support of the Nicaraguan Resistance. Costa Rica was among the first Latin American countries, however, to support the U.S.-led reestablishment of democratic order in Panama in 1989 and was a firm supporter of the U.S. position during the Persian Gulf crisis following Iraq's invasion of Kuwait in 1990. The United States and Costa Rica share a strong interest in promoting and strengthening democratic processes and in-

stitutions and enhancing free market oriented economic development in Central America and throughout the hemisphere.

The United States has responded to Costa Rica's economic needs through developmental assistance programs. The Peace Corps, with some 150 volunteers, has helped develop skills in agriculture, education, health, nutrition, and natural resources development. The U.S. Agency for International Development works not only to support Costa Rican efforts to stabilize the economy in the short term, but also to help broaden and accelerate economic growth through policy reforms and trade liberaliza-

TRADE

	1990	1991	1992
Total exports	1,448.2	1,590.1	1,227.4
Total imports	1,989.7	1,852.8	1,637.8
Exports to the U.S.	606.4	696.5	771.0
Imports from the U.S.	825.4	801.2	830.0
U.S. share of Costa Rican imports (%)	41.5	43.2	50.7
Imports of manufactured goods:			
Total from all countries	*	*	*
Projected average growth rate through 1994 (%)	*	*	*
From the U.S.	777.4	829.3	904.0
Projected average growth rate through 1992 (%)	9.6	6.7	9.0
U.S. share of manufactured imports (%)	*	*	*

Trade Balances with Four Leading Partners in 1991:

USA	−104.7
Japan	−90.5
Venezuela	−119.0
Germany	112.6

All figures are U.S. dollars millions.

Sources: USAID/Office of Economic Analysis (Central Bank).
U.S. Department of Commerce.
Foreign Economic Trends Report, Costa Rica, June 1992.

* Costa Rican imports of manufactured goods figures are not compiled in Costa Rica. The statistical information available is total imports, which includes manufactured goods.

tion. Low-income farmers are being helped toward self-sufficiency, and the urban poor are aided by industrial development, family planning, and increased educational opportunities. The private sector, as the primary engine for sustained economic growth, is also supported by U.S. assistance efforts.

Many other U.S. government agencies, including the U.S. Information Service and the Department of Agriculture, are active in Costa Rica. More than 20,000 American private citizens, mostly retirees, live in the country.

APPROACHING THE MARKET

Commercial Environment

Prospects for 1993 are optimistic, despite continuing pressure from international institutions and creditor countries to meet foreign debt payments and to maintain tight monetary and fiscal policies. Prices (CPI) are ex-pected to rise 20 percent, while unemployment will remain at the same level as 1991 (5.6 percent). The Central Bank announced a relative freeing of foreign currency restrictions starting March 1, 1992, followed by a freeing of the capital account on May 1. These changes are expected to ease import restrictions, improve the investment climate and set a more realistic exchange rate.

A government labor reduction plan has reduced the size of public sector employment by 9,000 employees and is continuing to cut costs. On the income side, public revenues are increasing through sales taxes which were raised from 10 to 13 percent. This tax will decrease by 1 percent annually until 1994. It is currently at 12 percent. With the combination of lower public spending and higher revenue, the government hopes to reduce its fiscal deficit to not more than one-half of 1 percent of GDP. A further government objective is to slow price increases to 12 percent. However, private sec-

Principal U.S. Exports (1991) by Tariff Line Item *

Oil (not crude) from petroleum and bitum mineral	HS Code 2710	57.1
Kraft paper and paper board	HS Code 4804	59.5
Corn (maize)	HS Code 1005	31.8
Polymers (ethylene), in primary forms	HS Code 3901	12.9
Fertilizers	HS Code 3100	26.2

Principal U.S. Imports (1991) by Tariff Line Item *

Bananas and plantains	HS Code 0803	201.0
Coffee (processed)	HS Code 0901	65.0
Meat of bovine animals	HS Codes 0201-0202	33.7
Dates, figs, pineapples, avocados	HS Code 0804	21.4
Melons and papayas	HS Code 0807	13.2

* Excludes offshore assembly (maquiladoras), mainly textile and apparel outputs.

All figures are U.S. dollars millions.

Source: U.S. Department of Commerce.

(Millions 1966 Colones unless otherwise indicated)

tor estimates put inflation likely in the range 18–20 percent.

Foreign Trade and Investment Decision-Making Infrastructure

Costa Rica announced its intention to begin lowering most tariffs to a maximum of 20 percent by second quarter 1993 with a minimum tariff of 5 to 10 percent.

Costa Rica signed a framework agreement on trade and investment with the U.S. in November 1990 under the Enterprise for the Americas Initiative. The Trade and Investment Council has met on three occasions as the main forum in which bilateral trade issues are discussed. Costa Rica is opening up its trade regime through trade agreements with Mexico, the CACM, and other bilateral and regional arrangements. A free-trade framework agreement was signed with Mexico in 1992.

On the export side, the government is committed to the promotion of Costa Rican exports, mainly nontraditional exports to third markets (other than Central America). However, in conformance with the GATT and anticipating a NAFTA, the government has modified the export subsidy system (CAT), which will be phased out by 1999.

The government of Costa Rica provides tax incentives to nontraditional exporters and to companies which generate foreign exchange, such as tourism. Costa Rica is reforming these incentives to remedy the economic distortions they cause, reduce their budget impact, and reduce their inconsistency with international practices. On October 7, 1991, a decree was published, whereby a 25 percent tax is levied on negotiable tax rebate certificates (CAT).

Implications for U.S. Exporters

Tariffs and taxes: Under the terms of Costa Rica's accession to the GATT, it agreed to implement a more transparent, unified, and lower tariff and tax system. Imports from other Central American Common Market (CACM) countries enter duty free, thus enjoying a significant advantage over similar U.S. goods. In addition to customs duties ranging from 1 to 100 percent ad valorem, U.S. goods are also subject to an array of taxes and surcharges including a 10 to 75 percent consumption tax levied on certain items, a 13 percent sales tax, a 2 percent surcharge, and border charges.

Since January 1, 1992, many U.S. basic grain exports face a Central American price band system, including the application of variable levies.

Central Bank import deposits: To purchase foreign currency (usually U.S. dollars), Costa Rican importers must deposit a set percentage of purchase value as an essentially interest-free loan to the Costa Rican Central Bank. The importer must then wait two weeks or more to receive the currency. The delay (known in Spanish as "la presa") and level is set by the Central Bank to help manage foreign currency reserves.

The Central Bank may also impose import surcharges to conserve foreign exchange. These surcharges do not require legislative approval and can be changed with relative ease.

Services barriers: Offshore banks may locate in Costa Rica, but operations are restricted to long-term (over 180 days) savings, bond issuance, and international services. These banks cannot offer checking accounts. Insurance of all types is provided exclusively by a state-owned monopoly, the National Insurance Institute, which specifies all charges and agent fees.

Government procurement practices: The Costa Rican government procures largely through open public bidding, although its law also permits private tenders and direct contracting of goods and services for small amounts or in cases of national emergency.

At times, tenders have contained unreasonable requirements prejudicial to otherwise qualified bidders, including U.S. companies, such as a requirement that a company must have previous Latin American experience in order to qualify or may not be the holding company of a parent company. While Costa Rica has agreed to review bids when arbitrary requirements were noted, there have been considerable delays in awarding the contracts. In addition, three appeals are permitted for each public tender, so that offers must be resubmitted after the resolution of each appeal, often with new specifications.

Original offers may not be resubmitted. In short, not only does the appeal system considerably delay the process, but it also involves costs to companies for the preparation of resubmissions.

Setting Up Business Operations

According to the Commercial Code of Costa Rica, foreign firms must contract a representative, agent, or distributor on an exclusive basis in order to sell in Costa Rica. The agent or distributor must have done business in Costa Rica for at least three years. Non-Costa Ricans must prove that they have been residing in Costa Rica for at least 10 years. Since the Costa Rican market is so small, U.S. exporters are advised to contract only one representative, although subagents can be designated for different product lines. Legitimate foreign representatives are generally members of the Chamber of Representatives of Foreign Firms (CRECEX).

Foreign products must be labeled in Spanish and denominated in the metric system. Cosmetics and chemicals must be registered every five years with the Department of Drugs, Narcotics, and Psychotropics Control. Food and beverages must be registered at the Food Control Department of the Ministry of Health. All manufacturers and importers must present a request for registration accompanied by a sample of the product. Medicines and cosmetics also need prior authorization/registration from the ministry, but the requirement for medicines may be waived in an emergency procurement by the Costa Rican Institute of Social Security, the centralized purchaser for the medical system.

To assist the U.S. exporter, the U.S. and Foreign Commercial Service offers the Agent-Distributor Search (ADS) for a customized presentation of qualified potential Costa Rican representatives. U.S. exporters may also order selected trade lists, industry sector analyses, and customized sales surveys (product-specific market research) from the Foreign Commercial Service, American Embassy San Jose, Unit 2508, APO AA 34020.

Business conducted in Costa Rica is largely based on personal relationships. Costa Rican business executives and government officials generally place great importance on personal contacts with foreign suppliers, who are expected to travel to Costa Rica routinely and follow up with correspondence and telephone calls. Costa Rica's communications systems are among the best in Latin America.

U.S. suppliers will quickly become aware of increased foreign competition in Costa Rica, since foreign competitors are extremely aggressive. U.S. executives interested in pursuing business in Costa Rica should approach local representatives in the same manner in which they approach prized clients in the United States. Suppliers must be prepared to explain how their products and services will complement existing products and systems.

In view of the proximity of Costa Rica to the United States, U.S. sales personnel should travel to the country. Such travelers are often surprised at the accessibility of key decision-makers and the openness and frankness of local buyers. (Note: The U.S.

and Foreign Commercial Service of the American Embassy in Costa Rica will arrange appointments and translator services for U.S. companies on a pay-basis through the Gold Key/Silver Key Services).

Promotional material should be in Spanish. Although many business people are fluent in English, the technicians and engineers often work only in Spanish. Costa Ricans are extremely receptive to technical presentations which are educational rather than sales-oriented.

Forms of Business Organization

The government of Costa Rica encourages foreign investment and actively seeks to promote the development of new export crops by foreigners. The Costa Rican constitution provides foreign investors the same legal guarantees as Costa Rican citizens, except for participation in political affairs. As this report was drafted, there were no legal restrictions on the repatriation of profits or on joint venture regulations that might represent barriers to direct foreign investment in Costa Rica. Foreigners may legally own Costa Rican companies, or equity therein, and may invest in all areas not expressly reserved for state or para-statal entities. Foreign corporations may be organized legally in several ways: as branches (except for banks), joint ventures, wholly owned subsidiaries, or locally incorporated companies. Any bona fide investment is encouraged in Costa Rica. The government is particularly interested in agro-industry and specialty or nontraditional agriculture for export, such as ornamental plants, spices, fruits, and nuts. Labor-intensive activities, such as food processing and light assembly operations, especially textile and electronics under drawback arrangements, are particularly attractive. U.S. companies with local operations mention the availability of bilingual qualified local engineers and managers as a

definite plus. Costa Rica is negotiating a bilateral investment treaty with the United States that would provide additional incentives and benefits to the citizens of both countries.

While U.S. corporations and persons may legally own equity in Costa Rican companies, several activities are reserved for the State, including public utilities, insurance, demand deposits (checking and short-term savings accounts), the production and distribution of electricity, hydrocarbons and radioactive mineral extraction, refining, and the operation of ports and airports. Investment in a few other enterprises is limited to national owners.

INVESTMENT CLIMATE

OPIC extends its insurance policies to U.S. citizens and corporate entities wishing to invest in Costa Rica. Costa Rica has signed an investment agreement with the Multilateral Investment Guarantee Agency (MIGA) of the World Bank. As of the drafting of this report, that agreement awaits ratification in the Legislative Assembly. Costa Rica has signed a bilateral Tax Information Exchange Agreement with the United States, which grants such benefits as access to U.S. Tax Code Section 936 fund loans from Puerto Rico, the ability of Costa Rican hotels to attract more conferences and conventions, and the possibility of establishing foreign sales corporations under Secs. 801–805 of the Deficit Reduction Act of 1984 and Sections 921–27 of the U.S. Tax Code.

Investors in private real estate should be aware that some foreigners holding property outside of the central valley region have been subject to squatter invasions and other disputes which have led to loss of certain property rights and in some cases loss of their land. Investment in rural land should be limited to circumstances where the investor intends to develop the property actively. Absentee land investment for speculative purposes, or investments through land developers not well known to the investor, may be ill-advised. We suggest U.S. citizens considering such investments check with the U.S. Embassy first.

Similarly, persons considering investment in development of certain tropical products for export should carefully investigate the bona fides of any such offer before investing. Please note that offerings made outside the United States are not subject to SEC or other U.S. guidelines. Potential investors should therefore exercise due caution before investment with firms with which they are unfamiliar.

Additional information regarding investments in Costa Rica can be obtained from the U. S. Embassy publication, "Investment Climate Statement: Costa Rica." The publication "Investor's Guide to Costa Rica" can be purchased from the Costa Rican-American Chamber of Commerce, San Jose, tel: (506) 202-200, fax: (506) 202-300.

Investment Barriers

Access to foreign exchange: Most difficulties faced by foreign investors stem from an inefficient bureaucracy which slows approval of documents necessary for many transactions. For example, even though no unusual restrictions are imposed on the repatriation of earnings, royalties, or capital, delays in receiving dollars for these transactions or for imports can be quite lengthy. These delays can add considerably to an investor's operating expenses.

Investment disputes: While there are no recorded cases of Costa Rican expropriation of commercial or manufacturing properties, individual landowners have lost their lands to squatters. In addition, Costa Rica has expropriated lands adjacent to national parks. The civil and commercial codes provide for arbitration of commercial disputes. How-

ever, the procedures as established by law are cumbersome and rarely used. In practice, cases are usually settled in court. Costa Rican law does not recognize the jurisdiction of other than Costa Rican courts.

Article 45 of the Costa Rican Constitution stipulates that no property can be expropriated without previous, prompt, and fair payment.

Costa Rican law does not discriminate between nationals and foreigners in this regard. However, when dealing with land disputes, conflicts take a long time to be resolved. Constitutional guarantees notwithstanding, almost all investment disputes involving U.S. citizens center on expropriation of American-owned land.

Tourism investment: Costa Rican Tourism Institute (ICT) is vested with the authority to declare areas within 200 meters of the coast "Touristic Zones." Once permission is obtained from the ICT, the developer then requests the concessions. According to this law, concessionaires must be Costa Rican citizens. Foreign tourism-related enterprises must have at least 50 percent Costa Rican capital in order to obtain concessions.

Extent of U.S. Investment in Goods-Producing Sectors

U.S. percent of total foreign direct investment (flow) has averaged 50 percent over the past several years.

Total Foreign Direct Investment*

	Stock	Flow
1987	—	89.0
1988	—	168.0
1989	—	143.0
1990	162.4	109.0
1991	142.0	120.0
1992	N/A	125.0**

* U.S. $ Millions
** Projected
Source: Central Bank of Costa Rica.

FINANCING AND CAPITAL MARKETS

General Policy Framework

Costa Rica's economic performance in 1991 has been mixed. The trade balance has improved, delays of 15 days or more for foreign exchange access eliminated, the Paris Club debt rescheduled, and international reserves increased. Costa Rica has not been able to meet the IMF program fiscal deficit target of 0.5 percent of GDP. This figure was 2 percent or more in 1991. Nevertheless, 2.0 percent is a significant improvement over the 5.2 percent GDP deficit in 1990.

Disappointingly, inflation has remained more than twice the program target, nearly 30 percent versus a hoped for 12 percent. The GDP is expected to grow no more than 1.5 to 2 percent in 1991 versus 3.4 percent in 1990.

Costa Rica implemented a tight monetary policy in 1991, increasing reserve requirements, raising interest rates for government bonds, imposing import deposits, and limiting local currency monetization of external funds. On the fiscal side, Costa Rica temporarily increased the sales tax from 10 percent to 13 percent, and increased the price of public sector services and petroleum products. Despite increased revenues, there is still a fiscal gap. Costa Rica has been unable to substantially control public expenditures to close the gap. Planned reductions in public sector employment were slowed by political and legal considerations. As a result, the structural fiscal deficit remains the fundamental cause of economic instability.

To control import growth, Costa Rica first sought to reduce the money supply by increasing reserve requirements. Costa Rica complemented this effort with substantial weekly mini-devaluations and the use of import deposits and surcharges. Import deposits (currently 30 percent) were scheduled to be eliminated at the end of December, but still remain; surcharges were reduced to 2 percent in August 1991.

From January–September of 1991, the trade deficit reached $148 million compared to $401 million in the same period of 1990. This reduction is due to a combination of higher exports and lower imports. The trade deficit for 1991 (about $300 million including the value added by "maquilla"), however, exceeded the IMF program deficit by U.S. $130 million.

Debt Management Policies

The 1991 IMF stand-by program seeks to reduce the Costa Rican current account deficit from 11 percent of GDP (1990) to 3.5 percent of GDP in 1991. This assumes an increase in net international reserves, including a reduction in arrears. Additional reserves should come from the Paris Club rescheduling (U.S. $136 million); bilateral credits from Mexico (U.S. $35 million), Venezuela (U.S. $35 million), and Taiwan (U.S. $30 million); multilateral financing (about U.S. $220 million, including U.S. $120 million from the World Bank); and AID ESF (U.S. $25 million).

On July 17, 1991, the government of Costa Rica reached an agreement to reschedule the Paris Club debt. Under the new terms of the Paris Club negotiation, Costa Rica will repay $175 million of the total debt ($893 million) over an extended 10-year period, with a five-year grace period.

The Currency and Exchange Rate Mechanisms

Costa Rica has a unified exchange rate for all commercial purposes. Since May 1990, Costa Rica has employed a system of mini-devaluations designed to offset the effect of domestic inflation vis-a-vis the value of the U.S. dollar. Although Central Bank authorities claim that the intent was also to devalue the colon slightly, internal inflation has grown at such a pace that there has been little real devaluation of the colon. As of November 1991, the weekly devaluations of the colon were 45 centimos a week, or approximately 1½ percent a month.

Foreign exchange is available from the Central Bank for the purchase of imports and the repatriation of profits and royalties. Purchasers must deposit 30 percent of the value of foreign exchange desired in local currency and wait from 10 to 60 days for its supply by the Central Bank.

Approximately 25 percent of all foreign currency needs are met in the parallel foreign exchange market where dollars receive a premium of 2 to 5 percent above the Central Bank rate. The parallel market is technically illegal but tolerated by local authorities.

Banking and Other Financial Institutions

Only one U.S. bank currently operates in Costa Rica (Citicorp) as an investment company ("financiera"). The National Banking System includes four state-owned commercial banks and 16 private banks. Private banks may currently accept funds from the public in the form of investment certificates with a minimum tenor of 180 days, if the bank is classified by Costa Rican Superintendent of Banks as an "A" bank with a minimum capital of 300 million colones (U.S. $1.25 million). This law is currently in contention. The nation's public banking system controls short-term lending as well as all savings and checking account holdings.

The Central Bank of Costa Rica has authorized the National Banking System to provide foreign currency for the import payment process.

New-to-market U.S. exporters are strongly advised to request payment by irrevocable, confirmed letter of credit. Experienced U.S. exporters to Costa Rica commonly use either the open credit or sight drafts. Both of these are more economical than letters of credit but are also riskier.

Tapping International Aid Institutions

The Trade Credit Insurance Program is a U.S. Export-Import Bank program guaranteed by USAID that provides lines of credit to Costa Rican importers of U.S. goods. This financing is administered through the government Central Bank and the Bank of Costa Rica. Allocation for Costa Rica in fiscal year 1992 was U.S. $25 million. However, this program has been suspended due to the fact that Costa Rica is in arrears on previous Ex-Im Bank loans. Additional information may be obtained through the U.S. Export-Import Bank in Washington, D.C. or the Office of Private Sector, USAID Costa Rica, tel: (506) 204-545.

The Private Investment Corporation (PIC) offers medium- to long-term financing and equity participation for Costa Rican export-oriented and tourism projects. In addition, PIC offers a variety of financial services to assist investors in developing financial packages that utilize other capital sources. PIC's total resources consist of equity capital and loan funds from USAID, the German Finance Company, and the Commonwealth Development Corporation. Since PIC's establishment in 1984, some of the projects have included the textile, non-traditional and traditional agricultural, seafood, footwear, and plastics sectors. Current PIC lending capacity for a single project ranges from U.S. $150,000 to U.S. $2 million. All loans and repayments are made in U.S. dollars.

Contact:

Private Investment Corporation
Apartado Postal 8609-1000
San Jose
COSTA RICA
Tel: (506) 336-422
Fax: (506/) 36-541

The Industrial Development Fund

(FODEIN) provides medium- and long-term credit to manufacturing, tourism, and agro-industry projects. Since its 1981 establishment through World Bank funding, the subsidized funds have originated from the World Bank, the Inter-American Development Bank, CABEI, and the government's Central Bank counterpart funds. The terms of the loans are competitive when measured against "average" local commercial rates. Grace periods up to three years may be granted by individual lending institutions. FODEIN resources are channeled through all private and state banks.

The Export Financing Fund (FOPEX) was created in 1983 primarily through World Bank and Inter-American Development Bank loans. Its purpose is to offer financing to increase Costa Rica's nontraditional exports. FOPEX funds are available for the financing of the importation of raw materials, spare parts, and packing materials, among other uses. FOPEX financing is available for companies established in Costa Rica which export at least 10 percent nontraditional products.

OPIC extends its insurance policies to U.S. citizens and corporate entities wishing to invest in Costa Rica. Costa Rica has signed an investment agreement with the Multilateral Investment Guarantee Agency (MIGA) of the World Bank. Currently, that agreement awaits ratification in the Legislative Assembly. Costa Rica has signed a bilateral Tax Information Exchange Agreement with the United States, which grants such benefits as access to U.S. Tax Code Section 936 fund loans from Puerto Rico, the ability of Costa Rican hotels to attract more conferences and conventions, and the possibility of establishing foreign sales corporations under Secs. 801–805 of the Deficit Reduction Act of 1984 and Sections 921–27 of the U.S. Tax Code.

Financial Market Operations and Structural Policies

Pricing policies: The Costa Rican government has authority to set producer, wholesale, and retail prices and margins for virtually all goods.

In practice, Costa Rica sets the prices for a number of agricultural products including milk, eggs, rice, corn, wheat, flour, and beans.

Currently, prices for basic grains are equal to or exceed world prices and thus do not impair the competitiveness of U.S. exports. Costa Rica has indicated that it intends to eliminate the fixing of certain prices and margins over time. They propose to fix only the prices of public services and goods and services produced under monopolistic conditions, and up to 15 products included in the "basket of essential goods."

Regulatory policies affecting automobiles and light trucks: Passenger cars imported into Costa Rica are subject to four levies: 1) a 25 percent tariff on pickups and a 100 percent tax on automobiles; 2) a Central Bank surcharge of 17 to 152 percent of CIF based on a government of Costa Rica determination of the car's market value; 3) a consumption tax of 0 to 75 percent based on the dollar value and engine size; and 4) a 13 percent sales tax levied on the customs determined value plus levies 1–3 above.

As applied, these levies keep large cars out of the market and discriminate against U.S. autos and light trucks. U.S. vehicles are assessed higher duties and tax rates. Light trucks, although having identical capacities and meeting identical U.S. standards, are classified differently in Costa Rica and assessed markedly different taxes. For example, Costa Rica taxes Japanese pickups, classified as weighing more than one ton, 46.38 percent. U.S. pickups, classified as 3/4 ton trucks, are taxed 187.63 percent. The U.S.

has suggested that Costa Rica adopt a standard, either Japanese or American, by which like vehicles will be classified and treated the same. On October 21, 1991, the Costa Rican government stated that, to remedy the discriminatory aspects of the taxation system on U.S. automobiles, it would explore a unified ad valorem tariff on vehicle CIF price without any distinctions made on the basis of engine size.

Chapter 8
ECUADOR

	Total	Urban	
Population (1993)	11,252,000	55.0%	

Main Urban Areas	Population	Percentage of Total	International Calling Code
Guayaquil	1,699,000	15.1	593-4
QUITO	1,234,000	11.0	593-2
Cuenca	218,000	1.9	593-7
Machala	159,000	1.4	593-4
Portoviejo	156,000	1.4	593-4
Riobamba	150,000	1.3	593-2
Ambato	134,000	1.2	593-2
Manta	130,000	1.2	593-4
Esmeraldas	115,000	1.0	593-2

Land Area	276,840 square kilometers
Comparable U.S. State	Slightly smaller than Nevada
Language	Spanish 93%
	Quechua 7%
Common Business Language	Spanish
Currency	1 sucres (S/) = 100 centavos
Exchange Rate (May 1993)	U.S. $1.00 = 1,871 sucres
Best Nonstop Air Connection via U.S.	Miami to Quito: 4 hours
	American Airlines (800) 433-7300
	Saeca Ecuadorean Airlines (800)328-2367
	Both offer two nonstops daily.
Best Hotel	12 de Octobre 1820 and Luis Cordero
	Quito
	Tel: (593-2) 566-497
	Fax: (593-2) 569-189

INTRODUCTION AND REGIONAL ORIENTATION

Ecuador's population is ethnically mixed. The largest ethnic groups are Indian and mestizo (mixed Spanish and Indian). Africans, Spanish and other Europeans, and some Asians form smaller groups.

Two kinds of internal migrations are occurring in Ecuador, from the highlands to the coast and from the countryside to the cities. Although Ecuadorians were concentrated in the mountainous central highland region a few decades ago, the population today is divided about equally between that area and the coastal lowlands. The cities now contain about 55 percent of the population. The tropical forest region to the east of the mountains remains sparsely populated and contains only about 3 percent of the population.

History and Political Conditions

After the War of Independence from Spain ended in 1822, Simon Bolivar joined Ecuador with the Republic of Greater Colombia. In 1830, Ecuador seceded and became a separate republic.

Until 1948, the republic was marked by a succession of presidents, dictators, and juntas. Stability was reestablished from 1948 to 1960, as presidents were elected under free elections. Unstable civilian and military rule alternated for almost 20 years until 1979.

Jaime Roldos was inaugurated in 1979, beginning a new era of civilian rule. Roldos, a populist, brought Christian Democrat Osvaldo Hurtado with him as vice-president. In May 1981, Roldos was killed in an airplane crash, and Hurtado ascended to the presidency.

During his three-year tenure, Hurtado pursued a course of moderate change and economic development marked, at times, by financial difficulties. Floods did enormous damage to the country's agriculture and roads and sparked social unrest.

Social Christian Leon Febres Cordero won the 1984 presidential elections by a narrow margin. Much of his tenure was characterized by bitter wrangling between the executive and the other branches of government, which were often dominated by the opposition, led by Social Democrat Rodrigo Borja. Febres Cordero implemented free-market economic policies, sought to diversify Ecuador's exports, and pursued close ties to the United States. He also took a strong stand against drug trafficking and terrorism. A devastating earthquake in March 1987 set back development plans.

In August 1988, Rodrigo Borja became president after a landslide victory the previous spring that gave his party (Democratic Left-ID) almost an absolute majority in Congress. He instituted a government characterized by respect for human rights and economic restructuring. The government reached an accord with the main terrorist group (AVC) under which it was to become law abiding.

Despite initial success, efforts to control inflation failed to bring it below 50 percent, and in mid-term congressional elections (June 1990), the ID lost more than half its seats. Nevertheless, Borja pledged to continue economic restructuring, tight credit control, and efforts to attract foreign investment.

CRACKING THE MARKET

Demographics

Ethnic groups: Indian 25%, mestizo (mixed Indian and Spanish) 65%, Caucasian and others 7%, African 3%.

Religion: Predominantly Roman Catholic.

Languages: Spanish (official), Indian languages, especially Quechua.

Education: Years compulsory—ages 6–12. Attendance (through 6th grade)—76% urban, 33% rural. Literacy—88%.

Work force (3.4 million): agriculture 39%; services 42%; industry 11%; other 8%.

Central government budget (1990 est.): $1.4 billion.

Economy

Agriculture is the cornerstone of Ecuador's economy. The coastal region produces most of Ecuador's export crops, such as bananas and coffee, while the highlands grow most of the country's food crops and are beginning to export flowers and vegetables. Although only 15 percent of GPD, petroleum constitutes half of Ecuador's exports and of government revenue. Therefore, international oil prices have a major effect on overall economic performance. The small industrial sector produces largely for a protected domestic market.

Pursuing a policy of gradual economic reform, the Borja administration achieved notable improvements in the economy in 1989. It tightened public sector spending and slowed monetary growth, reducing inflation from 86 percent at the end of 1988 to 54 percent at the end of 1989. It also improved the external accounts, raising net international reserves from negative $176 million to a positive $203 million. However, growth in 1989 was only 0.2 percent.

Progress stalled in the first half of 1990. Public spending increased, monetary growth remained high, and inflation stabilized at just under 50 percent. In response, the government cut spending for the second half of the year by the equivalent of 11 percent of the original budget. This, coupled with increased revenue from higher oil prices, may reduce the deficit and moderate inflation.

Although the government has made structural reforms, much remains to be done, including a reduction of direct government control of the economy, movement toward free-market interest rates, privatization of some companies, further liberalization of trade, reform of labor laws, and promotion of domestic and foreign private investment.

The government has regularized its relations with the multilateral banks and bilateral creditors. The IMF approved a stand-by program for Ecuador in 1989 and renewed it in 1990, and the World Bank and IBD have resumed lending. In October 1989 the government rescheduled principal and interest due to official bilateral creditors (the Paris Club). Ecuador began discussions with commercial bank creditors in August 1989 but was unable to reach agreement. The original round of talks stalled, but discussions were resumed in November 1990. In June 1989 the government began paying about 30 percent of interest due. At the end of 1989, total outstanding external debt was $11.3 billion.

Natural resources: Petroleum, fish, shrimp, timber, gold, limestone.

Agriculture (17% of GDP): Products—bananas, seafood, coffee, cacao, sugar, rice, corn, and livestock.

Industry (16% of GDP): Types—food processing, wood products, textiles, chemicals (pharmaceuticals).

Political/Institutional Infrastructure

The Republic of Ecuador gained its independence on August 10, 1809.

The constitution provides for concurrent four-year terms of office for the president, the vice-president, and the 12 congressmen (of a total of 72) who are elected as "National" (at large) legislators. The remaining 60 legislators, representing the country's 21 provinces, serve for two years. No president can be reelected, and outgoing legislators must sit out a term before running for Congress again.

ECUADOR
Key Economic Indicators

	1989	1990	1991
Income, Production, and Employment			
GDP (billions U.S. $)[1]	10.1	10.9	11.5
GDP growth rate (%)	0.6	2.3	2.5
GDP/capita (U.S. $)[1]	963	1,007	1,038
GDP by sector (%)			
Agriculture, fishing	13.7	13.2	N/A
Petroleum, mining	11.8	15.1	N/A
Manufacturing	22.7	22.8	N/A
Construction	4.6	3.7	N/A
Services	43.5	41.7	N/A
Other	3.7	3.5	N/A
Size of labor force (millions)	3.4	3.5	3.6
Unemployment rate[2]	8.0	12.0	N/A
Money and Prices			
Money supply (M1, % growth)	32.2	44.6	50.0
Commercial interest rates (est.)	50.0	53.0	53.0
Savings rate (% GDP)	17.1	19.0	19.0
Inflation (CPI, year-end)	54.2	49.5	0
Official exchange rate[3]	527	768	1,040
Parallel exchange rate[3]	568	822	1,080
Balance of Payments and Trade			
(Millions of U.S. dollars unless otherwise noted)			
Exports (FOB)	2,354	2,714	2,925
Imports (CIF)	1,693	1,711	1,950
Exports to U.S.[4]	1,474	1,377	1,485
Imports from U.S.[4]	643	680	780
Aid from U.S.[5]	32.3	23.0	21.0
Aid from other countries	N/A	N/A	N/A
External public debt (bil.)	11.2	11.7	12.4
Annual debt service payments (bil)	1.8	1.5	1.5
Balance of payments			
Current account	−472	−136	−150
Trade account	661	1,003	975
Service balance[6]	−1,230	−1,239	−1,225
Transfers	97	100	100
Capital account	854	538	178
Investment	80	82	N/A
External debt	402	−455	N/A
Arrears	492	823	N/A
Other	−120	88	N/A
Change in reserves	379	400	−28

1. Sucres converted at the average intervention rate for the year. Because of real appreciation of the sucre against the dollar in 1990 and 1991, dollar figures overstate growth of GDP and GDP/capita.
2. Open unemployment. Underemployment estimated at 40–60 percent.
3. Exchange rates cited are annual averages.
4. U.S. data, may vary from Ecuadorian data.
5. Data are for fiscal year.
6. Includes interest accrued but not fully paid.

Each year legislators elect from among themselves a president and vice-president of Congress. Congress begins its annual two-month regular session on Independence Day, August 10. For the remainder of the year, unless an extraordinary plenary session is called, all legislative business is transacted by the 20 members of the Congress who constitute its four permanent committees.

Ecuador has a three-tiered court system. Congress appoints justices of the Supreme Court for four-year terms. The Supreme Court names the members of the superior (provincial) courts, who in turn choose ordinary civil and penal judges. The power of judicial review rests with the Tribunal of Constitutional Guarantees (TGC), a 15-member body representing executive, legislative, and judicial branches, as well as the private sector. All TGC decisions must be submitted to the Congress, which has ultimate authority to interpret the constitution.

The executive branch includes 12 ministries and several cabinet-level secretariats headed by presidential appointees. The president also appoints Ecuador's 20 provincial governors (the capital district of Pichincha Province has no governor), who represent the central government at the local level.

Principal Government Officials

President
   Rodrigo BORJA Cevallos

Vice-President
   Luis PARODI Valverde

Foreign Minister
   Diego CORDOVEZ Zegers

Ambassador to the U.S.
   Jaime MONCAYO Garcia

Ambassador to the OAS
   Miguel Antonio Vasco

Ambassador to the UN
   Jose AYALA

Ecuador maintains an embassy in the United States at:

2535 15th Street, NW
Washington, D.C. 20009
Tel: (202) 234-7200

Consulates are established in Chicago, Dallas, Houston, Los Angeles, Miami, New Orleans, New York, and San Francisco.

Defense

The armed forces include about 50,000 troops, and the national defense budget for 1990 was $154 million.

Current Political Conditions

Historically, Ecuador's political parties have been small, loose organizations dependent more on populist, often charismatic, leaders than on programs or ideology. Frequent internal splits produced extreme factionalism.

To encourage the development of strong, stable political parties, the constitution permits only candidates affiliated with registered political parties to run for elective office. To be certified, a party must file a petition signed by a number of unaffiliated citizens equal to at least 1.5 percent of the number of valid votes cast in the last national election.

The party must then field candidates in at least 10 of the country's provinces, including two of the three most populous.

The 1990 congressional and local elections revealed that political fragmentation continues to exist: 15 parties, including two communist parties, contested the election. Eleven political parties are represented in the Congress. The opposition, made up of independents, the center-right, and populist parties, remains loosely organized, with former leaders of the Febres Cordero administration among the chief spokesmen.

Foreign Relations

Ecuador traditionally has maintained good relations with East and West and emphasizes multilateral approaches to international problems.

One of Ecuador's basic foreign policy objectives is a revision of the 1942 Rio Protocol of Peace, Friendship, and Boundaries, which ended a short war between Peru and Ecuador. Ecuador holds that the protocol awarded disputed territory to Peru. Geographical features along a 78-kilometer (49 mi.) stretch of land that do not match topographical descriptions in the protocol have, according to Ecuador, made a complete boundary demarcation between the two countries "inexecutable." Most Ecuadorians would welcome a revision of the protocol (a move Peru opposes) to gain sovereign access to the Maranon river, a main tributary of the Amazon.

This long-running border dispute has erupted into armed conflict along the undemarcated section. The most recent and serious episode occurred in 1981. Ecuador has requested that the four guarantors of the Rio protocol (Argentina, Brazil, Chile, and the United States) help end formal differences over the border. In his inaugural address, Borja expressed interest in reaching a negotiated solution, and relations between the two countries have warmed.

In addition to international financial institutions, Ecuador looks primarily to the United States, Western Europe, and Japan for assistance in addressing social and economic development. The government has indicated it will seek to attract private foreign investment and has begun to remove trade impediments. Ecuador is not a member of GATT (General Agreement on Tariffs and Trade).

U.S.-Ecuadorian Relations

The United States and Ecuador have close ties based on mutual interests in maintaining democratic institutions; fighting narco-traf-ficking; building trade, investment, and finance; fostering Ecuador's economic development; and participating in inter-American organizations. The United States assists Ecuador's economic development through its Agency for International Development program in Ecuador and through multilateral organizations such as the Inter-American Development Bank and the World Bank. In addition, the U.S. Peace Corps operates a sizable program in Ecuador.

Both countries are signatories of the 1947 Rio treaty, the Western Hemisphere's mutual security treaty. Ecuador shares U.S. concern over increasing narcotics trafficking and terrorism. Ecuador has condemned terrorist actions, eliminated coca production since the mid-1980s, and developed a vigorous program of combating money laundering and narcotics trafficking.

Differences have arisen over the breadth of the territorial sea claimed by a coastal state and its rights over highly migratory fish traveling through its claimed territorial waters. Although the United States claims jurisdiction for the management of coastal fisheries up to 320 kilometers (200 mi.) from its coast, it excludes highly migratory species such as tuna. Ecuador, on the other hand, claims a 320-kilometer (200-mile) wide territorial sea and has implemented that claim by imposing license fees and fines on foreign fishing vessels, with no exceptions made for the catch of migratory species.

Trade

Exports (1990)—$2.4 billion: petroleum and petroleum products, shrimp, bananas, coffee, cocoa.

Major markets—U.S., Latin American Integration Association (ALADI), EC.

Imports (1990)—$1.7 billion: agricultural and industrial machinery, industrial raw materials, agricultural commodities, chemical products, transportation and communication equipment, petroleum products.

Major suppliers: U.S., EC, Japan, ALADI.

Trade and Investment Policies

For 1991, tariffs for most products ranged from 2 to 35 percent. Some agricultural inputs enter duty free, while automobiles carry a 50 percent tariff, although the importation of cars and light trucks is prohibited. Tariffs were to be reduced in 1992, as part of either Ecuador's three-year program to reduce tariffs or the Andean Pact's efforts to establish a common external tariff for the Pact members.

Ecuador's tariff schedule is based on the GATT's Harmonized System of Nomenclature, although Ecuador is not a member of the GATT. Most nontariff fees on imports have been eliminated; there are plans to eliminate the remaining fees, which total 3 percent.

All imports must have a prior import license, which is issued by the Central Bank. Licenses are usually made available for all goods, although obtaining them can be a bureaucratic hassle. All foreign exchange transactions for imports and exports must take place through the Central Bank at the intervention rate.

Foreign ownership of banking is limited to 49 percent, although three banks with 100 percent foreign ownership (including one U.S. owned bank) are allowed to operate. The operations of these banks are somewhat more restricted than those of local banks. Foreign airlines (including one U.S. cargo and two U.S. passenger carriers) operate in Ecuador, but the government limits their operations to protect the state-owned airline.

In 1991 Ecuador's foreign investment regime was liberalized. Foreigners may invest in most sectors without prior govern-mental approval. Foreign investment is prohibited in the media and limited to 49 percent of bank shares. Foreign investment in public services must obtain prior governmental approval. Cargo preference laws require use of Ecuadorian flag vessels where available. Ecuador has lagged in implementing Andean Pact decisions favoring freer competition in air and maritime services. The government has been slow, and sometimes reluctant to resolve investment disputes.

Government procurement practices do not usually discriminate against U.S. or other foreign suppliers. However, bidding for government contracts can be cumbersome and time-consuming. Many bidders object to the requirement for a bank-issued guarantee to ensure execution of the contract. Shipments to Ecuadorian government agencies must be made via Ecuadorian flag vessel or airlines.

Customs procedures can be difficult but are not used to discriminate against U.S. products.

Trade Financing Environment and Options

The government subsidizes exporters through an exchange rate program known as the "Advanced Sale of Foreign Exchange." Under the program, exporters sell dollars (usually borrowed) to the Central Bank in anticipation of earning those dollars at a later date through exports. The dollars are converted at the intervention rate prevailing at that time. When the exportation actually takes place, the Central Bank compensates for any depreciation of the sucre against the dollar that has taken place since the dollars were sold to the Central Bank.

This complex procedure provides exporters with local currency working capital at dollar interest rates. Since local interest rates exceed 50 percent, and dollars can be borrowed for about 15 percent, the indirect

---

INVESTMENT CLIMATE
Extent of U.S. Investment in Goods-Producing Sectors
U.S. Direct Investment Position Abroad on a Historical-Cost Basis—1990
(Millions of U.S. dollars)

Category		Amount
Petroleum		121
Total manufacturing		174
Food and kindred products	30	
Chemicals and allied products	16	
Metals, primary and fabricated	18	
Machinery, except electrical	0	
Electric and electronic equipment	18	
Transportation equipment	14	
Other manufacturing	78	
Wholesale trade		35
TOTAL PETROLEUM/MANUFACTURING/WHOLESALE TRADE		330

Source: U.S. Department of Commerce, *Survey of Current Business*
(August 1991, vol. 71, no. 8, table 11.3).

---

subsidy is large. The government has reduced the program by limiting the advance sales of dollars to 60 days before exporting; previously it had been 270 days. There are no other direct subsidies or preferential interest rates for exporters.

FINANCING AND CAPITAL MARKETS

General Policy Framework

The Ecuadorian economy grew 2.3 percent in 1990, below the population growth rate but an improvement over 1989 when growth was 0.6 percent. Growth in 1991 was expected to be around 2.5 percent. The balance of payments performance in 1990 was strong as net international reserves increased threefold to $603 million. In 1991, reserves fluctuated around $550 million (three months of imports). In 1990 both growth and reserves were boosted by higher oil revenues because of the Gulf crisis. On the down side, inflation has remained at around 50 percent as the effort to bring it down lost momentum. In addition, Ecuador has accumulated over $1.6 billion of arrears to commercial banks since early 1987.

Government spending patterns have been uneven in the past three years, with periods of fiscal austerity alternating with increased spending. In recent years the government has run small public sector deficits or surpluses, but the uneven spending cycles have contributed to inflation.

Deficits are usually financed by foreign borrowing, limited sales of government securities, and accumulation of arrears. The Central Bank has not financed the government deficit in recent years, although it has indirectly financed some para-statals through loans from national development banks.

Monetary creation on the part of the Central Bank has been a major source of inflation. The Central Bank has incurred significant losses in recent years because of a wide variety of subsidies that it offers, and has printed money to cover the losses. For 1991, the money supply increased at the rate of 50 to 60 percent, higher than inflation. Since the Central Bank cannot control its own sources of monetary growth, it has pressured private sector banks, with limited success, to limit private sector credit expansion.

Debt Management Policies

Ecuador and the International Monetary Fund negotiated a stand-by agreement in December 1991 to cover the following year. The previous stand-by expired in February 1991. Ecuador rescheduled 1991 and 1992 interest and amortization payments to the Paris Club in early 1992.

Ecuador's previous rescheduling agreement with the Paris Club expired in 1990.

Ecuador stopped servicing its debt to the commercial banks in 1987, and began paying about 30 percent of interest due in June 1989.

It began discussions with commercial bank creditors in August 1989, but they have been unable to reach agreement.

At the end of 1990, total outstanding external debt was 11.8 billion dollars, with accumulated interest arrears accounting for 1.6 billion dollars. Over half the debt, 6.8 billion dollars, and almost all the arrears, are owed to commercial banks.

The Currency and Exchange Rate Mechanisms

Ecuador has two functioning exchange rates, the intervention and free-market rates. Public sector transactions, as well as private sector imports and exports, are conducted at the intervention rate, which is set by the government. Exporters are required to surrender their foreign exchange earnings to the Central Bank for sucres. Foreign exchange is allocated to importers on a weekly basis; usually there is sufficient foreign exchange available so importers do not need to resort to the free market. Residual transactions are conducted in the free market. Foreign currency is readily available in the free market, and there are no restrictions on the movement of foreign currencies into or out of Ecuador.

There is a weekly mini-devaluation of the intervention rate against the U.S. dollar, with an occasional larger devaluation (usually three to six percent) to make up for any slippage. This policy has, for the most part, kept the sucre competitive, although there has been some real appreciation against the dollar in the last two years. The spread between the intervention and free rates in late 1991 has been less than five percent. At times in the past year the spread has widened to 10–15 percent. This policy has kept the sucre relatively competitive.

Tapping International Aid Funds

US Assistance (FY90): Economic $16.7 million; Military $1.2 million.

Financial Market Operations and Structural Policies

Since taking office the Borja government has made a number of structural reforms, introducing several changes each year. The most current reforms are particularly notable because many observers did not expect the Borja government to undertake many initiatives in the second half of its term. Even with these reforms, domestic and foreign investment probably will be limited for some time, since more needs to be done to liberalize the economy and encourage investment.

The most notable reforms have been in

the area of trade. Maximum tariffs and trade dispersion have been reduced and most non-tariff surcharges have been eliminated. Ecuador agreed to enter Andean free trade in July 1992, six months behind the other members of the Andean Pact. Other major reforms include a new tax law, an in-bond industry law, liberalized foreign investment regulations, and a revised mining law.

A bill that would make Ecuador's highly restrictive labor code somewhat more flexible was sent to Congress. The administration also drafted a number of other important reforms and submitted them to Congress in 1991. The draft laws should have simplified procedures for exporters, reduced loss-making demands on the Central Bank, unified the public sector budget, and provided the basis for a more modern capital market.

VISITING AND LOCATING

General Travel Checklist

Immigration and customs: A valid Ecuadorian visa is required to enter the country; however, visas can be obtained from immigration authorities upon arrival in Ecuador. Tourist visas are valid for up to 90 days per calendar year. Those wishing to study or work in Ecuador should request visas from the nearest Ecuadorian Consulate or the Ecuadorian Embassy in Washington, D.C.

Clothing and climate: Temperatures vary with altitude, not season. Spring and fall clothing is useful all year in the Sierra, while summer clothes are necessary in the Costa and Oriente. Rainwear is necessary during the rainy season in Quito and Guayaquil (roughly November-March).

Health: Inoculations against typhoid, polio, tetanus, and hepatitis are recommended throughout the country. In addition, malaria suppressant and yellow fever inoculation are recommended in the lowlands. Travelers must take precautions against contaminated food and water.

Tap water is not potable in all areas.

The high altitude of the Sierra may cause problems, especially for older people and those with heart problems.

Telecommunications: Domestic telephone, telegraph, and fax services are available between major cities in Ecuador. Long-distance telephone service, cables, and telex are available.

Ecuador is in the eastern standard time zone but does not observe daylight savings.

Transportation: Flights are available from the United States, with the best connections through Miami and Los Angeles. Domestic airlines serve most large- and medium-sized cities in Ecuador. Intercity railroad passenger service is limited, but inter-city buses are frequent. In the major cities, buses and taxis are plentiful and reasonably priced.

Chapter 9
EL SALVADOR

	Total	Urban
Population (1993)	5,638,000	43.0%

Main Urban Areas	Population	Percentage of Total	International Calling Code
SAN SALVADOR	460,000	8.2	503
Santa Ana	138,000	2.4	503
San Miguel	87,000	1.5	503
Nueva San Salvador	52,000	0.9	503
Sonsonate	47,000	0.8	503
Cojutepeque	31,000	0.5	503

Land Area   20,720 square kilometers
    Comparable U.S. State   Slightly smaller than Massachusetts

Language   Spanish   100%
    Common Business Language   Spanish

Currency   1 colon (C) = 100 centavos
    Exchange Rate (May 1993)   U.S. $1.00 = 7.70 colons

Best Nonstop Air Connection via U.S.   Miami to San Salvador: 2 hours
    American Airlines (800) 433-7300
    Two nonstops daily

Best Hotel   Camino Real
    Boulevard des Los Heroes 05-44
    San Salvador
    Tel: (503) 233-344
    Fax: (503) 235-660

INTRODUCTION AND REGIONAL ORIENTATION

El Salvador has been battered by eleven years of civil war. The costs, perhaps 75,000 killed and material damages of at least U.S. $2 billion, are steep for a tiny country with a population of little over five million, and per capita gross domestic product (GDP) of about $1,000. During the early years of the conflict, between 1978 and 1982, real GDP fell by 22 percent; but thanks to U.S. $3 billion in U.S. economic assistance, the economy since then has experienced modest growth. The war has been the major impediment to economic reactivation, but El Salvador has also had to contend with weak international commodity prices, especially of coffee, and with an ill-advised government policy framework.

Fortunately, the government of President Alfredo Cristiani, which took office in June 1989, has opted for ambitious free market economic policies.

The government has adopted a market-determined exchange rate regime, eliminated import licenses and most other administrative impediments to imports, compressed tariffs, eliminated nearly all price controls, abolished the marketing monopolies for coffee, sugar, and cotton, and embarked on a plan to privatize the nationalized banking system. The government has also followed orthodox fiscal and monetary policies. As a result of its comprehensive economic adjustment program, El Salvador signed a stand-by agreement with the International Monetary Fund (IMF) in 1990. The IMF program led, in turn, to a rescheduling of El Salvador's official bilateral debt through the Paris Club, and approval in 1991 of large policy-based loans by the World Bank and the Inter-American Development Bank (IDB). El Salvador also acceded to the international trading organization, the GATT, in 1991.

The policies initiated in 1989 are having a major positive impact. Real output grew by 3.4 percent in 1990. The recovery was led by the agricultural sector, which grew by 7.4 percent. Most other sectors, including manufacturing, expanded by about 3.0 percent. Inflation, despite oil price increases associated with the Gulf crisis, was held to 19.3 percent in 1990, among the lowest rates in Latin America. There were also improvements in the external sector: imports increased by U.S. $100 million; nontraditional exports to extra-regional markets grew 34 percent and contributed to a 17 percent growth rate for exports overall; and remittances from Salvadorans abroad and strong private capital inflows helped increase Central Bank net international reserves by U.S. $117 million. The government's official 1991 growth estimate is 3.0 percent, and that may well be conservative.

Guerrillas have hampered economic activity, principally by targeting the electrical system. However, UN-sponsored negotiations between the government and guerrillas went on intermittently startimg in 1989, and in 1991 prospects for a cease-fire appeared fairly good. With a cessation of hostilities, the economy would be a major beneficiary, and it was positioned for major expansion.

CRACKING THE MARKET

Economy

The government is meeting the challenge of maintaining strong growth without high inflation. Preliminary estimates predict a growth rate of 3.5 percent in 1991. Inflation was contained at 9.8 percent in 1991, very low for Latin America, and the government met its austere fiscal targets. On the trade side, in 1991 the tariff schedule was narrowed to a 5–35 percent range, with a few exceptions for luxury goods. The maximum tariff rate was scheduled to drop to 20 percent by 1993.

The foreign exchange market was also completely liberalized and all controls on dollar transactions eliminated. The colon floats at a market-determined exchange rate and dollars are freely available at private or bank exchange houses with no controls. Buoyed by international assistance and dollar remittances sent by family members in the U.S., the colon stabilized at about eight colones to the dollar in August 1990, and has shown only minor fluctuations since.

The private sector dominates the economy. However, some vestiges of the nationalization trend of the early 1980s remain. Privatization of several state-owned assets remains a major policy challenge facing the Cristiani administration. Only the complex bank privatization process has already begun. Shares in two of the largest state-owned banks are more than 70 percent sold, and the Central Bank planned to privatize four more commercial banks in 1992–93.

Early indicators for 1991 provided grounds for optimism. Inflation continued to fall, imports in the first quarter were up strongly, and business confidence in the government's handling of the economy remained high.

Agriculture is the economic wellspring of El Salvador, providing approximately two-thirds of the nation's exports and employing one-third of its labor force (see Table 9-1 for GDP growth components). The combination of the removal of price controls, the elimination of monopolies on coffee and sugar trade, and a sharp depreciation of the exchange rate boosted real prices in the sector and led to increased plantings. Improved incentives plus generally favorable weather conditions were reflected in the major gains registered in nearly all agricultural categories in the 1989–90 crop year. Another encouraging signal of the recovery in the agricultural sector is the fact that some temporary farm workers were able to command wages above the government-decreed minimum during the most recent harvest season.

Coffee is by far El Salvador's most important export and cash crop. In calendar year 1990, coffee output and exports increased by 19 and 13 percent, respectively. This, however, was primarily the result of the excellent 1989–90 crop.

TABLE 9-1
Main Components of GDP in 1990

Origin of GDP	Real Growth (%)	At Current Prices
Agriculture	7.4	11.2
Manufacturing	3.0	18.6
Construction	−12.8	2.6
Transport/communications	6.3	4.6
Commerce	3.3	34.8
Government	1.6	7.6
Personal services	1.8	10.4
Other	3.0	10.2
TOTAL	3.4	100.0

Second after coffee, sugar normally provides 15–25 million dollars in foreign exchange earnings annually, and more importantly generates employment. In 1990, sugar exports surged in response to stable world prices and a major increase in the U.S. quota for El Salvador. Cane production rebounded from a bad crop in 1989, increasing by 26 percent, and favorable weather and improved yields resulted in a 45.5 percent jump in sugar production. Higher domestic prices have sparked sharp increases in sugar cultivation.

Continuing a decade-long decline, El Salvador produced only 26,000 bales of cotton in 1990–91, compared to 365,000 bales in 1977–78. Seventy percent of the traditional production area is located in the eastern region of the country, where the effects of the insurgency have been the most severe. The failure of cotton has exacerbated the economic problems in the east, where nearly half of all arable land is abandoned. However, the cotton sector is now guardedly optimistic that economic liberalization and increased yields will spark a gradual increase in cotton planting and production in the 1990s.

Basic corn and grains production, up 4.5 percent in 1990–91, has clearly benefited from economic reform. Favorable weather conditions and higher real prices led to record harvests in corn and beans. With improved yields and greater areas under cultivation, bean production rose more than 30 percent, sorghum 11 percent, and the corn harvest, while showing only 2.4 percent growth, bettered its earlier record. In 1990 a new flexible tariff rate system went into effect on corn and rice, allowing for tariffs to be adjusted based on fluctuations in world prices. While recent increases in food consumer food prices present a short-term hardship for urban consumers, they provide a long-delayed incentive for small farmers to cultivate abandoned farmland.

Recognizing the need to diversify the agricultural economy, development planners have focused on nontraditional agricultural exports, such as fresh fruits, frozen vegetables, and sesame seeds. Favored by the exchange rate liberalization, these investments are playing an increasingly important role in El Salvador's economy. In 1990, nontraditional agricultural exports outside the region increased to U.S. $26.6 million compared to U.S. $22.4 million in 1989. This sector is still in a nascent stage, however, and is subject to the vagaries of weather and international prices. In the first quarter of 1991, nontraditional agricultural export earnings dropped nearly 20 percent from the same period in 1990.

Manufacturing

In the 1970s, El Salvador was the most industrialized nation in Central America, though 11 years of war have eroded this position. In 1990, manufacturing accounted for 18.0 percent of GDP, produced 36 percent of total exports, and employed about 15 percent of the work force. Based primarily in the capital city of San Salvador, the industrial sector is oriented largely toward the domestic and Central American market, although that is gradually changing. In 1989 the government began to dismantle the protectionist trade policies that had allowed a generation of inefficient, import-substituting industries to prosper.

The industrial sector must now cope with heightened international competition. Imported raw materials have become more dear as a result of the currency devaluation, and lower tariffs on finished goods have encouraged import competition. In addition, the government has pledged to further narrow the tariff schedule over the next three years. The industrial sector, however, is adapting admirably to the new environment; producers are focusing on competitive exports and increasing productivity.

Improved productivity has come naturally; perhaps the nation's most important resource is its abundant and energetic labor force. The Salvadoran work ethic is often cited by foreign investors as the primary consideration in the decision to locate manufacturing operations in El Salvador.

Predictably, reduction of bureaucratic obstacles to export and the devalued colon have provided potent incentives for export-oriented firms. The most import growth in El Salvador's manufacturing sector has occurred in apparel assembly. Several foreign investors have recently located textile drawback plants in San Salvador to exploit preferential U.S. trade treatment to El Salvador as a CBI beneficiary. Drawback exports jumped an estimated 50 percent in 1990. The free trade zone, where most drawback operations are located, is completely filled. However, several new free trade zones are planned and two should be ready to accommodate potential investors within one year. Other growth industries include shoes and pharmaceuticals.

Commerce

Commercial activity has been the single dynamic growth sector in the past decade. It increased its share of GDP (measured in current prices) from 22.9 percent in 1980 to 34.8 percent in 1990. The pace of commerce in El Salvador is inextricably linked to the crop cycle; commerce peaks during the November-March coffee harvesting season, tending to decline throughout the rest of the year. Merchants report strong sales in early 1991, linked to the abundance of foreign exchange which is permitting substantial growth in merchandise imports. Merchandise imports grew by 8.7 percent in 1990. Import growth in 1990 was led by consumer goods, which surged 35.4 percent. Raw material imports were up 9.0 percent, but much of that was attributable to the nearly 40 percent hike in the country's petroleum bill, all of which must be imported.

Capital goods imports actually fell, by 16.2 percent in 1990, as most manufacturers concentrated on increasing plant utilization rates and productivity. The situation should be somewhat different in 1991, as there are indications that consumer goods imports are leveling off. Consequently, the commerce sector is expected to grow in line with the rest of the economy in 1991.

Construction

Construction was the economy's weak link in 1990, contracting by 12.8 percent. The construction slump is attributable to a decline in public sector investment spending, tight bank credit, rising raw materials prices, and lower demand for mid- to upscale residential housing. Nevertheless, the outlook for 1991 looked considerably better. The best indicator is probably cement production, which has increased by 6.5 percent in the first quarter, compared to the same period of 1990.

Trade

The trade deficit widened only slightly from U.S. $663.8 million in 1989 to U.S. $682.2 million in 1990, as the U.S. $83 million improvement in exports was more than offset by a U.S. $101 million dollar jump in imports (see Tables 9-2, 9-3, 9-4, and 9-5). A strong coffee harvest, booming sugar exports, and a noteworthy 34 percent growth in non-traditional exports outside the Central American Common Market lifted exports by a robust 16.6 percent. At the same time, however, the rapid economic expansion and trade liberalization stimulated an 8.7 percent growth in imports. Preliminary 1991 data show that while imports continue to rise, exports have slackened due to a smaller 1990–91 coffee harvest, the U.S.

EL SALVADOR
Key Economic Indicators

	1989	1990	1991
Domestic Economy			
Population (millions)	5.1	5.2	5.2
GDP (millions of current colones)	32,230.0	41,057.0	47,621.7
Real GDP growth (%)	1.1	3.4	3.0
GDP (millions of dollars)[1]	5,309.0	5,367.0	5,528.0
GDP per capita (1990 dollars)	1,041.0	1,032.0	1,063.0
Consumer price index (% change)	23.5	19.3	12.0
Central govt revenues, before grants			
(millions, current colones)	2,660.0	3,498.0	4,590.0
Central govt expenditures			
(millions, current colones)	4,233.0	4,776.0	5,760.0
Central govt deficit			
(before grants, as a % of GDP)	4.9	3.1	2.5
External Sector (millions of dollars)			
Exports	497.5	580.2	640.0
of which: Coffee	228.6	258.9	250.0
Shrimp	10.1	14.3	16.0
Sugar	13.5	20.3	39.0
Imports	1,161.4	1,262.5	1,260.0
Current account balance	−183.8	−136.6	−80.0
Current account balance[2]	−466.2	−359.8	−300.0
External debt (year-end)	2,089.0	2,142.0	2,336.0
Debt-service Ratio[3]	31.8	27.9	29.1
Net international reserves (year-end)	2,46.5	363.6	433.6
Prevailing exchange rate (colones/dollars)	5.9	8.0	8.0
Money and Credit (millions of colones)			
Money supply (M1)	3,153.6	3,863.2	4,360.0
Quasi-money	7,622.2	9,748.9	1,210.0
Credit to private sector	7,080.0	7,836.8	9,169.9
Credit to public sector	2,850.1	2,856.1	3,326.4
U.S.–El Salvador Trade (millions of dollars)			
U.S. exports to El Salvador (FAS)	513.9	547.0	575.0
U.S. imports from El Salvador (CIF)	243.9	237.5	260.0
U.S. assistance (fiscal year)			
Direct economic	341.0	262.2	235.1
Military	87.0	81.2	84.0

Notes:

1. Using 1990 exchange rate (7.46 colones/dollar) as base
2. Excluding official transfers
3. As percent of export of goods and services; and before rescheduling

Source: American Embassy San Salvador (July 1991).

TABLE 9-2
El Salvador's Principal Exports
(U.S. $ millions)
January–September

	1990	1991
Traditional Exports		
Coffee	249.7	201.5
Sugar	20.2	30.9
Shrimp	9.5	16.4
Cotton	1.3	0.7
Nontraditional Exports		
to Centam Common Market	140.3	159.0
to rest of world	96.6	106.2
Total exports FOB	517.6	514.6

Note that these figures do not include approximately U.S. $100 million FOB in maquila exports.

Source: BCR Central Reserve Bank (January 1992).

TABLE 9-3
Leading U.S. Exports to El Salvador: Jan.–Sept. 1991
(U.S. $ millions)

Oil (not crude)	23.6
Vegetable oils	16.8
Wheat	14.3
Animal oils and fats	13.7
Electronic capacitors	
(for assembly and reexport)	10.9
Fertilizers	9.4
Women's and girls' coats	8.3
Military equipment and apparel	6.0
Polymers of ethylene	5.6
Food preparations	5.6

Source: American Embassy San Salvador (January 1992).

recession, and an increasingly overvalued colon.

The economic reforms and higher interest rates have created an attractive environment for returning capital; new private capital inflows surged to U.S. $173 million in 1990. Family remittances from Salvadorans living in the U.S. of perhaps U.S. $500–600

TABLE 9-4
El Salvador's Imports: Top 10 Suppliers
(January–September 1991)

	Imports (U.S. $ Millions)	Exports (U.S. $ Millions)
Total	1,056.0	461.0
United States	410.7	154.6
Guatemala	122.3	79.0
Mexico	121.7	6.8
Venezuela	48.5	0.1
Japan	46.8	14.6
Germany	42.4	97.9
Costa Rica	29.3	33.3
Brazil	25.4	N/A
Great Britain	15.3	1.3
Canada	9.5	3.7

Note: Official El Salvador statistics underestimate or exclude a large volume of the country's imports.

Source: BCR Central Reserve Bank (January 1992).

million per year, provide foreign assistance averaging U.S. $400 million per year, and provide additional hard currency to finance imports. Overall, the balance of payments registered a surplus of nearly U.S. $100 million dollars in 1990, a dramatic improvement compared to the deficit of the same magnitude in 1989.

APPROACHING THE MARKET

Commercial Environment

El Salvador's small but dynamic economy offers surprisingly good opportunities for U.S. exporters. In 1989, El Salvador embarked on the free market path, which has inspired greater business confidence and stimulated higher output. The positive results of the reforms are helping El Salvador climb out of the economic stagnation caused by a decade of civil war and years of economic mismanagement. El Salvador's economy expanded by 3.4 percent in 1990, the highest rate since the start of the civil war in 1979.

Demand for Goods and Services

The Salvadoran market is extremely receptive to U.S. products. Many Salvadoran businessmen were educated in the U.S. and enjoy doing business the American way, and consumer tastes are strongly oriented to U.S. products. Salvadoran importers often prefer U.S. to Asian or European suppliers because the proximity of U.S. ports means quicker delivery.

Importers also note that rapid turnaround time on spare parts and servicing is another advantage to doing business with the U.S. Individuals or companies planning to

TABLE 9-5
El Salvador's Imports: Principal Groups
(U.S. $ millions)
January–October

	1990	1991	% Change
Consumer goods	315	297	(5.8)
Nondurable	286	257	(10.1)
Durable	29	40	36.6
Intermediate goods	497	586	18.4
Industry	370	445	20.3
(of which petroleum)	88	105	19.3
Agriculture	52	62	17.7
(of which fertilizer)	28	28	N/A
Construction	68	72	6.1
Other	5	7	48.8
Capital goods	200	263	31.1
Industry	62	70	13.9
Transportation	87	124	42.7
Agriculture	8	9	13.1
Construction	6	9	54.8
Others	38	50	32.7
Total imports	1,012	1,147	13.4

Source: BCR Central Reserve Bank (January 1992).

make large purchases, especially first-time buyers, will also frequently travel to the source to personally visit distributors and manufacturers. Thus the proximity of the U.S. and the greater likelihood of finding a Spanish-speaking trade contact make the U.S. especially convenient.

With foreign exchange now freely available and the pre-import deposit requirement dropped, importing goods has become easier for the Salvadoran businessperson. Tariff rates are expected to fall to 20 percent by 1993. The Salvadoran market, however, remains relatively small.

U.S. companies hoping to take advantage of the export opportunities offered in El Salvador would be best served by a finding a competent local representative. Because the business community is small and highly concentrated, companies looking for investment opportunities are also recommended to work closely with a Salvadoran partner or institution with the contacts and expertise to make it work.

Implications for U.S. Exporters

The United States continues to be El Salvador's single most important trading partner. One-third of all Salvadoran imports came from the U.S. in 1990. The Salvadoran market is extremely receptive to U.S. products, and with foreign exchange freely available and import procedures liberalized, importing became easier for Salvadorans in 1990. The U.S. also enjoys a built-in advantage in that many products are purchased through U.S. economic assistance programs and must be U.S.-sourced.

The most important U.S. shipments to El Salvador include grain, animal and vegetable oil, fertilizer, chemicals, electrical machinery, and paper products. Excellent export opportunities also exist for power generation and distribution equipment, machine tools, telecommunications and computer technology, medical equipment, and used transport vehicles. U.S. exporters should also be alert to recent growth in the production of nontraditional agricultural goods. Opportunities exist in sales of agro-processing, irrigation, and agricultural technology.

In 1990, U.S. imports from El Salvador slipped 3 percent to U.S. $237.5 million, due to lower coffee prices. However, this figure masks the surge in nontraditional exports to the U.S. in 1990. Apparel exports increased 28 percent due largely to new investment in assembly operations, and exports of footwear to the U.S. grew by a spectacular 52 percent. Other important Salvadoran exports to the U.S. include shrimp, sugar electronic capacitors, and cotton thread.

Best Prospects

1. Telecom equipment

The American Embassy San Salvador estimates the market at U.S. $26 million (1991), of which the U.S. supplies roughly 80 percent.

ANTEL, the national telecommunications agency, embarked in 1989 on a five-year plan to double the number of lines in El Salvador. Other than wires and cables, virtually all telecommunications equipment used in El Salvador is imported from outside the Central American region. U.S. suppliers compete mainly with Siemens, Ericson, and NEC Japan. Under the current administration, the telecom agency is one of the most profitable and transparent of the government institutions. The expansion, combined with ANTEL plans to restructure and modernize its advanced technology system, should provide excellent opportunities for U.S. firms.

2. Electrical power generation equipment

The market is estimated at U.S. $25 million, of which the U.S. share is roughly U.S. $23.3 million. An annual growth rate of 8 percent is predicted through 1993.

More than 90 percent of the electrical generation equipment used in El Salvador is imported. The electric utility (CEL) predicts an increase in electricity demand of at least 5 percent annually. Because of the war, for the last decade all improvements on electrical power grid have been only stop-gap measures; with peace, CEL will be able to invest in real improvement/expansion.

3. Agricultural fertilizers

The market demand is estimated at U.S. $39 million, of which the U.S. supplies U.S. $32.3 million.

With the liberalization of most agricultural prices in El Salvador, agricultural production is booming. Imports of fertilizer should rise in the short term. El Salvador is also promoting exports of nontraditional agricultural goods, such as melons and winter vegetables.

4. Consumer goods

Total market is estimated at U.S. $355 million, of which the U.S. supplies U.S. $108 million. Demand is projected to grow at 14 percent per year.

Consumer tastes are strongly oriented towards U.S. consumer goods. El Salvador's own consumer goods industry is quite small, and with trade liberalization, consumer goods manufacturers are shifting increasingly to importing.

The most promising subsectors include: foods, home electronics, sports and leisure equipment, cosmetics, and costume jewelry.

5. Medical equipment and supplies

The market is estimated at U.S. $21 million, of which the U.S. currently supplies U.S. $6.4 million.

The Social Security Institute (ISS) planned to expand medical coverage in 1991–92 to cover two new segments of the population: children aged two to six and agricultural cooperative workers. The ISS was also completing work on a cardiovascular unit which would need to be equipped. The private sector's share of imports in this field is approximately 20–30 percent. A sizable amount of equipment and supplies has been donated or financed by soft loans from U.S. or European countries.

The most promising subsectors include: used medical equipment, cardiovascular equipment, X-ray equipment, and electronic apparatus.

6. Major infrastructure projects

Major projects financed by the U.S. and international donors, particularly the Inter-American Development Bank, provide excellent export opportunities for U.S. firms. Other areas offering exceptional opportunities are telecom and electric power generation.

It is extremely useful for U.S. firms seeking to win contracts in El Salvador to be represented by a local agent who can pick up market intelligence on upcoming projects and handle the logistics of bid openings.

Lead times on procurement tenders are often very short, making it difficult for bidders outside the area to obtain the bid documents and submit proposals. All correspondence regarding procurement opportunities and bids should take place by telephone and fax, because the local mail system is slow and unreliable. Consultants and other interested firms are also reminded that in Latin America, business often hinges on personal contacts, and visiting El Salvador to meet personally with potential buyers is highly recommended. See below for names of procurement officials in government institutions and major projects planned in El Salvador.

ELECTRIC ENERGY:
Ing. Alfredo Calderon, Technical Sub-Director
Comision Ejecutiva Hidroelectrica del Rio Lempa—CEL
(State Electric Utility)
1a. planta, Edificio CEL
Centro de Gobierno
San Salvador
EL SALVADOR
  Tel: (503) 710-855
  Fax: (503) 710-855

TELECOMMUNICATIONS:
Hector Efrain Aguila, Procurement Officer
Administracion Nacional de Telecomunicaciones—ANTEL
(National Telecommunications Company)
Centro de Gobierno, 3a. planta
San Salvador
EL SALVADOR
  Tel: (503) 717-815
  Fax: (503) 213-463

CIVIL AVIATION:
Oscar Giron, Procurement Officer
Direccion General de Aeronautica Civil
Aeropuerto de Ilopango
San Salvador
EL SALVADOR
  Tel: (503) 270-026
  Fax: (503) 271-962

MILITARY SALES:
Colonel Ismar Roque, Procurement Officer
Ministerio de Defensa
Carretera a Santa Tecla
San Salvador

EL SALVADOR
  Tel: (503) 230-233
  Fax: (503) 982-035

MILITARY HOSPITAL:
Major Victoria Guevara de Salinas, Procurement Officer
Hospital Militar
Alameda Roosevelt
San Salvador
EL SALVADOR
  Tel: (503) 237-855
  Tlx: 20641

RAILROADS:
Ing. Tulio Omar Vergara, Manager
Ferrocarriles Nacionales de El Salvador—FENADESAL
Edificio Torre Roble
San Salvador
EL SALVADOR
  Tel: (503) 229-000, 715-632
  Fax: (503) 715-650

ELECTRIC POWER DISTRIBUTION:
Ing. Oscar Edgardo Quan, Purchasing—Technical Division
Compania de Alumbrado Electrico de San Salvador—CAESS
(Electric Power Distribution Company)
Frente Hotel Camino Real
Boulevard de los Heroes
San Salvador
EL SALVADOR
P.O. Box 186
  Tel: (503) 236-033
  Fax: (503) 240-787

WATER AND SEWAGE:
Mr. Jose Ricardo Cruz Diaz, Procurement Officer
Administracion Nacional de Acueductos y Alcantarillados—ANDA
(National Administration of Sewage and Water)
Final Avenida Peralta
Plantel El Coro
San Salvador

EL SALVADOR
  Tel: (503) 229-780
  Fax: (503) 714-531

HEALTH AND MEDICINE:
Lic. Nuria de Munoz, Procurement Officer
  Instituto Salvadoreno del Seguro Social—ISSS
(Salvadoran Institute of Social Security)
Final Pasaje Cipactly, Colonia Atlacatl
San Salvador
EL SALVADOR
  Tel: (503) 268-467, 268-857
  Fax: (503) 761-414

HEALTH AND MEDICINE:
Lic. Mario Manuel Martinez, Procurement Officer
Ministerio de Salud Publica y Asistencia Social
(Ministry of Public Health and Social Security)
Calle Arce 827
San Salvador
EL SALVADOR
  Tel: (503) 221-590

PORTS:
Ing. Jose Guillermo Merlos
Comision Ejecutiva Portuaria Autonoma—CEPA
(Ports and Railways Commission)
Edificio Torre Roble
San Salvador
EL SALVADOR
  Tel: (503) 241-423, 250-007
  Fax: (503) 241-355

AGRICULTURE:
Lic. Ana Maritza Fernandez, Purchasing Agent
Ministerio de Agricultura y Ganaderia
(Ministry of Agriculture and Livestock)
83 Avenida Norte y 11 Calle Poniente
San Salvador
EL SALVADOR
  Tel: (503) 791-984, 791-985
  Fax: (503) 242-944

INVESTMENT CLIMATE

For sophisticated investors, cognizant of the political risks, El Salvador represents a promising investment opportunity. El Salvador invites foreign investment; its recently implemented free market economic reforms have considerably enhanced prospective returns for foreign investors and the regulatory landscape is extremely favorable. One of the most comprehensive foreign investment statutes in Latin America, the 1988 Foreign Investment Promotion and Guarantee Law, allows 100 percent repatriation of dividends and profits for manufacturing operations. The Export Promotion Law of 1990, targeted particularly towards maquila and assembly-type investments, provides generous tax incentives to foreign investors interested in export ventures.

Foreign investors in El Salvador are not required by law to operate through joint ventures. Similarly local management and control are not required by law, but in El Salvador's small and highly concentrated local economic environment, local participation is generally desirable. Despite favorable investment regulations, however, many potential investors are deterred by the continuing guerrilla conflict. Foreign investment levels remain low, although an increasing number of foreign firms are setting up apparel assembly operations in El Salvador for export to the U.S.

Some promising investment opportunities include apparel and electronic assembly, processing and production of vegetables and fruit, and shrimp aquaculture. The government is also interested in privatizing several state-owned enterprises, although the pace of privatization has been slowed by bureaucratic inertia. Included among these are: a luxury hotel in San Salvador, several sugar mills, a fishing complex in southeastern El Salvador, a silver mine, and various port and airport services.

Foreign investment, still the weak link in the Salvadoran economic picture, made an impressive turnaround in 1991. Foreign investment in the apparel assembly industry exceeded five million dollars, and overall foreign investment returned to prewar levels for the first time in ten years.

However, the signing of a peace agreement in early 1992 should add fuel to the growing flicker of international investor interest in El Salvador.

FINANCING AND CAPITAL MARKETS

General Policy Framework

The government allowed private sector credit to expand in 1991 in nominal terms. Credit is readily available in soon-to-be-privatized commercial banks, although primarily for working capital. Lending rate ceilings for colon-denominated loans are currently at about 17.5 percent, but in 1992 the government announced plans to establish market-determined interest rates. In 1990–91, with the growing international business confidence in El Salvador and the reestablishment of commercial contacts, the use of letters of credit saw a sharp drop-off. Bankers estimate that in 1987–88, 80 percent of international purchases were made through letters of credit, whereas now approximately 70 percent use open accounts or collections.

Debt Management Policies

Supported by large-scale concessional loans by multilateral development agencies, El Salvador has avoided the crushing debt burdens of most developing countries. Preliminary data show that total external debt in 1990 rose only 4.4 percent, to approximately U.S. $2.2 billion. More than 90 percent of all external debt is owed to official and multilateral lenders, and 80 percent of this is owed to the United States.

In August 1990, the International Monetary Fund approved a stand-by arrangement, which paved the way for a Paris Club debt rescheduling agreement in September 1990. The Paris Club agreement provides exceptional financing, via deferred payments, estimated at U.S. $135 million for the period through September 1991. El Salvador had no external debt arrears as of year-end 1990.

Tapping International Aid Institutions

Foreign assistance plays a vital role in the Salvadoran economy by helping to finance the balance of payments gap and the bulk of the capital budget for public sector infrastructure development projects. During fiscal year 1990, the United States provided U.S. $262.2 million in direct economic assistance (grants and loans). In FY91, USAID administered a program of approximately U.S. $235.1 million, comprising U.S. $55.0 million in development assistance, U.S. $39.8 million in PL-480 assistance, and 140.0 million in economic support funds (SF), of which U.S. $90 million was balance of payments assistance. Other international donors including the World Bank, the Inter-American Development Bank (IDB), Germany, and Taiwan also provided assistance, primarily in the way of development loans.

Chapter 10

GUATEMALA

	Total	Urban	
Population (1993)	9,735,000	39.0%	

Main Urban Areas	Population	Percentage of Total	International Calling Code
GUATEMALA CITY	1,057,000	10.9	502-2
Escuintla	77,000	0.8	502-9
Quezaltenango	73,000	0.7	502-9
Puerto Barrios	48,000	0.5	502-9
Retalhuleu	47,000	0.5	502-9
Coban	44,000	0.5	502-9
Chiquimula	43,000	0.4	502-9
Mazatenango	39,000	0.4	502-9

Land Area	108,430 square kilometers
Comparable U.S. state	Slightly smaller than Tennessee

Language		
	Spanish	66%
	Quiche	13%
	Cakchiquel	6%
	Mam	4%
	Kekchi	4%
	Mayan, other	7%
Common Business Language	Spanish	

Currency	1 quetzal (Q) = 100 centavos
Exchange Rate (May 1993)	U.S. $1.00 = 4.77 quetzals

Best Nonstop Air Connection via U.S.	Miami to Guatemala City: 1.5 hours American Airlines (800) 433-7300 Four nonstops daily

Best Hotel	Camino Real Reforma Avenue and 14th Street Zone 10 Guatemala City Tel: (502-2) 334-633 Fax: (502-2) 374-313

INTRODUCTION AND REGIONAL ORIENTATION

Guatemala is a predominantly mountainous tropical country comprising most of Mexico's southern border (962 kilometers). It has the largest population and economy in Central America and conducts most commercial affairs with the United States (destination for 39 percent of exports).

For much of the past decade, Guatemala's economy was adversely affected by the war in neighboring El Salvador (203-kilometer border). Now that the war has been resolved, the economic prospects look excellent.

The economy is based on family and corporate agriculture, which accounts for 26 percent of GDP, employs about 60 percent of the labor force, and supplies two-thirds of exports.

CRACKING THE MARKET

Economy

The two-year-old government of President Jorge Serrano has done an excellent job of economic stabilization. It has also enacted significant fiscal reform and is pursuing other economic reforms. Public investment in infrastructure and social services is the next priority, but still lagging.

Guatemala's economy is dominated by the private sector, which generates nearly 90 percent of gross domestic product. Agricultural production rose only 3 percent in 1991, reflecting the dual weight of drought and depressed world commodity prices. Commerce moved up 2.4 percent for the same period. The manufacturing sector again occupied third place, representing 14.8 percent of GDP. However, Guatemalan manufacturing continues to operate at low rates of capacity.

Local industrialists are actively engaged in shifting production from domestic to Central American and world markets. There is no heavy industry. Most manufacturing is devoted to light assembly and food processing operations, and is still geared largely toward the domestic and nearby Central American markets. However, a marked trend toward diversification, both in production and exports, has emerged since 1986. Textile and apparel exports to industrialized countries—especially to the United States—and nontraditional agricultural exports (NTAEs) are growing. (NTAEs are agricultural products other than traditional exports of coffee, cotton, bananas, sugar, cardamom, and meat.) Fast growing NTAEs now include winter fruits and vegetables and cut flowers; shipments are almost exclusively bound for the United States.

The Serrano government is also targeting key sectors of the small public sector for privatization, particularly telephone, airline, and railroad operations. The government has also welcomed large private investment in electricity generation.

All sectors recorded positive growth. Construction bounced back from negative growth in 1990 to post a healthy 8 percent gain. Transportation and services grew by 6.5 percent and 2.4 percent respectively; utilities climbed 4.1 percent, and public administration and defense, 5.1 percent.

Exports of products eligible for preference under the Caribbean Basin Initiative (CBI) continue to grow.

Guatemala's public sector is among the smallest in Latin America and the country's tax burden is among the lightest. Public spending on infrastructure and social services has lagged behind that of other countries in the region.

Tourism is projected to grow 10 to 30 percent annually, and thus represents a potential sector for economic diversification as well as an opportunity for U.S. investment (see Table 10-1).

The private sector is pressing policy makers to remove bureaucratic and legal barriers, such as protectionist aviation and transportation policies, that are constraining more rapid growth of nontraditional exports and tourism.

Trade

The United States is Guatemala's largest trading partner, purchasing 37 percent of Guatemala's exports and supplying 41 percent of the nation's imports in 1991 (see Table 10-2 for trade details). Guatemalan sales to other Central American countries

Table 10-1
Incoming Tourism Earnings

	1988	1989	1990	1991	1992
Number of tourists: (thousands)	405	437	508	600	690
Earnings (U.S. $M)	124	152	186	212	250

Source: American Embassy Guatemala City (September 1992).

Table 10-2
Guatemalan Trade

	1990	1991	1992
Total exports	1,163.0	1,202.0	1,405.0
Total imports	1,649.0	1,851.0	2,107.0
Exports to the U.S.	450.0	455.0	465.0
Imports from the U.S.	652.0	764.0	781.0
U.S. share of host-country imports (%)	39.0	41.0	37.0
Imports of manufactured goods (U.S.)			
Brussels Tariff Nomenclature—BTN (%)	29.0	29.0	31.0
Total (from all countries)	323.0	772.0	777.0
Projected average growth rate through 1994 (%)	9.3	9.3	9.3
From the U.S.			
Projected average growth rate through 1994 (%)	7.3	7.3	7.3
U.S. share of manufactured imports (%)	28.0	12.5	14.0
Trade balance with three leading partners in 1991			
Mexico		−60.0	
Japan		−87.0	
Germany		−41.0	

Source: American Embassy Guatemala City (September 1992).

GUATEMALA
Key Economic Indicators

	1990	1991	1992
Domestic Economy (U.S. $ millions, except as noted)			
GDP (current)[1]	7,620.0	9,286.0	9,611.0
GDP projected average growth rate through 1994 (%)	2.7	3.2	3.8
GDP per capita	828.0	983.0	1,017.0
Government spending as % of GNP	1.9	2.4	3.0
Inflation (%)	60.0	9.0	14.0
Unemployment (%)[2]	6.4	6.5	6.6
Foreign exchange reserves (U.S. $ million)	−233.0	383.0	400.0
Average exchange rate for U.S. $1.00	4.50	5.06	5.06
Foreign debt (U.S. $ million)	2,601.0	2,561.0	2,600.0
Debt service ratio (ratio of principal and interest payments on foreign debt to foreign income)	499.0	532.0	540.0
U.S. economic assistance (U.S. $ million)	120.0	94.0	72.8
U.S. military assistance (U.S. $ million)	3.0	0.0	0.0

1. Calculations based on average exchange rate for each year.
2. Excludes "underemployment."

Source: American Embassy Guatemala City (September 1992).

	1988	1989	1990	1991
Balance of Payments				
Exports	1,022	1,108	1,163	1,202
Imports	1,557	1,641	1,649	1,851
Trade balance	− 535	− 546	− 486	− 649
Current account balance	− 544	− 468	− 344	− 425
Foreign debt	2,599	2,732	2,601	2,561
Debt service	528	487	499	532
Debt service as % of exports	49	43	41	44
Net foreign exchange reserves	− 386	− 285	− 233	383
Average exchange rate (Quetzals per U.S. $1.00)	2.61	2.80	4.50	5.06

GUATEMALA
Key Economic Indicators

	1988	1989	1990	1991*
U.S.-Guatemala Trade				
U.S. exports to Guatemala (FAS)	580	601	652	764
U.S. imports from Guatemala, customs basis (FOB)	281	380	450	445
Trade balance	299	221	202	319
U.S. share Guatemalan exports (%)	26	34	37	37
U.S. share Guatemalan imports (%)	37	37	39	41
U.S. bilateral aid (fiscal year)	146	154	123	94
Economic	137	145	120	94
Military	9	9	3	0

Principal U.S. exports, 1991: machinery and electronics; petroleum products; chemicals; vehicles and transportation materials; plastics; paper products.

Principal U.S. imports, 1991: coffee; sugar; fruits and vegetables.

* Data for 1991 is estimated.
Calculations based on average exchange rate for each year.

increased nearly 13 percent in 1991, to reach U.S. $324 million, while exports to the United States (U.S. $445 million), the EC (U.S. $272 million), and Japan (U.S. $34 million) remained essentially unchanged.

For calendar year 1991, Guatemala's total imports reached U.S. $1.851 billion (up 12.3 percent), while total exports rose to U.S. $1.202 billion (up 3.4 percent).

The export performance of traditional commodities was disappointing in 1991. Only export earnings from sugar (U.S. $138 million, up 15.5 percent) and meat (U.S. $29 million, up 9.7 percent) increased. Export earnings from cotton (U.S. $10 million, −57.4 percent), cardamom (U.S. $29 million, −16.2 percent), coffee (U.S. $286 million, −11.5 percent), and bananas (U.S. $66 million, −1.9 percent) decreased. Low international price levels and the 1991 drought were contributing factors.

Happily, a surge in the growth of nontra-ditional exports (NTEs) offered significant compensation. Total NTE earnings surpassed coffee export revenues (Guatemala's number one foreign exchange earner) for the first time, pulling in a total of U.S. $399 million in 1991. This represents their sixth year of robust expansion, confirming the widespread belief that nontraditional exports offer the best hope for future economic growth and job creation. In 1991, NTE growth was led by manufacturing (U.S. $172 million, up 47 percent); nontraditional agricultural exports (U.S. $145 million, up 26 percent); minerals, fish, and handicrafts (U.S. $39 million, up 50 percent); and others (U.S. $43 million, up 19 percent).

Policies to Attract New Business

Guatemala's major problem in the investment area may be its inability thus far to organize investment promotion efforts.

Other countries in the Caribbean Basin, with assistance from the U.S. Agency for International Development (AID), have created entities in their private and public sectors to address the special needs of foreign investors. The government of Guatemala opened an investors' one-stop shop in May 1992.

Guatemala is aware of the fact that it must compete with other investment sites for available venture capital. Progress has been achieved in this area, and both the Enterprise Chamber and FUNDESA have a "one-stop" investment information center.

Basic issues that will confront potential U.S. investors and/or joint venture partners are:

1. Lack of basic infrastructure (communications, roads, water, electricity) for those opportunities in outlying, remote areas;

2. Cumbersome procedures to obtain government approval of OPIC political risk insurance applications.

APPROACHING THE MARKET

Commercial Environment

The Guatemalan market for imported goods has expanded rapidly since 1987. U.S. exporters are competitive in a wide variety of products. However, several Latin American, Asian, and European nations have adopted more aggressive trade attitudes, cutting into the U.S. share of exports to Guatemala.

U.S. exporters looking at Guatemala will find a relatively open market. All Guatemalan manufactured imports, except those imported under special industrial incentive programs and direct government imports, are subject to customs duties. Ad valorem rates have been reduced to between 5–20 percent. This range excludes a 3 percent surcharge made permanent in 1990. There is a value added tax of 7 percent to be paid on the sum

of ad valorem duty and the CIF value of the import. Guatemala became a full member of GATT in September 1991. Nonagricultural imports in every category are allowed into the market generally undisturbed by nontariff barriers.

U.S. exporters looking for long-term market development will find good opportunities in food processing equipment, agricultural chemicals, and textiles and other industrial machinery. Other "best prospects" for U.S. exports are a wide range of industrial chemicals, agricultural machinery, paper products, petroleum products, household consumer items, and agricultural products such as wheat, feed grains, and processed foods. The growth of assembly (maquila) industries under a drawback regime offers U.S. firms the opportunity to export partially finished items to Guatemala for assembly. During 1991, two trade mission and four catalog shows were supported by US&FCS Guatemala, introducing approximately 500 new U.S. firms to the Guatemalan market. As a result, over U.S. $10 million in initial export transactions were concluded.

Export of vegetables (broccoli, cauliflower, and snow peas) and fruits (strawberries and melons) continued strong growth in 1991. Prospects for additional investment in value added industries such as freezing, canning, and processing are excellent. The textile assembly industry has seen dramatic growth in the last five years, with over 250 firms now producing apparel for export. A "first ever" investment by a U.S. firm in an electronics drawback operation was announced in 1990. Agricultural chemicals is another area where the drawback regime has been successful.

Most business is conducted in Guatemala based on personal relationships. Guatemalan business executives and government officials place great importance on personal contacts with suppliers. U.S. suppliers should be prepared to travel to Guatemala and follow up visits with correspondence and telephone calls. Travelers often are surprised at the accessibility to key decision makers and by the openness and frankness of local buyers.

U.S. suppliers will quickly become aware of increased foreign competition in Guatemala. Foreign competitors are extremely aggressive. U.S. executives interested in pursuing business in Guatemala should approach local business persons in the same manner they approach prized clients in the United States. Suppliers should be prepared to explain how their products and services will complement existing products and systems.

Promotional material should be in Spanish. Though many private and public officials speak and read English, many technicians and engineers do not. Guatemalans are extremely receptive to technical presentations that are educational rather than sales oriented.

Implications for U.S. Exporters

U.S. industrial exporters and investors looking at Guatemala will find a relatively open market. Exporters of U.S. agricultural products, on the other hand, still face stiff import restrictions (i.e., quarantine, import permits, etc.). Guatemala appears to have few nontariff barriers worthy of concern. Products that are judged to impact the public health or the environment are usually controlled by local government entities. In most instances, these local government entities follow the lead of U.S. and European regulatory entities like the EPA and FDA.

Guatemalan Accession to GATT

Guatemala became a full member of GATT in September 1991. A bilateral trade and investment framework agreement under the Enterprise for the Americas Initiative was signed in October 1991.

Customs Valuation Procedures

Current customs valuation procedures are a potentially significant trade barrier. Established importers of U.S. products complain that underinvoicing of imports and outright contraband is widespread, damaging their relationship with the U.S. exporter.

Customs officials are sometimes subject by importers to pressure to underreport import values; in other cases, they arbitrarily charge duties at an artificial price above that on the commercial invoice. In sum, customs valuation procedures are arbitrary and not transparent. The new government has asked for U.S. government help.

Government Procurement Practices

Law requires all government purchases over U.S. $55,000 to be submitted for public competitive bidding, and no fewer than five bidders must participate. U.S. major project suppliers have recently expressed concern over increasing violations of this transparent government procurement procedure. They charge that in recent years public purchases increasingly are being made directly under the exemption allowed for emergency purchases, or even breaking up one project into amounts of less than U.S. $55,000 so as not to require public bidding.

These same U.S. suppliers complain that in recent years bilateral development assistance from other industrialized countries has been tied to commercial purchases made on a noncompetitive basis.

INVESTMENT CLIMATE

Guatemala's economic policy framework, physical proximity to the United States, large labor pool, and preferential access to the U.S. market through the Caribbean Basin Initiative (CBI) and Generalized System of Preferences (GSP) make it a promising site for potential investors.

Guatemala has traditionally welcomed foreign investment and few legal impediments confront investors, although bureaucratic red tape can be trying. The investor in Guatemala still enjoys relatively low labor costs.

In July 1989, the Guatemalan government adopted an export promotion/drawback law that provides fiscal incentives for investments in nontraditional export industries. There are no legal restrictions on repatriation of profits; although before 1991 delays have been experienced in currency conversion during times of foreign exchange shortage.

The 1989 Guatemalan decree permitting the establishment of Free Trade Zones provided for: (1) total exemption from import duties and customs charges on the importation of machinery, equipment, tools, and other construction materials used in the Free Trade Zones; (2) income tax exoneration for 15 years from Free Zone entity generated profits; (3) exoneration of property taxes for five years; (4) exoneration of import and consumption taxes and import duties on fuels when used for electric power generation within the zones; (5) total exemption of import duties and other customs charges on the importation of machinery, equipment, tools, raw materials, semifinished products, containers, packaging materials, and related items to be used in the production of goods or services; and (6) income tax exemption for a period of 12 years. These free zones may be private or government operated.

Foreign investors are generally granted national treatment by law. Foreigners can own as little as 1 percent or as much as 100 percent of a local firm. Wholly owned subsidiaries must be registered as local entities, and managers must be at least temporary residents of the host country.

These conditions are routinely fulfilled by an attorney in a short period of time. Several hundred small- to medium-sized companies have U.S. capital, but there is no reliable estimate of the total value of U.S. investment in Guatemala.

In order to assist the foreign investor in reducing red tape and obtaining vital information, the Fundacion para el Desarrollo de Guatemala (FUNDESA) has recently opened an investor services center. Contact can be made through:

Paul Weaver
Fundacion para el Desarrollo de
    Guatemala (FUNDESA)
Parque Las Margaritas
Diagonal 6, 10-65, Zona 10
01010 Guatemala, C.A.
    Tel: (502-2) 327-952 through
    327-957
    Fax: (502-2) 327-958

The Guatemalan Enterprise Chamber (Camara Empresarial), a private sector development group, also has an investor services center. Contact can be made through:

Lic. W. Rodolfo Ferber, Director
    Ejecutivo
Centro de Servicios al Inversionista
Camara Empresarial de Guatemala
Edificio Camara de Industria, Nivel 8
Ruta 6, 9-21, Zona 4
01004 Guatemala, C.A.
    Tel: (502-2) 346-878
    Fax: (502-2) 316-513

Unfortunately, this office will be phased out by 1994 and principal responsibilities will be transferred to FUNDESA.

FINANCING AND CAPITAL MARKETS

General Policy Framework

In January 1991, Jorge Serrano became the second consecutive democratically elected president of Guatemala. President Serrano's business- and market-oriented government

---

Foreign Investment in Guatemala

	1989	1990	1991
Total foreign direct investment (U.S. $ millions)	820.0	850.0	870.0
U.S. direct investment (U.S. $ millions)	616.0	637.0	652.5
and % share of total foreign investment	75.0	75.0	75.0

Figures are estimated. Guatemala has no official figures on foreign investment.

SOURCE: Bank of Guatemala, Economic Planning Council (March 1992).

---

inherited a 60 percent inflation rate, a rapidly depreciating currency, a practically empty Treasury, and debt service arrears of about U.S. $100 million. The new economic team moved immediately to tighten monetary and fiscal policies: net credit to the Bank of Guatemala was reduced by almost 140 percent, positive real interest rates were established, a policy of no net credit to the central government and government spending cuts were implemented, leading to a small fiscal surplus for 1991.

As a result of these policies, the nation's inflation rate fell from 60 per cent to 9.2 percent. Dollar holdings of the Bank of Guatemala swelled from U.S. $53 million in the beginning of 1991 to U.S. $578 million by year's end, while the exchange rate stabilized at approximately 5.0 quetzales to the dollar.

The government also eliminated its arrears to the Inter-American Development Bank and froze arrears to the World Bank at approximately U.S. $50 million. A special tax/bond levy was successful in raising Q660 million for debt arrears and priority infrastructure and social service projects.

Under present regulations the Guatemalan importer registers his transaction with the Bank of Guatemala and requests foreign exchange from the private banking system. During 1991 the Bank of Guatemala's governing Monetary Board had the foreign exchange mechanism functioning smoothly.

Under this regime, all exporters must deliver 100 percent of their foreign exchange earnings to the Bank. Buyers must deposit the day before the auction 100 percent of their bid in local currency converted at their bid rate. Currently, approximately U.S. $8 million is made available each day to purchasers.

A full range of payment schedules is available in Guatemala, including: prepaid orders, open account, letters of credit, and payment against shipping documents. In initial contacts, new-to-market and infrequent U.S. exporters prefer to deal in confirmed irrevocable letters of credit. As experience accumulates with the Guatemalan importer it is more common to observe open account sales despite the foreign exchange weakness described earlier.

All local banks, including the Central Bank, have correspondent banking relationships with well-known money centers and regional banks in the United States, Europe, and Japan. The common practice is for each bank to contract with a foreign bank in a private manner, as there is no government regulation of this business activity.

Trade Credit Insurance Project (TCIP): A significant amount of trade in recent years has been sustained by the TCIP. The original contract between the Bank of Guatemala and AID/Export-Import Bank was signed on March 11, 1985 for a five-year period. In fiscal year 1991 Guatemala received U.S.

$90 million for the import of U.S. agricultural inputs and raw materials destined for Guatemalan export industries. To apply, the U.S. exporters work with their U.S. banks and one of four participating U.S. banks (Chase, Citizens Southern, Manufacturers Hanover, and Bank of Boston).

There are no restrictions for the repatriation of royalties, dividends, or capital as long as the investor is properly registered with the appropriate authorities of the Central Bank and Ministry of Economy. In 1991 companies had little difficulty with the foreign exchange auction system.

The Currency and Exchange Rate Mechanisms

From the outset, the Serrano administration has sought to maintain exchange rate stability. This was achieved at an average exchange rate of 5.0 quetzales to the dollar throughout 1991—stark contrast to 1990, when the quetzal depreciated more than 60 percent against the U.S. dollar. By sharply raising interest rates on Bank of Guatemala bonds, the new Monetary Board was able to boost dollar holdings from virtually nothing to over U.S. $578 million by the end of 1991.

During the course of 1991, the Bank of Guatemala reduced its international debt service arrears to U.S. $62 million. As of April 1992, arrears were at U.S. $50 million. Once the government reaches agreement, as expected, on an IMF stand-by agreement, the release of U.S. $50 million in pending U.S. economic support funds will enable the government to pay off 100 percent of its external arrears.

Debt Management Policy

Guatemala's total external debt of U.S. $2.6 billion, while burdensome, is manageable. Debt service payments currently constitute a high 44 percent of export earnings. Most of the debt is held by the government and the Bank of Guatemala, and is owed principally to official lenders and multilateral institutions. The government of Guatemala has not restructured either its commercial or bilateral public international debt through the Paris Club or the London Club.

Banking and Other Financial Institutions

In Guatemala there are 21 privately owned banks, and three state-owned banks which operate with two departments (the commercial and the mortgage department). In addition there are six private financial corporations which operate as investment banks.

By March 1991, the privately owned banks had provided a total of U.S. $675 million for industry, agriculture, cattle, construction, commerce, financing, consumption, and other. The state banks had provided a total of U.S. $103 million for agriculture, cattle, construction, consumption, and commerce, and the financial corporation had provided U.S. $107 million for agriculture, industry, construction, consumption, commerce, and finance.

In sum, the financial sector in Guatemala, as in other small open economies, has been sensitive to macroeconomic disturbances arising from fiscal balances, exchange rate and monetary policies, and external shocks.

Tapping International Aid Institutions

Guatemala has benefited under the Caribbean Basin Initiative (CBI) since 1984. The CBI legislation seeks to spur economic activity and expand private sector opportunities in the region through a permanent, one-way free trade regime that allows duty-free access to the U.S. market for most CBI country products. Exceptions are canned tuna, petroleum and petroleum products, footwear, and certain textiles. Apparel products produced in CBI countries from cloth made and cut in the United States also benefit from a special program of guaranteed access to the U.S. market.

VISITING AND LOCATING

All U.S. citizens visiting Guatemala are required to obtain a tourist visa. Visas are issued free of charge by the Guatemalan Embassy or Consulate upon presentation of a valid passport. There are airport departure fees of Q50.00, or approximately U.S. $10.00.

The official currency unit is the quetzal. The exchange rate is approximately Q5.00 to U.S. $1.00. This rate may vary, but has been stable for two years. Major credit cards are accepted at principal hotels and restaurants.

Chapter 11

GUYANA

	Total	Urban	
Population (1993)	744,000	35.0%	

Main Urban Areas	Population	Percentage of Total	International Calling Code
GEORGETOWN	200,000	26.7	592-2
Linden	30,000	4.0	592-4
New Amsterdam	20,000	2.7	592-3
Corriverton	11,000	1.5	592
Mahaicony	5,000	0.7	592-21

Land Area	196,850 square kilometers
Comparable U.S. State	Slightly smaller than Idaho

Language	Creole English	78%
	Caribbean lang.	1%
	* English	—
	Hindi	
	Other	
	(*) Official language	
Common Business Language	English	

Currency	1 dollar (G$) = 100 cents
Exchange Rate (May 1993)	Unavailable

Best Nonstop Air Connection via U.S.	Miami to Georgetown
	New York to Georgetown
	BWIA (800) 327-7401
	Guyana Airlines (800) 242-4210

Best Hotel	Forte Crest Georgetown (U.S. $150)
	Seawall Road
	Tel: (592-2) 528-56
	Fax: (592-2) 605-32

INTRODUCTION AND REGIONAL ORIENTATION

After 15 years of economic decline, far-reaching policy reform began to pay off for Guyana in 1991. According to World Bank estimates, output in 1990 was only 60 percent of its 1976 level. Gross domestic product grew 6 percent, sugar production grew over 20 percent, rice was up 60 percent, and bauxite and timber output expanded more modestly.

Guyana's economy has been dramatically changed in recent years by the government's Economic Recovery Program (ERP). The reform program included a drastic reduction in the government's role in the economy, the promotion of foreign investment, and the sale of many government-owned businesses.

A key element of the reform program was the creation of a free market in foreign currency. The rate has remained stable at around 125 to 1 since the government linked the official rate to the free market rate in February 1991. Exchange rate stability has virtually halted inflation since mid-1991.

The government also continued its divestment of state enterprises. By mid-1992, the government had privatized the telephone utility and sold assets in the timber, rice, and fishing industries. Negotiations continued over the divestment of state-owned bauxite, sugar, and electric companies, and all three were due to be placed under independent management as a first step to privatization.

National parliamentary and regional elections were held in the latter part of 1992. The leader of the party winning the largest number of seats in the National Assembly becomes president. The two leading parties were led by incumbent President Desmond Hoyte and leader of the opposition Dr. Cheddi Jagan. Both leaders favored foreign investment and good relations with the U.S.

Dr. Jagan had, however, raised objections to some of the divestment projects and an opposition victory could have slowed or even halted further privatization.

The outlook for U.S. businesses is mixed. There are promising opportunities for investors in gold, agriculture, oil, seafood, and forestry. However, the low national income limits demand for most U.S. products. The three largest markets for U.S. products will be Guyanese exporters who need inputs to production, internationally financed development projects, and small-scale traders who buy consumer goods. Guyanese liquor, lumber, seafood, apparel, and tropical fruits, among other products, have the potential to supply U.S. importers. U.S. firms whose trade debt payments have been frozen should not expect prompt repayment.

Geographical Background

Guyana is slightly smaller than the state of Idaho. It hugs the Caribbean Sea bordered by Venezuela to the west and Suriname to the east, and Brazil inland to the south.

CRACKING THE MARKET

Demographics

Ethnic divisions: East Indian 51%, black and mixed 43%, Amerindian 4%, European and Chinese 2%.

Religion: Christian 57%, Hindu 33%, Muslim 9%, other 1%.

Language: English, Amerindian dialects.

Literacy: 95% (male 98%, female 96%) age 15 and over having ever attended school (1990 estimate).

Labor force (268,000): industry and commerce 44.5%; agriculture 33.8%; services 21.7%.

Public sector employment amounts to 60–80% of the total labor force (1985).

Organized labor: 34% of labor force.

Economy

After growing on average at less than 1 percent a year in 1986–87, GDP dropped by 3 percent a year in 1988–89. The decline resulted from bad weather, labor trouble in the cane fields, and flooding and equipment problems in the bauxite industry. Consumer prices rose about 35 percent in 1988 and by over 100 percent in 1989, and the current account deficit widened substantially as sugar and bauxite exports fell. Moreover, electric power is in short supply and constitutes a major barrier to future gains in national output. The government, in association with international financial agencies, seeks to reduce its payment arrears and to raise new funds. The government's stabilization program—aimed at establishing realistic exchange rates, reasonable price stability, and a resumption of growth—requires considerable public administrative abilities and continued patience by consumers during a long incubation period.

Production—agriculture: Guyana's sugar and rice industries rebounded in 1991 from extremely low 1990 production.

Sugar is one of Guyana's two largest exports. Total output exceeded 300,000 metric tons (mt) in 1981, but production declined to only 132,000 mt in 1990, before beginning to recover in 1991 to 162,000 mt. Guyana failed to fulfill lucrative quotas for sugar exports to the U.S. and Europe from 1988 to 1991, but expected to fill both quotas in 1992 and achieve total production of 217,000 mt.

The Guyana Sugar Corporation (GUYSUCO) remains government-owned, but Booker-Tate was hired to provide management in 1990, and privatization was expected by the end of 1992. The return of Booker-Tate, which owned GUYSUCO un-til nationalization in the 1970s, was an important symbol of the complete reversal of policy in Guyana. The World Bank and Inter-American Development Bank (IDB) are providing assistance to restore sugar production to the 250,000 mt level.

Guyana's rice production was expected to reach 170,000 mt in 1992, up from a low of only 93,000 mt in 1990. Recovery in the rice industry follows the privatization of the government-owned rice mills and the transfer of rice transactions to the cambio market for foreign currency. Rice prices tripled in March and April of 1991, and farmers brought abandoned fields back into cultivation. Guyana shares a European rice quota with Suriname, and if farmers can produce the high quality rice required for export markets, the industry should continue to contribute to Guyana's economic recovery.

Production—mining: Guyana's second major export is bauxite, and despite the problems of the government-owned mining company, Guymine, foreign investment in the bauxite sector has boosted production. Guyana produces extremely high quality refractory grade bauxite, and hopes that it can regain a once dominant market share for this commodity. A soft market and the inefficiency of Guymine have combined to create a serious debt problem, but if rescheduling is achieved, the World Bank is prepared to invest heavily in the rehabilitation of the company.

Gold production will expand dramatically in 1993 when a Canadian-owned mine goes into full operation and becomes the largest gold mine in South America. Officially recorded gold production reached 60,000 ounces in 1991, but it is widely believed that the majority of gold produced in Guyana is never reported. The new mine expects to produce 250,000 ounces a year for 10 years.

Production—other: Seafood will continue to account for over $15 million a year in foreign exchange earnings. The sector in Guyana which is likely to see the largest growth is the forestry industry. In 1992 international investors will double Guyana's 1991 timber export total of under $5 million, and in a few years the industry may generate over $60 million a year in export earnings. Guyana's nontraditional exports, both agricultural and manufactured, are unlikely to grow rapidly. Production is hampered by the competition in the local market from foreign goods brought in by traders who avoid duties and taxes.

Imports: Officially recorded Guyanese merchandise imports were $252 million in 1991. Fuel from Venezuela accounted for about a fourth of Guyana's merchandise imports, and imports from the U.S., primarily capital equipment and unprocessed food, accounted for a third. Much of the processed food sold in Guyana's street markets is smuggled into the country from the U.S., Venezuela, or Brazil. As part of Guyana's economic reform program, imports restrictions have been removed, although high import duties may make legal imports uncompetitive with smuggled products. Import licensing procedures have been simplified.

Electricity: Although service began to improve in 1992, the lack of a reliable supply of electricity in and around Georgetown is a severe constraint on national economic activity and is a leading factor in emigration. The Guyana Electricity Corporation (GEC) often cannot guarantee service to a particular area at a particular time, which complicates business planning. Blackouts occur frequently. Most greater Georgetown businesses have imported "standby" generators, increasing total fuel demand.

The IDB has provided short-term funding for the Guyana Electricity Corporation, and has projected a need for over $100 million in new investment in the medium term. The government of Guyana is interested in selling the utility, but negotiations have stalled.

Other infrastructure: Deterioration of other areas of the infrastructure has hampered Guyana's development. The deterioration of the seawall which protects the below-sea level coastal areas where the majority of Guyana's population lives has led to increased flooding and lost agricultural production in recent years. The drainage and irrigation system necessary for agricultural production and flood control has also been insufficiently maintained. The educational system has declined seriously in the last decade, and is often cited as a cause of emigration. Other factors which limit production and discourage potential investors include poor (but improving) air and ship service to Guyana, poor road conditions, and emigration of skilled personnel. Sale of the telephone company to a U.S. Virgin Island firm has resulted in investment in improved service, and decontrol of fuel prices in 1991 has eliminated fuel shortages.

In order to revitalize its economy, Guyana will need millions of dollars of new investment in its infrastructure and in production facilities. Some of these investments, such as in the telephone and electric utilities and in production for export, can be made by foreign investors, but most infrastructure investment must come from international financial institutions (IFIs) such as the World Bank, the International Monetary Fund (IMF), the Caribbean Development Bank (CDB) and the Inter-American Development Bank (IDB).

Political/Institutional Infrastructure

The Co-operative Republic of Guyana gained its independence from the United Kingdom in 1966; it was formerly known as British Guiana. Its current constitution was ratified on 6 October 1980. The capital is Georgetown.

GUYANA
Key Economic Indicators

(In millions of U.S. dollars unless noted)	1989	1990	1991	1992 Proj.
Population (thousands)	750	750	750	750
GDP in Guyana dollars (millions)	10,330	15,665	38,283	44,000
Nominal GDP (millions U.S. $)	325	313	330	350
Nominal GNP	223	204	212	217
Nominal GDP per capita (U.S. $)	433	417	440	465
Real GDP (% change)	−5	−4	+6	+5
Consumer price index (% change)	100	65	100	12
Unemployment rate	12	12	12	N/A
Current government deficit as % of GDP	8	19	20	21
Balance of Payments				
Exports, FOB	205	204	239	268
Imports, CIF	212	250	252	315
Trade balance	−7	−46	−13	−47
Current account balance	−113	−148	−136	−173
External public debt	1,853	1,940	2,063	2,189
Debt service	297	249	162	164
Debt service as % of exports	145	122	68	61
Foreign exchange reserves, year-end	15	27	123	84
Average exchange rate for year	32	50	116	125

Source: American Embassy Georgetown, June 1992.

The legal system is based on English common law with certain admixtures of Roman-Dutch law, and has not accepted compulsory ICJ jurisdiction.

National holiday: Republic Day, 23 February (1970).

Executive branch: executive president, first vice-president, prime minister, first deputy prime minister, cabinet.

Legislative branch: unicameral National Assembly.

Judicial branch: Supreme Court of Judicature.

Principal Government Officials

Chief of State—Executive President
    Hugh Desmond HOYTE
    (since 6 August 1985)

First Vice-President
    Hamilton GREEN
    (since 6 August 1985)

Head of Government—Prime Minister
    Hamilton GREEN
    (since August 1985)

Political parties and leaders:

People's National Congress (PNC)
Hugh Desmond HOYTE

People's Progressive Party (PPP)
Cheddi JAGAN

Working People's Alliance (WPA)
Eusi KWAYANA
Rupert ROOPNARINE
Moses BHAGWAN

Democratic Labor Movement (DLM)
Paul TENNASSEE

People's Democratic Movement (PDM)
Llewellyn JOHN

National Democratic Front (NDF)
Joseph BACCHUS

United Force (UF)
Marcellus F. SINGH

United Republican Party (URP)
Leslie RAMSAMMY

National Republican Party (NRP)
Robert GANGADEEN
Suffrage: universal at age 18

Elections

Executive President—Results of 1985 elections: Hugh Desmond HOYTE was elected president (the leader of the party with the most votes in the National Assembly elections).

National Assembly—Results of 1985 elections: PNC 78%, PPP 16%, UF 4%, WPA 2%; seats—(65 total, 53 elected): PNC 42, PPP 8, UF 2, WPA 1.

Communists: 100 (estimated) hardcore within PPP; top echelons of PPP and PYO (Progressive Youth Organization, militant wing of the PPP) include many Communists; small but unknown number of orthodox Marxist-Leninists within PNC, some of whom formerly belonged to the PPP.

Other political or pressure groups: Trades Union Congress (TUC); Guyanese Action for Reform and Democracy (GUARD) includes various labor groups as well as several of the smaller parties; Guyana Council of Indian Organizations (GCIO); Civil Liberties Action Committee (CLAC); the latter two organizations are small and active but not well organized; GUARD includes various labor groups, as well as several of the smaller political parties.

Diplomatic representation: Ambassador Dr. Cedric Hilburn GRANT. Chancery at:
2490 Tracy Place, NW
Washington, DC 20008
Tel: (202) 265-6900

There is a Guyanese Consulate General in New York.

Flag: Green with a red isosceles triangle (based on the hoist side) superimposed on a long yellow arrowhead; there is a narrow black border between the red and yellow, and a narrow white border between the yellow and the green.

Disputes: All of the area west of the Essequibo river claimed by Venezuela; Suriname claims area between New (Upper Courantyne) and Courantyne/Kutari rivers (all headwaters of the Courantyne).

Defense

Branches: Guyana Defense Force (GDF; includes Coast Guard and Air Corps), Guyana Police Force (GPF), Guyana People's Militia (GPM), Guyana National Service (GNS).

Manpower availability—males 15–49 years old: 148,477 fit for military service.

Defense expenditures: $5.5 million, 6% of GDP (1989 estimate).

Trade

Principal U.S. Exports 1991: machinery, motor vehicles, grain, steel goods.

Principal U.S. Imports 1991: bauxite, seafood, gold, garments, wildlife. See Table 11-1 for breakdown of U.S.-Guyana trade.

Exports: $234 million (FOB, 1991 esti-

Table 11-1
U.S.-Guyana Trade

	1989	1990	1991
(in millions of U.S. dollars unless noted)			
U.S. exports to Guyana (FAS)	78	76	86
U.S. imports from Guyana (CIF)	56	52	84
Trade balance	22	24	2
U.S. share of Guyana's exports	27	25	35
U.S. share of Guyana's imports	37	30	34
U.S. bilateral aid	7	8	8

Source: American Embassy Georgetown, June 1992.

mate); commodities—bauxite, sugar, gold, rice, shrimp, molasses, timber, rum.

Major partners (1989): UK 31%; U.S. 23%; CARICOM 7%; Canada 6%.

Imports: $319 million (CIF, 1991 estimate); commodities—manufactures, machinery, food, petroleum.

Major suppliers (1989): U.S. 33%; CARICOM 10%; UK 9%; Canada 2%.

APPROACHING THE MARKET

Demand for Goods and Services

Guyana is not a large or a prosperous market. Guyanese look to the United States as the principal source of their imports of consumer goods and inputs to production. A common language, physical proximity, the large Guyanese migration to the United States, and the size of the U.S. economy add to the Guyanese preference for U.S. products over those of other industrialized nations. U.S. exporters should obtain payment in advance or an irrevocable letter of credit before shipping products to Guyana.

Implications for U.S. Exporters

Multilaterally Financed Projects

There are three primary market opportunities for U.S. firms. One consists of the infrastructure projects funded by multilateral development agencies. The U.S. Commerce Department publicizes these opportunities among the U.S. business community. Guyana's primary source of funds for infrastructure improvement projects is the Inter-American Development Bank (IDB). IDB projects underway or soon to begin include $45 million for primary education, $50 million for agricultural rehabilitation, $19 million for renovation of Georgetown's public hospital, $20 million for water and sewage rehabilitation, $20 million for agricultural research and extension, $50 million for sea defenses, $15 million for urban development, $30 million for electricity expansion, and $20 million for road rehabilitation.

When Guyana repaid its World Bank arrears, it became eligible for World Bank project aid as well. Most of the initial World Bank aid was a cash credit to repay the arrears-clearing bridge loan, but the Bank

plans to fund a $25 million program to reha-
bilitate the sugar industry, a $10 million
health and nutrition project, and a $15 mil-
lion infrastructure rehabilitation project.

The International Foundation for Agricultural Development (IFAD) funds and carries out agricultural projects, and the UNDP
supports a variety of projects. The EEC
funds infrastructure projects, but usually restricts contractors to firms from Guyana or
EEC countries. The U.S. Agency for International Development does not finance
Guyanese infrastructure projects.

Guyanese Exporters

A second market for U.S. exports is made up
of the Guyanese firms that export. Those
firms need machinery, spare parts, raw materials, and other inputs to production. Guyanese exporters are expected to profit more
from the government's reforms than will
other Guyanese firms and will thus continue
to be a good market for U.S. products. Products most likely to be sold to these firms
include mining equipment, earthmoving
equipment, agricultural equipment, pesti-
cides, fertilizers, transportation equipment,
sawmilling equipment, power generating
equipment, specialized sewing machines,
personal computers, and spare parts.

Traders

A third group of purchasers of U.S. products
is the thousands of Guyanese traders who
buy goods in the United States to sell in
Guyana.

Traders buy principally consumer goods,
especially clothing, shoes, and electronic
items, and spare parts. These purchases may
not be included in official trade statistics.
The volume of trade at the cambios suggests
that about 100 million dollars more in foreign currency changes hands than official
figures indicate. Much of this probably
comes in as remittances from relatives and
goes out to pay for unrecorded imports.

Imports

Because of the small domestic market and
the lack of hard currency, Guyanese firms
are extremely interested in selling to the
United States. This creates opportunities for
United States importers and distributors.
Guyana's principal exports to the United
States in 1989 were bauxite, shrimp, gold,
sugar, clothing, and wildlife. Guyana is a
beneficiary of the Caribbean Basin Initiative
(CBI), which eliminated U.S. customs duties
on many Guyanese products.

INVESTMENT CLIMATE

The government of Guyana welcomes foreign investment in every sector. Investors
have been provided with generous concessions and tax holidays, but World Bank and
IMF advice may lead the Ministry of Finance to cut back on these fiscal incentives.
Although the law governing foreign exchange transactions does not explicitly discuss repatriation of profits, currency is available for all purposes. Divested state corporations and natural resource concessions
have attracted the most interest.

Many Guyanese products are eligible for
reduced duties under the CBI, GSP (United
States), Lome (EEC), and Caribcan (Canada) programs. The Overseas Private Investment Corporation (OPIC), a U.S. government agency, offers potential U.S. investors
loans, loan guarantees, and insurance
against war, civil strife, and expropriation.

The chief factors discouraging potential
U.S. investors are Guyana's inadequate infrastructure and a serious shortage of skilled
personnel. Most investors must provide their
own infrastructure and in many cases expa-
triate staff.

Extent of U.S. Investment in
Goods-Producing Sectors

The U.S. Virgin Islands firm Atlantic Tele-

Network purchased 80 percent of the telephone company in early 1991. Reynolds International is mining bauxite in a joint venture with the government of Guyana. Mobil is exploring for oil off shore, and Hunt Oil Company planned to drill its first well in southwestern Guyana in late 1993.

Georgetown Seafoods sells shrimp to its U.S. parent company. Green Mining, a subsidiary of a U.S. firm, has mined bauxite on contract for GUYMINE.

Esso, Texaco, Seaboard (flour), Colgate-Palmolive, DHL, and United Parcel Service have subsidiaries that sell to the domestic market.

FINANCING AND CAPITAL MARKETS

General Policy Framework

The government of Guyana announced a reversal of economic policy in 1988. In the place of a predominantly state-controlled, socialist economy, the Economic Recovery Program (ERP) called for a free market. A number of steps have been taken as a consequence, including reform of fiscal and monetary policy, the creation of a free market in foreign currency, divestment of state enterprises, elimination of price controls, and removal of import prohibitions. Assistance from multilateral and bilateral donors is an integral part of the ERP, and a Support Group was formed in 1989 to help Guyana clear arrears and qualify for new lending. Debt restructuring and forgiveness has been another outgrowth of economic reform.

To rein in fiscal deficits, Guyana has tried to rationalize tax collection by converting consumption taxes to an ad valorem basis, reducing income tax exemptions and marginal tax rates, and adopting Caricom's Common External Tariff. Tax avoidance remains a serious problem. On the expenditure side, since 1988 the government has reduced spending on salaries, goods, and services from over 30 percent of GDP to less than 13 percent. A heavy debt service burden has kept the fiscal deficit high.

Removal of price controls and rapid devaluation spurred inflation, which remained in the 60 to 100 percent a year range from 1989 to 1991. Price increases in 1991 were concentrated in the first half of the year. In the first six months of 1992, inflation came to a virtual halt, as the exchange rate stabilized.

One of the government's most visible reforms has been its effort to introduce private, usually foreign, management and capital into government corporations. The four most important divestment efforts are the so far unsuccessful electricity privatization, the creation in January 1991 of a new telephone company with majority ownership by the U.S. Virgin Islands firm Atlantic Tele-Network, the return to the Guyanese sugar industry of the British firm Booker-Tate and the negotiations for the sale of the government-owned bauxite company. Of these efforts, only the telephone divestment was completed by mid-1992, though Booker-Tate returned in October 1990 to manage the state-owned sugar company. Other divestments include the sale of Guyana Timbers Limited and Demerara Woods, the sale of the net-making firm Guyana Nichimo, the lease of most of the assets of Guyana Fisheries Limited, the sale of some of the assets of the government's largest trading firms, the sale of some of the assets of the national bus company, and sale of the rice mills of the Guyana Rice Milling and Marketing Authority. The divested firms have been acquired by both Guyanese and foreign interests.

Debt Management Policies

Despite rescheduling and debt forgiveness, in 1991 Guyana's debt exceeded 600 percent of GDP, and total debt service was two-thirds as large as export revenue. Around 30 percent of this debt is owed to the international financial institutions (IFIs), which do not reschedule debt. The policy reform embodied in the ERP is a necessary, but not sufficient, condition for the stabilization of Guyana's fiscal and current account deficits; additional debt relief will be required.

The Currency and Exchange Rate Mechanisms

Guyana legalized the parallel market for foreign exchange in 1990, and unified the exchange rate in early 1991. Foreign exchange is available on the free market, at currency exchange houses called cambios, for any transaction. The elimination of foreign exchange restrictions was followed by rapid devaluation. In March of 1990 when the cambios were created, the official exchange rate was 33 Guyana dollars to one U.S. dollar. By the end of 1990 the market rate was 100 to 1, and by April 1991 the rate was about 125 to 1. Since that time, except for brief exceptions, the rate has remained stable.

When hard currency became scarce, many Guyanese firms that had contracted hard currency debts were not allowed to buy hard currency. Their deposits of Guyana dollars in the value of their debts have been frozen by the Guyanese government in its External Payments Deposit Scheme (EPDS) for repayment when hard currency becomes available. The government has agreed to convert the currency at near the exchange rate existing at the time it was deposited, but has not committed to any time frame.

Banking and Other Financial Institutions

The government owns one commercial bank, and the Bank of Nova Scotia (Canadian) and the Bank of Baroda (Indian) are owned by foreign banks. Two commercial banks have public shareowners. The government also runs a development bank, a mortgage finance bank, and the central bank, the Bank of Guyana. When the government legalized cambios in March 1990, over a dozen businesses and the five commercial banks opened cambios.

Commercial banks are very profitable because spreads are large, and because banks are able to earn market rates on deposits at the Bank of Guyana and thus make few risky loans. The government has held up consideration of applications for new bank licenses pending revision of banking regulations.

Tapping International Aid Institutions

Economic aid: U.S. commitments, including EX-IM Bank (FY70–89), $116 million; Western (non-U.S.) countries, ODA and OOF bilateral commitments (1970–88), $244 million; Communist countries 1970–89, $242 million.

U.S. aid: When Guyana's arrears to the United States were rescheduled in September 1989, Guyana became eligible for U.S. Agency for International Development (USAID) assistance. The U.S. gave 995,700 dollars in mid-1990 as part of the IFI arrears-clearing effort and has provided $2 million in support of a free and fair electoral process.

The U.S. government has provided PL-480 loans for Guyanese commodity purchases since 1986, including $7 million per year for wheat since 1988. The United States also provides antinarcotics aid and training in many other fields for Guyanese.

Chapter 12
HONDURAS

	Total	Urban
Population (1993)	5,240,000	43.0%

Main Urban Areas	Population	Percentage of Total	International Calling Code
TEGUCIGALPA	641,000	12.2	504
San Pedro Sula	429,000	8.2	504
La Ceiba	66,000	1.3	504
Choluteca	65,000	1.2	504
El Progreso	61,000	1.2	504
Puerto Cortes	42,000	0.8	504
Comayagua	32,000	0.6	504
Tela	28,000	0.5	504
Siguatepeque	26,000	0.5	504
Santa Rosa de Copan	21,000	0.4	504
Danli	20,000	0.4	504

Land Area	111,890 square kilometers
Comparable U.S. State	Slightly larger than Tennessee
Language	Spanish 97%
	Black Caribbean 2%
	English, other 1%
Common Business Language	Spanish, English
Currency	1 lempiras (L) = 100 centavos
Exchange Rate (May 1993)	U.S. $1.00 = 5.32 lempiras
Best Nonstop Air Connection via U.S.	Miami to Tegucigalpa: 2 hours
	American Airlines (800) 433-7300
Best Hotel	Honduras Maya Hotel (U.S. $115)
	At Convention Center
	Colonial Palmira
	Tel: (504) 323-191
	Fax: (504) 327-629

INTRODUCTION AND REGIONAL ORIENTATION

Although a relatively small market, Honduras offers many opportunities for U.S. exporters. Honduras depends on imports of many raw materials, virtually all machinery, equipment and parts, agricultural inputs, and many consumer goods. As the economic recovery continues, demand for U.S. goods should grow. Although the Honduran government has recently liberalized the system by which importers acquire foreign exchange, Honduran businesses will continue to be constrained by foreign exchange scarcity.

Geographical Background

Honduras has an 820-kilometer Caribbean coastline facing Cuba, and is situated between Guatemala to the northwest and Nicaragua to the south. Mostly mountainous, tropical, and forested (34 percent of the landmass), it is inhabited predominantly by a rugged mestizo Indian population engaged in agriculture.

As noted in the June 6, 1992, edition of *The Economist,* "Honduras has a long way to go, but it is on the move." The political environment is favorable. Honduras continues to enjoy peace and stability and has been fortunate not to have been embroiled in the civil strife which, up until recently, seriously affected life in neighboring countries. Greater stability has been achieved with three consecutive terms of freely elected civilian governments.

The competitive advantages which Honduras has to offer for trade and investment are noteworthy. Located in the heart of Central America, Honduras has access to both the Atlantic and Pacific oceans. Its climate is ideal for agriculture. It has abundant forest and mineral resources. The tourism industry has excellent potential and there is a large supply of very good and low-cost labor. The most modern port in Central America (Puerto Cortes), within three days of the U.S. market, is located in Honduras. The country has four international airports and is the only Central American country to export electricity to its neighbors.

CRACKING THE MARKET

Economy

Honduras is well positioned to offer new and ample opportunities for trade and investment. Throughout 1991–92, the Honduran Government sustained an ambitious reform program launched in March 1990 in response to an economic crisis unmatched in recent decades. The government succeeded in trimming the size of its fiscal deficit, liberalized foreign exchange management while restoring confidence in a sharply devalued lempira, and removed most restrictions on commercial lending. It also managed to trim the overall size of its external debt, particularly to bilateral lenders, and to improve its relations with the international financial institutions. By January 1992, the maximum import tariff had been reduced to 20 percent.

As a result of these measures, the Honduran economy grew by 2.2 percent in 1991, inflation fell sharply, and net international reserves rebounded by approximately U.S. $90 million. Growth was strongest in the agricultural sector, which rebounded with 3.4 percent growth.

The good economic news was not felt throughout the economy. While nontraditional exports of shrimp and melons and north coast industrial parks continued to prosper, banana exports fell by approximately six million boxes due to a combination of weather and labor-related factors.

HONDURAS Key Economic Indicators			
	1990	**1991**	**1992**
Domestic Economy (U.S. $ millions, except as noted)			
GDP (current)	2,824.3	3,083.8	3,222.6
GDP projected average growth rate through 1994 (%)			5.5
GDP per capita (U.S. $)	600.3	636.9	671.4
Government spending as % of GDP	22.7	20.3	19.9
Inflation (%)	36.4	21.4	17.5
Unemployment (%)	13.0	12.0	11.5
Foreign exchange reserves	−112.4	−219.8	N/A
Average exchange rate for U.S. $1.00	4.4	5.3	5.4
Foreign debt[1]	2,786.9	2,445.6	N/A
Debt service ratio	18.3	15.5	N/A
U.S. economic assistance	192.0	102.9	N/A
U.S. military assistance	21.1	23.0	N/A

1. Excludes IMF short- and long-term debt.

Source: American Embassy Honduras (September 1992).

Coffee producers were hard hit by record low world prices. Total merchandise exports fell by 4.6 percent to U.S. $808 million, driving up the current account deficit to U.S. $350 million.

Trade

The U.S. is Honduras' leading trading partner (see Tables 12-1, 12-2, and 12-3). In 1991, U.S. exports to Honduras were U.S. $419.4 million, representing approximately 31.3 percent of the country's total imports. The outlook for 1992–93 was for a resumption of growth in U.S. exports as the Honduran economy continued to expand.

Since Honduras is a beneficiary of both the Caribbean Basin Initiative (CBI), and the Generalized System of Preferences (GSP), most of its exports enjoy duty-free entry into the U.S. This benefit, coupled with the devaluation of the lempira, has stimulated Honduran interest in exporting.

The most successful examples of new export products can be found in shrimp aquaculture, melon production, and apparel assembly.

Total apparel exports to the United States grew to U.S. $195 million in 1991, up U.S. $82 million over 1990. Honduras has no quotas for apparel at this time, enhancing its attractiveness for firms interested in the U.S. market. In 1989 and 1990, several private industrial parks were inaugurated and have

Table 12-1
Honduran Trade
(U.S. $ million)

	1990	1991	1992
Total exports	997.1	960.5	994.1
Total imports	1,342.6	1,338.2	1,304.7
Exports to the U.S. (FOB)	481.4	463.6	N/A
Imports from the U.S. (CIF)	421.8	419.4	N/A
U.S. share of host-country imports (%)	31.4	31.3	N/A
Imports of manufactured goods:			
Total (from all countries):			
Projected average growth rate through 1994 (%)			2.5
From the U.S.:			
Projected average growth rate through 1992 (%)			2.3
U.S. share of manufactured imports (%)	30.7	31.1	N/A

Trade balances with three leading partners in 1991 (U.S. $ millions):
U.S.—44.2
Mexico—47.8
Japan—10.1

Source: American Embassy (September 1992).

Table 12-2
Principal U.S. Exports to Honduras (1991)
(by tariff line item)

Product	HTS code
Rubber tire retreading materials	40.06.10.00
Wheat	10.01.90.00
Lubricating oils	27.10.00.00
Military aircraft fighters	88.02.30.00
Soybeans	12.01.00.00

Source: American Embassy (1992).

Table 12-3
Principal U.S. Imports from Honduras (1991)
(by tariff line item)

Product	HTS code
Bananas	08.03.00.00
Lobsters	03.06.11.00
Shrimp	03.06.13.00
Meat from bovine animals	02.02.30.00
Fresh melons and cantaloupes	08.07.10.00

Source: American Embassy (1992).

recruited a number of leading U.S. clothing manufacturers to establish foreign assembly operations.

Trade and Investment Policies

The government of Honduras is naturally solidly in favor of any effort to increase its export earnings and is supportive of efforts being made by important private sector promotion groups, e.g., the Foundation for Investment and Export Development (FIDE) and the Federation of Agricultural Producers and Exporters of Honduras (FPX). Both of these organizations are actively involved in attracting and developing international investment projects in Honduras. As a result of their important work, growth in nontraditional exports is proving to be an attractive new source of hard currency earnings.

The current administration is taking the bull by the horns and is seeking to create an atmosphere which is increasingly favorable to trade and investment. The most recent and significant action to date has been the May 29, 1992 passage of a new investment law for Honduras. In general terms, the law seeks to improve Honduras' competitive position in a global market by establishing clear and concise rules of the game for national and foreign investors. While too early to judge,

the feeling of most who are familiar with the dynamically changing events in Central America is that Honduras, cognizant of the business axiom to lead, follow, or get out of the way, has chosen to lead.

While the government generally espouses a verbal commitment to the principle of a "level playing field" for all comers, much remains to be done to correct an environment which historically has rewarded interests which were prepared to make offerings of "extra-official" goodwill in order to secure lucrative project work. However, in an accelerated effort to enhance prospects for Honduras as a site for expanded trade and investment, the government is taking to heart the fact that reputation is something other people give you.

APPROACHING THE MARKET

Commercial Environment

Honduras' relations with the United States are close and excellent. Lines of communication between both governments are open and there is much receptivity and understanding of each other's points of view.

The channels of distribution in Honduras are worth noting. The Honduran agent/distributor law includes a provision for penalties for wrongful termination which discourages exclusive distribution agreements.

Representatives and distributors tend to carry rather broad lines on a nonexclusive basis, and the number of full service local distributors which stock large inventories of parts and equipment is limited. In order to reduce costs (or because local reps are not sufficiently aggressive), many local buyers make direct contacts with U.S. suppliers at the factory or wholesale level. Store owners often buy consumer goods in small lots from stores, export brokers, and wholesalers in the U.S., particularly in Miami, New Orleans, and Houston, the principal gateway cities.

To participate in public tenders, foreign firms are required to act through a local agent. By law, local agency firms must be at least 51 percent owned by Hondurans.

U.S. suppliers are in the best position to fill the import requirements of Honduran businesses. With careful attention to effective distribution channels and the use of low-cost promotional techniques, U.S. suppliers should expand their sales to Honduras as the economy continues to improve.

While many Honduran business persons speak and understand English, Spanish is the preferred language for commercial correspondence. Any prospective U.S. provider of goods and services who appreciates this fact, will have one up on the competition.

In Honduras, two USAID-supported private sector groups promoting investment will be useful contacts for U.S. commercial interests. FIDE focuses on attracting assembly industries to Honduras' industrial parks and free zones, while FPX concentrates on agricultural projects (including aquaculture).

Their addresses are:

Foundation for Investment and Export Development (FIDE)
Apdo. Postal 2029
Tegucigalpa, D.C.
HONDURAS

Tel: (504) 320-937
Fax: (504) 321-808
Contact: Mr. Norman Garcia, President

Federation of Agricultural Producers and Exporters of Honduras (FPX)
Apdo. Postal 1442
San Pedro Sula, Cortes
HONDURAS
Tel: (504) 527-851, 526-794
Fax: (504) 527-852
Contact: Mr. Hernan Pineda, President

INVESTMENT CLIMATE

Honduras welcomes international investment and is growing more adept at marketing itself to overseas investors. Devaluation of the lempira and reduction of protective tariffs have increased Honduras' attractiveness to investors. On May 29, 1992, the Honduran Congress passed a new investment law which promises to be more responsive to investor needs. The United States-Honduras Treaty of Friendship, Commerce, and Consular Rights provides Most Favored Nation treatment for investors from both countries. In addition, the United States and Honduras have bilateral agreements for the Guarantee of Private Investments (1955), and for Investment Guarantees (1966). The U.S. Overseas Private Investment Corporation (OPIC) offers financing for U.S. investors in Honduras as well as insurance against war and expropriation.

Honduras faces an image problem. Many potential investors still view Central America and Honduras as an area suffering from political conflict and instability. Thus, they do not look closely enough to identify the very real opportunities for new business which exist here. The fact of the matter is that Latin America and the Caribbean are the fastest-growing regional markets for U.S. exports.

For the past five years, U.S. exports to the region have averaged 12 percent annual growth.

Honduran President Rafael Leonardo Callejas, a charismatic spokesman for Central American free trade, has committed his government to rapid reform. Since his election in 1989, he has been the preeminent spokesman not only for Honduras but for the region as well. His call to "Extend Free-Trade Accords Southward" carried in the January 31, 1992, edition of the *Wall Street Journal* provides an excellent review of his vision for the Americas.

The Honduran legal and regulatory regime is moving rapidly to reflect the new administration's open market principles. In the past, new laws affecting trade and investment have been passed by the Honduran Congress without provisions made for what are known as "implementing regulations." What this means is that, in most instances, any particular new law passed essentially has no teeth or legitimacy for enforcement without clearly published associated terms for implementation and enforcement. In the latter half of 1992, the government of Honduras has made great strides, with determined intention to minimize the passage of new laws without also ensuring the inclusion of implementing provisions as well.

It is safe to say that administration of justice in Honduras can be problematical. It is not unusual for foreign investors to find themselves caught up in a nasty web of legal bureaucracy whenever problems arise involving what they believe to be their legitimate rights under existing law. From time to time, persons who believe they are following or have followed prescribed legal procedures wind up finding themselves confronted by a legal system which is unable to render clear and timely adjudication of a dispute. Some of the problems encountered in this regard are a reflection of what is generally perceived to be an inherently weak judicial system, particularly handicapped by a severely overtasked and underpaid cadre of judges and clerks. And sometimes, "extrajudicial" activities prejudice attempts of investors to rights and privileges supposedly guaranteed under the law.

It is clear that the government is aware of problems involving the administration of justice and is trying to do its best to mitigate trade and investment problems caused by a weak judicial system.

Total foreign direct investment (1991): U.S. $320 million; U.S. direct investment (1991): U.S. $231.5 million; U.S. share of total foreign investment: 72.4%.

Principal foreign investors: United States, Japan, El Salvador.

FINANCING AND CAPITAL MARKETS

Lack of adequate financial resources is a severe impediment to Honduras' growth whether viewed as a market for U.S. exports or as a site for new investment. The banks in the financial system are very traditional and limited in their operations and tend to favor members of their own industrial groups when allocating credit or scarce foreign exchange.

Despite progress made in the last two years, access to external lines of credit is still limited because of a history of nonpayment and tight foreign exchange availability.

The Currency and Exchange Rate Mechanisms

In late 1991 and early 1992, the government implemented a series of regulations to liberalize foreign exchange controls. In June 1992, after a series of economic measures that included the devaluation of the local currency, the lempira, the introduction of a self-financing mechanism for importers, and the elimination of restrictions on the use of currency purchased in the free market for the acquisition of imports, through authorization of dollar denominated bank accounts, the Central Bank of Honduras eliminated all import permits and foreign exchange authorizations.

Importers, however, must still file a registration form with their commercial bank of preference for every import transaction.

Foreign exchange for imports is still limited. By law, all export earnings by companies operating in Honduras must be repatriated through the local commercial banking system. The use of these earnings is divided among the central bank, the commercial bank, and the exporter. According to current regulations, 30 percent of the earnings must be sold by the commercial bank to the central bank the following day after the foreign exchange is received. The commercial bank is allowed to use 40 percent of the earnings to meet its regular clients' needs. The remaining 30 percent is allocated to the exporter that generated the foreign exchange to purchase necessary imports for its operation. Since foreign exchange availability is limited, many importers resort to the free market as their source for dollars. In this instance, the dollars must be deposited with a commercial bank to be used later to pay for imports. An importer is not allowed to clear its products through customs unless it shows proof that the dollars needed to purchase the imports were acquired through the commercial banking system, regardless of their source.

Banking and Other Financial Institutions

All banks in Honduras maintain correspondent relationships with U.S. banks. In some instances, these relationships extend beyond the basic services offered by the U.S. banks, such as collections or opening of prepaid letters of credit. Some U.S. regional banks also offer specific lines of credit to their Honduran counterparts. Although limited in number and in amount, these lines have helped some local banks expedite the payment process between Honduran importers and their foreign suppliers.

Financial Market Operations and Structural Policies

Significant efforts made during 1990 to rationalize Honduran public finances as a result of the implementation of a structural economic reform program, were complemented during 1991 by a reduction in the government fiscal deficit. Tax administration was improved, utility tariffs were adjusted to halt costly subsidies, and expenditures on goods and services were cut. The government also avoided the end-of-year spending surge, apparent in 1990, that upset monetary aggregates and aggravated inflation. Current revenues rose by 41 percent, well above the current expenditure increase. As a result of these measures, the overall public sector deficit fell from 8.7 percent of GDP in 1990 to about 4.0 percent in 1991. The government has announced a fiscal deficit reduction target of 3.0 percent for 1992.

The government implemented a mix of conservative monetary policies and financial sector reforms during 1991 aimed at reining in inflation, stabilizing the currency, and building up its net international reserve position. High rediscount rates and strict rediscount line management rationalized the movement of credit within the financial system and lowered central bank credit to the banking sector. Central bank credit to the public sector also fell by 50 percent during 1991. Commercial bank interest rates were liberalized for all loan categories, with the exception of basic grain production and low-cost housing, which continue to receive subsidies. These policies proved effective, as inflation fell sharply, the Honduran lempira stabilized on the parallel market, and net international reserves rose by an estimated U.S. $90 million.

Also, as a result of the implementation of the structural economic reform program in March 1990, the government began a series of devaluations of the lempira, its first adjustments in over 70 years. These devaluations were made possible through the establishment of an "interbank" rate of exchange by the central bank. The central bank may modify the interbank rate of exchange from time to time according to the circumstances, including the supply and demand for dollars in the local commercial banking system.

On June 19, 1992, however, the central bank liberalized the rate of exchange by allowing commercial banks to buy and sell dollars in the open market at the best rate of exchange possible. By mid-July, the lempira had devalued by approximately 2.8 percent in the interbank market, from 5.40 lempiras to the dollar on June 19 to 5.55 on July 10.

The government's debt policy during 1990 focused on reducing the burden of public indebtedness and reopening vital credit lines from the international financial institutions (IFIs). Led by the U.S., a group of donor nations assisted Honduras in clearing U.S. $246 million in arrears to the IFIs in June.

This was followed in September by a Paris Club rescheduling of U.S. $295 million in bilateral debt. Relying on a variety of debt conversion instruments, commercial debt was reduced to U.S. $180 million.

The Honduran government continued to reduce its indebtedness during 1991, virtually eliminating external arrearages. An extension of the Paris Club consolidation period expanded the rescheduling to include a total of U.S. $345 million in bilateral debt in September. The Dutch and Swiss governments subsequently forgave U.S. $6.8 million and U.S. $10.7 million in official debt, respectively. The World Bank declared Honduras eligible for lending from its IDA affiliate on highly concessional terms. Finally, the government continued to reduce its commercial debt. By year-end 1991, Honduras' total external debt, including IMF short- and long-term debt, stood at U.S. $3.1 billion, down 9 percent from 1990.

U.S. firms interested in exploring participation prospects in multilateral development bank (MDB) project financing are urged to contact the following Trade Development officers at the U.S. Department of Commerce:

Michelle Miller, IDB Liaison
Tel: (202) 482-1246

Janice Mazur, World Bank Liaison
Tel: (202) 482-4332

Chapter 13

JAMAICA

	Total	Urban	
Population (1993)	2,534,000	51.0%	

Main Urban Areas	Population	Percentage of Total	International Calling Code
KINGSTON	525,000	20.7	809
Spanish Town	89,000	3.5	809
Montego Bay	70,000	2.8	809
May Pen	41,000	1.6	809
Mandeville	35,000	1.4	809
Savanna-la-Mar	14,000	0.6	809

Land Area	10,830 square kilometers
Comparable U.S. State	Slightly smaller than Connecticut

Language	Creole English	70%
	* English	27%
	Hindi	
	Other	
	(*) Official language	
Common Business Language	English	

Currency	1 dollar (J$) = 100 cents
Exchange Rate (May 1993)	U.S. $1.00 = 21.14 dollars

Best Nonstop Air Connection via U.S.	Miami to Kingston: 1.5 hours
	Air Jamaica (800) 523-5585
	American Airlines (800) 433-7300
	BWIA (800) 327-7401
	Four nonstops daily
	Nonstop service also from Atlanta, Baltimore and New York
	Nonstop service also to Montego Bay

Best Hotel	Pegasus Jamaica (Financial District)
	81 Knutsford Boulevard (U.S. $200)
	Kingston
	Tel: (809) 225-5843
	Fax: (809) 929-4062
	Wyndham Rose Hall Beach Hotel and Country Club (U.S. $145)
	P.O. Box 999
	Montego Bay
	Tel: (800) 822-4200

INTRODUCTION AND REGIONAL ORIENTATION

Jamaica is a multiracial society made up of people who primarily are of African origin, along with other diverse groups. Traditionally, Jamaica has enjoyed harmonious racial and cultural relations. Its national motto, "Out of many, one people," suggests this desire for harmony. Class distinctions from the colonial period are being reduced as social mobility increases through education and greater opportunities for property ownership.

Geographical Background

Jamaica is the third largest island in the Caribbean. Mountains cover about 80 percent of its surface. The highest, Blue Mountain, is 7,402 feet. The climate is humid and tropical most of the year, but temperatures from November to March are cooler, particularly along the north shore, where the range is 70–80 degrees fahrenheit. Rainfall is seasonal, with striking regional variations. Some northern regions receive up to 200 inches a year; the southern and southwestern plains receive much less. In September 1988, Hurricane Gilbert, one of the century's most powerful Caribbean storms, hit Jamaica. The storm affected the entire island and caused widespread damage to crops, vegetation, coastal properties, utilities, and roofs.

History and Political Conditions

Jamaica was discovered in 1494 by Christopher Columbus and settled by the Spanish during the early sixteenth century. In 1670 Great Britain gained formal possession through the Treaty of Madrid.

After a long period of direct British colonial rule, Jamaica gained some local political control in the late 1930s. During this period,

which was marked by social unrest and occasional violence, the groundwork was laid for Jamaica's major political parties, led by Norman Washington Manley (People's National Party—PNP) and his cousin, Sir Alexander Bustamante (Jamaica Labor Party—JLP).

Jamaica's first election with adult suffrage was held in 1944, and the JLP formed the first government. Since then, the two parties have alternated in power, with each serving two terms at a time.

In 1958, Jamaica joined nine other British territories in the West Indies Federation but withdrew when, in a 1961 referendum, Jamaican voters rejected membership. Jamaica gained independence from the United Kingdom in 1962 but has remained a member of the Commonwealth.

CRACKING THE MARKET

Demographics

Ethnic groups: African 76.3%; Afro-European 15.1%; Chinese & Afro-Chinese 1.2%; East Indian & Afro-East Indian 3.4%; European 3.2%; other 0.9%.

Religions: Anglican, Baptist and other Protestant, Roman Catholic.

Education: Years compulsory—to age 14. Literacy (age 15 and over)—82%.

Work force 855,100 (1987): industry 41%; agriculture 31%; services 27%; other 1%.

Economy

Agriculture: Products—sugar, bananas, citrus fruits, coffee, pimiento, allspice, coconuts.

Industry: Types—bauxite and alumina, garments, processed foods, sugar, rum, molasses, cement, metal, paper, chemical products, tourism.

Jamaica has natural resources, primarily

bauxite, and a climate conducive to agriculture and tourism. Although faced with some serious problems, the country has the economic base for growth and modernization.

The Jamaican economy traditionally was based on plantation agriculture, particularly sugar and bananas. However, the discovery of bauxite in the 1940s and the subsequent establishment of the bauxite-alumina industry became the dominant factors in the island's economic growth. During the 1960s, the expansion of tourism and establishment of local manufacturing industries were emphasized.

Foreign investment in bauxite and alumina production accelerated, and by the 1970s Jamaica had emerged as a world leader in exports of these minerals. Bauxite revenues fueled an economic expansion that began in 1965 but, in the 1970s, Jamaica's economic good fortunes were hurt by high oil prices and recessions in the economies of important trading partners.

The JLP, led by Edward Seaga, was elected in 1980 on a platform of economic revitalization, using a private sector and export-oriented strategy. The Seaga government sought foreign investment to help diversify the economy and reduce dependence on traditional export products.

The economy enjoyed positive growth rates in 1987–88, spurred by buoyancy in the tourist sector and recovery in the bauxite/alumina industry. Unemployment declined to 18.2 percent, and the inflation rate stabilized at under 10 percent.

In 1988, Hurricane Gilbert caused a temporary setback to a generally favorable economic climate. Jamaica has made an impressive recovery, and the economy appears to be back on a growth track. The major constraint on Jamaica's economic prospects is a heavy foreign debt of more than $4 billion.

Current economic policies encourage foreign investment in areas that earn or save foreign exchange, generate employment, and use local raw materials. The government provides a wide range of incentives to investors, including remittance facilities, tax holidays, and duty-free access for machinery and raw materials imported for approved enterprises. Free trade zones have stimulated investment in garment manufacturing, light manufacturing, and data entry by foreign firms. The "807A" program, which guarantees access in the United States for garments made in Caribbean Basin Initiative (CBI) countries from textiles woven and cut in the United States, has opened new opportunities for investment and expansion in Jamaica. More than 150 U.S. firms have operations in Jamaica, and total U.S. investment, including that in bauxite/alumina, is estimated at more than $1 billion.

The American Chamber of Commerce was formed in 1986 to enhance trade opportunities between Jamaica and the United States, promote Jamaican exports, attract new U.S. private investment to Jamaica, and provide Jamaican and American businessmen with a forum through which to advocate public policies enhancing the business climate.

Although Jamaica faces a difficult short-term economic situation, the long-term economic outlook is more promising. Increased tourism, a revival in the bauxite industry, duty-free trade benefits under the CBI, Canadian CARIBCAN, and access to the European Economic Community markets under the Lome Convention are likely to sustain continued economic progress.

Political/Institutional Infrastructure

Jamaica is a constitutional monarchy which obtained its independence from the United Kingdom on August 6, 1962. Its current constitution was adopted on that date.

Under Jamaica's British-style parliamentary system, Queen Elizabeth II, as head

JAMAICA
Key Economic Indicators
Domestic Economy (U.S. $ millions)

	1990	1991	1992
GDP current (U.S. $M)	3,915	3,578	3,478
GDP growth rate %	3.8	−2.0	−2.7
GDP per capita (U.S. $)	1,779	1,556	1,449
Government revenues	1,235	1,200	1,285
Government spending	1,494	1,474	1,675
Inflation %	29.8	80.2	N/A
Unemployment %	15.3	15.0	17.0
Foreign exchange reserves	−357	−380	350
Average exchange rate (per U.S. $1)	7.3	27.0	22.5
Foreign debt (U.S. $M)	4,152	4,147.5	4,157.5
Debt service as % of export	28	35	40
U.S. economic assistance (U.S. $M)	59	60	80
U.S. military assistance (U.S. $M)	6.9	1.2	2.2
National minimum wage J$(40 hours)	130	160	300

of state, appoints a governor general on the advice of the prime minister. The governor general's duties are largely ceremonial. Executive power resides in a 13-member cabinet led by a prime minister and responsible to Parliament. The prime minister is the leader of the majority party in the House of Representatives and is appointed by the governor general.

Elections for the 60 members of the House of Representatives are held at the discretion of the governor general on the advice of the prime minister for a five-year term.

Parliament is composed of an appointed Senate and an elected House of Representatives. Thirteen Senate members are nominated on the advice of the prime minister and eight on the advice of the leader of the opposition. The Senate may submit bills, and it also reviews legislation submitted by the House. It cannot delay money bills for more than one month or other bills for more than seven months.

The prime minister and the cabinet are selected from the Parliament.

Not less than two nor more than four members of the cabinet must be selected from the Senate.

The judiciary is modeled on the British system. The Court of Appeal is the highest appellate court in Jamaica. Under certain circumstances, cases may be appealed to the Privy Council of the United Kingdom.

Jamaica's parishes have elected councils that exercise limited powers of local government.

Principal Government Officials

Governor General
Sir Florizel Glasspole

Prime Minister and Minister of Defense
Persival J. Patterson

JAMAICA

	1989	1990	1991
Income, Production and Employment			
Real GDP(J$Millions) (1974 base year)	2,103.9	2,184.2	2,206.2
Real GDP growth rate	4.6	3.8	1.0
GDP By major sectors			
Agriculture, forestry, and fishing	152.7	170.7	N/A
Mining and quarrying	140.1	164.8	N/A
Manufacturing	355.2	369.8	N/A
Construction and installation	166.9	168.9	N/A
Distributive trade	327.3	330.6	N/A
Transportation, storage and communication	173.3	179.4	N/A
Real estate and business services	260.4	274.5	N/A
Government services	323.2	318.8	N/A
Real GDP per capita (J$ 1974 Base)	884.0	910.1	880
Size of labor force (000s)	1,062.9	1,058.5	N/A
Unemployment rate (avg)	18.0	15.3	N/A
Money and Prices			
Money supply (M1) (J$Millions) (Jul)	2,739.4	3,516.0	4,651.9
Avg. commercial interest rate (Aug)	31.0	36.03	31.65
Savings rate	18.0	18.0	18–21
Investment rate (gross fixed capital formation as % of GDP)	29.4	29.3	N/A
Consumer price index (Dec-Dec)	17.2	29.8	56.3
Wholesale price index	N/A	N/A	N/A
Exchange rate (J$/U.S. $)	5.75	7.28	12.03
Balance of payments and trade (Millions of U.S. Dollars)			
Total exports FOB	1,000.4	1,156.9	1,206.8
Total exports to U.S.	347.2	334.8	352.6
Total imports Cif	1,873.4	1,877.1	1,625.2
Total imports from U.S.	913.5	896.7	753.6
Aid from U.S. (FY90, FY91, FY92)	71.7	67.3	69.8
Aid from other countries	202.7	119.7	N/A
External public debt, (U.S. $ Millions)	4,038.4	4,152.4	4,147.5
Debt service payments, actual (U.S. $Millions)	670.0	652.3	652.8
Net official reserves (U.S. $Millions) end of year (Jun)	474.3	−383.4	−221.6

Source: American Embassy Kingston.

Deputy Prime Minister and Minister of Development, Planning and Production
P.J. Patterson (formerly)

Ministers

Finance and the Public Service
Seymour Mullings

Justice
Carl Rattray

Foreign Affairs and Foreign Trade
David Coore

National Security
K.D. Knight

Labor, Welfare and Sport
Portia Simpson

Construction
O.D. Ramtallie

Agriculture
Horace Clarke

Public Utilities and Transport
Robert Pickersgill

Local Government
Ralph Brown

Mining and Energy
Hugh Small

Industry and Commerce
Claude Clarke

Education
Carlyle Dunkley

Tourism
Frank Pringle

Youth, Culture, and Community Development
Douglas Manley

Health
Easton Douglas

Ministers without Portfolio
Paul Robertson
Kenneth McNeill

Ambassador to the U.S. and the OAS
Keith Johnson

Ambassador to the UN
Lloyd Barnett

Defense

The Jamaica Defense Force (JDF) was formed in 1962. Its mission includes defending the country against aggression and supporting, as required, the Jamaica Constabulary Force in maintaining law and order and essential services and protecting the civil population in the event of a disaster. It also is responsible for coastal surveillance and air-sea rescue operations. The JDF is a unified, composite military organization, the major components of which are the first, second, and third Battalions, the Support and Services Battalion, the Coast Guard, and the Air Wing. The ground elements are called the Jamaica Regiment, even though no regimental organization exists. The senior officer is the chief of staff, a major general who directs operations and is responsible to the prime minister/defense minister.

Current Political Conditions

The two major political parties are closely linked to the two major trade unions—the Jamaica Labor Party (JLP) with the Bustamante Industrial Trade Union (BITU) and the People's National Party (PNP) with the National Workers Union (NWU).

The JLP emphasized the role of the private sector, restructuring of the economy, reform of government, and the need for foreign private investment during its most recent term in office (1980–89) under party leader Edward Seaga. The JLP is affiliated with the International Democrat Union.

The PNP is a social democratic party. The party, now the government, pledges to improve social and educational conditions and to expand the private sector with the help of foreign investment. It is affiliated with the

Socialist International. Minor political movements do not play a significant role in Jamaican politics, although the small Communist Workers Party of Jamaica is affiliated with the expanding University and Allied Workers Union, now the country's third largest.

In the February 1989 general elections, the PNP won 45 seats, and the JLP won 15 in the House of Representatives. Major issues in the campaign included the state of social services, alleged centralization of decision making under the 1980–89 Seaga government, and the question of whether change was needed after more than 8 years of JLP rule. The election marked the return of a two-party parliament (the PNP boycotted the 1983 general election because of a dispute over voter registration) and continued the Jamaican tradition of alternating two-term governments. A preelection "peace accord" between the two parties helped minimize political campaign violence that was significantly reduced from the high level that characterized the 1980 general election.

Jamaica's political system is stable and backed by sound institutions. However, the country's serious economic problems have exacerbated social problems and have become the subject of political debate. Unemployment and shortages of foreign exchange are the most serious economic problems. Concentration of unemployed people in urban areas has produced shantytowns, contributing to a high crime rate, especially in Kingston.

Central government revenue (1988–89 estimate): $1.07 billion.

Defense (FY 1988–89 estimate): 0.8% of GDP.

Flag: Intersecting golden diagonal stripes form a saltire dividing the flag into four triangles. The top and bottom triangles are green, and the left and right are black.

Foreign Relations

Jamaica is a member of the British Commonwealth. Historically, it has had close ties with Britain, but trade, financial, and cultural relations with the United States and Canada are now predominant. Regionally, Jamaica is linked with the other countries of the English-speaking Caribbean through the Caribbean Common Market. As a member of the Nonaligned Movement, Jamaica has been active in the councils of primary-product countries, particularly with regard to their efforts to receive a better price for their exports in comparison with the prices of manufactured goods and over the question of Third World debt. Jamaica is active in the United Nations and in other international organizations.

Jamaica has diplomatic relations with most nations, and a wide range of countries and international organizations maintain missions in Kingston. Under the Seaga government, Jamaica severed diplomatic relations with Cuba in 1981, charging Cuba with interference in its internal affairs. The new Manley government has promised to restore diplomatic ties with Cuba.

U.S.-Jamaican Relations

The United States maintains close and productive relations with the government of Jamaica. Prime Minister Manley visited Washington shortly after his return to office in 1989, his first trip abroad as prime minister. He met with President Bush and other senior U.S. government officials. The United States is strongly supportive of the Jamaican government's efforts to revitalize the economy. The two governments are cooperating closely on narcotics control measures.

Trade

Trade (1987): Exports—$708.4 million: alumina, bauxite, sugar, bananas, garments, citrus fruits and products, rum, cocoa. Major markets—U.S. 37 percent, U.K. 18 percent, Canada 14 percent, Russia 4 percent, CARICOM 6 percent. Imports—$1.2 billion: machinery, transportation and electrical equipment, food, fuels, fertilizer. Major suppliers—U.S. 48 percent, U.K. 7 percent, Canada 6 percent, CARICOM 5 percent, Japan 4 percent, Venezuela 4 percent.

The Jamaican economy is heavily import dependent both for production and consumption. The United States continues to be Jamaica's leading supplier of goods and services. In 1991, U.S. exports to Jamaica amounted to $962.9 million, a decrease from the $1 billion it exported in 1989. The year 1992 showed a modest improvement in export market.

While traditional exports of minerals and agriculture remain important to the Jamaican economy, nontraditional exports have expanded significantly. Principal U.S. imports from Jamaica include bauxite/alumina, food, beverages, tobacco, and textiles.

Trade and Investment Policies

Since its election in February 1989, the Manley administration followed economic liberalization policies creating a largely open, market-oriented economy. His administration pursued a tariff reduction program and continued a successful divestment of state-owned properties. In March 1992, Prime Minister Manley resigned his post due to his deteriorating health.

The new prime minister, Persival J. Patterson, took office stating that the economic liberalization measures instituted under the Manley government would continue.

In 1991 Jamaica removed its most serious roadblock to trade by liberalizing foreign exchange transactions allowing the free flotation of the Jamaican dollar and the purchase of foreign currency in the open market. The resulting devaluation of the Jamaican dollar, however, is affecting the private sec-

tor's ability to finance imports and other types of financial transactions. Also, the government's need to service its international debt is crowding hard currency demand. Only the tourist and bauxite sectors have been spared currency problems due to their priority status. Despite these shortcomings, the government is not likely to impose new trade restrictions, leaving the way open to importers to initiate their own creative solutions toward foreign payments.

Policies to Attract New Business

The Caribbean Basin Initiative (CBI), initiated in 1984, encourages economic development in the Caribbean and Central America through export diversification led by the private sector. The CBI program provides duty-free access to the United States for most products manufactured in the Caribbean Basin. Jamaica is one of the countries in the region that has benefited the most from the opportunities available through CBI. In 1990, over half of Jamaican exports to the United States entered duty-free in part under the provisions of the CBI.

Under the CBI, manufacturers of apparel made from fabric cut and formed in the United States pay U.S. import duties only on the value added outside the United States. In 1990, the U.S. Congress added a provision to the CBI that extends similar treatment to footwear produced in CBI-beneficiary countries. As a CBI beneficiary and signatory to a Tax Information Exchange Agreement, Jamaica also has access to investment funds from Puerto Rico under Section 936 of the Internal Revenue Code, and is an eligible site for tax-deductible conventions for U.S. firms.

Nontraditional Jamaican products that offer good prospects for U.S. importers include data-processing services, apparel assembly, fruits and vegetables, horticulture, aquaculture, industrial minerals such as limestone and marble, beverages and to-bacco, light manufacturing, furniture, and handicrafts. In addition, the Caribbean mar-ket has expanded for U.S. exporters of prod-ucts essential to these new industries, includ-ing textiles and textile machinery, furnishings for tourism facilities, electronic components and computer equipment, and intermediate goods such as wood, chemi-cals, and fertilizers.

Articles excluded from CBI treatment are textiles and apparel already subject to textile agreements:

- footwear (except disposable items and parts such as uppers)

- handbags, luggage, flat goods, work gloves, and leather wearing apparel which is not covered by the Generalized System of Preferences

- canned tuna

- petroleum and petroleum products (pro-vided for in Part 10 of Schedule 4 of the U.S. Tariff Schedule)

- watches and watch parts, if any compo-nent originated in a communist country.

Ethanol, sugar, beef, and veal may be eligible for duty-free treatment but special conditions apply, such as import quotas.

Leading Trade Opportunities

Leading U.S. exports for the near term (1993–95) include mining equipment, infor-mation services, textiles, electric power sys-tems, construction equipment, agricultural and industrial chemicals, processed foods, hotel and restaurant equipment, and trucks, trailers, and buses.

APPROACHING THE MARKET

Commercial Environment

In 1992 the Jamaican economy continued to grow but at a reduced rate. Inflation in 1991 was 80.2 percent, the highest in the history of Jamaica since independence.

The incumbent government continues to profess and practice free enterprise. This includes "reducing the level of state inter-vention in market transactions, eliminating price controls, reducing the level of state involvement in the productivity sector and eliminating exchange controls."

Combined with government's efforts is that of the private sector and the Jamaican public at large. An initiative has been taken to halt the previously rapid devaluation of the Jamaican dollar and to provide a substan-tial and even flow of foreign exchange into the banking system.

These efforts have so far taken the JDol-lar from U.S. $1 = J$30 (35) to a level of U.S. $1 = J$22.6.

Should this economic stability continue, coupled with Jamaica's political stability, its traditional adherence to law and order, the government's commitment to market-ori-ented economic policies and its liberaliza-tion program, prospects for commercial op-portunities in Jamaica will be good.

The best barometers with which to track the commercial health of the Jamaican econ-omy are the world price of bauxite-alumina, the tourist entries into Jamaica, and the world price of oil. Bauxite and tourism earn U.S. $700,000,000 each plus the foreign ex-change necessary to pay the interest on the very heavy debt in these industries, as well as permit suppliers and investors to be paid their current account obligations. The oil account is a perpetual drain in foreign ex-change reserves. Jamaica brings in from 40–42,000 barrels a day. (One dollar a barrel a day increase equals over $15,000,000 U.S. $ per year).

The Jamaican government is committed to attract foreign investment in the island. The government agency Jamaican Promo-tions Ltd. (Jampro) is responsible for pursu-ing trade and investment opportunities. (Operating on the basis that trade should be bilateral, both the government and Jampro are very accommodating and cooperative on all matters of trade with the United States.)

The recent scaling down of Jampro by 20 percent is not expected to affect the level of mutually beneficial cooperation which now exists between USFCS Kingston and that organization.

Despite meager foreign exchange reserves, the government has not imposed new trade restrictions. More and more it seems to be leaving the way open for importers to initiate their own creative solutions toward foreign payments.

Jamaica is a consumer oriented country, which produces very little of its major necessities. In addition to a healthy appetite for imported consumer goods, the import content of manufactured goods ranges between 30–60 percent. The United States is the major supplier of most of the requirements of the Jamaican market.

In 1991 Jamaica moved its position from number 17 in the order of markets for U.S. exports to number 16. Overall world imports stood at U.S. $1.8 billion, 51 percent of which was from the United States.

The Common External Tariff (CET) implemented in February 1991 ought to have dramatically reduced duty rates to a maximum of 35 percent, but this has been offset by a 10 percent stamp duty, customs charges, a sliding scale of additional taxes of up to 200 percent, and the recently implemented consumption tax. These factors have boosted the effective minimum duty to 55 percent.

Under the guideline of agreements with the International Monetary Fund, efforts have been made to reduce import duties as follows:

a) 5% for utilities
b) 10% for raw materials
c) 20% for capital goods
d) 30% for consumer goods

However, in February 1990 a category of goods labeled as "luxury goods and heavy users of foreign exchange" were burdened with a consumption duty surcharge of 50 percent.

In spite of successive government efforts to simplify the trade regime, a prohibitive level of bureaucratic red tape and a cumbersome customs department continue to impede trade.

Inflation is currently running at a rate greater than 50 percent per year. Government's efforts to limit depreciation of the Jamaican dollar has led to higher interest rates and weak investment demand. Jamaican banks are currently charging up to 51 percent interest on loans and overdraft, when they are available.

There are, however, bright spots in the 1993–94 economic picture: sugar and banana exports, financial services, information services, and export of other nontraditional items are earning well needed foreign exchange.

With tourism on the upswing and other export sectors on a sound footing, prospects for the near term (1993–95) seem hopeful. The financial environment should also benefit from Government's ongoing IMF-supported economic reform program.

Implications for U.S. Exporters

Import licenses: Since 1987, the government has progressively eliminated quantitative import restraints. Currently only a few items, including certain chemicals, pharmaceuticals, vegetable saps and extracts, onions, prepared or preserved tomatoes, motor vehicles, and arms and ammunition are under import license. Excepting arms, licenses for these items are generally easily obtained. The ongoing depreciation of the Jamaican dollar is the single greatest barrier to imports.

Service barriers: The provision of power, water, and telephone services are performed by government-owned or -controlled monopolies. As pointed out above, the number of authorized foreign exchange dealers is strictly controlled. Non-Jamaicans seeking employment in Jamaica are required to obtain a work permit, which is granted at the discretion of the minister of labor.

Government procurement practices: Government procurement practices generally allow U.S. goods to compete freely. The range of manufactured goods produced in Jamaica is relatively small, so that instances of foreign goods competing with domestic manufacturers are very limited. A revised, five-year countertrade agreement between Russia and Jamaica began January 1991. Under the agreement, Jamaica is obliged to export to Russia one million metric tons of bauxite per year and receive 50 percent of the contract value in Russian goods and services and the remainder in hard currency. Due to foreign exchange shortages in Russia, only about 20 percent of the contracted amount for 1991 wasscheduled to be shipped.

Jamaica entered into a three-year countertrade agreement with a French company worth roughly U.S. $3 million per year. Under this agreement, which began January 1, 1991, Jamaica will export 150,000 tons of bauxite annually in exchange for Peugeot cars.

Customs procedures: Exporters and importers have expressed mounting concern with the slow and unpredictable service at Jamaican customs. In addition, procedures designed to stop narcotics exports are complex and can delay export shipments.

Foreign Trade and Investment Decision-Making Infrastructure

The Export Industry Encouragement Act allows approved export manufacturers access to imported raw materials and capital goods for a maximum 10-year period duty-free. As stated above, exporters are also exempted from the General Consumption Tax. Other benefits are available from the Jamaican government's Export-Import Bank, and include access to preferential financing through the Export Development Fund, lines of credit, and export credit insurance. Jamaica does not adhere to the GATT Subsidies Code.

INVESTMENT CLIMATE

U.S. companies have substantial investments in Jamaica. In 1991 the U.S. provided U.S. $70 million in grant and loan assistance. A similar amount was projected for FY92. Jamaica's financial climate also receives booster shots under the Enterprise for the Americas Initiative which has already led to a reduction in excess of U.S. $217 million in PL-480 debt.

Increased investment, particularly in the private sector, has been identified by government as an essential factor in the strategy for reviving and sustaining the economy. Government has therefore continued and initiated action in a number of areas which are intended to encourage investment.

In general the few foreign investment barriers which exist are endemic to an economy short of foreign exchange, and those areas of economic activities which up to now have been reserved as government "political" domains. Such barriers include: bureaucratic red tape and occasional bungling, restricted areas of operation, slowness of profit remittance due to tight foreign exchange situation, and competitiveness of certain local firms.

Jamaica wants and needs foreign investment. The government seeks to encourage it through various programs and incentives such as: (a) The Industrial Incentives Act—grants income tax exemptions of up to nine years to industries on the basis of local value added. (b) The Export Industries Encouragement Act—applicable to companies producing exclusively for sale outside of Jamaica and CARICOM countries. (c) The Hotel Incentives Act—provides income tax concessions for up to seven years to owners or tenant operators of resort cottages with no less than ten furnished bedrooms. (d) Guarantees against Appropriation and Naturalization—the constitution of Jamaica protects the property of local and foreign investors.

While foreign investment is welcomed and encouraged, the government would not approve participation or involvement in activities where profit does not accrue as a result of real increases in output. The government is also unlikely, except in special circumstances, to grant investment in areas where adequate capacity already exists, e.g., catering and restaurants, auditing and accounting, entertainment, advertising, and public relations. In the case of insurance companies, foreign companies are allowed to own a maximum of 49 percent of total shares. Further, there may be agreements in place between current investors and the government that provide exclusive rights to those investors.

FINANCING AND CAPITAL MARKETS

General Policy Framework

Over the last decade two successive Jamaican administrations have worked hard to dismantle elements of statist economic policies and government intervention in the economy. Through this process a largely open, market-oriented economy has been created. Since the internal economy is small, however, Jamaica depends on trade for its economic welfare, and is vulnerable to economic conditions overseas. At U.S. $1,500, Jamaica's per capita Gross Domestic Product puts it in the mid-range of developing countries.

The administration of Prime Minister Manley continued and expanded the free market policies begun by the former prime minister, Seaga. To reduce the role of the government in the economy and improve competitiveness, various sectors of the economy have been deregulated (e.g., petroleum products, motor vehicle imports) and a number of government entities have been privatized. In addition, the government has eliminated subsidies on basic food items.

These initiatives are also part of an ongoing government effort to cope with a chronic balance-of-payments problem, exacerbated by an exceptionally heavy official debt burden. The focus of this effort is a structural adjustment program which includes fiscal and monetary restraint, tax reform, lower external tariffs, and a market-based exchange rate.

These programs are producing encouraging results: the government budget deficit continues to fall as a proportion of GDP; prices, and the Jamaican dollar exchange rate, now better reflect supply and demand; and taxes are less likely to distort economic decisions.

Fiscal policy: The Jamaica fiscal year (JFY) 1991–92 budget (ending in March 1992) provides for continued spending austerity. The budget is designed to reduce the public sector deficit to 2.2 percent of GDP via a 2 percent real increase in tax revenues (including new and expanded taxes) and a 5 percent real decrease in central government expenditures.

Budgeted central government expenditure for JFY 1991–92 is J$14.7 billion, of which 41 percent is allocated to debt servicing. The sharp depreciation of the Jamaican dollar during the second half of 1991 has put pressure on government planners to cut spending on capital projects and to ensure better tax compliance to achieve its budget deficit goals.

Monetary policy: To control inflation

and to reduce the demand for scarce foreign exchange, the government continues to maintain a high cash reserve ratio and to sell new government securities. These policies have enjoyed only partial success, however. High interest (currently 30–35 percent) paid by the government on these securities is not balanced by new revenue inflows, and thus contributes to sharp increases in the money supply. Nevertheless, these policies have resulted in very high commercial bank lending rates, averaging 35 percent in October 1991. Aware of the effects of these policies, the Bank of Jamaica has indicated its intention to rely on more orthodox open market operations in the future.

Debt Management Policies

The government continues to service a large stock of official external debt. At the end of 1990, total external debt amounted to U.S. $4.15 billion representing 106 percent of GDP or 177.6 percent of exports of goods and services. Per capita debt amounts to U.S. $1,730. Debt-service payments obligations account for 37.6 percent of exports of goods and services, and hence continue to be a major burden on the government.

Jamaica completed its latest IMF stand-by program in March 1991 and has negotiated a new U.S. $59 million 12-month stand-by agreement for JFY 1991–92. Jamaica continues to benefit from a multi-year-rescheduling–debt/equity-swap arrangement concluded in 1987 with commercial banks. To date, about U.S. $85 million, or 21 percent of commercial debt, has been converted via the program. Under the Enterprise for the Americas Initiative, the U.S. government in 1991 reduced Jamaica's U.S. $271 million PL-480 debt to U.S. $57 million, an 80 percent reduction. A proposal to reduce other categories of Jamaica's debt to the U.S. is now before the U.S. Congress.

The Currency and Exchange Rate Mechanisms

Faced with declining inflows of foreign exchange into the interbank foreign exchange system and an expanding gap between the official and black market rates, the government removed virtually all controls on foreign exchange in 1991. Under the new system, persons or companies that earn or receive foreign exchange are free to retain it either in Jamaica or overseas, and payments in any currency acceptable to the buyer and seller are permitted. Jamaican residents can purchase foreign exchange freely and maintain foreign currency accounts in Jamaica or overseas. Also, capital flows, including dividends and portfolio investments, no longer require Bank of Jamaica approval. The main remaining restriction is that foreign exchange transactions must be effected through a licensed dealer, and licenses are tightly restricted. In addition, any company or person having payments to make to the government by agreement or law (such as the levy and royalty due on bauxite) will continue to make such payments directly to the Bank of Jamaica.

Banking and Other Financial Institutions

There are two full-service non-Jamaican banks: Citibank and the bank of Nova Scotia, both of which have all rights and offer all services as any Jamaican bank. Additionally, Jamaican banks act as correspondent banks for both the U.S. private banks as well as EX-IM and OPIC.

Services are also available through agencies of the following three Jamaican banks in Miami:

The Jamaica Citizens Bank
The National Commercial Bank Ja. Ltd.
Island Victoria Ltd.

Overseas Private Investment Corporation (OPIC) is on cover for Jamaica, and has in the past two years backed four successful ventures.

Jamaica may also benefit from a U.S. Ex-Im Bank import facility which is administered through the National Ex-Im Bank of Jamaica. The financial environment has some bright spots favorable to U.S. trade, despite negatives such as high inflation, a high debt service burden, and foreign exchange uncertainties.

The basic sale purchase system remains the same. The supplier provides an invoice which the purchaser uses to clear the goods. The purchaser then according to the sale terms attempts to purchase the foreign exchange from one or a number of banks. The fact that deregulation has made it unnecessary for importers to lodge these documents with the central bank, or an individual commercial bank, and to join a waiting list, has opened the way for a better relationship between exporter and importer.

There are at present no countertrade requirements imposed by the government of Jamaica.

Tapping International Aid Institutions

Economic and development assistance received: U.S. aid—$74 million (FY 1988). International Monetary Fund—SDR82 million (for 14-month period beginning September 1988). Multilateral organizations (1987)—$127 million. Bilateral countries (1987)—$129 million.

Contact points for the IDB and the World Bank are as follows:

Michelle D. Miller, Inter-American Development Bank Liaison
U.S. Department of Commerce
14th & Constitution Avenue, NW
Washington, D.C. 20230
Tel: (202) 482-1246
Fax: (202) 482-3954

Janice Mazur, World Bank Liaison
U.S. Department of Commerce
14th & Constitution Avenue, NW
Washington, D.C. 20230
Tel: (202) 482-4332

Financial Market Operations and Structural Policies

Prices in Jamaica are generally determined by the forces of demand and supply. Pursuant to Jamaica's 1990 agreement with the International Monetary Fund, the government has successfully removed all price controls, except for domestic kerosene, dark sugar, bus fares, and motor vehicle parts. Price increases for these items require the approval of a government minister. However, prices on an array of export agricultural products are controlled by various marketing authorities; namely, the Coffee Board, the Cocoa Board, the Citrus Growers Association, the Sugar Industry Authority, and the Banana Exporting Company.

Estimated tax receipts for JFY 1991–92 comprise 83.5 percent (J$10 billion) of total government revenue. Major taxes are income tax (J$4.5 billion), consumption duty (J$1.9 billion), stamp duties (J$1.1 billion), and customs duty (J$1 billion).

Jamaica implemented the Caribbean Common Market (CARICOM) Common External Tariff (CET) in 1991. Under this system, goods produced in CARICOM states are not subject to import duty. Goods coming into Jamaica from outside CARICOM are subject to import duties ranging between 5 percent and 45 percent, with higher rates applicable to "nonbasic" and finished goods, as well as goods competing with those produced in CARICOM states.

Suspensions granted to Jamaica include cod, mackerel, herrings, alewives, powdered milk, maize, soya beans, and rice. In addition to these duties, imports of some items bear special import duties: liquor, cigarettes, petroleum products, and certain vegetables.

Effective October 22, 1991, the government introduced a value-added style General Consumption Tax (GCT) at a flat ad valorem rate of 10 percent. The GCT replaced excise duties, consumption duties, additional stamp duties, retail sales taxes, telephone service taxes, entertainment taxes, and hotel taxes. There are a number of exemptions to the GCT: basic food staples, medical services, and residential rent payments are the most significant examples. Imports are subject to the GCT at the port of entry; all goods exported are exempt from the GCT.

With the exception of imports of milk solids, monopoly rights of the state Jamaica Commodity Trading Company (JCTC) ceased June 30, 1991. The U.S. Embassy is unaware of any government regulatory policy that would have a significant adverse impact on U.S. exports.

Chapter 14

MEXICO

	Total	Urban	
Population (1993)	94,011,000	71.0%	

Main Urban Areas	Population	Percentage of Total	International Calling Code
MEXICO CITY	8,831,000	9.4	52-5
Guadalajara	1,626,000	1.7	52-36
Monterrey	1,090,000	1.2	52-83
Puebla	836,000	0.9	52-22
Leon	656,000	0.7	52-471
Ciudad Juarez	567,000	0.6	52-16
Culiacan	560,000	0.6	52-671
Mexicali	511,000	0.5	52-65
Tijuana	461,000	0.5	52-66
Merida	425,000	0.5	52-99
Acapulco	409,000	0.4	52-748
Chihuahua	407,000	0.4	52-14
San Luis Potosi	407,000	0.4	52-481
Hermosillo	341,000	0.4	52-62
Mazatlan	250,000	0.3	52-678

Land Area	1,923,040 square kilometers
Comparable U.S. State	Slightly less than three times the size of Texas
Language	Spanish 91%
	(Largest Spanish-speaking population in the world)
	Nahautl 2%
	Yucatec 1%
	Amerindian, other 6%
Common Business Language	Spanish, English
Currency	1 new peso (Mex$) = 100 centavos
SPSP Exchange Rate (May 1993)	U.S. $1.00 = 2.86 new pesos
Best Nonstop Air Connection via US	Dallas to Mexico City: 1.5 hours
	American Airlines (800) 433-7300
	Seven nonstops daily
	Delta Airlines (800) 241-4141
	Two nonstops daily
Best Hotel	Nikko Mexico City (US$160-210)
	Campos Eliseos 204 Col. Polanco
	11560 Mexico City
	Tel: (905) 280-1111, (800) 645-5687
	Fax: (905) 280-919

INTRODUCTION AND REGIONAL ORIENTATION

Many of Mexico's abundant natural resources are still untapped and represent attractive opportunities for future growth and development.

Diversified soils and temperatures have enabled the country to produce a wide variety of agricultural products, such as grains, fruits and horticultural products, and timber. There are 57 million acres of arable land, of which 14 million currently are irrigated.

Mexico's waters offer great opportunities for the future. It is estimated that Mexico's waters potentially could yield nine million metric tons of fish per year. Despite the fact that Mexico currently only uses one-fifth of this capacity, it is the thirteenth largest fishing country in the world and is developing this sector rapidly.

The country is also rich in mineral deposits. The potential for growth in the exploitation of these resources is great, since it is estimated that only 1 percent is presently being extracted. Mexico is also a prominent oil and gas producer and exporter. Proven oil reserves total 66 billion barrels, about seven percent of the world's proven reserves. With crude oil production averaging 2.5 million barrels per day, Mexico ranks as the fifth largest oil producer in the world.

Mexico is the most populous Spanish-speaking country in the world. Its population of approximately 86 million inhabitants is the eleventh largest in the world and the third largest in Latin America after Brazil and Argentina. Mexico is a young country with 69 percent of its population under 30 years of age. The Mexican government has stressed the importance of education, health, and housing as top priorities to accelerate Mexico's development and is investing large amounts of resources in these areas.

According to 1987 estimates, the urban population of Mexico City may have grown to 20 million, which would make greater Mexico City the largest urban concentration in the world. The northwestern region which borders the United States also had a sharp rise.

Mexico has a relatively well developed industrial infrastructure, which will continue to provide support for steady growth in the leading economic sectors. This includes 57,000 miles of paved roads, 17,000 miles of railways, 43 national and 35 international airports, and 84 ports. Mexico has over nine million telephones and 108,000 GWH of electricity production capacity.

The country's industrial production is varied and dynamic. Some of its most important sectors include: food and beverages, such as milk and meat products; grain milling; fruit and vegetable preparations; sugar; oils; soft drinks; beer and other alcoholic beverages; textiles products, apparel, and footwear; petroleum refining, petrochemicals, chemicals, fertilizers, synthetic resins, and artificial fibers; pharmaceuticals, soaps and toiletries, rubber and plastic products; glass, cement, and nonmetallic mineral products; iron, steel, and other primary metal industries; metal products; machinery; electric appliances; electronics; electric apparatus; automobiles and other transportation equipment.

Geographical Background

Mexico is the thirteenth largest country in the world. Its territory of 1.978 million square kilometers (764,000 square miles) is larger than that of continental Western Europe. Its Atlantic, Pacific, and Caribbean coastlines measure 6,303 miles. Mexico is bounded on the north by the United States, with whom it shares a border of more than 2,000 miles.

The topography of Mexico ranges from low desert plains and jungle-like coastal strips to high plateaus and rugged mountains. Beginning at the Isthmus of Tehuantepec in southern Mexico, an extension of a South American mountain range runs north almost to Mexico City, where it divides to form the coastal Occidental (west) and Oriental (east) ranges of the Sierra Madre. Between these ranges lies the great central plateau, a rugged tableland 2,400 kilometers (1,500 miles) long and as much as 800 kilometers (500 miles) wide. From a low desert plain in the north, it rises to 2,400 meters (8,000 feet) above sea level near Mexico City.

Mexico's climate is generally more closely related to altitude and rainfall than to latitude. Most of Mexico is dry; only about 12 percent of the total area receives adequate rainfall in all seasons, while about one-half is deficient in moisture throughout the year. Temperatures range from tropical in the coastal lowlands to cool in the higher elevations.

History and Political Conditions

An advanced Indian civilization existed in Mexico before the Spanish conquest. Cortes conquered Mexico in 1519–21 and founded a Spanish colony that lasted nearly 300 years. Mexico's independent republic was established on December 6, 1822. Antonio Lopez de Santa Ana controlled Mexican politics from 1833 to 1855.

Santa Ana led Mexico during the conflict with Texas, which declared itself independent from Mexico in 1836, and during the war with the United States (1846–48). Benito Juarez was president of Mexico from 1858 to 1871. His terms, however, were interrupted when Napoleon III of France established Archduke Maximilian of Austria emperor of Mexico in 1864. The Archduke was deposed and executed by Juarez in 1867.

Mexico's drastic social and economic problems erupted in the revolution of 1910.

The Institutional Revolutionary Party, under various names and after a number of reorganizations (now known as the Partido Revolucionario Institucional—PRI), continues to be the most important political force in the nation.

CRACKING THE MARKET

Demographics

Ethnic groups: Indian-Spanish (mestizo) 60%; American Indian 30%; Caucasian 9%; other 1%

Religions: Roman Catholic 97%; Protestant 3%

Work force (26.3 million, 1989): agriculture, forestry, hunting, fishing 26%; manufacturing 12.8%; commerce 13.9%; services 31.4%; mining and quarrying 1.3%; construction 9.5%; electricity 0.3%; transportation and communication 4.8%.

Natural resources: petroleum, silver, copper, gold, lead, zinc, natural gas, timber.

Agriculture: Products—corn, beans, oilseeds, feed grains, fruit, cotton, coffee, sugarcane, winter vegetables.

Industry: Types—manufacturing, services, commerce, transportation and communications, petroleum and mining.

Trade (1989 estimate):

Exports (U.S. $22.8 billion): manufacturing 55.3%; petroleum and derivatives 33.8%; agriculture 8.2%; mining 2.7%.

Imports (U.S. $23.8 billion): intermediate goods 66.4%; capital goods 19.3%; consumer goods 14.3%; major trading partners U.S., EC, Japan.

Economy

Top macroeconomic priorities for the Mexican government during 1992 were controlling inflation, increasing government tax receipts, completing both the bank privatization process and negotiations of the North American Free Trade Agreement (NAFTA), promoting regulations to modernize industry and the Mexican financial system, and maintaining a viable external accounts position. The government was successful in all of those areas.

The long-term economic objectives of the Salinas administration are to renew sustained economic growth with inflation similar to levels in the industrialized countries, to make the economy more internationally competitive, to achieve greater North American integration, and to reduce poverty levels. During 1992, the government has pursued very restrictive fiscal and monetary policies and has been willing to sacrifice some economic expansion, in an effort to force a rapid decline of inflation.

Between 1982 and 1988 there was no overall expansion in the economy and real per capita income fell by more than 15 percent. The medium-term strategy is to progressively stimulate the economy by promoting increased availability of goods and services, while tempering growth of domestic demand in order not to induce inflationary pressures.

In the National Development Plan released in May 1989 the government projected average annual economic growth between 2.9 and 3.5 percent during the 1989–91 period, and between 5.3 and 6.0 percent annual growth for the 1992–94 period. The government was on target with its growth objectives for 1989 and surpassed its objectives in 1990 and 1991. However, growth will be significantly lower than projected for 1992.

With a government committed to streamlining the state and limiting its role in the economy, most of this growth is expected to come from the private sector. Structural reforms to improve domestic economic efficiency and further open the economy are helping to promote this expansion. During

the past year the government has encouraged private investment in infrastructure projects (such as highways and electrical plants) that were previously reserved for the public sector. It has modified the Mexican Constitution to permit private ownership of former communal farm lands. In July 1992, the state-owned oil monopoly, Pemex, was reorganized and may allow more private investment, and in June the mining law was modified to allow more foreign investment.

Over the past four and one-half years economic policy has been implemented under the Economic Solidarity Pact (ESP), begun in December 1987, and its successor, the Pact for Stability and Economic Growth (PSEG), which remained in effect through January 1993.

The ESP was developed at a time of economic uncertainty, characterized by accelerating inflation, speculation against the peso, problems in financing public sector expenditures, and collapse of the stock market. The ESP was a heterodox program, combining tight fiscal and monetary policies with price, wage, and exchange rate controls and rapid trade liberalization. The intent was to reduce inflation and restore confidence in Mexican macroeconomic policy without falling into a deep recession. The pact was formally signed by representatives of the government, labor, rural, and private sectors in order to maximize support for the tough economic program.

The ESP was largely successful. Over the course of 1988 inflation fell from 159 percent to 52 percent by the year's end, while economic growth was a modest 1.2 percent. International reserves grew to record levels, but declined in the second half of the year because of growing imports, falling petroleum prices, and the government's financing requirements. The public sector fiscal deficit dropped as a percentage of GDP, but fell somewhat short of its target.

In December 1988, the incoming Salinas

administration announced the extension of the ESP in a modified, renamed version—the Pact for Stability and Economic Growth (PSEG). The PSEG was similar to the ESP with the most important modification being a relaxation of the exchange rate policy, replacing the exchange rate freeze with a controlled exchange rate that devalued one peso per day against the dollar. The first phase of the PSEG ran from January 1 to July 31, 1989. During that period most controlled prices remained frozen, although some were revised, and the minimum import tariff was raised from zero to 10 percent. The minimum wage was increased 8 percent, and the government pledged continuation of tight fiscal policies.

The administration has extended the pact four times since mid-1989. The one peso per day devaluation policy remained in effect from January 1989 through May 1990. In late May the rate of devaluation was decreased to 80 centavos per day and in November 1990 it was again cut to 40 centavos per day. Under the pact which became effective November 10, 1991, and was to last through January 31, 1993, the controlled exchange rate was replaced by an exchange rate that floats within a band, the upper limit of which devalues by 20 centavos per day. The administration is using the exchange rate as a tool to control inflation, and by decreasing the rate of devaluation it hopes to limit the inflation caused by higher-priced imports and self-fulfilling higher inflationary expectations.

Recent versions of the pact have allowed for price adjustments to prevent shortages, and better align relative prices so as to help prevent repressed inflationary pressures from building excessively. The government relaxed some of the price and wage controls in 1989 and accelerated the process in 1990 and 1991. This was one of the major reasons for the temporary upswing in inflation in 1990. The government has continued to follow tight fiscal and monetary policies which have resulted in a sharp decrease in the public sector financial (overall) deficit and an increase in government revenues.

Two other important features of the November 1991 extension of the pact were a 12 percent increase in minimum wages and a reduction in the value-added tax from rates of 20 and 15 percent to a uniform rate of 10 percent.

Gross Domestic Product

GDP grew by an estimated 2.8 percent in the first half of 1992, down from 3.6 percent in 1991 and 4.4 percent in 1990 (see Table 14-1). Economic growth slowed significantly in the second quarter of 1992 due to high domestic interest rates and tight fiscal policies which have discouraged consumption. During the first half of 1992 compared to the same period in 1991, agricultural output increased 1.1 percent, industrial production increased 2.5 percent, and the services sector grew 3.3 percent. Construction, transportation and communications, and the metal products, machinery, and equipment subsector are still performing well despite the overall slowdown in the economy.

Investment was expected to increase during 1992 by almost 10 percent in real terms, spurred by an 11.4 percent increase in private sector investment and a 5 percent real increase in public sector investments. In light of the slowdown of the economy, this projection may have been somewhat high. However, Mexico should still enjoy a robust growth in investments, given that the private sector continues to make large investments to become more internationally competitive and take advantage of greater North American economic integration. Also, major infrastructure projects, such as the Mexico City to Acapulco Toll Road, are underway.

Inflation

The inflation rate for the first seven months

Table 14-1
Gross Domestic Product by Sector, 1988–1992
(Percent Change[1])

	1988[2]	1989	1990	1991	Jan.–Jun.[2] 1992
General index (1980 = 100)	1.2	3.3	4.4	3.6	2.8
Agriculture	−3.8	−3.9	6.1	0.5	1.1
Mining	0.4	−0.6	2.8	0.1	1.0
Manufacturing	3.2	7.2	5.8	3.7	2.1
Construction	−0.4	2.1	7.0	2.6	4.9
Electricity	6.0	6.5	2.6	4.1	3.8
Retailing, restaurants, hotels	1.6	4.1	4.6	4.5	2.9
Transportation, communications	2.3	4.0	7.0	6.0	7.6
Financial services	1.6	2.9	2.2	4.1	N./A.
Other services	0.5	1.3	1.9	3.7	N./A.
Selected manufacturing subindices					
Food, beverages, tobacco	0.2	7.7	3.0	2.0	0.9
Textiles and clothing	0.8	3.5	2.2	−3.4	1.1
Wood, wood products	−2.4	−1.5	−2.0	−1.1	−5.0
Paper, printing	4.1	7.0	4.4	−1.3	−6.4
Chemical, rubber, plastics	2.0	9.2	5.2	3.1	2.8
Non-metallic minerals	−1.6	4.8	6.3	1.3	6.8
Basic metals	5.2	2.5	7.4	−2.6	−7.4
Metal products, machinery	13.0	11.1	13.1	15.1	7.2

1. Percentage changes are with respect to the same period of the previous year.
2. Data from 1988 forward was revised.

Source: National Statistical Institute, "Cuaderno de Informacion Oportuna, 5/92." Data for January–June 1992 is from "El Economista, 8/24/92."

of 1992 (through July 31) was 7.1 percent, which is Mexico's lowest seven-month inflation figure since 1972 (see Tables 14-2, 14-3, and 14-4). Inflation was 18.8 percent in 1991 and 29.9 percent in 1990. The official inflation estimate for 1992 was 9.7 percent, but the actual figure was probably closer to 11 percent. Finance Minister Aspe said in July 1991 that 1992 inflation would likely run between 10 and 11 percent. Inflation tends to be high toward the end of the year both because of seasonal factors and

because of increases in the minimum wage and prices of key products, such as gasoline and electricity, that are announced when the Pact for Economic Growth and Stability is extended.

Since 1988, the Salinas administration has pursued a consistent and successful policy aimed at controlling inflation by:

• reducing public sector internal borrowing and expenditures so the government does not create inflationary pressure (between May 1991 and May 1992, the

Table 14-2
Consumer and Producer Price Indices[A]
(Percent Changes)

Consumer Price Indices	1991	1992	Producer Price Indices	1991	1992
	(Jan-July)			(Jan-June)	
General index	18.8	7.1	General index	11.0	7.2
Food	15.5	5.5	Agroindustry	17.7	13.9
Clothing	11.7	7.3	Mining	−7.0	0.6
Housing	23.9	8.1	Petroleum	−19.6	21.8
Household items	11.9	6.6	Food and Tobacco	15.9	3.7
Health care	16.7	9.3	Chemicals	13.3	5.8
Transportation	29.8	6.1	Machinery and equipment	7.9	4.3
Education	24.1	7.8	Construction	15.9	5.8
Other services	13.6	8.4	Electricity	45.5	−7.7

A. The consumer price index is calculated monthly based on 140,000 price quotes taken in 35 Mexican cities regarding 1,200 different products and services. Those price quotes are then separated among the 302 different generic products and services that comprise the Mexican consumer price index. The weighting given to each type of expenditure is based on a national survey taken in 1977.

Source: Bank of Mexico, "Indicadores Economicos 6/92."

Table 14-3
Evolution of Inflation in Mexico[A]
Percentages Increase in the National Consumer Price Index
(1978 = 100)

	Monthly Rate	Year to Date	Annual Index[1]
1987–Dec.	159.2	159.2	10,647.2
1988–Dec.	51.7	51.7	16,147.3
1989–Dec.	19.7	19.7	19,327.9
1990–Dec.	29.9	29.9	25,112.7

A. The consumer price index is calculated monthly based on 140,000 price quotes taken in 35 Mexican cities regarding 1,200 different products and services. Those price quotes are then separated among the 302 different generic products and services that comprise the Mexican consumer price index. The weighting given to each type of expenditure is based on a national survey taken in 1977.

1. Annual = (index in month i of year t / index in month i of year t-1) − 1.

Source: Bank of Mexico, "Indicadores Economicos 7/92," and the "Diario Oficial."

Table 14-4
Increase in the National Producer Price Index[B]
Including Petroleum (1980 = 100)

	Monthly Rate	Year to Date	Annual Index 1/
1987–Dec.	166.5	166.5	6,676.7
1988–Dec.	37.3	37.3	9,169.8
1989–Dec.	15.6	15.6	10,598.1
1990–Dec.	29.2	29.2	13,692.2

B. The producer price index is calculated monthly based on 6,000 price quotes taken from 1,500 companies located throughout Mexico. Those price quotes are then separated among the 592 generic articles that comprise the Mexican producer price index. The weighting given to each type of expenditure is based on a national survey taken in 1970.
1. Annual = (index in month i of year t / index in month i of year t-1) – 1.

Source: Bank of Mexico, "Incicadores Economicos 7/92."

amount of outstanding internal debt fell by 21 percent in real terms);

- controlling aggregate demand through tight fiscal and monetary policies (a balanced budget and high interest rates are evidence of these policies);

- keeping the rate of the devaluation of the peso low and predictable;

- closely monitoring wage and price increases throughout the economy;

- correcting relative price distortions to prevent shortages of critical goods and services;

- liberalizing the trade regime to lower import costs and increase price competition for domestic producers; and

- sterilizing a large portion of capital inflows (the Bank of Mexico sterilized about 40 percent of capital inflows in 1991 by issuing internal debt instruments).

Since the inception of the economic pacts the government has emphasized the exchange rate as a tool to control inflation. The government argues that an important part of Mexico's inflation is derived from the rise in foreign prices and the devaluation of the exchange rate. By decreasing the rate of devaluation of the peso the government hopes to limit the inflation caused by higher priced imports. This concern was not so important for 1992 since the U.S. accounts for almost 70 percent of Mexico's imports and U.S. consumer price inflation was expected to be only about 2.7 percent, compared to 3.1 percent in 1991.

A major factor in lowering inflation during 1992 was the Bank of Mexico's restrictive monetary policies that are keeping interest rates high. High real interest rates lower inflation because they encourage financial savings rather than consumption. Less consumption means lower demand for products, which tends to limit producers' and merchants' ability to raise prices. Higher interest rates also increase the borrowing costs of producers, which producers can pass on to consumers via higher priced products, but in Mexico they have been forced to absorb a portion of these increased costs because of reduced demand. Although Mexico seemed unlikely to achieve its 9.7 percent inflation target for 1992, a continuation of the trends may since have brought Mexico's inflation level down to a single digit. Bringing inflation down to the level of Mexico's major trading partners is extremely important, since low inflation will encourage financial savings, limit wage increases (thereby increasing productivity), and limit further the real appreciation of the peso which will make Mexican exports more competitive.

Monetary Policy and Interest Rates

The primary goal of Mexico's monetary policy is to create a stable, low inflation economic environment conducive to private-sector driven economic growth. The Bank of Mexico pursues this objective by:

- eliminating from the economy excess liquidity that could otherwise cause inflationary pressure;

- assuring it places enough domestic debt to meet the government's financing needs (which are rapidly decreasing, so this objective is not difficult to achieve);

- assuring there are sufficient capital inflows to finance Mexico's current account deficit; and

- assuring interest rates remain high enough to encourage financial savings.

The Bank of Mexico is able to eliminate excess liquidity from the economy and raise interest rates by increasing the size of its weekly primary auction of government securities and/or selling treasury bills in the secondary market. Both actions take money out of the economy and put upward pressure on interest rates. Alternatively, when credit is too tight, the Bank of Mexico can diminish the size of its weekly primary auction and/or buy treasury bills in the secondary market. Both actions put money into the economy and tend to lower interest rates.

In 1991 and the first half of 1992, nominal interest rates (as measured by the 28-day treasury bill rate) first declined steadily from a December 1990 average of almost 26 percent down to a December 1991 average of 16.65 percent, and finally a low of 11.0 percent in mid-March 1992. This dramatic fall in interest rates was due to both changes in regulatory policies and increased investor confidence in Mexico.

Policies that tended to reduce interest rates in 1991 were:

- a December 1990 announcement that foreigners could purchase Mexican treasury bills;

- tight fiscal policies that led to a real reduction of internal debt at the same time that the universe of buyers for that debt was expanded to include foreigners;

- a September 1991 decision to reduce the liquidity coefficient (a type of reserve requirement) for Mexican commercial banks from 30 percent of average daily deposits during each month to a fixed level of 25 percent of average daily deposits during August 1991; and

- a simultaneous September announcement that there would be no liquidity coefficient requirement for any increase in bank deposits above their August 1991 level.

The aforementioned policies led to an increase in the availability of credit. Meanwhile, a booming Mexican stock market in 1991, bright prospects for growth under NAFTA, and declining U.S. interest rates made investing in pesos extremely attractive to dollar-based investors. Foreign holdings of Mexican government debt increased from 9.1 trillion pesos (U.S. $3.1 billion) on February 22, 1991 to 10.2 trillion (U.S. $3.4 billion) on December 20, 1991 and 17.5 trillion pesos (U.S. $6.0 billion) as of March 20, 1992.

In April 1992, the previous trend of rapidly declining interest rates was reversed because of policy changes followed by a change in investors' perceptions of Mexico. On April 1, the Bank of Mexico announced that Mexican banks must limit their foreign borrowing to 10 percent of total liabilities. Although this was a necessary and prudent measure, it reduced capital inflows which caused a decrease in the availability of credit and an increase in interest rates.

To partly offset the decrease in liquidity, the Bank of Mexico undertook the following three measures involving government securities that commercial banks held at the Bank of Mexico to meet the 25 percent liquidity coefficient. First, the Bank of Mexico eliminated the obligation to purchase 10-year bonds with the government securities that had been frozen in accounts at the Bank of Mexico for that purpose. As soon as those securities mature, the money will be returned to commercial banks. Second, the Bank of Mexico began allowing banks to transfer part of their securities from frozen accounts to tradeable accounts. Third, the Bank of Mexico decided to slowly repurchase the outstanding 10-year bonds.

New Pesos

The most important change to affect Mexican money, effective January 1, 1993, was the introduction of a new monetary unit, called the new peso.

The new peso represents 1,000 old pesos and it was introduced into the economy in three phases.

During the first phase (June–December 1992) bills and coins were printed. The second phase (January 1, 1993–January 1, 1994) saw the introduction of the new currency and coins into circulation. All of the new bills have the phrase "new pesos" printed on them. The third phase, scheduled to begin in 1995, will see a new set of bills introduced that will simply be denominated "pesos" instead of "new pesos."

The new coins in circulation will be different in size, form, weight and color from those currently in circulation. The peso coins will be denominated in 1, 2, 5, and 10 peso units. Centavo coins will be introduced in 5, 10, 20, and 50 centavo units.

During the period when new pesos are being put into circulation and old pesos are being phased out, both new and old pesos will be completely interchangeable. Prices for all goods and services will be marked in both new and old pesos and both must be accepted for all kinds of payments. Once the Bank of Mexico believes that the time is appropriate, it will publish in the Diario Oficial (official gazette) the date on which old pesos will cease to circulate. However, the Bank of Mexico will continue to exchange new pesos for old pesos for two years following that date.

As the new currency is introduced there will clearly be the danger that unscrupulous merchants may try to disguise price increases or convince naive shoppers to pay with new pesos for an item whose price is listed in old pesos. However, such abuses are apt to be very limited. The government's success at requiring merchants to reduce the value-added tax from 15 to 10 percent in November 1991 shows that it can implement a new policy rapidly and with great success.

Balance of Payments

During the first 3 months of 1992, Mexico ran a U.S. $4.4 billion current account deficit and financed it with a U.S. $5.6 billion capital account surplus (see Tables 14-5 and 14-6). There was a U.S. $4.0 billion trade account deficit reflecting a 27.7 percent increase in imports and only an 0.6 percent increase in exports. Although manufactured exports performed well (they increased 16.8 percent versus first quarter 1991), all other exports were hurt by exogenous factors, such as declining international oil prices, a depressed minerals market worldwide, and an unusually cold, wet winter in Mexico.

Table 14-5
Mexico's Balance of Payments
(U.S. $ millions)

	1990	1991	Jan–Mar 1992
Current account blance	−7,113.9	−13,282.8	−4,389.6
Merchandise trade balance (net)	−4,433.5	−11,063.7	−3,999.6
Tourism (net)	1,464.4	1,905.1	741.5
In-bond	3,551.2	4,133.9	1,078.2
Frontier transactions (net)	−1,526.1	−1,712.3	−445.6
Interest payments	−6,527.6	−5,481.7	−1,493.6
Transfers (net)	3,465.0	2,241.9	552.8
Other items (net)	−3,117.1	−3,305.8	−823.3
Capital account balance	8,163.6	20,179.0	5,570.0
Liabilities	16,863.1	21,649.8	7,087.3
Debt	12,235.4	9,348.2	1,929.5
Development banks	4,995.1	2,340.7	764.4
Commercial banks	4,250.4	5,119.1	−14.7
Bank of Mexico	−365.1	−220.0	−194.0
Public nonbanking	1,859.0	−586.4	732.4
Private nonbanking	1,496.0	2,694.8	641.4
Foreign investment	4,627.7	12,301.5	5,157.9
Direct	2,633.2	4,761.5	1,421.0
Portfolio	1,994.5	7,540.0	3,736.9
Assets	−8,699.5	−1,470.8	−1,517.3
In banks abroad	760.7	496.7	61.0
Foreign credits	−529.5	−116.5	−40.0
Guarantees on external debt	−7,354.0	−604.3	−172.3
Other	−1,576.7	−1,246.6	−1,366.0
Errors and omissions	2,183.2	1,241.0	−431.1
Reserve change[1]	3,232.9	8,137.4	749.3

1. Reserves were valued using IMF criteria, plus silver. Gold was valued at U.S. $42.22 per ounce.

Source: Bank of Mexico, "Indicadores Economicos 7/92."

Gross international reserves amounted to U.S. $18.3 billion at the end of March and U.S. $18,023 million as of August 21, 1992. Enough capital to finance the current account deficit appears to be entering Mexico largely to take advantage of the high domestic interest rates and despite the precipitous decline of the Mexican stock index.

Since 1990, Mexico has run large current account deficits that have been more than offset by large capital account surpluses. As a result, Mexico has seen an impressive in-

Table 14-6
Mexico's Trade Balance
During the First Three Months of 1991 and 1992
(U.S. $ million)

	1Q91	1Q92	Change
Total exports	6,472	6,508	0.6
Petroleum exports	2,028	1,765	−13.0
Crude petroleum	1,747	1,541	−11.8
Others	281	224	−20.3
Nonpetroleum exports	4,444	4,744	6.7
Agriculture	893	681	−23.8
Mining	147	87	−40.6
Manufacturing	3,404	3,976	16.8
Total imports	8,229	10,508	27.7
Consumer goods	1,270	1,557	22.6
Intermediate goods	5,207	6,471	24.3
Capital goods	1,751	2,480	41.6
Trade balance	−1,757	−4,000	127.6
In-bond industries	909	1,078	18.6
Trade balance including in-bond	−848	−2,922	244.6

Source: Bank of Mexico "Indicadores Economicos 7/92."

crease in its foreign exchange reserves from U.S. $6.9 billion in 1989 to U.S. $10.3 billion in 1990, U.S. $17.5 billion in 1991, and U.S. $18.0 billion in August 1992.

The current account is composed of the trade account (exports minus imports) plus the nonfactor services account (which includes revenue from foreign tourists in Mexico and the maquiladora industry minus expenditures by Mexican tourists abroad and shipping and insurance costs on exports) plus the factor services account (which includes interest revenue paid by foreigners to Mexicans minus interest expenditures on Mexico's external debt) and the unilateral transfers account, which consistently is a large surplus due to workers' remittances to Mexico.

Since 1989 Mexico has been importing far more goods than it has been exporting and this is the major reason for Mexico's current account deficit. Prior to 1989 the primary reason for a current account deficit in Mexico was large interest payments on its external debt. Since the renegotiation of Mexico's external debt, although interest payments are still large, they are a far smaller burden due to both a decrease in the size of those payments and renewed growth of the economy.

Regarding Mexico's balance of payments figures, in June 1992 the Bank of Mexico made significant revisions to those figures dating back to 1985. The analysis in this report was made using the revised figures. The revisions did not change Mexico's foreign exchange reserves, but they did change the mix of capital inflows and outflows leading to the increase or decrease in those reserves.

For example, due to the revisions, Mexico's 1990 current account deficit increased by roughly U.S. $0.8 billion, the capital account surplus decreased by U.S. $1.5 billion, and errors and omissions increased by U.S. $2.3 billion. Also due to the revisions, for the first three quarters of 1991, Mexico's current account deficit increased by U.S. $0.5 billion, its capital account surplus decreased by U.S. $2.2 billion, and errors and omissions increased by U.S. $2.7 billion. Overall, Mexico's balance of payments figures are slightly weaker as a result of the revisions, showing a more rapid growth of the current account deficit and a somewhat less robust growth of the capital account surplus.

Petroleum Sector

The Mexican economy remains heavily reliant on petroleum production and exports, although this dependence has been reduced substantially in recent years. Pemex, the state oil company, provided 30 percent of Mexico's export earnings and 34 percent of all public sector income in 1991. Mexico's crude oil production averaged about 2.68 million barrels per day (mbd) in 1991 and 2.66 mbd during the first two months of 1992. In 1991 crude oil exports averaged 1.37 mbd compared to 1.28 mbd in 1990. In the spring of 1992 there was a catastrophic explosion in Guadalajara that prompted a thorough review of Pemex facilities and maintenance procedures and a reorganization of Pemex into a parent company and four subsidiaries. In August 1992, Mexico announced a sweeping reclassification of basic and secondary petrochemicals that will allow more private and foreign investment in the petrochemicals sector.

The tragic explosion along a sewage pipeline in the spring of 1992 destroyed many blocks of downtown Guadalajara and killed over 200 people. The causes of the explosion were still being evaluated at the time of this report, but press reports largely point the finger at Pemex for allowing gasoline to leak into the sewage system. In the wake of the Guadalajara explosion, President Salinas ordered both a complete reorganization of Pemex and a thorough review of Pemex facilities and maintenance procedures.

The reorganization plan was jointly drafted by top Pemex officials and advisors close to the president and became law the day after it was published in the Diario Oficial in mid-July. Pemex had until January 1, 1993 to fully implement the reorganization.

The reorganization plan reaffirmed state control of Petroleos Mexicanos (Pemex), the parent company, but splits its operations into four subsidiary companies:

- Pemex Exploration and Production is charged with exploration and exploitation of oil and gas;

- Pemex Refining will control the industrial refining processes, manufacture of petroleum products, and basic petroleum derivatives;

- Pemex Gas and Basic Petrochemical is in charge of processing of natural gas and natural gas liquids, and production of primary petrochemicals;

- Pemex Petrochemical will control production of secondary petrochemicals.

The draft text of the North American Free Trade Agreement (NAFTA), that was recently completed by negotiators from Mexico, the United States, and Canada, includes a chapter on energy. NAFTA fully respects the restrictions in the Mexican Constitution dealing with energy. As such, Pemex will retain its constitutional monopoly over petroleum exploration, production, refining, and basic petrochemicals. NAFTA does, however, provide access for U.S. firms to Mexico's petrochemical, gas, and energy services and equipment markets. NAFTA provides significant opportunities to sell to state-owned Pemex under open and competitive bidding rules. NAFTA immediately lifts trade and investment restrictions on most petrochemicals by lifting restrictions on 14 of the 19 previously restricted basic petrochemicals and on 66 secondary petrochemicals.

On August 16, 1992, Mexico announced a sweeping reclassification of basic and secondary petrochemicals that reduced the number of basic petrochemicals from 19 to eight and reduced the number of secondary petrochemicals from 67 to 13. In all, 11 formerly basic petrochemicals were reclassified as secondary; and three formerly basic and 66 formerly secondary petrochemicals were reclassified as tertiary petrochemicals. This is important because Mexican law limits investment in the petrochemical sector depending on the class of petrochemicals. Under Mexican law, production of basic petrochemicals is reserved for the state; secondary petrochemicals can be produced by private firms with up to 40 percent foreign participation; and tertiary petrochemicals can be produced by private sector firms that are up to 100 percent foreign owned.

Readers who wish additional information on Mexico's petroleum sector should obtain a copy of the American Embassy's Petroleum Report, which was completed in August 1992. This 33-page document covers the entire industry and includes eight pages of statistical tables.

Agriculture

Under the completed NAFTA text on agriculture, there are two bilateral agreements dealing with market access: U.S. and Mexico, and Mexico and Canada. U.S. and Canadian market access issues will remain as negotiated under the U.S.-Canadian Free Trade Agreement. Under the U.S.-Mexico bilateral, all tariff and nontariff trade barriers will be eliminated over periods of time ranging from immediate phase-out to fifteen years, with the most sensitive items also having access to safeguard measures. The agricultural agreement contains trilateral provisions concerning internal support, export subsidies, and a system for resolving private commercial disputes regarding transactions in agricultural products. There is also a U.S.-Mexico provision regarding grade and quality standards. Sanitary and phyto-sanitary texts mirror those that have been agreed to in the ongoing General Agreement on Tariffs and Trade negotiations. These will give traders more confidence in the rules governing national health standards for agricultural and food trade.

Considerable attention continues to be focused on the reforms made to Article 27 of the Mexican Constitution that address changes in the country's land tenure system and allow for corporate investment, joint ventures, and private ownership of ejido lands. Initially, there was some concern that peasants would rush to sell their newly obtained ownership rights and migrate to the cities. This has not occurred, but neither has there been an overwhelming investor response. However, there are some limited, high-profile Mexican corporate investments that have taken place since the reforms were instituted. For example, Agramex (a Mexican food company) invested in a former ejido (communal farm) land in Tamaulipas and arranged with ejido farmers to produce wheat for Agramex. The most significant short-term outcome of the land reform changes by the Salinas administration has been to legitimize long-standing financial relationships that have existed between individuals and/or companies, both foreign and domestic, in Mexican agriculture.

Reforms to Article 27 have not yet yielded significant foreign investment in production agriculture in Mexico. Foreigners are still not allowed to own land within 100 kilometers of Mexico's frontiers or 50 kilometers of either coast. A large portion of

Mexico's productive land falls within the restricted areas. In interior areas, foreigners may only possess a maximum of 49 percent of any land holding. As the economy improves, it is expected that additional domestic and foreign investment will be attracted into manufacturing and food processing throughout Mexico.

Mexican domestic agricultural production policy continues to heavily support corn and dry bean producers through guaranteed prices that are held substantially above world levels. For other commodities such as rice, oilseeds, grain sorghum, and cotton, prices are negotiated at approximately world levels, causing large amounts of land to be shifted to corn and dry bean production.

The USDA's Foreign Agricultural Service recently opened an Agricultural Trade Office (ATO) in Mexico City in order to take greater advantage of increasing market opportunities by supplying services to U.S. exporters and Mexican importers. The ATO has information on a wide range of products and markets in Mexico and can provide U.S. exporters with contact lists in their field of interest. In addition, through the "Trade Leads" program, the ATO provides information on current product needs from a range of interested Mexican importers. Also, the Foreign Agricultural Service held its third annual Food and Beverage Show in the summer of 1993. The 1992 show held in Mexico City was attended by over 150 U.S. exhibitors and was visited by almost 5,000 Mexican distributors, wholesalers, and retailers. Contact the Agricultural Trade Office through the American Embassy for more information about these activities.

Political/Institutional Infrastructure

The United Mexican States is a federal republic which first proclaimed its independence from Spain on September 16, 1810; the republic was formally established in 1822. The current Constitution was adopted on February 5, 1917.

The Constitution of 1917 provides for a federal republic with a separation of powers into independent executive, legislative, and judicial branches of government, similar to the U.S. Since 1929, the PRI has controlled Mexico's government and has won every presidential and gubernatorial race, except for the 1989 Baja California Norte contest.

To secure its power, the PRI has relied on extensive public patronage and massive government and party organizational resources.

The executive branch is the dominant branch of the government. Executive power is vested in the president, who promulgates and executes the laws of the Congress. The president also legislates by executive decree in certain economic and financial fields, using powers delegated from the Congress. The president is elected by universal adult suffrage for a six-year term and may not hold office a second time. There is no vice-president; in case of the removal or death of the president, a provisional president is elected by the Congress.

Congress is composed of a Senate and a Chamber of Deputies. Consecutive reelection to the Congress is prohibited. Sixty-four senators (two from each state and the federal district) are elected to six-year terms. Under constitutional and legislative reforms adopted in 1986, the Chamber of Deputies was enlarged in 1988 from 400 to 500 members. In the expanded lower chamber, 300 deputies are directly elected to represent single-member districts, and 200 are selected on an at-large basis by a modified form of proportional representation. The 200 at-large seats were created to give the opposition parties more of a voice in the Chamber of Deputies. Deputies serve three-year terms. The Mexican Congress may legislate on all matters pertaining to the national government.

MEXICO
Key Economic Indicators

	1990	1991	1992
Domestic Economy			
Population (year-end, millions)	82.4	84.0	85.6
Population growth (annual % change)	2.0	2.0	1.9
GDP, current U.S. $ (billions)[1]	241.9	283.6	319.0
GDP per capita, current U.S. $[1]	2,935.7	3,376.2	3,726.6
Real GDP growth (% annual change)	4.4	3.6	3.0
Real GDP per capita growth (% annual change)[2]			
	2.4	1.6	1.1
Consumer price index (% annual change)	29.9	18.8	11.0
Money supply (M-1) (% annual change)[3]	62.6	122.2	50.0
Production and Employment			
Labor force (year-end, millions)	26.2	26.8	27.4
Open unemployment (% of work force)	4.0	3.2	3.0
Real industrial production (% annual change)	5.5	3.1	3.0
Gross fixed investment (% of GDP)	18.8	19.7	20.5
Government financial deficit (% of GDP)	4.0	1.5	−0.8
Balance of Payments (U.S. $ billions)			
Exports (FOB)	26.8	27.1	28.7
Imports (FOB)	31.2	38.2	45.2
Trade balance	−4.4	−11.1	−16.5
Current account balance	−7.1	−13.3	−18.5
Foreign direct investment	2.6	4.8	5.5
Foreign portfolio investment	2.0	7.5	6.5
Capital account	8.2	20.2	20.0
Errors & omissions	2.2	1.2	−1.0
Foreign exchange reserves (end-of-period)	10.2	17.5	18.0
Foreign debt (end-of-period)	99.2	104.1	103.0
Foreign debt (% of GDP)	40.6	35.6	31.7
Average exchange rate (per U.S. $1)[4]	2,807.3	3,006.8	3,115.0
Foreign Direct Investment (U.S. $ billions)			
Total (cumulative)	30.3	33.9	39.0
U.S. (cumulative)	19.1	21.5	24.6
U.S. share (%)	63.0	63.4	61.7
U.S.-Mexico Trade (U.S. $ billions)			
U.S. exports to Mexico (FAS)	28.4	33.3	39.0
U.S. imports from Mexico (CUS)	30.2	31.2	34.0
Trade balance[5]	−1.8	2.1	5.0
U.S. share of Mexican exports (%)	69.8	70.0	70.0
U.S. share of Mexican imports (%)	64.6	67.0	67.0

Notes to Key Economic Indicators:
1. At average exchange rate for year; sharp fluctuations in dollar values are due to exchange rate movements.
2. Real GDP per cap growth = (1 + real GDP growth / 1 + population growth) − 1.
3. M-1 growth registered December 1990 excludes most interest-bearing checking accounts. M-1 growth registered in 1991 was unusually high since all interest-bearing checking accounts were incorporated into M-1.
4. Average controlled exchange rate up to November 10, 1991. Average interbank rate thereafter. Projected rate for 1992 assumes no change in exchange rate policy.
5. Based on U.S. data, which includes imports and exports for in-bond sector. U.S. data are calculated free alongside (FAS) for exports and customs basis (CUS) for imports. Mexican data are calculated free on board (FOB) for both imports and exports, and exclude the in-bond sector. Therefore, Mexican and U.S. trade data are not comparable.

Following federal elections in 1988, six parties gained representation in the Chamber of Deputies and two in the Senate—the latter a first in Mexican political history. The combined opposition won an unprecedented 237 seats out of 500 in the lower house of Congress and four of 64 in the upper. In municipal elections held through December 1989, the government recognized several opposition victories by both leftist and conservative parties. In the state of Michoacan, for example, the center-left Party of Democratic Revolution won almost half the state's municipalities, including the state's capital and most populous city, Morelia.

The judicial system is divided into federal and state court systems, with the federal courts having jurisdiction over most civil cases and those involving major felonies. Under the Constitution, trial and sentencing must be completed within 12 months of arrest for crimes that would carry at least a two-year sentence. Trial is by judge, not by jury, in nearly all criminal cases. Defendants have a right to counsel, and public defenders are available. Other rights include defense against self-incrimination, the right to confront one's accusers, and the right to a public trial.

Supreme Court justices are appointed by the president and approved by the Senate.

Mexico has 31 states and a federal district. Each state is headed by an elected governor. Powers not expressly vested in the federal government are reserved to the states.

Political Parties

Institutional Revolutionary Party (PRI), National Action Party (PAN), Mexican Socialist Party (PMS), Mexican Democratic Party (PDM), Popular Socialist Party (PPS), the Authentic Party of the Mexican Revolution (PARM), Mexican Workers Party (PMT), Revolutionary Workers Party (PRT), Party of the Cardenist Front of National Reconstruction (PFCRN).

Principal Government Officials

President
 Carlos SALINAS de Gortari

Ministers

Government (Interior)
 Fernando GUTIERREZ Barrios

Foreign Relations
 Fernando SOLANA Morales

National Defense
 General Antonio RIVIELLO Bazan

Navy
 Adm. Mauricio SCHLESKE Sanchez

Finance
 Pedro ASPE Armella

Programming and Budget
 Erenst ZEDILLO Ponce de Leon

Energy, Mines and Parastatal Industry
 Fernando HIRIART Balderrama

Commerce and Industrial Development
 Jaime Jose SERRA Puche

Agriculture and Water Resources
 Carlos HANK Gonzalez

Communications and Transportation
 Andres CASO Lombardo

Urban Development and Ecology, Public Education
 Patricio CHIRINOS Calero

Health and Public Assistance
 Jesus KUMATE Rodriquez

Labor and Social Welfare
 Arsenio FARELL Cubillas

Agrarian Reform
 Victor CERVERA Pacheco

Tourism
 Pedro JOUQUIN Coldwell

Fisheries
 Maria de Los Angeles MORENO Uriegas

Federal District
 Victor Manuel CAMACHO Solis

Attorney General
Enrique ALVEREZ Del Castillo

Attorney General for the Federal District
Ignacio MORALES Lechuga

Comptroller General
Maria Elena VAZQUEZ Nava

Ambassador to the U.S.
Gustavo PETRICIOLI Iturbide

Defense

Mexico's armed forces in 1989 totaled about 125,000 personnel. The army makes up about three-fourths of the total. One year of limited training is required of all males reaching age 18. A paramilitary force of communal landholders is maintained in the countryside.

Principal military roles include maintenance of public order and civic action assignments, such as road building and disaster relief. Military expenditures constituted less than 2 percent of the central government budget for the year ending December 31, 1989.

Branches: National Defense (including Army and Air Force), Navy (including Marines).

Manpower availability: males 15–49, 23,023,871; 16,852,513 fit for military service; 1,138,455 reach military age (18) annually.

Defense expenditures: exchange rate conversion—$1.6 billion, less than 1% of GDP (1982 budget).

Current Political Conditions

President Salinas de Gortari began his six-year term in 1988. Salinas, a Harvard graduate, was Secretary of Programming and Budget under President de la Madrid and played a prominent role in formulating economic policy. Significant political themes of the Salinas administration have included facilitating economic recovery by lowering inflation and reducing the foreign debt burden, liberalizing trade practices, increasing openness of the political system, reducing narcotic trafficking, and combating corruption among public servants.

Suffrage: Universal over 18.

Administrative subdivisions: 31 states and the federal district.

Flag: Green, white, and red vertical bands. An eagle holding a snake in its beak and perching on a cactus is centered.

Foreign Relations

The government of Mexico seeks to maintain its interests abroad and project its influence largely through moral persuasion and selective economic assistance. In particular, Mexico champions the principle of nonintervention, self-determination, and certain legal corollaries—the Estrada, Calvo, and Drago doctrines. In an effort to revitalize Mexico's economy and open it to international competition, the Salinas administration seeks closer relations with the United States, Western Europe, and the Pacific Basin.

Mexico is a strong supporter of the UN system and also pursues its interests through a number of ad hoc international bodies. Mexico has been selective in its membership in other international organizations. Mexico is not a member of the Organization of Petroleum Exporting Countries and the Nonaligned Movement. In 1986, Mexico acceded to the General Agreement on Tariffs and Trade (GATT).

U.S.-Mexican Relations

U.S. relations with Mexico are among the most important and complex that it has with any nation. They are shaped by a mixture of mutual interests, shared problems, growing interdependence, and differing national perceptions. Historical factors, cultural differences, and economic disparities add further intricacy to the relationship.

The scope of U.S.-Mexican relations includes extensive commercial, cultural, and educational ties. Along the U.S.-Mexican 3,200-kilometer (2,000-mile) border, state and local governments interact closely. The two countries cooperate to resolve many issues, including trade, finance, narcotics, immigration, environment, science and technology, and cultural relations.

An independent, strong, and economically healthy Mexico is a fundamental U.S. interest. Both governments actively discuss ways to improve cooperation on bilateral issues. Mexican and U.S. policy have differed over regional conflicts in Central America, but both countries agree on the ultimate goal of establishing a lasting peace and in recognizing that such a peace requires a redressing of the region's historic patterns of economic and social injustice.

Trade

Exports: U.S. $27.4 billion (FOB, 1991 estimate).

Commodities: Crude oil, oil products, coffee, shrimp, engines, motor vehicles, cotton, consumer electronics.

Major buyers (1990 estimate): U.S. 68%; EC 14%; Japan 6%.

Imports: U.S. $36.7 billion (CIF, 1991).

Commodities: Grain, metal manufactures, agricultural machinery, electrical equipment.

Major suppliers (1990): U.S. 69%; EC 13%; Japan 6%.

For the fifth year in a row, Mexico was among the top-performing markets for U.S. exports. Exports rose 17 percent to a record U.S. $33.3 billion in 1991. Since 1986 Mexico has been the third largest market for U.S. exports, behind only Canada and Japan and ahead of Germany. Imports from Mexico also rose to a record U.S. $31.2 billion, but export growth outpaced import growth by a factor of five to one. As a result of the dramatic growth in exports in 1991, the United States registered its first merchandise trade surplus with Mexico in a decade. Much of the increase in U.S. exports is attributed to manufactured goods. U.S. exports are projected to continue increasing rapidly during 1992 at a rate of 20 percent or more and to reach approximately U.S. $40 billion. Strong economic growth, reduced trade barriers, and the attention Mexico has garnered as a result of the negotiations to create a North American Free Trade Area have reinforced the interest of U.S. exporters in the Mexican market. Over the last five years, U.S. exports to Mexico have increased by well over 100 percent.

Intermediate goods, such as automotive and electronics parts, account for much of the United States' exports to Mexico. However, U.S. exports of primary products (such as synthetic resins and chemicals), agricultural products (such as corn, soybeans and meat), and even consumer goods continue to perform very well.

Mexico's dramatic liberalization of trade regulations and an increasing awareness on the part of U.S. firms as to the great opportunities offered by the Mexican market has caused an increase in U.S. exports to Mexico over the past five years. In December 1987, the Mexican government (GOM) cut tariffs from 40 percent to a maximum of 20 percent, with the current trade-weighted average tariff being 10.8 percent; eliminated the 5 percent export development tax on imports; reduced the number of products subject to prior import permit requirements to 198 out of the approximately 12,000 items in the tariff schedule; and discontinued the use of official prices for customs valuation purposes. In 1991, Mexico eliminated the prior import permit requirement for computer hardware, an industry previously protected from foreign competition.

United States-Mexico commercial relations have never been better and both governments remain committed to working together to achieve their shared goal of promoting mutually beneficial economic growth.

The U.S. Department of Commerce's offices in Mexico have identified the following areas in the order listed as the best prospects for exporting to Mexico in 1993 and 1994. While these products and services have been identified as the best prospects, many other products also have a good market in Mexico and are either being sold successfully or could be sold successfully in Mexico. A firm should not discount the possibility of doing business in Mexico if the products or services it offers are not included in this list.

1. Franchising
2. Automotive parts and services equipment
3. Chemical production machinery
4. Plastics materials and resins
5. Industrial chemicals
6. Machine tools and metalworking equipment
7. Laboratory and scientific equipment
8. Computers and peripherals
9. Telecommunications equipment and services
10. Oil and gas field machinery and equipment
11. Household consumer goods
12. Apparel
13. Textile fabrics
14. Industrial process controls
15. Medical equipment
16. Materials handling machinery
17. Pollution control equipment
18. Computer software
19. Textile machinery and equipment
20. Business equipment (noncomputer)
21. Agricultural machinery and equipment
22. Sporting goods and equipment
23. Cosmetics and toiletries
24. Food processing and packaging equipment
25. Processed foods
26. Plastics production machinery
27. Hotel and restaurant equipment
28. Printing and graphic arts equipment
29. Forestry and woodworking machinery
30. Packaging equipment
31. Electrical power systems
32. Mining industry equipment
33. Building products
34. Security and safety equipment
35. Jewelry
36. Architecture/engineering/construction services
37. Construction equipment
38. Dental equipment
39. Musical instruments
40. Electronic components

APPROACHING THE MARKET

Commercial Environment

Mexico has traditionally relied upon a policy of import substitution to encourage the development of the domestic industry. Protection from foreign competition has been accomplished primarily through a system of import permits and restrictive tariffs. During the 1956–1976 period, Mexico followed a highly protectionist policy. At its peak in 1974, 74 percent of imports were subject to nontariff barriers such as import permits.

The sector most protected during this period was manufacturing, in particular durable consumer goods and capital goods, which enjoyed an effective protection rate of 77 percent.

The first liberalization took place during the 1977–1980 period, as a result of the discovery of vast oil reserves and the improvement in Mexico's balance of payments. The total number of products subject to nontariff barriers was reduced from 90 percent of total import value in 1977 to 60 percent in 1980, with a simultaneous decrease in duty rates. This process was temporarily reversed in 1982 when, due to the severe economic crisis, quantitative protection was imposed on all imported items. During the past administration, a thorough restructuring of Mexico's industrialization and foreign trade patterns was undertaken. This plan was the beginning of Mexico's gradually increasing exposure to foreign competition, which is expected to make Mexican industry more competitive, both internally and externally.

The ultimate goal is to accelerate the development of markets for Mexican exports. On July 1985, the Mexican government eliminated the import licensing requirements on all but 900 of the 8,000 products in the tariff schedule. This requirement has historically been the most restrictive of Mexico's import substitution policies. On August 24, 1986, Mexico became a full member of the GATT. This action required the country to reduce tariff and nontariff barriers and to gradually bring its trade practices in conformity with established GATT principles, by substituting import permits with tariffs and reducing duty levels.

NAFTA and Trade Liberalization

By far the most important recent development in Mexico's trade policy was the August 12, 1992, announcement that negotiations for the North American Free Trade Agreement (NAFTA) were completed. For Mexico, this agreement culminated six years

of trade liberalization begun in 1986 when it joined the GATT. Canada, Mexico, and the U.S. expect the agreement to create jobs and generate economic growth in all three countries. When NAFTA takes effect on January 1, 1994, it will create a market of 360 million consumers with U.S. $6 trillion in combined gross domestic production. Meanwhile, Mexico has actively pursued free trade agreements with its other trading partners, including Chile (an agreement was signed in September 1991), five Central American countries, Venezuela, and Colombia. Mexico's average weighted tariff is about 10 percent and there are five different tariff rates.

On August 12, 1992, the presidents of the three countries announced that the NAFTA negotiations had been completed. The agreement covers a broad range of important issues. Some key provisions include:

- Tariffs. Tariffs on most industrial and agricultural goods produced by the NAFTA partners will be eliminated either when the agreement goes into effect or phased out over five to ten years. For certain sensitive products the phase-out period is 15 years.

- Rules of origin. NAFTA rules of origin are designed to ensure that NAFTA benefits are only given to goods produced wholly or principally in NAFTA countries. Goods from non-NAFTA countries may qualify for preferential treatment if they are sufficiently transformed in a NAFTA country. Special rules of origin apply to automotive goods, extiles, and apparel.

- Automobiles. NAFTA eliminates trade barriers for and investment restrictions on participating country autos, trucks, buses, and auto parts over a 10-year period. It also eliminates export performance and local con10t requirements over 10 years. The three countries will eliminate tariffs on auto parts over 10 years, but duties for most products will go to zero immediately, or over a five-year transition period. The Mexican auto decrees will terminate after 10 years.

- Agriculture. Mexico has separate agreements with the U.S. and Canada, both of which have safeguard mechanisms. The agreement with the U.S. includes elimination of import licensing and phase-out of tariffs over a maximum 15-year period for all types of agricultural, livestock, poultry, and dairy products. In the Mexico-Canada Agreement, the dairy, poultry, egg, and sugar sectors will continue to be protected.

- Energy. With the exception of five basic petrochemicals, Mexico will open this sector to foreign investment and eliminate import and export licenses. Mexico will allow foreign investors from NAFTA countries to own electric generating plants for their own use or for independent power generation to be sold to the Mexican Federal Electricity Commission. Service contracts may contain performance incentives. Mexico reserves to its government the oil, gas, refining, basic petrochemical, and nuclear sectors.

- Textiles. The three countries will eliminate immediately or phase out over a maximum 10-year period duties on textiles and apparel that meet NAFTA rules of origin. U.S. quotas on Mexican textile and apparel goods that meet NAFTA rules of origin are eliminated immediately. Quotas on sensitive products will be phased out in seven to 10 years.

- Services. The three countries agreed to the basic obligations of most-favored-nation and national treatment for trade in services. Service firms may establish operations in any of the three countries or sell their services across borders. Services such as engineering, construction, publishing, tourism, accounting, and telecommunications will no longer be subject to investment restrictions.

- Banking. Immediately, U.S. and Canadian banks may establish subsidiaries in Mexico that in aggregate represent at most 8 percent of the total net capital of the Mexican banking system. This capital limit rises to 15 percent over six years and to 25 percent over 10 years.

- Intellectual property rights. The agreement offers very strong protection of copyrights, trademarks, patents, and trade secrets, including computer programs, integrated circuit designs, and sound recordings. The agreement also prohibits compulsory licensing.

- Investment. NAFTA provides fair rules for investment in North America by ensuring nondiscrimination, ending local con10t requirements, and dropping export performance quotas.

- Dispute settlement. NAFTA establishes an effective dispute settlement mechanism among its members.

- Labor. To limit the displacement of workers, NAFTA provides a transition period for the opening of import-sensitive industries, safeguards to protect sectors against injury from imports, and tough rules of origin.

- Environment. NAFTA is the first trade agreement to include far-reaching provisions to protect and improve the environment. It maintains U.S. environmental, safety, and health standards, allows the U.S. to enact even tougher standards, and encourages partners to strengthen their standards.

U.S. Ratification Process

Now that the NAFTA negotiations are completed, the text must be approved. The fast track procedure prohibited Congress from amending the agreement. Fast track authority was to expire at midnight May 31, 1993. Therefore the president had to notify the Congress of his intention to sign NAFTA no later than February 27, 1993 (e.g., begin the 90 calendar day clock) in order to have NAFTA considered by Congress under the fast track rules.

Mexican Ratification Process

Mexico would approve the NAFTA as it would any treaty. President Salinas would sign the agreement and legislative action would be confined to the Mexican Senate. Once the treaty was ratified, any implementing legislation that was necessary would be presented to the Mexican legislature in the same fashion as other legislation.

There were no time limits for each stage of this process and the ruling PRI holds a majority of seats in the Senate, so passage was virtually assured.

Moreover, the Mexican Senate has never amended or vetoed an executive action. The treaty enters into force upon its publication in the "Diario Oficial." The president can call a special session, however, as he did before to consider agrarian reform.

Canadian Ratification Process

The Canadian parliamentary system does not have a separate process for approval of treaties. Approval of a major international treaty like the 1988 U.S.-Canada Free Trade Agreement or a NAFTA is accomplished by passing implementing legislation, which typically includes a clause approving the agreement as signed. The federal government is required to consult with the provinces on treaties which affect provincial interests, and it has done so on an ongoing basis regarding NAFTA. Like any federal bill in Canada, implementing legislation must pass through the following stages: drafting by the Department of Justice, approval by the Cabinet Committee, passage by both the House of Commons and the Senate, royal assent (a formality) and coming into force.

Foreign Trade and Investment Decision-Making Infrastructure

In September 1991 Mexico signed a free trade agreement with Chile that will eliminate tariffs on most traded goods over a four-year period that commenced in January 1992. Tariffs on more sensitive products will be phased out over six years. Although trade has quadrupled since the agreement was signed, it is still relatively small.

In January 1991 Mexico and five Central American countries (Guatemala, Honduras, El Salvador, Nicaragua, and Costa Rica) signed the Tuxtla Gutierrez Framework Agreement which outlined general guidelines for future bilateral trade agreements. Mexico held bilateral consultations with each country and in mid-August of 1992 signed a framework agreement to create a free-trade zone of 110 million people by 1996. The agreement will eliminate barriers for trade in goods and services while protecting sensitive industries. An agreement with Costa Rica was expected by year end and Panama was considering joining the group.

Mexico also is negotiating a free trade agreement with Venezuela and Colombia. Talks have slowed, however, due to concerns among other Latin countries that these types of agreements violate regional agreements such as the Andean Pact. Nevertheless, the three countries met on July 13 and an agreement was expected by year end. Mexico has also held trade consultations with Argentina, Brazil, and Bolivia.

Mexico signed a Cooperation Agreement

with the European Economic Community in April 1991. It is expected to promote and diversify Mexico's foreign trade, encourage economic, scientific, and financial cooperation, promote investment, and increase protection of intellectual property.

Mexico is also interested in joining the 15-nation Asia-Pacific Economic Cooperation (APEC) group. APEC members were expected to make a decision on Mexico's membership at their September ministerial meeting in Bangkok.

Along with increasing trade by opening its borders, Mexico has also made a concerted effort to help Mexican companies increase their export capacity (see Table 14-7).

Three of Mexico's most important government-administered export programs are ALTEX, ECEX and IPCA ("Importaciones por Cuenta Propria" which replaced the former PITEX program).

Any company that exports at least U.S. $2 million annually or directly exports at least 40 percent of sales or indirectly exports 50 percent of sales can qualify for ALTEX benefits, which include lower cost export financing from Bancomext (Mexican Export and Import Bank), simplified customs procedures, and accelerated reimbursement of eligible value-added tax payments. To qualify for the ECEX program which allows access to ALTEX benefits, a company must

Table 14-7
Mexico's Exports to the World
(January–October 1991)
(U.S. $ million)

Region	U.S. $ Amount	Percent of Total Exports
U.S.	15,743.2	69.53
European Community	2,801.3	12.37
Asia	1,343.6	5.94
Latin American Integration Association	813.7	3.59
Canada	501.7	2.22
Central American Common Market	326.7	1.44
Rest of Latin America	287.5	1.27
Rest of America	184.7	0.82
Caribbean	85.4	0.38
European Free Trade Association	169.2	0.75
Middle East	184.2	0.81
Eastern Europe	34.4	0.15
Africa	51.1	0.23
Oceania	62.9	0.28
Other	49.8	0.22
TOTAL	22,639.4	100.00

Source: National Statistical Institute, "Estadistocas del Comercio Exterior de Mexico, 11/91."

have at least U.S. $100,000 in fixed equity, at least U.S. $3 million in annual exports, and must run a positive commercial balance. The PITEX program allowed tax-free entry and duty-free importation of materials and machinery as long as they were used for the subsequent production of imports. Since there was some abuse of the PITEX program, the government reorganized it in June 1992 and renamed the program "Importaciones por Cuenta Propria." Mexico also offers preferred financing through Nafinsa (the National Development Bank) to help micro, small, and medium-sized firms export.

Implications for U.S. Exporters

Presently, approximately 320 of the nearly 12,000 items in the Mexican Harmonized System tariff schedule are subject to prior import permit requirements. In terms of effective coverage offered by these permit requirements, they represent roughly 20 percent of the value of the goods imported into the country.

During 1989, two major decrees were published liberalizing imports in the computer and automotive industry. All computers and peripherals are now allowed entry without prior import permit requirements and established car manufacturers are permitted to import new cars up to 15 percent of their production if they can show a surplus in their balance of payments.

The items still requiring an import permit are principally parts for the manufacture of machinery and equipment; a number of consumer items considered luxury goods, such as works of art and caviar; a few chemical and pharmaceutical products; products made in Mexico considered vital to its economy, such as corn, cocoa, oils, sugar, poultry, eggs, milk, cheese, beans, apples, pears, wheat, barley, malt, sesame and lemon oil, tobacco, paper, tapestries and used clothing, natural gas and other gases, petroleum and gasoline, trucks and tractors. There are additionally 17 items which are prohibited from being imported, such as drugs and arms.

Used machinery also requires a permit to be imported into the country. This includes most agricultural machinery, textile machinery and sewing machines, tractors, railroad wagons and containers, and electric automobiles.

A Prior Import Permit, as the license is officially called, is issued by the Secretariat of Commerce and Industrial Development (SECOFI) and must be applied for by the Mexican purchaser. The applicant must be registered in Mexico with the National Register of Importers and Exporters. The application is considered by one or more committees within SECOFI. The license is usually rejected if the product in question, or a close substitute, is available domestically. Committees often rely on industry associations and secretariats for advice on whether to grant the permit.

The processing time for import license applications is usually between one and two months, but longer delays are not uncommon. Once issued, a license is valid for nine months. Exporters should avoid shipping until the usance of the license has been confirmed.

Tariffs

On December 15, 1987, the maximum duty rate of 40 percent was reduced by the government to 20 percent on the CIF invoice value. The average duty rate in 1989 was 13 percent, down from 25 percent in 1985. The highest duties are generally applied to luxury and consumer goods. Industrial machinery and equipment and capital goods generally are subject to rates of 10 or 15 percent.

The product categories subject to the highest average rates are tobacco, apparel, alcoholic beverages, electric household appliances, soft drinks, fishing and hunting, corn and wheat grinding, beer and malt, wood products, processed food products, glass and glass products, soaps, detergents and cosmetics, textiles, plastic products, metal furniture and other products, electronic apparatus and equipment, footwear, and pharmaceuticals. The lowest duties are paid on petroleum and petroleum products, steel, sugar, petrochemicals, meat and milk products, fertilizers, minerals, oils, printers and editorials, agricultural products, and transportation equipment. Machinery and equipment imports pay average duties of 15 percent.

All customs duties are paid by the Mexican importer or by a customs broker on his behalf at the time the goods clear Mexican customs. Customs will not release the goods until the importer presents the import declaration proving payment of import duties and other taxes.

Mexico applies its tariffs on a most-favored nation (non-discriminatory) basis, with the exception of several preferential duty rates offered to fellow members of the Latin American Integration Association (ALADI), that is, Argentina, Bolivia, Brazil, Chile, Colombia, Ecuador, Paraguay, Peru, Uruguay, and Venezuela.

Tariffs on most industrial and agricultural goods produced by the NAFTA partners will be eliminated either when the agreement goes into effect or phased out over five to 10 years. For certain sensitive products the phaseout period is 15 years.

In the last five years, as President Salinas has dismantled many long-standing Mexican trade and investment restrictions, U.S. exports to Mexico have nearly tripled.

Official Prices

Until January 1, 1988, Mexico also employed a system of government-established official prices on certain items in the tariff schedule.

This measure was intended to establish a minimum base for the duty calculation on those products for which the government determined a threat of unfair dumping or export subsidies. Under this system, the ad valorem duty rate was applied on the official price times the weight of the shipment. Duties were assessed on the official value if it exceeded the commercial invoice value. As of January 1988, official prices have been eliminated. In order to avoid dumping or other unfair commercial practices, a system of compensatory quotas has been established.

Other Import Taxes

In addition to the general ad valorem import duty, the Mexican importer must pay some other taxes and surcharges. A customs processing fee of 0.6 percent is assessed on the CIF invoice value. A value-added tax (VAT or IVA in Spanish) of 15 percent is levied on the cumulative value of the invoice value plus all duties and taxes of most imported items. Finally, shipments by mail are subject to a 10 percent surcharge on the invoice value.

Duty Drawback

Mexican companies or individuals involved in exporting can, in some cases, be eligible for a refund or drawback of duties paid on imports of raw materials, parts, and components incorporated into merchandise for export. Components and raw materials imported for use in the maquiladora industry are also exempt from duties. The items eligible for these duty drawbacks change often and importers must meet complex requirements to qualify for these benefits. It is therefore important to check with the importer and the customs broker for specific product information.

Technical Standards

There are no official metric requirements applicable to imports into Mexico. However, since the metric system is the official standard of weights and measures in Mexico, importers will usually require metric labeling for packaged goods, although the English system is also often used. Dual labeling is acceptable. It is also important to note that the Mexican government has recently enforced three import requirements: a labeling regulation, the free sale certificate, and the certificate of quality.

The Mexican government has begun enforcing a law under which certain categories of products must be labeled in Spanish prior to importation into Mexico. As of November 1992, this list includes all textile and apparel products, all leather products, and refrigerators. Mexico requires that all other products have a Spanish-language label affixed prior to reaching the consumer. As of October 1992, Mexico permitted importers and distributors to affix these Spanish-language labels after importation into Mexico. However, because this practice may change, exporters may want to explore cost-effective ways to label their products in Spanish. Importers and customs agents can usually provide information on current and proposed labeling requirements.

Mexico has also recently begun requiring certificates of quality before certain products can be sold in Mexico. For a list of product categories requiring certificates of quality and complete labeling information, please consult the Tariffs, Permits, and Custom Regulations section of the Main Menu (document #0101) of the Office of Mexico's Flash Facts system at (202) 482-4464.

All the products entering into Mexico must have a free sale certificate.

This certificate proves that the imported goods are also sold in the country of origin. A letter from the local chamber of commerce stating the sale of this product in the local market is sufficient proof for this requirement.

This summary was based on the following publications and articles: *Sexto Informe de Gobierno,* Miguel de la Madrid 1988; *Trade Policy and Regulations—Mexico,* Monthly Digest, The Mexican Chamber of Commerce of the U.S.; *Economic Trends Report,* February 1992 and November 1992, American Embassy Mexico; *Aspectos de la Apertura Comercial, Revista de Comercio Exterior,* October 1987, BNCE Mexico; newspaper clippings, official bulletins, and other research.

Environment

The American administration has moved forward with a comprehensive bilateral environmental agenda to allay concerns that free trade could undermine U.S. environmental and food safety regulations or lead to environmental degradation on the U.S.-Mexico border. During the last year, substantial progress has been made.

Energy

With the exception of five basic petrochemicals, Mexico will open its petrochemical sector to foreign investment, over time. Except for basic petrochemicals, no import or export licenses will be required for petrochemicals.

Mexico will allow private foreign investors to own electric generating plants for their own use or for independent power generation to be sold to the Mexican Federal Electricity Commission.

Mexico reserves to its government the oil, gas, refining, basic petrochemical, nuclear and electricity sectors.

Restrictions on energy trade are limited to national security reasons or certain specific circumstances such as to conserve exhaustible natural resources, short supplies, or the need to stabilize prices.

Mining

The 1917 Mexican Constitution makes subsoil resources and minerals the property of the nation, and companies wishing to open mining operations must obtain a concession from the government. Such concessions are only granted to Mexican nationals or majority-owned Mexican firms.

Exploitation of some minerals, such as sulphur, iron, coal, and phosphoric rock, requires 66 percent Mexican ownership.

The mining industry received a boost from the 1992 Mining Law under which the private sector—including foreigners—will now be able to exploit sulphur, potassium, phosphorous rock, iron, and coal. The state will retain total or majority control over oil and hydrocarbons, salt, radioactive minerals, deep-sea suspended particles, and construction grade stone. The law also sets the stage for the privatization of three state-owned mining companies—Roca Fosforica Mexicana, Azufrera Panamericana, and Compana Exportadora del Istmo.

Agriculture, Fisheries, Forestry

A relatively large segment (about 25 percent) of the total working population continues to be employed in agriculture, cattle raising, forestry, and fishing. Direct foreign investment in these areas has been very limited due to constitutional and other restrictions. Only a small portion of the land can be considered as first-class agricultural land, particularly because of lack of rainfall in the northern part of the country. However, irrigation has considerably increased the amount of land under cultivation , and in a normal crop year Mexico is largely self-sufficient in food, except for recurring deficiencies of wheat and corn in recent years. The principal agricultural exports have been coffee, tomatoes, cauliflower, artichokes, and other vegetables.

Tourism

Largely because of the many lovely bays on its extensive coastline, its numerous archeological sites, and its tropical and semitropical climate, Mexico has developed a substantial tourist industry, handling over seven million foreign tourists per year, mainly from the United States, in addition to those who merely visit the border zone. Substantial foreign investments have been made in properties in the resort areas.

Service Industries

The service industries form a major part of the economy, with the commercial sector alone (including hotels and restaurants) accounting for a large percentage of GNP. Financial and business services represent a much smaller proportion.

Advertising agencies of Mexico include many that are partially owned by foreign agencies, although as with all phases of the service industries, it is somewhat difficult for non-Mexicans to obtain immigration papers authorizing them to work in service-oriented companies. Management consulting is practiced by the principal public accounting firms and some specialized firms, some of which are direct affiliates of foreign—principally U.S.—firms. Computer services are largely offered by producers of the equipment, mostly affiliates of foreign companies.

INVESTMENT CLIMATE

Extent of U.S. Investment in Goods-Producing Sectors

Foreign direct investment (as measured in the capital account of the balance of payments) totaled U.S. $4.8 billion in 1991 and U.S. $2.2 billion during the first half of 1992. During the same periods foreign portfolio investment totaled U.S. $7.5 billion and U.S. $3.7 billion, respectively. The United States is the leading source of direct foreign investment in Mexico with 61.7 percent of the accumulated total as of June 1992. A new Mining Law promulgated in 1992 allows the private sector, including foreigners, to exploit several minerals that were previously restricted to exploitation by the state, which may lead to more investment in that sector. Over the next several years foreign investment in Mexico is expected to increase rapidly due to the liberalization of Mexico's investment regime that is part of NAFTA.

However, not all authorized investment actually flows into the country during the year that it is approved. The balance of payments figures show actual direct foreign investment inflows to Mexico rather than approvals. During 1991 total inflows of direct investment recorded in the balance of payments were U.S. $4.76 billion, up from U.S. $2.63 billion in 1990. During the first three months of 1992, Mexico received U.S. $1.42 billion of direct foreign investment as recorded in the balance of payments, down from the U.S. $1.87 billion received during the first quarter of 1991.

Direct foreign investment is comprised of capital inflows made to purchase plant, equipment, land, and services in Mexico as well as capital injections from a foreign parent to its Mexican subsidiary. By contrast foreign portfolio investment is capital inflows that are used to purchase financial assets in Mexico, such as stocks, bonds, and treasury bills. Portfolio investment is potentially far more volatile than direct investment.

Foreign portfolio investment in Mexico has increased dramatically since 1989. Mexico received U.S. $493 million of portfolio investment in 1989, U.S. $2 billion in 1990, and U.S. $7.5 billion in 1991. Of the total portfolio investment received in 1991, U.S. $6.3 billion was invested in equity and U.S. $1.2 billion in debt.

Portfolio investment in Mexico has increased because of growing confidence in Mexico since the debt renegotiation, a dramatic increase in international issues of Mexican securities, and changes in Mexican regulations to facilitate the purchase by foreigners of almost all Mexican debt and equity instruments.

As of June 1992, accumulated direct foreign investment in Mexico amounted to about U.S. $36.0 billion. Of that total, 56.2 percent was invested in manufacturing, 34.5 percent in services (e.g., financial services, insurance, transportation, and communications), 7.5 percent in commerce (retail, restaurants, and hotels), 1.4 percent in mining, and 0.4 percent in agriculture and cattle breeding. Investment trends have changed markedly in recent years with the service sector now being the single largest recipient of direct foreign investment. The service sector averaged 50 percent of total new investment approvals in the 1986–90 period and it accounted for 60 percent of the total in 1991.

The United States is the leading source of direct foreign investment in Mexico with about 61.7 percent of the accumulated total as of June 1992. Following the United States is the United Kingdom (6.5 percent), Germany (5.8 percent), Switzerland (4.6 percent), Japan (4.4 percent), and France (4.1 percent). Several other countries have investments in Mexico, but each of those countries accounts for 1 percent or less of the total accumulated direct foreign investment in Mexico. It is notable that although the U.S. accounts for about two-thirds of foreign investment in Mexico, Mexico has only received about 4.5 percent of all U.S. investment abroad.

The Mexican government expected direct foreign investment to increase significantly in 1991 as investors exercised the U.S. $3.5 billion of debt/equity swap rights auctioned in July and October 1990, a portion of which were won or purchased by foreigners in the secondary market. However, the value of Mexican debt has increased so sharply that investors earned more by selling their debt in the secondary market than using it to invest in Mexico.

According to the "National Development Plan 1989–1994" and the "Agenda for Mexico," The Mexican government's target is to capture U.S. $25 billion in foreign investment during the Salinas administration, more than double the 1982–88 total. Moreover, the Salinas administration hopes to receive at least U.S. $5 billion per year of direct foreign investment by 1994.

Excluding portfolio investments, Mexico nearly achieved that target, with U.S. $4.8 billion, in 1991.

Strategic areas that are reserved for the state include: (1) petroleum and basic petrochemicals; (2) mining of radioactive materials (uranium); (3) power and nuclear energy generation; (4) railroads; (5) telegraphic and radio communications; (6) operation and ownership of satellites; and (7) the minting of coins.

For detailed information on Mexico's investment law and regulations as well as information on NAFTA, see the American Embassy's annual Investment Report.

Privatization Activities

The Mexican government has continued to streamline the para-statal sector by liquidating, merging, transferring, and selling companies, and by opening sectors to private investment that were previously reserved for the state, such as the construction and operation of highways. In 1982 there were 1,155 state-owned enterprises. As of August 1992 the number had dropped to 223, 87 of which were in the process of being privatized. The most important privatizations completed during the first eight months of 1992 were the sales of Mexico's 18 commercial banks (for which the government received U.S. $12.4 billion) and an international equity placement of Telmex stock that raised U.S. $1.4 billion. Some key enterprises for sale in 1992 are two state-owned television stations (channels 7 and 13), an insurance company (Asemex), and a newspaper (*El Nacional*).

Between 1983 and 1988, the Mexican

government privatized many relatively small firms. Privatizations took several forms, including liquidations, mergers, sales, and transfers of companies to state and local governments. During this period one of the government's primary goals was to gain experience on how to privatize enterprises, and to establish a transparent process that could later be applied to the privatization of large companies. Whereas the total revenues from the 33 privatizations completed in 1989 amounted to only U.S. $684 million, revenues from the 99 privatizations in 1990 were U.S. $2.7 billion, and revenues from the 39 privatizations during 1991 and the first six months of 1992 (excluding the sale of state-owned banks) were U.S. $5.1 billion.

Most notable among the firms that have been privatized since 1989 are: the telephone company, Telmex; Mexico's 18 commercial banks; the airlines, Aeromexico and Mexicana; two large copper mines, Cananea and Mexicana de Cobre; and two large steel companies, Sicartsa and AHMSA.

The most important companies that now are in the process of being privatized are:

- Aseguradora Mexicana (insurance company)
- Fertilizantes Mexicanos (four separate fertilizer companies)
- Leche Industrializada Conasupo (milk company)
- Almacenes Nacionales de Deposito (bonded warehousing company)
- Canal 7 (television station)
- Compania Operadora de Teatros (movie cinemas)
- Canal 13 (television station)
- Periodico *El Nacional* (newspaper)

Privatization of state-owned enterprises clearly has produced large one-time revenues for the government but it also has produced permanent benefits for the Mexican economy. First, the government has been able to reduce its role in the economy and garner savings by reducing its transfers to inefficient enterprises. Second, since private sector companies operate to make profits and the government can tax those profits, the government's income stream has increased. Third, private sector companies are better able to make capital expenditures so the privatizations are encouraging a rapid modernization of Mexican industry. Finally, most of the revenues from the privatization process have been used to retire internal and external debt, which has significantly improved the Mexican government's finances and allowed greater expenditure on social programs.

Given their size and importance to the Mexican economy, the privatization of Telmex and Mexico's 18 commercial banks deserve special mention.

Telmex

The privatization of Telefonos de Mexico (Telmex) took place in three stages. In December 1990, the government sold all its "AA" shares in Telefonos de Mexico (or 20.4 percent of the stock representing 51 percent of the voting power) to a consortium led by Grupo Carso and including Southwestern Bell and France Telecom. After the sale of its "AA" shares the government was left with a 26 percent equity stake in the telephone company. In May and June 1991 the government reduced its equity stake to 9.7 percent of the company through a simultaneous international stock offering, exercising of options by the underwriters, and the sale of 1.4 percent of the company to Telmex employees. Revenues from the privatization were huge (U.S. $4.027 billion): U.S. $1.757 billion for the controlling stake sold to the consortium, and U.S. $2.474 billion from the second stage sales.

In May 1992, the government sold another 4.7 percent of Telmex through an international equity offering that raised U.S. $1.2 billion abroad and 479 billion pesos (U.S. $155 million) in Mexico. The government still has a 5 percent stake in Telmex.

The Telmex privatization was an extraordinary success for the Salinas administration. The government planned for the privatization by renegotiating the union contract, revising the Telmex concession, reforming tariffs and taxes, and restructuring Telmex's capital to permit a Mexican investor (Grupo Carso) to control Telmex with just over 10 percent of the equity capital.

Commercial Banks

The first Mexican commercial bank was privatized in June 1991 and the eighteenth and last bank was sold just over a year later, in July 1992. As of August 1992, revenues from the sale of the 18 banks amounted to 37.8 trillion pesos (U.S. $12.4 billion). Total revenues will be even greater because the government still holds stock representing 8.8 percent of the total capital of the Mexican banking system, comprised of the following: 22.5 percent of the capital of Bancomer (Mexico's second largest bank by asset size), 15.9 percent of Serfin, and 21 percent of Banco Internacional (Mexico's third and fourth largest banks by asset size, respectively).

The average weighted price of the banks was 14.7 times earnings and 3.09 times book value. Fourteen of the 18 banks were purchased by financial groups or brokerage houses, and the remaining four banks were purchased by three private investor groups and one industrial company (Maseca), which all intend to form financial groups. A Mexican financial group must contain at least three different types of financial services companies (such as a bank, an insurance company, and a factoring company) and the group must own at least 51 percent of the equity capital of each of its parts.

There were several steps to the bank privatization process: (1) the Bank Divestiture Committee analyzed the proposals of interested bidders; (2) the committee conducted interviews with the prospective buyers; (3) the committee compiled a definitive list of candidates to participate in the bank securities auction; (4) the approved participants presented bids; (5) the government announced the new owners of the bank; (6) the new owners audited their bank and applied to the government for a refund if they discovered any undisclosed irregularities.

Infrastructure Projects

In addition to privatizations, the government has expanded the role of the private sector by allowing it to participate in activities previously restricted to the public sector, particularly infrastructure projects.

One of the most important programs has involved granting temporary concessions to the private sector for the construction and operation of highways. The concession holder is allowed to charge tolls on projects he develops until construction costs have been recovered and a reasonable profit made, at which time ownership of the highway reverts to the government.

During the Salinas administration, 724 kilometers of new highways have been opened and a further 1,900 kilometers are being built through this mechanism. The government estimates that it will grant concessions to build and operate another 3,046 kilometers of highways in 1992, including highways linking Mexico City-Guadalajara, Pachuca-Tampico, and Tehuacan-Oaxaca.

The government has also opened certain operations in ports and airports to private investment, such as loading and unloading of cargo, pilot services on tugboats, and the operation of storage facilities. The private sector has been able to participate in the building of electric plants and dams through leaseback schemes where a private sector company builds a turnkey plant, transfers it to the government upon completion, and the government repays the builder his costs and a profit through a lease.

FINANCING AND CAPITAL MARKETS

General Policy Framework

The government maintained tight fiscal control in 1991 and continued to do so in 1992. The public sector financial deficit has fallen markedly from 4.0 percent of GDP in 1990 to 1.5 percent of GDP in 1991. For 1992, the government projects that the financial deficit will become a surplus amounting to about 0.8 percent of GDP, excluding revenues from the sales of state-owned companies. The government has been able to improve its balances both by increases in income, due to a rigorous tax collection effort, and by dramatic decreases in expenditures.

Expenditures have declined primarily because of lower debt servicing costs reflecting both a reduction of interest rates and a real decrease in the balance of public sector debt outstanding. The reduction of interest expenses has allowed the government to increase spending on necessary capital investment and social projects.

The following section provides some preliminary numbers for the first half of 1992, but complete numbers for public sector finances are only available through the first quarter.

During the first quarter of 1992 compared to the first quarter of 1991, total public sector income, including revenues from the privatization process, increased 10.42 percent in real terms and total expenditures fell by 3.26 percent in real terms. The growth in income was due first to an increase in revenues from the privatization process, but also to improved tax revenues (which increased 3.1 percent in real terms). However, income

Extent of U.S. Investment in Goods-Producing Sectors
U.S. Direct Investment Position Abroad
on a Historical-Cost Basis—1990
(U.S. $ million)

Category	Amount
Petroleum	80
Total manufacturing	7,314
Food and kindred products	913
Chemicals and allied products	1,596
Metals, primary and fabricated	336
Machinery, except electrical	310
Electric and electronic equipment	562
Transportation equipment	1,749
Other manufacturing	1,849
Wholesale trade	503
TOTAL	7,897

Source: U.S. Department of Commerce, *Survey of Current Business*, (August 1991, vol. 71, no. 8, table 11.3.)

growth was hampered by a 42.4 percent real reduction in revenues from oil exports attributed to about a two dollar decline in the average per-barrel price of Mexican export oil during the first quarter of 1992 compared to the first quarter of 1991.

According to a report sent to the Mexican Congress in mid-August 1992, the overall financial surplus for the first half of 1992 amounted to 7.8 trillion pesos, excluding privatization revenues. Including those revenues, the surplus was 33 trillion pesos, or 3.3 percent of GDP, and up from the 13.9 trillion pesos surplus recorded through March 1992. Also, during the first half of 1992 compared to the same period in 1991, in real terms public sector income increased 3.8 percent and tax revenues increased 2.1 percent.

The 1992 increase in total tax revenues is particularly impressive since it occurred despite a reduction in revenues from the value-added tax (VAT).

VAT revenues decreased 27.7 percent in real terms between March 1991 and March 1992. When the Pact for Stability and Economic Growth was extended on November 10, 1991, the VAT was reduced from rates of 15 and 20 percent to a single rate of 10 percent. At the same time, compliance efforts were intensified and the prices of gasoline and utilities were increased. The overall increase in tax revenues between March 1991 and March 1992 was due to a 13.9 percent real increase in revenues from income taxes (income tax revenues increased 8.4 percent in the first half of 1992) and a 47 percent increase in gasoline tax revenues.

The Salinas administration has made a concerted effort to increase tax revenues by lowering tax rates, broadening the tax base, making the tax system more equitable, and increasing enforcement. Between 1988 and 1991, the maximum corporate tax rate was reduced from 39.2 to 35 percent, and the maximum marginal tax rate for individuals was lowered from 50 to 35 percent.

During the first quarter of 1992, about 40 percent of Mexico's public sector income came from tax collections, 22 percent from federal government nontax sources (including privatization revenues), 19 percent from state-owned companies, 13 percent from domestic petroleum sales, and 6 percent from exported petroleum.

On the expenditure side, during the first quarter of 1992 compared to the same period in 1991, total expenditures fell by 3.26 percent in real terms led by a 20.2 percent real reduction in interest payments. This was offset in part by a 12.4 percent real increase in personnel expenditures and a 5.5 percent real increase in capital expenditures. Interest rates on Mexican internal debt (as measured by 28-day Treasury bills) fell dramatically during the first quarter, from 16.65 to 11.0 percent.

Lower interest rates have meant enormous savings for Mexico. The government has been able to use money saved on interest servicing to improve its fiscal balances and spend on necessary capital investment and social projects. For example, in December 1991 the total internal debt was 170.3 trillion pesos (U.S. $55.5 billion). Therefore, each one percentage point fall in interest rates represented a 1.7 trillion pesos (U.S. $555 million) savings in debt servicing costs. Between December 1991 and March 1992 the interest rate on 28-day Treasury bills fell 4.8 percentage points, which represents over U.S. $2.6 billion in savings on an annualized basis. The comparable figure in 1991 was about U.S. $5.1 billion dollars. Actually, real savings were substantially less than the aforementioned figures because interest rates fell over a period of several months, the yields of all government instruments and cost of borrowing from the banks did not decline as sharply as that of 28-day Treasury bills, and the government retired internal debt so the savings was on a smaller balance than that recorded in December 1991.

Since mid-March 1992, interest rates have bounced back to between 15.5 and 18.0 percent. Higher interest rates will also hinder economic growth, which may lower the growth rate of tax revenues. At the same time, export oil revenues may be lower than projected. During the first four months of 1992, the average per-barrel price of Mexican export crude oil was U.S. $12.90, versus an annual budgeted average of U.S. $14.00 per barrel. Meanwhile, expenditures on salaries have increased and much needed capital expenditures on infrastructure are underway.

On a positive note, the February 1992 merger of the Programming and Budget Secretariat into the Finance Ministry should facilitate government efforts to better correlate spending decisions with revenue. This may allow the Finance Ministry to rapidly curb expenditures if interest savings and petroleum and tax revenues do not meet projected levels. Furthermore, the government's decision to use revenues from the privatization process to retire debt means that even if domestic interest costs are higher than projected, the balance on which interest is paid is smaller, so savings would still be realized. The government will also benefit from lower than projected interest costs on its external debt. During the first half of 1992, the six-month LIBOR interest rate averaged 4.0 percent, versus a government projected level of 6.5 percent.

During the first quarter of 1992, about 25 percent of Mexico's public sector expenditures went to salaries, 20 percent to interest payments, 12 percent to capital expenditures, and the remaining 43 percent to a variety of sources. By comparison, in 1988 about 43 percent of Mexico's public sector expenditures went to interest payments, 15 percent to salaries, and 11 percent were capital expenditures.

Under the Salinas administration, the government has made an enormous effort to balance its budget, limit and define its role in the economy, and reorient expenditures away from subsidies to ailing businesses and toward social programs. To that end, total public sector spending as a percentage of GDP fell from 40 percent in 1988 to 30 percent in 1991 and was expected to be an estimated 25 percent of GDP in 1992. During the same period, the financial deficit as a percentage of GDP fell from 12.4 to 1.5 percent, and a surplus was projected for 1992. The number of companies owned by the public sector has fallen from 1,155 in 1982 to 412 in 1988 and 223 as of August 1992. The government now views its primary role as creating a low-inflation environment conducive to economic growth and promoting social programs that target the poorest segments of society.

According to data from the Bank of Mexico, expenditure on social programs increased 41 percent in real terms between 1988 and 1991, including: health (43 percent increase), education (29 percent increase), PRONASOL (180 percent increase), and law and security (50 percent increase). The PRONASOL program deserves special mention since it targets the estimated 24 million Mexicans that live in extreme poverty and relies heavily on each community's involvement in designing and executing programs. Projects supported by PRONASOL funds usually address some immediate need of a community, such as potable water, sewage, and electrification. Funds also are used for worker training and primary school teaching materials. During 1991, the government spent 5.1 trillion pesos (U.S. $1.7 billion) on PRONASOL and 6.4 trillion pesos (U.S. $2.1 billion) was budgeted for 1992.

In January 1990 the governments of the United States and Mexico exchanged diplomatic notes which put into effect a tax exchange information agreement to assist the two countries in enforcing their tax laws. The agreement covers information that may affect the determination, assessment, and collection of taxes, and investigation and prosecution of tax crimes. In August 1992, the two governments concluded negotiations on a bilateral tax treaty—details of which will be released when the treaty is signed.

Debt Management Policies

Internal Debt

During 1991 and the first half of 1992, the government was able to decrease internal debt by both practicing fiscal restraint to limit the public sector's borrowing requirements and using revenues from the privatization process. Total internal debt amounted to 161.4 trillion pesos (U.S. $54.8 billion) in December 1990 and 170.3 trillion pesos (U.S. $55.5 billion) in December 1991 (as measured by the government obligations outstanding in the Bank of Mexico's "Indicadores Economicos"). Although there was a nominal increase in the amount of outstanding internal debt, in real terms (e.g. once the 18.8 percent inflation recorded in 1991 is factored out) internal debt declined by 11 percent.

During the first five months of 1992, there was a dramatic decrease in the internal debt and change in its composition towards (1) fewer types of instruments and (2) a larger percentage of ajustabonos (inflation indexed bonds with a three- to five-year maturity). Over the past year and a half, the following public sector internal debt instruments have been retired from circulation: petrobonos and pagafes. Peso-denominated bonds issued by state-owned companies have been transferred to the private sector since companies with those bonds were privatized.

The government believes that the best use of revenues from the privatization process is to retire internal debt, since a reduction in internal debt permanently benefits the economy by reducing the public sector's use of capital and lowering the government's debt servicing costs. In October 1991, the government used 20 trillion pesos (U.S. $6.56 billion) from the contingency fund (a special account into which proceeds from the sale of state-owned companies were channeled) to retire internal debt. According to data from the Finance Ministry, between January 1, 1992 and June 1, 1992, the government used another 35.7 trillion pesos (U.S. $11.5 billion) to retire public sector debt. This figure appears to have been applied to retirement of both internal and some external debt.

Due to tight fiscal policies, retirement of internal debt, and strong economic growth, Mexico's internal debt as a percentage of GDP fell from 24.1 percent in 1989 to 21.2 percent in 1990, 17.9 percent in 1991, and an estimated 14.5 percent of GDP in 1992. The average maturity of internal debt has also increased from 263 days in January 1990 to 417 days in January 1992. At the end of June 1992, the average maturity of Treasury bills was 127 days, up from 113 days in July 1991.

External Debt

Between January and August 1992, the most important factors to affect Mexico's external debt were:

- the April 1, 1992 decision by the Bank of Mexico to limit external borrowing by Mexican commercial banks to 10 percent of total liabilities;
- the U.S. $7.171 billion reduction in Mexico's public sector external debt, from U.S. $80.3 billion at the end of March to U.S. $76.1 billion as of June and U.S. $73.2 billion once Mexico receives all of the debt cancellation confirmations;
- the June announcement by Finance Min-

ister Aspe that Mexico entered into a risk insurance program (probably an interest rate swap) to ensure that Mexico will not have to pay more than 6.25 percent on its public sector external debt during 1992 and 1993; and

- the July 30 rating of Mexican government external debt as a "BB Plus" risk by Standard and Poor's.

Together, the aforementioned changes have acted to reduce Mexico's exposure to external shocks and lower its cost of borrowing abroad.

April 1, 1992 Limit on Foreign Borrowing

According to statistics from the Bank of Mexico, as of January 1992, 19.6 percent of the liabilities of the Mexican commercial banking system were denominated in foreign currency and contracted with external creditors (either through loans from foreign sources to Mexican banks, or deposits by nonresidents with Mexican banks). These foreign currency liabilities amounted to approximately 20.6 billion dollars, or 17 percent more than Mexico's December 1991 foreign exchange reserves.

The large amount of foreign borrowing by Mexican banks was potentially destabilizing because of:

- the sheer size of the commercial banks' foreign currency liabilities relative to Mexico's foreign exchange reserves;
- the composition of the foreign borrowing; and
- the use of the foreign funds.

Mexican banks used some of the money borrowed abroad to invest in peso-denominated loans and money market instruments. The influx of foreign funds increased Mexico's foreign exchange reserves but also caused an excessive decline in interest rates, which discouraged financial savings.

Therefore, in April 1992, the Bank of

Mexico established limits on foreign borrowings by Mexican commercial banks and requirements about how that money was to be invested. The April regulations stipulated that:

- over time banks must increase their peso-denominated liabilities so that only 10 percent of a bank's total liabilities are foreign currency denominated;

- at least 15 percent of a bank's foreign currency liabilities must be invested in top quality, liquid foreign securities; and

- no more than 85 percent of those foreign currency liabilities can be invested in foreign currency loans which can only be made to companies that have foreign currency earnings.

These measures limited the profitability of Mexican banks since their access to cheap foreign funding was reduced. However, the measures were necessary and prudent since they:

- increased the stability of Mexico's foreign exchange reserves by eliminating growth in reserves from new Euro-C.D. issues by Mexican banks;

- reduced the Mexican banking system's dependence on foreign funds by linking a bank's foreign currency borrowing to its foreign currency lending;

- reduced the Mexican financial system's exposure to exchange rate fluctuations by mandating that banks could only make foreign currency loans to companies with export earnings; and

- encouraged domestic financial saving by making domestic interest rates better reflect Mexican inflation rather than the profit expectations of dollar-based investors.

The April restrictions on foreign borrowing will impact Mexico's external debt balance over time since each Mexican bank cannot increase its foreign currency borrowing until that bank's peso liabilities have increased to 90 percent of total liabilities.

Other Developments

During the first eight months of 1992, five Mexican private sector companies issued U.S. $944 million worth of medium-term debt. The two largest placements were made by Femsa (brewery affiliated with Bancomer) and Volkswagen de Mexico for U.S. $300 million and Deutsch mark 400 million (U.S. $267 million equivalent), respectively. The third largest placement (U.S. $207 million) was backed by revenues from the Mexico City-Toluca toll road.

During the same period, four government agencies issued U.S. $789 million of medium-term debt.

The public sector debt issues are important both as funding sources and as benchmarks against which the prices of private sector debt issues can be compared. Since Mexico's return to the voluntary credit markets in June 1989, the government has pursued a consistent policy aimed at lowering the cost of borrowing abroad by Mexican entities, lengthening the maturity of debt, and diversifying financing sources. To that end, during 1992 the Mexican Export Bank (Bancomext) did a peseta five-year bond issue in Madrid, the National Development Bank (Nafinsa) did an ECU issue in Luxembourg and PEMEX (government-owned oil monopoly) did a French franc issue in Paris.

These transactions were a clear indication of increased confidence in Mexico among an expanding base of foreign investors.

Total external debt as a proportion of GDP fell from 58 percent in 1988 to 39.4 percent in 1990, 35.6 percent in 1991, and was expected to be an estimated 31.7 percent of GDP at the end of 1992. External debt servicing cost (amortization plus interest payments) as a percentage of GDP fell from

7 percent in 1988 to 5 percent in 1991. The finance ministry's decision to engage in a risk insurance program to ensure that Mexico would not have to pay more than 6.25 percent on its public sector external debt during 1992 and 1993 should mean additional savings for Mexico. During 1991, the average interest rate paid on Mexico's public sector external debt was 7.47 percent.

Mexico's External Debt Renegotiation

Mexico's debt package (negotiated in 1989 and early 1990) consisted of large new loans from the IMF, the World Bank, the Japanese Export-Import Bank, and a Paris Club agreement for government-to-government debt restructuring. The culminating portion of the package took place on February 4, 1990, when the Mexican government signed an agreement with the 15 banks of the Bank Advisory Committee, which represented the roughly 500 commercial banks that had exposure in Mexico. The agreement covered U.S. $48.2 billion. In exchange for accepting reduced principal or interest payments, banks received greater security. Mexico set up a fund totaling U.S. $7.12 billion which it used to guarantee the payment of principal on the new bonds and the 18-months interest on a rolling basis.

As a result of the debt agreement, Mexico's external debt fell by the equivalent of U.S. $14.4 billion (U.S. $7.2 billion through principal reduction and U.S. $7.2 billion through implicit principal reduction due to a lower interest rate paid on U.S. $22.4 billion of debt). Annual interest payments were reduced by U.S. $1.174 billion on average between 1990 and 1994 (see Table 14-8).

Principal payments on the new bonds were deferred to a single payment in 30 years and covered by the purchase of U.S. Treasury bonds. The debt agreement was retroactive to July 1989. However, until the agreement was finalized, Mexico serviced its debt under the previous terms. Thus, Mexico re-

ceived credit for these outlays in 1990 and 1991 against its first two scheduled payments on the new Mexican bonds.

The Currency and Exchange Rate Mechanisms

Mexico has had a managed floating exchange rate since November 1991. The rate at which large foreign exchange transactions are done fluctuates within a band that is defined by the rates at which banks will buy and sell U.S. dollars cash (e.g., small retail transactions).

Within the band the actual exchange rate is determined by market forces.

Dollar/peso foreign exchange is available on a same-day, 24 and 48 hour settlement basis. Most large foreign exchange transactions are settled in 48 hours.

When the current Pact for Stability and Economic Growth was announced on November 10, 1991, there was a 35 peso spread between the U.S. dollar cash buy and sell rates. At that time, the Bank of Mexico announced the spread would increase to 60 pesos. This was achieved by keeping the rate at which banks buy dollars constant at 3,051.2 pesos, and devaluing the sell rate by 0.2 pesos per day. The 60 peso spread between the buy and sell rates was reached on March 14, 1992, when the buy rate for one U.S. dollar cash was 3,051.2 pesos and the sell rate was 3,111.2 pesos. Under the original plan on March 15, banks should have begun devaluing both the U.S. dollar buy and sell rates by 0.2 pesos per day to keep the spread constant at 60 pesos.

However, the Bank of Mexico decided not to devalue the buy rate for dollars and to continue devaluing the sell rate by 0.2 pesos per day. Therefore the spread between the U.S. dollar cash buy and sell rates increases daily. It appears that the Bank of Mexico decided not to devalue the buy rate for U.S. dollars because:

Table 14-8
Mexico's External Debt, 1988–1991
(U.S. $ billions)

	1988	1989	1990	1991
Public sector	81.0	76.0	77.8	80.0
By creditor:				
Commercial banks	57.8	53.4	47.1	45.9
World bank and IDB	10.4	10.1	14.7	15.2
Official bilateral	8.7	8.3	11.5	12.8
Other	4.1	4.2	4.5	6.1
Mexican banks	8.1	9.0	7.7	8.7
Private sector	7.0	5.0	7.7	8.7
Bank of Mexico (IMF)	4.8	5.1	6.5	6.7
TOTAL	100.9	95.1	99.7	104.1

Source: Ministry of Finance, "Mexico Economic and Financial Statistics Data Book 3/31/92."

- The exchange rate for large transactions appreciated when the peso was allowed to float and was near the bottom of the band from February through mid-March. The Bank of Mexico would have had to intervene (buy dollars) daily to force a devaluation of the dollar buy rate.

- Foreign exchange reserves were at all time highs so the Bank of Mexico did not want to be forced to buy more dollars.

- If the exchange rate remained near the bottom of the band, Mexico would not "import inflation" from a devaluing currency, which the Bank of Mexico believes to be a significant source of inflationary pressure.

- By keeping the cash dollar buy rate constant, if the capital inflows remained large the government could, in practice, benefit from a constant exchange rate without the negatives of an actual fixing.

- Finally, if capital inflows slowed down (as they did in June and July) the band

within which the peso could adjust freely would be larger and therefore better able to reflect real demand and supply.

From an investor's point of view, the major impact of the March decision was to increase the potential volatility of the peso/dollar exchange rate since the spread within which the exchange rate can move freely, increases daily.

As of August 14, the bottom of the band was still fixed at 3,051.2 and the top was 3,141.8 pesos/dollar. This meant that the peso/dollar exchange rate could fluctuate 2.9 percent without intervention from the Bank of Mexico. If this policy was maintained (which appeared likely at least until the Pact for Stability and Economic Growth was renewed), on January 8, 1993 there should have been a 4 percent spread within which the peso/dollar exchange rate could fluctuate.

Under its floating exchange rate policy, Mexico saw a revaluation of the peso between November 1991 and late April 1992, with some volatility due to seasonal factors at year-end and the end of each quarter. However, at the end of April capital inflows diminished due to the limit on foreign borrowing by Mexican banks and uncertainty in the capital markets. Between April 13 and July 28 the peso devalued 1.7 percent from 3,060 to 3,113 pesos/dollar. During August the peso/dollar exchange rate has strengthened to about 3,080 pesos/dollar. This is due in part to foreign investment in the Mexican money markets.

The government believes that the exchange rate is a crucial tool in the fight against inflation and has stated that it eventually hopes to arrive at a fixed peso/dollar exchange rate. However, since inflation in Mexico has been consistently higher than in the United States and the devaluation of the peso has not compensated for the difference, the peso has appreciated in real terms against the dollar. The peso appreciated by 9.9 percent against the dollar in 1990, 9.3 percent in 1991, and another 4.1 percent during the first seven months of 1992.

Several Mexico analysts have expressed concern about Mexico's appreciating peso and large trade account deficit. They believe that the large trade account deficit is unsustainable and that Mexico will have to devalue its currency to make exports more competitive and discourage imports.

While the appreciation of the peso is clearly a pattern, a devaluation seems highly unlikely at this stage. The government believes a devaluation is unnecessary because many Mexican industries' exports are still very competitive, capital inflows remain large, and foreign exchange reserves are still at very high levels. Manufactured exports increased 17 percent during the first quarter of 1992 compared to the same period in 1991, which indicates that productivity gains are outpacing price rises due to the appreciation of the peso. Mexico's foreign

exchange reserves amounted to U.S. $17,547 million at the end of 1991 and U.S. $18,023 million as of August 21, 1992.

Since the U.S. dollar has depreciated significantly in relation to other world currencies (DM, Yen, etc.) and the peso is linked to the dollar, Mexico's exports to countries (except the U.S.) benefited from a weak currency during 1992. This is important in light of Mexico's aggressive effort to expand its trade relations worldwide.

Foreign Exchange Coverage

Mexico offers short-term dollar/peso foreign exchange coverage, up to one year. Formerly, the coverage was only available to Mexican corporations but the market was expected to be opened to foreigners and individuals (both Mexican and foreign) by the end of August 1992. Foreign exchange coverage in Mexico works as follows:

- On day one, an investor pays a premium for foreign exchange coverage, and

- On day two, the investor discovers what the reference rate is for that coverage. Any devaluation above the reference rate is refunded to the investor when the foreign exchange coverage contract matures.

The reference rate is determined by the Bank of Mexico each day and published the following day. The reference rate is the average sell rate of a group of foreign exchange dealers surveyed by the Bank of Mexico. Since the reference rate is an average and it is unknown to the investor at the time he purchases foreign exchange coverage, the reference rate usually differs from the investor's cost of pesos so a perfect hedge is not possible.

Tapping Multilateral Aid

Economic aid: U.S. commitments, including Ex-Im (FY70–89), $3.1 billion; Western (non-U.S.) countries, ODA and OOF bilateral commitments (1970–89), $7.7 billion; Communist countries (1970–89), $110 million.

Financial Market Operations and Structural Policies

The most important developments in the Mexican financial markets during the first eight months of 1992 were: (1) a deluge of international equity offerings by Mexican firms that saturated demand; (2) a sharp rise of the Mexican stock index through March followed by a precipitous decline of the index starting in June; (3) problems in the ajustabonos market which decreased liquidity and shook investor confidence in that instrument; and (4) an acceleration of regulatory efforts to modernize the Mexican financial markets.

During 1991 and the first three months of 1992, the international appetite for Mexican equity appeared insatiable. Over that period 21 different Mexican companies made highly successful international equity offerings and raised a total of U.S. $4.35 billion. Total foreign investment in the Mexican stock market and investment in the Mexico fund increased from U.S. $4.08 billion in December 1990 to U.S. $18.54 billion in December 1991, and U.S. $25.48 billion in March 1992. The Mexican stock index rose 33 percent between December 30, 1991, and March 3, 1992; and it rose 128 percent in 1991.

In April 1992, Cemex (Mexico's largest cement company) broke the trend with an unsuccessful international equity offering. The underwriters for the Cemex issue had to both decrease the size of the offering and price it below market. This was the first indication that foreign demand for Mexican equity could be saturated.

Most analysts believe that the Cemex offering was unsuccessful because Cemex itself (as well as other Mexican companies) had already done too many 144-A offerings. If an equity offering is made under the U.S. Securities Exchange Commission's 144-A rules, less disclosure is required about the company but the universe of investors is limited to only qualified institutional buyers that manage U.S. $100 million or more. Cemex had previously done successful 144-A offerings, but by April 1992, U.S. institutional investors were already loaded up with Cemex stock so demand for more of the same was limited. Furthermore, of the 21 Mexican companies that made international equity offerings in 1991 and the first three months of 1992, only three chose to be listed on an exchange and the rest did 144-A placements.

In May, Telmex (Mexico's telephone monopoly) placed another U.S. $1.4 billion worth of equity in international markets (including Mexico). A year prior, Telmex had placed U.S. $1.9 billion in international markets. The Telmex issue was listed on the New York stock exchange but its sheer size worried investors and depressed Mexican stock prices during the spring.

Before investors had a chance to digest the Telmex issue that was placed on May 12, the Banacci financial group (which includes Mexico's largest bank, Banamex), announced that it planned to do a 144-A international equity offering to raise an estimated U.S. $1.5 billion. The size of this offering was enormous and, as had happened with Telmex, anticipation of the Banacci issue depressed stock prices. Had the Banacci offering been successful, it would have been the largest 144-A offering ever, and could have been as large as the largest equity placement ever by a U.S. bank. As it turned out, the Banacci offering was withdrawn in June due to the decline of the Mexican stock index.

The aforementioned numerous equity offerings and spectacular rise of the index between December 1990 and March 1992 set the stage for profit-taking, which was triggered in early June by press reports that NAFTA negotiations were stalled and statements against NAFTA by presidential candidate Ross Perot. Between June 1 and June 24, the Mexican stock index plummeted from a high of 1,907.36 points (33.25 percent year-to-date [YTD] gain) to 1,562.71 points (9.17 percent YTD gain) on June 24.

In early July foreign investors, who felt they had been misled by Cemex as to the use of funds raised in its April equity offering, began a major sell-off of Cemex stock which continued into August. During July, the index seemed to consolidate around 1,640 points (14 percent YTD gain) but then declined sharply at month's end due to unfounded rumors that Telmex's second quarter earnings would be much lower than expected.

During the first three weeks of August, the Mexican stock index remained extremely weak and the volume of trading low. A hoped-for rally following the completion of the NAFTA negotiations on August 12 never materialized.

Analysts indicated that investors: (1) already discounted the completion of NAFTA negotiations; (2) were uncertain about which companies would benefit under NAFTA and therefore which stocks to buy; (3) were uncertain about the prospects for Mexican equity during the NAFTA ratification process; and (4) given that uncertainty and high interest rates in Mexico, preferred to invest in fixed-income securities.

As of August 25, the Mexican stock index registered 1,353.09 points (5.5 percent YTD loss). The index's weighted average price/earnings ratio was 9.58 and its weighted average price/book value ratio was 1.7.

At the end of July, total foreign investment in Mexican equity amounted to U.S.

$21.88 billion down from a high of U.S. $27.24 billion recorded in May.

While the equity markets suffered from a series of negative developments, rising interest rates between March and July hurt Mexican financial intermediaries that had taken large speculative positions in the money market on the assumption that interest rates would continue to decline.

Historically such speculation had been extremely profitable. The real yield of ajustabonos (inflation indexed government bonds) had fallen steadily from 19.5 percent in July 1989 to 2.0 percent in mid-March 1992, resulting in large trading gains for financial intermediaries. Between December 1990 and the end of February 1992, the monthly volume of trading in ajustabonos increased almost 300 percent to U.S. $18.5 billion equivalent. During the same period the real yield of ajustabonos fell from 4.6 percent to just over 2.0 percent.

Ajustabonos have a three- or five-year maturity so any movement in their yields is amplified. Therefore, when interest rates began to increase in the second half of March and continued to increase through July, rumors began to circulate of large trading losses accumulated by banks and brokerage houses on their ajustabonos positions. Demand for ajustabonos withered. The total volume of ajustabonos traded fell from U.S. $17.0 billion equivalent in March to U.S. $11.5 billion equivalent in April and bottomed out at U.S. $7.7 billion equivalent in May.

In July, the press drew attention to the mounting losses in the ajustabonos market and stated that: (1) at least 60 percent of Mexico's 18 banks and 26 brokerage houses purchased speculative positions in ajustabonos that were losing money, and (2) some financial intermediaries had dumped the losing ajustabonos positions into client-owned mutual funds.

The regulatory authorities responded by both warning investors about the losses and aggressively auditing banks' and brokerage houses' accounts.

Nonetheless, worries about the impact of those losses on an already weak stock market and concern about who would pay for the losses caused a decline of bank stocks and also may have caused the decline of investment in fixed-income mutual funds (which had begun in May) to continue. Between July 21, when the losses in the ajustabonos market made front page news, and July 27, the value of most bank stocks decreased about 20 percent. The total assets of all Mexican fixed-income mutual funds decreased from 55.2 trillion pesos (U.S. $18.0 billion) in April to 52.0 trillion pesos (U.S. $16.8 billion) in May, 46.9 trillion pesos (U.S. $15.0 billion) in June and 43.3 trillion pesos (U.S. $14.0 billion) in July.

Efforts to avoid negative perceptions of ajustabonos rubbing off on other government debt and restore confidence in that instrument are important since the market for Mexican government debt is by far the most active and liquid of all Mexican financial markets. During the first six months of 1992, trading in Mexican government securities accounted for 97 percent of the total volume of debt and equity traded on the Mexican stock exchange: approximately 92 percent of all trading on the Mexican stock exchange was concentrated in Treasury bills (50 percent in overnight Treasury bills and 42 percent in other Treasury bills), 4 percent was in ajustabonos, 2 percent was in stocks, and 1 percent each in government bonds and private sector debt instruments.

The Treasury bills' dominance of trading reflects a well developed secondary market (which other instruments lack), as well as investors' preference for short-term, liquid instruments. However, during the first six months of 1992 compared to the same period in 1991, trading in Treasury bills with more than a one-day maturity increased over 2,200 percent in dollar terms to U.S. $629.8 billion. This growth was due both to the introduction of longer-term Treasury bills (364-day Treasury bills were introduced in November 1990) and to increased investors' confidence in the economy and consequent willingness to hold longer-term securities.

Over the past three and one-half years the capitalization of Mexico's stock market has increased over 360 percent from U.S. $27 billion in December 1989 to U.S. $41.1 billion in December 1990, U.S. $101.7 billion in December 1991, and U.S. $126 billion in July 1992. The volume of equity trading has increased almost 400 percent over the same period. Between December 1990 and July 1992, the number of stocks listed on the exchange increased from 226 to 252 and the average daily value of stocks traded (excluding block trades and new offerings) increased from U.S. $16.6 million to U.S. $113.7 million. In nominal terms the Mexican stock index increased 98 percent in 1989, 50 percent in 1990, and 128 percent in 1991.

Mexican regulatory authorities have responded to this spectacular growth by accelerating their efforts to modernize the Mexican financial markets. To that end, following are highlights of some of the most important regulatory announcements made in the 1991–92 time frame.

- April 1991: the National Securities Commission (CNV) authorized short sales of highly liquid Mexican stocks.

- December 1991: CNV authorized the establishment of two new rating agencies for Mexican securities, which brought the total number of rating agencies in Mexico to three. The first rating agency

(CAVAL) began operations in May 1990.

- April 1992: CNV issued regulations which allow brokerage houses to trade variable income securities for their own account. Over time this change is expected to increase the volume of shares traded and to provide liquidity for more issues.

- June 1992: the Mexican banking and financial groups laws were amended so that Mexican banks and financial groups can issue "L" class shares which can constitute up to 30 percent of ordinary capital, can be owned by all investors including foreigners, and convey limited voting rights.

- August 1992: CNV issued regulations requiring firms to wait at least 30 working days from the date they receive authorization to do an initial public offering until the date the offering is made.

- August/September 1992: the CNV issued regulations that provide a legal framework for trading warrants on Mexican equity.

Warrants are the first derivative instruments ever in Mexico. A warrant gives the holder the right but not the obligation to buy or sell a predetermined quantity of stock at a specified price during a specified period of time in the future. Warrants are an important hedging mechanism whose introduction should increase the depth and stability of the Mexican market. According to information from the Mexican stock exchange, the key features of the Mexican warrants market are as follows:

- Warrants may be issued by brokerage houses and banks on individual highly liquid Mexican stocks, baskets of medium and highly liquid stocks, and on stock indices.

- There are no restrictions as to who may purchase warrants.

- Loans, short sales, or repurchase agreements with warrants are prohibited.

- Warrants must be registered with the CNV and settlement will take three days and be made through INDEVAL.

According to press reports, the government is considering the development of both financial and commodities futures. Also the Mexican stock exchange is trying to create a new index that will be easier to hedge and has a more even weighting of stocks listed on the exchange. As of August 25, Telmex alone accounted for 32 percent of the Mexican stock index.

Financial Savings

Current government estimates are that real financial savings as a percentage of GDP will grow from 40.0 percent of GDP in 1991 to 41.3 percent of GDP in 1992. There has been a dramatic growth in savings since 1989, when real financial savings represented only 29 percent of GDP. This growth has been due to the popularity of interest-bearing checking accounts, the introduction of new financial instruments, the repatriation of capital, and large amounts of foreign portfolio investment. The growth in savings and investment has helped to ensure the availability of additional resources for private sector financing. The February 1992 introduction of a mandatory private pension system (to supplement the government system) could rapidly become another major source of long-term savings, and will lead to an increase in overall savings during 1992. Commercial bank loans to the private sector expanded 33 percent in real terms between April 1991 and April 1992. Over the same period, in real terms, commercial bank loans to the public sector decreased 8 percent.

LICENSING, PATENTS, AND TRADEMARKS

Protection of U.S. Intellectual Property

Mexico is a member of the World Intellectual Property Organization, as well as the Berne Convention for the Protection of Literary and Artistic Works, the Paris Convention for the Protection of Industrial Property, the Universal Copyright Convention, the Geneva Phonograms Convention, and the Brussels Satellite Convention.

The Mexican government significantly increased its protection of intellectual property by means of a new Act for the Protection of Industrial Property (patents and trademarks) that came into effect on June 28, 1991, and reforms to the copyright act that became effective in August 1991. As a result, Mexico now provides intellectual property protection that is relatively strong in comparison with that afforded by other developing countries and even a number of industrialized countries.

Several U.S. concerns over Mexican intellectual property protection remain to be addressed in the ongoing NAFTA negotiations, such as patent protection for plant species, a statutory right of importation for copyrighted works, protection for semiconductor chip layout design, and general intellectual property rights enforcement issues. Whatever changes are negotiated in these areas will be strongly influenced by the outcome of the Trade Related Aspects of Intellectual Property (TRIPS) segment of the Uruguay Round/GATT negotiations, still in progress at the time of this report.

Product patent protection was extended to all processes and products, including chemicals, alloys, pharmaceuticals, biotechnology, and plant varieties. The patent protection term was extended from 14 to 20 years from the date of filing. Trademarks are now granted for 10-year renewable periods.

The enhanced copyright law provides protection for computer programs against unauthorized reproduction for a period of 50 years. Of particular importance to U.S. producers, sanctions and penalties against infringements have been increased. In addition, damages now can be claimed regardless of the application of sanctions. With the sweeping new legal framework only recently enacted, enforcement of the new regime will be the key intellectual property concern over the next year, as past losses to U.S. producers have been large.

VISITING AND LOCATING

General Travel Checklist

Customs: A passport or certified copy of a birth certificate and a tourist card are required for entry.

Climate and clothing: The high plateau area around Guadalajara and Mexico City is springlike throughout the year, a bit cooler in winter, and a little warmer in summer. The Yucatan Peninsula, the Monterrey area, and the U.S. border areas are very hot in summer and pleasant in winter. Business suits for men and street dresses or pantsuits for women are appropriate in the cities. Sport shirts are worn for all social occasions in the coastal zones.

Health: Cooked food is safe to eat; raw vegetables often are not. Tap water may not be potable. Medical facilities in the larger cities are good. A leisurely pace is recommended for the first few days in the higher altitudes.

Telecommunications: Long-distance telephone and telegraph service to major cities is good. Mexico City is one time zone behind eastern standard time.

Transportation: Direct international air service from many U.S. airports is available to Mexico City, Cancun, Guadalajara,

Merida, Monterrey, and other points. Bus service in Mexico is good, and the highway system is extensive. Auto rental is available.

Tourist attractions: About six million tourists, some 90 percent of them U.S. citizens, visit Mexico annually. Among the richest archeological sites are Teotihuacan (with its famous pyramids) and Tula near Mexico City, Monte Alban and Palenque in the south, and Chichen Itza and Uxmal in the Yucatan. The National Museum of Anthropology in Mexico City is one the world's finest. Other important museums include the Colonial Museum in Tepozotlan, Chapultepec Castle, and the Museum of La Venta at Villahermosa, Tabasco. The major coastal resorts are Acapulco, Puerto Vallarta, Ixtapa, Cozumel, and Cancun.

THE EXPATRIATE

Economic and Employment Factors

Mexican workers, with the exception of those earning the minimum wage, fared better in 1991 and 1992 than in the previous few years. Although minimum wages ran slightly behind inflation, despite the 13 percent increase in the minimum wage which was instituted in 1991, numbers of contractual workers in the manufacturing sector were able to post higher real wages during this period. The flexible freeze on wages, prices, and exchange rates effectively helped to keep inflation in check during 1991, although prices continued to be the most difficult element to control. The annual inflation rate for 1991 was held to 19 percent, but labor sector dissatisfaction continued to increase in light of worker impatience to recover previously lost purchasing power, even though the 1992 inflation rate had been projected to run at only about 12 percent.

Organized labor continues to accept the government's tough economic recovery program, in part because less than 15 percent of the labor force (mostly unorganized labor) earns the minimum wage, and most other workers (especially organized workers) have enjoyed income increases in line with or in excess of inflation. Real wages in the manufacturing sector grew by 2.8 percent in 1990 and by 4.8 percent in 1991.

Job creation has been and will continue to be a major challenge for the government. The government projects that the economy will grow by 3.5 percent in 1992. This is greater than the population growth rate, which is estimated to be in the range of 2 percent.

Employment in the manufacturing sector decreased by 1.6 percent between 1990 and 1991. Due to the slower devaluation of the peso against the dollar, competition from imports will intensify and will complicate potential expansion on the part of many companies and the rate of job creation. Still, employment in maquiladora industries, which declined slightly in 1991, showed signs of solid recovery in early 1992.

Unemployment remained a problem, despite the seemingly low unemployment figures released by the Mexican government. While unemployment figures are particularly difficult to come by, with between 2 and 4 percent as generally accepted figures under the more narrow Mexican definition of unemployment as "persons actively looking for work," many observers would say the unemployment rate is considerably higher. Since the definition Mexico uses for unemployed workers is different than that used by the U.S. and most other OECD countries, unemployment numbers quoted by the Mexican government should not be compared with figures for OECD countries. Underemployed Mexicans, the largest numbers of whom are to be found in the informal economy, and those "seeking employment," are estimated by the Mexican government to be numbered in the range of 12 to 15 percent. Again, given the differences in definition,

Mexican underemployment rates should not be compared directly with other countries using different criteria.

The maquiladora or in-bond assembly industry continued its steady growth and expansion, and by 1991 there were close to 2,000 plants employing nearly 500,000 workers. The full employment of the Mexican border states, where most maquiladora industries are located, contrasts starkly with the pronounced unemployment and underemployment problem of states in most other parts of Mexico. At the same time, the magnet of the maquiladora industries in the border states has exacerbated the dearth of housing, social services, and other infrastructure services, thus lowering the quality of life in these areas which offer almost full employment. Some of the pressures are easing somewhat with the gradual shift of maquiladoras away from the border areas. The percentage of maquiladoras on the border has declined from 92 percent in 1985 to approximately less than 87 percent by 1991. Unionization of workers varies along the border with the density of labor organization generally decreasing as one goes from east to west. Most nonunion entry-level maquiladora workers earn the minimum wage but receive additional benefits such as free lunches, transportation, etc.

Although rates vary historically, turnover among workers in the maquiladora industry tends to be fairly high as workers shop around for better benefits or make their way into the U.S. economy.

Wages and Labor

The minimum wage increased 12.0 percent in 1991 while falling over six percent in real terms (the increase was in mid-November and it did not compensate for inflation which was 18.8 percent for the year).

1991 was the ninth consecutive year that the minimum wage has fallen in real terms. Between January 1983 and July 1992, the minimum wage deteriorated by 54 percent in real terms. As of August 1992, the minimum wage in Mexico City was 13,330 pesos (about U.S. $4.35) per day.

Although minimum wages have been falling since 1982, they have progressively diminished in importance as a yardstick for measuring labor compensation in Mexico. Less than 10 percent of the labor force in the sixteen major urban areas earns the minimum wage, and most other workers have enjoyed income increases in line with or in excess of inflation.

For example, in 1991 the average increase in contractual wages was 21 percent compared with inflation of just under 19 percent. Contractual wages that were negotiated between January and June 1992 increased 16.6 percent on average. During the first half of 1992, the highest contractual wage increases were in the food and beverage sector (20.0 percent), and the lowest increases were in the mining sector (15.0 percent). On May 15, President Salinas announced a 20 percent increase in teachers' salaries, which brought a teacher's average salary to 3.5 times the minimum wage (U.S. $15.25 per day).

Nonetheless, the minimum wage is important to the overall economy since many items are indexed to it, and it is used as a reference for other wages. For example, pensions, employer contributions to the social security system, and some liability insurance payments are indexed to the minimum wage. The annual increase in the minimum wage is announced when the Pact for Stability and Economic Growth is extended (usually November) and acts as a benchmark against which contractual wage increases are compared.

Table 14-9 shows the distribution of wages among economically active people in Mexico's 16 largest urban areas for the first quarters of 1989, 1991 and 1992.

In addition to wages, most Mexican

workers receive fringe benefits which, in the case of manufacturing, amount to 30–35 percent of a worker's total compensation package. Total compensation in the manufacturing sector registered an average annual real growth of 3.9 percent during 1991 compared to 4.9 percent in 1990, and 9.9 percent in 1989. Between March 1991 and March 1992, total compensation in the manufacturing sector increased 2.7 percent in real terms. During 1991 average compensation per worker in the industrial and construction sectors was 6.0 and 2.5 times the minimum wage (U.S. $26.00 and U.S. $10.90 per day), respectively.

In February 1992, the executive branch of the Mexican government sent a legislative proposal to the Congress to create a private pension system, the first contributions to which were made in May. The private pension system is funded by a tax deductible 2 percent employer contribution. Individual accounts are established for each worker and Mexican commercial banks administer the accounts. The new pension plan also includes a 5 percent tax that is channeled into workers' housing. Mortgages of up to 30 years are now available, thereby greatly facilitating the ability of moderate income families to purchase houses.

In May 1992, the CTM (Mexico's largest labor union with over five million members) and other Mexican labor unions joined a tripartite (government/employers/labor) voluntary National Accord for Raising Productivity and Quality (ANEPC). The government and employers both pledged to invest more in upgrading workers' skills, while organized labor agreed to negotiate workplace understandings with management on improving productivity. Employers also pledged to reward workers for productivity increases. The ANEPC may be a first step in modernizing Mexico's labor-management relations system so that it is more attuned to businesses facing competition in a free-market economy.

According to data from the National Statistical Institute, 30 percent of the Mexican population was economically active as of

Table 14-9
Income Distribution, 16 Urban Areas

Wage	Percent of Urban Workers Receiving Said Wage During First Quarter		
	1989	1991	1992
Less than 1 minimum wage	18.6	10.8	9.1
1 to 2 minimum wages	49.3	46.2	42.6
More than 2 minimum wages	20.0	27.6	30.8
More than 5 minimum wages	4.8	7.8	8.2
No income	4.8	4.2	5.2
Not specified	2.5	3.4	4.1
	100.0	100.0	100.0

Source: National Statistical Institute (INEGI), "Cuaderno de Informacion Oportuna, 6/92 and 1/91."

1990 (the most recent statistics available). Of those 24 million economically active people, 22 percent were employed in agriculture, 19 percent in manufacturing, 13 percent in the wholesale and retail trade, 8 percent in community services, 7 percent in construction, 4 percent in transport and communications, and 27 percent in other sectors. At the same time, roughly 12 million workers were enrolled in one of Mexico's social security systems. Despite progress in job creation, unemployment and underemployment remain serious problems in Mexico.

Between March 1991 and March 1992, there was an 5.2 percent increase in the number of workers registered in the Mexican Social Security System (IMSS).

This brought the total number of registered workers up to 11.3 million, of which 10 million were employed full time and 1.3 million part time.

Employment in the in-bond industries (AKA maquiladora sector) totaled 475 thousand in August 1991, about the same as a year earlier, but this figure has increased significantly since then. As of May 1992, the maquiladora sector employed just over 500 thousand workers. Due to strong demand for a qualified, stable work force, remuneration in the maquiladora sector has increased more rapidly than salaries in other sectors. For example, total remuneration for maquiladora workers in real terms increased 4.9 percent in 1991 and 11.8 percent between February 1991 and February 1992.

Worker Rights

Under the Constitution, specified worker rights are guaranteed, and may not be diminished in any way. These include the right of association, the right to bargain, and the right to strike. Mexico also has signed and ratified most ILO conventions dealing with worker rights. However, worker rights may be augmented in various ways, including individual labor contracts, collective bargaining agreements, or law contracts. If a firm's survival is threatened, some worker benefits could be justifiably reduced, modified, or eliminated after an agreement or collective judgment by a Conciliation and Arbitration Board. Still, the level of worker rights may never go below the floor set by the FLL (Federal Labor Law).

The right of association: The Mexican Constitution guarantees workers and employers the right to form unions and professional associations. Unions must register with the Labor Secretariat, though registration requirements are not onerous. Leftist labor activists complain, however, that their effects to register new unions are rejected unjustifiably. Mexico enjoys a well-developed trade union movement with close to 30–35 percent of a work force of an estimated 23–26 million organized into union confederations (largely affiliated with the ruling Institutional Revolutionary Party) and a small number of independent unions. Almost all public sector employees are unionized, and have the right to strike, although this is rarely exercised.

The right to organize and bargain collectively: Both the right to organize and bargain collectively are guaranteed by Mexican labor law and generally honored in practice. Collective bargaining is common, particularly in industry and commerce, less so in the public sector. The right to organize is respected in the in-bond (maquila) industry, although relatively few workers of the firms belong to unions.

Generally speaking, nonunion in-bond firms provide benefits and working conditions that match or exceed those established by union contracts.

Workers are protected by law from antiunion discrimination but this law is unevenly enforced, especially in states with a low degree of unionization.

Prohibition of forced or compulsory labor: The Constitution prohibits forced or compulsory labor. There have been no credible reports for many years of forced labor in Mexico.

Minimum age of employment of children: Mexican law sets the minimum age of employment for children at 14 years of age, with those 14 and 15 permitted to work a maximum of six hours daily in nonhazardous areas. Fourteen- and 15-year-olds also may not work at night or do overtime. Child labor laws are strictly enforced in large and medium-sized manufacturing and commercial establishments. Enforcement is less effective in smaller shops and factories, and even less still among street vendors or others engaged in the underground economy.

Acceptable conditions of work: Mexican labor legislation provides substantial protection for workers with respect to occupational safety and health, though again, compliance with the law varies in accordance with the size and formal organization of the establishment. The law provides for a maximum work week of 48 hours. Minimum wage legislation is often revised to account for inflation, but has not kept up with actual rises in the cost of living. Unionized workers generally enjoy a somewhat higher standard of living than that provided by the legislated minimum wage, and for the past two years their wages and benefits have kept pace with inflation.

Rights in sectors with U.S. investment: The following sectors have U.S. investment: Food and related products, chemicals and related products, primary and fabricated metals, machinery (except electrical and electronic equipment), transportation equipment, other manufacturing, wholesale trade. (N.B. petroleum is a state monopoly.) In all of the above sectors, the rights of association and to organize and bargain collectively, a prohibition on the use of forced or compulsory labor, a minimum work age, and acceptable working conditions exist and are re-

spected. As stated earlier, the majority of Mexican workers at in-bond plants have not been unionized, and there have been accusations that unionization has been discouraged and other worker rights, such as minimum age restrictions, violated. Such accusations have not, by and large, held up to scrutiny, with the exception of smaller plants (10–100 workers) which are more likely to be locally rather than foreign-owned.

Working Conditions

Hours of work: The work shift may be a day shift (eight hours maximum), mixed shift (7½ hours maximum), or night shift (seven hours maximum). A 48-hour work week including one full day of rest with full pay is the standard set out by the FLL. Workers must be paid twice their hourly wage for overtime, and three times the hourly wage for any more than nine hours of overtime worked.

Special limitations apply to minors age 14 and 15. They are not allowed to work in nonindustrial establishments after 10:00 p.m. and industrial night labor is forbidden. The work shift for minors may not exceed six hours, divided into two periods of maximum of three hours divided by a rest period of at least one hour. Minors may not work overtime, on holidays, or on mandatory rest days.

Holidays

The FFL established seven mandatory holidays per year, as well as one additional day when a new president is installed and another when there are federal or local elections. Work performed on holidays must be paid at twice the normal hourly wage.

Vacations

By law, employees are entitled to six working days vacation after one year of service. After that, the number of days increases.

Employees are also entitled to a vacation bonus during their vacation days equivalent to 25 percent of their salary.

Salary

The minimum salary is set by a tripartite National Commission for Minimum Salaries and is the least amount an employer may pay. Salaries may be set based on a unit of time (day, week, month or year—but not by the hour); a unit of work (piece-rate); lump sum; in the form of commissions; or any other mutually-agreed manner. A yearly bonus, equal to two-weeks' pay, must be paid to workers in December of each year.

Profit Sharing

Employees are granted the right to a share of the profits of each establishment. The shares are determined by the National Commission for Employee Profit Sharing in Enterprise. Currently, 10 percent of gross profits must be reserved for profit sharing. Fifty percent of the employees' share of profits is distributed to individual workers on the basis of salary and the number of days worked during the year. The remaining 50 percent is distributed equally among all employees, according to the number of days each worked. There are numerous exceptions to profit sharing, exempting newly formed firms from sharing profits with employees and disqualifying executive officers and the like from sharing in profits.

Vocational Training and Instruction

Under the FLL workers are entitled to employer-provided training and instruction in their work which permits them to "raise their standards of living and productivity, in accordance with the plans and programs developed by mutual agreement between the employer and the union or the employees, and as approved by the Secretariat of Labor and Social Welfare." For years this provision has

been widely ignored but given the challenge of a competitive global economy, the government is urging employers and unions to observe it.

Social Security System

By law, employers and employees contribute to a national social security system. One institution, IMSS, covers the private sector; another, ISSSTE, covers government employees; and, a third, PEMEX Institute, covers oil workers. The more than 12 million system enrollees constitute what is considered the formal sector work force. The system provides retirement and disability benefits, and full medical care for the worker, spouse, minor children, and live-in parents. Social security hospitals and clinics thus cover over half the national population. IMSS also collects the payroll deductions that fund the worker housing fund, INFONAVIT, and the retirement savings program, SAR. IMSS charges employers for health care by their experience ratings.

Housing

Mexico also established a National Housing Fund (INFONAVIT), which is funded by a 5 percent payroll tax. The fund assists employees in financing housing or improvements. It proved unable to keep pace with worker housing needs, especially in the northern states along the U.S. border. In 1992, it underwent major revisions.

Labor Relations

Mexico's labor relations situation during 1991 and 1992 was dominated by the impact of continued restructuring of the national economy and the expectation that Mexico soon would join the United States and Canada in NAFTA. Employers placed pressure on the government to revise the FLL with an eye to removing alleged obstacles to productivity and product quality. The CTM (Confederation of Mexican Workers), the country's largest labor organization, objected, fearing a loss of hard-won gains for workers.

In May 1992, an alternate approach was agreed upon among government, employers, and organized labor in the form of a voluntary National Accord for Raising Productivity and Quality (ANEPC). In it, government and employers pledged to invest more in upgrading worker skills while organized labor agreed to negotiate workplace understandings with management on improving productivity. Employers also pledged to reward workers for gains achieved.

The creation of ANEPC reflects the growing preoccupation of government, employers and, belatedly, organized labor with addressing changes needed in a still largely corporatist labor-management relations system.

Continued government austerity and the proceeds of privatization sales enabled Mexico to balance its federal budget by 1992, drastically reduce its debt, and achieve a more than 3 percent GDP real growth rate for the fourth straight year. The inflation rate dropped to 19 percent in 1991 and may have reached 10-12 percent by the end of 1992. The CTM and the other now 37 members of the umbrella Labor Congress (CT) continued to back the economic policies of President Carlos Salinas de Gortari, although often criticizing the manner of their application. While the workers on minimum wage, less than 15 percent of the work force, suffered another slight decline in purchasing power in 1991, the rest—including trade union members—made modest gains. Badly paid teachers got a 25 percent catch-up wage increase in 1991 and a 20 percent increase in 1992.

By 1992 some stresses over change were apparent within the Labor Congress. The small labor central known as FESEBES

(Federation of Unions in Business Providing Goods and Services), led by the telephone union STRM, often voiced strong criticism of CT leadership. It claimed the dominant Labor Congress leaders had no agenda for addressing the challenges of labor-management relations in a free market economy and were stifling union democracy. SNTE, the large teachers' union, agreed. These critics' views were more in step with governmental economic restructuring policies than those of the dominant CT leaders.

The mainstream labor organization lost strength within the ruling party, PRI (Institutional Revolutionary Party). After the August 1991 federal legislative elections, thanks to fewer than usual PRI labor candidates, the percentage of CT senators and deputies in the federal congress was less than 10 percent. In 1992, only one labor leader was named as a PRI gubernatorial candidate. In May 1992 PRI reorganized its sectors, resulting in a merger of the labor and campesino sectors into a National Workers Front. The public sector, renamed National Citizens Front, was subdivided into four units: public sector workers, schoolteachers, the middle class, and a group of professionals and technicians. A territorial sector, Popular Territorial Movement, was added. With this, the era of the dominant labor sector formally ended and a possible middle class era for PRI was begun.

In early 1991, CT labor organizations backed Mexico's decision to negotiate a NAFTA with the U.S. and Canada. This cast a chill on CTM's normally good relations with the AFL-CIO, which, along with the CLC in Canada, opposed the NAFTA negotiations.

The CTM, AFL-CIO, and CLC are all members of the Mexico City-based ORIT (Inter-American Regional Organization of Workers) of the ICFTU (International Confederation of Free Trade Unions). In late 1991, ORIT adopted a policy of asking hemispheric governments to include labor in the negotiations of regional trade pacts, which must include labor protection provisions. The CTM supported this policy but said it applied only when the trade union movement of an involved country considered it necessary. The CTM concluded that Mexican law, including ratified ILO conventions, already provided adequate protection for labor so that inclusion of an EC-style social character in NAFTA was unnecessary.

In May 1991, the U.S. Labor Department (DOL) and Mexico's Secretariat of Labor and Social Welfare (STPS) agreed on an unprecedented bilateral procedure for consultation and cooperation on mutual labor concerns. By September 1992, the two labor ministries had undertaken a number of important joint activities in several fields. These included studies of important issues (child labor, employee safety and health, labor law and industrial relations systems, and the informal economy) and a program to foster full compliance with health and safety standards by maquiladoras (in-bond export plants) in northern Mexico. DOL and STPS also announced a new bilateral cooperation measure in mid-September. The new initiative created a Consultative Commission to facilitate ongoing cooperation, as well as expanded activities in the areas of worker safety and hygiene.

STPS signed a separate bilateral cooperation program with Canada's labor ministry, Labour Canada, in May 1992. A year earlier, STPS became an official observer in the OECD Labor and Employment Committee and pledged to apply OECD labor standards within Mexico.

Mexican Industrial Relations System

Mexican labor law and the country's industrial relations system is derived from Article 123 of the 1917 Mexican Constitution, which enumerated specific worker rights and protections, as well as principles governing industrial relations. To carry out this constitutional mandate in a comprehensive fashion, in 1931 the Mexican Congress passed the Federal Labor Law (FLL), which was revised in 1970.

During his campaign for election in 1988, then candidate Salinas promised to consider another revision of the FLL. Trade unions sought a 40-hour work week and other benefits while employers sought changes to give companies flexibility in workplace rules so as to become more competitive. After the election, a brief, unsuccessful attempt was made to find common ground for a FLL revision. Ever since, employers have taken the initiative for removing FLL revisions while the CTM and other trade unions, fearing an unfavorable outcome, have resisted.

Application of the Federal Labor Law (FLL)

The FLL applies in both federal and state jurisdictions, although state authorities implement it within their own jurisdictions. The FLL created a tripartite Federal Conciliation and Arbitration Board (JFCA), chaired by the government member, which handles most day-to-day governmental functions regarding industrial relations. The state governments have comparable Conciliation and Arbitration Boards to apply FLL provisions to businesses under state jurisdiction. Following a federalist principle familiar in the U.S., in Mexico all businesses come under state jurisdiction except those specified as under federal control. Federal jurisdiction covers several industries including:

Textiles
Electricity
Cinematography
Rubber
Sugar
Mining
Metals and steel
Exploration of basic minerals

Smelting and processing of minerals

Production of steel and steel products

Hydrocarbons

Petrochemicals

Cement

Lime

Automobiles and parts

Chemicals

Pharmaceutical

Cellulose and paper

Oils and vegetable fats

Packed, canned, or packaged foods

Bottled or canned beverages

Railroads

Wood products, including sawdust, plywood, and particle board

Flat, smooth, or etched glass and glass bottles

Tobacco, including cultivation and production

Also covered by federal jurisdiction are companies administered directly or indirectly by the federal government, that act by virtue of a contract or a federal grant and related industries, or work in federal zones or are under federal jurisdiction, in territorial waters, or in those included in the exclusive economic zone of the nation.

Finally, work-related conflicts that affect two or more states, collective contracts which are declared to be mandatory in more than one state, employer obligations in the area of education, and obligations of employers with regard to worker training and education as well as occupational safety and health fall under federal jurisdiction. With regard to the latter, the federal government relies on the assistance of the states when dealing with branches or activities under local jurisdiction.

Mexican Trade Union Organizations

The Congress of Labor (CT)

The Congress of Labor (CT) is an overall loose coordinating body grouping 37 PRI-affiliated labor confederations and independent unions under its umbrella. The Congress, which was established in the mid-1960s, claims to group an estimated 10 million members under its aegis, even though the estimated total organized labor force in Mexico is roughly 9.5 million workers. It is estimated that the Congress of Labor represents as much as 85 percent of Mexico's union members. The Labor Congress also includes all of the major trade union confederations in the country, including the CTM, the government-employee federation FSTSE, the CROC, the CROM, and various lesser confederations, in addition to a number of independent, but PRI-affiliated, individual unions within its ranks. The presidency of the Congress of Labor is changed among the Congress' 37 members for seven-to nine-month periods.

In early 1990, Rafael Rivapalacio Pontones of the National Institute Fund for Workers Housing Union became the Congress president. He was succeeded by Lorenzo Duarte Garcia of the Railroad Workers Union (STFRM). Rafael De Jesus Lozano of the powerful Federation of Unions of State Employees (FSTSE) became president of the Labor Congress in 1991, and he was followed by Ignacio Cuahtehmoc Paleta of the Regional Confederation of Mexican Workers (CROM). On July 1, 1992, Mario Suarez Garcia of the moderate-sized Revolutionary Confederation of Workers (CRT) began a seven-month term of office.

Suarez is said to be acceptable to CTM leader Don Fidel Velazquez, who, until the selection of Rafael Rivapalacio Pontones, was assumed to be able to dominate the choice of the largely symbolic Labor Congress presidency. The 1992 selection process showed growing differences within the Labor Congress. The ambitious new labor federation, FESEBES, comprised of several service worker unions including the telephone workers union STRM, had stated its preference for teacher's union (SNTE) president Elba Esther Gordillo Morales.

Each of the CT members traditionally has some form of linkage with the PRI. Although the teachers' union, SNTE, in May 1992 declared itself politically unaffiliated, its leader remains a strong PRI supporter. The main role of the Labor Congress seems to be to embody institutionally a labor alliance with the PRI. By itself, the Congress has little direct impact on labor relations. However, by being affiliated with the Labor Congress, which represents about 85 percent of organized labor, members become part of the official voice of labor.

Labor has been a pillar of the PRI and historically a dominant sector in the party's structure. It has lost much of its influence, however, and today it has less than 10 percent of the seats in Congress and only one state governorship. The labor sector has questioned and resisted a number of proposals for major changes in the party, particularly with regard to the party's sectoral organization. The structure of the PRI will continue to be a major issue of concern to the CTM and organized labor.

At the PRI's fifteenth National Assembly in May 1992, significant changes to the party's organizational structure were approved. The number of secretaries was reduced from 20 to seven. The National Political Council now consists of 157 members. Half these seats are distributed territorially, meaning senators, deputies, and regional party leaders. The remaining half are distributed sectorally, with representatives from the labor, campesino, popular, women's, and youth sectors. The role and power of labor in the National Political Council has diminished considerably as popular groups have ascended to more active positions in the PRI. The formation of two new popular movements, Popular Territorial Movement (Movimiento Popular Territorial) and the National Citizens Front (Frente Nacional Ciudadana) exemplified the shift of power from labor dominance to a more popular-dominated PRI. An important outcome of the fifteenth National Assembly was the labor-farmer pact (Pacto Obrero-Campesino), which attempts to merge labor and agricultural concerns under this umbrella group. The creation of the pacto along with the new prominence of popular movements is viewed by many in the labor movement as a significant reduction in labor's voice in the PRI.

The CTM

The CTM (Confederacion de Trabajadores de Mexico) remains the predominant trade union confederation in Mexico, with a claimed total membership of about five million members. It alone constitutes more than half the total membership of the Labor Congress.

Other Trade Union Organizations

The FSTSE

The second largest trade union confederation in Mexico, with estimated membership between 1.5 and 1.8 million, is the FSTSE, Federation of Government Employee Unions (or Federacion de Sindicatos de Trabajadores al Servicio del Estado). The FSTSE's membership consists exclusively of federal government workers.

The CROC

The CROC, or Revolutionary Workers and Peasants Confederation (Confederacion Revolucionaria de Obreros y Campesinos) continued its rivalry with the much larger CTM. The rivalry appears in large part to be encouraged by the government to ensure that the CTM does not exert an inordinate share of power. The CROC has a particularly strong following in the state of Jalisco, where it virtually shares power in a more or less cooperative relationship with the CTM. The CROC membership remains at an estimated 600,000 individuals, although the confederation's leaders claim more than one million.

The CROM

In recent years, the CROM (Confederacion Regional Obrera Mexicana) or Mexican Regional Workers Confederation, appears to have had some slight membership gains at the expense of both the rival CROC and the CTM; its membership may now be around 250,000.

CGT, CRT, COR, and Other Confederations in the Congress of Labor

There are several other smaller trade union confederations in the Congress of Labor which have from 30,000 to 50,000 members each. These include the CGT, or General Confederation of Workers (Confederacion General de Trabajadores), which stems from the Mexican Revolution and is reputedly the oldest existing trade union confederation in Mexico; the CRT, or Revolutionary Confederation of Workers (Confederacion Revolucionaria de Trabajadores); and the COR, or Revolutionary Workers Confederation (Confederacion Obrera Revolucionaria).

FESEBES

In early 1990, the Telephone Workers Union, STRM, spearheaded the founding of a new confederation. The Federation of Unions in Businesses Providing Goods and Services (Federacion de Sindicatos de Empresas de Bienes y Servicios), or FESEBES, is comprised of the individual CT unions of telephone workers, electricians, pilots, flight attendants, and cinematographic technicians. FESEBES is a new force in the labor movement, embodying much of the new thinking and challenging the entrenched labor establishment.

FESEBES has cooperated to a great extent with the opening of the Mexican economy and the need to become more competitive.

Independent Trade Unions within the Labor Congress

In addition to the aforementioned CT trade union confederations, the Congress also has more than 20 independent individual unions within its ranks. These include such large and important unions as the SNTE, the huge teachers' union, the 150,000-member Railroad Workers Union of the Mexican Republic, and the 100,000-member National Union of Mining and Metallurgical Workers, as well as numerous medium- and small-sized independent unions. An important addition on July 1, 1992, was the bank employees union, FENASIB, formerly a public sector union within FSTSE but thanks to the reprivatization of the banks, now an autonomous private sector union.

The SNTE

The principal public sector union is not, however, a FSTSE member but autonomous. This is the SNTE national teachers union, with a reported 1.3 million members. The SNTE's strong leftist dissident movement, which calls itself the CNTE, increased its agitation in 1989 and caused significant problems for both the union leadership and the government. The CNTE continues to agitate for more power within the union and higher wages for teachers and administrative personnel. Its efforts to force wage hikes in early 1991 through short work stoppages failed, however.

The SUTIN

The most leftist, and even Marxist, independent union in the Congress of Labor is the 30,000-member Sole Union of Workers in the Nuclear Industry (or SUTIN).

Independent Unions outside the Labor Congress

There are also numerous independent movements, trade unions, and one large labor confederation, FNSI, which exist outside the Congress of Labor. One of the largest unions is the CTC, described below, which withdrew from the Labor Congress a few years ago. Most other independent unions tend to be small plant- or company-level unions. There are, however, several thousand such independent unions, and in the aggregate they have over one million members. These unions are usually of three different types, i.e., genuine "bread and butter" unions that shun politics and instead focus on improving their members' wages and working conditions; classic "company unions" set up and manipulated by company managements— frequently called "sindicatos blancos" or "white unions"; and Marxist and/or leftist-oriented unions which have refused to join any of the PRI-affiliated trade union organizations inside the Congress of Labor because they consider those unions reactionary and government controlled.

FNSI

Among the apolitical independent unions, there exists one large independent trade union confederation known as the FNSI, or National Federation of Independent Unions (Federacion Nacional de Sindicatos Independientes). The FNSI claims some 200,000 dues-paying members, more than three-quarters of whom are in Monterrey and its surrounding areas. It dominates the industrially important state of Nuevo Leon, where its members comprise more than 70 percent of workers covered by collective bargaining agreements. The FNSI avoids involvement in politics and concentrates on improving the lot of its members and on providing them with a variety of social services and benefits.

The CTC

The CTC, or Confederation of Workers and Peasants (Confederacion de Trabajadores y Campesinos), is a trade union confederation numbering between 100,000 and 200,000 members; most are located in the State of Mexico and the Federal District. The CTC has had a fair degree of success in organizing workers in the State of Mexico, most of whom it has taken away from the CTM. Although the CTC is also PRI-affiliated, it is no longer a member of the Congress of Labor. The CTC is strongly competitive with the mainstream union confederations, particularly the CTM and CROC, in the areas where it operates.

The FAT

The FAT (Frente Autentico de Trabajadores) claims a membership of some 30,000, although that figure appears to be exaggerated. It is at the far left end of the Mexican political and trade union spectrum and in the past has issued pronouncements against the Mexican government, against the PRI, and against U.S. policies in Latin America. In 1991 and 1992 it became the leading labor organization, along with the MPI, to oppose the formation of NAFTA.

The MPI (formerly UOI)

The MPI, or Independent Proletarian Movement (Movimiento Proletario Independiente), is an organization which changed its name during 1987 from UOI, or United Independent Workers (Unidad de Obreros Independientes), the name by which it had been known since its founding in 1972. It is not a trade union confederation but a loose umbrella coordinating mechanism embracing a group of extreme leftist independent unions. Trotskyite in orientation, it is anti-PRI, anti-establishment, and often anti-United States but also strongly condemns Mexico's traditional Communists as well. It is made up of a number of small and insignificant Trotskyite unions, but it also does have one large and important union within its ranks. The 20,000-member union called SUTUAR-100, or Union of Workers of the Route 100 bus route, is made up of drivers and workers on one of Mexico City's extensive bus routes.

The Mesa de Concertacion Sindical

The Mesa de Concertacion Sindical (or, roughly translated, the "Table of Trade Union Harmony") is also not a trade union confederation. Neither, despite its name, is it an organization limited exclusively to trade unions, although some trade unions are among its component elements. Rather, it is an amorphous broad umbrella coordinating mechanism which groups leftist trade unions, political parties, student and university groupings, neighborhood groups, groups of "victims" of the September 1985 Mexico City earthquake, and other loose organizations under its aegis. It was founded some seven years ago, principally by elements of the old Mexican Communist Party. It has a loose collegial structure, and there is no one leader who stands out, but the domination of the Communists has been evident. In many respects, the "Mesa" resembles a classic Communist-dominated "popular front" organization. It was, however, largely inactive in 1991 and early 1992.

The PRD and Small Leftist Political Parties

Cuautehmoc Cardenas' political party, the Democratic Revolutionary Party (PRD) formed in May 1989, has made only limited inroads on the labor scene.

In an effort to broaden the party's labor support, the PRD has attempted to appeal to CTM-affiliated unions. Although little evidence of these efforts was apparent in 1991, several union disputes in 1990 demonstrated that dissidents sympathetic to the PRD had found some fertile ground among the workers of the Ford Motor Assembly Plant in Cuautitlan, Mexico state, and the Modelo Beer Brewery. Rank and file dissatisfaction with leadership and compensation issues facilitated these toeholds in otherwise firmly PRI-oriented union ranks. The dissidents have had their most significant gains with the COR labor confederation and the teachers' union, SNTE, where they have a recognized faction known as the CNTE.

International Trade Unions in Mexico

The ORIT (ICFTU)

The main international trade union organization active in Mexico is the ORIT (or Organizacion Regional Interamericana de Trabajadores), which is the inter-American organization of the anti-Communist ICFTU (International Confederation of Free Trade Unions), headquartered in Brussels. The ORIT headquarters, in fact, have always been in Mexico City, in office space provided by the CTM in the CTM's headquarters building.

The CPUSTAL

The CPUSTAL (or Confederacion Panamericana Unico de Sindicatos de Trabajadores de America Latina) is the Latin American regional organization of the disintegrating Communist WFTU (World Federation of Trade Unions) in Prague. The CPUSTAL has maintained its headquarters in Mexico City since 1978. Unlike the ORIT, the CPUSTAL maintains an extremely low profile in Mexico City. It reportedly only has three to four employees at its Mexico City headquarters, led by CPUSTAL Secretary General Roberto Priego, a Cuban.

The CLAT

The CLAT (or Confederacion Latina Americana de Trabajadores), which is the Latin American regional organization of the once-

Christian WCL (or World Confederation of Labor) in Brussels, has no office and little activity in Mexico. The Caracas-headquartered CLAT, however, does have one small Mexican affiliate, known as the FAT (or Frente Autentico de Trabajadores).

Mexican Employer Organizations

Nonunion organized groups who influence labor policy and politics include employer organizations. These groups are comprised of Mexican employers who coalesce to lobby government, to represent their members and to advise their members about labor-management issues. Important employer organizations include:

- Corporate Coordinating Council (CCE)
- Confederation of Industrial Chambers of the United Mexican States (CONCAMIN)
- Employers' Confederation of the Mexican Republic (COPARMEX)
- National Chamber of the Manufacturing Industry (CANACINTRA)
- Confederation of National Chambers of Commerce (CONCANACO)
- American Chamber of Commerce of Mexico (AMCHAM)

AMCHAM Mexico is the largest American Chamber of Commerce outside the United States. Its membership includes about 85 percent of U.S. companies operating in Mexico. It has committees that deal with maquiladoras and with labor affairs.

Special Voluntary Agreements among Government, Employers and Organized Labor

The PECE

A pillar of the Salinas government's economic policy and a major influence govern-

ing labor relations continued to be the operation and evolution of the voluntary Pact for Stability and Economic Growth (PECE). The PECE, the successor to the Economic Solidarity Pact initiated in December 1987, is essentially a package of tight fiscal and monetary policies, price and wage controls, and control of the exchange rate. It has been effective in controlling inflation through braking price and wage increases. Since December 1987 the PECE has required labor and management to operate under a government-managed voluntary minimum wage and price restraint pact that has curtailed wage increases sharply but has contributed substantially to the rapid drop in inflation (150 percent in 1987, 19 percent in 1991, estimated 12–13 percent for 1992).

The PECE is part of an economic program that President Salinas characterized in 1992 as social liberalism, meaning a free market economy that also justly addresses the social needs of society. However, the PECE seems to be more on the austere side from the perspective of Mexican workers. The launching of Salinas' National Solidarity program (PRONASOL) in December 1988 is a more appropriate example of the Mexican government's attempt to keep economic liberalism alive while meeting the basic social needs of the populace. The Solidarity program targets communities with basic infrastructure needs, and allocates funds locally for specific projects. Projects range from building bridges to health centers.

The CTM has been increasingly restive and critical of the PECE. It has repeatedly criticized the PECE for holding down wages and forcing workers to bear an unfair share of sacrifice for the country's economic restructuring program.

National Accord for Raising Productivity and Quality (ANEPC)

On May 25, 1992, after almost two years of discussion, the National Accord for Raising

Productivity and Quality (ANEPC) was signed. The accord is a tripartite agreement to attempt to raise productivity and quality in Mexican industry. The ANEPC is not law and there are no penalties for companies or employees who do not cooperate. Instead, it is a voluntary pact to begin finding ways to become more productive and improve quality. Still, it includes a government-led tripartite oversight committee that meets weekly to monitor progress, and the government might consider stronger measures if ANEPC achieves little progress.

Under the accord, the Mexican government, state governments, and employers committed themselves to making greater investments in human resources, e.g., upgrading worker skills, in return for union flexibility on work rules and other productivity and quality-related concerns.

Although there was concern among some labor leaders that the ANEPC would undermine the FLL, the CTM managed to alter enough wording of the draft accord to make sure it did not. In many respects, among both labor and management, the ANEPC is being viewed as a substitute for immediate changes in the FLL. It is unclear how employers will go about negotiating productivity and quality improvements under the new accord in 1992–1993.

Changes in Mexican Social Security System

In February 1992, the Mexican government initiated a new pension system including retirement and reformed housing provisions for workers.

Under the new system, each individual account will have two subaccounts. One is for retirement pensions and one for deposits under the new National Housing Fund (INFONAVIT) program.

The housing contribution is, as before, 5 percent of an employee's salary. The new rules for housing deductions represent an important departure from past regulations.

Now the employee owns his or her account. Before the new rules were promulgated, the 5 percent housing contribution went directly into the coffers of INFONAVIT. The money was never accounted for and not enough workers received housing.

Under the new system, INFONAVIT will no longer construct houses. Instead, the organization's role will be to help finance the building of houses and provide mortgage guarantees. What role exactly INFONAVIT will play, is still being decided.

Labor Secretariat Developments
In 1992, Labor Secretary Arsenio Farell Cubillas entered his tenth year as head of the Secretariat of Labor and Social Welfare (STPS). He has a reputation as a stern and tough orchestrator of labor-management relations, bearing down hard on employers and trade unions alike to negotiate differences without strikes and to keep economic settlements within a range that does not fuel inflation.

In the past Farell received strong criticism from leftists and some trade unionists for tough government attitudes during major strikes, such as at AeroMexico, the Modelo brewery, and the 1989–90 labor disturbances at a Ford plant outside Mexico City. In 1990, and again in 1991, a dissident faction of the COR associated with the Ford plant upheavals sought his removal from office.

STPS is focusing its resources on the promotion of improved worker training through its own National Program for Training and Productivity, partly funded through a World Bank loan. Although Mexico enjoys a comparative advantage with low-cost labor, which has attracted heavy foreign investment in-bond export industries (maquiladoras), this is a diminishing advantage for industries seeking literate, skilled workers who must deal with computer age technology. Such workers are in short supply and the prognosis is that continued industrial and commercial expansion will drive up skilled labor costs considerably during the remainder of the 1990s. The broader problem of an inadequately prepared industrial and commercial work force also was addressed in President Salinas' bold decision in early 1992 to reform education and to require young persons to complete nine years of schooling, instead of only six years.

STPS' international focus in 1991 and early 1992 was regional and functional rather than global. In both years no STPS official attended the annual ILO Conference, where Mexico was represented by its Permanent Mission to UN agencies in Geneva. Instead, in keeping with President Salinas' goal of attaining a first world economy for Mexico, STPS embarked on unprecedented initiatives in respect of the OECD, the United States, and Canada. In January 1992 Mexico participated for the first time as an official observer in an OECD labor ministers' meeting in Paris, having been accepted as an observer in the OECD's Labor and Employment Committee in 1991. Mexico seeks full OECD membership and has pledged to meet OECD standards, including those for labor.

In recognition of the importance of the rapidly growing Mexican-U.S. economic partnership and of the likely impact of a North American free trade pact, STPS and the U.S. Department of Labor (USDOL) signed in May 1991 a memorandum of understanding (MOU) on cooperation in labor affairs and an additional agreement forming a Consultative Commission in mid-September. For details, see below. For similar reasons, STPS signed a labor cooperation MOU with Canada's labor ministry in May 1992.

NAFTA in the Labor-Management Context

In June 1990, the United States and Mexico announced their intention to negotiate a Free Trade Agreement that would eliminate tariffs and most nontariff barriers to trade between the two countries. Canada joined the process in 1991, thus creating negotiations for a full North American Free Trade Agreement (NAFTA). U.S. Trade Representative, Ambassador Carla Hills announced in late 1990 that labor issues would not be specifically addressed in the agreement. However, with growing concern and activity by organized labor in the U.S. as well as in the U.S. Congress, President Bush announced in his May 1, 1991 letter to Congress his strategy for addressing labor issues related to the NAFTA.

First, the President described three aspects within the agreement and one outside the NAFTA that, among other things, would address some labor concerns:

- Transition period: Parts of the agreement will be phased in over a period of 10 or more years to allow especially vulnerable industries to adjust to reduced tariffs and possible corresponding increases in imports.

- Rules of origin: This part of the NAFTA will reduce pressure from imports from outside NAFTA, by insuring that only the products produced using mostly North American components are given preferential access to each other's markets.

- Safeguards: A special safeguards chapter within the NAFTA will provide a recourse for workers and companies to deal with injurious surges in imports as a result of tariff reductions in the NAFTA.

Second, the May 1, 1991 presidential letter also promised to provide a worker adjustment program that is adequately funded and ensures that workers who may lose their jobs as a result of NAFTA will receive prompt, comprehensive, and effective services. The president suggested that any changes to U.S. law to implement such worker adjustment assistance would be addressed through the legislation implementing NAFTA.

Third, the president said the United States and Mexico would establish a special bilateral mechanism for addressing labor concerns separate from the trade agreement itself. The Memorandum of Understanding (MOU) on labor issues between the U.S. and Mexican governments was signed on May 3, 1991 (discussed next).

Mexican Labor Congress member confederations and trade unions have supported the NAFTA. Overall, they accept the Mexican government's assurances that Mexico stands to benefit from a net gain in job creation. Complaints from U.S. unions about possible job losses from the U.S. to Mexico have, if anything, only reinforced the positive perception of the NAFTA for Mexican workers and trade unions.

In late 1991 ORIT, the ICFTU hemispheric regional labor organization to which both the CTM and the AFL-CIO (USA) belong, adopted a common inter-American trade union policy regarding the negotiation of economic integration or free trade pacts. It calls for the inclusion of an EC-style social charter on worker rights. Mexico's CTM supports this policy but defines it as applying only when a country's trade union movement sees the need for it. In the case of Mexico, the CTM feels that with the protection of the 1917 Constitution, the Federal Labor Law, and the many ILO conventions Mexico has ratified, Mexican workers are sufficiently protected. The CTM therefore does not support including a social charter in the NAFTA, nor has any other CT member expressed a need for a NAFTA social charter.

The Memorandum of Understanding on Labor Issues between the United States and Mexico

As a result of the concern expressed by

organized labor and members of Congress after the announcement of the intention to negotiate a free trade agreement with Mexico, the U.S. and Mexico embarked on a cooperative effort to learn about each other's labor systems and look for areas to improve both systems. On May 3, 1991, Secretary of Labor Lynn Martin and her Mexican counterpart, Secretary Arsenio Farell Cubillas, signed a Memorandum of Understanding (MOU) dealing with cooperation and information exchange. The areas agreed to be covered under the MOU at the time were:

- health and safety measures
- general work conditions, including labor standards and their enforcement
- resolution of labor conflicts
- collective bargaining agreements for improvement of work conditions
- social security systems
- credit institutions for workers to purchase consumer durables and housing
- labor statistics
- other areas of mutual concern

Actions taken under this cooperation framework are under the auspices of the U.S.-Mexico Binational Commission. By September 1992 its multifaceted achievements included:

- The preparation of a joint DOL-STPS study of U.S. and Mexican work place health and safety systems, released in September 1992.
- DOL/OSHA assistance to STPS in establishing hygiene testing laboratories, and training for STPS personnel on various health and safety matters.
- DOL/OSHA assistance for STPS and Mexican social security (IMSS) teams of experts who met in late 1991 and early 1992 with maquiladora plant officials throughout northern Mexico to advise

them of their obligations under Mexican health and safety regulations and to assist them with overcoming obstacles to full compliance.

- The preparation of a joint DOL-STPS study of the two countries' labor law and labor relations systems, expected to be released in October 1992. Top legal officials of DOL, the National Labor Relations Board (NLRB), and the Federal Mediation and Conciliation Service (FMCS) met with STPS and JFCA counterparts in June 1992. They compared their respective systems and agreed on organizing a bilateral labor law conference of leading practitioners in October 1992.

- Several meetings were held between DOL/BLS experts and those of STPS and Mexico's centralized statistical agency, INEGI, to organize the sharing of labor statistics between the two governments and to provide BLS training in a few areas.

- A joint DOL-STPS study of child labor in both countries, expected to be released in October 1992. Officials from the Department of Labor's Employment Standards Administration and their Mexican counterparts worked on the study, which is a first step to addressing child labor problems in both countries.

- The preparation of joint DOL-STPS studies of the informal economy in both countries which were expected to be released in October 1992. Officials from the Office of International Economic Affairs, at the U.S. Department of Labor, and their Mexican counterparts, as well as academics, contributed to the reports.

Based upon the initial success of the MOU, on September 14, 1992, the U.S. and Mexican governments expanded and improved the MOU by signing a new bilateral agreement creating a Consultative Commission on Labor Matters. The commission establishes an ongoing mechanism to manage and oversee new and ongoing cooperative activities. The Consultative Commission will operate under the auspices of the U.S.-Mexico Binational Commission and the May 3, 1991 MOU, and will provide a permanent forum to promote the rights and interests of working people in both countries. The commission will meet at least once a year, but more frequent or emergency meetings will be held, as necessary.

In addition to establishing the Consultative Commission, the U.S. and Mexico negotiated two new "pillars" of cooperation in the areas of industrial hygiene and workplace safety. The two countries have agreed to work toward a more common scheme in industrial hygiene by upgrading their respective systems where necessary. In the area of workplace safety, the U.S. and Mexico have agreed to forge closer links in the development and application of regulations protecting workers. A number of activities in training, education, prevention, and closer cooperation have been agreed to between the two countries to step up the improvement of industrial hygiene and workplace safety in both countries.

Labor Relations Outlook for 1994 and Beyond

The outlook for 1993 was for few overt changes but growing tensions within the Mexican house of labor. The elderly leadership of the three largest private sector labor confederations, CTM, CROC, and CROM, was reelected to new six-year terms of office, which certainly provided continuity. This continuity pertains, however, to leaders whose experiences and attitudes were shaped by the traditional corporatist system of politics, economics, and labor-management relations. Their usual levers of influence over the government, ruling party, and employers are steadily eroding and are not, so far, being replaced with new ones. This may spawn strong internal pressures for real changes within the mainstream labor organizations, including the CTM.

The PRI appears to be edging its formerly dominant labor sector, now merged with the campesino sector, to a secondary role within the ruling party. The new party center is distinctly middle class. The remaining PRI populist element is the new, and far more credible, PRONASOL organization, rather than the trade unions. Old time union leaders may find it difficult to be favored as potential PRI office holders by party managers seeking electable candidates in elections with honest counts. This is not to say union manpower will be shunned by the PRI at election times but, on balance, organized labor seems destined to continue to suffer a weakening of its already greatly diminished political clout.

Recent government economic and financial policies have undermined labor power, and probably will continue to do so. The 1992 decision to set up individual worker accounts at banks by their employers so as to build up individual employee credits for housing (INFONAVIT) and retirement savings (SAR) took the trade unions out of these loops. Future changes in social security procedures could further undermine union influence.

Union negotiators may find they are going to have to justify their demands for more wages or other improvements on convincing expert arguments about economic factors, health and safety considerations, and other concerns.

This will not be easy when employers are preoccupied with the impact of free market and global competition. Yet workers should remain impatient to regain more lost purchasing power and their voices cannot be ignored forever by union leaders. With greater political democracy occurring each year, workers may be emboldened to insist upon greater internal democracy within trade unions.

It is hard to see how Mexico's traditional leaders will be able to adjust to these challenges. This, at least, is the thrust of the criticism of the so-called Labor Congress dinosaurs by the head of the telephone union STRM, the electricians' union, SME, and other leaders in the controversial new labor confederation FESEBES. In 1992, FESEBES leaders often made common ground with the teachers' union, SNTE, which is the largest in Mexico. These naysayers may or may not offer viable solutions but, in 1991 and 1992, they voiced criticisms that defined much debate within the labor movement through 1993 and beyond.

For the government, it will be important to see how long it is desirable and politically feasible to extend the four-year-old voluntary minimum wage and price restraint program, PECE. CTM leader Fidel Velazquez has stated that the PECE may have outlived its usefulness and complained of an unjustified de facto ceiling on contract wage increases. It is an open question whether or not the government will try to extend the successful but shopworn PECE into 1993. One factor influencing its decision may be the success by November 1992 of the new voluntary program, ANEPC, which seeks to tie wage increases to productivity gains.

As long as he is mentally fit, the recently reelected Don Fidel Velazquez, age 92, will continue to lead the CTM. He has outmaneuvered potential rivals since the 1940s and shows no signs yet of losing his touch. If he should have left the scene through death or incapacity, it was not a foregone conclusion that his interim replacement would be Senator Emilio Manuel Gonzalez Parra, age 78, who was or is next in line. While still fit, as Senate president, he was loath to abandon this position, which is important to organized labor. Since Senator Blas Chumacero Sanchez, age 87, was too ill, the alternative was third CTM Undersecretary, Senator Leonardo Emilio Rodriguez Alcaine, age 72. He was/is Secretary General of SUTERM, the CTM's electrical workers' union. In 1991 Don Fidel Velazquez hinted that Rodriguez Alcaine mostly likely would take temporary control of the CTM in the event of his own incapacity.

If NAFTA was approved and implemented in 1993, organized labor in Mexico would have found its perceived shortcomings under great scrutiny by highly vocal critics in the U.S. CTM and AFL-CIO relations were distant in 1991 and early 1992 due to differences over NAFTA but, if NAFTA has become a fact, this could change.

The AFL-CIO and its unions would have a greater incentive to seek common ground with effective Mexican union leaders, within the CTM or even elsewhere. In 1992 the Communications Workers of America (CWA) signed a cooperation accord with the non-CTM telephone workers' union, STRM.

Francisco Hernandez Juarez, the outspoken STRM leader who heads the maverick labor confederation FESEBES, also visited with AFL-CIO leaders in Washington. In the first half of 1992, the AFL-CIO also drew closer to Mexico's single labor federation for federal workers, FSTSE.

Congress of Labor Organizations

Congreso del Trabajo (CT)
C. Ramiro Ruiz Madero
Ave. Ricardo Flores Magon #44, 7o Piso
Col. Guerrero
06300 Mexico, D.F.
583 57 79
583 38 17
583 97 60 FAX

Confederacion de Trabajadores de Mexico (CTM)

C. Fidel Velazquez
Vallarta No. 8
Col. Tabacalera
06030 Mexico, D.F.
535 06 58
703 31 12

Confederacion Revolucionaria de Obreros y Campesinos (CROC)
Sen. Alberto Juarez Blancas
Hamburgo No. 250
Col. Juarez
06600 Mexico, D.F.
584 54 44
584 54 44 Ext. 139 FAX

Federacion de Sindicatos de Trabajadores al Servicio del Estado (FSTSE)
Sen. Carlos Jimenez Macias
Gomez Farias No. 40
Col. San Rafael
06470 Mexico, D.F.
566 82 15
592 25 11
566 02 41 FAX

Confederacion Regional Obrera Mexicana (CROM)
Dip. Lic. Ignacio Cuauhtemoc Paleta
Republica de Cuba No. 60
Col. Centro
06010 Mexico, D.F.
512 88 50
512 14 79

Confederacion Obrera Revolucionaria (COR)
Gilberto Escalante Medina
Czda. de la Viga No. 9, 1er Piso
Col. Transito
06820 Mexico, D.F.
542 45 05
542 41 35
522 80 79 FAX

Sindicato de Trabajadores Ferrocarrileros de la Republica Mexicana (STFRM)
Dip. Praxedis Fraustro Esquibel
Ave. Ricardo Flores Magon No. 206

Col. Guerrero
06300 Mexico, D.F.
597 10 78
597 10 11
583 70 65 FAX

Sindicato Nacional de Trabajadores Mineros, Metalurgicos y Similares de la Republica Mexicana (MINEROS)
Dip. Napoleon Gomez Sada
Dr. Vertiz No. 668
Col. Narvarte
03020 Mexico, D.F.
519 56 90
519 56 91
519 19 61 FAX

Federacion de Trabajadores del Distrito Federal (FTDF)
Lic. Joaquin Gamboa Pascoe
Vallarta No. 8, 7o Piso
Col. Tabacalera
06030 Mexico, D.F.
535 73 68
535 73 32

Sindicato Mexicano de Electricistas (SME)
C. Jorge Sanchez Garcia
Antonio Caso No. 45
Col. San Rafael
06470 Mexico, D.F.
705 14 38
705 18 13
535 70 46 FAX

Sindicato de Trabajadores Petroleros de la Republica Mexicana (STPRM)
C. Profr. Sebastian Guzman Cabrera
Zaragoza No. 15
Col. Guerrero
06300 Mexico, D.F.
546 09 12
592 41 31
535 68 03 FAX

Confederacion General de Trabajadores (CGT)
Carlos Rivas Ramirez

Dr. Rio de la Loza No. 6, Desp. 11
Col. Doctores
06720 Mexico, D.F.
578 73 17
761 33 49

Sindicato de Telefonistas de la Republica Mexicana (STRM)
C. Francisco Hernandez Juarez
Rio Neva No. 16, 1er Piso
Col. Cuauhtemoc
06500 Mexico, D.F.
592 01 24
592 35 50
546 45 05 FAX

Sindicato Nacional de Trabajadores de la Educacion (SNTE)
Elba Esther Gordillo Morales
Venezuela No. 44
Col. Centro
06020 Mexico, D.F.
702 00 05
702 19 35
702 12 67
702 03 03 FAX

Federacion de Agrupaciones Obreras (FAO)
C. Jose Garcia S. Almaguer
Eje Lazaro Cardenas No. 85, 3er Piso
Col. Centro
06020 Mexico, D.F.
529 51 14

Confederacion Revolucionaria de Trabajadores (CRT)
C. Mario Suarez Garcia
Dr. Jimenez No. 218
Col. Doctores
06720 Mexico, D.F.
578 92 15

Sindicato Nacional de Trabajadores del Seguro Social (SNTSS)
C. Dr. Miguel Angel Saenz Garza
Zamora No. 107
Col. Condesa
06140 Mexico, D.F.

553 80 78
553 28 00
286 22 93 FAX

Asociacion Sindical de Pilotos Aviadores
(ASPA)
C. P.A. Celso Dominguez Galvez
Calle Palomas No. 110
Lomas de Sotelo
11650 Mexico, D.F.
020 32 98
202 30 23
202 90 05 FAX

Sindicato de Trabajadores del INFONAVIT
(SIND. INFONAVIT)
C. Arq. Rafael Riva Palacio Pontones
Minerva No. 30
Col. Credito Constructor
03940 Mexico, D.F.
524 97 09
534 47 17

Asociacion Nacional de Actores (ANDA)
C. Ing. Julio Mendez Aleman
Altamirano No. 126, 1er Piso
Col. San Rafael
06470 Mexico, D.F.
535 40 19
705 06 24
546 51 60 FAX

Sindicato de Trabajadores de la Produccion
Cinematografica de la
Republica Mexicana (STPCRM)
C. Lic. Arnulfo Mayorga
Plateros No. 109
Col. San Jose Insurgentes
03900 Mexico, D.F.
593 59 90
559 90 86 FAX

Federacion Nacional de Uniones Teatrales y
Espectaculos Publicos (FNUTEP)
C. Rafael Solana
Gomez Farias No. 47
Col. San Rafael
0647 Mexico, D.F.
492 54 86

Sindicato de Trabajadores Tecnicos y
Manuales de Estudios y Laboratorio de la
Produccion Cinematografica, Similares y
Conexos de la Republica Mexicana (TEC. Y
MANUALES)
Fresas No. 12
Col. Del Valle
03100 Mexico, D.F.
575 06 55
559 90 867 FAX

Confederacion Nacional "Martin Torres"
(TEXTILES)
C. Gustavo Estrada Urbina
Mercado No. 26
Col. Guerrero
06300 Mexico, D.F.
583 87 00

Federacion Revolucionaria de Obreros Textiles (FROT)
C. Benjamin Lara Aguilar
Isabel la Catolica No. 68, Desp. 201
Col. Centro
06000 Mexico, D.F.
709 30 49
709 32 55

Asociacion Sindical de Sobrecargos de
Aviacion (ASSA)
C. Lic. Carlos Larios Macedo
Patricio Sanz No. 751
Col. Del Valle
543 94 56
543 39 09
683 99 00 FAX

Federacion Nacional de Caneros (FNC)
C. Vicente Andrade Meza
Ricardo Flores Magon No. 44, 40 Piso
Col. Guerrero
06300 Mexico, D.F.

Confederacion de Obreros y Campesinos del
Estado de Mexico (COCEM)
C. Jesus Moreno Jimenez
Cuauhtemoc No. 90
13410 Tlalnepantla, Estado de Mexico
565 07 69

565 42 69
565 94 82

Union Linotipografica de la Republica
Mexicana (ULRM)
C. Luis Hoyos Aguilar
Calle 311 No. 7
Fracc. El Coyol
757 34 65

Alianza de Tranviarios de Mexico (ATM)
C. Francisco Munguia Alejos
Dr. Lucio No. 29
Col. Doctores
06720 Mexico, D.F.
588 15 71
588 15 72
539 26 69 FAX

Sindicato Industrial de Trabajadores del
Ramo de Lana y Conexos (SIND. IND.
LANA)
C. Rogelio Reyes Nunez
Tacuba No. 37 Desp. 330
Col. Centro
06000 Mexico, D.F.
521 74 47

Sindicato de Trabajadores de Novedades
Editores (STNE)
C. Alberto Serrano Serrano
Independencia No. 101 Desp. 33
Col. Centro
06050 Mexico, D.F.
521 74 24

Federacion de Sindicatos de Trabajadores al
Servicio de los Gobiernos de Los Estados,
Municipios e Instituciones Descentralizadas
de Caracter Estatal de la Republica Mexi-
cana (FSTSGEMY)
C. Juana Consuelo Mendez Vazquez
Ricardo Flores Magon No. 44, 5o Piso
Col. Guerrero
06300 Mexico, D.F.
583 56 99

Sindicato Nacional de Redactores de la

Prensa y Trabajadores de Actividades Similares y Conexas (REDACT. PRENSA)
C. Carlos Santa Ana Alavez
Filomeno Mata No. 8
Col. Centro
06000 Mexico, D.F.
510 00 48
510 03 05

Federacion de Sindicatos de Trabajadores al
Servicio de los Gobiernos de los Estados,
Municipios e Instituciones Descentralizadas
de los Gobiernos Estatales y Municipales de
la Republica Mexicana (FSTSGEM)
C. Lic. Agueda Galicia Jimenez
Lafragua No. 3, 7o Piso
Col. Tabacalera
06030 Mexico, D.F.
592 31 50
592 38 83

Sindicato Unico de Trabajadores de la Industria Nuclear (SUTIN)
C. Ing. Hector Cuapio Ortiz
Viaducto Rio Becerra No. 139
Col. Napoles
03810 Mexico, D.F.
523 80 48
687 63 53

Sindicato Nacional de Empleados de FON-
ACOT (SINEF)
C. Antonio Reyes
Oriente 170 No. 96
Col. Moctezuma, 28 Seccion
15500 Mexico, D.F.
762 79 11
762 71 98

Employer Organizations

Confederacion de Camaras Nacionales de
Comercio (CONCANACO)
Lic. Hugo Villalobos Gonzalez
Baderas No. 144, 3er Piso
06079 Mexico, D.F.
709 15 59

709 03 73
709 11 38 FAX

Confederacion de Camaras Industriales de
Los Estados Unidos (CONCAMIN)
Lic. Armando Cobos Perez
Manuel Ma. Contreras No. 133, 2o Piso
06597 Mexico, D.F.
703 27 28
703 27 72
535 68 71 FAX

Camara Nacional de la Industrial de la
Transformacion (CANACINTRA)
Lic. Vicente Gutierrez Camposeco
Ag. San Antonio No. 256
03849 Mexico, D.F.
563 34 00
598 58 88 FAX

Consejo Coordinador Empresarial (CCE)
Francisco R. Calderon
Homero 527, Piso 7
Col. Polanco
11570 Mexico, D.F.
520 69 77
531 93 16
250 69 96 FAX

Confederacion Patronal de la Republica
Mexicana (COPARMEX)
Insurgentes Sur 950, Primer Piso
Col. Del Valle
03110 Mexico, D.F.
687 28 21
687 64 93
536 21 60 FAX

Camara de Comercio Americana (AM-
CHAM)
John Bruton
Lucerna 78
Col. Juarez
06600 Mexico, D.F.
724 38 00
705 09 95
703 29 11 FAX
703 39 08 FAX

Camara Nacional de Comercio de la Ciudad
de Mexico
Lic. Eduardo Garcia Villasenor
Paseo de la Reforma No. 42, 3er Piso
705 04 24
705 05 49
705 53 10 FAX

Camara Nacional de la Industria Quimica y
Farmaceutica
Ing. Victor Manuel Diaz
Av. Cuauhtemoc No. 1481
03310 Mexico, D.F.
688 94 77
688 98 17
604 98 08 FAX

Camara Nacional de la Industria Electronica
y de Comunicaciones Electricas
Arq. Federico Ruiz Sacristan
Guanajuato No. 65
Col. Roma
06700 Mexico, D.F.
574 74 11
574 77 00
584 50 83 FAX

Camara Nacional de Industria Editorial
Mexicana
Lic. Rafael Servin Arroyo
Holanda No. 13
04120 Mexico, D.F.
688 22 21
688 20 11
604 43 47 FAX

Camara Nacional de la Industria de Radio y
Television
Lic. Cesar Hernandez Espino
Horacio No. 1013
Col. Polanco
11550 Mexico, D.F.
250 25 77
250 28 96
545 67 67 FAX

Camara Nacional del Cemento
Arq. Raul Arredondo Gonzalez

Leibnitz No. 77, 1er Piso
Col. Anzures
11590 Mexico, D.F.
533 24 00
533 01 34
203 41 02 FAX

Camara Nacional de la Industria de la Construccion
Ing. Mario Padilla Orozco
Periferico Sur No. 4839
Col. Parques del Pedregal
14010 Mexico, D.F.
665 15 00
665 21 67
606 83 29 FAX

Asociacion Mexicana de la Industria Automotriz, A.C.
Lic. Cesar Flores
Ensenada No. 90
Col. Condesa
06100 Mexico, D.F.
515 25 42
272 11 44
272 71 39 FAX

Asociacion de la Industria Nacional de Autopartes
Sor Juana Ines de la Cruz No. 344
Col. Centro
04030 Tlalnepantla, Estado de Mexico
390 56 19
390 53 31

390 73 03 FAX

Camara Nacional del Aerotransporte
Ing. Guillermo Heredia Cabarga
Paseo de la Reforma No. 76, 17o Piso
Col. Juarez
06600 Mexico, D.F.
592 44 72
535 14 58 FAX

Camara Nacional de la Industria Naval
Ing. Mario Uribe
Acapulco No. 35—702
06700 Mexico, D.F.
211 55 06
286 76 64 FAX

Camara Nacional de Autotransportes de Carga
Lic. Francisco Jose Davila Rodriguez
Pachuca No. 158—Bis
06140 Mexico, D.F.
553 98 09
553 26 82
211 55 68 FAX

Camara Nacional de Autotransporte de Pasaje y Turismo
Versalles No. 16
Col. Juarez
06600 Mexico, D.F.
566 54 21
566 54 14
566 56 36 FAX

Chapter 15

NICARAGUA

	Total	Urban	
Population (1993)	3,965,000	57.0%	

Main Urban Areas	Population	Percentage of Total	International Calling Code
MANAGUA (Metro)	2,000,000	50.4	5451
MANAGUA	682,000	17.2	505-2
Rosita	325,000	8.2	505
Leon	101,000	2.5	505-311
Granada	89,000	2.2	505-55
Masaya	75,000	1.9	505-52
Chinandega	68,000	1.7	505-341
Matagalpa	37,000	0.9	505-61
San Carlos	34,000	0.9	505
Esteli	31,000	0.8	505-71

Land Area   120,254 square kilometers
    Comparable U.S. State   Slightly larger than New York

Language

Spanish	95%
Miskito	4%
Creole English	1%

    Common Business Language   Spanish, English

Currency   1 cordoba (C$) = 100 centavos
    Exchange Rate (May 1993)   U.S. $1.00 = 5.51 cordobas

Best Nonstop Air Connection via U.S.   Miami to Managua: 3 hours
American Airlines (800) 433-7300
Aviateca (800) 327-9832
Nica (800) 831-6422
Sahsa (800) 327-1225

Best Hotel   InterContinental (U.S. $115)
101 Octava Calle S
Tel: (505-2) 623-531
      (800) 327-0200
Fax: (505-2) 625-208

INTRODUCTION AND REGIONAL ORIENTATION

History and Political Conditions

Before 1979, Nicaragua's economy was among the most advanced in Central America, characterized by a robust agricultural export sector, well-developed financial institutions, and reasonably well-managed domestic industries. Despite a severe blow from the 1972 Managua earthquake, the economy continued to grow throughout the 1970s. Following a long insurgency against the heavy-handed Anastasio Somoza regime, the Sandinistas came to power in 1979.

Eleven years later, Sandinista mismanagement, political repression, and a prolonged civil war had taken their toll on Nicaragua. On April 25, 1990, President-elect Violeta Barrios de Chamorro assumed charge of an economy scarred by hyperinflation, sharply reduced per-capita income levels, high rates of unemployment, inoperative banking and financial institutions, inefficient, overstaffed, and debt-burdened state-owned enterprises, and record per-capita levels of foreign debt. Nearly 15 percent of Nicaragua's population, including most skilled workers and professionals, now make their homes outside of Nicaragua.

During the election campaign, Chamorro promised to revitalize Nicaragua's economy, privatize state-owned enterprises, return illegally confiscated properties, reduce the government deficit, permit private sector imports and exports, and introduce a new currency to break inflationary expectations. The government passed decree 11–90 shortly after taking power, creating a confiscation revision commission to review illegal confiscations which took place during Sandinista rule. The deadline for filing with the commission was December 31, 1990.

Making good on promises to "rule from below," the Sandinistas paralyzed the government twice in 1990. In May, Sandinista activists shut down the government by locking employees out of their offices. In July, the Sandinistas seized all major intersections and constructed well-guarded paving-stone barricades. Although the government restored order after both incidents, it was able to do so only by granting concessions to state and para-statal employees.

In September 1990, the government entered into national dialogue ("concertacion") with all sectors of the economy. Although the Sandinistas initially refused to participate, they later joined the negotiations. The government and sector representatives signed the "concertacion" agreement on October 26, 1990. COSEP (the Superior Council of Private Enterprise—an umbrella organization for Nicaragua's Chambers of Commerce) declined to sign the accord.

Under the "concertacion" accord, the government agreed to retain most government employees, maintain public sector wages, reactivate the economy, and legislate a minimum wage. In return, the accord committed labor and the Sandinistas to six months of "social peace."

To develop international support for its program, Nicaragua presented its economic plan to a group of donors at Rome in June 1990. The donors held a second consultative group meeting in Paris in December 1990 to consider Nicaraguan arrears with international financial institutions (approximately U.S. $350 million). The government and donors agreed that a joint World Bank/ International Monetary Fund/ Inter-American Development Bank team would visit Nicaragua in January/February 1991. A follow-up donors meeting was held in March to reconsider arrears clearing.

Between May and September 1990, the government made important progress in reducing the domestically financed budget deficit and cutting inflation. By November

1990, however, the government domestically financed deficit shot back up. Inflation also edged back up in November and December 1990.

At the end of 1990, Nicaragua's economy remained at a crossroads. The government estimated 1990 GDP growth at minus 5.7 percent and 1990 annual inflation at more than 13,500 percent. Unemployment continued at approximately 25 percent of the work force. At 1990 year end, the government's foreign debt amounted to approximately U.S. $10–11 billion including principal and interest, more than six times GDP.

Despite the unsettled economic and political outlook, Nicaragua offers opportunities for U.S. firms seeking to do business overseas. The United States lifted a five-year-old trade embargo on Nicaragua in March 1990.

Nicaragua represents a potential market for U.S. capital equipment and consumer goods. Foreign exchange availability presents a problem for importers. Significant investment opportunities may arise as state-owned firms are privatized.

CRACKING THE MARKET

Economy

The agricultural sector represents the cornerstone of Nicaragua's economy. In 1989, agriculture employed 30.0 percent of Nicaragua's work force, accounted for 23.0 percent of GDP, and generated approximately 75 percent of Nicaragua's export earnings.

Nicaragua's agricultural sector fared poorly under the Sandinistas. Between 1978 and 1990 agricultural exports fell from over U.S. $450 million per year to under U.S. $300 million per year.

Overall agricultural production rose by 3.9 percent in 1989. Production of the nontraditional export crop sesame grew by 475 percent, while tobacco, coffee, and sugar cane production increased by 35.3, 7.9, and 6.4 percent respectively. Production of grains fell by 2.5 percent as a result of Hurricane Joan (1988) and a drought in 1989.

President Violeta Barrios de Chamorro signed a decree on January 28, 1991, repealing a government monopoly on the export of most commodities. Nicaragua's export earnings may get a boost as a result. The government has announced plans to reactivate the agricultural sector and revitalize agricultural exports. The Chamorro administration plans to increase cotton production by 188 percent by 1996, coffee production by 134 percent, and banana production by 118 percent.

In December 1990, the government drafted export promotion legislation. In its present form, the legislation would provide certain benefits to exporters of nontraditional items, including both agricultural and nonagricultural products. Nontraditional exporters will enjoy an income tax exemption on up to 80 percent of profits.

Based on preliminary statistics, 1990 agricultural production fell sharply. Continued drought, floods, and politically motivated strikes combined to reduce cultivated acreage in 1990. Delays in settling demobilized Nicaraguan resistance members, tight credit, and the unsettled land tenure situation also played a part in lower agricultural activity.

Overall the area under cultivation decreased by 24.5 percent in 1990 compared with 1989. The outlook for Nicaragua's export crop production for 1990–91 also appeared cloudy. As of November 1990, government officials were predicting a sharp 18.5 decline in coffee production, Nicaragua's leading export crop.

Manufacturing: Nicaragua's industrial sector also fared poorly under the Sandinistas. Industrial production fell by 8 percent in 1989 compared with 1988. A Sandinista government austerity program resulted in sharply reduced investment in all sectors in

1989, with expenditures in equipment and machinery falling by 41.9 percent compared with 1988.

During the Sandinista era, the government nationalized almost all strategic industries and firmly controlled the economy, even though only 40 percent of industrial assets were directly state-owned. As of December 1990, the government owned some 350–450 corporations, most of these administered through government holding company CORNAP (Nicaraguan Corporation of Public Companies).

Many government corporations are poorly managed, overstaffed, and inefficient. Public sector wages are consistently higher than wages for comparable private sector firms. Accounting information on the firms is almost nonexistent; complete balance sheets exist for a fraction of the firms.

CORNAP issued a privatization plan for the 350–450 state-owned enterprises in early 1991. Officials say that the policy will emphasize three factors: transparency, orderliness, and economic democracy. Economic democracy implies that all sectors participating in production (labor, suppliers) must have an opportunity to participate in ownership. The government says it wishes to move quickly on privatization, although concrete achievements to date are few and Sandinista opposition continues to present difficulties. The government was counting on raising U.S. $20 million in privatization proceeds in 1991.

In an effort to attract increased foreign investment, the government has introduced more liberal foreign investment legislation in the National Assembly. The foreign investment legislation calls for the creation of a high-powered investment committee which would include the Minister of Economy and Development, the Minister of Finance, the President of the Central Bank, and the Minister for External Cooperation. The draft law guarantees that foreign investors will be able to freely repatriate earnings and capital. The government also planned to introduce free trade zone and export promotion legislation in 1991.

Despite efforts to make the economic environment more attractive, preliminary statistics indicate that the industrial sector performed poorly in 1990. Sandinista-led labor actions in May and July 1990 resulted in significant lost output. Foreign exchange shortages and continued tight monetary and fiscal policy also contributed to depressed demand and lower industrial production.

U.S.-Nicaraguan Relations

Following the electoral victory of Violeta Barrios de Chamorro in March 1990, the United States lifted its five-year-old trade embargo on trade with Nicaragua. At the time of this writing, no figures are available on 1990–92 U.S. trade with Nicaragua.

Trade

In April 1990, the government of Nicaragua liberalized its import regime, permitting private sector imports for the first time in 11 years. Nicaragua slashed import duties on July 1, 1990, with the top rate cut from 61 to 20 percent. While the government continues to require import licenses, the licensing process is little more than a formality. Chronic foreign exchange shortages slow imports.

Imports were projected to fall 6.4 percent in 1990, to U.S. $592 million. Depressed domestic demand and Nicaragua's continued tight foreign exchange position contributed to lower imports. Higher oil prices resulting from the Persian Gulf crisis have placed and will continue to place additional strain on an already difficult balance of payments position.

Starting in 1989, nontraditional exporters had access to 100 percent of their foreign

NICARAGUA
Key Economic Indicators

	1989	1990	1991 (est)
Income, Production and Employment			
GDP (millions U.S. $)[1]	1,323	1,339	1,421
Percent Growth in Real GDP[2]	−2.8	−4.4	1.0
GDP by sector (%)			
Agriculture	15.9	15.6	14.7
Mining	0.6	0.6	0.4
Manufacturing	21.0	20.3	20.8
Construction	3.4	3.1	2.7
Government	13.0	13.5	12.9
Other services	46.1	46.9	48.5
GDP per capita (U.S. $)	353	347	N/A
Population (millions)[3]	3.73	3.86	3.99
Labor force (millions)[3]	1.28	1.33	1.39
Unemployment rate (%)[3]	8.4	11.1	13.3
Underemployment rate[3]	39.4	44.6	49.9
Population growth (%)[3]	3.4	3.8	3.1
Money and Prices			
Money supply (U.S. $ million)	46.6	68.5	78.1
Commercial interest rate	N/A	18.0	18.0
Savings rate	−22.2	−26.8	−13.2
Investment rate[4]	26.1	24.7	N/A
CPI (% change)[5]	4,770	7,485	2,741
Exchange rate (year-end)[6]	38,150	3,000,000	5
Balance of Payments & Trade (U.S. $ millions)			
Exports FOB	290.1	326.9	302.5
Exports to U.S.[7]	0.0	25.0	70.0
Imports CIF	−547.1	−567.1	−583.8
Imports from U.S.[7]	0.0	77.7	110.0
Aid from U.S.[8]	5	277	275
Total foreign aid (disbursed)	169	202	482
External public debt	9,597	10,585	9,996
Debt service paid (%)	172.7	177.4	265.3
Foreign reserves (as months of imports – gross)	2.1	1.3	1.3
Balance of payments	−630.1	−811.5	−1,118.7

Sources: International Monetary Fund (IMF) and World Bank unless otherwise indicated. All indicators are for calendar years unless otherwise indicated.

1. Source: World Bank. The IMF estimate of GDP is significantly lower, while the Nicaraguan Central Bank estimate is much higher.
2. The IMF projects −0.4 growth.
3. Source: Nicaraguan government Ministry of Labor.
4. Investment rates appear unrealistically high. This may result in part from state-owned companies claiming that loans obtained from the state banks were used for investments, when they were likely used for current operating expenses.
5. Reflects average inflation. Figures included in the 1990 report were year-end.
6. 1989 and 1990 figures are for the old currency. Complete conversion to the new currency, the gold cordoba, was effected by May 1991.
7. Source: Central Bank of Nicaragua
8. Source: U.S. Agency for International Development. These indicators correspond to funds obligated in U.S. government fiscal years (FY), e.g., FY 91 ran from October 1, 1990, to September 30, 1991.

exchange earnings for inputs and capital equipment purchases.

The Chamorro administration has made the reactivation of Nicaragua's agricultural export sector one of its primary objectives.

On January 28, 1991, President Chamorro signed a decree authorizing the Ministry of Economy to issue private export licenses for all major commodities. Foreign trade was previously the exclusive preserve of government marketing companies. Some private exporters could experience difficulty obtaining financing for their operations. If the government follows through with plans to privatize state-owned enterprises and liberalize the economy, export performance will likely improve under the Chamorro government. The lifting of the U.S. trade embargo in March 1990 and the admission of Nicaragua to the Caribbean Basin Initiative II program should boost exports. The World Bank projected 1990 exports at U.S. $321 million, up about 10 percent over 1989 exports.

Trade Prospects

Nicaragua remains, at best, a small emerging market and will remain a small market for imports, including U.S. imports. A long absence by U.S. firms from Nicaragua due to the five-year U.S. embargo has placed U.S. firms at a disadvantage as Nicaragua shifted its trade pattern to Eastern Europe, Japan, and elsewhere during those years. Despite this problem, U.S. exports to Nicaragua have increased from zero in 1989 to U.S. $110 million in 1991. Total import/export data and foreign aid for these years are given below:

Trade Results
(U.S. $ million)

	1989	1990	1991
Exports FOB	290	327	303
Imports CIF	547	567	583
Foreign aid	169	202	482

Specific Trade Opportunities

Medical equipment and supplies: Medical equipment and medical instrumentation are obsolete after 11 years of reliance on the Eastern bloc and Cuba for medical care and an exodus of qualified doctors. Medical supplies are scarce. New and refurbished equipment and supplies can find a good market here. As is true for all other best prospects, sources of financing are still a problem.

Suggested market entry strategy: Trade mission. This is a very small market and trade missions would be more cost-effective if they were to cover Nicaragua as part of their itinerary through Central America.

Consumer products: Many Nicaraguans lived permanently in the U.S.; some are returning to their former homeland. Others have traveled to the U.S. and acquired a taste for U.S. consumer products. As the Nicaraguan economy moves toward a free market, opportunities for sales of U.S. consumer products will increase.

Suggested market entry strategy: Trade mission; video catalogue show. Despite the devaluation, Nicaragua remains a very expensive place. A successful catalogue show here would cost several times what is normally budgeted for events of this nature.

Construction equipment: The Nicaraguan construction machinery base is obsolete or unreliable as Nicaragua has relied on Eastern Europe for over 11 years. Some local observers comment that Nicaragua needs in excess of 250,000 dwellings to satisfy the current housing crisis. The government of Nicaragua initiated a U.S. $280 million public investment program in 1992.

Much of these bids will be used to repair Nicaraguan infrastructure, housing, and transportation.

Suggested market entry strategy: Agent distributor service. U.S. suppliers could profit from association with known Nicaraguan firms which have adequate channels of distribution.

Hardware tools and equipment: Although linked to construction equipment through the lack of houses, hardware tools and equipment can be targeted separately. Nicaraguans are rebuilding their inadequate and deteriorated dwellings. As foreign economic assistance programs are beginning to place emphasis on employment creation and on rebuilding, Nicaraguans desperately need tools to do the job.

Suggested market entry strategy: Agent or distributor.

Agro-Industry: Despite difficulties in the countryside, Nicaragua's competitive advantage remains agriculture. A strong effort is being made to increase nontraditional exports. The county needs farm equipment and fertilizers now and will begin to increase demand for food processing equipment with the expected increase of fruits and vegetable exports.

Suggested market entry strategy: Agent or distributor, direct sales.

International airport improvement: The U.S. Trade Development Agency (TDA) funded a definitional mission and a subsequent U.S. $250,000 grant for a feasibility study to support a multilaterally funded construction project. Agreement is near completion but it has been delayed in the Nicaraguan clearance process. U.S. companies will be invited to bid for the feasibility project and subsequent implementation project.

Geothermal plant: A U.S. firm which tried to obtain a contract to build a plant of over 100 mw withdrew from the market due to a slow local bureaucracy and lack of assurances of a proper return on their investment, and because OPIC does not offer inconvertibility insurance in Nicaragua.

Great potential for geothermal development exists in Nicaragua. The best strategy to follow by U.S. companies interested in this sector is first to contact the economic/commercial section for a status report on Nicaragua's energy planning and then to expect to move through a very slow process as Nicaragua creates the legal and institutional environment that can make possible large infrastructure investment with pay-off far in the future.

APPROACHING THE MARKET

Commercial Environment

After years of "suspended animation," the Nicaragua commercial environment began to perk up. A newly revitalized Nicaraguan-American Chamber of Commerce (AmCham) increased its membership from 50 to 150 during 1991. AmCham also cooperated with the American Embassy in assuring the success of a State Department organized government approved (SOGA) 24-company Florida mission to Managua in November 1991. Mission members sold U.S. $1.5 million during the visit and projected U.S. $10.5 million in additional sales through November 1992.

COSEP, the Nicaraguan umbrella organization covering the entire spectrum of private sector associations, although still facing problems on the property rights front, remains a key player in the revitalization of the Nicaraguan economy.

The U.S. Agency for International Development (USAID) has implemented programs aimed at energizing the private sector and plans to provide technical support to COSEP and other private organizations to improve their effectiveness in promotions and trade. USAID's economic assistance to Nicaragua is also moving away from stabilization support and towards foreign exchange support for enterprises to purchase raw materials and capital goods for the export and agro-industry sector to capitalize on Nicaragua's agriculture competitive advantage.

During the Sandinista period, as many as 500,000 Nicaraguans moved to foreign countries, taking much wealth and expertise with them. The American Embassy estimates that as many as 150,000 have come back and small investments are becoming visible (small stores, restaurants, boutiques, etc.). Some of these investments are being made also by those who stayed behind and know what is politically possible in a still confused, uncertain, and risky economic environment. Some of the big family business groups stayed and even thrived in the Sandinista period. These groups are best positioned to successfully undertake sizable investments, at least in the short run. U.S. companies interested in sizing up the market for high-profile investments would fare better in association with these groups.

Many problems remain. Recent labor/political instability worries many private investors (both foreign and domestic). Perhaps the most significant negative event was the burning of Managua's city hall by Sandinista mobs in November 1991. A visiting trade delegation from Florida was nearly canceled as a result of disturbances. Mission members arrived the day after the disturbances, but the mission was ultimately successful.

Recalcitrant labor unions are still a problem, particularly with regard to their behavior towards companies which were nationalized and may be privatized in the next few years. Potential U.S. investors should keep a watchful eye on the role to be played by unions and workers in their enterprises. Disenchanted recontras (those who fought the Sandinistas) and recompas (those who fought on the Sandinista side) add another degree of uncertainty to the agro-business and agro-industrial sector.

The informal sector is very dynamic, fueled by an estimated U.S. $100 million per year overseas remittances. Small U.S. traders could take advantage of the informal economy on investments between U.S. $5–50,000 in consumer goods, which can be

turned over several times a year. They can do so, as long as they do not make vulnerable investments and as long as the government allows the exchange of cordobas for dollars in the marketplace. Repatriation of profits from investments registered with the Ministry of Economy and Development are still a problem for all investors not covered by the new investment law (which allows for repatriation of profits). The regulations on the law are yet to be published. Given the uncertainties and opportunities still remaining in Nicaragua, U.S. investors with a high tolerance for risk could be very successful in this market.

Demand for Goods and Services

Numerous opportunities for U.S. commercial sales exist in Nicaragua. After 11 years of economic stagnation, Nicaragua's capital equipment and machinery are badly run down and in need of repair or replacement. During the 1980s, the government relied heavily on the former Soviet Union and Eastern Europe to provide technology and equipment. Much of Nicaragua's capital stock is substandard as a result. Nonavailability of foreign exchange and competition from foreign competitors are likely to present the greatest obstacles to U.S. commercial sales in Nicaragua.

Nicaragua is in the process of clearing its U.S. $350 million arrears with the World Bank and the Inter-American Development Bank. Once arrears have been cleared, these institutions will resume lending to Nicaragua. Significant commercial opportunities for U.S. firms may arise, supplying World Bank and Inter-American Development Bank projects.

Business opportunities are likely to be best in the capital goods, agro-business, energy, and consumer goods industries. The government has put together a program aimed at doubling agricultural exports within five years. To boost agricultural output Nicaragua will need to import quantities of agricultural inputs, including fertilizer, farm machinery, and transportation equipment.

The energy sector is also an area of promise for U.S. firms. At present Nicaragua obtains one-half of its 350 megawatt electric generating capacity from inefficient thermal generating plants. Significant geothermal potential exists, waiting to be tapped. One geothermal electric plant is currently in operation—an Italian-built 70-megawatt unit on the slopes of the Momotombo volcano.

While not a large market, at just under four million inhabitants, Nicaragua is a potentially lucrative market for U.S. consumer goods. Many Nicaraguans developed a taste for U.S. products while in exile in Miami. In addition, after the five-year U.S. trade embargo, there exists a large unmet demand for U.S. consumer goods in Nicaragua.

Implications for U.S. Exporters

The Chamorro government has significantly reduced trade barriers, mainly by cutting tariffs and eliminating state monopolies. The result has been widespread availability of U.S.-produced consumer goods in several newly established Managua supermarkets. While import licenses are required, these are little more than a formality, with one notable exception. In September 1991 the Nicaraguan government's Ministry of Economy used the licensing procedure to restrict U.S. imports of chicken parts. In order to meet World Bank conditionality, the government has committed itself to removing this barrier and all quantitative restrictions by March 1992.

Legislation passed in 1991 allowed the establishment of private banks in Nicaragua. Previously, banking had been a state monopoly, as the insurance industry continues to be. At least one U.S. bank showed interest in starting operations in Nicaragua. However, it is unclear whether the current banking law allows foreign banks to open branches and accept deposits. Two private Nicaraguan banks were established in 1991.

In the absence of a bilateral aviation treaty, U.S.-Nicaraguan aviation relations are based on comity and reciprocity. In 1990–91 the Nicaraguan government granted landing rights to four U.S. carriers, while two Nicaraguan carriers were granted landing rights in the U.S. However, Nicaragua has not acted on a long-standing request for scheduled all-cargo service by another U.S. airline.

A new investment law was passed in 1991. The new law allows 100 percent foreign ownership in all areas. However, some U.S. investors still have difficulty repatriating profits due to foreign exchange shortages.

Export Subsidies Policies

The March 1990 lifting of the U.S. trade embargo and the November 1990 inclusion of Nicaragua in the Caribbean Basin Initiative II program, the latter allowing a wide range of Nicaraguan products duty-free access to U.S. markets, set the stage for export oriented policy changes.

In August 1991, President Chamorro signed an export promotion decree, establishing a package of fiscal exonerations and incentives for exports.

The legislation favors nontraditional exporters, who will be exonerated from paying 80 to 60 percent of income tax on a sliding scale from 1991 to 1996, with the benefit dropping to zero in 1997 and thereafter. All exporters are to be allowed to import inputs duty free and to be exonerated from paying value-added taxes over the same period, again on a sliding scale. In addition, the law promised preferential access to foreign exchange for exporters.

INVESTMENT CLIMATE

President Chamorro's administration has committed itself to an export-led strategy for economic development. In order to spur economic growth and attract foreign investment, the government introduced legislation in the National Assembly in December 1990 to revamp Nicaragua's foreign investment regime. The draft legislation compares favorably with foreign investment laws in other countries in Latin America. The government of Nicaragua introduced legislation into the National Assembly in early December to permit the operation of private financial institutions and insurance companies. The exact details of the operation of the private financial institutions will be subject to regulation by the central bank. The government is also considering legislation to reactivate its free trade zone and to provide increased export incentives.

The government has announced plans to privatize the bulk of its 350–450 state-owned enterprises within the next three years. While many of these firms are over-staffed, debt burdened, inefficient, and in very poor shape, some privatization candidates may offer significant opportunities. Investment opportunities in agro-business and other export areas may be very attractive.

Many U.S. firms maintained a presence in Nicaragua throughout the Sandinista period, if only to protect their assets from confiscation. U.S. investment is concentrated in the manufacture and/or marketing of petroleum and chemical products, office equipment, and other products. Although at least one U.S. bank continues to maintain its license to operate in Nicaragua, no U.S. banks or insurance companies actively operate at present. Current banking law prohibits domestic banking activity and strongly discourages foreign banks from operating.

Despite the opportunities, some U.S. firms currently doing business in Nicaragua continue to have difficulties repatriating earnings in a timely fashion. The U.S. Overseas Private Investment Corporation (OPIC) reopened for business in Nicaragua in 1990. At present OPIC is unable to offer convertibility coverage.

FINANCING AND CAPITAL MARKETS

General Policy Framework

Violeta Chamorro assumed control of Nicaragua's civilian government and an economy devastated by 11 years of Sandinista repression, economic misrule, and civil war. Control of the police, military, and intelligence services remained in the hands of the Sandinistas, with General Humberto Ortega staying on as army chief. Espousing a policy of national reconciliation, the Chamorro government achieved the disarmament of the Nicaraguan resistance and declared an end to obligatory military service in 1990, thereby fostering widespread peace. Little, however, was accomplished on the economic front in 1990. The new government was hindered by the economic sabotage of the outgoing Sandinistas, who looted the treasury and government offices, increased the wages of the bloated public sector by 800 percent in nominal terms, and financed the resulting deficit with the printing press.

The new government continued to use this method of deficit financing until January 1991.

Focusing on stabilization and structural adjustment, the main challenges for the Chamorro government in 1990 and 1991 were bringing inflation under control, clearing arrears with international financial institutions, and defining property rights. As of November 1991 the government had experienced success in the first two areas, with the third remaining an obstacle to restarting agricultural production and encouraging foreign investment. The legal status of large numbers of homes and businesses as well as large areas of land confiscated without compensation by the Sandinista government remained unclear. In the face of Sandinista opposition, the Chamorro government has been unable to define property rights and put in place a broadly accepted legal procedure for settling property rights.

Central government expenditures rose by only two percentage points of GDP in 1990, despite a more than two-fold increase in the wage bill due to the eleventh-hour Sandinista regime pay raise. With assistance from the International Monetary Fund (IMF), the government prepared a stabilization program, implemented on March 3, 1991, to reduce the public sector deficit to a level that can be financed by external grants and concessionary assistance, without recourse to domestic credits. The program calls for strict constraints on domestic bank credit.

Although public revenue is far less, government spending amounts to almost one-third of GDP. Government ownership of assets in all sectors and heavy public sector use of resources crowd out the private sector.

State-owned companies are said to account for 30–40 percent of GDP. By late 1991 the government had targeted some 350 state-owned enterprises for privatization. A short-term goal, in accordance with Wcrld Bank conditionality, is the divestiture of 25 such enterprises by March 1991.

Opportunities for U.S. firms will present themselves as this privatization process gains speed. The first invitations for bids, on mining and fishing concerns, in September 1991 saw solid U.S. private sector participation. In sum, the Nicaraguan government made considerable progress in stabilizing

the economy and undertaking structural reform in 1991.

Debt Management Policies

The Chamorro administration inherited a heavy burden of foreign debt from the previous government. In June 1991 total debt stood at U.S. $10.8 billion, of which over U.S. $6 billion was owed to the former Soviet Union and former East bloc countries. The government's first priority was to clear its U.S. $330 million arrearages with the World Bank and the Inter-American Development Bank, in order to obtain fresh funds from these institutions. This was achieved in September 1991 with U.S. $135 million in grant contributions from the international donor community (of which U.S. $75 million was given by the United States) and U.S. $193 million in short-term bridge loans from Mexico, Venezuela, Spain, and Colombia. The government's second priority has been to renegotiate bilateral debt. The most notable debt reductions in 1990–91 were with Mexico, which virtually pardoned the approximately U.S. $1 billion owed to it; the United States, which forgave U.S. $294.5 million in official debt; Venezuela, which gave terms amounting to forgiveness of the U.S. $140 million due it; and Colombia, which effectively forgave almost U.S. $50 million.

Nicaragua's foreign debt burden, which was between six and 10 times its GDP, has been somewhat relieved by a Paris Club rescheduling of Nicaragua's debt in January 1992. Nicaragua was the first country to receive a Paris Club rescheduling on the basis of the new "Trinidad Terms" framework. It should be noted that Nicaragua's debt problems do not parallel the general Latin American crisis, which began in 1982. In 1979, the Sandinistas inherited less than

U.S. $2 billion in debt from the Somoza regime. By the end of the 1980s they had run this up to almost U.S. $11 billion.

Last on the Nicaraguan government's list of priorities are commercial creditors. In July 1991 the Central Bank presented a representative of U.S. private banks documents recognizing Nicaragua's U.S. $1.8 billion debt and extending the statute of limitations expiration date of August 1991. This avoided the immediate necessity of U.S. banks' suing Nicaragua in the U.S. court for nonpayment, but left the option open. At the same time it showed the good faith of the Nicaraguan government.

The Currency and Exchange Rate Mechanisms

In May 1990, the Chamorro government introduced a second currency, the gold cordoba, which remained pegged to the U.S. dollar for all of 1990 and the first three months of 1991. This new currency was used largely as a unit of account for the first 10 months of its existence, as small amounts of gold cordoba notes were slowly introduced into circulation. On March 3, 1991, the government dramatically devalued the new currency from parity to five gold cordobas to the dollar. Complete conversion took place by the end of April 1991, with the withdrawal of the old currency. Because prices increased 261 percent in March, the real effect of devaluation was in the range of 30 percent. Inflation during the period April through October 1991 averaged 1 percent a month.

Despite the devaluation, the currency still appears to be overvalued, as indicated by price levels generally higher than in other Central American countries. Higher prices are also due in part to a generalized inefficiency in the economy, born of central planning, a steady brain drain, and Sandinista intervention in the economy. Another indicator is the continuing trade deficit. Following the March 1990 implementation of the stabilization plan, with its attendant drop in demand for imports, importers have had no difficulty gaining access to foreign currency. One reason foreign exchange is freely available is that Nicaragua has received infusions of foreign assistance, mostly from the U.S. in the form of fast-disbursing balance of payments support. The overvalued cordoba gives U.S. exports an advantage, but if not corrected may lead to balance of payments and foreign exchange reserve difficulties, which would impair Nicaragua's sustained ability to import U.S. goods.

Financial Market Operations and Structural Policies

The new government lifted price controls in general, with the exception of prices on fiscal goods (e.g., tobacco, soft drinks, alcoholic beverages), petroleum products, and public utilities. The government also continues to set prices on staple goods (e.g., beans, rice, corn) in government-owned outlets as part of the strategy to reduce inflation. Private operators are not required to sell at these prices; but they are required to post government prices in a conspicuous place. Retailers have been temporarily closed for failing to do so. Government officials have also tried jawboning to keep prices down. In addition, they have lowered the prices of inputs produced by state-owned companies and sold donated commodities at less than international prices.

In order to meet conditionality for World Bank loans, the government announced plans to cease these practices by March 1992. The freeing up of the market has allowed greater access for U.S. exports.

Tax policies: Measures taken by the government of Nicaragua in 1990 to reduce tariffs were a small step in the right direction. However, no substantial cuts were effected until July 1991. Following this latest round of cuts, Nicaragua had a maximum combined duty on most imports of 38 percent. This figure includes a tariff (20 percent maximum on most goods), a selective consumption tax (15 percent maximum on most goods), and revenue stamps (a flat 3 percent on all goods). Sixty-six percent of tariffs vary between 3–40 percent. While several categories of goods retain effective protection ranging up to 143 percent (e.g., vehicles, firearms, and alcoholic beverages), the government estimated that the July 1991 measures would reduce the cost of imported consumer goods by 10 percent. In a 1991 report the IMF estimated average protection to be 18 percent. The government announced that by December 1993 nominal import protection will be reduced to the 10–20 percent range. The government of Nicaragua receives about two-thirds of its revenue from indirect taxes, such as sales/excise taxes and customs duties. In 1990 the highest income tax rate was reduced from 60 percent to 38.5 percent (for taxpayers earning more than 180,000 gold cordobas, the equivalent of U.S. $36,000 at five cordobas to the U.S. dollar). The government plans to reduce the top rate to about 33 percent. Taxpayers earning less than 25,000 gold cordobas (U.S. $5,000) are exempt from the income tax. The other rates are: 10 percent between 25,000 and 60,000 gold cordobas; 20 percent between 60,000 and 120,000 (U.S. $24,000) gold cordobas; and 30 percent between 120,000 and 180,000 gold cordobas. Corporations pay the same tax rate as individuals.

Regulatory policies: In 1989 Nicaragua's state-owned trading companies administered trade with the Eastern bloc accounting for 56 percent of total imports, including a monopoly on imports of oil and fertilizers. Private parties were marginally involved in foreign trade in a system which included discretionary allocation/retention of foreign exchange, multiple exchange rates, and arbitrary trade credit rationing. Nominal import protection was nontransparent and widely differentiated. It ranged from 4 percent to 253 percent, averaging 48 percent. In February 1991, President Chamorro deregulated the import and export of most products. All except cotton and coffee exporters have full access to the foreign exchange that they generate. The government allows the use of foreign exchange for most current account transactions, but not for capital account transactions. One U.S. investor has over U.S. $50 million in blocked profits with the Central Bank. The Central Bank has refused to permit existing foreign companies to repatriate profits fully. An investment law passed in 1991 provides for the repatriation of new capital three years after the initial investment.

Chapter 16

PANAMA

	Total	Urban	
Population (1993)	2,581,000	52.0%	

Main Urban Areas	Population	Percentage of Total	International Calling Code
PANAMA	688,000	26.7	507
David	51,000	2.0	507
La Chorrera	39,000	1.5	507
Santiago	23,000	0.9	507
Tocumen	22,000	0.9	507
Colon	20,000	0.8	507

Land Area   75,990 square kilometers
    Comparable U.S. State   Slightly smaller than South Carolina

Language
Spanish	81%
Creole English	14%
Guaymi	2%
Kuna	2%
Other	1%

    Common Business Language   English

Currency   1 balboa (B) = 100 centesimos
    Exchange Rate (May 1993)   U.S. $1.00 = 1.00 balboas
    Note: Panama accepts U.S. dollars as its official tender.

Best Nonstop Air Connection via U.S.   Miami to Panama City: 2.75 hours
    New York to Panama City: 5 hours
    Los Angeles to Panama City: 7 hours
    American Airlines (800) 433-7300
       One nonstop daily

Best Hotel   Riande Continental Airport (U.S. $72)
    P.O. Box 8457
    Avenue Eusebio Amorales
    Tel: (507) 637-477
    Fax: (507) 640-930

INTRODUCTION AND REGIONAL ORIENTATION

Panama is the third largest target of U.S. investment in Latin America after Mexico and Brazil. U.S. investment dominates all foreign investment in Panama, accounting for U.S. $398.3 million of the U.S. $491.7 million total as of December 31, 1990. Most U.S. investment has been concentrated in petroleum products and the pipeline, agriculture and fishing, banking and commerce. With the exception of the pipeline, investment opportunities in these areas remain favorable. In addition, U.S. investors may find attractive prospects in export processing zones and in state-owned enterprises marked for privatization by the Panamanian government. In the long term, prospects may exist in the areas scheduled for reversion under the Panama Canal Treaties. Panama's use of the U.S. dollar as its national currency (Panama does not print its own paper currency), with no restrictions on conversion or repatriation of profits and capital, is also conducive to U.S. investment.

Panama's geographical location has been its comparative advantage for over 500 years. The Panama Canal—connecting the Pacific Ocean with the Atlantic—provides efficient transportation services and attracts a great number of international businesses. With the Panamanian government's recent decision to make the economy more competitive through privatization and commercialization, the country's trading and investment climate is favorable.

Panama's prospects for sustained economic growth will depend on the government's ability to implement economic reform programs that improve public sector efficiency and eliminate widespread market distortions.

Reduction in corporate income tax rates to 30–34 percent by 1994, together with the reduction in personal income tax rates to 4–30 percent on 11 brackets beginning in 1992, should stimulate incentives to work, save, and invest. A pick-up in the pace of privatization would promote economic growth and reduce the size of the public sector. To attract increased domestic and foreign private sector investment, the Panamanian government must also strengthen public sector investment to improve the country's aging infrastructure. Finally, government leaders must meet the challenge of planning for the reversion of the Panama Canal and related areas at the end of the decade.

Geographical Background

Panama is a mountainous, tropical wilderness (including rain forests), bordered to the northwest by Costa Rica (330 kilometers), and to the southeast by Colombia (225 kilometers). Its highest elevation is the Cerro Volcano (3,475 meters—11,468 feet). Its natural resources include: copper, mahogany forests, and shrimp.

Most of the territory is forest and woodland (54 percent), followed by meadows and pastures (15 percent). Only a small amount of the land is arable (6 percent), of which only one-third is cultivated with permanent crops.

History and Political Conditions

Panama's history has been shaped by the evolution of the world economy and the ambitions of great powers. Vasco Nuñez de Balboa's tortuous trek from the Atlantic to the Pacific in 1513 demonstrated that the isthmus was indeed the path between the seas, and Panama quickly became the crossroads and marketplace of Spain's empire in the New World.

In the early 1500s, gold and silver were brought by ship from South America, hauled across the isthmus, and loaded aboard ships for Spain. The route became known as the Camino Real, or Royal Road.

In November 1903, after Colombia rejected a treaty permitting the United States to build a canal, Panama proclaimed its independence from Colombia and concluded the Hay/Bunau-Varilla Treaty with the United States. The treaty authorized the United States to build a canal through a zone 10 miles wide and to administer, fortify, and defend it "in perpetuity." In 1914, the United States completed the existing 83-kilometer (52-mile) lock canal. The early 1960s saw the beginning of sustained pressure in Panama for the renegotiation of this treaty.

From 1903 until 1968, Panama was a constitutional democracy dominated by a commercially oriented oligarchy. In 1968 the military ousted the president and a military junta governed. The commander of the National Guard, Omar Torrijos, emerged as the principal power in Panamanian political life. Torrijos was a charismatic leader whose populist domestic programs and nationalist foreign policy appealed to the rural and urban constituencies largely ignored by the oligarchy.

Torrijos' death in a 1981 plane crash altered the tone but not the direction of Panama's political evolution. Despite 1983 constitutional amendments which appeared to proscribe a political role for the military, the Panama Defense Forces (PDF) continued to dominate Panamanian political life behind a facade of civilian government. The presidential election of 1984 resulted in the election of the promilitary coalition candidate, amid widespread voting irregularities and charges of fraud. Progovernment parties also won a majority of Legislative Assembly seats in races tainted by charges of corruption. By this time, General Manuel Noriega was firmly in control of both the PDF and the civilian government.

Traditional elites joined middle-class elements in organized opposition to the PDF's economic and political power. Prompted by government restrictions on media and civil liberties and the 1985 murder of a prominent opposition leader, business, civic, and religious groups formed a loose coalition that organized widespread antigovernment demonstrations in the summer of 1987.

Panama's developing domestic crisis was paralleled by rising tensions between the Panamanian government and the United States, which were caused in part by the regime's crackdown on civil liberties and its harassment of U.S. citizens.

The United States froze economic and military assistance to Panama in the summer of 1987 in response to the political crisis and an attack on the American Embassy. The government of Panama countered by ousting the U.S. Agency for International Development in December 1987. The U.S. Congress cut off all assistance to Panama. The indictment of General Noriega in U.S. courts in 1988 on drug-trafficking charges sharpened the political crisis in Panama and tensions between Panama and the United States. In early March, President Eric Arturo Delvalle's attempt to remove Noriega as PDF commander led to a government takeover by the PDF and domination of the Legislative Assembly by Noriega forces.

In April 1988, President Reagan invoked the International Economic Powers Act, freezing Panamanian government assets in U.S. banks and prohibiting a variety of payments by American agencies, firms, and individuals to the Noriega regime. Efforts to negotiate a resolution of the crisis failed in May 1988, when Noriega refused to abide by the terms of an agreement negotiated with his representatives for him to relinquish his authority.

The May 1989 presidential and legislative elections were widely understood by

Panamanians to be a referendum on Noriega versus democracy. Panamanian voters turned out in overwhelming numbers and voted by a margin of more than three-to-one for the anti-Noriega candidates. The size of the opposition victory and the presence of international observers thwarted regime efforts to control the outcome of the vote. The regime annulled the election and embarked on a new round of repression.

By the fall of 1989, the Noriega regime was clinging to power through fear and force. An unsuccessful PDF coup attempt in October produced bloody reprisals. Deserted by all but a small number of cronies, distrustful of a shaken and demoralized PDF, Noriega began increasingly to rely on irregular, paramilitary units. The climax of the crisis came in December 1989, with a regime declaration of war against the United States and attacks on U.S. military personnel. On December 20, President Bush ordered the U.S. military into Panama to protect U.S. lives and property, to fulfill U.S. treaty responsibilities to operate and defend the canal, to assist the Panamanian people in restoring democracy, and to bring Noriega to justice.

The U.S. troops involved in Operation Just Cause achieved their primary objectives quickly, and the withdrawal of troops sent into Panama on December 20 began on December 27. Noriega eventually surrendered voluntarily to U.S. authorities.

Panamanians moved quickly to begin rebuilding a civilian, constitutional government. On December 27, Panama's Electoral Tribunal—whose members were appointed by Noriega—invalidated the Noriega regime's annulment of the May 1989 election and confirmed the victory of opposition candidates Guillermo Endara (president), Ricardo Arias Calderon (first vice-president), and Guillermo Ford (second vice-president). As its priority objectives, the Endara govern-

ment identified economic recovery and the transformation of the Panamanian military into an apolitical police force under civilian control.

CRACKING THE MARKET

Demographics

Ethnic groups: Mestizo 70%; West Indian 14%; White 10%; Indian 6%.

Religions: Roman Catholic 93%, Protestant (Evangelical) 6%.

Languages: Spanish (official); 14% speak English as their native tongue; various Indian languages.

Literacy rate—87% overall: urban 94%, rural 62%.

Work force—820,000 (1990): government and social services 27%; agriculture 25%; commerce, restaurants and hotels 15%; manufacturing and mining 10%; transportation and communications 6%; construction 4%; finance, insurance and real estate 4%; canal area 2%; electricity, gas and water 1%; other 5%.

Economy

Panama's economy continued to grow in 1992 following two years of strong recovery from the adverse effects of the last years of the Noriega regime and U.S. sanctions. Private sector activity (particularly construction and the Colon Free Zone) is driving the expansion.

The Endara government has passed major reform legislation to modernize its tax code, facilitate privatization, and strengthen the social security administration. The government has also normalized its relations with the international financial institutions and can expect new financing for infrastructure and other development needs. The outlook for economic growth is favorable for the medium term. Sustainable long-term growth will require further government action to liberalize the trade regime, follow through on privatization of state enterprises, and foster job creation through labor code reforms.

Economic Performance

Panama's Gross Domestic Product (GDP) grew 9.3 percent in real terms in 1991, making Panama's economic growth one of the most impressive in the Western Hemisphere for the year. Strong internal demand for goods and services and better use of installed capacity were key factors in the 1991 performance. The year's showing places Panama's real GDP now nearly on par with the historical peak reached in 1987. Preliminary estimates for 1992 indicate a probable repeat of strong real growth at or above 8 percent.

Trends in Primary GDP Sectors

Panama's economy is highly dependent on a well-developed services sector which comprises approximately 75 percent of total GDP.

Service activities include the Panama Canal, banking, insurance, government, the transisthmian oil pipeline, and the Colon Free Zone. Agriculture contributes another 11 percent to GDP. Principal products include bananas, sugar, shrimp, coffee, cacao, meat, dairy products, rice, corn, and beans. The manufacturing sector—which contributes roughly 9 percent to GDP—is geared largely towards the domestic market, producing such items as clothing, processed foods, chemical products, and construction materials.

During 1991, almost all GDP sectors, with the exception of transportation services (e.g., the petroleum pipeline), showed increases over previous-year levels. 1992 saw improvements in all but the petroleum pipeline and government services sectors. The government services sector in particular was expected to decline as the Endara government carried out its commitment to reduce the size of the public sector. Construction activity and Colon Free Zone trade, along with the relevant complementary sectors (e.g., manufacturing, commerce, and tourism), led 1992 growth.

Agriculture: Agriculture, including livestock, forestry, and fisheries, contributes roughly 11 percent to GDP. Agricultural products are a major component of merchandise exports, though some products—principally corn and rice—are geared for the domestic market. In 1991, this sector maintained a 5 percent growth rate despite earthquake and flood damages to banana production, the most important agricultural export. Increases in nontraditional agricultural exports as well as remarkable growth in the poultry sector accounted for much of the growth. The year 1992 saw additional growth in agriculture. Beef, some tropical fruits, and nontraditional vegetable production were expected to expand. However, some of this growth may have been offset by declines in Panama's allotment of the decreasing U.S. sugar import quota and losses due to overfishing and increased foreign competition in the fisheries subsector.

Industry: Geared largely for domestic consumption, industrial activity is concentrated in the manufacture of clothing, consumer products, capital and intermediate goods, food products, beverages, and construction materials.

Production increased by 11.2 percent in 1991 as a result of increased demand—especially for construction materials—and more efficient use of installed capacity. While future construction activity growth rates will be more modest than the 104.2 percent shown for 1991, the continuing construction boom will generate additional expansion of industrial sector output.

The Endara government planned to reduce tariffs on industrial goods to 40 percent by March 1993. It had already reduced tariffs for industry to 60 percent. It aims to reorient production toward export markets and is promoting investment in industry by offering special incentives to businesses which establish manufacturing operations in export processing zones.

Banking: Panama's international banking center consists of 104 banks, of which 60 are general license banks, 27 are international license banks, and 17 are representative offices. Two of the general license banks—the National Bank of Panama and the National Savings Bank—are government-owned. U.S. banks with a presence in Panama include Citibank, Chase Manhattan, Bank of America, and First National Bank of Boston. The National Banking Commission estimates Panama's banking center employed 7,326 people and had a direct payroll of about U.S. $72 million in 1991.

Total banking center deposits increased by U.S. $2 billion in 1991. Individual and corporate deposits accounted for about two-thirds of this increase, interbank deposits for the remainder. Total assets expanded by U.S. $2.3 billion. Banks increased liquid (mainly external) claims by U.S. $1.5 billion and lending to the domestic private sector by U.S. $533 million. The latter was mainly to finance commerce (U.S. $334 million), consumer spending (U.S. $83 million), financial services (U.S. $44 million), and housing (U.S. $39 million).

USAID's Private Sector Reactivation Program supported expansion of domestic lending with disbursements of U.S. $76 million in 1991. Offshore banking declined slightly in 1991. Banking center activity is expected to grow in line with GDP in 1992. Banking system deposits were expected to grow by about 8 percent and total assets by 6–7 percent, to some U.S. $22 billion, by end-1992.

Panama Canal: Reversing the declining trend of the previous two years, fiscal year

(FY) 1991 registered substantial improvement in the most important elements of Panama Canal traffic and toll revenue. Oceangoing transits, Panama Canal (PC) net tonnage, and commercial cargo reached the highest levels since 1982. This unusually strong performance mostly occurred during the first half of the year and can be attributed primarily to changes in world trade patterns resulting from the Persian Gulf War. The rise in transit numbers and average ship size resulted in toll revenue reaching a record U.S. $374.6 million, up 4.4 percent from the amount collected in FY 1990.

In 1991, commercial cargo rose for the second consecutive year, increasing 3.6 percent to 162.7 million long tons. The increase was primarily concentrated in dry-bulk type commodities. All-time highs were registered in such commodities as phosphates, lumber, refrigerated products, containerized cargo, and others. The gains in these commodities more than offset the losses registered in petroleum and petroleum products, automobiles, and ores and metals.

As expected, canal traffic and toll revenue performed below FY 1991 levels during the first eight months of FY 1992. Oceangoing transits decreased 0.7 percent to 8,590 or 35.2 daily, toll revenue fell 1.5 percent to U.S. $250.2 million, and commercial cargo tonnage declined 0.5 percent to 107.6 million long tons. Year-end toll revenue was anticipated to total about U.S. $370.0 million, 1.2 percent below the U.S. $374.6 million registered in FY 1991.

Petroleum pipeline: Panama's pipeline (Petroterminal de Panama, S.A.) is a joint U.S.-Panamanian venture. Forty percent is owned by the government of Panama while 60 percent is owned by two American companies. The pipeline's contribution to GDP has fallen steadily over the past several years—from 6.9 percent in 1987 to 3.4 percent in 1990 to 2.5 percent in 1991—primarily because of a decrease in Alaskan oil

PANAMA
Key Economic Indicators
(millions of U.S. dollars, unless noted)

	1989	1990	1991 (est)	1992 (proj)
Domestic Economy				
Population (000s)	2,370	2,417	2,466	2,510
Nominal GDP	4,581.6	4,948.7	5,472.3	6,032.0
Real GDP (1970 prices)	1,786.1	1,868.4	2,042.7	2,206.1
Real GDP growth rate	(0.4)	4.6	9.3	8.0
Nominal per capita GDP	1,933	2,048	2,219	2,403
CPI (% change)	0.1	0.8	1.3	2.0
Employment				
Labor force (000s)	820.0	836.5	856.2	883.3
Unemployment rate (%)	16.3	16.0	15.7	15.7
Balance of Payments				
Trade deficit	567.2	999.1	1,158.5	1,289.0
Merchandise exports (FOB)	322.6	340.1	360.5	382.0
Merchandise imports (FOB)	889.8	1,339.2	1,519.0	1,671.0
Colon Free Zone (net)	50.8	390.1	220.9	200.0
Services balance (net)	882.3	828.1	918.9	947.0
Current account balance	365.9	219.1	(18.7)	(142.0)
Foreign investment flows	56.0	(30.0)	N/A	N/A
External Debt*				
Debt outstanding	5,039	5,355	5,414	5,250
Debt outstanding/GDP	110	108	99	87
Banking				
Assets (banking center)	15,395	18,384	20,682	21,993
Foreign	10,440	12,771	14,679	15,510
Domestic	4,955	5,613	6,003	6,483
Deposits (banking center)	11,527	15,072	17,119	18,212
Public Sector Finances				
Public investment as % of GDP	1.2	1.2	2.2	3.5
Public sector deficit as % of GDP**	(10.8)	(2.8)	(2.5)	(2.2)
Panama Canal*				
Number of transits	12,075	12,052	12,763	12,360
Toll revenues (thousands)	329.8	355.6	374.6	370.0

*   Includes interest arrears
**   Includes interest due
*** U.S. fiscal year data

Sources: Comptroller's Office, IMF, Panama Canal Commission, National Banking Commission, Panamanian Trade Development Institute, American Embassy Panama City estimates.

PANAMA
(millions of U.S. dollars, unless otherwise noted)

	1989	1990	1991 (est)
Income, Production, Employment			
Real GDP (1970 prices)	1,786.0	1,868.0	1,952.0
GDP growth (%)	−0.4	4.6	4.5
GDP by sector (% of total)			
Agriculture/forestry/fisheries	11.8	11.8	11.6
Manufacturing	8.7	9.0	9.4
Utilities	4.2	4.1	4.0
Construction	1.4	1.7	2.3
Commerce/hotels/restaurants	10.7	11.6	12.2
Panama Canal	10.5	10.0	10.0
Oil pipeline	4.4	3.4	2.9
Colon Free Zone	4.9	5.5	5.9
Transport/communications	6.1	6.2	6.2
Finance/insurance/real estate	15.2	14.9	14.9
Government services	14.7	13.3	12.0
Other	7.3	8.5	8.6
Real GDP/capita (1970 prices)	754	773	791
Labor force (thousands)	820	845	870
Unemployment (rate)	16.3	17.7	17.3
Money and Prices			
Money and quasi-money	1,600.0	2,184.0	2,556.0
Commercial interest rates			
Fixed deposit (%)	8.5	10.0	7.5
Average lending (%)	13.0	15.0	11.0
Savings rate (% GDP)	4.4	9.3	10.9
Investment rate (% GDP)	2.8	16.6	15.2
Consumer prices (%, annual average)	−0.1	0.5	2.0
Wholesale prices (%, annual average)	2.5	9.5	9.0
Exchange rate (Balboa:dollar)	1:1	1:1	1:1
Balance of Payments and Trade			
Total merchandise exports (FOB)	297	317	350
Exports to U.S. (%)	47	46	44
Total merchandise imports (CIF)	986	1,489	1,500
Imports from U.S. (%)	45	43	37
Aid from U.S. government[1]	0	89	211
External public debt[1]	5,039	5,358	5,099
Debt service paid	0	225	250
Foreign assets[1]	119	406	200
Balance of payments			
Current account	70	−356	−225
Capital account	−881	663	481

1. For 1991, data based on assumption that Panama clears arrears with international financial institutions by year-end.

production and an increase in consumption of this oil in California. The outlook for 1992 and beyond was for further decline despite occasional spot contracts negotiated with the pipeline's users.

Colon Free Zone: Established in 1948, the Colon Free Zone (CFZ) is the largest of its kind in Latin America and rivals Hong Kong in overall activity. Total trade (imports plus re-exports) set yet another all-time record in 1991, reaching U.S. $7.6 billion as traders took advantage of the opportunities the CFZ provided with regard to access to growing regional markets. Total CFZ trade is poised for another strong performance in 1992 despite inefficient port services and disturbances in Colon. First quarter 1992 data show imports of $999.9 million and re-exports of U.S. $1.05 billion.

On the balance of payments side, the CFZ's net shipments (re-exports less imports) declined to U.S. $221 million in 1991 from U.S. $390.1 million in 1990.

Movements in exchange rates and inventories caused the value of CFZ imports to grow faster than the value of CFZ re-exports in 1991, and continue to affect the level of net CFZ shipments in 1992.

Commerce and tourism: Commerce and tourism, which include restaurants, hotels, and wholesale and retail activities, registered 12.7 percent growth in 1991. Brisk sales by local businesses and strong patronage of restaurants by the average Panamanian accounted for a good portion of this increase. The average hotel occupancy rate increased by almost one-quarter, to 44.9 percent in 1991 from 36.6 percent in 1990, as hotels benefited from a large volume of business travelers.

Political/Institutional Infrastructure

The Republic of Panama gained its independence from Colombia on November 3, 1903; independence from Spain was granted to Colombia (including the territory of Panama) on November 28, 1821.

Panama is governed as a constitutional democracy; the current Constitution was adopted on October 11, 1972 (amended 1978 and 1983, new amendments pending).

Panama's legal system is based on civil law system; judicial review of legislative acts go before the Supreme Court of Justice. Panama accepts compulsory ICJ jurisdiction, with reservations.

Panama's Constitution separates the government into executive, legislative, and judicial branches. The president is elected to a five-year, nonrenewable term in a direct popular election. The legislative branch consists of a 67-member Legislative Assembly. The judicial branch is organized under a nine-member Supreme Court and includes all tribunals and municipal courts. An autonomous Electoral Tribunal supervises voter registration and political party and election law activities. Everyone over the age of 18 is required to vote, although those who fail to do so are not penalized.

The Legislative Assembly is considering a number of proposed constitutional amendments. While most of the proposed amendments are of a relatively minor nature, there are a number which would establish a permanent legal basis for the demilitarization reforms carried out by the Endara government in 1990 and 1991. They would prohibit the existence of an army, divide the public security forces into separate branches, and prohibit them from intervening in Panama's political life. Following approval by the Legislative Assembly, these constitutional changes will be submitted to popular ratification in a plebiscite.

Panama has a rather fragmented multiparty system; 16 parties took part in the 1984 elections, and more than 12 participated in the 1989 elections.

Each political party must have at least 30,000 members in order to acquire full legal status. The current government was elected under the aegis of the Civil Democratic Opposition Alliance (ADOC), which was a coalition of the Authentic Liberal Party (PLA), the Christian Democratic Party (PDC), and the National Liberal Republican Movement (MOLIRENA).

President Endara ran as the candidate of the Authentic Liberal Party because his own political party—the Authentic Panamanista Party—had been taken away by the regime's Electoral Tribunal and awarded to a Noriega supporter. In 1990, Endara reorganized his followers as the Arnulfista Party, which is now part of the governing coalition.

In April 1991, after a series of disagreements over policy and patronage issues, President Endara removed Arias Calderon from his cabinet position as Minister of Government and Justice, prompting the other members of the PDC to resign from government. Arias Calderon retains his elected position as first vice-president. The PDC, which holds a plurality in the legislature, has stated that it will act as a responsible opposition party, working in cooperation with the Endara government on issues to benefit the country.

The Democratic Revolutionary Party (PRD) leads the COLINA coalition of labor, revolutionary, and communist parties, and is made up primarily of former Noriega supporters; COLINA holds the "swing vote" in the national legislature with 12 seats. The Tendencia faction of the PRD is a strong-arm battalion with ties to Cuba and Libya. Tendencia's influence is declining because of internal frictions and public opposition.

Elections

President: last held on 7 May 1989, annulled but later upheld (next to be held May 1994).

Legislative Assembly: last held on 27 January 1991 (next to be held May 1994); results: seats—(67 total) progovernment parties—PDC 28, MOLIRENA 16, PA 6,

PLA 5; opposition parties—PRD 10, PALA 1, PL 1. (Note: the PDC went into opposition after President Guillermo Endara ousted the PDC from the coalition government in April 1991.)

Communists: People's Party (PdP), pro-Soviet mainline Communist party, did not obtain the necessary 3 percent of the total vote in the 1984 election to retain its legal status; about 3,000 members.

Other political or pressure groups: National Council of Organized Workers (CONATO); National Council of Private Enterprise (CONEP); Panamanian Association of Business Executives (APEDE); National Civic Crusade; National Committee for the Right to Life.

Principal Government Officials

President
Guillermo ENDARA

First Vice-President
Ricardo ARIAS Calderon

Second Vice-President and Minister of Planning and Finance
Guillermo "Billy" FORD

Minister of Foreign Affairs
Julio LINARES

Ambassador to the U.S.
Jaime "Jimmy" FORD

Ambassador to the UN
Dr. Carlos AROSEMENA

Ambassador to the OAS
Lawrence CHEWNING Fabrega

Flag: divided into four equal rectangles; the top quadrants are white with a blue five-pointed star in the center (hoist side) and plain red, the bottom quadrants are plain blue (hoist side) and white with a red five-pointed star in the center.

Defense

The Panamanian government has converted

the former Panama Defense Forces into a civilian police organization called the Public Forces, which is subordinate to civilian officials and is responsive to human rights concerns. Personnel strength has been cut from 16,000 to about 13,000.

Virtually all former PDF senior officers were removed from the Public Forces, and personnel discovered to have been involved in corruption or other criminal activity are being removed. The old, centralized command structure has been broken up into four independent units: the Panamanian National Police, the National Maritime Service (coast guard), the National Air Service (official transportation), and the Institutional Protective Service (VIP security).

The Public Forces are fully accountable to civilian authority under the Minister of Government and Justice. Investigative and other units that have been separated from the Public Forces, such as the Technical Judicial Police, are also directly subordinate to civilian authorities. The Public Forces budget—in contrast to that of the former PDF—is on public record and under control of the executive, decreasing from U.S. $97 million, plus at least U.S. $45 million in off-budget spending, under Noriega in 1989 to U.S. $76 million in 1990.

The United States, with congressional approval, is providing assistance to establish a truly professional law enforcement institution, dedicated to delivering adequate protection to the citizens of Panama while fully respecting human rights, democracy, and the law. The United States is providing police skills training and technical assistance in civilian law enforcement development through a U.S. $13.2 million program managed by the U.S. Department of Justice's International Criminal Investigative Training Assistance Program (ICITAP). In addition, U.S. $8 million is being spent to assist the Panamanian government to improve the administration of justice.

Manpower availability: males 15–49, 644,895; 444,522 fit for military service; no conscription.

Defense expenditures: U.S. $75.5 million, 1.5% of GDP (1990).

Foreign Relations

The government of Panama is nonaligned. Panama is a member of the UN General Assembly and most major UN agencies, and it has served three terms as an elected member of the UN Security Council. It maintains membership in several international financial institutions, including the World Bank, the Inter-American Development Bank, and the International Monetary Fund.

Panama is a member of the Organization of American States (OAS) and was a founding member of the now-defunct Contadora group, which during the mid-1980s sought peaceful settlement of Central American disputes. It is one of the founding members of the Union of Banana Exporting Countries and also belongs to the Inter-American Tropical Tuna Commission.

Although not yet a member of the Central America Common Market, Panama is affiliated with several other Central American regional organizations and, under the Endara government, has participated actively in Central American regional meetings. Panama has not participated in the Latin American Economic System, known informally both as the Group of Eight and the Rio Group, since it was suspended in early 1988 due to its internal political situation under Noriega. Panama is not a member of the General Agreement on Tariffs and Trade (GATT) but has established a commission to negotiate accession to the GATT.

U.S.-Panamanian Relations

The United States has traditionally maintained friendly relations with the people of

Panama and, with the exception of the later Noriega years, has cooperated with the Panamanian government in promoting economic, political, and social development through U.S. and international agencies. Cultural ties between the two countries are strong, and many Panamanians come to the United States for higher education and advanced training.

The presence of U.S. armed forces in Panama has generated some friction, however, and Panama's relationship with the United States has been a recurring political issue throughout Panamanian history. Severe strains were placed on the relationship by the Noriega regime during the late 1980s, but the renewal of democracy and stability in Panama has shown that the bilateral relationship remains fundamentally strong.

In addition, the Panama Canal Treaties have provided the foundation for a new partnership. The United States and Panama remain committed to the smooth implementation of these treaties, including the departure of U.S. armed forces, the reversion of U.S. military bases, and the turnover of the canal to Panamanian control on December 31, 1999.

Panama is also committed to the fight against illegal narcotics. The country's proximity to major cocaine producing nations and its role as a commercial and financial crossroads make it a country of special importance in this regard. Although Panamanian antinarcotics institutions lack trained personnel and blueprints for action, concerted efforts against the drug problem are being made by the Endara administration in cooperation with the United States. Several bilateral antinarcotics agreements have been signed, the United States is providing needed resources and training, and Public Forces joint operations with the Drug Enforcement Agency and other U.S. agencies have resulted in unprecedented seizures of cocaine and other narcotics. The conversion

of the PDF into the professional Public Forces has further demonstrated the government's resolve to strengthen democracy and to continue the fight against drug-trafficking and money-laundering in Panama.

The Panama Canal Treaties

The 1977 Panama Canal Treaties replaced the 1903 Hay/Bunau-Varilla Treaty between the United States and Panama and all other United States-Panama agreements concerning the Panama Canal which were in force on that date. The treaties comprise:

- a basic treaty governing the operation and defense of the canal from October 1, 1979, to December 31, 1999 (Panama Canal Treaty); and

- a treaty guaranteeing the permanent neutrality of the canal (Treaty on the Permanent Neutrality and Operation of the Panama Canal).

In negotiating the Panama Canal Treaties, the United States acted to protect a fundamental national interest in long-term access to a secure and efficient canal. Panama's cooperation is fundamental to this objective. By meeting Panamanian aspirations for eventual control of the canal, the United States sought a new relationship with Panama based on friendship and mutual respect.

The treaties make Panama a partner in the continued safe and efficient operation of the canal. In serving the best interests of both nations, the treaties serve the interests of all users of the canal.

Basic Provisions of the Treaties

The United States has primary responsibility for the operation and defense of the canal until December 31, 1999. U.S. rights to station military forces and maintain military bases also terminate with the canal treaty. After that date, the United States and Panama will maintain a regime of neutrality for the canal, including nondiscriminatory access and tolls for merchant and naval vessels of all nations.

U.S. warships will be entitled to expeditious passage of the canal at all times, however, and the United States will continue to have the right to ensure that the canal remains open and secure.

The United States operates the canal through the Panama Canal Commission (PCC), which is a U.S. government agency supervised by a board of directors consisting of five American and four Panamanian members appointed by the president; the Panamanian members are initially nominated by their government. Until 1990, the canal administrator was an American and the deputy administrator was Panamanian; these nationalities reversed for the final decade of the treaty on September 20, 1990, when Gilberto Guardia was installed as the first Panamanian administrator. Pursuant to treaty obligations, the PCC is training Panamanians in all areas of canal operations prior to the transfer of the canal in 1999. Panamanian citizens currently comprise over 87 percent of the PCC work force.

Trade

Panama's trade balance (1991) with: U.S.A –657.0; Mexico –18.0; Japan –112.2.

Principal U.S. exports (U.S. $ millions): industrial chemicals (39.02); agricultural chemicals (38.11); paper, carton (48.01); computers (84.53); soybean cake (23.04).

Trade (excluding Colon Free Zone): Exports (1991 estimate)—U.S. $385 million, of which bananas 25%; shrimp 13% (other seafood 4%); sugar 8%; clothing 5%; coffee 4%; other 41%

Major markets: U.S. (90%), Europe. Imports (1991 estimate)—U.S. $1.5 billion, of which consumer and intermediate goods 65%; capital goods 18%; food 9%; crude oil 7%.

Major suppliers: U.S. (35%), Japan, Europe, Mexico.

Trade and Investment Policies

In May 1991, a Bilateral Investment Treaty between the United States and Panama entered into force. In June 1991 the two countries signed a Bilateral Framework Agreement on Trade and Investment in the context of President Bush's Enterprise for the Americas Initiative (EIA). Representatives from both governments have begun discussions on eliminating trade and investment barriers under the auspices of the framework agreement.

The market for specific U.S. goods—paper products, packaging materials, telecom equipment, foodstuffs, spare parts for U.S. equipment and machinery, automobiles and associated parts, computers and related equipment—remains excellent. In addition, the Colon Free Zone continues to offer import and export opportunities for U.S. firms interested in gaining access to additional regional markets for luxury and consumer items.

Agricultural products are subject to widespread quantitative restrictions. Import quotas on 42 products and import permits on 23 products are the most important non-tariff mechanisms used to protect national production beyond levels afforded by tariffs. All quotas and import licensing are scheduled to be eliminated in 1993, but some duties may be raised in compensation.

While the government of Panama does not officially present any barriers to U.S. suppliers of banking, insurance, travel/ticket, motion picture, and air courier services, some professionals can expect certain technical/procedural impediments, e.g., architects, engineers, and lawyers have to be certified by Panamanian boards.

Standards: All imported packaged and bottled foods and beverages must be registered by the Ministry of Health. Pharmaceuticals, drugs, vitamins, cosmetics, and other like products are also subject to similar regulations.

Although Panama does not have an investment screening mechanism, the Panama Trade Development Institute (IPCE) does attempt to attract investment to priority areas. Under the terms of its Bilateral Investment Treaty with the United States, Panama places no restrictions on the nationality of senior management. Panama does restrict foreign nationals to 10 percent of the blue collar work force, however, and specialized foreign or technical workers may number no more than 15 percent of all employees in a business.

Disinvestment may be difficult for foreign (and Panamanian) companies because of labor code regulations, which restrict dismissal of employees and require large severance payments.

Panama decided to join the GATT in 1991. The government is preparing its Foreign Trade Memorandum in order to negotiate accession with the GATT contracting parties. Government policy action has produced a schedule for the reduction and elimination of tariff and nontariff barriers. Panama has committed to a maximum tariff of 50 percent for agro-industrial goods and 40 percent for industrial goods by March 1993. The government of Panama's trade liberalization policy aims to increase efficiency, reduce market distortions, and encourage exports.

Export Subsidy Policies

Export subsidy policies benefit both foreign-owned and domestic export industries. The tax credit certificate (CAT) is a major export subsidy. CATs are given to firms producing nontraditional exports when the exports' national content and national value-added both meet minimum established levels. Exporters receive CATs equal to an amount that is 20 percent of the exports' national value-added. The certificates are transferable and may be used to pay tax obligations to the government. They can also be sold in secondary markets at a discount.

A number of industries that produce exclusively for export are also exempted from paying certain types of taxes and import duties. The Panamanian government uses these exemptions as a way of attracting investment to the country. Companies that benefit from these exemptions are not eligible to receive CATs for their exports, however.

Exports

In recent years, the principal markets for Panamanian products have been North America, Western Europe, and Central America while the majority of Panamanian imports have come from North America, South America, and Japan.

Panama's principal exports to the U.S. include traditional products such as shrimp, sugar, coffee, bananas, and tropical fruits. Most of its U.S. imports consist of paper products, automotive parts, wheat, soy products, and natural gas and fuel oils.

Panama's goods and services export earnings have traditionally been among the largest in the world relative to GDP (35–40 percent) because of the country's strong services sector—the Panama Canal, Colon Free Zone, U.S. military presence, business tourists, and the oil pipeline. After declining sharply during 1988–89, goods and services exports recovered steadily during 1990 and 1991: passenger and other services export receipts increased by 7 percent per year, travel receipts by 10 percent per year, and other services by 6 percent per year. In the latter category, U.S. Department of Defense (DOD) expenditures in Panama (payroll outlays for Panamanian employees and purchases of local goods and services) grew from U.S. $213 million in 1990 to U.S. $273 million in 1991.

Given the prospect of continued decline in oil pipeline earnings, slow growth in Canal revenues, and the U.S. military drawdown in the 1990s, Panama is under pressure to implement structural adjustment measures to strengthen exports of services based on its comparative advantage—such as international transportation (ports) and related services (ship supplies and tourism)—and to encourage efficient substitution of high value-added industrial and/or commercial activity for U.S. military revenue.

Exports of bananas, shrimp, coffee, and sugar comprise roughly 46 percent of merchandise exports, excluding Colon Free Zone re-exports. Although bananas remained Panama's number one export in 1991, an April earthquake and August floods in banana-producing Bocas del Toro province led to a 3.6 percent decrease in sales of that commodity. Prospects for growth in the banana industry were clouded by the European Community's proposed 1993 single market quota.

Shrimp is Panama's second most important foreign revenue generating commodity after bananas. While exports grew from U.S. $44.4 million in 1990 to U.S. $50.4 million in 1991, they were still below the levels reached in the late 1980s. The outlook for shrimp export earnings appears bleak because of overfishing by the shrimp industry, inefficient management of aquaculture farms, adverse climatic conditions, and Far East products undercutting Panamanian shrimp prices in U.S. markets.

In 1991, the value of sugar exports fell one-third below the 1990 level. Earnings are expected to decline even further as the U.S. global sugar import quota continues to fall because of increased U.S. production and product substitution. The Endara government has targeted the state-owned sugar mills for privatization.

APPROACHING THE MARKET

Commercial Environment

The commercial environment in Panama became attractive following the 1989 U.S. military action. The local and international business community in Panama welcomed this change and responded with positive actions such as the repatriation of capital, start-up of new business ventures, and the upgrading and expansion of existing activities. 1991 was a year of growth and recovery and this recovery trend which started in 1990 is expected to continue throughout 1993–94.

Business interests are agreeing to participate in special activities that will help shape policies and legislation in ways to improve the business environment and its prospects. Panamanian resourcefulness is likely to identify more and better ways to address the country's most pressing problems. The Privatization Framework Law, deemed vital for future economic growth, was approved and signed by President Endara in 1992.

Panamanians are traders. The Colon Free Zone is better than the Orient Free Zone, business leaders say. A reasonable mark-up over Asian prices guarantees three- to seven-day delivery on products that would require months for delivery if ordered from the manufacturers, who are chiefly in the Pacific Rim.

Korean and Japanese companies have been particularly effective in using the Free Zone and its marketing networks to introduce innovations and complete product lines into markets like Venezuela, Chile, Brazil, Colombia, Dominican Republic, and Ecuador. The Free Zone's showrooms are always ready for visiting buyers, and the larger enterprises keep sales staffs that travel regularly to Central and South America and the Caribbean. American companies have not been as aggressive in using the Free Zone's unique capabilities, but Japanese and Korean success stories should be real eye openers, particularly for the small and mid-size U.S. exporter that aims for a share of the region's market without the cost, risk, or trouble of expanding its own organization in having to appoint individual agents in many Western Hemisphere countries. With a minimum of red tape, Free Zone businesses are ready for licensing and distribution arrangements and joint ventures.

The Free Zone ended 1991 with total transactions in the vicinity of the U.S. $7.0 billion mark. Free Zone authorities estimate that this total will be exceeded in 1992.

Demand for Goods and Services

Panama's domestic market serves a 2.4 million population with fairly sophisticated consumption patterns. U.S. products and equipment are appreciated and in great demand. Panama's dollar denominated economy helps the marketing of U.S. goods and services while it minimizes risk for U.S. suppliers. Most U.S. brand names are already represented in Panama, but aggressive marketing networks are always eager to consider innovations and new product lines.

Panama has had uniquely close ties with the U.S. since the early part of this century. The Panama Canal and the U.S. Southern Command headquarters in Panama have been responsible for an uninterrupted presence of thousands of Americans. Many Panamanian professionals, trained and educated in the U.S., have brought and established American management systems and marketing concepts in Panama's domestic marketplace. Thousands of Panamanians travel to the U.S., each year for business and pleasure. Panamanian professionals routinely participate in major conferences, seminars, and trade events in the U.S..

U.S. business representatives traveling to Panama soon discover the significance of close ties between the two countries. These include: an abundance of bilingual personnel, knowledge and appreciation of American brand names, styles, and standards. Whether the sport is basketball, baseball, or football, Panamanian fans cheer for an American team every season. American political and business leaders are often familiar to Panamanians who also appreciate American music, literature, and arts. Two U.S. colleges with campuses in Panama offer U.S. education and degrees to Panamanian students. Businesses, professionals, and workers who for decades have worked with U.S. military and canal authorities feel at home with American ways.

Panamanians are proud of their unique heritage and culture. However, unlike many in Latin America, most Panamanians have room in their pride for a continued special relationship with the U.S.

Implications for U.S. Exporters

All things considered, Panama still offers the easiest market access in the region for most products. In addition to export opportunities available in the Colon Free Zone (where no product restrictions and a minimum of regulation apply), Panama offers a dynamic domestic market for services, franchises, processed food products, electronics, housewares, textiles, apparel, novelties, and new products in most product sectors.

Panamanians love what is new and different, and like Americans, are willing to pay for it.

Trade barriers remaining from the 25-year-old Economic Commission For Latin America (ECLA) import substitution strategy still affect some industries.

Poultry, beef, selected processed foods

and agricultural products, construction materials, and a few other industrial goods fall in this category. The Panamanian Ministry of Commerce and Industry (MCI) has been hard at work to minimize these market distortions since the Endara administration came to power. The MCI has already negotiated multisectoral agreements to significantly reduce the tariff burden on food products, apparel, and construction materials. The MCI is also committed to a strategy for the gradual elimination of price controls and quotas, which limit market access, discourage domestic production, and increase consumer prices.

By 1993, import duties were expected to be lowered to a maximum of 50 percent on agricultural products and 40 percent on industrial products, based on customs value of products.

Agricultural products such as corn, beef, and dairy products are controlled by the Ministry of Agriculture and the Agriculture Marketing Institute (IMA). These government entities have not matched MCI's commitment to market liberalization and often support protectionist measures. Local agro-industrial interests working together with the MCI are trying to change this situation.

Working together with the AMCHAM committee on trade and investment, the American Embassy in Panama City (USFCS) has already initiated contacts with the Ministry of Health (MH) to review food product registration requirements and food additive controls. In this area, the government of Panama has again displayed a sincere commitment to market liberalization.

Product registration requirements, which were previously applied prior to market entry (by customs authorities) now become effective six months after initial product entry. Thus, importers can establish product sales potential prior to an investment of financial and staff resources in the registration process.

Regulations affecting color and other food/cosmetics additives will be more difficult to deal with. Many of these regulations were borrowed from similar regulatory codes of trading partners in Europe and South America. Importers of affected American products have proposed to the MH authorities a new system based on reciprocity. Under this proposal, unless a specific additive is directly associated with adverse health effects, the product containing the additive will be allowed into the market on the basis of a "certificate of free sale" issued by the authorities of the producer country. The MH is currently reviewing this proposal. Because most applicable legislation in this sector is very old and often obsolete, the Panamanian legislature was expected to complete the review of existing regulations in 1992.

INVESTMENT CLIMATE

The government of Panama officially promotes foreign investment and affords foreign investors national treatment. Panama's focus on the service sector has left countless investment opportunities in the industrial and agricultural sectors. The present administration, accepting the challenge of diversifying the national economy, is actively promoting specific investment opportunities in agriculture, industry, tourism, and an expanded range of services.

Since the military action of December 1989, trade and investment missions from Texas, Alaska, Florida, and North Carolina have visited Panama. The U.S. Overseas Private Investment Corporation (OPIC) once again offers risk insurance and financial support to Americans considering direct investment and joint ventures in Panama. In addition to the U.S. trade investment missions, Panama has hosted visiting business groups from Spain, Japan, Hong Kong, Taiwan, and South Korea.

The Panamanian Foreign Trade Institute (government) and the ANDE Foundation (private sector) are ready to support and assist organized investment missions. In May 1991, the U.S.-Panama bilateral investment treaty entered into force, aimed at offering additional protection and alternatives to those seeking investment opportunities.

As a beneficiary of the now permanent Caribbean Basin Initiative (CBI), Panama has much to offer the foreign investor. Even greater opportunities will be available when the Enterprise for the Americas Initiative is fully implemented.

The government of Panama has traditionally controlled or excluded foreign and national private sector investments in selected sectors like telecommunications, energy generation, and distribution. The government is currently reconsidering these policies. A privatization committee appointed by the government has been involved in analyzing its participation in all sectors of the economy, and has recommended privatization of state-owned entities. The government plans a gradual liberalization of the sectors based on the specific circumstances of each sector. Concrete actions have already been taken to stimulate private sector involvement in energy generation, waste disposal, airline operations, dock facilities, and in the expansion of telecommunication services (e.g., cellular telephony).

The so-called Reverted Areas will also offer great possibilities for foreign investment. Reverted Areas consist of huge extensions of land, buildings, roads, warehouses, etc., currently being used by U.S. military organizations that, according to the U.S.-Panama Canal Treaties, are gradually being transferred to Panama in a process that will be completed by the year 2000.

Current Panamanian plans call for leasing/sales of these areas to foreign or local investors to set up manufacturing plants, maquila industries, tourist resorts, or export oriented activities.

FINANCING AND CAPITAL MARKETS

General Policy Framework

The Panamanian economy continued to recover in 1991 after rebounding in 1990 from two years of U.S. sanctions and 20 years of poor economic policies under a military dictatorship. Delay in coming to terms with international financial institutions on policies to implement structural reform in Panama generated uncertainty in the private sector and tempered the pace of business expansion somewhat during 1991. Nevertheless, the Panamanian government remains committed to economic reform supported by international financial institutions and to strengthening domestic and foreign business confidence.

Panama's relatively small market (nominal GDP of U.S. $5 billion), the low share of agriculture and manufacturing in GDP (approximately 12 and 10 percent, respectively), and the concentration of economic activity in banking, commerce, and transportation services limit the opportunities for traditional U.S. industrial and intermediary product exports.

Nevertheless, the government's desire to attract export processing zone investment, privatize state-owned entities, and develop Canal territories reverting to its control suggests the prospects for U.S. businesses in these areas are good. In addition, Panama's traditional appetite and ability to pay dollars for imported consumer items, especially U.S. products, means the market for these products will continue to be favorable. Panama has traditionally had a greater demand for U.S. goods than other countries in the region, and its consumers are accustomed to having access to the latest products.

The use of the U.S. dollar as Panama's currency means that fiscal policy is the government's principal macroeconomic policy instrument.

Because Panama does not "print" a national currency, government spending and investment are strictly bound by tax and nontax revenues (including Panama Canal receipts) and the government's ability to borrow. The latter is extremely limited at present because of massive arrears to internal and external creditors built up by the previous regime as a means of financing large deficits.

The government of President Endara maintained a tight fiscal policy in 1990 and 1991 in order to reduce fiscal deficits and stabilize the growth of public debt.

Private fixed capital formation, inventory rebuilding, and consumption are believed to have led to real GDP growth of 4 to 5 percent in 1991. Merchandise imports associated with continued private sector expansion are expected to reach new highs and be easily financed through private capital flows. As Panama's economic reforms begin to take hold, the main sources of private sector growth in the 1990s are expected to be in traditional exports (bananas, shrimp), maquila industries, the Colon Free Trade Zone, financial services, insurance, tourism, and transportation. Domestic and foreign investment in these areas should boost associated imports substantially over time.

Debt Management Policies

Panama's total external public debt stood at U.S. $5.4 billion at end-1990, of which U.S. $3.1 billion represented principal and interest arrears. Foreign commercial banks held 54 percent of external debt, international financial institutions 28 percent, bilateral official creditors 12 percent, and suppliers and short-term creditors six percent.

External debt represented 113 percent of GDP at end-1990. External debt service due represents some 15 percent of GDP and 40 percent of goods and services exports; external debt service actually paid amounted to some 5 percent of GDP and 13 percent of goods and services exports in 1991.

The government of Panama began the process of reestablishing normal relations with external creditors in early 1990. It has made current payments to the International Monetary Fund (IMF), the International Bank for Reconstruction and Development (IBRD), and the Inter-American Development Bank (IDB) since May 1, 1990. The IMF Board approved an 18-month Fund-monitored program for Panama on September 12, 1990, and the government has performed fully under the program. The government held extensive discussions with the IMF/IBRD/IDB in 1990-1991 before reaching agreements in principle with these institutions in September 1991. The government was expected to reach final agreements and clear its arrears with the IMF/IBRD/IDB in early 1992. A U.S. government-led support group of friendly nations, together with a U.S. government bridge loan against initial disbursements from the IMF/IBRD/IDB, is expected to mobilize sufficient funds to clear the arrears. Once the arrears are cleared, the IMF will convert its Fund-monitored program to an IMF standby arrangement, and the IBRD and IDB will resume lending to support structural adjustment.

Future IDB disbursements will depend on adequate treatment of the privatization issue.

On the basis of the Fund-monitored program approved in September 1990, Panama rescheduled bilateral official debt in the Paris Club on November 14, 1990. Panama and the United States signed a bilateral agreement implementing the Paris Club accord on August 21, 1991, and the bilateral agreement entered into force on September 27, 1991.

Panama maintained communication with the Bank Advisory Committee of foreign commercial banks in 1990–1991 and expected to initiate formal discussions in 1992. The government of Panama expects to pursue a comprehensive solution to the external debt issue that will involve commercial bank debt and debt service reduction operations.

The government of Panama's steadily accumulating arrears with external creditors has eliminated public sector access to international financial markets. External financing for public sector imports is expected to come from official and bilateral sources for the foreseeable future.

Normalization of relations with official and multilateral creditors should have paved the way for official and bilateral financing in 1992. The public sector's lack of creditworthiness limited access of some private sector Panamanian borrowers to international financial markets during 1990. In 1991, however, foreign lenders began to restore normal trade and interbank lines for creditworthy private borrowers. Improved financial conditions for the private sector should have permitted growing private sector imports in line with continued economic growth in 1992.

Budget: revenues $1.7 billion; expenditures $1.8 billion, including capital expenditures of $70 million (1990 est.).

The Currency and Exchange Rate Mechanisms

Panama's official currency, the balboa, is pegged to the U.S. dollar at B/1.00 equals U.S. $1.00. The fixed parity means the price and availability of U.S. products in Panama depend on transport costs and tariff and nontariff barriers to entry. At the same time, the fixed parity means that U.S. exporters have zero risk of foreign exchange loss on sales to Panama.

Banking and Other Financial Institutions

Panama has evolved into a major financial center in the Latin American region. Of the 110 banks officially registered in the country, 66 provide a full range of banking services, 29 are international licensed banks with activities restricted to international operations, and 15 have representative license offices. The import payment process in Panama is quite simple due to the fact that the U.S. dollar circulates freely as legal tender. The payment process is limited to the ability of a particular company or individual to qualify for the opening of a letter of credit in any bank of the system. No foreign exchange limitations exist in the country as a consequence of its U.S. dollar-based economy. The way international payments are met depends upon the arrangements between buyers and sellers, with no government intervention in the process. A typical commercial transaction involves the use of sight letters of credit, although open account and prepayment are also common among companies which have had a favorable history of working together.

There are no limitations regarding the correspondent relationship that Panamanian banks can maintain with U.S. or other banks. Countertrade requirements are almost nonexistent, with only a few cases reported during the crisis period (1988–89), which represented an insignificant share of total trade.

The financing possibilities for companies engaged in local and international trade in Panama used to be ample and flexible. During the economic crisis of 1988–89, as a consequence of the U.S. sanctions and banking restrictions, the financing environment became very tight. After December 1989, with a legitimate democratic government and the lifting of the U.S. sanctions, the financing possibilities gradually returned to normal. The Panamanian banking sector remains very sensitive to signals of instability from political and socioeconomic developments. Activities in higher risk sectors (such as agriculture) may experience difficulties in securing needed financing.

Sources of financing include both Panamanian and foreign-owned banks. U.S. banks like Chase Manhattan, Citibank, and the Bank of Boston have local representation. All financial arrangements are performed directly between banks and companies or individuals, without any government intervention or restrictions. Other sources of financing include programs by bilateral and multilateral donors such as USAID, which offers specific financing programs for small and medium size enterprises and the U.S. Ex-Im Bank. Multilateral donors like the World Bank and the Inter-American Development Bank are ready to reestablish ties with Panama. The Overseas Private Investment Corporation (OPIC) has again included Panama in its program, which opens new financing possibilities for American companies interested in doing business in Panama. Another potential source of financing is the Panamanian Stock Exchange, which started operations two years ago and is growing in importance as a financing source.

Tapping International Aid

U.S. economic assistance: FY 1990–91, U.S. $451 million; FY 1992, U.S. $10 million. Cumulative U.S. commitments, including Ex-Im (FY70–89), U.S. $516 million; Western (non-U.S.) countries, ODA and OOF bilateral commitments (1970–88),

U.S. $575 million; Communist countries (1970–89), U.S. $4 million.

Financial Market Operations and Structural Policies

Panama has traditionally relied on the private sector to supply most goods and services. The Panamanian government seeks to promote export industries and has streamlined its investment promotion and industrial zone facilities toward this end with special tax exemptions and liberalization of the Labor Code. In addition to providing direct investment opportunities for U.S. firms, these developments offer export opportunities to U.S. producers of basic industrial and intermediary goods needed to develop light industry. The government's decision to privatize a number of state-owned firms and operations will also benefit U.S. suppliers of goods and services.

The Endara government is reducing tariff protection on a large number of products with the purpose of achieving greater efficiency in production. It reduced specific tariffs on a core group of industrial and agro-industrial products to a maximum of 60–90 percent on an ad valorem basis in 1991 and reduced quantitative restrictions, eliminated specific duties, and lowered maximum tariffs to 40–50 percent in 1992. The Panamanian government is also in the process of negotiating its accession with General Agreement on Tariffs and Trade (GATT) contracting parties.

Panama's use of the U.S. dollar and inability to print money preclude the rampant inflation usually associated with massive public sector deficits such as those Panama has generated. As a consequence, increases in prices are generally linked to that of the United States and to the prices which imports command. The Panamanian government also controls the price of certain staple and essential items to protect the purchasing power of low-income households, as import controls would otherwise allow importers, producers, and distributors to increase prices excessively given the small size of the market. As part of its economic program, however, the government will progressively eliminate import restrictions and price controls and substitute an office of consumer protection for the existing office of price regulation.

The openness of the Panamanian system and its dollar-based economy has led to the absence of a central monetary regulating system. Panama's money supply is determined primarily by its trade in goods and services and by changes in international interest and exchange rates. Panama imposes no restrictions on repatriation of profits and capital. There are no exchange rate regulations. The foreign assets of the National Bank of Panama are in some instances considered the country's official reserves. Otherwise, there is no official reserve organization or mechanism.

1992 Budget Law: The Legislative Assembly approved an overall public sector budget of U.S. $2.8 billion for 1992, down slightly from U.S. $2.9 billion for 1991. The 1992 budget law allocated 68 percent of total expenditures for operations, 17 percent for debt service, and 15 percent for investment. It increased spending on health, education, and government and justice, and expanded the budgets of key state-owned utilities.

Fiscal performance: As measured by performance of the nonfinancial public sector (the overall public sector less public banks and certain other government entities), Panama's public finances remained strong in 1991.

Revenues exceeded projections and more than compensated for higher-than-expected wage and salary outlays. Public investment strengthened in the latter part of 1991 and climbed to an estimated U.S. $120 million (2.2 percent of GDP) by year-end. Central government revenues continued to exceed expectations in the first half of 1992; public investment was expected to increase to U.S. $213 million (3.5 percent of GDP) by year-end.

Nonfinancial public sector revenues were expected to remain at about 30 percent of GDP in 1992, but public sector current expenditures (including interest due on foreign commercial debt) were expected to decline to 28–29 percent of GDP in 1992 to make room for continued expansion of public investment. Key to current expenditure reduction is reduction in the public wage bill. The number of public sector employees has declined by 9,294 (6.4 percent) since December 1989, but public sector wage increases mandated by law, plus restoration of the thirteenth month bonus for public sector employees in September 1991, have limited the reduction in the wage bill to 2.7 percent during this period.

Chapter 17

PARAGUAY

	Total	Urban	
Population (1993)	5,081,000	47.0%	

Main Urban Areas	Population	Percentage of Total	International Calling Code
ASUNCION	729,000	14.3	595-21
Puerto Stroessner	110,000	2.2	595-61
Pedro Juan Caballero	80,000	1.6	595-36
San Lorenzo	80,000	1.6	595-22
Fernando de la Mora	72,000	1.4	595
Encarnacion	31,000	0.6	595-71
Pilar	26,000	0.5	595-86
Concepcion	26,000	0.5	595-31
Coronel Oviedo	22,000	0.4	595-521
Villarrica	22,000	0.4	595-541
Caaguazu	20,000	0.4	595-522

Land Area   397,300 square kilometers
    Comparable U.S. State   Slightly smaller than California

Language

* Guarani	89%
* Spanish	6%
Portuguese	3%
German	1%
Other	1%

(*) Official languages

    Common Business Language   Spanish

Currency   1 guarani (G) = 100 centimos
    Exchange Rate (May 1993)   U.S. $1.00 = 1,430 guarants

Best Nonstop Air Connection via U.S.   No nonstops offered
Miami to Asuncion via Sao Paulo: 10.5 hours
American Airlines (800) 433-7300

Best Hotel   Hotel Casino Yacht and Golf Club
Paraguayo (U.S. $160)
P.O. Box 1795
Asuncion
Tel: (595-21) 36-117 or 36-121
Fax: (595-21) 36-120 or 36-133

INTRODUCTION AND REGIONAL ORIENTATION

Paraguay, with a population of 4.27 million, an annual population growth rate of 2.9 percent, and total land area of 154,047 square miles, has a small domestic market and limited but expanding access to world markets through the Paraguay/Parana river system. Asuncion is the political, financial, administrative, and commercial center of the country. The capital city with its suburbs has a population of about 1.7 million people, nearly 40 percent of the total population of the country.

Paraguay's population is distributed unevenly throughout the country. The vast majority of the people live in the east, most within 160 kilometers (100 miles) of Asuncion, the capital and largest city. The Chaco, which accounts for about 60 percent of the territory, is home for less than 4 percent of the population.

Ethnically, culturally, and socially, Paraguay probably has the most homogeneous population in South America. About 95 percent of the people are of mixed Spanish and Guarani Indian descent. Little trace is left of the original Guarani culture except the language, which is understood by 90 percent of the population. About 75 percent of all Paraguayans speak Spanish. Guarani and Spanish are both official languages.

A number of foreign groups, primarily Germans, Japanese, Koreans, Brazilians, and Argentines, have settled in Paraguay. About 1,500 nonofficial U.S. citizens live there.

History and Political Conditions

Paraguay declared its independence by overthrowing the local Spanish authorities in 1811.

Throughout the 1930s and 1940s, Paraguayan politics were characterized by the Chaco war, civil war, dictatorships, and periods of extreme political instability. Gen. Alfredo Stroessner assumed power in May 1954. He was elected to complete the unexpired term of his predecessor and was subsequently reelected president in 1958 and remained in power until 1989.

He ruled the country almost continuously under the state-of-siege provision of the constitution. When invoked, usually in political cases, state-of-siege measures effectively set aside habeas corpus and other legal guarantees. The Colorado Party, the military, and the government bureaucracy were the pillars of the Stroessner regime. A new constitution was promulgated in 1967.

On February 3, 1989, General Stroessner was overthrown in a military coup headed by General Andres Rodriguez, who scheduled presidential and congressional elections for May 1. He was nominated as Colorado Party candidate and easily won. Seven other political parties ran candidates even though some of the parties were new to the democratic process and had little time to organize effective campaigns. The next general elections were scheduled for 1993.

CRACKING THE MARKET

Demographics

Ethnic groups: Mixed Spanish and Indian descent (mestizo) 95%.

Religions: Roman Catholic 97%, Mennonite, and other Protestant denominations.

Languages: Spanish, Guarani.

Education: Years compulsory 7; attendance 83%; literacy 92%.

Work force (1.6 million): agriculture 44%; idustry and commerce 34%; service 18%; government 4%.

Economy

Paraguay is predominantly an agricultural country with no known significant mineral or petroleum resource. Agricultural commodities account for a major share of the country's exports.

Particular obstacles to Paraguay's development include fluctuating prices for major export items, the long and expensive river or land routes that foreign trade must traverse, a small domestic market, and internal- and external-trade barriers.

Despite these limitations, agricultural production has grown rapidly, especially cotton and soybeans for export. The economy has enjoyed relative price stability (inflation was held at 2 percent and 3 percent in the 1960s), but the cost of living has begun to rise. During 1988, the inflation rate was 27.3 percent and the rate for 1989 was higher.

Construction of the massive Itaipu hydroelectric project with Brazil greatly accelerated Paraguay's economic development. Work on the Yacyreta hydroelectric project with Argentina should further spur the economy and make Paraguay the world's largest exporter of hydroelectric energy.

Per capita GDP declined in the early 1980s before rising to $978 in 1988. Paraguay's economy, while still heavily dependent on agricultural output, has grown steadily during the last several years and registered a solid 6.4 percent growth in 1988. Inflation accelerated in 1989, partially from some of the economic reforms undertaken by the Rodriguez government. The most dramatic reform taken in February 1989 was to eliminate the multiple exchange rate system and to adopt a floating, free market rate. With the elimination of this hidden subsidy to the para-statal corporations, the government has been forced to raise prices for gasoline, water, electricity, telephone service, and bus fares.

Paraguay's external debt reached $2.4 billion by the end of 1988, equivalent to 56 percent of GDP. Debt service payments by the government during 1988 totaled $341 million, equivalent to 69 percent of recorded merchandise exports. Registered exports were expected to surge in 1989 as a result of record harvest of cotton and soybeans and the elimination of the multiple exchange rate system that provoked exporters to smuggle their products out of Paraguay in previous years. Still, the debt service ratio (scheduled debt service to registered exports) in 1989 was about 50 percent.

The government of Paraguay negotiated in early 1989 a rescheduling of the $436 million it owed the Brazilian government to stretch payments over 20 years with an eight-year grace period. It hopes to reschedule an additional $811 million of debt, of which $602 million was owed to other governments, mainly the Federal Republic of Germany and Japan, and $209 million was owed to foreign commercial banks. The balance of the government debt, $771 million, is owed to the World Bank, the IMF, and the Inter-American Development Bank. Paraguay also is interested in negotiating an IMF stand-by program and a debt reduction or rescheduling agreement.

Agriculture (1988—27% of GDP): Products—meat, corn, sugarcane, soybeans, lumber, cotton. Arable land—9 million hectares, of which 30% is cultivated.

Industry (1988—16% of GDP): Types—sugar, cement, textiles, beverage, and wood products.

Political/Institutional Infrastructure

Paraguay is a constitutional republic which gained its independence from Spain in May 1961.

Paraguay's highly centralized government is based on the constitution promulgated in August 1967. The preponderance of power rests with the executive branch. The president, popularly elected for a five-year term, is assisted by an appointed cabinet.

The bicameral Congress consists of a 36-member Senate and a 72-member Cham-

PARAGUAY
Key Economic Indicators

	1989	1990	1991[1]
Income, Production, Employment			
Real GDP[2]	6,614	6,818	7,022
Real GDP growth rate	5.8	3.1	3.0
Sectorial GDP (%)			
Agriculture, forestry, cattle	27.8	27.5	27.2
Manufacturing	16.2	16.1	16.7
Construction	5.4	5.2	5.4
Transport and communications	4.6	4.6	4.9
Commerce and finance	26.3	26.4	27.5
Central government (wages)	4.5	4.5	4.8
Other	15.2	15.7	13.5
Real per capita income[3]	1,259	1,301	N/A
Labor force (thousands)	1,337	1,377	1,418.4
Unemployment rate[1]	12.0	13.0	13.0
Underemployment rate[1]	23.0	25.0	25.0
Money and Prices			
Money supply[4]	609	808.2	1,006
Commercial banks (lending rates %)	28.0	36.0	37.0
Savings rate (as a % of GDP)	17.1	16.9	18.3
Investment rate (% of GDP)	23.8	23.0	N/A
Consumer price index	28.5	44.1	15.0
Wholesale price index	26.1	67.2	5.0
Annual average exchange rate	1,200	1,225	1,323
Balance of Payments and Trade			
Total exports FOB[5]	1,097	1,215.1	641.84
Total exports to U.S.[5]	40.81	39.40	32.70
Total imports CIF[5]	759.6	1,349.8	1,850
Total imports from U.S.[5]	93.8	146.7	208.8
Aid from U.S.[5]	1.3	1.5	2.5
Aid from Japan[1, 5]	27	20.2	N/A
Aid from Germany[1]	5	10.3	7.1
External public debt[5]	2,490	2,433	1,690
Annual debt service payments.[5]	141.9	147.8	151
Gold and foreign exchange reserve[5]	447.4	673	994.9
Balance of payments[1, 5]	5	123	170

1. Estimates or Projections
2. Millions of 1982 dollars
3. Dollars of 1982
4. Billions of Guaranies
5. Millions of dollars

ber of Deputies. Deputies and senators are elected concurrently with the president. Under Paraguayan electoral law, the party polling the largest number of votes in the congressional elections receives two-thirds of the seats in each chamber. The remaining seats are divided proportionately among the other contending parties.

In the three-month period when Congress is not in session, the president may issue decree-laws that must be submitted to the Congress for approval when it reconvenes. A Council of State composed of representatives from various sectors of the society advises the president on the issuance of decree-laws. Paraguay's highest court is the Supreme Court of Justice. Its five judges are presidentially appointed. For administrative purposes, Paraguay is divided into 19 departments, each headed by a government delegate appointed by the president.

Branches: executive—president; legislative—Senate and Chamber of Deputies; judiciary—Supreme Court of Justice.

Political parties: Colorado, Authentic Radical Liberal, Radical Liberal, Febrerista, and numerous smaller parties not represented in Congress. Suffrage: Adults age 18 and older.

Central government budget (1990): $655 million.

National holiday: Independence, May 15; other holidays celebrated Jan. 1, Feb. 3, Mar. 1, Mar. 27–28, May 1, June 12, Aug. 15, Dec. 8 and 25.

Flag: Horizontal stripes of red, white, and blue; one side bears the national coat of arms; the other, the treasury seal.

Principal Government Officials

President
General Andres Rodriguez

Ministers

Foreign Affairs
Luis Maria Argana

Interior
Gen. Orlando Machuca Vargas

Finance
Enzo DeBernardi

Education and Culture
Dionisio Gonzalez Torres

Agriculture and Livestock
Hernando Bertoni

Public Works and Communications
Porfirio Pereira Ruiz Diaz

National Defense
Gen. Angel Juan Souto Hernandez

Public Health and Social Welfare
Juan Manuel Cano Melgarejo

Justice and Labor
Alexis Frutos Vaezquen

Industry and Commerce
Antonio Zuccolillo

Minister without Portfolio
Juan Ramon Chaves

Ambassador to the U.S. and the OAS
Marcos Martinez

Ambassador to the UN
Alfredo Canete

Paraguay maintains an embassy in the United States at:
2400 Massachusetts Avenue, NW
Washington, D.C. 20008
Tel: (202) 483-6960

Consulates are in Miami, New York, New Orleans, Chicago, Detroit, and Los Angeles.

Defense

The military consists of three branches: army, navy, and air force. The army, with about 15,000 personnel, is organized into three corps areas with six infantry divisions and three cavalry divisions. The navy's 4,000 personnel are divided among three service branches. The air force, the newest and smallest of the services, has approximately 2,000 personnel. Military service is compulsory.

Defense accounts for 10.7 percent of the national budget (1990).

Current Political Conditions

Paraguay's two major traditional political parties, the Colorado and the Liberal Parties, have each ruled the country for prolonged periods. Fundamentally, little ideological difference exists between the two parties.

Following his 1989 coup, General Rodriguez immediately began implementing his promises of bringing democracy and a respect for human rights to Paraguay. Newspapers and radio stations closed by Stroessner were allowed to reopen and broadcast freely. Previously unrecognized and newly created political parties were given legal status. Dozens of independent labor unions were recognized.

Candidates for congressional seats and the presidency were allowed to campaign freely. All of the major opposition parties decided to participate in the May 1 elections.

The Colorado Party, as the highest vote getter, received two-thirds of the seats in each house of congress, 24 out of 36 seats in the Senate, and 48 out of 72 seats in the Chamber of Deputies. The PLRA received 19 percent of the ballots cast, thus obtaining 11 seats in the Senate and 21 in the chamber. The Febreristas obtained one seat in the Senate and two seats in the chamber while the Radical Liberal Party won a single seat in the chamber. All other parties were shut out.

Foreign Relations

Paraguay is a member of the United Nations and several of its specialized agencies, the Organization of American States, and the Latin American Integration Association. Its foreign policy has been strongly pro-Western and anticommunist. Located between two larger powers, Argentina and Brazil,

Paraguay strives to maintain a balanced and positive relationship with each.

U.S.-Paraguay Relations

The U.S. government, through the Agency for International Development (AID) and its predecessor agencies, has assisted Paraguayan development since 1946. Because of Paraguay's rapid economic development, the AID bilateral assistance program has been phased out. Modest funding for U.S. training, however, has been retained. Peace Corps and U.S. Information Service programs are active in Paraguay. Cooperation between Paraguay and the United States in international organizations traditionally has been good. According to the American Embassy, Paraguay has made substantial progress in the three areas of most concern to the United States: democracy, human rights, and narcotics.

Trade

Exports (1989)—$1.3 billion estimated (of which $506 million is registered): meat and meat products, lumber, cotton, soybeans, vegetable oil, coffee, tobacco, tannin, yerba mate. Major markets—Brazil, Argentina, EEC (50 percent), U.S. (3.4 percent).

Imports (1989)—$1.2 billion estimated (of which $767 million is registered): machinery, fuels and lubricants, transportation equipment. Major suppliers—Argentina, Brazil, EEC (18 percent), U.S. (16.7 percent), Japan.

U.S. Exports

Best prospects for U.S. exporters over the coming years include the following categories: quality consumer goods, electronic components, computers and peripherals, telecommunications equipment, medical and scientific instruments, and lumber/paper working machinery.

Trade and Investment Policies

Although Paraguay is a small country with a relatively small manufacturing sector, it generally has not sought to erect protective trade barriers. In practice, Paraguay's market policies are among the most liberal in the Southern Cone.

Import licenses requirements: None are presently imposed on potentially importable items. However, foreign goods competing with goods manufactured by local producers may be subject to special tariff treatment. Such tariff treatment consists of temporary, prohibitive, or restrictive measures to protect or promote the economic and social development of the country, maintain a sound trade balance, or offset dumping of foreign goods. In practice, such import bans most often are imposed on seasonal agricultural products competing with domestic production.

Service barriers: A regulation from the Ministry of Interior requires that non-Paraguayan owners of guard service firms should have resided a minimum of 10 years in Paraguay. Only Paraguayan nationals are authorized to operate commercial broadcasting stations.

Investment barriers: Paraguay maintains an open door policy to attract foreign investment. Paraguayan laws on foreign investment are among the most liberal in Latin America. In general, foreign investors enjoy all the same rights accorded to Paraguayan nationals and may take advantage of special investment incentive programs.

Government procurement practices: Public sector procurement is based on a competitive bidding process. Assuming no more than one firm bids on a particular purchase proposal, the government must call two more bids to attract additional bidders. If no other bidders appear after the third bid, the government agency can authorize the purchase on a noncompetitive basis. For all contracts for the construction of public works projects or for the supply of services to the government, preference must be given to local suppliers of domestic goods and services (Decree 31609/82). Such preference in the award of bids and tenders consists of a price differential of up to 15 percent compared to foreign goods and services.

Customs procedures: Probably the main obstacle to smooth export operations to Paraguay is the cumbersome bureaucratic procedures practiced by local customs. The long delay by customs dispatchers in clearing shipments is as much of a handicap for Paraguayan exporters as to importers, and is not seen as a discriminatory measure against imports.

Preferential financing for major crops: The central bank provides preferential financing to growers of soybeans, cotton, and wheat. Paraguay's economic activity is highly dependent on the performance of these crops. Exports of soybeans and cotton represent approximately 70 percent of 1990 total export earnings.

Tax exemption to encourage and promote manufactured products: The government has introduced incentives for the export of manufactured products that incorporate added value to domestic or imported raw material, using local manpower, services, and energy resources. Consequently, such exports are free from export fees and related taxes. Moreover, imported raw materials used in the production of goods for export are exempted from customs duties and import surcharges.

General Import Policy

Generally, the Paraguayan import system has been designed to facilitate imports needed by industry and to restrict imports of products considered nonessential or products that can be supplied locally. There are only minor quantitative import controls, but high tariffs do prevail on "nonessential" imports or on goods which could be produced in sufficient quantities domestically.

Starting in 1989, the Paraguayan government has taken some small steps to reduce the average tariff rate, but the need for revenues has slowed this effort. The dispersion of the tariff rates is considered excessive. The government planned to deal with this issue as part of its tax reform efforts in 1990 and also as part of the application process for joining the GATT. In particular, the Paraguayan government has made efforts to expand trade with Brazil and Argentina by providing preferential access to these countries in return for concessions on Paraguay's exports to them.

In September 1990, Paraguay was accepted into the regional integration pact composed of Brazil, Argentina, and Uruguay. As a less developed country member of the Latin American Integration Association (ALADI), Paraguay also offers trade concessions on certain products negotiated with other member countries.

Government Procurement

Role of the State in the Economy

State-owned companies play a major role in the Paraguayan economy. Over the past few years, about 45 percent of the sales of the top 40 companies in Paraguay were made by state companies. Even more pronounced is the concentration among the largest companies. In 1989, the largest state-owned enterprises were: ANDE (electric power utility), ANTELCO (telecommunications), PETRO-PAR (petroleum refinery), INC (cement plant), ACEPAR (steel plant), CORPOSANA (water utility).

Tenders

Law 1045 establishes that all contracts for undertaking projects of public works or for the supply of services must be awarded through the public tender system, subject to prior approval by governmental decree, whenever their value exceeds the equivalent of U.S. $60,000.

Bid Submissions

Contracts may be awarded through the price bidding system under the following circumstances:

- whenever the value of the contract is equivalent to less than U.S. $60,000;
- if no bids were received after public tenders have been called for twice;
- whenever the tenders submitted are considered unacceptable to the government.

Whenever there is an emergency and, in order to avoid great damage to public services, contracts may be awarded directly (without tenders or bids) subject to prior approval by the government.

Consulting firms: There is growing emphasis on the use of local contracting and consulting firms. Therefore, it is becoming more difficult for foreign consultants and contractors to obtain access to a public project unless associated with a local firm. Law 1045 regulates the promotion and contracting for consulting services by state agencies. The law equates the contracting for consulting services with contracting for goods and allows a 10 percent rebate to national firms winning international awards. In some instances it limits the degree of foreign participation. In a situation where two or more foreign firms show equal merit, preference will be given to the foreign firm with the largest amount of local participation.

Defense sales: These normally are handled through the Estado Mayor Militar (Military Procurement Office).

Marketing: Personal contact is considered a key element in dealing with state agencies. Written correspondence, while necessary, simply does not carry the weight of visits on the part of foreign business executives.

APPROACHING THE MARKET

Foreign suppliers are urged whenever possible to visit the offices of state-owned companies in Asuncion, make contacts with the chiefs of procurement, and make presentations relating to their companies' technical capabilities.

Increased awareness of new or improved technological capabilities can be reflected in specifications and can make a difference in a contract award. U.S. firms interested in developing a contact for a particular project are urged not to contact the secretariat but rather the specific state company officer managing the project. The appropriate government secretariat can provide guidance on the overall planning in its responsible sector.

Setting Up Business Operations

The following lists some of the major state-owned companies in Paraguay, all headquartered in Asuncion. Also listed are government ministries and secretariats, and official banks:

State-Owned Companies and Government Agencies Active in International Procurement

Administracion Nacional de Electricidad (ANDE)
(Electric Power Utility)
Calle Padre Cardozo 360 (Esq. Avenida Espana), Asuncion, Paraguay
> Tel: 22-713/6 and Telex 142 PY ANDE

Administracion Nacional de Navegacion y Puertos (ANNP)
(National Ports and Rivers Administration)
Plazoleta Isabel La Catolica, Asuncion, Paraguay
> Telex 790 PY ANNP

Administracion Nacional de Telecomunicaciones (ANTELCO)
(National Telecommunications Company)
Calle Alberdi (Esq. General Diaz), Asuncion, Paraguay
> Telex 178 PY ADMGRAL

CORPOSANA (Water Utility)
Calle Jose Berges 516, Asuncion, Paraguay
> Telex 172 PY CORPOSANA

Ministerio de Obras Publicas y Communicaciones
(Ministry of Public Works and Communications)
Calle General Diaz (Esq. Alberdi), Asuncion, Paraguay
> Tel: 444435 and Telex 162 PY MOPC

Estado Mayor General (Military Procurement Office)
Avenida Mariscal Lopez y Vice Presidente Sanchez, Asuncion, Paraguay
> Tel: 206180/9

Corpus Project (with Argentina) (Corpus hydro-project)
Calle General Diaz 488, Asuncion, Paraguay
> Tel: 492161/4

Entidad Binacional Yacyreta (EBY)
(Yacyreta hydroelectric project)
Calle Humaita 145, Asuncion, Paraguay
> Tel: 497462/3 and Telex 268 PY YACYRETA

Itaipu Binacional Project (with Brazil)
(Itaipu hydro-project)
Casilla Postal 691, Calle de la Residenta 1075, Asuncion, Paraguay
> Tel: 207161/9 and Telex 176 PY ITAIPU

Advertising, Market Research, and Business Services

Paraguay has a few advertising agencies and some management consultants, but only the largest firms offer complete services. The leading agencies are members of the Asociacion Paraguaya de Agencias de Publicidad (Paraguayan Association of Publicity Agencies). Several U.S. advertising agencies have branches or affiliates in Paraguay.

Advertising in the print media is the most widely used method, although television and radio advertising are highly effective and generally aimed at the Asuncion market. Asuncion has a wide range of radio programming, featuring American popular music, sports (particularly soccer), and news. Radio 1ro. de Marzo is the leading station in Asuncion, with over 50 percent of the listening audience. Paraguay has two TV stations, both privately owned. Local programming is similar to U.S. TV with a slightly larger component of live programming. Many programs are imported from Argentina and Brazil.

The following daily newspapers (and estimated circulating figures) are widely used by local advertisers:

ABC Color (50,000)
Calle Yegros 745
Asuncion, Paraguay
   Tel: 491166/9
   Telex: 275 PY
   Fax: 493059

Ultima Hora (50,000)
Calle Benjamin Constant 658
Asuncion, Paraguay
   Tel: 496261/8
   Telex: 446 PY UHORA
   Fax: 447071

Diario Hoy (20,000)
Avenida Mariscal Lopez 2984
Asuncion, Paraguay
   Tel: 603400/4
   Telex: 355 PY HOY

El Diario Noticias (20,000)
Avenida Artigas y Brasilia
Asuncion, Paraguay
   Tel: 292721/4
   Telex: 5175 PY EL DIARIO

Paraguayan business and industrial interests are represented by a few industry and trade associations. The Union Industrial Paraguaya is an umbrella organization representing many industry-specific manufacturers associations. The Paraguayan Chamber of Commerce is also very active and offers a variety of business services. The Paraguayan-American Chamber of Commerce offers advisory services to its members and visiting U.S. business people.

INVESTMENT CLIMATE

Paraguay offers a basically open climate for foreign investors both in a legal sense and in terms of underlying market potential. In general, foreign investors enjoy all the same rights as do national investors and may take advantage of special investment incentive programs. Still, general economic uncertainties and specific measures such as price controls have had a negative impact on the investment climate.

The Rodriquez administration has assigned a high priority to boosting investment and the introduction of the necessary macroeconomic framework. Since 1989, the government has made a major effort to encourage foreign investment in the manufacturing sector. Another effort has been to develop the agricultural sector through joint ventures between Paraguayan and foreign firms. The government has sought significant new investment commitments from the EEC.

In 1989, the Rodriguez government moved quickly to encourage investment, both foreign and domestic. The decree law sets out clear legal criteria for the application of investment incentives. It is also based on the principle of national treatment, makes no distinction between domestic and foreign investors, and provides for exemptions from many types of taxes and customs duties for a period of up to five years. The law applies to all sectors of the economy without distinction.

For the last 20 years, there is no knowledge of any foreign investment expropriation outside of land investments expropriated for use in the government land reform program. In these cases, the government and landowner arrive at a purchase price which is then paid out in installments.

Paraguay is not a member of the International Center of the Settlement of Investment Disputes (ICSID).

Extent of U.S. Investment in Goods-Producing Sectors

During 1980–89, a total of $1.135 billion in foreign direct investments was approved. The United States was the leading source of applications, with $218 million or 30 percent of the total. In 1989, Texaco entered into an exploration contract with the Paraguayan government to develop geologic data and to explore oil and gas in the central-north area of Paraguay. There are indications of oil deposits, but the extent and commercial viability are extremely uncertain.

FINANCING AND CAPITAL MARKETS

General Policy Framework

Paraguay is predominantly an agricultural country with vast hydroelectric potential but no known significant mineral or petroleum resources. The economy is highly dependent on production and exports of soybeans and cotton, which together accounted for nearly 70 percent of total exports in 1990.

The change in government in February 1989 marked the end of 34 years of Stroessner's repressive regime. The new administration implemented a sweeping economic liberalization program. In February 1989, the government of President Andres Rodriguez eliminated the multiple exchange rate system and adopted a free floating market rate. The move greatly reduced economic distortions, particularly in the trade area and in the public sector. The Rodriguez administration has also implemented a number of monetary measures to control inflation and to free interest rates. At the same time, the government eliminated price controls on basic products, reduced export taxes, and provided fiscal incentives to encourage investment and attract foreign investors.

The decision to reinstate Paraguay as a beneficiary of the U.S. Generalized System of Preferences (GSP) program effective February 6, 1991, led to Paraguay's restoration as a beneficiary of the Overseas Private Investment Corporation (OPIC) programs in August 1991.

Fiscal policy: The Rodriguez administration has made control of government expenditures one of its chief goals. The central government ran a budget surplus in 1989, 1990, and 1991. Despite the budget surplus, many public enterprises still present deficits and are heavily indebted. No progress has been achieved to privatize these public enterprises. Currently, the Congress is considering two bill · on the privatization of public enterprises

Monetary policy: During 1989, inflation accelerated, fueled by the shock of the exchange rate adjustment and expansionary pressures on the Central Bank. Since January 1991, the government has given top priority to the fight against inflation. This has been achieved through the implementation of highly restrictive monetary measures. As a result, the annual inflation rate has been reduced from 44.1 percent in 1990 to an expected 15 percent in 1991. In order to control the money supply, the Central Bank has restricted credit by maintaining relatively high reserve requirements for banks and other financial institutions.

These monetary measures have raised real interest rates, making access to credit difficult for most producers, particularly farmers. As a result, economic growth has declined in recent months. In order to control the situation and stimulate economic growth, on July 30, the Central Bank eased its restrictive monetary policy by reducing reserve requirements for deposits in local currency.

Debt Management Policy

The Paraguayan external debt increased substantially between 1976 and 1981, and from 1982 until 1987 the foreign debt burden was a serious problem for the Paraguayan economy. During this period the debt servicing ratio was about 92 percent. In 1990 the foreign debt service burden began to decline. In 1990, the servicing of the public debt represented 28.3 percent of total export earnings, and the level of the total external debt represented 29.3 percent of the 1990 GDP.

Paraguay's total external debt amounted to $1,670 million at the end of June 1991. Paraguay's external debt is divided as follows: $638 million (38.2 percent) with the member governments of the Paris Club; $819 million (49 percent) with the multilateral institutions (World Bank, Inter-American Development Bank, other institutions), and $214 million (12.8 percent) with the commercial banks.

The debt structure: Of the $1.67 billion registered external debt, approximately 40 percent is held by the central government; 47 percent is owed by public enterprises. Finally, debts of the financial institutions represent 13 percent of the total foreign debt.

In 1989, Paraguay negotiated a rescheduling agreement with its largest creditor, Brazil, whereby Paraguay could service its bilateral debt with the purchase of Brazilian debt on the secondary market. During 1990, Paraguay purchased Brazilian debt at an average discount of 75 percent and thus retired its entire $436 million obligation with Brazil. This operation reduced Paraguay's total foreign debt from about $2.1 billion down to

about $1.7 billion. Nevertheless, Paraguay's arrears to other creditors continued to climb, reaching some $460 million by the end of the third quarter of 1991. Meanwhile, the government has been intermittently seeking a stand-by agreement with the International Monetary Fund (IMF) since 1990. It appeared possible that a stand-by arrangement would be negotiated in 1992, if the government of Paraguay made a decision to do so. Negotiations to reschedule official debt with the Paris Club would have begun thereafter.

The Currency and Exchange Rate Mechanisms

Currently, Paraguay does not have controls on foreign currency exchange transactions. Foreign currency may be freely acquired at banks and exchange houses. While the foreign exchange rate is free to float, the Central Bank is authorized to participate in the market to avoid unusual fluctuations in the exchange rate. During 1991, the Central Bank has played an active role in the exchange market by buying dollars in order to prevent overvaluation of the local currency. High interest rates offered in the local market have attracted millions of speculative dollars to Paraguay, contributing to the appreciation of the guarani against the dollar.

Despite the massive purchase of dollars by the Central Bank to maintain the value of the guarani, since the change of government in February 1989 through the end of October 1991, the local currency has been depreciated only 22.7 percent against the dollar. Meanwhile, the accumulated inflation rate reached 81.7 percent during the same period.

Banking and Other Financial Institutions

The Paraguayan Central Bank is the chief institution through which the government manages domestic credit policies and implements monetary policy. The Bank regulates available credit and also controls currency circulation. In addition, the Bank closely supervises banking and other financial institutions, manages clearinghouses, operates in the foreign exchange market on behalf of the Treasury, and advises the government on economic matters.

The government has moved toward a more market-oriented banking system over the past couple of years. Reserve requirements have been reduced, and banks have more freedom to take deposits and make loans. The government took a major step in May 1989 by eliminating most controls on interest rates. In addition, foreign exchange markets were freed of controls.

Medium- and long-term capital and large project financing are generally provided by the official banks. The Inter-American Development Bank and the World Bank are active in Paraguay in providing long-term financing for major development projects. Only one U.S. bank, Citibank, is active in Paraguay. In addition, the U.S. Export Import Bank (Ex-Im Bank) offers its financing and insurance programs in Paraguay. Paraguay is seeking to be reinstated in the U.S. GSP program and OPIC may be expected to offer its financing and insurance programs in the near term.

Financial Market Operations and Structural Policies

Pricing policies: The economic system in Paraguay favors free enterprise. Economic incentives and resource allocation in general are guided by the price mechanism. Recent progress has been made by the Rodriguez administration in order to liberalize prices for certain basic products, such as sugar, bread, and liquid gas for cooking. Nevertheless the government still maintains price controls on some strategic goods and services such as gasoline and medicines. Prices of utilities, including telephone, electricity, and water, are established by the government.

Likewise, the Asuncion city government has power to set the price of public transportation. The minimum monthly wage is also fixed by the government.

Tax policy: The current tax system relies primarily on indirect taxes. The proposed FY1991 budget indicated that about 30 percent of estimated central government revenues would be derived from sales and stamp taxes, 22.6 percent from the royalties produced from Itaipu, 13 percent from taxes and duties on imports and exports (mainly imports), 8.3 percent from income taxes (mainly corporate taxes), 1.5 percent from real state taxes, and the remaining from miscellaneous revenue sources. Corporate income is taxed at progressive rates, reaching a maximum rate of 30 percent. The government provides tax incentives for exports of manufactured products. Law No. 90/90, effective December 1990, introduced incentives for the export of manufactured products, including the elimination of export duties and related taxes. Law No. 60/90 established fiscal incentives for domestic and foreign investment, providing exemptions from many types of taxes and custom duties for a period of up to five years.

Tax reform: Tax evasion has been widespread in Paraguay. To reduce tax evasion and simplify the current complex and obsolete tax system, in June 1991, the Ministry of Finance presented to the Paraguayan Congress a tax reform proposal. The proposal includes the imposition for the first time of a value-added tax, but does not include the controversial personal income tax.

Regulatory policies: Paraguay does not have significant discriminatory import restrictions such as quotas and other administrative restrictions that may impact negatively on U.S. exports. The government has maintained a two-tier import tariff structure. Rates between 5 and 35 usually are designed for revenue generation, rates over 35 percent usually are applied to items competing with goods produced by local manufacturers or to items considered as luxury imports. Currently, the top rate is 70 percent, but this level is rarely applied. Imported goods are not subject to prior licensing. However, foreign goods competing with goods manufactured by local producers may be subject to special treatment, such as prohibition or temporary import restriction. A large percentage of U.S. exports to Paraguay is destined for third countries, mainly Brazil and Argentina.

VISITING AND LOCATING

General Travel Checklist

Entrance requirements: U.S. citizens traveling to Paraguay may purchase a tourist card upon arrival ($3) which is valid for up to 90 days. Tourist cards are valid for one entry only and may not be extended beyond 90 days. Visitors planning to make multiple entries or to stay beyond 90 days should have a valid visa. No immunizations are required to enter Paraguay.

Business customs: Business dress and appearance, as well as one's general approach to business relations, can be fairly informal. A prior appointment for a business call is usually necessary and considered a customary courtesy. The pace of negotiation is slower than it is in the United States and is based much more on personal contact.

Office hours: Government offices are open from 07:00 to 13:00, Monday through Friday. Banking hours are 08:45 to 14:00 Monday through Friday. Appointments with bank officials outside regular banking hours frequently can be arranged. In addition to the holidays listed below, all banks are closed December 30. While business hours are generally 08:00 to 17:30, executives usually begin work later in the morning and stay later in the evening. Other than business lunches, appointments with companies generally are not made between noon and 15:00.

Business holidays and vacation periods: The best months for business travel to Paraguay are April through November. Paraguayans take vacations in January and February (the summer season). Some firms close for a time during these periods.

The following are the holidays when businesses are closed: Jan. 1 (New Year's), March 1 (Heroes Day), Holy Thursday and Good Friday, May 1 (Labor Day), May 15 (Independence Day), June 12 (Chaco Armistice), Aug. 15 (Founding of the City of Asuncion), Dec. 8 (Virgin of Caacupe), Dec. 25 (Christmas).

Climate: Climate is semitropical with strong humidity. Air conditioning is very necessary for those not accustomed to the climate. Asuncion's climate is similar to that of Atlanta, Georgia, except that the winter is less severe and it does not snow. Travelers should bear in mind that the seasons are reversed (for example, the weather in January in Asuncion is like July in Atlanta).

Language: Spanish is the language of the country. English is spoken by a limited but growing number of people, especially among urban business and professional people. Business cards in English are acceptable but cards in Spanish and English are more welcome.

Health: Asuncion has no particular health risks and no special precautions need be taken. Sanitary conditions are generally adequate, but care should be taken. Tap water may be used for drinking purposes in Asuncion. There are competent doctors, dentists, and specialists available in Asuncion, but outside the capital care should be taken.

Telecommunications: International services are adequate, although phone calls can meet with delays. The local telephone network is believed to be overburdened. Asuncion is one time zone ahead of eastern standard time.

Transportation: Asuncion has plenty of taxis and a bus system does exist, but it is generally inadequate for business purposes. Fares are quite reasonable. Small tips are customary, though not always expected. Taxi fares from the airport should be established prior to use.

Hotels (Asuncion)

Deluxe:

Hotel Excelsior
Calle Chile 980
Asuncion, Paraguay
Tel: 495632
Telex: 5192 PY HOTELEX

Hotel del Yacht y Golf Club
Av. del Yacht y Av. del Cerro
Ita Enramada, Paraguay
Tel: 37161/5
Telex: 5337 PY HCP

First Class:

Hotel Chaco
Calle Caballero y Mcal. Estigarribia
Asuncion, Paraguay
Tel: 492066/9
Telex: 281 PY

Hotel Guarani
Calle Oliva e Independencia Nacional
Asuncion, Paraguay
Tel: 491131/9
Telex: 277 PY GUARANI

Hotel Cecilia
Calle Estados Unidos y 25 de Mayo
Asuncion, Paraguay
Tel: 210365/7
Telex: 5251 PY CECI HOTEL

Hotel Casino Ita Enramada
Ita Enramada, Paraguay
Tel: 33041/9
Telex: 309 PY

Chapter 18

PERU

	Total	Urban	
Population (1993)	23,265,000	69.0%	

Main Urban Areas	Population	Percentage of Total	International Calling Code
LIMA	4,605,000	19.8	51-14
Arequipa	592,000	2.5	51-54
Callao	560,000	2.4	51-14
Trujillo	491,000	2.1	51-44
Chiclayo	395,000	1.7	51-74
Piura	297,000	1.3	51-74
Chimbote	279,000	1.2	51-44
Cuzco	255,000	1.1	51-84
Iquitos	248,000	1.1	51-94
Huancayo	199,000	0.9	51-64
Sullana	146,000	0.6	51
Pucallpa	141,000	0.6	51-6457

Land Area   1,280,000 square kilometers
    Comparable U.S. State   Slightly smaller than Alaska

Language

* Spanish   68%
* Quechua   27%
Aymara   3%
Other   2%
(*) Official languages

    Common Business Language   Spanish, English

Currency   1 nuevo sol (S/.) = 100 centavos
    Exchange Rate (May 1993)   U.S. $1.00 = 18.90 nuevo sol

Best Nonstop Air Connection via U.S.   Miami to Lima: 5.5 hours
AeroPeru (305) 572-0955
American Airlines (800) 433-7300
Ecuatoriana (800) 328-2367
Faucett (305) 592-5330
One nonstop daily.
Los Angeles to Lima: 8.5 hours
Avianca (800) 284-2622

Best Hotel   Sheraton Hotel and Towers (U.S. $100)
Paseo de la Republica 170
Tel: (51-14) 333-320
       (800) 334-8484
Fax: (51-14) 336-344

INTRODUCTION AND REGIONAL ORIENTATION

The Peruvian economy is basically capital-istic, with a large dose of government welfare programs and government management of credit. In the 1980s the economy suffered from hyperinflation, declining per capita output, and mounting external debt. Peru was shut off from IMF and World Bank support in the mid-1980s because of its huge debt arrears. An austerity program implemented shortly after the Fujimori government took office in July 1990 contributed to a third consecutive yearly contraction of economic activity, but was able to generate a small recovery in the last quarter. After a burst of inflation as the program eliminated government price subsidies, monthly price increases eased to the single-digit level for the first time since mid-1988. Lima has restarted current payments to multilateral lenders and, although it faces $14 billion in arrears on its external debt, is working toward an accommodation with its creditors.

CRACKING THE MARKET

Demographics

Ethnic composition: Indian 45%; mestizo (mixed Indian and European ancestry) 37%; white 15%; black, Japanese, Chinese, and other 3%.

Religion: predominantly Roman Catholic.

Language: Spanish and Quechua (both official), Aymara.

Literacy: 85% age 15 and over can read and write (1990 est.).

Labor force 6,800,000 (1986): government and other services 44%; agriculture 37%; industry 19% (1988 est.).

Organized labor: about 40% of salaried workers (1983 est.).

Budget: revenues $1.3 billion; expenditures $2.1 billion.

Economy

The government of President Alberto Fujimori has adopted orthodox, market-oriented economic policies to an extent previously unknown in Peru.

The objective is to stabilize the economy and create conditions for sustainable economic growth. In policy terms, the results to date have been impressive: markets have been liberalized, the economy has been opened, and reinsertion into the international financial community has begun. With the exception of a major reduction in inflation, however, the main macroeconomic aggregates have not yet begun to register significant improvement. In fact, the economy remained depressed in the first year of major structural reform.

When President Fujimori took office on July 28, 1990, he inherited a severe recession, hyperinflation, huge external debt arrears, and a rapidly deteriorating economy. During his predecessor's five years in office, the price level rose by almost 2 million percent. Per capita GDP had fallen in 1988 and 1989. By 1990, less than 20 percent of the work force was adequately employed. Tax revenues (under 4 percent of GDP) did not keep up with inflation, and the government maintained itself through the printing press, exhausting reserves. Peru was almost totally isolated from the international financial community.

In its first year, the Fujimori government initiated a tough stabilization program; corrected many price distortions; liberalized the trade, investment, and foreign exchange regimes, as well as labor and land markets; opened the economy to greater foreign competition; and began to reduce the size of the public sector. Inflation, which had been 3,040 percent in the final 12 months under

Alan Garcia, has registered less than 10 percent monthly since February 1991.

Under the austere monetary and fiscal regimen and the stress of forced structural adjustment, the economy continues in a deep recession. Real wages have dropped sharply. Public social spending is minimal. In addition, the Sendero Luminoso (SL) and the Tupac Amaru Revolutionary Movement (MRTA) terrorist organizations continue to damage the economy physically and by discouraging economic activity and investment in Peru.

Growth in industry and manufacturing: Peru's manufacturing output fell 4.6 percent in 1990, the third straight year of negative growth. The first half of 1991 registered a drop of 4.8 percent in GDP, in comparison with the first half of 1990.

Despite the serious problem of overvalued exchange rates, all export sectors did relatively well in 1990. They have done less well since January 1991.

Sectors dependent on internal demand (agriculture and manufacturing) have suffered from the recessionary contraction and the sharp drop in household purchasing power. Construction activity rose 3.1 percent in 1990, but dropped by over 20 percent in the first half of 1991. Production of capital goods, consumer durables, and intermediate goods have been particularly hard hit, falling markedly from even 1990's depressed levels. Utilization of existing plant remains at around 50 percent of capacity and a number of firms have closed. Private industrial plant and equipment, as well as the transportation system and public utilities, have deteriorated badly over the past several years, due to lack of investment and maintenance.

Mining and petroleum: The Peruvian mining sector contracted 4.6 percent during 1990. Production goals were unmet, largely because of financial disincentives from the overvalued exchange rate, lack of financing for improvements, continued (but diminished) labor unrest, and increased terrorist attacks. During 1990, copper production fell 12.8 percent, lead 2.6 percent, zinc 2.3 percent, silver 4.3 percent, and iron ore 26.3 percent.

Crude petroleum production fell 1.2 percent in 1990. Domestic prices of gasoline and other derivatives were raised by the new government to over 200 percent of the world price. Total production averaged 128,904 barrels per day, slightly below 1989 levels. Petroperu's financial problems continued to cause delays in payment to Occidental Petroleum, producer of about half of Peru's oil, forcing Occidental to lower production levels.

To encourage investment in oil and gas exploration and production, an August 6, 1991, Petroleum Law eliminated all of Petroperu's and its subsidiaries' monopolies or exclusivities in the hydrocarbon industry, including commercialization, imports of crude and by-products, refining, and basic petrochemicals, all of which can now be carried out freely by any Peruvian or foreign firm. A number of foreign oil companies have indicated interest in exploration.

Occidental Petroleum has plans to expand activities in its northern concession and is exploring in the Ucayali River Basin in the eastern jungle.

Mobil signed a final contract with Petroperu in 1989 for exploration/production in the Upper Huallaga Valley (UHV). The contract specifies that Mobil will invest at least $107.5 million over the first six years of exploration. If production equals Mobil's expectations, total investment in the project could reach $1 billion. A Sendero Luminoso (SL) attack on the Mobil UHV site in December 1990 delayed construction by six months. The government is discussing with Shell and other international firms a development contract to exploit a major gas find at Camisea in Peru's southeastern jungle.

The compensation claim by Enron Corporation and its U.S. insurer American International Group (AIG) for assets of Enron's Belco subsidiary seized by Peru in 1985 was resolved in 1991. A complex dispute related to investment recovery at Southern Peru Copper Corporation's Cuajone mine remained outstanding.

Agriculture and fisheries: Agricultural production fell by an average of 9.0 percent in 1990, primarily as a result of severe drought. Peruvian production of rice fell 11.9 percent; potatoes 28.4 percent; wheat 43.4 percent; cotton 24.6 percent; coffee 24.7 percent; sugar cane 3.1 percent; yellow corn 41.2 percent; sorghum 64.1 percent; and soybeans fell 45.8 percent.

During the 1989–90 sowing and harvest seasons, the severe drought led to sharply lower crop yields. Yields were further lowered because agricultural producers were unable to obtain credit necessary for the purchase of expensive imported fertilizers and agricultural chemicals. The government no longer provides direct or indirect financial subsidies for agriculture.

Government credit to agriculture, through the Banco Agrario, has been slashed by more than over two-thirds in real terms since the Fujimori government took office.

The 1990–91 harvest was somewhat better. In March 1991, however, most import quotas and licensing restrictions on agricultural imports were eliminated. These had kept the price of such goods in Peru at around twice world levels. Despite the fact that Peru imports most wheat and significant amounts of rice, sugar, corn, and soybean meal, agricultural imports (mostly bulk commodities) declined by one-third (to $168 million) in 1990.

Simultaneously, food consumption per capita fell dramatically. Calorie consumption fell 14 percent in the second half of 1990, while protein consumption fell 21 percent. As a result, childhood malnutrition and mortality levels are up sharply.

The U.S. market share remains relatively strong for wheat and rice, but the U.S. share of Peru's corn and soybean meal imports has been hurt by easier credit from other South American countries.

The fisheries sector is essentially an export-oriented industry, whose main product is fish meal (90 percent of which is sold overseas). Peru's catch in 1990 amounted to 6 million metric tons, down 1.6 percent from 1989.

Peru's 1991 cholera epidemic cut sharply into exports of fresh and frozen fish and seafood, as well as fresh fruits and vegetables. This affected both sectors negatively throughout 1991.

Transportation and communications: The transport sector has deteriorated rapidly over the last few years. Construction of Lima's mass-transit electric train project, a priority of the Garcia government, is continuing slowly. Private and public bus systems offer poor service, due to the age and poor condition of vehicles, the cost of spare parts and labor for repairs, and the lack of overall planning and organization in the sector. A chronic lack of funds for road repair and construction has led to deterioration and, in places, disappearance of Peru's land transport infrastructure. Import of new and used buses and taxis has increased since early 1991.

In 1990, the government granted the Peruvian Telephone Company (CPT), serving the Lima-Callao area, permission to offer facsimile, telex, data transmission, international long-distance telephone, and cellular telephone service. Panamsat satellite was launched in June 1988. Cellular telephone service is also offered by one private sector company. However, it should be noted that there are only 2.4 telephones per 100 Peruvian households.

Natural resources: copper, silver, gold, petroleum, timber, fish, iron ore, coal, phosphate, potash.

PERU
Key Economic Indicators
(millions of U.S. dollars unless otherwise noted)

	1989	1990	1991 (est)
Income, Production, Employment			
Real GDP (1979 U.S. $)	15,268	14,520	14,927
Real GDP growth rate	−11.6	−4.9	2.8
GDP by sector: (millions of 1979 intis)			
Agriculture	465.2	423.3	429.6
Fisheries	42.2	40.4	39.1
Mining	337.6	323.5	313.5
Manufacturing	749.5	706.4	741.7
Electricity	50.0	47.9	N/A
Construction	186.4	192.5	200.2
Commerce	456.5	438.7	N/A
Government	247.5	227.3	N/A
Others	895.8	864.2	N/A
Per capita GDP (1979 U.S. $)	701	650	652
Labor force (thousands)	7,429	7,500	7,450
Unemployment (%)	7.9	8.3	N/A
Money and prices (End of Year)			
Money supply (M1-thousands of soles)	7,739	392,769	706,400
Bank lending rate (nom.)	1,064	1,586	782
Bank savings rate (nom.)	706	820	153
Consumer prices (% chg.)	2,775	7,649	132
Wholesale Prices (% chg.)	1,918	6,534	130
Exchange rate (official)	0.01	0.53	1.10
Exchange rate (parallel)	0.01	0.53	1.10
Balance of Payments and Trade			
Total exports FOB	3,488	3,276	3,240
Total exports to U.S.	815	803	800
Total imports FOB	2,291	2,885	3,265
Total imports from U.S.	690	778	780
Aid from U.S.	51.4	83.1	187.9
Aid from other countries	N/A	N/A	N/A
External public debt[1]	15,796	16,301	15,857
Debt service paid	174	150	683
Debt service due	N/A	N/A	N/A
Foreign exchange reserves	357	531	1,100
Balance of payments	863	287	400

1. Excludes interest due on arrears.

Source: Central Reserve Bank, National Institute of Statistics, Ministry of Labor and Embassy estimates.

Land use: arable land 3%; permanent crops NEGL%; meadows and pastures 21%; forest and woodland 55%; other 21%; includes irrigated 1%.

Environment: subject to earthquakes, tsunamis, landslides, mild volcanic activity; deforestation; overgrazing; soil erosion; desertification; air pollution in Lima.

Note: shares control of Lago Titicaca, world's highest navigable lake, with Bolivia.

Agriculture: accounts for 12% of GDP, 37% of labor force; commercial crops—coffee, cotton, sugarcane; other crops—rice, wheat, potatoes, plantains, coca; animal products—poultry, red meats, dairy, wool; not self-sufficient in grain or vegetable oil; fish catch of 4.6 million metric tons (1987), world's fifth-largest.

Illicit drugs: world's largest coca leaf producer with about 121,000 hectares under cultivation; source of supply for most of the world's coca paste and cocaine base; about 85% of cultivation is for illicit production; most of cocaine base is shipped to Colombian drug dealers for processing into cocaine for the international drug market.

Political/Institutional Infrastructure

Peru gained its independence from Spain on July 28, 1821.

Administrative divisions: 24 departments (departamentos) and one constitutional province (provincia constitucional).

Constitution: July 28, 1980 (often referred to as the 1979 Constitution because the Constituent Assembly met in 1979, but the Constitution actually took effect the following year); reestablished civilian government with a popularly elected president and bicameral legislature.

Legal system: based on civil law system; has not accepted compulsory ICJ jurisdiction.

Executive branch: president, two vice-presidents, prime minister, Council of Ministers (cabinet).

Legislative branch: bicameral Congress (Congreso) consists of an upper chamber or Senate (Senado) and a lower chamber or Chamber of Deputies (Camara de Diputados).

Judicial branch: Supreme Court of Justice (Corte Suprema de Justicia).

Principal Government Officials

Chief of State (since July 28, 1990)
President Alberto FUJIMORI

Vice-President (since July 28, 1990)
Maximo SAN ROMAN

Vice President (since July 28, 1990)
Carlos GARCIA

Head of Government
Prime Minister (since February 15, 1991)
Carlos TORRES Y TORRES Lara

Ambassador to U.S.
Roberto G. MACLEAN
Chancery at:
1700 Massachusetts Avenue, NW
Washington, D.C. 20036
Tel: (202) 833-9860 through 9869

Peruvian Consulates General are located in Chicago, Houston, Los Angeles, Miami, New York, Paterson (New Jersey), San Francisco, and San Juan (Puerto Rico).

Suffrage: universal at age 18.

Flag: three equal, vertical bands of red (hoist side), white, and red with the coat of arms centered in the white band; the coat of arms features a shield bearing a llama, cinchona tree (the source of quinine), and a yellow cornucopia spilling out gold coins, all framed by a green wreath.

Defense

Branches: Army (Ejercito Peruano), Navy (Marina de Guerra del Peru), Air Force (Fuerza Aerea del Peru), Peruvian National Police.

Manpower availability: males 15–49, 5,704,684; 3,859,123 fit for military service; 241,792 reach military age (20) annually.

Defense expenditures: $430 million, 2.4% of GDP (1991).

Current Political Conditions

Political parties and leaders: Change 90 (Cambio 90), Alberto FUJIMORI; Democratic Front (FREDEMO), a loosely organized three-party coalition—Popular Christian Party (PPC), Luis BEDOYA Reyes; Popular Action Party (AP), Fernando BELAUNDE Terry; and Liberty Movement; American Popular Revolutionary Alliance (APRA), Luis ALVA Castro; National Front of Workers and Peasants (FRENATRACA), Roger CACERES; United Left (IU), run by committee; Socialist Left (IS), Enrique BERNALES.

Elections

President—next to be held April 1995.

Senate—next to be held April 1995; results from 1990—percent of vote by party NA; seats—(60 total) FREDEMO 20, APRA 16, Change 90 14, IU 6, IS 3, FRENATRACA 1.

Chamber of Deputies—next to be held April 1995; results from 1990—percent of vote by party NA; seats—(180 total) FREDEMO 62, APRA 53, Change 90 32, IU 16, IS 4, FRENATRACA 3, other 10.

Communists: Peruvian Communist Party-Unity (PCP-U), pro-Soviet, 2,000; other minor Communist parties.

Other political or pressure groups: leftist guerrilla groups—Shining Path, leader Abimael GUZMAN; Tupac Amaru Revolutionary Movement, Nestor CERPA and Victor POLLAY.

Trade

Exports: $3.01 billion (FOB, 1990 est.).

Commodities—fishmeal, cotton, sugar, coffee, copper, iron ore, refined silver, lead, zinc, crude petroleum and byproducts.

Partners: EC 22%; U.S. 20%; Japan 11%; Latin America 8%; Russia 4%.

Imports: $2.78 billion (FOB, 1990 est.). Commodities—foodstuffs, machinery, transport equipment, iron and steel semimanufactures, chemicals, pharmaceuticals.

Partners: U.S. 23%; Latin America 6%; EC 12%; Japan 7%; Switzerland 3%.

Broad market outlook: Severe recession and declining domestic demand continued throughout 1990 and 1991. MRTA and Sendero Luminoso terrorism continues to threaten productive investment in Peru. Exports in 1990 were higher than expected, yielding an estimated trade surplus of $391 million for the year.

The United States remained Peru's largest trading partner in 1990, despite a drop in U.S. share of both the import and export markets. Highest value U.S. exports to Peru in 1990 were cereals (wheat and rice), refined oil, machinery parts and equipment, organic chemicals, electrical machinery, sound equipment, and TV equipment and parts.

The best prospects for U.S. exports are mining equipment, agricultural machinery and equipment, oil and gas field machinery and equipment, food processing and packaging equipment, commercial fishing equipment, security and safety equipment, computers and peripherals, telecommunications equipment, medical equipment and supplies, automobile parts and equipment, and electrical power systems and equipment. Among agricultural exports, demand is highest for corn and wheat. The deteriorating security situation has increased demand for all types of security-related products. The increasing demand for low-income housing in the larger Peruvian cities has created a potential market for low-cost housing components.

As long as the inti continues to be highly overvalued, imports will be competitive. A serious devaluation could alter this outlook.

Countertrade and debt-for-product swaps are of growing importance. Peruvian importers are creating export trading companies to market Peruvian products internationally. International banks use debt-for-product swaps to recover debt obligations. Compensation trade is also increasingly prevalent. The American Embassy Commercial Section's extensive report on Compensation Trade Practices is available upon request.

Obstacles to trade: Before 1991, most agricultural imports were subject to import quotas and licensing restrictions supervised by state trading agencies which controlled the bulk of the agricultural import market. The government has eliminated ECASA, one of these two food import marketing firms. ENCI, the remaining company, continues in operation, but without its previous monopoly on wheat and wheat flour imports.

Peruvian tariffs on imported goods are officially 25 and 15 percent, depending on the type of good. The average tariff is approximately 17 percent, down from 80 percent at the end of the Garcia administration.

Foreign investment: The Fujimori government is committed to encouraging foreign investment in Peru. A September 1990 legislative decree liberalized Peruvian foreign investment regulations to grant national treatment to foreign investors. The decree guarantees foreign investors the right to remit freely all profits, royalties, and invested capital. An agreement with the World Bank's MIGA investment guarantee organization was signed in late 1990, and ratified by Peru's Senate in early 1991. An OPIC investment guarantee agreement with the United States is currently in force.

Major projects: The most interesting potential major project is the Camisea natural gas fields, with usable reserves estimated at 10.8 trillion cubic feet of gas and 720 million barrels of natural gas liquids (condensates).

Required financing for the Camisea project is estimated at $1.2 billion to develop the field and build two pipelines to Lima. Despite extensive negotiations, Shell and the government failed to agree to terms and broke off talks in September 1988. Camisea authorities are now studying the advantage to breaking down the project into smaller implementation units. Petroleum exploration possibilities abound and terms for mineral exploration are favorable. As privatization advances, foreign investors have been assured of equal opportunities to bid.

Trade and Investment Policies

The key barriers to U.S. exports to Peru have been systematically dismantled by the Fujimori government over the past few years. Import licensing requirements, the list of banned imports, and nearly all quantitative import restrictions have been eliminated. Import tariff surcharges remain, however, on dairy products and some agricultural commodities. Although almost all Peru's imports have a uniform 15 or 25 percent ad valorem duty, a tariff surcharge is levied on 10–18 key farm commodities to protect local producers. This surcharge is a variable import levy, based on a "band of prices" determined weekly by the Minister of Agriculture. Imposed in May 1991, the government of Peru describes these surtaxes as anti-dumping duties to protect Peruvian farmers from subsidized international competition. The surcharge regime effectively limits U.S. farm products access to the Peruvian market.

The Peruvian government has eliminated the government monopoly on reinsurance and on providing insurance to state entities. There are no longer any restrictions on foreign investment in financial services, mass communication, or transport. Foreign investment in Peru is guaranteed treatment equal to that provided to national investment under the 1979 Constitution. A prohibition on foreign investment remains in areas considered essential for national security. All restrictions on remittances of profits, royalties, and capital have been eliminated.

The 1985 expropriation of the assets of Belco, a U.S. oil producer, was resolved in December 1991. The government of Peru and American International Group (AIG), Belco's insurer, signed a framework agreement for the government of Peru to pay AIG $185 million in compensation.

Government procurement is ordinarily handled by public international tender. Exceptions are permitted for government entities declared in a state of emergency. The state of emergency determination has been used in the past to avoid tender requirements.

Peru has simplified import tariffs to two rates: 15 and 25 percent ad valorem. The average tariff rate is 17 percent, down from 80 percent at the end of the previous government. Tariffs may be lowered further, either in the Andean Pact context or unilaterally. In an effort to improve export performance, the Fujimori government has taken a number of steps to liberalize port and shipping operations, including elimination of cargo preference requirements. In recent years, the country's main port of Callao has been the most expensive on the west coast of South America.

Export Subsidies Policies

The Fujimori government has eliminated the CERTEX program of financial incentives to exporters of nontraditional products. Peru no longer has any export subsidies.

INVESTMENT CLIMATE

Economic Factors: Reform, Stability, and Growth

A successful arrears-clearing exercise with the international financial institutions, and International Monetary Fund (IMF)-approved economic stabilization and adjustment program, and an unprecedented rescheduling agreement with the Paris Club marked Peru's reinsertion into the international financial community. Missions from the IMF, World Bank (IBRD), and Inter-American Development Bank (IDB) are working closely with appropriate stabilization and adjustment measures.

Public finance, money, and prices: Peru's annual inflation reached 7,649.7 percent in 1990, one of the highest levels in the world and an increase over the 1989 level of 2,775.3 percent. In the first eight months of 1991, inflation totalled 102.1 percent.

Peru's inflation has been a consequence of, among other factors, chronic large fiscal and quasi-fiscal deficits financed by monetary emission, lagged adjustment of public tariff rates to market levels, and successive exchange rate adjustments—as well as widespread lack of confidence in their domestic currency. Past governments have attempted to stabilize the economy, reduce inflation, and correct price distortions through a series of partial and ineffective adjustment measures. The Fujimori government began implementation of a more coherent and comprehensive adjustment package in 1990. This led to immediate and severe price increases and a sharp drop in household purchasing power, but also served to eliminate many price distortions and put the government on a sounder fiscal footing.

The Fujimori government has pledged to eliminate Peru's fiscal deficit, which in 1990 was 5.4 percent of GDP. In fact, since September 1990, the government has run on a cash basis, with monthly expenditures dependent on revenues. Peru's chronic fiscal problems continue, however, aggravated by structural problems such as excess public employment and widespread tax evasion. A November 1990 reform of Peru's tax code cut the number of taxes and eliminated many exemptions. A radical restructuring of the tax administration is being carried out, and more reforms are anticipated. As a result, revenues have grown from below 4 percent of GDP in July 1990 to 8 percent in mid-1991. The government estimates, however, that at least 16 percent is needed for effective operations.

Privatization of public sector firms has been far slower than expected. In the first year, Fujimori's government had sold only its minority interests in Sogewiese Leasing and Minas Buenaventuras.

Credit available to the private sector rose 20.6 percent in real terms between July 1990 and July 1991. Of this, U.S. dollar credit rose by 67.8 percent, while inti/sol credit fell 16.6 percent. Inflation, capital flight, and tight government monetary policies have compressed domestic currency liquidity (M2 or money plus quasi-money). Nominal/real interest rates rose in January 1991 and surged higher by July 1991. Interest rates on domestic currency loans averaged nearly 17.5 percent per month (up from 15.8 in December and positive in real terms), while savings account interest rates rose to around 8 percent (6 percent in December and less negative in real terms). The spread between lending and savings rates has increased because of low levels of financial intermediation and high operating costs.

Interest rates on dollar-denominated credit have followed a similar trend, averaging 2 percent monthly for loans, and 1 percent monthly for savings accounts.

The domestic money supply (M1) contracted 25.4 percent in real terms from July 1990 to July 1991, although nominally it grew by 1,609.2 percent. Quasi-money (intis/sols in demand deposits) contracted 46.5 percent in real terms and grew 1,125.1 percent nominally. Meanwhile, holdings in foreign currency grew 174.4 percent in real terms, as portfolio decisions favored foreign over domestic currency.

Balance of payments: During 1990, Peru experienced a trade and capital surplus, but a deficit in the current account. Exports fell, while imports grew largely due to overvalued exchange and because government subsidies promoting exports were eliminated. This trend continued during 1991.

In 1990, Peru achieved an estimated trade surplus of $391 million, but suffered a current account deficit of $649 million. Peru's net reserve position improved in 1990, with an increase of $146 million. As of December 31, 1990, the Central Bank's (BCR) net international reserves were $531 million. Reserves rose to $820 million by July 22, 1991.

The Central Bank's (BCR) tight monetary policy since July 1990 has caused an increasing shortage of intis/soles in the economy. The Fujimori government's adjustment program, BCR monetary policy, and inflows of narco-dollars have contributed to the increasing overvaluation of Peru's domestic currency since August 1990. Current policies of monetary and fiscal contraction are creating an ever-greater scarcity of domestic currency and increasing its artificial overvaluation relative to the dollar. The steady inflow of narcotics revenues continues, adding to the excess dollar supply in Peru.

Foreign debt: The Fujimori government achieved Peru's reinsertion into the international financial system during 1991. Not only have arrears to the IMF, World Bank, and IDB been cleared, but the IMF has approved Peru's economic stabilization and adjustment program. The Paris Club rescheduled bilateral debt in September 1991, in an unprecedented agreement.

Negotiations with the commercial banks Steering Committee were held in early 1992.

Peru resumed debt service payments to

the IMF in October 1989, to the World Bank in October 1990, and to the IDB in November 1990. U.S. economic assistance and PL-480 programs continue, subject to receipt of payments on past assistance.

Peru's public external debt on December 31, 1990, was about $17.3 billion (excluding interest on arrears). Including interest on arrears, the total amounts to $22 billion (equal to 62 percent of 1990 GDP and over six times the value of 1990 exports).

Peru's government has promoted, since 1987, countertrade agreements to repay its large debt to the former U.S.S.R. and Eastern European creditors. Several agreements have also been approved by which commercial banks and other corporate creditors accept debt service payments in the form of exports such as textiles and processed food. The Garcia government approved debt-equity conversion legislation in late 1988, and

a limited debt-for-donation scheme in April 1989, but few projects were approved. The Fujimori government has not yet elaborated a policy on debt-equity or other debt conversion schemes.

FINANCING AND CAPITAL MARKETS

General Policy Framework

The Fujimori government inherited a country without international reserves and shunned by the international financial community. The economy was in deep recession, inflation was accelerating alarmingly, and the infrastructure had deteriorated over the previous 10 years. The government was supporting a diverse portfolio of unprofitable public sector companies.

Extent of U.S. Investment in Goods-Producing Sectors
U.S. Direct Investment Position Abroad
on a Historical-Cost Basis—1990
(millions of U.S. dollars)

Category		Amount
Petroleum		−2
Total Manufacturing		78
Food and kindred products	13	
Chemicals and allied products	27	
Metals, primary and fabricated	(D)	
Machinery, except electrical	0	
Electric and electronic equipment	−1	
Transportation equipment	0	
Other manufacturing	(D)	
Wholesale trade		73
TOTAL PETROLEUM/MANUFACTURING/WHOLESALE TRADE		149

(D) -Suppressed to avoid disclosing data of individual companies

Source: U.S. Department of Commerce, *Survey of Current Business* (August 1991, vol. 71, no. 8, table 11.3).

On August 8, 1990, the Fujimori administration eliminated price controls on basic food items and raised fuel and energy prices by as much as 3,000 percent in an effort to have prices reflect production costs. The end of subsidized public services, such as mass transit, was part of the antiinflationary effort, combined with the realignment of key relative prices. August 1990 inflation reached an historic high of almost 400 percent, but has since fallen to below 5 percent monthly. Since September 1990, the government has imposed tough fiscal austerity policies, requiring current spending to be paid out of (and not exceed) current revenues. The slight fiscal deficit is due to capital expenditure and external debt payments. The key fiscal priority is tax reform to boost revenues.

Government revenues are currently inadequate to fund basic health, education, law enforcement, and defense. The government has proposed a simplified system of taxes on income, wealth, sales, and imports, but the desperate need for revenues has led to "special," "temporary," and "extraordinary" taxes. A tax administration reform, initiated in early 1991, has already restored much public trust in the tax system and doubled government of Peru revenues to 8 percent of GDP. The lack of external credit, and the size of the fiscal deficit, drove monetary policy in earlier governments. The Central Bank's key challenge now is to allow enough liquidity to financial markets so that economic growth can resume, but not so much as to contribute to a surge of inflation. Open market operations are used frequently to inject liquidity into the system.

The Central Bank has eliminated interest rate ceilings and lowered reserve requirements. As of July 1, 1991, Peru's domestic currency is the New Sol.

The improved fiscal situation, lower household purchasing power, and the continued lack of liquidity led to a severe depression in late 1990. The first half of 1991 saw some recovery, with real growth of close to 3 percent expected for the year. U.S. exports to Peru have benefited from significantly liberalized trade and investment regimes and from the overvalued Peruvian currency.

Debt Management Policies

External debt: $20.0 billion (December 1990).

In September 1991, the IMF agreed to an arrangement to clear Peru's nearly $900 million in arrears to that institution by the end of 1992, and approved Peru's economic stabilization and adjustment program. Peru's roughly U.S. $400 million in debts to the Inter-American Development Bank were paid. An agreement to clear Peru's $900 million in arrears to the World Bank was expected soon. Also during September, the Paris Club agreed to reschedule Peru's debts to official creditors.

The Currency and Exchange Rate Mechanisms

The Fujimori government has liberalized the exchange rate regime, eliminating multiple rates, licensing requirements, and other cumbersome mechanisms. The exchange rate is determined by market forces, subject to Central Bank intervention. No restrictions exist on the purchase, use, or remittance of foreign exchange. Exporters are no longer required to channel foreign exchange earnings through the Central Reserve Bank (BCR), nor are importers required to obtain foreign exchange from the BCR.

Currency transactions are conducted freely by exporters and importers on the open market.

The Central Bank has intervened frequently in the market, usually in an effort to keep devaluation of the New Sol on a gradual course. On the basis of purchasing power parity, the New Sol remains at least 30 percent overvalued, according to the most conservative estimate. The government's overriding concern, however, is to avoid a resurgence of inflation, which many fear would be the inevitable result of too abrupt a devaluation.

Tapping International Aid Institutions

Economic aid: U.S. commitments, including Ex-Im Bank (FY70–89), $1.7 billion; Western (non-U.S.) countries, ODA and OOF bilateral commitments (1970–88), $3.95 billion; Communist countries (1970–89), $577 million.

Financial Market Operations and Structural Policies

Deep structural reforms are underway in Peru, although much remains to be done. One of the most fundamental measures taken so far was the elimination of subsidized prices for the goods and services provided by government enterprises and the removal of subsidies. Other important measures have been taken to liberalize the trade, exchange rate, financial system, and labor regimes.

The government of Peru has announced its intention to privatize or liquidate many of its para-statals. This would eliminate the government's responsibility for continuing losses and should increase efficiency. The terms of a proposed Inter-American Development Bank loan for financial sector adjustment commit Peru to combine its four development banks into one and to privatize other state-held banking interests.

Chapter 19

URUGUAY

	Total	Urban	
Population (1993)	3,159,000	89.0%	

Main Urban Areas	Population	Percentage of Total	International Calling Code
MONTEVIDEO	1,248,000	39.5	598-2
Salto	81,000	2.6	598-732
Paysandu	75,000	2.4	598-722
Las Piedras	61,000	1.9	598-322
Rivera	56,000	1.8	598-622
Melo	42,000	1.3	598-462
Tacuarembo	40,000	1.3	598-632
Mercedes	37,000	1.2	598-532
Minas	35,000	1.1	598-442

Land Area	173,620 square kilometers
Comparable U.S. State	Slightly smaller than Washington

Language	Spanish 100%
Common Business Language	Spanish, English

Currency	1 peso (N$Ur) = 100 centesimos
Exchange Rate (May 1993)	U.S. $1.00 = 3.94 new pesos

Best Nonstop Air Connection via U.S.
Miami to Montevideo: 9.5 hours
American Airlines (800) 433-7300
Ladeco (800) 825-2332

Best Hotel
Victoria Plaza (U.S. $100)
Plaza de la Independencia 759
Montevideo 11100
Tel: (598-2) 914-201
Fax: (598-2) 921-628

INTRODUCTION AND REGIONAL ORIENTATION

Uruguayans share a Spanish linguistic and cultural background, even though 25 percent of the population is of Italian origin. Most are Roman Catholics. Church and state are officially separated. Uruguay is distinguished by its high literacy rate and large urban middle class.

The overall drop in real income since the 1960s has increased poverty, but the average Uruguayan standard of living still compares favorably with that of most other Latin Americans. Metropolitan Montevideo, with about an estimated 1.41 million inhabitants, is the only large city. The rest of the population lives in about 20 towns.

During the past two decades, an estimated 500,000 Uruguayans have emigrated, principally to Argentina and Brazil. As a result of the low birth rate and relatively high rate of emigration of younger people, Uruguay's population is quite mature.

History and Political Conditions

In early Uruguayan history, Spain, Portugal, and later Brazil and Argentina struggled for control of the area. Batlle y Ordonez, president from 1903 to 1907 and again from 1911 to 1915, set the pattern for Uruguay's modern political development. He established widespread political, social, and economic reforms, such as an extensive welfare program, government participation in many facets of the economy, and a plural executive. Many of these programs continue today.

In 1973, amid increasing economic and political turmoil, the armed forces closed the Congress and established a civilian-military regime. A new constitution drafted by the military was rejected in a November 1980 plebiscite. Following the plebiscite, the armed forces announced a new plan for return to civilian rule, with national elections scheduled in 1984. Colorado Party leader Julio Maria Sanguinetti won the 1984 presidential election with 31.4 percent of the vote.

In the 1989 presidential election, Blanco Party leader Luis Alberto Lacalle gained the presidency with 27 percent of the vote. Since taking office on March 1, 1990, President Lacalle has concentrated on economic and social reform programs. The Lacalle administration is vigorously pursuing budget deficit reduction, foreign debt reduction, privatization of state enterprises, civil service reform, and education and labor reform. To achieve these ambitious goals, the Lacalle administration has sought the legislative cooperation of the Colorado Party by appointing several Colorado Party members to his cabinet. He also has continued the previous government's policies of reserving some directorship positions in the autonomous state entities for opposition parties.

In the 1989 election, the Leftist Broad Front Coalition won the seat of the Intendente (Mayor) of Montevideo. Next to the presidency, this is the most important elective post in the country, as Montevideo contains 44 percent of the country's population. The Communist Party/Socialist Party/Radical Left coalition hopes to use this five-year term as a springboard for future electoral gains at the national level.

Uruguay's economic difficulties, and the Lacalle administration's privatization and the labor reform proposals have led to increased tension between the Labor Federation, the PIT-CNT, and the national government. The tempo of labor protest, which had declined after the first year of the Sanguinetti administration, rose with the approach of the 1989 elections and will likely increase in the short term as the Lacalle administration's economic program progresses through parliament. The Lacalle administration is seeking through new labor legislation to regulate what currently is an almost unlimited right to strike, and to require that strikes be approved by a secret, obligatory vote of the membership.

CRACKING THE MARKET

Demographics

Ethnic groups (estimate): 90% white, 7% mestizo, 3% black.

Religions: Roman Catholic 66%, Protestant 2%, Jewish 2%, nonprofessing or other 30%.

Language: Spanish.

Literacy-96%.

Work force (1990) 1.4 million: manufacturing 22%; government 20%; agriculture 13%; commerce 17%; utilities, construction, transport and communications 12%; other services 16%.

Economy

Agriculture (11.8% of GDP, 1989): Products—beef, wool, grains, fruits, vegetables.

Industry (21% of GDP, 1989): Types—meat processing, wool and hides, textiles, shoes, handbags, leather apparel, tires, cement, fishing, petroleum refining.

Even though agriculture provides only 11 percent of the GDP and employs only 12 percent of the labor force, the government sees it as the engine of Uruguayan growth. In 1988 Uruguay's beef and sheep herds totaled 36 million head. Uruguay's manufacturing derives significantly from its agricultural sector, with meat processing, leather production, fish and fish products, and textile, shoe, handbag, and leather apparel production. The government is aggressively urging export diversification, and textiles and leather goods are appearing in export statistics along with meat products, hides and leather, and wool.

The government has adopted an export-based strategy to achieve economic growth and meet its debt service obligations. The trade surplus for 1989 exceeded $450 mil-

lion as exports rose 14 percent over 1988 and imports of capital goods declined by the same amount.

Because of the importance of exports, Uruguayan tariffs have been reduced. Trade promotion and tariff reduction agreements have been signed with Argentina and Brazil; ties with the United States and Western Europe are being strengthened; and through a program of new embassies and trade offices, new markets, such as Africa, the Middle East, and Asia are being explored.

Uruguay is committed to a floating exchange rate and has declared that it will intervene in the exchange market only in order to adjust seasonal fluctuations in foreign exchange inflows and outflows.

While Uruguay has one of the highest per capita external debts in the hemisphere, it has remained current on interest payments ($552 million in 1989).

The Lacalle administration has introduced a package of reforms aimed at modernizing the economy and reducing its debt burden, fiscal deficit, and inflation. Some parts are in place, but privatization measures and social security reforms are still pending.

Uruguay is negotiating with the International Monetary Fund for a stand-by agreement based on reduction of the federal budget deficit and lower inflation (nearly 100 percent throughout 1992). It also is negotiating a debt reduction agreement with commercial lenders. Completion of these negotiations will help reduce interest payments on its debts.

Political/Institutional Infrastructure

The Republic of Uruguay gained its independence from Spain on August 25, 1825.

Uruguay's 1967 Constitution institutionalizes a strong presidency, subject to legislative and judicial checks. Twelve cabinet ministers, appointed by the president, head the regular executive departments.

URUGUAY
Key Economic Indicators

	1989	1990	1991 (Est)
Income, Production, Employment			
GDP in current dollars (millions)[8]	7,818	8,218	9,136
Real GDP (mill. 1983 pesos)[1]	207,857	209,747	213,942
Real GDP growth rate (%)[1]	0.5	0.9	2.0
Breakdown of GDP by sector (% of total)[2]			
Agriculture	10.6	10.8	11.0
Fishing	0.2	0.1	0.2
Mining	0.2	0.2	0.2
Manufacturing	25.5	25.0	24.5
Utilities	3.0	3.4	3.3
Construction	3.0	2.8	2.5
Commerce, restaurants, and hotels	11.1	10.9	11.0
Transport, warehousing, and communications	6.7	6.6	6.8
Financial, insurance, housing, and services to companies	22.6	22.9	23.3
Government, social, and personal services	17.1	17.3	17.2
Real per capita GDP (U.S. $)[3]	2,541	2,656	2,935
Size of labor force (millions)[4]	1.341	1.355	1.369
Unemployment rate[5]	8.0	8.5	8.5
Money and Prices			
Money supply (M1) (nominal % increase at the end of CY)[1]	67.0	103.2	100.0
Interest rates			
Commercial			
Peso accounts[1]	127.6	174.4	140.0
Dollar accounts[1]	14.1	14.0	12.0
Savings deposits			
Peso accounts[1]	27.6	31.0	30.0
Dollar accounts[1]	4.6	4.5	4.3
Certificates of deposits (180 days)			
Peso accounts[1]	84.7	97.8	80.0
Dollar accounts[1]	6.9	6.5	5.0
Investment rate % of GDP[2]	10.9	10.3	11.0
Consumer price inflation (%)[5]	89.2	129.0	90.0
Wholesale price inflation (%)[1]	80.7	120.7	75.0

Table continues

URUGUAY
Key Economic Indicators
(Continued)

	1989	1990	1991 (Est)
Exchange rate (interbank floating selling rate) (New Pesos/U.S. $1)[1]	805.0	1,594.0	2,515.0
Balance of Payments and Trade			
Total exports—FOB (U.S. $ million)[1]	1,599	1,693	1,630
Total exports to U.S.—FOB (U.S. $ million)[1]	177	163	165
Total imports—CIF (U.S. $ million)[1]	1,203	1,343	1,680
Total imports from U.S.—CIF (U.S. $ million)[1]	113	137	190
Aid from U.S. (U.S. $ million)[6]	0.2	3.9	10.9
Aid from other countries[7]	10.0	10.0	15.0
Total U.S. direct investment (stock) (U.S. $ million)[9]	132.0	150.0	160.0
Net external debt—end of year, (U.S. $ million)[1]	3,245	3,120	2,650
Annual total debt service payment (U.S. $ million)[1]	802	784	1,317
Gold and foreign exchange reserves (U.S. $ million)[1]	1,018	1,098	890
Balance of payments (U.S. $ million)[1]			
Merchandise trade	463	426	45
Net nonfinancial services	40	120	250
Net financial services	−349	−322	−280
Current account	153	224	15
Capital account	−59	−143	−225
Net international reserves	−94	−82	210

Sources:

1. Central Bank of Uruguay.
2. U.S. Embassy computation based on Central Bank data.
3. U.S. Embassy computation based on Central Bank and Office of Statistics and Census data.
4. Embassy computation based on Office of Statistics and Census data.
5. Office of Statistics and Census.
6. Agency for International Development.
7. United Nations Development Program.
8. Current New Pesos converted at the average U.S. $ exchange rate for each year.
9. Survey of Current Business, U.S.DOC, August 1991.

In addition, a number of "autonomous entities" and "decentralized services" are important in government administration.

The constitution also provides for a bicameral General Assembly responsible for enacting laws and regulating the administration of justice. The General Assembly consists of a 30-member Senate and a 99-member Chamber of Deputies.

The highest court is the Supreme Court; below it are appellate and lower courts and justices of the peace. In addition, there are electoral and administrative ("contentious") courts, an accounts court, and a separate military judicial system.

Uruguay has 19 administrative departments organized similarly to the central government and four military regions.

Political parties: Colorado, Blanco (National), Broad Front Coalition, New Space Party, Civic Union.

Suffrage: Universal, 18 and over.

Central government budget (1989): $1.5 billion.

Principal Government Officials

President
Luis Alberto Lacalle

Minister of Foreign Affairs
Hector Gros Espiell

Ambassador to the U.S.
Eduardo Macgillycuddy

Ambassador to the UN
Felipe Paolillo

Ambassador to the OAS
Didier Operti

Uruguay maintains an embassy in the United States at:
1919 F Street, NW
Washington, D.C. 20006
Tel: (202) 331-1313
Consulates are located in Miami, Los Angeles, and New York.

Flag: Nine horizontal stripes—five white and four blue with a yellow sun in the left corner. The flag was adopted in 1830.

Membership in International Organizations

United Nations and some of its specialized and related agencies; INTELSAT; Latin American Integration Association (ALADI); Organization of American States (OAS); the Antarctic Consultative Group; Latin American Economic System (SELA); the Group of Eight, which is now known as the Group of Rio (informal group of Latin American states which deals with multilateral regional issues).

Defense

The armed forces are constitutionally subordinate to the president through the minister of defense. The approximate size of the armed forces is 19,800 for the army, 5,000 for the navy, and 3,300 for the air force. National defense accounts for 1.4 percent of GDP (1989).

Foreign Relations

Uruguay has strong political and cultural links with the democratic countries of the Americas and Europe. With these countries, it shares basic values, such as support for constitutional democracy, political pluralism, and individual liberties. Its international relations have been historically guided by the principles of nonintervention, respect for national sovereignty, and reliance on the rule of law to settle disputes. The new government has an active international relations program, seeking to find export markets and support for its financial needs.

Uruguay's location between Argentina and Brazil makes close relations with these two larger neighbors particularly desirable.

The three countries have been working closely on integrating their economic systems and improving relations across the spectrum. Uruguay also has been working with Brazil, Argentina, Paraguay, and Bolivia on an economic integration plan whose centerpiece is the development of the River Plate basin as a major shipping and commercial transportation link between the countries of the basin.

Uruguay is a party to the Inter-American Treaty of Reciprocal Assistance, General Agreement on Tariffs and Trade, Latin American Nuclear Free Zone, and River Plate Basin Treaty.

U.S.-Uruguayan Relations

U.S.-Uruguayan relations have traditionally been based on a common outlook and dedication to democratic ideals. Consequently, during the military regime, the United States expressed deep concern for human rights there and welcomed Uruguay's return to democracy.

Uruguay is cooperating with U.S. regional efforts to reduce drug trafficking, which is increasing there, and to limit the exploitation of Uruguay's strict bank secrecy regulation for money-laundering purposes.

The Uruguayan government places a high priority on debt renegotiation, and Uruguay has set an exemplary record of full compliance in its debt principal and interest payments. It works with the United States bilaterally and in international trade liberalization to foster economic and political cooperation and to improve regional cooperation.

While agreeing with U.S. policies to promote democracy, Uruguay sometimes differs on how this should be accomplished. This is particularly evident concerning U.S. policies in Latin America, where Uruguay is influenced by its aspirations for Latin solidarity and integration.

Trade

Exports $1.6 billion (FOB 1989): meat, wool, hides, leather and wool products, fish, rice, furs.

Major markets: U.S. 11%; EC 23%; Germany 8%; ALADI 37% (Argentina 5%, Brazil 28%).

Imports $1.2 billion (CIF 1989): fuels, chemicals, machinery, metals.

Major suppliers: U.S. 10%; EC 19.2%; Germany 6%; ALADI 51% (Argentina 16%, Brazil 26%).

Trade and Investment Policies

Certain imports require special licenses or customs documents. Among them are drugs, certain medical equipment and chemicals, firearms, radioactive materials, fertilizers, vegetable materials, frozen embryos, livestock, bull semen, anabolics, sugar, seeds, hormones, meat, and vehicles. To protect Uruguay's important livestock industry, imports of bull semen and embryos also face certain numerical limitations and must comply with animal health requirements, a process which can take years. In the case of automobiles, the enforcement of local content requirements makes the final price of an imported vehicle very high. Bureaucratic delays also add to the cost of imports, although importers report that a "debureaucratization" commission has improved matters.

The Uruguayan government maintains a legal monopoly in most aspects of the insurance industry, but few significant restrictions exist in other services. U.S. banks continue to be very active in off-shore banking. There are no significant restrictions on professional services such as law, medicine, or accounting. Similarly, travel and ticketing services are unrestricted. A new civil aviation agreement has provided equal treatment for foreign carriers.

There have been significant limitations on foreign equity participation in certain sectors of the economy. Investment in areas regarded as strategic require government authorization. These include electricity, hydrocarbons, banking and finance, railroads, strategic minerals, telecommunications, and the press. Uruguay has long owned and operated state monopolies in petroleum, rail freight, telephone service, and port administration. It has extensive holdings in other key areas, including fishing, free zones, and air transport. However, under legislation passed in September 1991, private investment is allowed in telecommunications, rail services, air transport, and electricity. Other pending legislation will allow privatization of port operations and possibly insurance.

Government procurement practices are well-defined, transparent, and closely followed. Tenders are generally open to all bidders, foreign or domestic. A government decree, however, establishes that in conditions of equal quality or adequacy to the function, domestic products will have preference over foreign ones. Among foreign bidders, preference will be given to those who offer to purchase Uruguayan products. The government favors local bidders even if their price is up to 10 percent higher.

Following a recent reduction in the top rate, Uruguay's tariff structure now varies between 0 and 30 percent. The only exemptions to tariff regulations, in the context of antidumping legislation, are reference prices and minimum export prices, fixed in relation to international levels and in line with commitments assumed under GATT.

These are applied to neutralize unfair trade practices which threaten to damage national production activity or delay the development of such activities. They are primarily directed at Argentina and Brazil.

Export Subsidies Policies

The government had provided a 12 percent subsidy to wool fabric and apparel using funds from a tax on greasy and washed wool exports. This subsidy was reduced progressively to 6 percent in 1992.

Uruguay is a signatory of the GATT Subsidies Code.

FINANCING AND CAPITAL MARKETS

General Policy Framework

Uruguay has a small, relatively open economy. The historical basis of the economy has been agriculture, particularly livestock production.

Agriculture remains important both directly (wool and rice) and indirectly for inputs for other sectors (textiles, leather, and meat). Industry is now the largest sector and has diversified beyond agro-industry into chemicals and consumer goods for local consumption. Services have assumed greater importance recently, particularly tourism and financial services which benefit from Uruguay's open financial system.

The government has been relatively successful in reducing its fiscal deficit from 6.1 percent in 1989 to under 2 percent in 1990 and 1991.

Principal sources of the deficit are losses by the Central Bank on nonperforming loans purchased from private banks, foreign debt payments, and transfers to the social security system. Inflation peaked at 129 percent in 1990, and was expected to fall to 90 percent in 1991.

Seeking to reverse a long-term economic deterioration and prepare itself for the formation of the Southern Common Market (MERCOSUR) being formed by Brazil, Argentina, Uruguay, and Paraguay, the government has started to implement a program of economic reform. Major elements of this program are partial privatization of state enterprises, financial sector reform, and reform of the costly social security system.

Uruguay is the beneficiary of large inflows of capital, principally from neighboring Brazil and Argentina. The government has been able to finance a substantial portion of its deficit through the issuance of dollar-denominated treasury bills.

Debt Management Policies

Uruguay is a heavily indebted middle-income country with a strong commitment to servicing its debt obligations. As of March 1991, its total external debt was $7.149 billion. Of this amount, approximately one billion dollars was owed by the public sector to foreign commercial bank creditors. Of the remainder, $2.365 billion are foreign currency deposits of nonresidents (mostly Argentines). Dollar-denominated Uruguayan government bills and bonds make up $1.359 billion, $910 million is owed to international financial institutions, and the balance of $942 million is mostly commercial credits. Total debt service in 1990 was $784 million, equivalent to 46.3 percent of total merchandise exports; 33 percent of combined merchandise and service exports and 9.5 percent of GDP.

Uruguay has always sought cooperative solutions to its debt problems, and has never defaulted, preferring instead to reach agreement with its creditors. The government and its commercial bank creditors signed a Brady Plan debt reduction agreement in January 1991, which resulted in a $634 million dollar buyback of commercial bank debt. A stand-by agreement negotiated with the International Monetary Fund in 1990 was suspended because Uruguay failed to meet its IMF targets.

Exchange Rate Policies

The Uruguayan government is committed to a floating exchange rate, but has intervened extensively in the market by buying dollars and selling pesos in an attempt to maintain some degree of competitiveness for its exports. However, in 1991, devaluation lagged well behind inflation, making dollars cheaper and improving the prospects for U.S. exports.

Uruguay has no foreign exchange controls. The peso is freely convertible into dollars for any transaction.

Tapping Multilateral Aid

Economic aid received: IBRD $693 million (to June 1988); IFC $35 million (to June 1988); IDB $716 million (1966–88); U.S. $205 million (FY 1946–88). Military aid $67 million (1950–87).

Financial Market Operations and Structural Policies

Price controls are limited to a small set of products and services for public consumption such as bread, milk, passenger transportation, utilities, and fuels. The government relies heavily on consumption taxes (value-added and excise) and taxes on foreign trade (export taxes and tariffs) for its general revenues. A substantial social security tax, sometimes equal to 50 percent of the base wage rate, is assessed on workers and employers. The top tariff rate was lowered from 40 percent to 30 percent in September 1991. This should have a positive effect on U.S. exports.

Imported fertilizers are charged a 12 percent value-added tax which is not charged on locally produced fertilizers.

VISITING AND LOCATING

Climate and clothing: Seasonal clothing, as in the U.S., is recommended. Although the temperature seldom drops below freezing and snow is rare, warm clothing is essential in winter months (June–August). Rainwear is useful.

Customs: No visa is required for a visit of less than 90 days. No inoculations are required. There are no currency restrictions.

Health: No particular health risks exist. Food handling and sanitation standards are relatively high, and the water supply is well maintained. Montevideo has several good private hospitals and many well-trained doctors.

Telecommunications: International telephone and telegraph service is efficient, although delays may be encountered; however, the local telephone network is overburdened. International telegraph-telex systems are available. Uruguay is two time zones ahead of eastern standard time.

Transportation: Several airlines have frequent service to Montevideo's Carrasco International Airport from the U.S., Europe, and other parts of Latin America. Internal transportation is mainly by car or bus; air service is available to a number of towns in the interior; there is no passenger railway service. Within Montevideo, bus service is inexpensive. Taxi service is reasonably priced, good, and readily available. Main roads are good, and secondary roads are adequate.

Holidays:
January 6—Three Kings' Day
April 19—Landing of the 33
May 1—Labor Day
May 18—Battle of Las Piedras
June 19—Artigas' Birthday
July 18—Constitution Day
August 25—Independence Day
October 12—Columbus Day
November 2—Memorial Day

Chapter 20

VENEZUELA

	Total	Urban	
Population (1993)	21,170,000	83.0%	

Main Urban Areas	Population	Percentage of Total	International Calling Code
Maracaibo	1,330,000	6.3	58-61
CARACAS	1,276,000	6.0	58-2
Valencia	1,181,000	5.6	58-41
Maracay	891,000	4.2	58-43
Barquisimeto	741,000	3.5	58-51
Ciudad Guayana	510,000	2.4	58-68
San Cristobal	347,000	1.6	58-76
Ciudad Bolivar	268,000	1.3	58-85
Maturin	261,000	1.2	58-91
Merida	259,000	1.2	58-74
Cumana	255,000	1.2	58-93
Barcelona	237,000	1.1	58-81
Cabimas	217,000	1.0	58-64

Land Area	882,050 square kilometers
Comparable U.S. State	Slightly more than twice California
Language	Spanish 97%
	Amerindian 1%
	Other 2%
Common Business Language	Spanish, English
Currency	1 bolivar (Bs) = 100 centimos
Exchange Rate (May 1993)	U.S. $1.00 = 86.24 bolivars
Best Nonstop Air Connection via U.S.	Miami to Caracas: 3.5 hours
	New York to Caracas: 5.5 hours
	American Airlines (800) 433-7300
	Two nonstops daily
Best Hotel	Sheraton Macuto Resort (U.S. $210)
	P.O. Box 65
	Urb La Guaira
	Tel: (58-31) 944-300
	(800) 334-8484
	Fax: (58-31) 944-318

INTRODUCTION AND REGIONAL ORIENTATION

Coming off of the hemisphere's highest real growth rate of 10.4 percent in 1991, Venezuela was rocked by an attempted military coup on February 4, 1992, and was shaken by political events which followed. Despite the heightened political uncertainty, the economy remained resilient and was expected to record solid real economic growth in 1992. Most importantly, except for minor modifications at the margins, the economic reform program remains intact.

In 1991, the government recorded a fiscal surplus equivalent to 0.7 percent of GDP for the consolidated public sector. The drop in international oil prices, however, contributed to an expected fiscal deficit equivalent to 3 to 5 percent of GDP in 1992. The Central Bank has moved aggressively to control bolivar liquidity. Interest rates were positive and M-2 remained about the same over the first six months of 1992.

Venezuela recorded an overall balance of payments surplus of U.S. $3.3 billion in 1991 but an overall deficit of about U.S. $1.0 billion was expected in 1992 because of lower oil prices and recent political events.

For U.S. exporters, Venezuela remains a significant market. It ranks behind Mexico and Brazil as the third largest in Latin America. The outlook for the export of U.S. goods and services into Venezuela remains quite positive. In 1991, U.S. exports totaled U.S. $4.6 billion; moreover, for the first two quarters of 1992, U.S. exports reached U.S. $2.7 billion, an increase of 22 percent over the same period of 1991.

CRACKING THE MARKET

Demographics

Ethnic composition: Mestizo 67%, white 21%, black 10%, Indian 2%.

Religion: Nominally Roman Catholic 96%, Protestant 2%.

Language: Spanish (official); Indian dialects spoken by about 200,000 Amerindians in the remote interior.

Literacy: 88% age 15 and over can read and write (1981 estimate).

Labor force: 5,800,000; services 56%, industry 28%, agriculture 16% (1985).

Organized labor: 32% of labor force.

National budget: revenues $8.4 billion; expenditures $8.6 billion, including capital expenditures of $5.9 billion (1989).

Economy

Domestic real economy: The Venezuelan economy continues to register strong positive real rates of growth. Following the 1989 recession, real GDP expanded by 6.5 percent in 1990 and 10.4 percent in 1991, the highest in the hemisphere. The strong 1991 performance was led by the petroleum sector, which grew by 10.3 percent in real terms. The nonpetroleum sector increased by 8.5 percent; sectors with dramatic expansion were construction with 30.8 percent, and commerce with 7.9 percent.

According to preliminary data, strong real growth continued through the first quarter of 1992, when GDP surged by about 10 percent as compared to the same period of 1991. That strong GDP growth stemmed from public sector investment chiefly in the petrochemical and energy sectors and expansion of aggregate demand due in large part to increases in the minimum wage and public sector salaries. Senior government officials estimate 1992 real growth at about 5 percent; however, private economists' forecasts range from about 2–6 percent. Given the strong first quarter performance and the buoyancy exhibited by some sectors, 1992 real growth was expected to reach the 4–6 percent range.

Fiscal policy and taxation: Since the initiation of the economic reform program in 1989, the government has made progress with its fiscal accounts.

But, fiscal equilibrium has not yet been achieved. In 1991, a fiscal surplus equivalent to 0.7 percent of GDP was recorded for the consolidated public sector. This result was due neither to fiscal restraint, nor enhanced tax collections, but largely to a large inflow of privatization revenues. The outlook for 1992 was not as favorable, however. It was widely anticipated that the government would record a deficit. Senior officials estimated the deficit at about 3 percent of GDP. This estimate may have been slightly low. The Treasury, in conjunction with the Central Bank which is acting as its financial agent, was selling 40 billion bolivares in short-term instruments to finance its temporary cash imbalances. Final fiscal results would depend on several factors, including the government's ability to find and implement cuts in the PDVSA budget, to pass legislation raising additional revenues, and to implement spending cuts proposed by President Perez on August 23, 1992.

The government remains very dependent on the petroleum sector for tax revenues. Petroleum provides about 82 percent of total revenues while income tax generates only a small share. Personal and corporate income taxes represented almost 5.5 percent of total current revenues in 1991.

The administration has proposed several new taxes, including a value-added tax (VAT) and a tax on business assets. Deliberations are underway with the Congress. The VAT is an element of Venezuela's Extended Fund Facility (EFF) with the International Monetary Fund (IMF).

Reliance on the petroleum sector to finance the public sector burdens the state oil company PDVSA at a moment when it is embarking on a major investment program. Joint ventures with PDVSA for the develop-ment and refining of heavy and extra-heavy crudes and the development and processing of unassociated natural gas are excluded from the special 67.7 percent tax applied to oil companies and are subject to the 30 percent corporate tax rate. Moreover, they are subject to the export reference value (ERV), which is the amount by which export revenues are inflated for tax calculation purposes. Until recently, the ERV was set at 20 percent; this meant that U.S. $100 of oil exports had been taxed at U.S. $120. (In May, the government decided to reduce gradually the ERV by cutting it to 19 percent on June 1, 1992 and to 18 percent as of October 1, 1992.)

The Central Bank maintains a unified, freely floating exchange rate; however, in practice, it is a managed float. To moderate depreciation of the bolivar after the coup attempt, the Central Bank has absorbed bolivar liquidity and, at times, has sold dollars heavily. In the first seven months of 1992, the bolivar has fallen 8.5 percent against the dollar.

Although progress has been made, inflation remains stubbornly high. Prices (year-end to year-end) increased 36 percent in 1990—a sharp decline from the 81 percent recorded in 1989. The downward trend continues. Inflation was 31 percent in 1991. Over the first seven months of 1992, prices rose 18.5 percent. Inflation was expected to be about the same as 1991; however, price performance in the next few months would have determined whether or not the government's economic measures were able to prevent 1992 inflation from exceeding that recorded in 1991. Except for a basic basket (public sector transportation, sardines, and basic medicines), price controls have been eliminated. In early March of 1992, in his response to the attempted coup and political events, President Perez suspended planned gasoline price hikes, froze electrical utility rates temporarily, and imposed a temporary price "stabilization" scheme on basic foodstuffs.

Stock market: The Caracas Stock Exchange, which recorded substantial gains over the past two years, has slumped following the attempted coup. The broad market index which climbed by 64 percent in 1991 fell by 10 percent during the first two quarters of 1992. Market valuation has fallen from U.S. $12.3 billion in February to U.S. $10.4 billion at the end of July. Several private sector firms trade their shares as American Depository Receipts (ADRs) in New York and Global Depository Shares in several markets.

Despite the attempted coup in 1992, several key sectors have performed well, recording growth rates of between 10–20 percent. For example, the appliance sector is having a record year due in part to an increase in residential construction and the 10-year cycle of replacement of old equipment. Construction, which clipped along at 20 percent growth through March, dipped in April and May, but has regained its earlier momentum in recent months. Spurred by the new domestic automobile policy to allow the imports of new vehicles at reduced tariff rates, this industry estimates sales of over 128,000 units this year with imports accounting for one-fourth of the total. Since April, monthly sales have climbed over 20 percent.

Telecommunications Sector Strong

Because of privatization of the national telephone company, the telecommunications sector has grown substantially. The government of Venezuela has granted several concessions, all of which have involved U.S. participation and/or equipment. Other sectors which have experienced strong growth or have recently shown an upward trend

include advertising, processed food, and pharmaceuticals.

Tourism—Rough Sledding

Because of the coup attempt, tourism has suffered; however, business travel was expected to run 6 to 8 percent above 1992 due to continued economic liberalization. Another sector experiencing a slowdown is engineering services, hard hit by an 11 percent reduction in the expansion plans of Petroleos de Venezuela, S.A. (PDVSA), the national oil company.

Petroleum Sector Is Supreme

The country's economic future relies heavily on the rapid expansion of its oil sector, which requires substantial investments during this decade.

Some economists predict that even if Congress passes value-added and asset taxes, Venezuela will be hard pressed to cover its 1992 deficit, estimated at about 5 percent GDP. Added to that concern is a rise in inflation, originally estimated to run between 25–30 percent. This development, coupled with a currency which is considered overvalued by as much as 11 percent, could lead the government to carry out a sudden, large devaluation of the Bolivar, a measure it has taken in the past in order to close the fiscal deficit.

Political/Institutional Infrastructure

Administrative divisions: 20 states, 2 territories, 1 federal district, and 1 federal dependence; note—the federal dependence consists of 11 federally controlled island groups with a total of 72 individual islands.

Independence: July 5, 1811, from Spain.
Constitution: January 23, 1961.

Legal system: Based on Napoleonic code; judicial review of legislative acts in

VENEZUELA
Key Economic Indicators

	1990	1991	1992	1993
Domestic Economy				
GDP (U.S. $ billion)	48.3	53.4	58.6	
GDP projected average growth rate through 1993:	6.5	10.4	5.0	5.0
GDP per capita (U.S. $)	2,485	2,686	2,923	
Government spending as % of GNP	0.2	0.7	(3.0)	
Inflation	36.5	31.0	31.0	
Unemployment	9.9	8.7	8.6	
Foreign exchange reserves (U.S. $1 billion)	11.8	14.1	13.1	
Average exchange rate (U.S. $=)[1]	47.2	56.9	68.4	
Foreign debt (U.S. $ billion)[2]	25.7	26.8	28.9	
Debt service ratio (ratio of principal and interest payment on foreign debt to foreign income)	23.5	20.1	19.5	
U.S. economic assistance (no aid)				
U.S. military assistance			0.6	
Minimum monthly wage rate (Bs)	4,000	6,000	9,000	

Sources: U.S. Department of Commerce, Banco Central de Venezuela, International Monetary Fund, CORDIPLAN, VenEconomy estimates.

1. Annual average
2. Public sector

Cassation Court only; has not accepted compulsory ICJ jurisdiction.

National holiday: Independence Day, July 5 (1811).

Executive branch: president, Council of Ministers (cabinet).

Legislative branch: Bicameral Congress of the Republic (Congreso de la Republica) consists of an upper chamber or Senate (Senado) and a lower chamber or Chamber of Deputies (Camara de Diputados).

Judicial branch: Supreme Court of Justice (Corte Suprema de Justica).

Principal Government Officials

Chief of State and Head of Government—

President

Carlos Andres PEREZ
(since February 2, 1989)

Political parties and leaders: Social Christian Party (COPEI), Eduardo FERNANDEZ, secretary general; Democratic Action (AD), Gonzalo BARRIOS, president, and Humberto CELLI, secretary general; Movement Toward Socialism (MAS), Argelia LAYA, president, and Freddy MUNOZ, secretary general.

Suffrage: universal and compulsory at age 18, though poorly enforced.

Elections: President—last held December 4, 1988 (next to be held December 1993); results—Carlos Andres PEREZ

VENEZUELA
Key Economic Indicators

	1989	1990	1991[1]	% Chg 90–91
National Income (Bs millions)*				
GDP at current prices	1,510,361	2,279,261	3,036,275	33.2
GDP at 1984 prices	449,262	478,320	527,927	10.4
Disposable national income	1,333,354	2,114,699	2,749,109	30.0
Central government surplus/deficit (–)	−14,783	−47,387	83,479	
Public sector surplus/deficit (–)	−16,543	3,660	19,741	
Net domestic investment	147,697	164,107	300,591	83.2
Investment rate (% of GDP)	9.8	7.2	9.9	
Population and labor (000)				
Population	18,972	19,429	19,890	2.4
Labor force	6,901	7,081	7,418	4.8
Total employment	6,239	6,379	6,769	6.1
Unemployment rate (%)	9.6	9.9	8.7	
Production				
Petroleum/LNG/condensates (000 b/d)	2,015	2,249	2,492	10.8
Aluminum (000 MT)	1,826	1,951	1,974	1.2
Steel finished products (000 MT)	462	454	448	−1.3
Cement (000 MT)	5,259	5,996	6,326	5.5
Motor vehicle sales (000 units)	28	43	71	65.1
Petrochemicals (000 MT)	2,546	2,917	3,124	7.1
Money and prices (End of period)				
Money supply M2	463,816	746,477	1,116,103	49.5
Public external debt ($ millions)	26,427	25,671	26,821	4.5
Public domestic debt (Bs millions)	126,396	155,796	267,151	71.5
Bank lending rate (annual average)	34.1	34.9	37.7	8.0
Consumer price index (1984=100)	454.5	620.3	812.7	31.0
Caracas Stock Exc. Ind. (1971=100)	2,767.9	17,937.6	29,316.6	63.4
Exchange rate (Bs/$)	43.1	50.6	61.7	21.9
Balance of payments ($ millions)				
Merchandise imports (FOB)	7,283	6,807	10,101	48.4
Merchandise exports (FOB)	12,915	17,444	14,892	−14.6
Petroleum exports	9,862	13,912	12,122	−12.9
Merchandise trade balance	5,632	10,637	4,791	−55.0
Current account balance	2,161	8,279	1,663	−79.9
Current-capital account balance	−1,055	3,225	3,327	3.2
Central Bank reserves (Dec 31)	7,411	11,759	14,105	20.0
U.S.-Venezuela Trade ($ millions)				
U.S. exports to Venezuela (FAS)	3,025	3,107	4,668	50.4
U.S. imports from Venezuela (C.V.)[2]	6,771	9,446	8,228	−13.9
U.S. (%) share of Venezuelan exports	52.4	54.2	55.3	
U.S. (%) share of Venezuelan imports	41.5	45.6	46.2	

*Local currency (Bolivares = Bs)

1. Preliminary figures   2. Customs value

(AD) 54.6%, Eduardo FERNANDEZ (COPEI) 41.7%, other 3.7%.

Senate—last held December 4, 1988 (next to be held December 1993); results—percent of vote by party NA; seats—(49 total) AD 23, COPEI 22, other 4; note—three former presidents (one from AD, two from COPEI) hold lifetime senate seats.

Chamber of Deputies—last held December 4, 1988 (next to be held December 1993); results—AD 43.7%, COPEI 31.4%, MAS 10.3%, other 14.6%; seats—(201 total) AD 97, COPEI 67, MAS 18, other 19.

Communists: 10,000 members (1992 estimate).

Other political or pressure groups: FEDECAMARAS, a conservative business group; Venezuelan Confederation of Workers, the Democratic Action-dominated labor organization.

Flag: three equal horizontal bands of yellow (top), blue, and red with the coat of arms on the hoist side of the yellow band and an arc of seven white five-pointed stars centered in the blue band.

Diplomatic Representation

Ambassador to U.S.: Simon Alberto CONSALVI Bottaro
Chancery at:
    2445 Massachusetts Avenue, NW
    Washington, D.C. 20008
    Tel: (202)797-3800
There are Venezuelan Consulates General in Baltimore, Boston, Chicago, Houston, Miami, New Orleans, New York, Philadelphia, San Francisco, and San Juan (Puerto Rico).

Defense

Branches: Ground Forces (Army), Naval Forces (including Navy, Marines, Coast Guard), Air Forces, Armed Forces of Cooperation (National Guard).

Manpower availability: males 15–49,

5,220,183; 3,782,548 fit for military service; 216,132 reach military age (18) annually.

Defense expenditures: $1.9 billion, 4.3% of GDP (1991).

Trade

Main U.S. exports (1991): machinery, transport equipment, auto parts, chemicals, wheat, feed grains. Main U.S. imports (1991): crude oil/products, aluminum, steel products, iron ore, cement, shellfish, tuna, coffee. (Sources: Central Bank of Venezuela, VenEconomy, Metroeconomica, U.S. Department of Commerce.)

Major export partners (1989): U.S. 50.7%; Europe 13.7%; Japan 4.0%.

Main import commodities (1989): foodstuffs, chemicals, manufactures, machinery, and transport equipment.

Major import suppliers (1989): U.S. 44%; Germany 8.0%; Japan 4%; Italy 7%; Canada 2%.

Table 20-1 further details the trade flows between Venezuela and the U.S.

Implications for U.S. Trade

The Venezuelan economic reforms which began in March 1989 are transforming Venezuela from a traditionally state-dominated, oil-driven economy, towards a market-oriented, diversified, and export-oriented economy. The outlook for the near future is a positive one, which offers continued opportunities for increased U.S. trade and investments.

Substantial trade and investment reforms have been implemented by the government of Venezuela since 1989. Some of the new reforms are:

- Quantitative import restrictions have been virtually eliminated on nonagricultural goods and there are fewer restrictions on agricultural commodities.

- Tariffs are being reduced and simplified. Most rates are already below 20 percent,

Table 20-1
VENEZUELA
Trade Flows
(U.S. $ billions)

	1990	1991	1992
Total exports (FAS $ billion)	14.7	14.9	13.3
Total imports (FAS $ billion)	6.8	10.1	11.0
Exports to U.S. (customs value U.S. $ billion)	9.5	8.2	6.9
Imports from U.S. (FAS U.S. $ billion)	3.1	4.7	4.8
U.S. share Venezuelan imports (%)	45	46	44
Imports of manufactured goods			
Total (from all countries) (FOB U.S. $ billion)	5.3	7.9	8.6
Projected average growth rate through 1994—3%			
From the U.S.			
Projected average growth rate through 1994—3%			
U.S. share of manufactured imports (%)	50	49	47
Venezuela's trade balances with three leading trading partners in 1991 (U.S. $ billion)			
U.S.	6.1	3.2	1.9
Canada	.3	.3	.2
Germany	.1	.2	.2

Principal U.S. exports: oil and gas machinery (7300), transport equipment (8703–4), auto parts (8708), chemicals (3800), wheat and feed grains (1000–1).

Principal U.S. imports: crude oil and petroleum products (2709–10), aluminum (7601), steel products (7200), iron ore and other ores (2601).

e.g., capital goods pay a tariff of 0–10 percent (if not produced in Venezuela).

- Foreign investors can now have a 100 percent ownership in most types of enterprises as a result of government decree 727, and later by decree 2095.

- Restrictions on remittances of interest, dividends, and capital were eliminated.

Promising business opportunities for U.S. investment and trade are offered as Venezuela moves forward in its efforts to privatize over 70 state-owned enterprises such as banks, cement companies, agrobusiness firms, hotels and ports.

Some of the best prospects for U.S. exporters to Venezuela are:

- Oil and gas filled machine and equipment/services

- Telecommunication equipment

- Computer and peripherals

- Medical equipment

- Security and safety

Trade and Investment Policies

The manufacturing sector continued to recover from the 1989 recession and grew at 5.4 percent in real terms in 1991, which was slightly higher than 1990's 4.9 percent. The industrial capacity utilization rate climbed through 1991. Industrial employment expanded by 104,000 jobs in 1991, an increase of 10.3 percent over 1990. Performance between sectors has varied. Sales of cement, major appliances, and motor vehicles have risen while others, e.g., aluminum, have remained flat.

Both tariff and nontariff barriers have been reduced significantly over the past two-and-a-half years, as a result of the government's economic liberalization program and GATT entry process. Areas which still need to be addressed are:

Venezuela recently revised its tariff schedule, and in fact exceeded its GATT commitments by directly implementing the Andean Pact Common External tariff which has a maximum tariff of 20 percent. One exception is on automobiles where all new vehicles are taxed at 25 percent. If a vehicle exceeds $15,000, an additional 60 percent surcharge on the 25 percent tariff is also paid. The import of used vehicles is still prohibited.

Venezuela has indicated plans to improve protection for intellectual property (IPR) through implementation of Andean Pact Decision 313 and passage of an improved copyright law.

The preparatory work has been completed so that negotiations can now begin on a Venezuelan-United States bilateral subsidies agreement. Key issues to be discussed during the negotiations include whether the government of Venezuela is still providing illegal export subsidies. Venezuela wants to receive the injury test back as a result of a successful agreement.

The Venezuelan government plans to establish internationally accepted product standards, and a supporting measures capability to enhance industrial quality control and economic competitiveness. Inappropriate product standards could become a nontariff barrier to U.S. products.

Import license requirements: Import license requirements have been reduced pursuant to the government's reform program. Only poultry, pork, feed grains, soybean meal, sugar, and milk are currently subject to import license requirements. Poultry, pork, and feed grains were scheduled for liberalization in January 1992. Import prohibitions have been removed from some agricultural products.

Sanitary certificates from the Ministries of Health and Agriculture and from the country of origin are required to import certain agricultural products and pharmaceuticals. In August 1990, the government imposed a requirement for sanitary certificates from the country of origin on 203 agricultural items for which certificates had not previously been required, and for which the U.S. government issues no sanitary certificates. However, the Venezuelan customs authorities have been accepting state or federal certification that the United States does not issue sanitary certificates for these items.

Service barriers: Foreign equity investment in banking, insurance, guard and security services, television, radio, Spanish language newspapers, and all professional services subject to licensing, is limited to 20 percent. A comprehensive package to reform the financial sector was introduced in the Congress in July 1991. The proposed legislation would allow foreign firms to enter the banking and insurance/reinsurance sectors. Foreign financial institutions would be permitted to open fully owned branches and to acquire an equity position in existing domestic institutions. Full national treatment would be phased in gradually.

A U.S.-Venezuela maritime agreement in October 1991 eased terms of certain cargo preference requirements in the bilateral trades and will encourage more competitive service.

Investment barriers: In January 1990, the Venezuelan government issued Executive Decree 727, liberalizing foreign investment rules. The decree allows total foreign ownership of companies engaged in retail sales, telecommunications, and water and sewage services (all formerly reserved to national companies) and eliminates barriers to dividend and capital repatriation. The decree strips the Superintendency for Foreign Investment (SIEX) of discretionary authority in registering foreign investment. Foreign companies may establish branches without prior approval from SIEX. Prior approval by SIEX for trademark and patent licenses, distribution agreements, technical know-how, and technical assistance agreements has also been eliminated. Only royalties in excess of 5 percent which are paid by a foreign company to its foreign parent require prior approval by SIEX.

In the petroleum sector, the exploration, exploitation, refining, transportation, storage, and foreign and domestic sales of hydrocarbons are reserved to the Venezuelan government or to its entities. When in the public interest, the government may enter into agreements with private companies as long as the agreements guarantee state control of the operation, are of limited duration, and have the previous authorization of the legislature meeting in joint session.

Local content requirements: Pursuant to Executive Decree 1095, published September 4, 1990, auto assemblers and parts manufacturers must meet a percentage foreign exchange contribution, intended to offset foreign exchange spent on imports, by fulfilling a combination of local content and export requirements. Companies which fail to meet established norms are fined. The new policy removes the requirements that specified parts be incorporated in the vehicle, and that motors be assembled in the country.

Government procurement practices: A new government Contract Law was passed by the Congress on July 20, 1990. The government of Venezuela may procure goods and services in three ways: (1) for goods and services estimated to cost over 10 million bolivars, and construction works estimated to cost more than 30 million bolivars, general tender is required (Article 29); (2) for goods and services estimated to cost between one million and 10 million bolivars, and for construction works estimated to cost between 10 and 30 million bolivars, and where the national registry certifies that there are no more than 10 companies technically and financially qualified to provide the goods or perform the service or construction, then a selective tender process may be used (Article 32); (3) for goods and services estimated to cost less than one million bolivars, the contract may be awarded directly (Article 33).

Trade Financing Environment and Options

Recent U.S. countervailing duty investigations have determined that in the case of certain specific products, some Venezuelan government programs, which included preferential input pricing, short-term financing by Finexpo (the Central Bank Export Financing Agency), interest-free loans, and an export bonus, effectively conferred subsidies on these products. The Venezuelan government has replaced the export bonus for manufactured products with a so-called duty drawback scheme. The organic customs law provides for full or partial rebate of import taxes paid on an exported product. On May 20, 1991, the Venezuelan government published Executive Decree 780, implementing the partial duty drawback. It provides for rebates equivalent to 2 percent of the FOB value of exports through the special suspended duty regimes, such as the temporary admissions program (maquila), stock replenishment program, or customs warehousing program. It also provides for a rebate of 5 percent of the FOB value of all other exports. Agricultural products continue to be covered under the export bond program. The government has said that it intends to phase out the partial rebate.

Decree 1597 dated June 13, 1991, provides for a bond of 10 percent (formerly 6 percent) for exports of agricultural products.

Finexpo, the Central Bank's export financing arm, increased the interest rates on its loans in December 1990. The rate of interest is 90 percent of the average national rate of interest measured by the operations of Venezuela's principal commercial banks. Dollar loans are issued at London Interbank Offer Rate (LIBOR) plus 1 percent. Interest on financing for foreign importers of Venezuelan goods is the rate charged by the Inter-American Development Bank (IDB) plus a 1 percent handling fee. Venezuela has not yet signed the GATT subsidies code which would require broad elimination of export subsidies.

APPROACHING THE MARKET

The economic reforms initiated in 1989 have stripped away many of the barriers to trade and investment. Venezuela allows 100 percent foreign equity participation in many activities and grants foreign investors the same rights as local investors, except in those areas reserved for national companies as expressly provided for in legislation. Sectors reserved and/or restricted by law in one form or another include hydrocarbons, steel, aluminum, iron ore, coal, banking and insurance, media, and professional services (e.g.,

legal, accounting, architecture, engineering, consulting/management services).

Foreigners may buy shares in national or mixed companies and purchase shares on the stock market; unrestricted freedom to remit earnings, dividends, and capital abroad is also authorized. Intangible technological contributions are accepted as direct foreign investments, and the payment of royalties from a subsidiary to its parent is allowed without limit. Foreign company registration has been greatly simplified—prior approval to invest is no longer required, although foreign investors must register their investments with the Superintendency of Foreign Investment (SIEX) or the Ministry of Energy and Mines (MINISIEX) in the case of mining ventures.

Foreign investors may export their products to other Andean Pact member countries with the benefit of liberated tariffs.

Venezuela has significantly liberalized its trade regime by eliminating most quantitative restrictions, abolishing import licensing requirements, and lowering tariffs. In early 1992, Venezuela lowered the tariff ceiling to 20 percent (down from 40 percent) with few exceptions, notably new passenger cars which bear a duty of 25 percent. (Note: Passenger car imports valued over $15,000 are also assessed a 60 percent surcharge of the payable duty.) The average import tariff is approximately 9 percent. Payments for trade transactions are unrestricted and can be made through the free exchange market at current rates. Multiple exchange rates and exchange permits have been eliminated. Due to these sweeping economic reforms, foreign traders from all over the world have swarmed to Venezuela in the past few years. Although many have been anxious to succeed quickly, those who have achieved success have approached the market carefully and taken time to secure sound legal advice locally and a bona fide agent, distributor, or joint venture partner.

In many fields, such as suppliers to the oil and gas industry, minerals and metallurgy, tourism, and a host of others, identifying a joint venture partner who knows the workings of local industry is very important.

In searching for an agent or distributor, it is useful to keep in mind that few Venezuelan businessmen touch a project unless they can earn at least 100 percent, and markups of 400 percent are not unknown. An agent usually operates on a commission basis, typically ranging from 5–30 percent. These can be higher if the agent is expected to provide services to the end-user. Contracts for agents and distributors should be written in Spanish and signed by an attorney to indicate that they comply with Venezuelan law.

Exporters should ensure in the contract that the agent or distributor is not placed on one's payroll since this person would then be entitled to several benefits under the Venezuelan labor law.

Although financing is covered in another section, it should be noted here that letters of credit, confirmed by a U.S. or Venezuelan bank, are the most common form of payment for import transactions. Venezuelan dealers would rather deal on an open account basis because of the high interest rates associated with letters of credit, but until the dealer is well-known to the exporter, this approach is not recommended.

Establishing a business in Venezuela, although not overly complicated, will require the services of a local law firm. A list of attorneys is available through the U.S. Embassy or the Venezuela Desk Officer at the Department of Commerce. The maximum corporate tax rate is 30 percent, and there is no difference in tax treatment between a fully-owned subsidiary and a joint venture.

The purchase of goods and services by government agencies is ruled by a complex system of laws, presidential decrees, regulations, and other policies. Venezuelan government officials are not permitted to conduct business in any language other than Spanish. The tendering process, both for government and the private sector, is relatively transparent, with some totally open and others by invitation only.

A major concern of most companies dealing in Venezuela is the lack of intellectual and industrial property protection. Although the Andean Pact version of patent and trademark protection (Decision 313) has been published in the government's Official Gazette, it falls short of world-class standards and controversy surrounds the entire issue, including copyright protection. The Patent and Trademark Office is woefully underfunded and poorly staffed, and enabling legislation for an autonomous office is still required, as is a strong copyright law.

INVESTMENT CLIMATE

New foreign investment continues to flow into Venezuela. According to the Superintendency for Foreign Investment (SIEX), in 1991, new investment totaling U.S. $224.3 million entered Venezuela and brought the stock of registered foreign investment to U.S. $4.1 billion, with about U.S. $2 billion accounted for by U.S. investors. In 1992, through June 30, new foreign investment flows reached U.S. $555 million, which exceeds that of the same period of 1991.

Investment in 1991

Total foreign direct investment: U.S. $4.1 billion.

U.S. direct investment: U.S. $2.0 billion or 50% of total.

Principal foreign investors: U.S.A; United Kingdom; Switzerland.

Privatization: The government has embarked on an ambitious privatization program. Revenues from privatizations totaled about U.S. $2.1 billion in 1991. In December, a private sector consortium, which includes GTE and ATT, acquired 40 percent of the state telephone company, CANTV, for U.S. $1.9 billion. A consortium including Iberia purchased 60 percent of Venezuela's largest state airline, VIASA. Other proposed privatizations include hotels, sugar mills, the Aeropostal Airline, and electrical generation and distribution facilities. With assistance from the World Bank and the Inter-American Development Bank (IDB), the government plans to restructure the national electrical system. The controversial privatization of the Caracas water system received a setback when no qualified bids were submitted. A new privatization law specifies how the government may spend revenues from privatizations; the bulk of revenues is earmarked for social spending with some for payment of Venezuelan external debt.

FINANCING AND CAPITAL MARKETS

General Policy Framework

Venezuela is a major oil producer/exporter and a founding member of OPEC. After nearly three decades of relative economic and political stability, the country has a moderately well-established economic infrastructure, and an impressive potential for economic growth. Major economic resources include petroleum, natural gas, hydroelectric power, iron ore, coal, bauxite, and gold. Venezuela is in the process of modifying its macroeconomic model and economic policies to diversify from depend-

---

Extent of U.S. Investment in Goods-Producing Sectors
U.S. Direct Investment Position Abroad
on a Historical-Cost Basis—1990
(millions of U.S. dollars)

Category		Amount
Petroleum		278
Total manufacturing		963
Food and kindred products	228	
Chemicals and allied products	240	
Metals, primary and fabricated	82	
Machinery, except electrical	−2	
Electric and electronic equipment	83	
Transportation equipment	8	
Other manufacturing	323	
Wholesale trade		155
TOTAL PETROLEUM/MANUFACTURING/WHOLESALE TRADE		1,396

Source: U.S. Department of Commerce, *Survey of Current Business* (August 1991, vol. 71, no. 8, table 11.3).

ence on petroleum exports (although the petroleum sector still dominates the economy) and to develop nontraditional basic export industries such as petrochemicals, aluminum, steel, cement, forestry, manufactured consumer products, and mining (gold, iron ore, bauxite, and coal).

Venezuela encourages foreign investment in most sectors, but foreigners are still largely excluded from the petroleum sector. The bulk of foreign investment is from the United States. The United States is Venezuela's chief trading partner, accounting for 55 percent of Venezuelan exports and 48 percent of its imports in 1990.

The Venezuelan economy has recovered from the 1989 recession. According to preliminary figures, real GDP grew 5.3 percent in 1990, principally driven by a 13.6 percent increase in the oil sector, and was expected to expand by over 9 percent in 1991. The government recorded a small fiscal surplus of about 1 percent for the consolidated public sector in 1990. That performance was due to the Iraq war oil revenue windfall and not fiscal restraint. The government hoped to achieve a surplus equal to 1.3 percent of GDP in 1991.

Monetary policy continues to reflect the fundamental objectives fixed by the government at the beginning of 1989, which are to reduce inflation rates, maintain positive interest rates, and ensure a competitive exchange rate. Monetary liquidity (M2), however, grew 61 percent in nominal terms in 1990 as a result of sharply increased public spending and a rise in international reserves, mainly during the last four months of 1990. The component of the money supply which increased the most was quasi-money because prevailing high interest rates encouraged the public to put its liquidity into savings and time deposits. The expansion of liquidity continued into 1991. For the first six months of the year, M2 grew by 21 percent. At mid-year, however, the Central

Bank undertook a more aggressive program to control liquidity. The Central Bank increased its sale of short-term bills (zero coupon bonds) and announced a gradual increase in the bank reserve requirements, and consequently, M2 grew by only 2 percent in the third quarter.

The government has made much progress in reducing inflation. Prices increased 41 percent in 1990—a sharp decline from the 85 percent jump recorded in 1989. The downward trend is continuing and 1991 inflation was estimated at 31 percent.

Debt Management Policies

In December 1990, the government and the commercial banks closed a deal which reduced the debt and debt service obligations on $19.8 billion within the context of the Brady Plan. The most popular option (32 percent) was a 30-year par bond with a fixed interest rate of 6.75 percent whose principal is backed by U.S. Treasury "zero-coupon" bonds. The second most popular option (31 percent) was a 17-year, new-money bond. The deal enabled the government to reduce principal by $2 billion, reduce interest payments by approximately $470 million per year, raise $1.2 billion in new money, and obtain more favorable repayment terms on the remaining debt.

As of December 1990, Venezuela's public sector external debt totaled $27.1 billion. Medium-term registered private sector debt totaled an additional $3.8 billion. External debt represents almost 70 percent of GDP. Roughly 90 percent of the external debt is owed to commercial banks. In 1990, Venezuela's debt service payments totaled $4.1 billion, or 23.5 percent of total exports.

The government has entered the third year of a three-year Extended Fund Facility with the International Monetary Fund. The World Bank and Inter-American Development Bank are providing multi-year sectoral loans to assist the economic restructuring process.

The Currency and Exchange Rate Mechanisms

The Venezuelan government unified the exchange rate on March 13, 1989. The Central Bank of Venezuela intervenes in the exchange market to correct abrupt fluctuations, but its stated policy is that the exchange rate will remain competitive and be set by market forces. In 1990, the bolivar fell by 17.4 percent against the dollar to close the year at 50.6 bolivars to the dollar. During the January–October 1991 period, the bolivar depreciated 18.9 percent and closed at Bs60.15/U.S. $1.0. (Inflation was 25 percent over the same period.)

The Central Bank's foreign exchange reserves have grown substantially in the past few years. They climbed from $7.4 billion at the end of 1989 to $11.6 billion at the end of 1990 and totaled about $12.5 billion at the end of October 1991. With the advent of exchange unification, prior exchange authorizations and preshipment inspections have been eliminated.

Banking and Other Financial Institutions

The banking system is comprised of 41 commercial banks, of which five are government-owned (and tend to be specialized). The largest commercial banks by asset size are: (1) Banco Provincial; (2) Banco de Venezuela; (3) Banco Latino; (4) Banco Mercantil; (5) Banco Union; (6) Banco Consolidado. All six have international operations by which a customer can send and receive U.S. dollar transfers; all have offshore branches to service L/Cs (letters of credit).

There are approximately 80 foreign banks with either agencies or representative offices in Venezuela. With the exception of Citibank and certain Latin American banks, foreign institutions are not permitted to establish retail branches; however, they can operate as nonbank financial institutions, such as investment banks, leasing companies, or representative offices. (Twelve U.S. banks have representative offices in Venezuela.) Under these conditions, foreign banks cannot take deposits nor give bolivar loans (but can grant loans in dollars). Foreign banks are restricted to an intermediary role between the parties they represent and the companies that are the recipient of the credits granted.

On the whole, Venezuelan banks tend to be very conservative, with strict credit criteria in lending, primarily because of the difficulties experienced in 1983 when the bolivar was drastically devalued. Venezuelan banks are strictly regulated by the Central Bank. Foreign exchange is freely available and there are no restrictions on converting bolivars to dollars.

New banking legislation is pending before the Congress of Venezuela which, as presently drafted, will permit more participation in the local financial sector by foreign banks.

Banking sources indicate that most imports are being financed on 90-day terms, or in cash—even though the supply of short-term trade credits available from the U.S. and other countries' commercial banks exceeds demand. Local banks are very selective about assuming new debt, even short-term. The six largest Venezuelan banks selectively finance imports, usually collateralized. Unfamiliarity with the new floating exchange rate system, and lack of a foreign exchange forward market have contributed to a reluctance on the part of importers to finance by letter of credit (L/C). High interest rates and undercapitalized local banks, along with their clients' diminished financial strength after the severe recession in 1989, have also limited L/C demand. Applications are beginning to increase, however, in line with renewed economic activity and the growing improvement in Venezuela's balance of payments position. Several U.S. money center banks are offering pre-export financing to "select" customers, collateralized by future export receipts.

Tapping International Aid

Economic aid: U.S. commitments, including Ex-Im (FY70–86), $488 million; Communist countries (1970–89), $10 million.

Structural Policies

The Perez administration eliminated price controls on most goods and services early in 1989. Price controls remain in effect on a "basic basket" of goods and services considered of primary necessity. Government producer subsidies have also been reduced.

A major income tax reform designed to lower tax rates and ultimately increase revenues by reducing widespread tax evasion entered into force on September 1, 1991. The maximum tax rate for individuals and corporations fell to 30 percent. Joint ventures with the state oil company, PDVSA, for the development and refining of heavy and extra-heavy crudes and the development and processing of unassociated natural gas are excluded from the special tax of 67.7 percent and, therefore, are subject to the 30 percent rate; however, these two categories are still subject to the export reference value of 20 percent. Foreign corporations operating in Venezuela receive the same tax treatment as Venezuelan firms. In order to stimulate the formation of a "maquiladora" export industry, the government has eliminated taxes and duties on imported goods used in the production of exports. Nonresidents pay a 10 percent tax on hotel rooms and lodging.

The government intends (with congressional approval) to introduce a value-added tax.

In June 1989, the government initiated a multi-year trade liberalization program. Maximum tariff rates were reduced in 1989 from 130 to 80 percent, to 50 percent in 1990, and to 40 percent in 1991. Maximum tariffs were scheduled to be reduced to 30 percent in 1992, and 20 percent in 1993. Customs duty collections were expected to increase because of virtual elimination of tariff exemptions and exonerations. Venezuela acceded to the General Agreement on Trade and Tariffs (GATT) on September 1, 1990.

The government's regime for managing imports through licenses changed dramatically in 1989 and 1990. Overall the entry of imports has been freed considerably; virtually all manufactured products can enter Venezuela without quantitative restrictions. Import licenses are still required on some agricultural items, and a few import prohibitions still exist. Preshipment inspection is no longer required for imported items.

Chapter 21

KEY CONTACTS AND RESOURCES

U.S. DEPARTMENT OF STATE

Key Offices of Foreign Service Posts

The Key Officers Guide lists key officers at Foreign Service posts with whom American business representatives would most likely have contact.

American embassy staff are an invaluable resource to all U.S. companies and individuals operating abroad. In general, they are the best way to get an up-to-the-minute assessment of the "lay of the land"—for example, what impact will the elections have on commercial dealings; are the official economic growth projections realistic; who is the best person at a certain ministry to address a specific issue; what is the reputation of a company doing business in the country.

On the other hand, there are substantial constraints on embassy staff—namely time and money. Commercial section staff are universally oversubscribed with workload. Consequently, establishing a good working relationship with embassy staff is often vital to accomplishing in-country objectives. Do not wait for a commercial problem to arise—invest in the relationship as early as possible for the maximum benefit.

At the head of each U.S. diplomatic mission are the chief of mission (with the title of ambassador, minister, or charge d'affaires) and the deputy chief of mission. These officers are responsible for all components of the U.S. mission within a country, including consular posts.

Commercial officers assist U.S. business through: arranging appointments with local business and government officials, providing counsel on local trade regulations, laws, and customs; identifying importers, buyers, agents, distributors, and joint venture partners for U.S. firms; and other business assistance. At larger posts, trade specialists of the USFCS (Foreign and Commercial Service) perform this function. At smaller posts, commercial interests are represented by economic/commercial officers from the Department of State.

Commercial officers for tourism implement marketing programs to expand inbound tourism, to increase the export competitiveness of U.S. travel companies, and to strengthen the international trade position of the United States. These officers are employees of the U.S. Travel and Tourism Administration (USTTA), an agency of the U.S. Department of Commerce with offices in various countries. Additional important markets in Europe, Asia, the Pacific, and Latin America are covered by the Foreign Commercial Service and the private sector under USTTA leadership.

Economic officers analyze and report on macroeconomic trends and trade policies and their implications for U.S. policies and programs.

Financial attaches analyze and report on major financial developments.

Political officers analyze and report on political developments and their potential impact on U.S. interests.

Labor officers follow the activities of labor organizations and can supply information on wages, nonwage costs, social security regulations, labor attitudes toward American investments, etc.

Consular officers extend to U.S. citizens and their property abroad the protection of the U.S. government. They maintain lists of local attorneys, act as liaison with police and other officials, and have the authority to notarize documents. The State Department recommends that business representatives residing overseas register with the consular officer; in troubled areas, even travelers are advised to register.

Administrative officers are responsible for normal business operations of the post, including purchasing for the post and its commissary.

Regional security officers are responsible for providing physical, procedural, and personnel security services to U.S. diplomatic facilities and personnel; their responsibilities extend to providing in-country security briefings and threat assessments to business executives.

Security assistance officers are responsible for Defense Cooperation in Armaments and foreign military sales to include functioning as primary in-country point of contact for U.S. defense industry.

Scientific attaches follow scientific and technological developments in the country.

Agricultural officers promote the export of U.S. agricultural products and report on agricultural production and market developments in their area.

Agency for International Development (AID) Mission Directors are responsible for AID programs, including dollar and local currency loans, grants, and technical assistance.

Public affairs officers are the post's press and cultural affairs specialist and maintains close contact with the local press.

Legal attaches serve as representatives to the U.S. Department of Justice on criminal matters.

Communications programs officers are responsible for the telecommunications, telephone, radio, diplomatic pouches, and records management programs within the diplomatic mission. They maintain close contact with the host government's information/communications authorities on operational matters.

Information systems managers are responsible for the post's unclassified information systems, database management, programming, and operational needs. They provide liaison with appropriate commercial contacts in the information field to enhance the post's systems integrity.

Animal and plant health inspection service officers are responsible for animal and plant health issues as they impact U.S. trade and in protecting U.S. agriculture from foreign pests and diseases. They expedite U.S. exports in the area of technical sanitary and phytosanitary (S&P) regulations.

Business representatives planning a trip overseas should include in their preparations a visit or telephone call to the nearest U.S. Department of Commerce District Office. The District Office can provide extensive information and assistance as well as a current list of legal holidays in the countries to be visited. If desired, the district officer can also provide advance notice to posts abroad of the representative's visit.

The Department of State, Bureau of Diplomatic Security, can also provide current data on the security situation to interested persons planning trips abroad. American business representatives desiring this information should contact the Diplomatic Security Service, Overseas Support Programs Division, tel: (202) 647-3122.

Some of the services jointly provided by the Departments of State and Commerce to U.S. business firms interested in establishing a market for their products or expanding sales abroad include:

- The Trade Opportunities Program (TOP), which provides specific export sales leads of U.S. products and services;
- World Traders Data Report (WTDR), which provides detailed financial and commercial information on individual firms abroad upon request from U.S. companies;
- Agent Distributor Service (ADS), which helps U.S. firms find agents or distributors to represent their firms and market their products abroad; and
- Information about foreign markets for U.S. products and services and U.S.-sponsored exhibitions abroad in which American firms can participate and demonstrate their products to key foreign buyers.

In all matters pertaining to foreign trade, the nearest U.S. Department of Commerce District Office should be your first point of contact. Foreign trade specialists at these facilities render valuable assistance to U.S. business representatives engaged in international commerce.

CONTACT: For additional information about Foreign Service assistance to American business overseas, or for specialized assistance with unusual commercial problems, you are invited to visit, telephone, or write the Office of Commercial, Legislative, and Public Affairs, Bureau of Economic and Business Affairs, U.S. Department of State, Washington, D.C. 20520-5816. Tel: (202) 647-1942.

American Embassies in Latin America

ARGENTINA—Buenos Aires
Tel: (54-1) 772-1041, 773-1063
Fax: (54-1) 775-6040
Senior Commercial Officer:
Arthur Alexander

Foreign Service National:
Carlos Gutierrez

BRAZIL—Brasilia
Tel: (55-61) 321-7272
Fax: (55-61) 225-5381
Senior Commercial Officer:
Richard Ades
(resident in Sao Paulo)
Foreign Service National:
Renata D'Almeida

CARIBBEAN—Regional Office in Santo Domingo, Dominican Republic
Tel: (809) 221-2171
Fax: (809) 688-4838
Senior Commercial Officer:
Larry Eisenberg

CHILE—Santiago
Tel: (56-2) 671-0133, 695-2661
Fax: (56-2) 697-2051
Senior Commercial Officer:
Ricardo Villalobos
Foreign Service National:
Isabel Valenzuela

COLUMBIA—Bogota
Tel: (57-1) 285-1300, 285-1688
Fax: (57-1) 288-5687
Senior Commercial Officer:
Richard Lenahan
Foreign Service National:
Consuleo Alarcon

COSTA RICA—San Jose
Tel: (506) 20-3939
Fax: (506) 20-2305
Senior Commercial Officer:
Maria Galindo
Foreign Service National:
Rodrigo Rojas

DOMINICAN REPUBLIC—
Santo Domingo
Tel: (809) 541-2171

Senior Commercial Officer:
Larry Eisenberg

ECUADOR—Quito
Tel: (593-2) 562-890
Fax: (593-2) 502-052

Senior Commercial Officer:
Ralph Griffin

Foreign Service National:
Nadia Ordonez

GUATEMALA—Guatemala City
Tel: (502-2) 311-541
Fax: (502-2) 318-885

Senior Commercial Officer:
Henry Nicol (Acting)

Foreign Service National:
Raul Villagran

HONDURAS—Tegucigalpa
Tel: (504) 32-3120
Fax: (504) 32-0027

Senior Commercial Officer:
Michael McGee (Acting)

Foreign Service National:
Lizbeth Martell

MEXICO—Mexico City
Tel: (52-5) 207-8837, 211-0042
Fax: (52-5) 511-9980

Senior Commercial Officer:
Roger W. Wallace

Foreign Service National:
Javier Flores

PANAMA—Panama City
Tel: (507) 271-777
Fax: (507) 271-713

Senior Commercial Officer:
Americo Taden

Foreign Service National:
Enrique Tellez

PERU—Lima
Tel: (51-14) 338-000
Fax: (51-14) 316-682

Senior Commercial Officer:
Dean Anderson

Foreign Service National:
Guillermo Thais

VENEZUELA—Caracas
Tel: (58-2) 285-3111, 285-2222
Fax: (58-2) 285-0336

Senior Commercial Officer:
Edgar Fulton

Foreign Service National:
Robert Bucalo

OTHER AGENCIES: CONTACTS AND INFORMATION

U.S. DEPARTMENT OF COMMERCE
14th and Constitution Avenue, NW
Washington, D.C. 20230
Tel: (202) 482-2000 (Main switchboard)

International Trade Administration (ITA)

Office of Latin America

Regional Affairs
Carrie Clark, (202) 482-0477

Andean Division
Janice Bruce (202) 482-4726

Caribbean Basin
William Dowling (202) 482-1648

Southern Cone
Carlos Montilieu (202) 482-1743

Argentina
Randy Mye (202) 482-1548

Belize
Michelle Brooks (202) 482-2527

Bolivia
Paul Moore (202) 482-1659

Brazil
Larry Ferris (202) 482-3871

Chile
Roger Turner (202) 482-1495

Colombia
Paul Moore (202) 482-1659

Costa Rica
Jay Dowling (202) 482-1658

Cuba
Mark Seigelman (202) 482-5680

Dominican Republic
Mark Seigelman (202) 482-5680

Ecuador
Paul Moore (202) 482-1659

El Salvador
Helen Lee (202) 482-2528

Guatemala
Helen Lee (202) 482-2528

Haiti
Mark Seigelman (202) 482-5680

Honduras
Helen Lee (202) 482-2528

Jamaica
Mark Seigelman (202) 482-5680

Mexico
Regina Vargo (202) 483-0300

Nicaragua
Jay Dowling (202) 482-1658

Panama
Jay Dowling (202) 482-1658

Paraguay
Randy Mye (202) 482-1548

Peru
Laura Zeiger-Hatfield (202) 482-4303

Puerto Rico
Mark Seigelman (202) 482-5680

Trinidad and Tobago
Michelle Brooks (202) 482-2527

Uruguay
Roger Turner (202) 482-1495

Venezuela
Laura Zeiger-Hatfield (202) 482-4303

Virgin Islands (US)
Mark Seigelman (202) 482-5680

Latin America/Caribbean Business Development Center

Publishes an outstanding free monthly newsletter on significant events and activities of interest to American firms seeking business in the region, including calendar of events, announcements of U.S. government programs, and abstracts of trade and investment opportunities identified by the commercial section of American embassies in the region. To request being put on the mailing list, fax your request to (202) 482-2218.

General Information
(202) 482-0703

Tourism
Jim Phillips (202) 482-0841

Infrastructure
Maria de la Guardia (202) 482-0841

Infrastructure
Carlos de Quesada (202) 482-0703

Editor (Newsletter)
Walt Schaffer (202) 482-0841

Mexico Flash Facts Information Hotline

The Office of Mexico has initiated a 24-hours-a-day seven-days-a-week automated information retrieval system which transmits documents directly to your fax machine. To access the files, call (202) 482-4464 and follow the pre-recorded instructions. First time users may wish to obtain the main menu (document selection 0101) to get started.

Electronic Bulletin Board (EBB)

The EBB is an affordable on-line source for trade leads as well as the latest statistical releases from the Bureau of Economic Analysis, the Bureau of the Census, the Bureau of Labor Statistics, the Federal Reserve Board, the Department of the Treasury, and other federal agencies. The EBB provides periodic government reports such as foreign exchange rates, consumer and producer price indices, and trends in wages and population. All that is needed to browse or download data is a basic personal computer equipped with a modem (speeds 300–9600). For more information, call (202) 482-1986.

National Technical Information Service (NTIS)
Operates as a clearinghouse for useful U.S. government publications, including maps and economic assessments produced by the Central Intelligence Agency (CIA), country profiles and other business tips prepared by the commercial section of American embassies abroad, and industrial/competitive commercial assessments for most countries prepared by the ITA. For a free listing of what is available, call (703) 487-4660.

National Trade Data Bank (NTDB)
A monthly CD-ROM compiling the most significant publications and databases produced by the U.S. government. The NTDB contains over 100,000 documents including basic export information, country-specific information, industry-specific information, and industry-country information (Market Research Reports, generally prepared by the commercial section of American embassies). Anyone with a 386-IBM-compatible computer and a basic skill of word processing can utilize the NTDB—the cost of a single copy of the CD-ROM is U.S. $95, the annual subscription (updated monthly) is U.S. $360. CD-ROM playback units are now well under U.S. $400 (for example, from DAK mail order, (800) 325-0800 or (818) 888-8220). Otherwise, the NTDB is available for spot research at 600 federal depository libraries around the world. For further information, call: (202) 482-1986.

Information Sources for the NTDB

Central Intelligence Agency (CIA)
World Factbook
Country Profiles

Congressional Budget Office
The Economic and Budget Outlook FY93–97

Council of Economic Advisors
Economic Report of the President, 1993

Department of Commerce
Economics and Statistics Administration, Bureau of the Census
  Summary Demographic Data—
    1990 Decennial Census
  Census of Manufacturers, 1987
  Pollution Abatement Costs and
    Expenditures
ESA, Bureau of Economic Analysis
  Business Cycle Indicators
  Annual Input-Output Tables
  Business Statistics
  Fixed Tangible Wealth of the U.S.
  Gross State Product Originating
  National Income and Product
    Accounts
  Pollution Abatement Expenses
  Regional Projection to 2040
ESA, Office of Business Analysis
  Capital Stocks Database
  National Energy Accounts
International Trade Administration
  (ITA)
  1992–93 Industrial Outlook
  Country Marketing Plans
  Country Economic Profiles
National Oceanic and Atmospheric
  Administration (NOAA)
  National Environmental Data Service
    Weather Condition at Stations in the
      U.S.
    Fisheries in the U.S.
    Wholesale Fish Price Information

Department of Education, National Center for Education Statistics
Digest of Educational Statistics

Department of Energy, Energy Information Administration
Annual Energy Review
Energy Information Directory

Department of Health and Human Services
Centers for Disease Control
Health Statistics, 1992

Department of Justice, Bureau of Justice Statistics
Crime and the Nation's Households
School Crime

Department of State
Country Background Notes
Directory of Foreign Service Officers

Department of Transportation
Airline On-Time Arrival and Departure Data

Environmental Protection Agency
Toxics in the Community
Toxic Release Data for U.S. Counties and Businesses

Federal Reserve Board
New England Economic Indicators
Composite Quotations for U.S. Government Securities

General Accounting Office
Reports and Testimony

Office of Management and Budget
Budget of the U.S.

Small Business Administration
State Profile
Current Economic Indicators
Disaster Assistance Information
Women in Business

Trade Information Center

The "one-stop-shop" for export support for Latin America. Provides: export counseling, seminars and conferences, overseas buyers and representatives referrals, overseas events calendar, export financing referral, and technical assistance. Tel: (800) USA-TRADE (800) 872-8723). Fax: (202) 482-4473.

Export Hotline

The U.S. Department of Commerce, AT&T, and the international accounting firm KPMG Peat Marwick have initiated a 24-hours-a-day seven-days-a-week fax retrieval system to assist exporters with basic information on export markets. Call: (800) USA-EXPORT—(800) 872-3978.

MULTILATERAL FINANCIAL INSTITUTIONS

Each year, multilateral financial institutions such as the World Bank, the International Finance Corporation (IFC), and the Inter-American Investment Corporation (IIC) provide billions of dollars in loans and guarantees to less developed countries (LDCs) around the world. For the most part, these funds go to large-scale infrastructure projects such as transport (ports, railways, airports), energy (electric power plants, petroleum pipelines, mining), urban development (mass transit, housing), and information technology (telephones and computerization).

Projects typically range from U.S. $40–500 million and take multiple years to implement. Substantial opportunities exist for American suppliers in all aspects of project execution, including planning, equipment supply, and installation. Virtually all projects require international competitive tender, supervised by the lending institution. While most opportunities are suitable for only Fortune 500 sized enterprises, there are plenty of supporting contracts ideal for smaller firms with a high degree of technical expertise, including planning, engineering, logistics, and training.

The U.S. Trade and Development Agency (TDA) is also an excellent possibility for American firms to get a piece of the multilateral pie. TDA provides grants to support multilaterally funded infrastructure projects, ranging from U.S. $25,000 to U.S. $1 million in size—depending on the ultimate procurement value of the infrastructure project. Additional information is cited under the U.S. government section, above.

World Bank Contact List

General Institutional Issues
    Tim Cullen (202) 473-1782
    Chief Spokesperson

Debt, Trade, Economics
    Bill Brannigan (202) 473-1784

Environmentally Sustainable Development, Agriculture, Transportation, Water, and Urban Development
    Alan Drattell (202) 473-1787
    Leandro Coronel (202) 473-1788
    Lesley Simmons (202) 473-1785

Industry and Energy
    Marjorie Sheen (202) 473-1789

Human Resources Training and Operations Policy
    Ellen Tiller (202) 473-1790
    John Mitchell (202) 473-2475

Private Sector Development
    Marjorie Sheen (202) 473-1789

Brazil, Peru, Venezuela
    Antonio Pimenta-Neves (202) 473-8722

Other Latin American and Caribbean Countries
    Ciro Gamarra (202) 473-8721

International Finance Corporation (IFC)

General Institutional Issues
    Jack Garrity (202) 473-9119

Multilateral Investment Guarantee Agency (MIGA)

General Institutional Issues
    Moina Varkie (202) 473-6170

OTHER MULTILATERAL AND REGIONAL DEVELOPMENT BANKS

Latin America

Inter-American Development Bank (IDB)
1300 New York Avenue, NW
Washington, D.C. 20577
    Tel: (202) 623-3900
    Fax: (202) 623-2360

Central American Bank for Economic Integration
Apartado Postal 722
Tegucigalpa
HONDURAS
    Tel: (504) 372-253

Andean Development Corporation
P.O. Box 5086 Carmelitas
69011-69012 Altamira
Caracas
VENEZUELA
    Tel: (58-2) 285-5555

Caribbean Development Bank
Wildey, P.O. Box 408
St. Michael
BARBADOS
    Tel: (809) 426-1152
    Fax: (809) 427-8106

Europe

European Bank for Reconstruction and Development (EBRD)
6 Broad Gate
London EC 2M2QS
UNITED KINGDOM
    Tel: (44-71) 496-0060
    Fax: (44-71) 638-2375

Centre for the Development of Industry
Rue de l'Industrie 28
1040 Brussels
BELGIUM
    Tel: (32-2) 513-4100
    Fax: (32-2) 511-7593

European Investment Bank (EIB)
100, Boulevard Konrad Adenauer
L-2950 Luxembourg
LUXEMBOURG
    Tel: (352) 437-91
    Fax: (352) 437-704

Banque Francaise de Commerce Exterior
21, Boulevard Haussmann
75427 Paris Codex 09
FRANCE
    Tel: (33-1) 4800-4800

Nordic Investment Bank
Unioninkatu 30
P.O. Box 249
SF-00171 Helsinki
FINLAND
    Tel: (358-0) 1800-1
    Fax: (358-0) 1800-309

German Agency for Technical Cooperation
(GTZ)
Dag-Hammarskjold-Weg 1
P.O. Box 5180
6236 Eschborn 1
GERMANY
    Tel: (49) 6196-790

Industrial Fund for Developing Countries
P.O. Box 2155
Bremerholm 4
DK-1016 Copenhagen K
DENMARK
    Tel: (45-33) 142-575
    Fax: (45-33) 323-524

Caisse Centrale de Cooperation
Economique
Cite du Reito

35-37 rue Boissy d'Anglas
F-75379 Paris Cedex 08
FRANCE
    Tel: (33-1) 4006-3131
    Fax: (33-1) 4266-0331

De Nederlandse Investeringsbank voor
Ontwikkelingslanden NV
P.O. Box 380
Camegieplein 4
NL-2501 BH The Hague
NETHERLANDS
    Tel: (31-70) 342-5425

SWEDECORP (Swedish International En-
terprise Development Corporation)
P.O. Box 3144
S-10362 Stockholm
SWEDEN
    Tel: (46-8) 667-6600
    Fax: (46-8) 249-290

Commonwealth Development Corporation
1 Bessborough Gardens
London SW1 V2JQ
UNITED KINGDOM
    Tel: (44-71) 828-4488
    Fax: (44-71) 828-6505

Australia

Commonwealth Development Corporation
of Australia
Prudential Building, First Floor
39 Martin Place
G.P.O. Box 2719
Sydney NSW 2001
AUSTRALIA
    Tel: (61-2) 227-711

Asia

Asian Development Bank (ADB)
P.O. Box 789
1099 Manila
PHILIPPINES

Tel: (63-2) 711-3851
Fax: (63-2) 741-7961

Japan Development Bank
9-1, Otemachi 1-chrome
Chiyoda-ku
Tokyo 100
JAPAN
Tel: (81-3) 270-3211, 244-1770
Fax: (81-3) 245-1938

Overseas Economic Cooperation Fund
Takebashi Godo Building
4-1, Otemachi, 1-chrome
Chiyoda-ku
Tokyo 100
JAPAN
Tel: (81-3) 215-1311
Fax: (81-3) 201-5982

Canada

Canadian International Development
Agency (CIDA)
Place du Centre
200 Promenade du Portage
Hull, Quebec K1A 0G4
CANADA
Tel: (819) 997-7901

Africa

African Development Bank
P.O. Box 1387
Abidjan 01
COTE D'IVOIRE
Tel: (255) 20-4907

West African Development Bank
P.O. Box 1172
Lome
TOGO
Tel: (228) 214-244, 215-906
Fax: (228) 215-267

Banque Algerienne de Developement
12, Boulevard Colonel Amirouche
Algiers
ALGERIA
Tel: (213) 638-895, 638-950, 638-146
Arab Bank for Economic Development in
Africa
P.O. Box 2640
Khartoum
SUDAN
Tel: 73647, 73709, 70498
Fax: 22248, 22739
(No direct dial available)

East African Development Bank
4 Nile Avenue
P.O. Box 7128
Kampala
UGANDA
Tel: (256-41) 230-021

Banque de Developement des Estates de
l'Afrique Centrale (BDEAC)
P.O. Box 1177
Brazzaville
CONGO
Tel: (242) 810-212

ECOWAS Fund for Cooperation, Compen-
sation and Development
P.O. Box 2704
Lome
TOGO
Tel: (228) 216-864

Fonds de Solidarite Africain (FSA)
P.O. Box 382
Niamey
NIGER
Tel: (227) 727-632, 727-633, 727-634

Fonds de Solidarite et D'Intervention Pour
le Developement de CEAO
(FOSIDEC)
P.O. Box 2529
Ouagadougou
BURKINA FASO
Tel: (226) 334-794, 334-733

Middle East

OPEC Fund for International Development
Parkring 8
A-1010 Vienna
AUSTRIA
    Tel: (421) 515-640
    Fax: (421) 513-9238

OTHER RESOURCES

Enterprise Development International
    Foundation
5619 Bradley Boulevard
Bethesda, MD 20814
    Tel: (301) 652-0141
    Fax: (301) 652-0149
Contact: Allyn Enderlyn, President

Institute of the Americas
10111 North Torrey Pines Road
La Jolla, CA 92037
    Tel: (619) 453-5560, 277-0600
    Fax: (619) 453-2165
Contact: Ambassador Paul H. Boeker, President

Latin American Development Corporation
4903 Edgemoor Lane #L-03
Bethesda, MD 20814
    Tel: (301) 652-0179
    Fax: (301) 652-0177
Contact: Oliver Dziggel, President

Latin American Manufacturing Association
419 New Jersey Avenue, SE
Washington, DC 20003
    Tel: (202) 546-3803

Caribbean / Latin America Action
1211 Connecticut Avenue, NW #510
Washington, DC 20036
    Tel: (202) 466-7464
    Fax: (202) 822-0075
Contact: Douglas Maguire, Director

Council of the Americas

An Affiliate of the Americas Society, Inc.
1625 K Street, NW #1200
Washington, DC 20006
    Tel: (202) 659-1547
    Fax: (202) 659-0169

Mexico Faxline

The Mexican Investment Bank (MIB) has initiated a 24-hours-a-day seven-days-a-week faxline for information on investing in Mexico. The 29 menu options offer statistical and economic data plus detailed information on various aspects of doing business in Mexico, including profiles of specific industries and a roster of foreign companies operating in Mexico. To receive a menu call (800) MIB-2434 (800) 642-2434) or call the MIB faxline directly at (602) 930-4802 and follow the recorded instructions.

U.S. Trade Promotion Organizations

American Association of Exporters and
    Importers (AAEI)
11 W. 42nd Street
New York, NY 10036
    Tel: (212) 944-2230

Federation of International Trade
    Associations (FITA)
1851 Alexander Bell Drive
Reston, VA 22091
    Tel: (703) 391-6108

World Trade Center Association
One World Trade Center
55th Floor
New York, NY 10048
    Tel: (212) 313-4600

National Council on International Trade
    and Documentation (NCITD)
350 Broadway #205
New York, NY 10013
    Tel: (212) 925-1400

United States Council for International
    Business

1212 Avenue of the Americas
New York, NY 10036
Tel: (212) 354-4480

United States Chamber of Commerce
1615 H Street, NW
Washington, DC 20062
Tel: (202) 463-5488
Fax: (202) 463-3114

Newsletters

Caribbean Update
(Monthly—U.S. $150/year)
52 Maple Avenue
Maplewood, NJ 07040
Tel: (201) 762-1565
Fax: (201) 762-9585

Latin America Monitor
(Monthly—U.S. $195/year)
56-60 St. John Street
London EC1M 4DT
Tel: (44-71) 608-3646
Fax: (44-71) 608-3620

Latin America Index
(Biweekly—U.S. $249/year)
Welt Publishing
1413 K Street, NW
Washington, DC 20005
Tel: (202) 371-0555

Mexico Business Monthly
(U.S. $150/year)
52 Maple Avenue
Maplewood, NJ 07040
Tel: (201) 762-1565
Fax: (201) 762-9585

Washington Letter on Latin America
(Biweekly—U.S. $250/year)
1117 North 19th Street
Arlington, VA 22209-1798
Tel: (703) 783-1717

U.S.-Mexico Free Trade Reporter
(Biweekly—U.S. $597)
1725 K Street, NW #200

Washington, DC 20006
Tel: (202) 785-8851

Multilateral Development Bank (MDB) Liaison Team

ITA/U.S. Department of Commerce

The Office of International Major Projects' MDB Team promotes U.S. exports by keeping U.S. engineers, equipment manufacturers, and consultants aware of opportunities arising from MDB project lending to developing countries. The team counsels firms, retrieves project information, maintains outreach efforts, advises on procurement disputes and reviews procurement policies at the various MDBs.

Contacts: Commerce contact for World Bank, Janice Mazur, (202) 482-4332; for Inter-American Development Bank and European Bank for Reconstruction and Development, Michelle Miller, (202) 482-1246; for African Development Bank, Barbara White, (202) 429-5160; for Asian Development Bank, Mary Alice Healey, (202) 377-4333; FAX for all contacts, (202) 377-3954 and (202) 377-4643

Trade and Investment Services

Bureau for Private Enterprise/Agency for International Development

Under the TIS program, PRE engages the resources of the International Executive Service Corps (IESC) to support, worldwide, a range of industry-specific trade and investment services designed to link businesses in the U.S., developing countries, and the emerging democracies. TIS activities are designed to assist in the expansion of U.S. and developing country business through development of joint and co-ventures, including the sale or licensing of U.S. equipment and technology, long-term sales and co-production agreements, free zone operations, etc.

Contact: Ed Wise, Office of International Business Development, (202) 647-3805, FAX (202) 647-1805

International Executive Service Corps

Agency for International Development

AID has a multi-year commitment totaling $20 million to support IESC activities. Composed of retired senior U.S. corporate executives, IESC provides technical assistance to businesses and organizations worldwide.

Contact: Russ Anderson, Office of Emerging Markets, (202) 647-5806, FAX (202) 647-1805

Technical Assistance Trust Funds for U.S. Consultants

Trade and Development Program

Funds available to finance consultancies and feasibility studies. To qualify as a consultant eligible for this work contact:

African Development Bank:
Abidjan, Ivory Coast, 011-22-5-204015,
    FAX 011-22-5-332172
Contact: Eael Haj Merghoub, (202) 473-3145, FAX (202) 477-3046.
World Bank/International Bank for Reconstruction: Funds are available to finance preparation and appraisal activities.
Contact: Carol Stitt, Business Affairs Advisor, (202) 473-1795, FAX (202) 676-0637.
International Finance Corporation: The IFC finances project-related activities (e.g., sector surveys, feasibility studies).
Contact: Ursula Schmitz, Office of Consultant Liaison, (202) 473-0642, FAX (202) 334-8705.

Definitional Missions

Trade and Development Agency

After receiving a request to fund a major study for a new project, TDA usually hires a technically qualified U.S. consultant to visit the country and discuss the plan with the project sponsors. In addition to making recommendations as to whether the project should be funded or not, the Definitional Missions consultant works with the project sponsor to define the work program for the proposed feasibility study.

Contact: Della Glenn, (703) 875-4357, FAX (703) 875-4009.

Feasibility Studies

Trade and Development Agency

Feasibility Studies assess the economic, financial, and technical viability of a potential project. The host countries must hire U.S. firms to undertake the detailed studies of the technical and economic feasibility of the proposed projects. The average size of a feasibility study grant was nearly $400,000.

Contact: Carol Stillwell, (703) 875-4357, FAX (703) 875-4009.

Financing Assistance

Working Capital Guarantee Program

Export-Import Bank

The program helps small businesses obtain critical pre-export financing from commercial lenders. Ex-Im Bank will guarantee 90 percent of the principal and a limited amount of interest on loans or revolving lines of credit which are extended to eligible exporters. The funds may be used for such pre-export activities as buying raw materials or foreign marketing.

Contact: James Crist, U.S. Division (202) 566-8819, FAX (202) 566-7524.

Export Credit Insurance

Export-Import Bank

Through its agent, the Foreign Credit Insurance Association Management Company, Ex-Im Bank offers insurance which covers political and commercial risks on export receivables.

The New-to-Export-Policy is available to firms just beginning to export or with average annual export credit sales of less than $750,000 for the past two years. The policy offers enhanced coverage and a lower premium than usually found in regular insurance policies.

The Umbrella Policy is available to commercial lenders, state agencies, export trading companies, and similar organizations to insure export receivables of their small and mid-sized clients.

The Bank Letter of Credit Policy insures commercial banks against loss on irrevocable letters of credit issued by foreign banks for U.S. exporters.

The Multi-Buyer Policy insures all or a reasonable spread of an exporter's short-term or medium-term export credit sales.

The Financial Institution Buyer Credit Policy insures individual short-term export credits extended by financial institutions to foreign buyers.

The Short-Term Single-Buyer Policy and the *Medium-Term-Single-Buyer Policy* allow exporters to insure their receivables against loss due to commercial and specified political risks on a selective basis.

Lease Insurance Policies offer a lessor the opportunity to expand its overseas leasing program by providing comprehensive insurance for both the stream of lease payments and the fair market value of the leased products.

Contact: Robert Charamella, Insurance Division, (202) 566-8955, FAX (202) 566-7524.

Guarantee Program
Export-Import Bank

The program provides repayment protection for private sector loans to credit-worthy buyers of U.S. capital equipment and services exports. Coverage is available for loans of up to 85 percent of the U.S. export value, with repayment terms of one year or more. Most guarantees provide comprehensive coverage of both political and commercial risks, but political-risk-only coverage is also available. Ex-Im Bank's guarantee is available for fixed or floating rate export loans in dollars or convertible foreign currencies.

Contact: James Sharpe, Export Finance Group, (202) 566-8187, FAX (202) 566-7524.

Loan Program
Export-Import Bank

The program provides competitive, fixed interest rate financing for U.S. export sales of U.S. capital equipment and related services. Ex-Im Bank extends direct loans to foreign buyers of U.S. exports and intermediary loans to responsible parties that make loans to foreign buyers. Coverage is available for loans of up to 85 percent of the U.S. export value. The interest rates are the official minimum matrix rates agreed on by members of the Organization for Economic Cooperation and Development (OECD) and depend on the repayment period and the classification of the buyer's country.

Contact: James Sharpe, Export Finance Group, (202) 566-8187, FAX (202) 566-7524.

Lease Guarantees
Export-Import Bank

Ex-Im Bank offers lease guarantees for finance and operating leases to foreign entities covering U.S. manufactured goods. The guarantees cover large transactions only, such as commercial jet aircraft or offshore drilling rigs.

Contact: Arthur Pilzer, Latin America Division, (202) 566-8943, FAX (202) 566-7524.

Engineering Multiplier Program
Export-Import Bank

The program stimulates exports of U.S. architectural, industrial design, and engineering services. Ex-Im Bank will extend loans or guarantees for up to 85 percent of the U.S. export value of services involving projects with the potential of generating U.S. export orders of $10 million or double the original export contract, whichever is greater. It also will guarantee commercial financing for approved project-related costs in the host country of up to 15 percent of the U.S. export value.

Contact: John Wisniewski, Engineering Division, (202) 566-8802, FAX 202) (566-7524.

Operations and Maintenance Contracts Program

Export-Import Bank

The program helps U.S. firms competing for overseas contracts to operate and maintain new or established projects. Ex-Im Bank will provide loans or guarantees for up to 85 percent of the U.S. export value of operations and maintenance transactions with repayment terms of up to five years. The contract must provide a long-term benefit to the owner, such as training local personnel to take over operation or establishing permanent procedures to assure good operation of the project.

Contact: John Wisniewski, Engineering Division, (202) 566-8802, FAX (202) 566-7524.

Export-Import Bank Contact: Raymond Albright, Asia Division, (202) 566-8885, FAX (202) 566-7524.

Agency for International Development Contact: Fred Zobrist, John Mullin, Bureau for Private Enterprise, (202) 647-7474, FAX (202) 647-6901.

Market Promotion Program

U.S. Department of Agriculture

Authorized by the Food, Agricultural, Conservation, and Trade Act of 1990 and administered by USDA's Foreign Agricultural Service, the Market Promotion Program (MPP) promotes a wide variety of U.S. commodities in almost every region of the world. Surplus stocks or funds from the Commodity Credit Corporation are used to partially reimburse agricultural organizations conducting specific foreign market development projects on eligible products in specified countries. Proposals for MPP programs are developed by trade organizations and private firms; they are then submitted to USDA by a deadline specified in the program announcement which is published annually in the Federal Register.

Contact: Sharon McClure, Marketing Operations Staff, (202) 720-4327, FAX (202) 720-8461.

Federal International Energy and Trade Development Opportunities Program

U.S. Department of Energy
Agency for International Development
Trade and Development Agency

This interagency program offers financial support to U.S. firms for prefeasibility studies leading to potential energy trade and development opportunities.

Contact: Peter Cover, Office of Fossil Energy, (202) 586-7297, FAX (202) 586-1188.

Export Revolving Line of Credit Program

Small Business Administration

The program guarantees loans up to $750,000, for export-related purposes, including: (1) pre-export financing of labor and materials used in the manufacture of goods for export, or to purchase goods or services for export; (2) specific expenses related to the penetration and development of foreign markets; and (3) insured accounts receivable generated from sales of goods and services for export. The maximum maturity is generally 12 months but may be renewed twice for a total of 36 months.

Contact: Sheldon Snook, Office of International Trade, (202) 205-6720, FAX (202) 205-7272.

International Trade Loan Guarantee Program

Small Business Administration

The program offers loan guarantees up to $1 million for facilities and equipment and up to $250,000 for working capital (1) to small businesses that can significantly expand existing export markets or develop new export markets; or (2) to those adversely affected by import competition. Maturities of loans may extend up to 25 years.

Contact: Sheldon Snook, Office of International Trade, (202) 205-6720, FAX (202) 205-7272.

7(a) Business Loan Guarantee Program
Small Business Administration

Financing for fixed-asset acquisition or general working capital purposes may be obtained; the program encourages private lenders to make loans of up to $750,000 to borrowers who could not borrow on reasonable terms without government help.

Contact: Mike Dowd, Office of Financial Assistance, (202) 205-6490, FAX (202) 205-7064.

Private-Sector Revolving Fund
Bureau for Private Enterprise/Agency for International Development

PRE will consider loans or guarantees for projects in developing countries that have a substantial developmental impact by (1) sustaining sound environmental development, (2) generating net employment opportunities, (3) earning net foreign exchange, and (4) developing managerial and technical skills, or transferring technologies. Specific replicable programs supporting leasing, privatization, small business, U.S. exports, franchising, and expansion of financial markets are available. Financing/guarantees are available from up to 50 percent of the total project cost, usually in the range of $150,000 to $6,000,000. The maximum term is 10 years.

Contact: Steve Eastham, Office of Investment, (202) 647-9842, FAX (202) 647-1805.

Forfeit Guarantee Program
Agency for International Development

This nonrecourse financing guarantee program assists U.S. firms in obtaining financing for the export of durable goods and manufactured goods to AID-assisted developing countries. In forfeiting, the importer's bank usually guarantees a series of promissory notes, given to the exporter at the time of shipment, which can be sold to a third party (a forfeit house) at a discount for immediate cash payments. Fifty (50) percent financing guarantees are available for exports with a maximum value of $1,000,000 on terms of up to 5 years.

Contact: Dan Roberts, Office of Investment, (202) 647-9842, FAX (202) 647-1805.

Development Funds
Overseas Private Investment Corporation

Five investment funds have been established to promote development in various regions and business sectors; these Growth Funds cover Africa, Asia Pacific, Latin America, and Eastern Europe as well as Environmental Investment.

Contact: Daven Oswalt, Public Affairs, (202) 457-7087, FAX (202) 223-1088.

Investment Insurance
Overseas Private Investment Corporation

OPIC offers a number of programs to insure U.S. investments in friendly, less developed countries against the risks of (1) political violence of assets and business income, (2) expropriation, and (3) inconvertibility of local currency. Coverage is available for new investments, expansion or modernization of existing plants, and additional working capital needs. OPIC will insure 90 percent of the investment. Special programs are also available for contractors, exporters, and lessors.

Contact: Daven Oswalt, Public Affairs, (202) 457-7087, FAX (202) 223-1088.

Finance Programs
Overseas Private Investment Corporation

Medium- to long-term financing for overseas investment projects is made available through loan guarantees and direct loans. Direct loans generally range from $50,000 to $6 million and are reserved exclusively for projects significantly involving U.S. "small businesses" or cooperatives. Guarantees, from $2 million to $50 million, are available for projects sponsored by any U.S. company, regardless of size. OPIC's financing commitment may range up to 50 percent of total project costs for new ventures and up to 75 percent for expansion of existing successful operations, with final maturities of five to 12 years or more. A special small contractor's guarantee program is also available.

Contact: Daven Oswalt, Public Affairs, (202) 457-7087, FAX (202) 223-1088.

Lease Financing Program
Overseas Private Investment Corporation

The program offers loans and guarantees to foreign leasing companies in which there is a significant U.S. private business interest.

Terms of the guarantees are typically from four to seven years.

Contact: Daven Oswalt, Public Affairs, (202) 457-7087, FAX (202) 223-1088.

Small Contractor's Guarantee Program
Overseas Private Investment Corporation

The program will guarantee an eligible financial institution for up to 75 percent of an on-demand stand-by letter of credit or other form of payment guarantee issued on behalf of a small business construction or service contractor.

Contact: Daven Oswalt, Public Affairs, (202) 457-7087, FAX (202) 223-1088.

AMERICAN EMBASSY STAFF
Abbreviations Used

AMB:	Ambassador	ECO:	Economic
DCM:	Deputy Chief of Mission	EDO:	Export Development Officer
CHG:	Charge d'Affairs	EX-IM:	Export-Import Bank of the United States
ADM:	Administration	FAA:	Federal Aviation Administration
AGR:	Agriculture		
APHIS:	USDA—Plant Health Inspection Service	IO:	Information Officer
		IRS:	Internal Revenue Service
APO:	Army Post Office	ISM:	Information Systems Officer
AID:	Agency for International Development	LAB:	Labor
		MILGP:	Military Group
CDC:	Centers for Disease Control	ODA:	Office of Defense Attache
COM:	Commercial	PAO:	Public Affairs Officer (USIS)
CON:	Consular Section	POL:	Political
CPO:	Communications Program Officer	RSO:	Regional Security Officer
		SCI:	Scientific Attache
CUS:	Customs (Treasury Department)	USA:	United States Army
		USN:	United States Navy
DOE:	Department of Energy		

AMERICAN EMBASSY STAFF
(September 1993)

Argentina

Buenos Aires (E)
4300 Colombia, 1425, Unit 4334
APO AA 34034
  Tel: [54] (1) 774-7611/8811/9911
  Fax: [54] (1) 775-4205
  Fax: [54] (1) 775-6040—FCS
Telex 18156 AMEMBAR

AMB:	Terence A. Todman
DCM:	James D. Walsh
POL:	Timothy J. Dunn
ECO:	Peter D. Whitney
COM:	Arthur Alexander
CON:	Barbara Hemingway
ADM:	Bernardo Segura Giron
RSO:	Victor G. Dewindt, Jr.
PAO:	Ernesto Uribe
CPO:	George J. Solomon
ISM:	Vincent J. Ryan
SCI:	Paul C. Maxwell
AID:	Robert Asselin
	(resident in Montevideo)
ODA:	Col. Wayne C. Fisher, USAF
MILGP:	Col. John C. Woolshlager, USA
AGR:	Max F. Bowser
APHIS:	Thomas L. Andre, Jr.
LAB:	William L. Lofstrom
FAA:	Larry Bruce
IRS:	Stanley Newman
	(resident in Sao Paulo)

Bahamas

Nassau (E)
Mosmar Building, Queen Street
P.O. Box N-8197
  Tel: (809) 322-1181 and 328-2206
  Tlx: 0-138 AMEMB NS138
  Fax: (809) 328-7838
  Nonimmigrant Visa Section
    Tel: (809) 328-3496

AMB:	Chic Hecht
DCM:	Lino Gutierrez

POL:	Bruce E. Thomas
ECO/	
COM:	Diana F. Brown
CON:	Curtis Stewart
ADM:	James Griffin
RSO:	Stephen P. Burchyns
PAO:	Mary K. Reeber
CPO:	Elwood Rische
NAU:	Denise Malczewski
NLO:	LCdr. Doug Bird
CGLO:	Cdr. Claude Hessel
AGR:	Ray I. Miyamoto
APHIS:	David Q. Tollett
CUS:	Leon A. Casey, Sr.
DEA:	John R. Pulley
FAA:	Thomas Martin
	(resident in Miami)
LAB:	Lester P. Slezak
	(resident in Washington, D.C.)
INS:	James M. Ward
IRS:	Louis Hobbie

Bolivia

La Paz (E)
Banco Popular Del Peru Building
Corner of Calles Mercado and Colon
P.O. Box 425
APO AA 34032
  Tel: [591] (2) 350251, 350120
  Tlx: AMEMB BV 3268
  Fax: [591] (2) 359875

AMB:	Charles R. Bowers
DCM:	David B. Dloughy
POL:	W. Lewis Amselem
ECO/	
COM:	J. Michael Shelton
CON:	Kevin F. Herbert
ADM:	Daniel A. Johnson
RSO:	Jeffrey Pursell
PAO:	John S. Williams
CPO:	Kenneth L. Hill
ISM:	Joseph Smith
FBO:	Joseph W. Toussaint
AID:	Carl H. Leonard
ODA:	Col. David Hunt, USAF
MILGP:	Col. Claude Shelverton, USA

AGR: William Emerson
(resident in Lima)
FAA: Victor Tamariz
(resident in Miami)
LAB: Casey H. Christensen
IRS: Stanley Newman
(resident in Sao Paulo)
IAGS: Lawrence J. Jungman
NAU: James J. Kessinger

Brazil

Brasilia (E)

Avenida das Nacoes, Lote 3
Unit 3500
APO AA 34030
   Tel: [55] (61) 321-7272
   Tlx: 061-1091 and 61-2318
   Fax: [55] (61) 225-9136
   COM Fax: [55] (61) 225-3981
   USIS Fax: [51] (61) 321-2833
   GSO Fax: [55] (61) 226-2938

AMB: Richard H. Melton
DCM: Mark Lore
POL: Stanley T. Myles
ECO: Jack P. Orlando (Acting)
COM: Richard Ades
(resident in Sao Paulo)
CON: Margaret Ann Murphy
ADM: Robert Austin, Jr.
RSO: Barry M. Moore (Acting)
PAO: Carl Howard
IMO: Nicodemo Romeo
ISM: Thomas Smith
SCI: Leroy C. Simpkins
AID: John D. Pielemeier
ODA: Capt. Isidore Larguier, Jr., USN
ODA/
SA: Col. Dennis J. McMahan,
USAF
MLO: Col. Dennis J. McMahan,
USAF
AGR: John J. Reddington
FIN: Christopher P. McCoy
NAU: Norma V. Reyes

Rio de Janeiro (CG)

Avenida Presidente Wilson, 147
APO AA 34030
   Tel: [55] (21) 292-7117
   Tlx: 21-22831
   USIS Tlx: 21-21466
   Fax: [55] (21) 220-0439
   COM Fax: [55] (21) 240-9738

CG: A. Donald Bramante
DPO/
ECO: (Vacant)
ECO: Curtis M. Stewart (Acting)
POL: John D. Fernandez
COM: Walter Hage
CON: Layton Ross Russell
ADM: Harry E. Young, Jr.
RSO: Stephen P. Baker
BPAO: Katherine Lee
CPO: Anthony J. Skok
ODA: Cdr. Rafael L. Polo, USN
ODA/
SA: LCdr. Holly L. Nye, USN
MLO: Cdr. Holly Nye, USN
RES: Curtis Stewart
AGR: John J. Reddington
(resident in Brasilia)
FAA: Santiago Garcia
LOC: James Armstrong
IAGS: Angus C. Jones
VOA: Roger Wilkison

Sao Paulo (CG)

Rua Padre Joao Manoel, 933, 01411
P.O. Box 8063
APO AA 34030
   Tel: [55] (11) 881-6511
   Fax: [55] (11) 852-5154
   Tlx: [55] (11) 31574
   USIS Tlx: 21-21466
   COM Fax: [55] (11) 853-2744

CG: Philip B. Taylor III
POL: Earle Scarlett
ECO: Thomas J. White
COM: Richard Ades
CON: Patricia Ann Murphy

ADM: Craig S. Tymeson
RSO: Keven Durnell
BPAO: Susan A. Clyde
CPO: James H. Porter
ODA: Maj. Thomas J. Solitario
AGR: Alan D. Hrapsky
LAB: Charles B. Smith, Jr.
IRS: Stanley Newman

Commercial/Agricultural Offices
Edifico Eloy Chaves Avenida Paulista, 2439
Sao Paulo
APO AA 34030
   Tel: (11) 853-2011) 2411/2778
   Fax: (11) 853-2744
   Tlx: 11-25274

COM: Richard Ades

Porto Alegre (C)
Rua Coronel Genuino, 421 (9th Floor)
Unit 3504
APO AA 34030
   Tel: [55] (51) 226-4288) 4697
   Fax: [55] (51) 221-2148, 221-2213

PO: Brent E. Blaschke
CON: Lesslie C. Viguerie
BPAO: Joao M. Ecsodi

Recife (C)
Rua Goncalves Maia, 163
APO AA 34030
   Tel: [55] (81) 221-1412) 1413
   Tlx: 81-1190
   Fax: [55] (81) 231-1906

PO: Maria Sanchez-Carlo
CON: Richard T. Reiter
BPAO: Neil Klopfenstein

Commercial and Agricultural offices are also located at:

Belo Horizonte (USIS and COM Branch)
Av Alvares Cabral, 1600 3 Andar—Belo Horizonte

MG CEP 30170
   Tel: [55] (31) 335-3555, 3670, 3250 3930
   Tlx: [55] (31) 1817
   COM and USIS Fax: [55] (31) 335-3054

PAO: Vacant
COM: John Kuehner
     (resident in Sao Paulo)

Belem (CA)
Rua Osvaldo Cruz 165,
66017-090 Belem Para, Brazil
   Tel: [55] (91) 223-0800 and 223-0613
   Tlx: 91-1092
   Fax: [55] (91) 223-0413
CA: Christine M. Serrao

Manaus (CA)
Rua Recife 1010
Adrianopolis, CEP 69057-001
Manaus, Amazonas, Brazil
   Tel: [55] (92) 234-4546
   Tlx: [55] (92) 2183
   Fax: [55] (81) 231-1906
CA: James R. Fish

Salvador da Bahia (CA)
Av. Antonio Carlos Magalhaes
S/N -Ed. Cidadella Center 1, Sala 410
40275-440 Salvador, Bahia, Brazil
   Tel: [55] (71) 358-9166 or 9195
   Tlx: [55] 71-2780 EEVA
   Fax: [55] (71) 351-0717
CA: Heather May Marques

Chile

Santiago (E)
Codina Building, 1343 Agustinas
Unit 4127
APO AA 34033
   Tel: [56] (2) 671-0133
   Tlx: 240062-USA-CL
   Fax: [56] (2) 699-1141
   COM Fax: [56] (2) 697-2051

AID Fax: [56] (2) 638-0931
FAS Fax: [56] (2) 698-9626
FBO Fax: [56] (2) 233-4108
CON Fax: [56] (2) 632-32336

AMB: Curtis W. Kamman
DCM: Michael W. Cotter
POL: Alejandro D. Wolff
ECO: Richard W. Behrend
COM: Ricardo Villalobos
CON: Laurence M. Kerr
ADM: F. Coleman Parrott
RSO: Jeffrey L. Bozworth
PAO: James T. L. Dandridge II
CPO: Cliff Brozowski
ISM: Steven G. Valdez
ODA: Capt. Thomas H. Smith, USN
MLO: Col. Wayne R. Erwin
AID: Paul W. Fritz
APHIS: Herbert L. Murphy
IRS: Stanley Newman
         (resident in Sao Paulo)
AGR: Richard B. Helm
FAA: Santiago Garcia
         (resident in Rio de Janeiro)
LAB: Joseph G. McLean

Colombia

Bogota (E)
Calle 38, No. 8-61
P.O. Box A.A. 3831
APO AA 34038
   Tel: [57] (1) 285-1300/1688
   Tlx: 44843
   Fax: [57] (1) 288-5687
   COM Fax: [57] (1) 285-7945

AMB: Morris D. Busby
DCM: John B. Craig
POL: Janet L. Crist
ECO: Joel F. Cassman
COM: Richard Lenahan
CON: Thomas L. Randall, Jr.
ADM: James A. Weiner
RSO: C. Stephen Craigo
PAO: (Vacant)

CPO: Bradford W. Ham
ISM: Gary T. Greene
AID: Edward Kaduna
ODA: Col. William S. Justus, USA
MAAG: Col. Arturo Rodriguez, USA
AGR: John W. Harrison
APHIS: Gary T. Greene
FAA: Victor Tamariz
         (resident in Miami)
FAA/   Victor H. Echevarria
CASLO: (resident in Caracas)
LAB: Kathleen W. Barmon
NAU: Brian R. Stickney
IRS: Charles Shea
         (resident in Caracas)

Barranquilla (C)
Calle 77 Carrera 68
Centro Comercial Mayorista
P.O. Box A.A. 51565
APO AA 34038
   Tel: [57] (58) 45-7088/7560
   Tlx: 33482 AMCOCO
   Fax: [57] (58) 45-9464

PO: Carmen M. Martinez
ADM/
CON: Sylvia D. Johnson
ISM: Leon G. Galanos

Costa Rica

San Jose (E)
Pavas, San Jose
APO AA 34020
   Tel: [506] 20-39-39
   Fax: [506] 20-23-05
   COM Fax: [506] 31-47-83

AMB: Luis Guinot, Jr.
DCM: Robert O. Homme
POL: Donald B. Harrington
ECO: Stephen V. Noble
COM: Maria Galindo
CON: (Vacant)
ADM: Robert L. Graninger
RSO: Frederick Byron

PAO: Louise K. Crane
CPO: Gilbert M. Harcum
ISM: David S. Fleming
AID: Ronald F. Venezia
ODC: Ltc. Raul J. Colon, USA
AGR: David B. Young
APHIS: Mark E. Knez
FAA: Thomas Martin
 (resident in Miami)
FAA/ Victor H. Echevarria
CASLO: (resident in Caracas)
LAB: (Vacant)
IRS: Daniel R. Dietz
 (resident in Mexico City)

Ecuador

Quito (E)
Avenida 12 de Octubre y Avenida Patria
P.O. Box 538
Unit 5309
APO AA 34039-3420
 Tel: [593] (2) 562-890
 Fax: [593] (2) 502-052
 COM Fax: [593] (2) 504-550

AMB: (Vacant)
CHG: James F. Mack
POL: Charles E. Costello, AID
ECO: Paul E. Simons
COM: Ralph Griffin
CON: Dennis P. Harrington
ADM: Ned E. Morris
RSO: Scott A. Tripp
PAO: Guy Burton
CPO: Alton P. Gorbett
ISM: Stephen A. Jasak
AID: Robert H. Kramer
ODA: Col. Walter Loendorf, USA
MILGP: Col. Steven Hightower
IAGS: James P. Hutchings
PC: Robert Drickey
AGR: Bill Emerson
 (resident in Lima)
FAA: Victor Tamariz
 (resident in Miami)

FAA/ Victor H. Echevarria
CASLO: (resident in Caracas)
LAB: James H. Benson
NAU: Robert E. Snyder
IRS: Charles Shea
 (resident in Caracas)

Guayaquil (CG)
9 de Octubre y Garcia Moreno
APO AA 34039
 Tel: [593] (4) 323-570
 Fax: [593] (4) 325-286
 COM Fax: [593] (4) 324-558

CG: Gwen C. Clare
CON: Larry D. Huffman
ADM: Jeffrey C. Irwin
CPO: John E. Alston

El Salvador

San Salvador (E)
Final Boulevard Station Antiguo Cuscatlan
Unit 3116
APO AA 34023
 Tel: (503) 78-4444
 Fax: (503) 78-6011
 USAID Tel: (503) 98-1666
 USAID Fax: (503) 98-0885
 ECO/COM Fax: (503) 79-0569
 Tlx: 20657
 GSO Fax: (503) 78-6012

AMB: (Vacant)
CHG: Peter F. Romero
DCH: Phillip T. Chicola
POL: Alyce Tidball
ECO/
COM: Albert G. Nahas
CON: Leslie A. Gerson
ADM: Russell F. King
RSO: Arthur W. Jones
PAO: Michael Hahn
CPO: Michael W. Meyers
IFM: Heywood Miller
ODA: Col. Jose Ocasio, USA
AID: John Sanbrailo

MILGP: Col. Rudolph M. Jones, Jr., USA
AGR: Grant Pettrie
(resident in Guatemala City)
APHIS: Steve C. Smith
FAA: Thomas Martin
(resident in Miami)
FAA/ Victor H. Echevarria
CASLO: (resident in Caracas)
LAB: Kevin M. Johnson
IRS: Daniel R. Dietz
(resident in Mexico City)

Guatemala

Guatemala City (E)

7-01 Avenida de la Reforma, Zone 10
APO AA 34024
Tel: (502) (2) 31-15-41
Fax: (502) (2) 31-88-85
COM Fax: (502) (2) 317-373

AMB: (Vacant)
DCM: John F. Keane
POL: George A. Chester, Jr.
ECO: Geraldeen G. Chester
COM: (Vacant)
CON: Sue H. Patterson
ADM: Russell L. Keeton
RSO: Seymour C. DeWitt
PAO: James B. Carroll
CPO: Raymond L. Norris
AID: Terrence J. Brown
ROCAP: Irenemaree Castillo
ODA: Col. Allen C. Cornell, USA
MILGP: Col. Paul A. Scharf, USA
AGR: Grant Pettrie
APHIS: Gordon Tween
NAU: David C. Becker
IAGS: Glenn T. Ramsey
PC: Peter A. Lara
FAA: Thomas Martin
(resident in Miami)
FAA/ Victor H. Echevarria
CASLO: (resident in Caracas)
LAB: Donald R. Knight
IRS: Daniel R. Dietz
(resident in Mexico City)

Guyana

Georgetown (E)

99-100 Young and Duke Streets
Kingston, Georgetown, Guyana
P.O. Box 10507
Tel: [592] (2) 54900-9 and 57960-9
Tlx: 213 AMEMSY GY
Fax: [592] (2) 58497

AMB: George F. Jones
DCM: Manuel Barrera
POL: Edgar L. Embrey
ECO/
COM: Michael G. Heath
CON: Maria I. Philip
ADM: Julio T. Perez
RSO: Bruce T. Mills
PAO: Michael D. Thomas (Acting)
CPO: Carrie A. Ullman
ODA: Ltc. Gustavo Perez-Poveda
(resident in Caracas)
AGR: Lynn Abbott
(resident in Caracas)
LEGAT: Paul F. Nolan
(resident in Bridgetown)
FAA: Thomas Martin
(resident in Miami)
FAA/ Victor H. Echevarria
CASLO: (resident in Caracas)
LAB: Mary Ann Singlaub
(resident in Bridgetown)
IRS: Charles Shea
(resident in Caracas)

Honduras

Tegucigalpa (E)

Avenido La Paz
AMEMB, Unit 2924
APO AA 34022
Tel: (504) 32-3120
Fax: (504) 32-0027
COM Fax: (504) 38-2888

AMB: Cresencio S. Arcos
DCM: James C. Cason
POL: Thomas Ochiltree

ECO:	Hugo L. Llorens
COM:	Michael McGee
CON:	Fernando Sanchez
ADM:	John W. Fuhrer
RSO:	Nanette A. Krieger
PAO:	Andrew Schlessinger
CPO:	Harvey Eidenberg
ISM:	John F. Carper
AID:	Marshall Brown
ODA:	Col. Charles E. Hogan, USAF
MILGP:	Col. Larry L. Gragg, USA
AGR:	Grant Pettrie
	(resident in Guatemala City)
APHIS:	James E. Novy
FAA:	Thomas Martin
	(resident in Miami)
FAA/	Victor H. Echevarria
CASLO:	(resident in Caracas)
PC:	Kate C. Roftery
	(resident in Miami)
LAB:	Kathleen J. Croom
IRS:	Daniel R. Dietz
	(resident in Mexico City)

Jamaica

Kingston (E)

Jamaica Mutual Life Center
2 Oxford Road, 3rd Floor
  Tel: (809) 929-4850 through 4859
  Fax: (809) 926-6743
  USIS Fax: (809) 929-4850 ext. 1042

AMB:	(Vacant)
DCM:	Lacy A. Wright, Jr.
POL:	Robert A. Proctor
ECO:	John P. Riley
COM:	Laurence Eisenberg
	(resident in Santo Domingo)
CON:	John W. Vessy III
ADM:	George H. Haines III
RSO:	Douglas K. Roberts
PAO:	Virginia Farris
CPO:	Fedrick J. Vinson
ISM:	Anita D. Banks
AID:	Robert S. Queener
ODA:	Ltc. Norman Wiggins, USMC

MLO:	Ltc. Mark Daniel, USA
AGR:	Forrest K. Geerken, Jr.
	(resident in Santo Domingo)
APHIS:	Osvaldo E. Perez-Ramos
NAU:	Walter N. Davenport, Jr.
PC:	Janet P. Simoni
FAA:	Thomas Martin
	(resident in Miami)
LAB:	Edmond E. Seay III
IRS:	Louis Hobbie
	(resident in Nassau)

Mexico

Mexico City, D.F. (E)

Paseo de la Reforma 305
Colonia Cuauhtemoc, 06500
Mexico, D.F.
Mail: P.O. Box 3087,
Laredo, TX 78044-3087
  Tel: [52] (5) 211-0042
  Tlx: 17-73-091 and 017-75-685
  Fax: [52] (5) 511-9980, 208-3373
  COM Fax: [52] (5) 207-8938

AMB:	John D. Negroponte
DCM:	Allen L. Sessoms
POL:	Theodore S. Wilkinson, III
ECO:	Donald F. McConville
COM:	Carlos Poza
CON:	Patricia A. Langford
CG:	Kathcrine J. Mullen
ADM:	Thomas J. Fitzpatrick
RSO:	Anthony J. Walters
PAO:	William J. Dieterich
CPO:	Russell Edgett
ISM:	Charles D. Wisecarver, Jr.
AID:	Arthur H. Donart
ODA:	Capt. Edward K. Andres, USA
SCI:	S. Ahmed Meer
AGR:	Richard L. Barnes
APHIS:	Wilmer E. Snell
ATO:	Marvin Lehrer
FAA:	Auerlio V. Rendon
LAB:	John W. Vincent
INS:	Luis Garcia
NAS:	Robert Retka

CUS: Alfredo Villarreal, Jr.
MLO: Col. Ralph E. Duncan, USAF
EPA: Anne L. Alonzo
IRS: Daniel R. Dietz
USTTA: William M. Tappe
FIN: Jack V. Sweeney

U.S. Export Development Office
Liverpool 31
06600 Mexico, D.F.
  Tel: [52] (5) 591-0155
  Tlx: 01773471
  Fax: [52] (5) 566-1115

DIR: Robert W. Miller

U.S. Travel and Tourism Office
Plaza Comermex
M. Avila Camacho 1-402
11560 Mexico, D.F.
  Tel: [52] (5) 520-2101
  Fax: [52] (5) 202-9231

DIR: William M. Tappe

Ciudad Juarez (CG)
Chihuahua Avenue Lopez Mateos 924N
Mail: Box 10545
El Paso, TX 79995-0545
  Tel: [52] (16) 134048
  Tlx: 033-840
  Fax: [52] (16) 16-9056

CG: Richard R. Peterson
CON: Dale L. Shaffer, Jr.
ADM: Rufus A. Watkins
RSO: Wolfgang Fuchs
          (resident in Monterrey)
CPO: Paul W. White
INS: Ramona Flores

Guadalajara (CG)
JAL; Progreso 175
Mail: Box 3088
Laredo, TX 78044-3088
  Tel: [52] (3) 625-2998, 625-2700
  Tlx: 068-2-860 AGDME
  Fax: [52] (3) 626-6549

COM Fax: [52] (36) 26-3576

CG: John P. Jurecky
POL/   Manfred G. Schweitzer
ECO:
COM: Bryan Smith
CON: Ronald J. Kramer
ADM: Nancy Jane Cope
RSO: Mark G. Hoffman
BPAO: Marjorie Coffin
CPO: Jimmy R. Barrett
AGR: Nathaniel Perry
APHIS: Nathaniel Perry
INS: James McClain

Monterrey (CG)
Nuevo Leon
Avenida Constitucion 411 Poniente
64000 Monterrey, N.L.
Mail: Box 3098
Laredo, TX 78044-3098
  Tel: [52] (83) 45-2120
  Tlx: 0382853 ACMYME
  Fax: [52] (83) 45-7748
  COM Fax: [52] (83) 42-5172

CG: Jake M. Dyels, Jr.
POL: Deborah M. Odell
ECO: Mary Lee K. Garrison
COM: John Harris
CON: Patsy G. Stephens
ADM: Isiah L. Parnell
RSO: Wolfgang G. Fuchs
BPAO: Robert R. Gibbons
CPO: Simon M. Guerrero
INS: Yvette La Gonterie
CUS: Dale F. Wisley

Tijuana (CG)
B.C.N.; Tapachula 96
Mail: P.O. Box 439039
San Diego, CA 92143-9039
  Tel: [52] (66) 81-7400
  Fax: [52] (66) 81-8016

CG: Edwin P. Cubbison
CON: Edwin L. Beffel
ADM: John P. Markey, Jr.

PAO: Peter Samson
CPO: Arnold Olivo, Jr.
INS: Raul Ozuna

Hermosillo (C)
Son; Monterrey 141
Mail: Box 3598
Laredo, TX 78044-3598
   Tel: [52] (62) 172375
   Fax: [52] (62) 172578

PO: Gregory T. Frost
CON: Donald Heflin
CPO/
GSO: Russell Edgett
CUS: Javier G. Vasquez
AGR: Wilmer E. Snell
APHIS: Wilmer E. Snell

Matamoros (C)
Tamaulipas Ave. Primera 2002
Mail: Box 633
Brownsville, TX 78520-0633
   Tel: [52] (891) 6-72-70 /1/2
   Fax: [52] (891) 3-80-48

PO: Janice L. Jacobs
CON: William H. Duncan
ADM: Larry J. Kay
APHIS: Lazaro Q. Holguin

Mazatlan (C)
Sinaloa; Circunvalacion 120, Centro
Mail: Box 2708
Laredo, TX 78044-2708
   Tel: [52] (69) 82-1659
   Tlx: 066-883 ACMZME
   Fax: [52] (69) 82-0036

PO: Edward H. Vazquez
CON: (Vacant)
ADM: Michael R. Schimmel
RSO: Mark G. Hoffman
       (resident in Guadalajara)

Merida (C)
Yucatan; Paseo Montejo 453
Mail: Box 3087
Laredo, TX 78044-3087

Tel: [52] (99) 25-5011
Tlx: 0753885 ACMEME
Fax: [52] (99) 25-6219

PO: Stephanie A. Smith
CON: Otto H. Van Maerssen
CUS: Robert Gracia

Nuevo Laredo (C)
Tamps; Calle Allende 3330, Col. Jardin
88260 Nuevo Laredo, Tamps
Mail: P.O. Box 3089
Laredo, TX 78044-3089
   Tel: [52] (871) 4-0512
   Fax: [52] (871) 4-0696 x128

PO: Mary M. Daniel
CON: (Vacant)
CPO/
ADM: (Vacant)

Nicaragua

Managua (E)
Km. 4-1/2 Carretera Sur
APO AA 34021
   Tel: [505] (2) 666-010, 666-013,
   666-015 through 18, 666-026 through
     27, 666-032 through 34
   Fax: [505] (2) 666-046
   USIS Fax: [505] (2) 663-861

AMB: (Vacant)
CHG: Ronald D. Godard
POL: Robert A. Millspaugh
ECO: Paul Trivelli
COM: Richard Lenahan
CON: Kay Daly
ADM: Roger E. Burgess, Jr.
RSO: Richard J. Watts
PAO: Steven Monblatt
CPO: Michael F. Ingram
ISM: Frederick R. Sadler
AID: Janet C. Ballantyne
ODA: Ltc. Ellis Perkins, USA
AGR: David B. Young
       (resident in San Jose)
APHIS: Alan Terrell

FAA: Thomas Martin
(resident in Miami)
FAA/ Victor H. Echevarria
CASLO: (resident in Caracas)
LAB: Donald R. Knight
(resident in Guatemala City)
IRS: Daniel R. Dietz
(resident in Mexico City)

Panama

Panama City (E)
Apartado 6959, Panama 5
AMEMB Panama, Unit 0945
APO AA 34002
Tel: (507) 27-1777
Afterhours and Weekends
Tel: (507) 27-1778
Fax: (507) 27-1964
GSO/FBO Fax: (507) 27-2128
COM Fax: (507) 27-1713

AMB: Deane R. Hinton
DCM: Oliver P. Garza
POL: Stephen G. Wesche
ECO: Maureen F. Quinn
COM: Americo Taden
CON: Robert T. Raymer
ADM: William P. Francisco III
RSO: Mark C. Boyett
PAO: Peter DeShazo
ISM: Michael Hoftel
AID: Kevin Kelly
ODA: Col. Paul F. Joseph, USA
AGR: William W. Westman
APHIS: Kelly Preston
FAA: Victor Tamariz
(resident in Miami)
FAA/ Victor H. Echevarria
CASLO: (resident in Caracas)
LAB: (Vacant)
CUS: Raphael G. Lopez
CPO: Joseph E. Zeman
ICITAP: Patrick H. Lang
NAU: Paul Belmont

LEGAT: Luis Fernandez
PC: Joseph W. Hindman
IRS: Charles Shea
(resident in Caracas)

U.S. Delegation to the Commission for the
Study of Alternatives to the Panama Canal
(CASC)
c/o USEMB Panama, Apartado 6959, Panama 5
Unit 0945
APO AA 34002-0008
Tel: (507) 27-1777
Fax: (507) 27-1970

USREP: Joseph A. Byrne
USDEL: David F. Bastian

Paraguay

Asuncion (E)
1776 Mariscal Lopez Ave.
Casilla Postal 402
APO AA 34036-0001
Tel: [595] (21) 213-715
Fax: [595] (21) 213-728

AMB: Jon David Glassman
DCM: Gerald C. McCullough
POL: Stephen Geis III
ECO/
COM: Luis E. Acosta
CON: Denise Boland
ADM: Carlos Perez
AGR: Max Bowser
(resident in Buenos Aires)
RSO: Maximiliano A. Salazar
PAO: Patrick D. Duddy
CPO: Harold Muroaka
AID: Richard B. Nelson
ODA: Ltc. Alfonso Gomez
ODC: Col. Leon Morand
FAA: Santiago Garcia
(resident in Rio de Janeiro)
PC: (Vacant)

IRS: Stanley Newman
(resident in Sao Paulo)

Peru

Lima (E)
Corner Avenidas Inca Garcilaso de la
Vega and Espana
P.O. Box 1991, Lima 1
Unit 3822
APO AA 34031
  Tel: [51] (14) 33-8000
  Fax: [51] (14) 31-6682
  Tlx: 25212 PE
  GSO Fax: [51] (14) 33-4588

Consular Section:
Grimaldo Del Solar 346, Miraflores Lima
18
  Tel: [51] (14) 44-3621
  Fax: [51] (14) 47-1877

COM Section:
Larrabure Y Unanue 110, Lima 1
  Tel: [51] (14) 33-0555
  Fax: [51] (14) 33-4687
  USAID Tel: [51] (14) 33-3200
   Fax: [51] (14) 33-7034
  USEMB ADM, AGR, and
    USIS Tel: [51] (14) 33-0555
  USIS Fax: [51] (14) 33-4635
  AGR Fax: [51] (14) 33-4623

AMB: (Vacant)
CHG: Charles H. Brayshaw
POL: Stephen G. McFarland
ECO: Douglas C. Hengel
COM: Richard M. Lenahan
CON: Royce J. Fichte
ADM: David A. Roberts
RSO: Wallace Ray Williams
PAO: Pamela Corey Archer
CPO: Gregory J. Tyson
ISM: Susan H. Swart
AID: Craig G. Buck
ODA: Capt. Manuel Y. Durazo, USN

MAAG: Col. Roy Trumble, USA
DMA: John O. Gates
AGR: Bill Emerson
FAA: Victor Tamariz
(resident in Miami)
FAA/ Victor H. Echevarria
CASLO: (resident in Caracas)
NAS: Sherman N. Hinson
IRS: Stanley Newman
(resident in Sao Paulo)

Uruguay

Montevideo (E)
Lauro Muller 1776
APO AA 34035
  Tel: [598] (2) 23-60-61 and 48-77-77
  Fax: [598] (2) 48-86-11

AMB: Richard C. Brown
DCM: Gerald J. Whitman
POL: Gerard R. Pascua
ECO/
COM: (Vacant)
ADM: John R. Baca
CON: Paul M. Doherty
RSO: James R. Prietsch
PAO: Cynthia F. Johnson
CPO: Kenneth E. Parton
AID: Robert J. Asselin, Jr.
ODA: Col. Thomas N. Almojuela,
USA
MAAG: Col. Curtis S. Morris, USAF
AGR: Max Bowser
(resident in Buenos Aires)
CUS: William C. Kavanaugh (Acting)
DEA: David A. Garcia
LAB: Judy M. Buelow
IRS: Stanley Newman
(resident in Sao Paulo)
FAA: Santiago Garcia
(resident in Rio de Janeiro)
PC: Robert L. Blenker
LEGAT: Samuel C. Martinez

Venezuela

Caracas (E)
Avenida Francisco de Miranda and
Avenida Principal de la Floresta
P.O. Box 62291
Caracas 1060-A
APO AA 34037
Tel: [58] (2) 285-2222
Tlx: 25501 AMEMB VE
Fax: [58] (2) 285-0336
COM Fax: [58] (2) 285-2558 and
285-0336

U.S. Agricultural Trade Office:
Centro Plaza, Tower C, Piso 18, Los Palos
Grandes, Caracas
Tel: [58] (2) 283-2353 and 283-2521
Tlx: 29119 USATO VC

AMB: Michael M. Skol
DCM: Robert C. Felder
POL: William Millan
ECO: Frank S. Parker
COM: Edgar Fulton
CON: Thomas Holladay
ADM: Arnold A. Munoz
RSO: Kevin Barry
PAO: Stephen M. Chaplin
CPO: Richard Gunn

ISM: Marion I. Middlebrooks
ODA: Col. Michael J. Kenna, USAF
MILGP: Col. Albert Brownfield, USA
FBO: Knox Burchett
AGR: Lynn Abbott
ATO: Alfred Persi
APHIS: Nicholas Gutierrez
CUS: Robert Benavente
FAA: Victor Tamariz
           (resident in Miami)
FAA/
CASLO: Victor H. Echevarria
LAB: George Dempsey
IRS: Charles Shea
NAU: Dianne H. Graham
LEGAT: Rinaldo A. Campana

Maracaibo (C)
Edificio Sofimara, Piso 3, Calle 77 Con
Avenida 13
Unit 4974
APO AA 34037
Tel: [58] (61) 83-054, 83-055,
      84-253, 84-254
Tlx: 62213 USCON VE
Fax: [58] (61) 524-255

PO: Darrell A. Jenks
ADM: Edward R. Munson

Appendix 1
REGIONAL ORIENTATION

Latin American Integration Association Asociacion Latinoamerican de Integracion—ALADI

Members: All of South America plus Mexico

ALADI has introduced the Regional Tariff Preference System to promote intra-regional trade. In June 1990, ALADI members agreed to increase the average level of regional tariff preferences from 10 percent to 20 percent. ALADI is in a state of flux as members await development of other Western Hemisphere trade blocs.

Andean Free Trade Zone

Members: Venezuela, Colombia, Bolivia, Peru, and Ecuador

Members intend to implement a free trade zone by the end of 1993, and a full-fledged common market by 1995. A common external tariff has yet to be determined, but the tariff could be set as low as 5–20 percent. Rules of origin would be scheduled to come into effect in the mid-1990s.

Mercosur—Southern Cone Market

Members: Argentina, Brazil, Paraguay, Uruguay, with negotiations underway to admit Chile

Established in early 1991, Mercosur's goal is to create a common market among its members. By the beginning of 1995, a completely free market of goods, services, and labor is to be in place for Argentina and Brazil, with Uruguay and Paraguay to come

in line a year later. To date, Mercosur has yet to determine a common external tariff rate, nor has it determined the extent or character of preferential arrangements.

Argentina-Brazil Agreement

In 1987, Argentina and Brazil announced a duty-free status for 600 capital goods. Twenty more agreements are pending that would cover food, energy, and nuclear cooperation. Tariffs and duties have been lowered on 350 manufactured goods. Overall, tariffs are decreasing at the rate of 20 percent per year.

Group of Three

Members: Colombia, Mexico, and Venezuela

The goal of these three oil-producing countries is to create a free-trade "energy basin." By the end of 1993, they plan to have in place a series of guidelines for the liberalization of trilateral trade. The members have yet to establish maximum tariffs, yet have a goal of zero tariffs on manufactured goods to be implemented by January 1994.

Chile-Mexico Free Trade Agreement

This agreement is viewed as a preliminary mechanism that will eventually be subsumed under a North American FTA.

Caricom (Caribbean Community)

Members: Antigua and Barbuda, Bahamas,

Barbados, Belize, Dominican Republic, Grenada, Guyana, Jamaica, Monserrat, St. Kitts and Nevis, St. Vincent and the Grenadines, St. Lucia, Trinidad, and Tobago

Caricom's common external tariff reduces the top tariff rate from 70 percent to 45 percent, the higher rates reserved for imports that would harm domestic industry.

Caribbean Basin Initiative (CBI)

Covers: Antigua, Aruba, Bahamas, Barbados, Belize, British Virgin Islands, Costa Rica, Dominica, Dominican Republic, El Salvador, Grenada, Guatemala, Guyana, Haiti, Honduras, Jamaica, Monserrat, Netherlands Antilles, St. Kitts and Nevis, St. Vincent and the Grenadines, St. Lucia, Trinidad, and Tobago

The 22 Central American and Caribbean economies in the CBI encourage U.S. export and investment by making the U.S. a favored supplier and offering a variety of tax incentives and subsidies. The CBI Caribbean Economic Recovery Act (CBERA) allows waiver of U.S. duties on products that meet certain local content and local manufacturing requirements.

U.S.-Mexico Free Trade Agreement

Already, less than 4 percent of goods imported from the U.S. now come under quota, and only 20 percent of U.S. exports are subject to any form of nontariff barrier. Mexico has cut import duties to a maximum of 20 percent (with an average rate of 11 percent), eliminated the 5 percent export development tax on imports and reduced by 97 percent the number of products subject to prior import permit requirements. Custom valuation procedures have been liberalized.

Central American Common Market

Members: Costa Rica, El Salvador, Guatemala, Honduras, Nicaragua

This bloc is to be reestablished by 1994.

Appendix 2
STATISTICS

The U.S. Department of State establishes allowable per diem expenses for government employees traveling abroad. These figures are useful as benchmarks for the low to medium end of the accommodation spectrum—generally, a standard single bed in a hotel in the vicinity of the American embassy. Rates are established periodically, published annually, and supplemented monthly. The latest edition can be obtained from the Government Printing Office (GPO) Bookstore, Tel: (202) 653-5075 or (202) 512-0132, Fax: (202) 376-5055.

Locality	Maximum Lodging	Maximum Meals and Incidentals	Combined Total	Date
ANTIGUA AND BARBUDA				
Antigua				
(5/1–11/30)	81	70	151	12/90
(12/1–4/30)	103	74	177	12/90
Other				
(5/1–11/30)	31	25	56	12/90
(12/1–4/30)	38	32	70	12/90
ARGENTINA				
Bariloche	51	45	96	6/91
Buenos Aires	95	65	160	11/91
Mar del Plata	43	43	86	6/91
Mendoza	43	43	86	6/91
Other	39	31	70	6/91
BAHAMAS				
Andros Island	20	10	30	12/90
Grand Bahama Island				
(5/1–12/14)	160	76	236	4/92

Locality	Maximum Lodging	Maximum Meals and Incidentals	Combined Total	Date
(12/15–4/30)	179	78	257	4/92
Nassau				
(5/1–12/14)	105	72	177	4/92
(12/15–4/30)	154	76	230	4/92
Other	105	72	177	4/92
BARBADOS				
(4/16–12/14)	98	59	157	10/91
(12/15–4/15)	144	63	207	10/91
BELIZE	78	54	132	10/91
BERMUDA				
(12/1–3/15)	100	81	181	1/91
(3/16–11/30)	143	85	228	1/91
BOLIVIA				
Cochabamba	61	37	98	12/90
La Paz	52	33	85	2/92
Santa Cruz	63	38	101	12/90
Other	52	33	85	2/92
BRAZIL				
Belem	55	40	95	4/92
Belo Horizonte	59	61	120	1/92
Brasilia	79	43	122	4/92
Campinas	66	40	106	4/92
Campo Grande	60	46	106	3/92
Curitibe	82	44	126	4/92
Florianopolis	80	48	128	4/92
Fortaleza	102	47	149	4/92
Foz de Iguacu	92	45	137	4/92
Goiania	63	42	105	3/92
Joao Pessoa	82	39	121	4/92
Manaus	140	48	188	3/92
Natal	98	46	144	4/92
Porto Alegre	82	61	143	4/92
Recife	87	48	135	4/92
Rio de Janeiro	77	41	118	4/92

Locality	Maximum Lodging	Maximum Meals and Incidentals	Combined Total	Date
Salvador d Bahia	74	46	120	3/92
Sao Luis	73	49	122	4/92
Sao Paulo	86	44	130	4/92
Teresina	78	43	121	4/92
Viracopos Airport	86	44	130	4/92
Other	55	37	92	8/91
BRITISH WEST INDIES				
Anguilla				
(5/1–11/30)	120	100	220	12/90
(12/1–4/30)	139	115	254	12/90
Cayman Islands				
(5/1–11/30)	95	53	148	12/90
(12/1–4/30)	138	58	196	12/90
Monserrat				
(5/1–11/30)	68	55	123	12/90
(12/1–4/30)	103	58	161	12/90
Virgin Islands				
(5/1–11/30)	76	57	133	12/90
(12/1–4/30)	125	62	187	12/90
Other				
(5/1–11/30)	68	55	123	12/90
(12/1–4/30)	103	58	161	12/90
CHILE	106	59	165	3/92
COLOMBIA				
Barranquilla				
(2/3–12/14)	76	35	111	4/92
(12/15–1/31)	105	38	143	3/92
Bogota	116	41	157	3/92
Cali	57	33	90	12/90
Cartagena	98	43	141	4/92
Other	38	37	75	12/90
COSTA RICA	77	45	122	8/91
CUBA				
Havana	93	57	150	4/91
Other	26	32	58	12/90

Locality	Maximum Lodging	Maximum Meals and Incidentals	Combined Total	Date
DOMINICA	66	44	110	12/90
DOMINICAN REPUBLIC				
La Romana				
(4/16–11/15)	53	43	96	12/90
(11/16–4/15)	94	78	172	12/90
Puerto Plata				
(4/16–11/15)	90	46	136	3/92
(11/16–4/15)	116	49	165	3/92
Santo Domingo	73	44	117	9/91
Sosua				
(4/16–11/15)	90	46	136	3/92
(11/16–4/15)	116	49	165	3/92
Other	32	32	64	12/90
EASTER ISLAND	66	55	121	12/90
ECUADOR				
Guayaquil	54	28	82	8/91
Quito	60	25	85	6/91
Other	27	24	51	2/92
EL SALVADOR	56	30	86	7/91
FALKLAND ISLANDS	29	23	52	12/90
FRENCH GUIANA				
(4/1–10/31)	83	64	147	4/92
(11/1–3/31)	117	85	202	4/92
GRENADA				
(4/16–12/15)	68	58	126	12/90
(12/16–4/15)	94	60	154	12/90
GUADELOUPE				
St. Martin (FR)				
(5/1–12/14)	121	38	159	12/90
(12/15–4/30)	162	46	208	12/90
Other	83	93	176	2/92

Locality	Maximum Lodging	Maximum Meals and Incidentals	Combined Total	Date
GUATEMALA				
Guatemala City	94	41	135	4/92
Other	25	24	49	12/90
GUYANA	80	44	124	12/90
HAITI				
Cap–Haitien	34	27	61	12/90
Petionville	51	38	89	9/91
Port–au–Prince	51	38	89	9/91
Other	20	16	36	12/90
HONDURAS				
Bay Island	70	30	100	3/91
Puerto Cortes	29	29	58	12/90
San Lorenzo	20	28	48	12/90
San Pedro Sula	58	27	85	10/91
Tegucigalpa	70	30	100	3/91
Tela	33	30	63	12/90
Trujillo	40	23	63	12/90
Other	20	23	43	12/90
JAMAICA	90	50	140	4/91
MARTINIQUE				
(4/16–12/14)	144	101	245	4/92
(12/15–4/15)	157	102	259	4/92
MEXICO				
Acapulco				
(4/15–12/15)	45	43	88	5/91
(12/16–4/14)	63	46	109	12/90
Aguascalientes	82	44	126	11/91
Cabo San Lucas (BCS)				
(4/15–12/15)	79	43	122	12/90
(12/16–4/14)	95	44	139	12/90
Campeche	45	44	89	5/91
Cancun	151	74	225	5/91
Chetumal	52	44	96	5/91
Chihuahua	71	47	118	6/91
Ciudad de Carmen	58	50	108	5/91

Locality	Maximum Lodging	Maximum Meals and Incidentals	Combined Total	Date
Ciudad Juarez	45	45	90	5/91
Ciudad Obregon	53	46	99	5/91
Coatzacoalcos	45	41	86	5/91
Cozumel				
(4/15–12/15)	96	57	153	10/91
(12/16–4/14)	127	60	187	10/91
Durango	71	46	117	6/91
Ensenada	58	42	100	12/90
Guadalajara	104	59	163	4/92
Guanajuato	45	44	89	5/91
Guaymas	51	39	90	5/91
Hermosilio	71	48	119	2/91
Ixtapa Zihuatanejo				
(4/15–12/15)	67	65	132	12/90
(12/16–4/14)	99	67	166	12/90
La Paz	53	35	88	12/90
Leon	56	34	90	5/91
Los Mochis	48	43	91	5/91
Manzanillo	67	47	114	5/91
Matehuala	45	51	96	5/91
Mazatlan	69	46	115	5/91
Merida	69	65	134	2/92
Mexicali	51	34	85	5/91
Mexico City	99	42	141	1/92
Monclova	55	63	118	5/91
Monterrey	105	71	176	3/92
Morelia	55	34	89	5/91
Nogales	47	43	90	5/91
Piedras Negras	63	49	112	7/91
Puerto Vallarta	72	43	115	5/91
Saltillo	64	41	106	11/91
San Carlos	51	39	90	5/91
San Felipe	49	37	86	12/90
San Jose Del Cabo				
(4/15–12/15)	48	40	88	12/90
(12/16–4/14)	63	42	105	12/90
San Luis Potosi	51	34	85	5/91
San Luis RC	57	37	94	5/91
San Miguel de Allende	79	39	118	2/92
Tapachula	65	46	111	2/92
Tijuana	58	40	98	12/90

Locality	Maximum Lodging	Maximum Meals and Incidentals	Combined Total	Date
Torreon	60	47	107	5/91
Villahermosa	70	61	131	5/91
Zacatecas	64	47	111	2/92
Other	45	34	79	5/91
NETHERLANDS ANTILLES				
Aruba				
(5/1–12/14)	90	54	144	12/90
(12/15–4/30)	154	60	214	12/90
Bonaire				
(5/1–12/14)	97	34	131	12/90
(12/15–4/30)	124	37	161	12/90
Curacao				
(5/1–12/14)	72	65	137	12/90
(12/15–4/30)	96	68	164	12/90
Sint Maarten (Dutch)				
(5/1–12/14)	121	38	159	12/90
(12/15–4/30)	162	46	208	12/90
Other				
(5/1–12/14)	54	25	79	12/90
(12/15–4/30)	61	26	87	12/90
NICARAGUA				
Managua	105	61	166	2/91
Other	20	35	55	2/90
PANAMA				
Canal Area	75	57	132	12/90
Colon	75	57	132	12/90
Contadora				
(5/1–12/14)	79	55	134	12/90
(12/15–4/30)	94	55	149	12/90
Panama City	75	57	132	12/90
Volcan	65	63	128	12/90
Other	41	41	82	12/90
PARAGUAY				
Asuncion	59	47	106	4/92
San Bernadino	30	30	60	12/90
Other	25	19	44	12/90

Locality	Maximum Lodging	Maximum Meals and Incidentals	Combined Total	Date
PERU				
Cuzco	65	51	116	10/91
Lima	84	64	148	10/91
Other	65	35	100	10/91
SAINT KITTS AND NEVIS				
(5/1–11/30)	76	66	142	12/90
(12/1–4/30)	116	70	186	12/90
SAINT VINCENT AND THE GRENADINES				
(5/1–11/30)	66	57	123	12/90
(12/1–4/30)	85	56	141	12/90
SURINAME	95	103	198	12/91
TRINIDAD AND TOBAGO				
Tobago	56	52	108	12/90
Trinidad	64	48	112	12/90
TURKS AND CAICOS IS-LANDS				
Providenciales Island				
(4/14–12/14)	113	81	194	12/90
(12/15–4/14)	131	84	215	12/90
Other				
(4/14–12/14)	117	74	191	12/90
(12/15–4/14)	124	76	200	12/90
URUGUAY				
Montevideo	57	53	110	4/92
Punta del Este				
(3/16–12/14)	116	81	197	4/92
(12/15–3/15)	177	86	263	4/92
Other	57	53	110	4/92
VENEZUELA	90	36	126	3/92

Table A-2
LATIN AMERICA
Political, Financial, and Economic Risk
(August 1991)

	Political	Financial	Economic	Composite
Argentina	63.0	30.0	23.0	58.0
Bahamas	66.0	39.0	36.5	71.0
Bolivia	52.0	34.0	32.0	59.0
Brazil	67.0	34.0	23.0	62.0
Chile	67.0	42.0	30.5	70.0
Colombia	60.0	41.0	34.0	67.5
Costa Rica	71.0	35.0	32.0	69.0
Cuba	54.0	16.0	12.0	41.0
Dominican Republic	53.0	23.0	30.5	53.5
Ecuador	58.0	29.0	26.0	56.5
El Salvador	37.0	18.0	32.0	43.5
Guatemala	41.0	24.0	30.5	48.0
Guyana	51.0	29.0	20.5	50.5
Haiti	28.0	12.0	26.5	33.5
Honduras	49.0	28.0	28.0	52.5
Jamaica	66.0	37.0	24.0	63.5
Mexico	71.0	41.0	28.5	70.5
Nicaragua	44.0	27.0	17.0	44.0
Panama	47.0	28.0	34.0	54.5
Paraguay	59.0	39.0	34.5	66.5
Peru	45.0	28.0	21.5	47.5
Suriname	44.0	23.0	28.0	47.5
Trinidad and Tobago	59.0	35.0	31.5	63.0
Uruguay	66.0	39.0	32.0	68.5
Venezuela	75.0	40.0	36.0	75.5
USA	78.0	49.0	39.5	83.5

Note: The composite risk rating is calculated as follows:
Composite rating (country X) = 0.5 (political risk + financial risk + economic risk ratings).

Source: International Country Risk Guide
Tel: (212) 685-6900 Fax: (212) 685-8566

Table A-3
LATIN AMERICA
**Political, Financial and Economic Risk
Ranked by Lowest Composite Risk Rating
(August 1991)**

	Political	Financial	Economic	Composite
USA	78.0	49.0	39.5	83.5
Venezuela	75.0	40.0	36.0	75.5
Bahamas	66.0	39.0	36.5	71.0
Mexico	71.0	41.0	28.5	70.5
Chile	67.0	42.0	30.5	70.0
Costa Rica	71.0	35.0	32.0	69.0
Uruguay	66.0	39.0	32.0	68.5
Colombia	60.0	41.0	34.0	67.5
Paraguay	59.0	39.0	34.5	66.5
Jamaica	66.0	37.0	24.0	63.5
Trinidad and Tobago	59.0	35.0	31.5	63.0
Brazil	67.0	34.0	23.0	62.0
Bolivia	52.0	34.0	32.0	59.0
Argentina	63.0	30.0	23.0	58.0
Ecuador	58.0	29.0	26.0	56.5
Panama	47.0	28.0	34.0	54.5
Dominican Republic	53.0	23.0	30.5	53.5
Honduras	49.0	28.0	28.0	52.5
Guyana	51.0	29.0	20.5	50.5
Guatemala	41.0	24.0	30.5	48.0
Peru	45.0	28.0	21.5	47.5
Suriname	44.0	23.0	28.0	47.5
Nicaragua	44.0	27.0	17.0	44.0
El Salvador	37.0	18.0	32.0	43.5
Cuba	54.0	16.0	12.0	41.0
Haiti	28.0	12.0	26.5	33.5

Note: The composite risk rating is calculated as follows:
Composite rating (country X) = 0.5 (political risk + financial risk + economic risk ratings).

Source: International Country Risk Guide
Tel: (212) 685-6900 Fax: (212) 685-8566.

Table A-4
TOP 50 MARKETS FOR U.S. EXPORTS (1990)
(Domestic and Foreign Merchandise, FAS U.S. $millions)

Rank 1990	Rank 1980	Country	1990	% Change 1989–90
1	1	Canada	83,866	9.5
2	2	Japan	48,585	9.2
3	3	**Mexico**	**28,375**	**13.6**
4	4	United Kingdom	23,484	12.7
5	5	Germany	18,752	10.6
6	11	South Korea	15,983	7.0
7	7	France	13,652	17.9
8	6	Netherlands	13,016	14.5
9	14	Taiwan	11,482	1.3
10	8	Belgium/Luxembourg	10,448	22.6
11	15	Australia	8,535	2.4
12	19	Singapore	8,019	9.2
13	10	Italy	7,987	10.7
14	20	Hong Kong	6,840	8.7
15	18	Spain	5,208	8.6
16	13	**Brazil**	**5,062**	**5.4**
17	16	Switzerland	4,944	0.7
18	17	China	4,807	−16.5
19	9	Saudi Arabia	4,035	12.9
20	32	Malaysia	3,425	19.3
21	26	Sweden	3,404	8.4
22	23	Israel (incl. Gaza)	3,201	13.2
23	12	**Venezuela**	**3,107**	**2.7**
24	30	USSR	3,088	−27.9
25	33	Thailand	2,991	30.7
26	39	Ireland	2,539	2.3
27	28	India	2,486	1.2
28	24	Philippines	2,472	0.8
29	45	Turkey	2,253	12.5
30	25	Egypt	2,249	−13.8
31	27	**Colombia**	**2,038**	**17.3**
32	29	Indonesia	1,897	52.1
33	22	South Africa	1,732	−93.0
34	31	**Chile**	**1,672**	**18.2**
35	40	**Dominican Republic**	**1,658**	**108.5**
36	37	Denmark	1,311	24.8
37	38	Norway	1,281	23.5
38	21	**Argentina**	**1,179**	**13.5**

Table A-4
TOP 50 MARKETS FOR U.S. EXPORTS (1990)
(Domestic and Foreign Merchandise, FAS U.S. $Millions)
(Continued)

Rank				% Change
1990	1980	Country	1990	1989–90
39	42	Pakistan	1,143	0.8
40	43	New Zealand	1,133	1.4
41	46	Finland	1,126	16.2
42	35	United Arab Emirates	998	−19.4
43	47	**Costa Rica**	**992**	**99.1**
44	44	Algeria	948	25.4
45	50	**Jamaica**	**944**	**−6.2**
46	36	Portugal	922	−0.3
47	48	Austria	873	0.1
48	41	**Panama**	**867**	**19.8**
49	49	**Bahamas**	801	3.8
50	34	**Peru**	**778**	**12.0**

Source: U.S. Department of Commerce

Table A-5
LATIN AMERICA
Top Destinations for U.S. Travelers (1991)

Caribbean

1   U.S. Virgin Islands
2   Bahamas
3   Aruba
4   Jamaica
5   Saint Maarten/St. Marten
6   Bermuda
7   Cayman Islands
8   Martinique
9   Puerto Rico
10   St. Lucia
11   Trinidad

South America

1   Sao Paulo, Brazil
2   Buenos Aires, Argentina
3   Caracas, Venezuela

Successful Meetings, July 1992
355 Park Avenue South, NYC, NY 10010
Tel: (212) 592-6438   Fax: (212)592-6409.

Table A-6
LATIN AMERICA
Per Capita GNP, 1991

	Per Capita GNP (U.S. $)	Population (thousands)
Antigua and Barbuda	4,330	80
Argentina	2,790	32,646
Bahamas	11,750	259
Barbados	6,630	258
Belize	2,010	193
Bolivia	650	7,356
Brazil	2,940	153,164
Chile	2,160	15,360
Colombia	1,260	32,873
Cuba	—	10,712
Dominica	2,440	72
Dominican Republic	940	7,197
Ecuador	1,000	10,503
El Salvador	10,080	5,308
French Guiana	—	96
Grenada	2,180	91
Guadeloupe	—	390
Guatemala	930	9,466
Guyana	430	802
Haiti	370	6,603
Honduras	580	5,259
Jamaica	1,160	2,440
Martinique	—	364
Mexico	3,030	87,821
Nicaragua	460	3,975
Panama	2,130	2,460
Paraguay	1,270	4,441
Peru	1,020	22,135
Puerto Rico	6,320	3,554
St. Kitts and Nevis	3,960	39
St. Lucia	2,490	152
St. Vincent	1,730	108
Trinidad and Tobago	3,670	1,249
Uruguay	2,840	3,110
Venezuela	2,730	20,191
United States	22,240	252,040

Source: The World Bank, *World Bank News*, April 29, 1993.

Table A-7
LATIN AMERICA
Per Capita GNP, 1991
Ranked by Per Capita GNP

	Per Capita GNP (U.S. $)	Population (thousands)
Bahamas	11,750	259
Barbados	6,630	258
Puerto Rico	6,320	3,554
Antigua and Barbuda	4,330	80
St. Kitts and Nevis	3,960	39
Trinidad and Tobago	3,670	1,249
Mexico	3,030	87,821
Brazil	2,940	153,164
Uruguay	2,840	3,110
Argentina	2,790	32,646
Venezuela	2,730	20,191
St. Lucia	2,490	152
Dominica	2,440	72
Grenada	2,180	91
Chile	2,160	15,360
Panama	2,130	2,460
Belize	2,010	193
St. Vincent	1,730	108
Paraguay	1,270	4,441
Colombia	1,260	32,873
Jamaica	1,160	2,440
El Salvador	1,080	5,308
Peru	1,020	22,135
Ecuador	1,000	10,503
Dominican Republic	940	7,197
Guatemala	930	9,466
Bolivia	650	7,356
Honduras	580	5,259
Nicaragua	460	3,975
Guyana	430	802
Haiti	370	6,603
Cuba	—	10,712
French Guiana	—	96
Guadeloupe	—	390
Martinique	—	364
United States	22,240	252,040

Source: The World Bank, *World Bank News,* April 29, 1993.

Table A-8
LATIN AMERICA
Per Capita GNP, 1991
Ranked by Population

	Per Capita GNP (U.S. $)	Population (thousands)
Brazil	2,940	153,164
Mexico	3,030	87,821
Colombia	1,260	32,873
Argentina	2,790	32,646
Peru	1,020	22,135
Venezuela	2,730	20,191
Chile	2,160	15,360
Cuba	—	10,712
Ecuador	1,000	10,503
Guatemala	930	9,466
Haiti	370	6,603
Bolivia	650	7,356
Dominican Republic	940	7,197
El Salvador	1,080	5,308
Honduras	580	5,259
Paraguay	1,270	4,441
Nicaragua	460	3,975
Puerto Rico	6,320	3,554
Uruguay	2,840	3,110
Panama	2,130	2,460
Jamaica	1,160	2,440
Trinidad and Tobago	3,670	1,249
Guyana	430	802
Guadeloupe	—	390
Martinique	—	364
Bahamas	11,750	259
Barbados	6,630	258
Belize	2,010	193
St. Lucia	2,490	152
St. Vincent	1,730	108
French Guiana	—	96
Grenada	2,180	91
Antigua and Barbuda	4,330	80
Dominica	2,440	72
St. Kitts and Nevis	3,960	39
United States	22,240	252,040

Source: The World Bank, *World Bank News*, April 29, 1993.

Index

A